International Conference on Advances in Pattern Recognition

Springer
London
Berlin
Heidelberg
New York
Barcelona
Hong Kong
Milan
Paris
Santa Clara
Singapore
Tokyo

Sameer Singh (Ed.)

International Conference on Advances in Pattern Recognition

Proceedings of ICAPR '98, 23-25 November 1998, Plymouth, UK

With 199 Figures

Springer

Dr Sameer Singh, PhD
Dept. of Computer Science
University of Exeter
Exeter EX4 4PT
UK

ISBN-13:978-1-4471-1214-3 Springer-Verlag London Berlin Heidelberg

British Library Cataloguing in Publication Data
International conference on Advances in Pattern Recognition
: proceedings of ICAPR 98, 23-25 November 1998, Plymouth
1. Pattern recognition systems - Congresses
I. Singh, Sameer II. International Conference on Advances in
Pattern Recognition (1998 : Plymouth, England)
006.4
ISBN-13:978-1-4471-1214-3

Library of Congress Cataloging-in-Publication Data
International conference on Advances in Pattern Recognition (1998 :
Plymouth, England)
International conference on Advances in Pattern Recognition :
proceedings of ICAPR 98, 23-25 November 1998, Plymouth / Sameer Singh, (ed.).
p. cm.
Includes bibliographical references.
ISBN-13:978-1-4471-1214-3 e-ISBN-13:978-1-4471-0833-7
DOI:10.1007/978-1-4471-0833-7

1. Pattern recognition systems - Congresses. 2. Image Processing - Congresses.
3. Optical pattern recognition - Congresses.
I. Singh, Sameer, 1970- . II. Title.
TK7882.P3I56 1999 98-42078
006.4-dc21 CIP

Typesetting: Camera ready by contributors

34/3830-543210 Printed on acid-free paper

INTERNATIONAL CONFERENCE ON ADVANCES IN PATTERN RECOGNITION
23-25 November, 1998

COPTHORNE
PLYMOUTH

Conference and Program Chair
Sameer Singh, University of Exeter, UK

Programme Committee
Adnan Amin, University of New South Wales, Australia
Bir Bhanu, University of California at Riverside, USA
Michael Brady, University of Oxford, UK
Dov Dori, Israel Institute of Technology, Israel
Marco Gori, University of Siena, Italy
Hans Guesgen, University of Auckland, New Zealand
Robert Haralick, University of Washington at Seattle, USA
Gabor Herman, University of Pennsylvania, USA
Xuedong Huang, Microsoft Corporation, USA
Joseph Kittler, University of Surrey, UK
Jussi Parkkinen, Lapeenranta University of Technology, Finland
Ching Y Suen, Concordia University, Canada

Organising Chair
Elizabeth Stuart, University of Plymouth, UK

Organising Committee
Subbiah Baskaran, NASA, USA
Martin Brown, University of Southampton, UK
John Macintyre, University of Sunderland, UK
Derek Partridge, University of Exeter, UK
Maria Petrou, University of Surrey, UK
Noel Sharkey, University of Sheffield, UK
Babis Theodoulidis, UMIST, UK

INTERNATIONAL CONFERENCE ON ADVANCES IN PATTERN RECOGNITION
23-25 November, 1998

COPTHORNE
PLYMOUTH

Sponsors
Kodak Limited, UK
SmithKline Beecham Pharmaceuticals, UK
British Computer Society Specialist Group on Pattern Analysis and Robotics

Aims and Scope of the Conference
The main aim of the conference was to bring together invited researchers of repute to an important meeting in 1998. The conference includes contributions in applied domains including, but not limited to:
Vision and Image Processing
Medical Analysis
Neural and Evolutionary Computing
Speech Recognition
Document and Character Analysis
Pattern Recognition

Journal Special Issue
A special issue on the conference will appear in **Pattern Analysis and Applications** journal by Springer in 1998.

Enquiries
Enquiries on the conference including the purchase of proceedings at a reduced price should be directed to: Sameer Singh, Department of Computer Science, University of Exeter, Exeter EX4 4PT, UK.

INTERNATIONAL CONFERENCE ON ADVANCES IN PATTERN RECOGNITION

23-25 November, 1998

COPTHORNE

PLYMOUTH

The conference wishes to thank the following referees for their services to the conference.

Adnan	Amin	University of New South Wales	Australia
Subbiah	Baskaran	NASA-Huntsville	USA
Bir	Bhanu	University of California-Riverside	USA
Horst	Bischof	Technical University of Vienna	Austria
James	Boyce	King's College London	UK
Michael	Brady	University of Oxford	UK
Martin	Brown	University of Southampton	UK
Guido	Bugmann	University of Plymouth	UK
Kathryn	Burn-Thornton	University of Plymouth	UK
Neil	Cade	GEC Marconi	UK
Terry	Caelli	University of Ohio at Columbus	USA
Andreas	Dengel	German Research Centre for AI GmbH	Germany
Dov	Dori	Israel Institute of Technology	Israel
James	Duncan	Yale University	USA
Alexander	Franz	Sony US Research Laboratories	USA
Marco	Gori	University of Siena	Italy
Hans	Guesgen	University of Auckland	New Zealand
Gregory	Hager	Yale University	USA
Gabor	Herman	University of Pennsylvania	USA
Evor	Hines	University of Warwick	UK
Kurt	Hornik	Technical University of Vienna	Austria
Xuedong	Huang	Microsoft Corporation	USA
Joseph	Kittler	University of Surrey	UK
Ravi	Kothari	University of Cincinnati	USA
Andras	Lorincz	Eotvos Lorand University	Hungary
David	Lowe	Aston University	UK
John	MacIntyre	University of Sunderland	UK

Peter	Marcer	European Institute for Quantum Computing	UK
Ruggero	Milanese	University of Geneva	Switzerland
Melanie	Mitchell	Santa Fe Institute	USA
Mari	Ostendorf	Boston University	USA
Jussi	Parkkinen	Lappeenranta University of Technology	Finland
Derek	Partridge	University of Exeter	UK
Maria	Petrou	University of Surrey	UK
Henri	Prade	Universite Paul Sabatier	France
Steven	Renals	University of Sheffield	UK
Steven	Salzberg	The Institute for Genomic Research	USA
Eric	Saund	Xerox Palo Alto Research Center	USA
Noel	Sharkey	University of Sheffield	UK
Sameer	Singh	University of Plymouth	UK
Richard	Staunton	University of Warwick	UK
Ching Y	Suen	Concordia University	Canada
Jasjit	Suri	Transurgical Inc.	USA
Chew Lim	Tan	National University of Singapore	Singapore
Babis	Theodoulidis	UMIST	UK
Tardi	Tjahjadi	University of Warwick	UK
Roland	Wilson	University of Warwick	UK

Preface

International Conference on Advances in Pattern Recognition (ICAPR 98) at Plymouth represents an important meeting for advanced research in pattern recognition. There is considerable interest in the areas of image processing, medical imaging, speech recognition, document analysis and character recognition, fuzzy data analysis and neural networks. ICAPR 98 is aimed at providing an international platform for invited research in this multi-disciplinary area. It is expected that the conference will grow in future years to include more research contributions that detail state-of-the-art research in pattern recognition.

ICAPR 98 attracted contributions from different countries of the highest quality. I should like to thank the programme and organising committee for doing an excellent job in organising this conference. The peer reviewed nature of the conference ensured high quality publications in these proceedings. My personal thanks to Mrs. Barbara Davies who served as conference secretary and worked tirelessly in organising the conference. I should also thank the organising chair for the local arrangements and our key-note, plenary and tutorial speakers for their valuable contributions to the conference. I also thank Springer-Verlag for publishing these proceedings that will be a valuable source of research reference for the readers. Finally, I thank all participants who made this conference successful.

SAMEER SINGH

ICAPR 98 Conference Chairman

Contents

MEDICAL ANALYSIS

NEURAL AND EVOLUTIONARY COMPUTING

SPEECH RECOGNITION

DOCUMENT AND CHARACTER ANALYSIS

PATTERN RECOGNITION

TUTORIALS

PLENARY SESSIONS

LOOKING FOR AWARENESS IN THE BRAIN.

J.G Taylor, Department of Mathematics, King's College London, UK.

ABSTRACT

New windows on the mind (PET, fMRI, MEG and EEG) are being used to image the brain as it creates awareness. Recent new data analysis techniques (structural modelling, independent component analysis or ICA and magnetic field tomography) are allowing us to determine how brain sites are interacting to create awareness. Some of these signal processing techniques and the experimental results derived by their use are briefly described. A global model of awareness based on these results, involving posterior 'slave' working memory and anterior control sites as well as memory 'convergence' zones, is presented as a conclusion to the paper.

1. INTRODUCTION

The problem of understanding consciousness requires several avenues to be followed in parallel:

1) to analyse the nature of consciousness as an inner experience by the each of us;
2) to build a data-base of the detailed activities and interactions of the various components of the brain while consciousness is experienced, and relate these regions of activity to the various components of consciousness as they are experienced;
3) to construct neural network models which help explain these features.

This paper does not contribute much to the first task; it assumes that the various states of consciousness can be taken from internal report from subjects. We will consider very briefly later how to categorise these states and thence label active brain sites according to the category of consciousness they are involved in. Otherwise we take from psychology the many results investigating awareness. We will only consider the third part rather briefly, due to limitations of space; it is considered in much more detail elsewhere [1]. Here we discuss at greater length the second of the above approaches. At the level of human cognitive processing the appropriate data-base is of the modules used to solve cognitive tasks, with their concomitant levels of consciousness. This is to be seen as an important first step in building the associated neural models, since the associated modelling consists in explaining the manner in which the observed modules interact and the detailed functions they perform. We are involved in what may be termed 'brain topography', leading later to 'neural modelling'. This paper is thus to be seen as a contribution to the ongoing attempt in the second and third avenues above, and to indicate their relevance to the search for awareness in the brain.

There is increasing information becoming available on functional brain topography from the discipline of functional brain imaging as to the specific brain modules active while human subjects solve various cognitive tasks. The data show that there are networks of modules active during task solution, with a certain amount of overlap between the networks involved in different problems. The experimental paradigms used to obtain the functional brain imaging data already contain partial descriptions of the functions being performed by the various areas.

I propose to start by briefly surveying the various machines now being used for studying brain activity at a global level. I will then consider in the following section some of the techniques of data analysis that allow us to better understand what these results imply. A brief overview of the results obtained from PET on the distribution of activity in the brain during various tasks is then given in section 4. In section 5 results from a recent fMRI study on the Motion-After-Effect are used to develop an understanding of some of the modules involved in the creation of consciousness in such a phenomenon. A simple model of the emergence of consciousness is then proposed in the following section which is consistent with known data, and support it by a specific task in the following section. The final section discusses future work.

2. A SURVEY OF BRAIN IMAGING MACHINES

PET and fMRI machines investigate the underlying neural activity in the brain indirectly, the first by measuring the 2 photons emitted in the positron annihilation process occurring during the radio-active decay of a suitable radio-nuclide such as $H_2\,^{15}O$ injected into a subject at the start of an experiment, the second from the uneven distribution of nuclear spins (effectively that of the proton) when a subject is in a strong magnetic field (usually of 1.5 Tessla, although a 12 T machine is being built especially for human brain imaging studies). The PET measurement allows determination of regions of largest blood flow, corresponding to the largest 2-photon count. The fMRI measurement is termed that of BOLD (blood oxygen-level dependent). This signal stems from the observation that during changes in neuronal activity there are local changes in the amount of oxygen in tissue, which alters the amount of oxygen carried by haemoglobin, thereby disturbing the local magnetic polarisibility.

The sensitivity of the two types of machines is not at all comparable. Spatially they have a few millimetres accuracy across the whole brain. However temporally they are far less effective. PET measurements need to be summed over about 60-80 seconds, limiting the temporal accuracy considerably. fMRI is far more sensitive to time, with differences in the time of activation of various regions being measurable down to a second or so by the 'single event' measurement approach. This has already produced the discovery of startling dissociations in the time domain between posterior and anterior cortical sites in working memory tasks [2].

Many cognitive studies have been performed using PET; there are now as many using fMRI, some duplicating the PET measurements. These results show very clear localisation of function and the involvement of networks of cortical and subcortical sites in normal functioning of the brain during the solution of tasks. At the same time there has been considerable improvement in our understanding of brain activity in various mental diseases, such as schizophrenia, Altzheimer's and Parkinson's diseases. There have also been studies of patients with brain damage, to discover how the perturbed brain can still solve tasks, albeit slowly and inefficiently in many cases.

The magnetic field around the head due to neural activity, although very low, is measurable by sensitive devices, such as SQUIDs (superconducting quantum interference devices). Starting from single coils to measure the magnetic field at a very coarse level, MEG measurements are now being made with sophisticated whole-head devices using 148 [3] or even 250 measuring coils [4]. Such systems lead to ever greater spatial sensitivity, although they have a decided number of problems before they can be fully exploited. In particular it is first necessary to solve the inverse problem, that of uncovering the underlying current sources producing the magnetic field. This is non-trivial, and has caused MEG not to be as far advanced in brain imaging as PET and fMRI systems. However that situation is now changing. There is good reason to bring MEG up to the same standard of data-read-out simplicity as PET and fMRI since, although it does not have the same spatial sensitivity as the other two it has far better temporal sensitivity - down to a millisecond. Thus MEG fills in the temporal gap on the knowledge gained by PET and fMRI. This is also done by EEG, which is being consistently used by numbers of groups in partnership with PET or fMRI so as to determine the detailed time course of activation of known sites already implicated in a task by the other machines [5].

3. DATA ANALYSIS

3.1 STATISTICAL PARAMETER MAPS (SPMs)

The data arising from a given experiment consists of a set of data points - a time series collected during an experiment - for a given position in the head (a pixel). This is reasonably immediate for PET and fMRI, although there must be careful preprocessing performed in order to remove movement artefacts and to relate the site being measured to its co-ordinates in the head according to some standard atlas. All the machines now use a static MRI measurement of the brain of a subject as a template, to which the data being measured are referred.

The data at a given pixel is a set of activation levels. These have been obtained from a number of measurements taken under a set of known conditions. For example, I am involved in studying the motion after-effect (MAE) by fMRI [6]. This occurs in a subject due to adaptation to movement in one direction, and arises, for example, if the subject looks at a waterfall for a period of about 20 or so seconds and then turn their gaze to the side. The static rock face then seems to move upwards for about 10 seconds afterwards. Our measurements were taken using an 'on-off' paradigm, with a set of moving bars being observed by a subject during 10 measurements (each lasting 3 seconds) , then 10 with static bars, then 10 with the bars moving up and down, then another 10 with static bars. The MAE occurs at the end of a period of movement in one direction only, so the purpose of the study was to determine the change of BOLD signal after the one-way movement, in comparison to the two-way movement. Regions were searched for with a suitably high correlation of their activation with the 'box-car' function, equal to +1 during movement and just afterwards and -1 during other static periods and the up-and-down movement. This correlation at each pixel in the head leads to the statistical parameter map of the heading of this sub-section. Significance levels can then be attached to the value at any one point in terms of the variance of the signal during that period. This leads to the standard t-test and to maps of t- or z-parameters throughout the brain. More sophisticated analysis can then be performed to detect regions of interest (a number of adjacent pixels with significant z-scores) and their significance. There are now a number of software packages available to perform such analysis, and they have been recently been compared [7]. Fast data analysis techniques are now available so that on-line results can be obtained and thereby allow for optimisation of paradigms being employed [8].

3.2 THE INVERSE PROBLEM

There is a hard inverse problem - to determine the underlying current distribution causing the observed field strengths - for both EEG and MEG. That for the former is more difficult due to the conduction currents that 'wash out' the localisation of deep sources. This does not occur for MEG, but there is still the problem that certain currents, such as radial ones in a purely spherical head, are totally 'silent', leading to no external magnetic field. Modulo this problem, the standard approach to uncovering the underlying neural generators has been to assume that there is a limited set of current dipoles whose parameters (orientation, strength and position) can be varied to optimise the mean square reconstruction error (MSE) of the measured data. Such approaches are limited, especially when fast temporal effects are being investigated. More recently magnetic field tomography (MFT) has been developed to give a distributed source representation of the measurements [9]. This uses the idea of a lead field, $\phi_m(r)$, which is the value of the measurement at the m'th coil due to a unit current source at the position **r** in the brain. If **j(r)** is the current distribution in the brain then the measurement condition is

$$d_m = \int \phi_m(\mathbf{r}).\mathbf{j}(\mathbf{r})\, d\mathbf{r} \qquad (1)$$

Then a 'lead field' expansion of the unit vector **j^(r)** of source current is assumed:

$$\mathbf{j}\hat{}(\mathbf{r}) = \sum_m A_m\phi_m(\mathbf{r})\, w_p(\mathbf{r})\, ||\mathbf{j}(\mathbf{r})||^p \qquad (2)$$

where p is not specified, $||\mathbf{j}(\mathbf{r})||$ is the Euclidean length of the source current at **r** and the weight function $w_p(\mathbf{r})$ has also to be determined. Solving (1) and (2) leads to the value for the unknown coefficients in the lead field expansion (1)

$$A = (L(||\mathbf{j}||^{p+1})^{-1}\, d \qquad (3)$$

where

$$L_{mn}(||\mathbf{j}||^{p+1}) = \int (\phi_m(\mathbf{r}).\phi_n(\mathbf{r}))\, ||\mathbf{j}(\mathbf{r})||^{p+1}\, w_p(\mathbf{r})d\mathbf{r} \qquad (4)$$

The condition that the unit current (2) has unit length then leads to the infinite system of equations

$$1 = j(r_0)^{2p}(d^T(L(||\mathbf{j}||^{p+1})^{-1}M(r_0)\, L(||\mathbf{j}||^{p+1})^{-1}d) \qquad (5)$$

where j is the length of **j** and

$$M(r) = (\phi_m(\mathbf{r}).\phi_n(\mathbf{r}))\, w_p^2(\mathbf{r}) \qquad (6)$$

It is then possible to reduce the system of equations (5), (6) to a finite set, as shown in the following lemma.

Lemma

The system of equations (5) can be reduced to the NxN set of non-linear equations for the matrix Δ (where N is the number of sensors) as

$$\Delta_{mn} = \int(d^T\Delta^{-1}M(\mathbf{r})^{-1}\Delta^{-1}d)^{-1/2p}(\phi_m(\mathbf{r}).\phi_n(\mathbf{r}))\, d\mathbf{r} \qquad (7)$$

where j(**r**) may be reconstructed from a matrix solution Δ of (7) as

$$j(\mathbf{r}) = (d^T\Delta^{-1}M(\mathbf{r})^{-1}\Delta^{-1}d)^{-1/2p} \qquad (8)$$

provided $p \neq 0$.

Proof. If the matrix Δ is defined as

$$\Delta_{mn} = L_{mn}(j^{p+1}) = \int j(\mathbf{r})^{p+1}\, (\phi_m(\mathbf{r}).\phi_n(\mathbf{r}))\, d\mathbf{r} \qquad (9)$$

then equation (7) immediately gives (8), whilst equation (7) is also immediate on replacing j(**r**)| in the integrand on the right hand side of (9) by the value just obtained from (8).The lemma is proved.

The lemma shows that there is considerable structure in the system of equations (5) and (6) that can be explored along the above lines. However the lemma and resulting approaches only apply for the cases $p \neq 0$. The value p=0 turns out to be the most interesting one since it is the most stable under perturbations of the measurement data [10], as compared to the other cases. Thus MFT proper is restricted to this case of p=0, although the values of p near zero give valuable information about putative source distributions in the brain. The equations (5) in this case are used in the form

$$||\mathbf{j}(\mathbf{r_0})||^2 = ||\mathbf{j}(\mathbf{r_0})||^2\, (d^T(L(||\mathbf{j}||)^{-1}M(\mathbf{r_0})\, L(||\mathbf{j}||)^{-1}d) \qquad (10)$$

so as to be iterated from the right to the left-hand side of (10). The resulting solutions are very stable, although a regularisation parameter must also be introduced to prevent singularity arising from dependence between rows or columns in the matrix $L(||\mathbf{j}||)$.

The use of MFT and similar systems is now becoming more commonplace in MEG, so that high-quality data are now becoming available for an increasing number of cognitive tasks similar to those from fMRI and PET but with far greater temporal sensitivity.

3.3 STRUCTURAL MODELLING

Initially the results of PET and fMRI studies have uncovered a set of active brain sites involved in a given task. This is usually termed a 'network', although there is no evidence from the given data that a network is involved but only an isolated set of regions. It is possible to evaluate the correlation coefficients between these areas, either across subjects (as in PET) or for a given subject (in fMRI). There is great interest in using these correlation coefficients to determine the strength of interactions between the different active areas, and so uncover the network involved. Such a method involves what is called 'structural modelling', in which a linear relation between active areas is assumed and the path strengths (the linear coefficents in the relation) are determined from the correlation matrix.

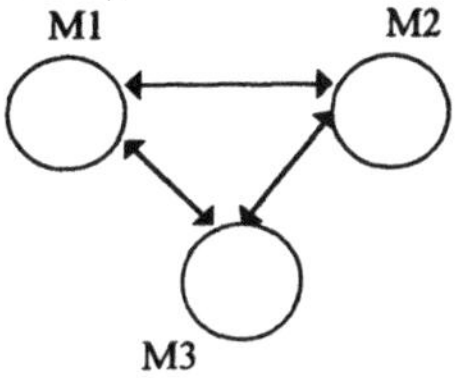

Figure 1. A set of three interacting modules in the brain, as a representative of a simple structural model. The task of structural modelling is to determine the path strengths with which each module effects the others in terms of the cross-correlation matrix between the activities of the modules.

Corresponding activities z_i (i =1,2,3) of the modules of figure 1 satisfy a set of linear equations

$$z_i = \Sigma\, a_{ij}\, z_j + \eta_i \qquad (11)$$

where the variables η_I are assumed to be independent random noise variables. It is then possible to calculate the coefficients a_{ij} from the correlation coefficients C(i,j) between the variables z. This can be extended to comparing different models by a chi-squared test so as to allow for model significance testing to be achieved.

An important question is as to how to bridge the gap between the brain imaging data and the underlying neural network activity. In particular the interpretation of the structural model parameters will then become clearer. One is by the mean field approximation, so that the particular label of a neuron in a given module is averaged over. The averaged equations for the membrane potentials u(i ,t) for the mean neuron in the i'th module at time t then results as:

$$\tau\, du(i,t)/dt = -\, u(i,t) + \sum_j c(i,j)\, f[u(j,\, t-t(i,j))] \qquad (12)$$

where c(i ,j) is the mean connection strength between the modules i and j and t(i ,j) the associated time delay . In the limit of $\tau = 0$ and for linearly responding neurons with no time delay there results the equations:

$$u(i,t) = \sum_j C(i,j)\, u(j,t) \qquad (13)$$

which are the structural equations of the form of equation (11) now being used to analyse the data of PET and fMRI. The path strengths are thus to be interpreted as the average connection weights between the modules. Moreover the path strengths can be carried across instruments, so as to be able to build back up to the original neural networks. This involves also inserting the relevant time delays as well as the connection strengths to relate to MEG data.

4. STATIC ACTIVATION STUDY RESULTS

There are many psychological paradigms used to investigate cognition, and numbers of these have been used in conjunction with PET or fMRI machines. These paradigms overlap in subtle ways so that it is difficult at times to 'see the wood for the trees'. To bring in some order we will simplify by considering a set of categories of cognitive tasks. We do that initially along lines suggested by Cabeza and Nyberg [11], who decomposed cognitive tasks into the categories of:

- attention (selective/sustained)
- perception (of object/face/space/top-down)
- language (word listening/word reading/word production)
- working memory (phonological loop/visuospatial sketchpad)
- memory (semantic memory encoding & retrieval/episodic memory encoding & retrieval)
- priming
- procedural memory (conditioning/skill learning)

So far the data indicate that there are sets of modules involved in the various cognitive tasks. Can we uncover from them any underlying functionality of each of the areas concerned? The answer is a partial 'yes'. The initial and final low-level stages of the processing appear more transparent to analysis than those involved with later and higher level processing. Also more study has been devoted to primary processing areas. Yet even at the lowest entry level the problem of detailed functionality of different regions is still complex, with about 30 areas involved in vision alone, and another 7 or 8 concerned with audition. Similar complexity is being discerned in motor response, with the primary motor area being found to divide into at least two separate subcomponents. The details of these many areas are slowly being unravelled.

5. THE MOTION AFTER-EFFECT (MAE)

This effect was already introduced in section 3.1. We used fMRI for the study, as compared to PET, since it allowed determination of the timing of the emergence and continuation of activity time locked to the motion-after effect period [6]. The possibility of observing such time-courses depends crucially on using a suitable paradigm to enable the timing to be specified. We used a moving stimulus (in our case a set of moving bars) which ceased their motion at a certain time so that we had an offset point from which to time any changes of activity. It was also necessary to compare with activations brought about by exposure of the subject to a control condition, such as the bars moving up and down. For that stimulus there would have been no after-effect. This was the basis of the method used in [12] (although with a different stimulus composed of moving and static rings), and was used more extensively in our study. We searched for activations, especially in prefrontal sites, which were timed exactly with the offset of either bars moving in one direction (we only used bars moving down in this study), or up and down successively. Any region which had activation which commenced as the stimulus movement ceased at the end of the motion down period, and which then decayed over about the expected time for the MAE experience, was a candidate for the network of areas subserving the MAE experience itself. The signal after the one-way movement, as compared to that in the up and -down case, gave the net MAE effect. That characteristic was the main signal for which we searched in the fMRI data.

There were also other characteristics of signals expected from regions involved in the overall processing. Thus we expected to see sites involved in analysis of the static bars during the period just after the downward motion. This period itself can be split into one during which the MAE is being experienced and a period in which there are only static bars, together with the fixation cross, being observed and experienced. In order to achieve the highest attention during the whole period of exposure of the subject we did not tell them not to expect to experience any MAE after the up-and-down motion period So there was also the putative MAE period after the up-and-down motion period. We will also considered those areas which were especially active during one or more of downward MAE, putative up-and-down MAE and at other times when the bars were static as well as during either motion period. It turned out, on further questioning, that different subjects used different strategies.

Our main findings [13] were that there were some remarkable time courses in both posterior and prefrontal cortical areas which differed significantly across these periods and across the different areas. Some sites (such as the frontal ones in BA 40, 44, 47 or the cingulate gyrus) were only active during either of the possible MAE periods (for a few seconds after the cessation of either the movement down of the bars or that in both directions). Other time courses (also in BA 44 or 47) were only or mainly active during downward-caused MAE. Yet others (such as in MT/V5) were active both during either motion period and during the downward MAE. These results indicate that there are different networks involved in different stages of the total experience. Some areas have different components involved in different stages and very likely in different networks.

The overall picture uncovered of the modus operandi of the brain areas involved in processing the MAE is one of different networks of sites involved in different tasks. These are:

a) responding to the static or to the moving stimuli,

b) checking for the occurrence of MAE,

c) creating the experience of MAE itself.

The networks involved in these various tasks are found to be overlapping to a certain extent. Thus checking MAE and creating the experience both involve BA44, BA40, cingulate gyrus and BA46/47/10. This was supported by calculation of the correlation matrix of activities between the different sites; the correlation values were large (>0.5) for the separate anterior and posterior nets separately with only one or two key areas joining the two networks together, and then only with correlation coefficients at about 0.5. The overall picture of this set of networks is shown in figure 2. This indicates that there are two main networks which

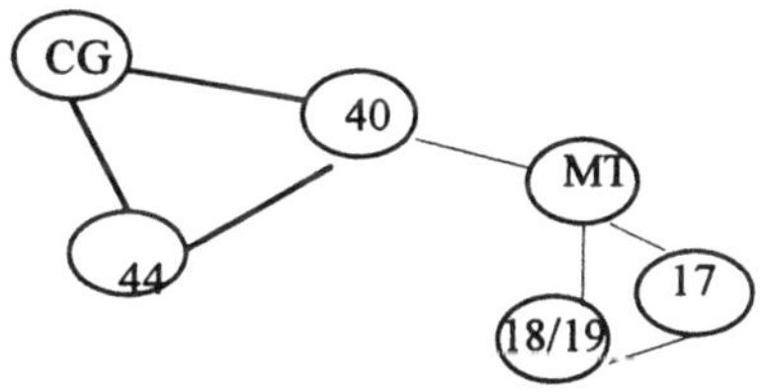

Figure 2. The two networks: BA 40, 44 and cingulate gyrus (CG) and BA 18/19, MT and 17, with the path strengths greater than 0.5 shown by connecting lines. MT and BA 40 are the two key areas which carry information from one network to the other.

communicate to each other via MT and BA 40.

Which of these is involved in the creation of awareness of the MAE experience itself (task (c) in our above list)? Up until now MT was regarded as the site of such experience. Our data indicate that another candidate for the creation of this experience is also BA 40. Use of independent component analysis [14] singles out two separate signals, one especially involved with MT as an overall motion detector, and the other contained mainly in the anterior sites BA 44/40/47 (not shown explicitly in the figure 2 but part of the anterior network) and CG [15]. The second independent component is exactly timed to the MAE signal. Thus it would appear as if the experience of the MAE is based more frontally than posteriorly, although there is a part of the MAE signal detectable in MT (as the first experimental results of [12] on this showed convincingly). Thus consciousness is created in a network of sites, although not all of cortex is directly used in such activation. Early cortical processing, such as in V1, does not have a distinctive MAE signal, so is not involved (as it is not in other early processing, such as orientation sensitivity [16]).

6. THE THREE-STAGE MODEL OF CONSCIOUSNESS

Thus we arrive at the three stage model of consciousness creation [17] of figure 3, in which a further third stage is added for attentional processing (which may be independent of consciousness):

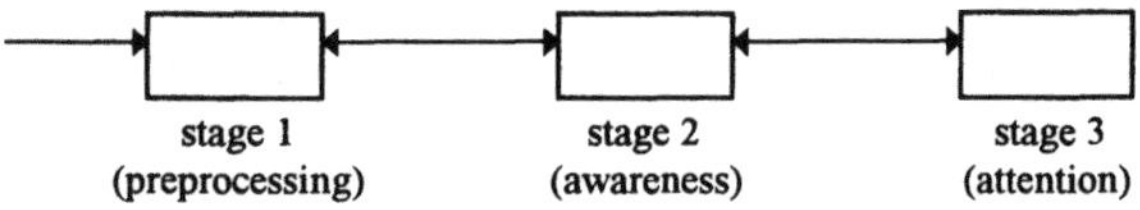

Figure 3. The 3 stages of the emergence of awareness. Stage 1 is only involved with preprocessing, as in early visual or auditory cortex. In stage 2 simple awareness of the environment emerges, whilst in stage 3 attentional processes allow memory of the conscious experience to be built as well as filter and control input and later processing.

The relation between the three stages of figure 3 and the two networks of figure 2 is still to be worked out. Further evidence was presented for the three stage model of figure 3 in [17] as applied to awareness and attention of auditory stimuli. Subjects were exposed to sequences of syllables and had to listen to them under the three conditions of a) inattention, when they were required to detect flickering of visual inputs, b) awareness, when they listened to the syllables with no other distractor but were not required to process them strongly, c) attention, when they had to count the number of times the syllable /ta/ was spoken. In proceeding from condition a) to c), with increasing attentional load, increasing numbers of cortical areas became active as detected by fMRI. These areas were in expected regions, with those for inattention involving primary auditory areas, those for awareness sited more posteriorly in inferotemporal cortex (mainly left) and finally the attentional sites were predominantly in frontal cortex. Nor were there strong changes of activity in the old areas still being used in the higher attentional load cases as compared to the lower attentional ones. In all the sets of areas observed under the conditions a), b) and c) can be identified with the modules of stages 1, 2 and 3 respectively of the three-stage model of figure 3.

The three-stage model has a further extension, supported by considerable psychological and brain imaging data that helps to fill in some of the details as to how awareness arises in the first instance in stage 2 modules. This involves the inclusion in the stage 2 modules of cortical areas specialised by the long duration of their neural activity. These are the 'slave' working memory sites proposed as part of the model of working memory of Baddeley and Hitch [18]. These sites have now been observed directly by brain imaging techniques [19]. It has also been suggested [20] that the cortical sheet can be approximated as a continuous sheet and then neural field models can be considered which predict the existence of 'bubbles' of continued activity. The more precise characteristics of the neural systems needed to create phenomenological awareness were explored in [20]; they seem to be in agreement with the neuroanatomical properties of the slave working memory sites just mentioned.

There is also increasing understanding of the source of attentional activation in the stage 3 modules. There has been observed even more extended duration of activity in frontal areas than that in the posterior slave sites. The cause of this activity has been suggested as arising from the functioning of 'loops' of activity flowing through the cortex-basal ganglia-thalamus-cortex loops [21], for which there is strong neuroanatomical support. The resulting so-called ACTION network can be seen to provide a platform for explanation of the numerous functions performed by the frontal lobes, such as the storing of goals, inhibition of prepotent responses, planning, thinking, control of social responses [22]. We thus extend the global circuitry of figure 2 to consist of the following:

stage 1 modules: preprocessing sites (up to semantic level) in the posterior cortex;

stage 2 modules: buffer 'working memory' sites, such as the phonological store, the visuospatial sketchpad, the body matrix, and so on;

stage 3: a set of coupled ACTION nets in the frontal cortex, including their associated basal ganglia and thalamic sites.

We should also not neglect the subcortical (thalamic and other nuclei) support systems for both the stage 1 and stage 2 modules. They also play their important roles to support the complete functioning of the preprocessing and awareness stages.

The possibilities of dissocation between activities in these various sites is clearly considerable, caused by too heavy a load, damage to various of the sites or drug and other biochemical interferences. This is an indication of the complexity of consciousness itself, so that it is thereby not easy to give a definition of consciousness. It is composed of a number of components of which one division can be into the parts:

- posterior or passive,
- anterior or active,
- self,
- emotional.

Each of these major subdivisions can themselves be subdivided into further components, as seen from analysis of the effects of brain defects on experience as well as from more detailed brain imaging studies.

That there is a unity of the totality of consciousness, as we experience it in our normal waking lives, is a miracle, given the above divisibility. However there may be global control circuits able to give unity to what would otherwise be a confusing chaos of inputs in an inner activations. This is considered elsewhere [1].

6. DISCUSSION

We have considered various approaches to analysing results on brain activity during conscious experience as now being probed by brain imaging machines (PET, fMRI, EEG and MEG). The paper started by briefly describing brain imaging and some aspects of the associated data analysis. I then went on to describe experimental results relevant to the search for consciousness in the brain. In particular results obtained from global brain activity observed by fMRI during the Motion After-Effect were used to lead into the three-stage model of brain activity and consciousness. This model divides cortical (and associated sub-cortical) regions into those involved only with preprocessing (up to semantic level), those creating awareness at the lowest level and those involved with attentional processing and the sense of self. This subdivision was also supported by further fMRI data, and is also strongly supported by data coming from patients suffering brain damage of a variety of sorts.

The three-stage model is only the beginning stage of the process of constructing more complex models allowing analysis of more complex activities involved in perceiving and reacting in numerous situations. Thus the development of object percepts and of episodic memory is needed to be modelled in order to allow the inner content of consciousness to be filled in, as well as to allow more detailed predictions to be made of brain activities expected to be observed during the solution of a range of tasks. Such a program has already been begun, and must go hand in hand with that of brain imaging itself in order to make sense of the wealth of such imaging data in respect of our own miraculous inner experience of consciousness.

REFERENCES

[1] Taylor JG The Race for Consciousness, MIT Press, Cambridge, MA, 1998.

[2] Ungerleider LG, Courtney SM and Haxby JVA. Neural system for human visual working memory. Proceedings of the National Academy of Sciences (USA) 1997; 95: 883-890.

[3] Bti Ltd, San Diego, CA.

[4] NEC, private communication from AA. Ioannides.

[5] Posner M and Raichle ME, Images of Mind, Freeman and Co, San Francisco, 1994.

[6] Schmitz N, Taylor JG, Shah NJ, Ziemons K, Gruber O, Grosse-Ruyken ML and Mueller-Gaertner H-W. The Search for Awareness by the Motion After-Effect. Proceedings of the Conference on Human Brain Mapping '98, NeuroImage.

[7] Gold S, Christian B, Arndt S, Zeien G, Cizadio T, Johnson DL, Flaum M and Andreason NC. Functional MRI Statistical Software Packages: A Comparative Analysis. Human Brain Mapping 1997; 6: 73-84.

[8] D Gembris, S Posse, JG Taylor, S Schor et al (1998) Methodology of fast Correlation Analysis for Real-Time fMRI Experiments, submitted.

[9] Ioannides AA (1995) in Quantitative & Topological EEG and MEG Analysis, Jena: Druckhaus-Mayer GmbH

[10] Taylor JG, Ioannides AA, Mueller-Gaertner H-W (1998) Mathematical Analysis of Magnetic Field Tomography, Human Brain Mapping Conference '98, Abstract.

[11] Cabeza R & Nyburg L (1997) Imaging Cognition. J Cog Neuroscience 9, 1-26

[12] Tootell RB, Reppas JB, Dale AM, Look RB, Sereno MI, Malach R, Brady TJ and Rosen BR, Visual motion aftereffect in human cortical area MT revealed by functional magnetic resonance imaging, Nature, 1995, 375: 139-141.

[13] Taylor JG, Schmitz N, Shah NJ, Ziemons K, Gruber O, Grosse-Ruyken M-L and Mueller-Gaertner H-W, The Network of Brain Areas Involved in the Motion After-Effect, in preparation.

[14] Karhunen J, Oja E, Wang L, Vigario R and Joutsenalo J, A class of neural networks for independent component anlaysis, IEEE Transactions on Neural Networks, 1997, 8(3)

[15] Taylor JG, Schmitz N, Fellenz W, in preparation.

[16] He S, Cavanagh P and Intrilligator J, Attentional resultion and the locus of visual awareness, Nature , 1996, 383: 334-337.

[17] Taylor JG. Jaencke L, The Three Stage Model for Awareness: Formulation and Experimental Support, NeuroReport, 1998 (in press).

[18] Baddeley A, Working Memory, Oxford University Press, Oxford, 1986.

[19] Smith EE, Jonides J, Marshuetz C & Koeppe RA (1998) Components of verbal working memory: Evidence from neuroimaging, Proc Natl Acad Sci USA 95, 876-882

[20] Taylor JG, Cortical Activity and the Explanatory Gap, Consciousness and Cognition, 1998, (in press).

[21] Taylor JG (1995) Modelling the Mind by PSYCHE, Proceedings International Conference on Artifical Neural Networks '95, ed F Soulie and P Gallinari, Paris: EC2 & Co.

[22] Bapi R, Bugmann G, Levine D & Taylor JG (1997) Analysing the Executive Function of the Prefrontal System: Towards a Network Theory. Behaviour and Brain Sciences (submitted)

PATTERN CLASSIFICATION: FUSION OF INFORMATION

J Kittler,
Centre for Vision, Speech and Signal Processing
School of Electronic Engineering, Information Technology and Mathematics
University of Surrey, Guildford GU2 5XH, United Kingdom
E-mail: J.Kittler@ee.surrey.ac.uk

ABSTRACT

Improvements in the performance of pattern recognition systems can be brought about by fusing as many sources of information as possible. These include multiple cues, multiple opinions of experts, prior contextual knowledge and measurement context. Tools for fusing such diverse sources of information are reviewed. In particular, we show that the use of multiple cues can be formulated as a problem of fusing the opinions of multiple experts employing distinct representations. This contrasts with the methods aimed at improving estimates of decision function values, which can be viewed as fusion of opinions of experts using identical representations. Spatial and temporal context can be incorporated by taking into account measurements on neighbouring objects and modelling the distributions over their relations. This is shown to involve two basic components: a measurement process model and a prior world knowledge model. Depending on formulation, contextual decision making leads either to compound classification or to estimation of Maximum Aposteriori Probability of joint labelling [1].

1 INTRODUCTION

Over the years, an extensive effort has been invested in the development of the methodology for the design of pattern classifiers using statistical, structural and neural network approaches. Although considerable advances can be claimed, it has become transparent that any significant improvements in the performance of pattern recognition systems can be brought about only by fusing other sources information pertinent to each recognition task. The possible sources of additional information include multiple cues, multiple opinions of experts, prior knowledge and context. In this paper the main tools for fusing such diverse sources of information are reviewed. They include schemes for fusing multiple cues, strategies for fusing multiple experts, and techniques for combining measurement and contextual information. The first two categories are discussed in the next section under the heading classifier combination. Contextual decision making methods are the subject of Section 3. The paper concludes with a brief summary in Section 4.

2 CLASSIFIER COMBINATION

2.1 INTRODUCTION

The goal of multiple expert fusion is to improve the accuracy of pattern classification. Instead of relying on a single decision making scheme, several designs (experts) are used for decision making. By combining the opinions of the individual experts, a consensus decision is

[1]This work was supported by the Engineering and Physical Sciences Research Council Grant GR/J89255.

derived. Various classifier combination schemes have been devised and it has been experimentally demonstrated that some of them consistently outperform a single best classifier.

An interesting issue in the research concerning classifier ensembles is the way they are combined. For a recent review of the literature see Kittler [8, 31, 32]. From the point of view of their analysis, there are basically two classifier combination scenarios. In the first scenario, all the classifiers use the same representation of the input pattern. In this case each classifier, for a given input pattern, can be considered to produce an estimate of the same aposteriori class probability.

In the second scenario each classifier uses its own representation of the input pattern. In other words, the measurements extracted from the pattern are unique to each classifier. An important application of combining classifiers in this scenario is the possibility to integrate physically different types of measurements / features. In this case it is no longer possible to consider the computed aposteriori probabilities to be estimates of the same functional value, as the classification systems operate in different measurement spaces.

In the following sections the theoretical framework for classifier combination approaches for these two scenarios will be overviewed.

2.2 DISTINCT REPRESENTATIONS

It has been observed that classifier combination is particularly effective if the individual classifiers employ different features (see Xu [7], Ho [5]). Consider a pattern recognition problem where pattern Z is to be assigned to one of the m possible classes $\{\omega_1, ..., \omega_m\}$. Let us assume that we have R classifiers each representing the given pattern by a distinct measurement vector. Denote the measurement vector used by the i-th classifier by $\mathbf{x}_i$. In the measurement space each class ω_k is modelled by the probability density function $p(\mathbf{x}_i|\omega_k)$ and its a priori probability of occurrence is denoted $P(\omega_k)$. We shall consider the models to be mutually exclusive which means that only one model can be associated with each pattern.

Now according to the Bayesian theory, given measurements $\mathbf{x}_i, i = 1, ..., R$, the pattern, Z, should be assigned to class ω_j, i.e. its label θ should assume value $\theta = \omega_j$, provided the aposteriori probability of that interpretation is maximum, i.e.

$$assign \qquad \theta \rightarrow \omega_j \qquad if$$

$$P(\theta = \omega_j|\mathbf{x}_1, ..., \mathbf{x}_R) = \max_k P(\theta = \omega_k|\mathbf{x}_1, ..., \mathbf{x}_R) \tag{1}$$

Assuming the measurement vectors are conditionally statistically independent the decision rule in (1) can be shown to simplify to

$$assign \qquad \theta \rightarrow \omega_j \qquad if$$

$$P^{-(R-1)}(\omega_j) \prod_{i=1}^{R} P(\theta = \omega_j|\mathbf{x}_i)p(\mathbf{x}_i) = \max_{k=1}^{m} P^{-(R-1)}(\omega_k) \prod_{i=1}^{R} P(\theta = \omega_k|\mathbf{x}_i)p(\mathbf{x}_i) \tag{2}$$

where $p(\mathbf{x}_i)$ is the unconditional probability density at measurement $\mathbf{x}_i$. The decision rule (2) quantifies the likelihood of a hypothesis by combining the aposteriori probabilities $P(\theta = \omega_k|\mathbf{x}_i)$ generated by the individual classifiers by means of a product rule. It is effectively a severe rule of fusing the classifier outputs as it is sufficient for a single recognition engine to inhibit a particular interpretation by outputting a close to zero probability for it. It has been shown in Kittler [8] that under certain assumptions this severe rule can be developed into a benevolent information fusion rule which has the form of a sum. Benevolent fusion rules are less affected by one particular expert than severe rules. Thus even if the soft decision outputs of a few experts for a particular hypothesis are close to zero, the hypothesis may be accepted provided it receives a sufficient support from all the other experts. Denoting the weights associated with the respective experts by $w(\mathbf{x}_i)$, the benevolent decision rule can be expressed as [8]

$$assign \qquad \theta \rightarrow \omega_j \qquad if$$

$$(1-R)P(\omega_j) + \sum_{i=1}^{R} w(\mathbf{x}_i)P(\omega_j|\mathbf{x}_i) = \max_{k=1}^{m}[(1-R)P(\omega_k) + \sum_{i=1}^{R} w(\mathbf{x}_i)P(\omega_k|\mathbf{x}_i)] \qquad (3)$$

The main practical difficulty with the weighted average classifier combiner as specified in (3) is that not all classifiers will have the inner capability to output such information. For instance, it would not be provided by a multilayer perceptron and many other classification methods. However, one can limit one's objectives somewhat and identify the weights $w(\mathbf{x}_i) = w_i$ which will reflect the relative confidence in the classifiers in expectation. These can easily be found by an exhaustive search through the weight space.

It can readily be shown that the decision rules (2) and (3) simplify to the commonly used combination strategies such as *Product rule, Sum rule, Min rule, Max rule, Majority vote.*

2.3 IDENTICAL REPRESENTATIONS

In many situations we wish to combine the results of multiple classifiers which use an identical representation for the input pattern $\mathbf{x}$. A typical example of this situation is a battery of k-NN classifiers which employ different numbers of nearest neighbours to reach a decision. Alternatively, neural network classifiers trained with different initialisations or different training sets (Wolpert (1992),Cao et al (1995)) also fall into this category. The combination of ensembles of neural networks has been studied in Hashem and Schmeiser (1995), Cho and Kim (1995) and Hansen and Salamon (1990).

By means of classifier combination one is able to obtain a better estimate of the aposteriori class probabilities and in consequence a reduced classification error. A typical estimator is the averaging estimator

$$\dot{P}(\omega_i|\mathbf{x}) = \frac{1}{N}\sum_{j=1}^{N} \hat{P}_j(\omega_i|\mathbf{x}) \qquad (4)$$

where $\hat{P}_j(\omega_i|\mathbf{x})$ is the aposteriori class probability estimate given pattern $\mathbf{x}$, delivered by the $j-th$ estimator and $\dot{P}(\omega_i|\mathbf{x})$ is the combined estimate based on N observations.

The weighted estimator

$$\dot{P}(\omega_i|\mathbf{x}) = \sum_{j=1}^{N} w_{ij}(\mathbf{x})\hat{P}_j(\omega_i|\mathbf{x}) \qquad (5)$$

represents a general case with the weights $w_{ij}(\mathbf{x})$ satisfying $\sum_{j=1}^{N} w_{ij}(\mathbf{x}) = 1$.

Note that the estimator (5) is defined as a linear combination of the individual estimates. This immediately suggests that it may be possible to obtain even a better combined estimate of the class aposteriori probabilities by means of a nonlinear combination function as

$$\dot{P}(\omega_i|\mathbf{x}) = F(\hat{P}_1(\omega_i|\mathbf{x}), ..., \hat{P}_N(\omega_i|\mathbf{x})) \qquad (6)$$

In fact estimators which aim to enhance their resilience to outliers by adopting a rank order statistic such as the median, i.e. $\dot{P}(\omega_i|\mathbf{x}) = med_{j=1}^{N}\hat{P}_j(\omega_i|\mathbf{x})$ fall into this category. Such nonlinear estimators do not require any additional training. However, if sufficient additional training data is available, a suitable nonlinear function may be found by means of general function approximation (i.e. neural network methodology) or by other design alternatives. The effective local variance of the resulting estimator could be estimated from the input variances by function linearisation techniques.

2.3 CONCLUSIONS

The problem of classifier combination was considered in the context of the two main fusion scenarios: fusion of opinions based on identical and on distinct representations. We showed that in both cases (distinct and shared representations), the expert fusion involved the computation of a linear or nonlinear function of the aposteriori class probabilities estimated by the individual experts. Classifier combination could therefore be viewed in a unified way as a multistage classification process whereby the aposteriori class probabilities generated by the individual classifiers are considered as features for a second stage classification scheme.

3 FUSION OF CONTEXTUAL INFORMATION

3.1 INTRODUCTION

Perhaps the most dramatic developments in object classification have recently been witnessed on the front of contextual methods. The conventional techniques base the decision about class membership of an object simply on the information contained in the measurements. However, objects by definition do not exist in isolation. Thus the distinguishing feature of object labelling problems in machine perception is that we deal with a large network of objects which interact with each other. The a priori world knowledge or context can be used to help to disambiguate decisions based simply on noisy features of individual objects. For instance in text recognition individual characters are an integral part of larger objects such as words or sentences formed by character groups. Word dictionary and rules of grammar dictate which combinations of characters and implicitly which individual characters are possible. In contextual labelling we effectively associate with each object a decision making process which attempts to combine evidence from observations made on the object together with the contextual information conveyed by the other objects in the network to deduce which label assignment is most appropriate from the point of view of the available measurement information, local constraints and global labelling consistency.

The following subsections concentrate on cooperative decision making processes for pattern interpretation. First, two basic formulations of the problem of labelling networks of objects are introduced in Section 3.2. Examples of the various methods based on these two formulations are given in Section 3.3.

2.1 PROBLEM FORMULATION

Let us consider a set of measurement vectors $\mathbf{x}_j$, representing respectively objects $a_j, j = 1, ..., N$ arranged in a network with a particular neighbourhood system.

We wish to assign each object a_j a label θ_j. Following the conventional Bayesian approach object a_i would be assigned to class ω_r based on the information conveyed by measurement vectors $\mathbf{x}_i$ according to the minimum error decision rule [11]. In contrast here we wish to decide about label θ_i using not only the information contained in unary relation measurements relating to object a_i but also any context conveyed by the network. In other words we wish to utilise also the binary relation measurements, i.e. the full measurement vector $\mathbf{x}_i$ plus all the information about the other objects in the network contained in $\mathbf{x}_j$, $\forall j \neq i$. This is a general statement of the problem but in order to develop contextual labelling schemes our formulation will have to be somewhat more precise.

The first important issue to settle is whether we wish to aim at *object centred* or *message centred* interpretation. In object centred interpretation the emphasis is on one node at a time. Contextual information is used to reduce the ambiguity of labelling a single object. Note that object centred interpretation does not guarantee that the global interpretation makes sense. For example, individually most likely object categories in a character recognition problem will not necessarily combine into valid words. The use of context merely reduces the chance of the global labelling being inconsistent.

In contrast, message centred interpretation is concerned with getting the message conveyed by sensory data right. In our text recognition problem the main objective of message centred labelling would be to label characters so that each line of text gives a sequence of valid words.

The choice between object centred and message centred interpretation will depend in the first instance on the application in hand. For example, if we search for a specified object in a network without requiring to understand the entire content of the network, object centred interpretation might be most appropriate. On the other hand, if global understanding of sensory data is at stake, the labelling task should be posed as a message centred interpretation problem.

Generally speaking, in message centred interpretation we search for a joint labelling $\theta_1 = \omega_{\theta_1}, \theta_2 = \omega_{\theta_2}, \ldots\ldots, \theta_N = \omega_{\theta_N}$ which explains observations $\mathbf{x}_1, \mathbf{x}_2, \ldots\ldots, \mathbf{x}_N$ made on the objects in the network. The most appropriate measure of fit between data and interpretation (but by no means the only one) is the aposteriori probability $P(\theta_1 = \omega_{\theta_1}, \ldots, \theta_N = \omega_{\theta_N} | \mathbf{x}_1, \ldots\ldots, \mathbf{x}_N)$. For the sake of brevity we shall denote this probability function as $P(\theta_1, \ldots, \theta_N | \mathbf{x}_1, \mathbf{x}_2, \ldots, \mathbf{x}_N)$ whenever this short hand notation does not compromise the clarity of exposition. The Bayesian approach of maximising aposteriori probability (MAP) of joint labelling which is referred to in the literature as MAP estimation amounts to the following decision rule:

$$assign \qquad \theta_1 \to \omega_{\theta_1}, \ldots, \theta_N \to \omega_{\theta_N} \qquad if$$

$$P(\theta_1 = \omega_{\theta_1}, \ldots, \theta_N = \omega_{\theta_N} | \mathbf{x}_1, \ldots\ldots, \mathbf{x}_N) = max_{\Omega_1, \ldots, \Omega_N} P(\theta_1, \ldots, \theta_N | \mathbf{x}_1, \ldots\ldots, \mathbf{x}_N) \tag{7}$$

where Ω_i is the set of labels admitted by object a_i. For simplicity we shall assume that

$$\Omega_i = \{\omega_0, \omega_1, \ldots, \omega_M\} = \Omega \qquad \forall i$$

where ω_0 is the null label used to label objects for which no other label is appropriate.

The object centred counterpart computes instead $P(\theta_i = \omega_{\theta_i} | \mathbf{x}_1, \mathbf{x}_2, \ldots\ldots, \mathbf{x}_N)$, the aposteriori probability of label θ_i given all the observations. The main difference between message and object centred interpretation can be brought out by expressing both probabilities using the Bayes formula. Starting with the aposteriori probability of joint labelling

$$P(\theta_1, \ldots\ldots, \theta_N | \mathbf{x}_1, \mathbf{x}_2, \ldots\ldots, \mathbf{x}_N) = \frac{p(\mathbf{x}_1, \ldots\ldots, \mathbf{x}_N | \theta_1, \ldots\ldots, \theta_N) P(\theta_1, \ldots\ldots, \theta_N)}{p(\mathbf{x}_1, \ldots\ldots, \mathbf{x}_N)} \tag{8}$$

we note that for given observations the joint probability density function value in the denominator is fixed and therefore the left hand side is proportional to the product in the numerator. The first term of the product, the conditional joint probability density function of measurement vectors $\mathbf{x}_1, \ldots\ldots, \mathbf{x}_N$ models the measurement process whereas the second term embodies our a priori knowledge of the likelihood of various combinations of labels occurring. It is our global, world model.

For the object centred labelling we can write

$$P(\theta_i = \omega|\mathbf{x}_1, ...,\mathbf{x}_N) = \frac{p(\mathbf{x}_1, ...,\mathbf{x}_N|\theta_i = \omega)\hat{p}\,(\theta_j = \omega)}{p(\mathbf{x}_1, ...,\mathbf{x}_N)} \tag{9}$$

where $\hat{p}\,(\theta_j = \omega)$ is the a priori probability of label θ_i taking value ω. Again the denominator in (9) can be dismissed. Expanding the first term of the numerator over all possible labellings in the usual fashion, i.e.

$$p(\mathbf{x}_1, ...,\mathbf{x}_N|\theta_i = \omega) = \sum_{\Omega_1}..\sum_{\Omega_j}..\sum_{\Omega_N} p(\mathbf{x}_1, ...,\mathbf{x}_N, \theta_1, ..\theta_j.., \theta_N|\theta_i = \omega) =$$

$$= \sum_{\Omega_1}..\sum_{\Omega_j}..\sum_{\Omega_N} p(\mathbf{x}_1, ...,\mathbf{x}_N|\theta_1, ..\theta_i = \omega.., \theta_N)P(\theta_1, ..\theta_j.., \theta_N|\theta_i = \omega) \qquad \forall j \neq i \tag{10}$$

we find

$$P(\theta_i = \omega|\mathbf{x}_1, ...,\mathbf{x}_N) =$$
$$= \frac{\sum_{\Omega_1}..\sum_{\Omega_j}..\sum_{\Omega_N} p(\mathbf{x}_1, ...,\mathbf{x}_N|\theta_1, ..\theta_i = \omega.., \theta_N)P(\theta_1, ..\theta_i = \omega.., \theta_N)}{p(\mathbf{x}_1, ...,\mathbf{x}_N)} \tag{11}$$

Thus computing the probability of a particular label ω on a single object a_i amounts to scanning through all the possible combinations of labels $\theta_1, ..., \theta_N$ with label θ_i set to ω and summing up the corresponding products of the respective joint measurement and label probabilities.

The inspection of the expressions for the probabilities $P(\theta_1, ..., \theta_N|\mathbf{x}_1, \mathbf{x}_2, ...,\mathbf{x}_N)$ and $P(\theta_i = \omega|\mathbf{x}_1, ...,\mathbf{x}_N)$ in (8) and (11) respectively reveals that they are both defined in terms of the same ingredients, namely the a priori probability distribution of joint labelling, $P(\theta_1, ..., \theta_N)$ and the conditional probability density function $p(\mathbf{x}_1, ...,\mathbf{x}_N|\theta_1, ..., \theta_N)$. It is apparent that for any practical value of N and M it will not be feasible to apply techniques of statistical inference to estimate these probability distributions.

It is evident that to obtain workable models some assumptions will have to be introduced which will allow us not only to specify these global probability distributions functions but also to use them for solving practical problems. An important role in this respect is the assumption of Markov property which permits characterisation of global dependence in terms of local interactions. More specifically, let without any loss of generality, $\xi_i, i = 1, ..., N$ be a discrete random variable associated with the i-th node of a network of objects with neighbourhood system $I_i, i = 1, ..., N$. The Markov property states that

$$p(\xi_i|\xi_j, \forall j \neq i) = p(\xi_i|\xi_j, \forall j \in I_i^*)$$

where I_i^* denotes the index set of the immediate neighbours to ξ_i, i.e. set I_i with the ith node removed. In other words, the conditional probability of a particular outcome or state of variable ξ_i given all the other observations $\xi_j, \forall j \neq i$ is completely determined by the values of ξ_i's neighbours. This assumption facilitates the maximisation of (7) by means of local updates of the object labels.

Alternatively, one may employ a dictionary of label configurations. The approach exploits the fact that the number of permissible label configurations on a network of objects is usually very small in comparison with the number of all combinatorial labellings. If the size of the dictionary is reasonable, an exhaustive scan through all its items becomes feasible.

Finally, an important and physically realistic assumption regarding the unary measurement process distribution is that the outcomes of measurements are conditionally independent.

$$p(\mathbf{x}_1, ..., \mathbf{x}_N | \theta_1, ..\theta_i, .., \theta_N) = \Pi_{i=1}^{N} p(\mathbf{x}_i | \theta_i = \omega_{\theta_i}) \tag{12}$$

All the contextual classification methods that have been developed commence from one of the above formulations and a choice of model for the prior world knowledge and the measurement process. They are briefly reviewed in the following section.

2.3 A REVIEW OF CONTEXTUAL DECISION MAKING METHODS

In the message centred interpretation category, the deterministic methods exploiting the Markov random field models include the iterative conditional modes technique (ICM) of Besag [12], Blake and Zisserman [16], Koch, Marroquin and Yuille [17], and Witkin, Terzopoulos and Kass [18]. Their stochastic optimisation counterpart is represented by the method developed by Geman and Geman [13] which is based on the simulated annealing technique [15]. More recent are the attempts to use the mean field theory [14] to simplify and speed up the discrete optimisation process.

The message centred approach combined with the dictionary representation of the prior world knowledge leads to the classical discrete relaxation algorithm of Waltz [25]. However, the seminal qualities of Waltz's algorithm were not matched by practical utility because of its computational complexity (effectively requiring an exhaustive search in a combinatorial optimisation space). A computationally feasible technique of discrete relaxation has been developed by Hancock and Kittler [26] which introduces the idea of a label error process to cope with the two fundamental problems of the original algorithm [25]: i) inadmissible label configurations introduced by initial object labelling and ii) the optimisation process deadlock, which was the consequence of the (binary) labelling performance criterion used by Waltz.

For the object centred formulation linked with the Markovian assumption, only Markov models of special type can be employed to develop effective contextual classification techniques. Haslett [27] resorted to the Pickard random field model and Devijver [28] succeeded in developing a recursive compound decision scheme for images that can be modelled by a Markov mesh process.

Finally, the object centred formulation combined with the dictionary model of the world knowledge are the germ of a family of algorithms known as probabilistic relaxation. The method was conceived by Rosenfeld, Hummel and Zucker [19] in 1976 and since its publication it has attracted sustained interest. The effectiveness of the approach has been demonstrated on numerous applications including line and edge detection [29], [30]. For a comprehensive list of applications the reader is referred to the review article of Kittler and Illingworth [20].

Notwithstanding its practical potential, the early applications of probabilistic relaxation unveiled many theoretical problems, including inherent bias of the updating process which was exhibited in no information experiments, questions relating to convergence, interpretation of the computed probabilities, and the specification of the compatibility coefficients and support functions [20]. Most of these problems were overcome in two key papers published in the nineteen eighties [21], [22]. In [21] Hummel and Zucker laid down the theoretical foundations of probabilistic relaxation by formally defining the notion of consistency and by showing that under certain assumptions the optimisation of a simple functional was synonymous with improving the consistency of object labelling.

In spite of this progress the relaxation process design methodology remained very heuristic until the publication of the work of Kittler and Hancock [22] which was aimed at providing theoretical underpinning of probabilistic relaxation using the Bayesian framework. It led to the development of an evidence combining formula which fuses observations and a priori contextual information in a theoretically sound manner. The polynomial combinatorial complexity of the approach has been avoided by means of introducing and developing the concept of label configuration dictionary. The methodology has been validated on problems of edge and line postprocessing [23].

The outstanding criticisms of probabilistic relaxation, namely that the process does not utilise measurement information with the exception of the initialisation stage, and that the richest source of contextual observational information contained in object relations (binary relations) has never been tapped, have been overcome most recently [24].

4 CONCLUSIONS

Any significant future improvements in the performance of pattern recognition systems can be brought about only by fusing other sources information pertinent to each recognition task. The possible sources of additional information include multiple cues, multiple opinions of experts, prior knowledge and context. In this paper the main tools for fusing such diverse sources of information have been reviewed. They include schemes for fusing multiple cues, strategies for fusing multiple experts, and techniques for combining measurement and contextual information. A pointers to literature where the reviewed methodology has been successfully applied have be given.

References

[1] J. Cao, M. Ahmadi, and M. Shridhar, Recognition of handwritten numerals with multiple feature and multistage classifier, *Pattern Recognition*, vol. 28, no. 2, 1995, 153-160.

[2] S.B. Cho and J.H. Kim, Multiple network fusion using fuzzy logic, *IEEE Transactions on Neural Networks*, vol. 6, no. 2, pp. 497-501, 1995.

[3] L.K. Hansen and P. Salamon, Neural network ensembles, *IEEE Transactions on Pattern Analysis and Machine Intelligence*, vol. 12, no. 10, 1990, pp. 993- 1001.

[4] S. Hashem and B. Schmeiser, Improving model accuracy using optimal linear combinations of trained neural networks, *IEEE Transactions on Neural Networks*, vol. 6, no. 3, 1995, 792-794.

[5] T.K. Ho, J.J. Hull, and S.N. Srihari, Decision combination in multiple classifier systems, *IEEE Transactions on Pattern Analysis and Machine Intelligence*, vol. 16, no. 1, 1994, pp. 66-75.

[6] D.H. Wolpert, Stacked generalization, *Neural Networks*, vol. 5, no. 2, 1992, 241-260.

[7] L. Xu, A. Krzyzak, C.Y. Suen, Methods of combining multiple classifiers and their applications to handwriting recognition, *IEEE Trans. SMC*, vol. 22, no. 3, 1992, pp. 418-435.

[8] J. Kittler, M. Hatef and R.P.W. Duin, Combining classifiers, *Proceedings 13th International Conference on Pattern Recognition*, Vienna, 1996, Volume II, Track B, 897-901.

[9] J Kittler, A Hojjatoleslami and T Windeatt, Weighting factors in multiple expert fusion, *Proc British Machine Vision Conference*, Colchester, pp 41-50, 1997.

[10] T S Huang and C Y Suen, Combination of multiple experts for the recognition of unconstrained handwritten numerals, *IEEE Trans Pattern Analysis and Machine Intelligence*, **17**, pp 90-94, 1995.

[11] P A Devijver and J Kittler, Pattern recognition: A statistical approach, Prentice-Hall, Englewood Cliffs, NJ, 1982.

[12] J Besag, On the satatistical analysis of dirty pictures, *Journal Royal Statist. Society*, **48**, Series B, 259-302, 1986.

[13] S Geman and D Geman, Stochastic relaxation, Gibbs distributions and the Bayesian restoration of images, *IEEE Trans. Pattern Analysis and Machine Intelligence*, **PAMI-6**, 721-741, 1984.

[14] D Geiger and F Girosi, Parallel and deterministic algorithms from MRF's: Surface reconstruction, *IEEE Trans. Pattern Analysis and Machine Intelligence*, **PAMI-13**, 181-188, 1991.

[15] S Kirkpatrick, C D Gellatt and M P Vecchi, Optimization by simulated annealing, *Science*, **220**, 671-680, 1983.

[16] A Blake and A Zisserman, Visual reconstruction, MIT Press, Cambridge MA, 1987.

[17] C Koch, J Marroquin and A Yuille, Analog neuronal networks in early vision, *Proc Nat. Academic Science*, **83**, 4263-4267, 1986.

[18] A Witkin, D Terzopoulos and M Kass, Signal matching through scale space, *Intern. Journal Computer Vision*, 133-144, 1987.

[19] A Rosenfeld, R Hummel and S Zucker, Scene labeling by relaxation operations, *IEEE Trans System Man and Cybernetics*, **SMC-6**, 420-433, 1976.

[20] J Kittler and J Illingworth, A review of relaxation labelling algorithms, *Image and Vision Computing*, **3**, 206,216, 1985.

[21] R Hummel and S Zucker, On the foundations of relaxation labeling process, *IEEE Trans. Pattern Analysis and Machine Intelligence*, **PAMI-5**, 267-286, 1983.

[22] J Kittler and E R Hancock, Combining evidence in probabilistic relaxation, *Intern. Journal of Pattern Recognition and Artificial Intelligence*, **3**, 29-51, 1989.

[23] E R Hancock and J Kittler, Edge labeling using dictionary-based relaxation, *IEEE Trans. Pattern Analysis and Machine Intelligence*, **PAMI-12**, 165-181, 1990.

[24] W J Christmas, J Kittler and M Petrou, Structural matching in computer vision using probabilistic relaxation *IEEE Trans. Pattern Analysis and Machine Intelligence*, **PAMI-17**, 749-754, 1995.

[25] D L Waltz, Understanding line drawings of scenes with shadows, in *The Psychology of Computer Vision*, P H Winston, ed., McGraw-Hill, New York, 1975.

[26] E R Hancock and J Kittler, Discrete relaxation, *Pattern Recognition*, **23**, 711-733, 1990.

[27] J Haslett, Maximum likelihood discriminant analysis on the plane using a Markovian model of spatial context, *Pattern Recognition*, **18**, 287-296, 1985.

[28] P A Devijver, Probabilistic labelling in a second order Markov mesh, in *Pattern Recognition in Practice, Vol. 2*, E S Gelsema and L Kanal, eds., North Holland, 1986.

[29] S Peleg and A Rosenfeld, Determining compatibility coefficients for curve enhancement relaxation processes, *IEEE Trans Systems, Man and Cybernetics*, **SMC-8**, 548-555, 1978.

[30] S Zucker, R Hummel and A Rosenfeld, An application of relaxation labelling to line and curve enhancement, *IEEE Tranc Computers*, **C-26**, 394-404, 1977.

[31] J Kittler, M Hatef, R P W Duin and J Matas, On combining classifiers, *IEEE Transactions on Pattern Analysis and Machine Intelligence*, vol. 20, pp 226-239, 1998.

[32] J Kittler, Combining classifiers: A theoretical framework, *Pattern Analysis and Applications* , vol. 1, pp 18-27, 1998.

DATABASE-RETRIEVAL ORIENTED APPROACH FOR MODEL-BASED OBJECT RECOGNITION [1]

G. Sudhir, College of Engg., Univ. of California, Riverside, U.S.A.
Bir Bhanu, College of Engg., Univ. of California, Riverside, U.S.A.

ABSTRACT

Model-based recognition of objects when the number of model objects becomes large is a challenging problem which makes it increasingly difficult to view the object recognition problem as – "find *the* best match" problem. We present a database-retrieval oriented approach for this case wherein the goal is to index, retrieve, rank and output a few top-ranked models, according to their similarity with an input query object. The approach consists of three stages: (1) feature-based representation of model objects and object-feature correspondence analysis; (2) clustering and indexing of the model objects in the factor space; and (3) ranking indexed models based on mutual information with query object. We believe that this approach has practical advantages for large model databases where the best-match approach can be unreliable. It also finds applications in semi-automatic object recognition tasks which involve interaction with humans. Experimental results are presented using a variety of data to demonstrate the merits of our approach.

1 INTRODUCTION

Model-based object recognition is a powerful approach which involves invariant feature domain representations of models of different objects to generate a model database, and matching these to the features of a new observation of an object, to select the best match. However, as the number of models in the model database increases, it becomes increasingly difficult to view the object recognition problem as – "find *the* best match" problem. There are two main reasons for this: (1) Firstly, the discriminating power of a set of known features becomes increasingly insufficient for the purpose of finding *the* correct matching model, for all the objects. Moreover, there may be a lack of knowledge about the *optimal* set of features; and (2) Secondly, the sensitivity of features to changes in object pose, image formation geometry, sensor parameters, etc. adds to the problem of correct recognition.

In this context, the model-based object recognition problem shares similarity with the *content-based retrieval* problems where the insufficiency of features arises in capturing the notion of *content*. However, the database retrieval approach – wherein, the goal is index, retrieve, rank and output a few top-ranked models as the most probable matches – has proved to be useful for various practical tasks [1]. Hence, for the case of large model databases, taking a database-retrieval stance to model-based recognition is a practically useful one for various interactive applications. One such case is that of model-based recognition of targets in Synthetic Aperture Radar (SAR) images. As has been observed and quantified in our earlier research efforts [2], one of the main characteristics of SAR images of objects is the sensitivity of features (scattering centers) to *azimuthal variation* (pose variation). That is,

[1]This research was supported in part by DARPA/AFOSR grant F49620-97-1-0184. The contents do not necessarily reflect the position or the policy of the U.S. Government.

for a given depression angle, there is very low invariance for the scattering centers (features which are local maxima) when the azimuth of an object is changed even by a couple of degrees. This requires that one model object be used for each azimuth thus totaling a set of 360 models for a single object. Thus, the number of models in the model-database will easily run into thousands even when a few targets are considered. This paper presents a database-retrieval oriented approach for the problem using a feature-based representation, classification and ranking of the models, and provides experimental results for several SAR image databases.

2 RELATED RESEARCH AND CONTRIBUTIONS

Recently, Pun *et al.* [3] have used correspondence analysis (CA) for statistical structuring of pictorial databases for content based retrieval. They represent images using aggregate features based on multiple cues, and do CA on images and attributes. However, in the factor space generated by CA, they use the feature projections only to explain the dominant factors and not as seeds for clustering objects. They propose an Ascendant Hierarchical Classification method [4, 5] for structuring the projections of the images in the factor space and report their experiments on example image database of 54 images. For large model databases consisting of thousands of objects with sensitive and noisy features (like the SAR target database we have used), the projections of objects are spread out almost randomly in the factor space, and as a result, a tree based classification may not be appropriate. Hence, we propose the combination of feature-based clustering of objects in factor space and a triangle-inequality based indexing of the objects inside each cluster. We believe that it is a useful alternative to hierarchical clustering and indexing approaches.

Triangle-inequality (TI) based indexing schemes take advantage of the triangle inequality of distance measures to reduce the number of direct comparisons in a threshold search[2]. This indexing scheme has recently gained a lot of attention in the context of content-based retrieval from image databases [6, 7]. Barros *et al.* [6] have applied the idea to a real image database and Berman *et al.* [7] have reported the performance of different algorithms for the selection of *key* objects as well as handling multiple distance measures on a set of image features. However, application of the TI using the distance between objects in the feature space has the limitation of not dealing with any redundancies of feature set in capturing a description of the database objects. Our approach deals with it in a systematic manner, since it considers all the distances in the factor space after object-feature correspondence analysis. An important advantage of computing distance in factor space (instead of feature space) is that, undesirable *weighting bias* towards a large set of *redundant* features is clearly avoided. This is because, CA eliminates the effect of a set of redundant features by grouping them together in the feature space. Exploiting this, our approach computes the distance of the model objects from the "feature-group" as one entity.

Berman *et al.* [7] have reported on ranking the retrieved model objects according to the computed lower bounds on distances, in the context of content-based retrieval of images. However, in the context of object recognition, since the feature based representation of model objects is usually insufficient to capture *all* the properties of objects, the ordering based on lower bounds may not be accurate. Hence, we propose the use of feature based

[2]Given an object database O, a query object Q, and a distance measure $d(\cdot)$, the threshold search for a given threshold T is to search for all objects $o \in O$ such that the distance $D(Q,o) \leq T$.

representation only to quickly index a set of model candidates for a query object which can be further ranked based on mutual information which is a robust measure of similarity between the query and model objects. Recently, mutual information (MI) has been reported to be a more robust measure than normalized cross correlation, for its relative insensitivity with respect to variations in illumination [8]. Viola *et al.* [8] use MI measure in their algorithm for alignment of a model object to a new observation, assuming that the new observation belongs to the same model object. In our context, we use the MI measure for comparing a *candidate* model object to a query object. Our motivation to use MI is to compare the model and query objects according to their statistical dependencies, in order to robustly rank a set of candidate models for a query object. For the empirical estimation of MI, we have used the technique reported in [9].

The main contribution of our paper is that it presents a new, systematic approach to model-based object recognition from the database-retrieval point of view. The advantages of our approach are, (*i*) it deals with feature redundancies using CA, (*ii*) it proposes feature-based clustering of model objects in factor space, followed by TI based indexing of objects for each cluster, as an useful alternative to standard hierarchical clustering and tree-based indexing methods, and (*iii*) advocates a robust approach for ranking the initial retrievals using mutual information between a query object and a candidate model object. Our approach compares the query and model objects by considering their information content first in the feature domain (in TI based indexing in factor space generated by CA), and then in the original data domain (in mutual information based ranking of initial retrievals). The former step helps in quickly pruning a large number of models from consideration for a query object and the latter step ranks the candidates in a more robust manner.

3 TECHNICAL APPROACH

Figure 1 illustrates our conceptual approach. There are two phases: (1) Database construc-

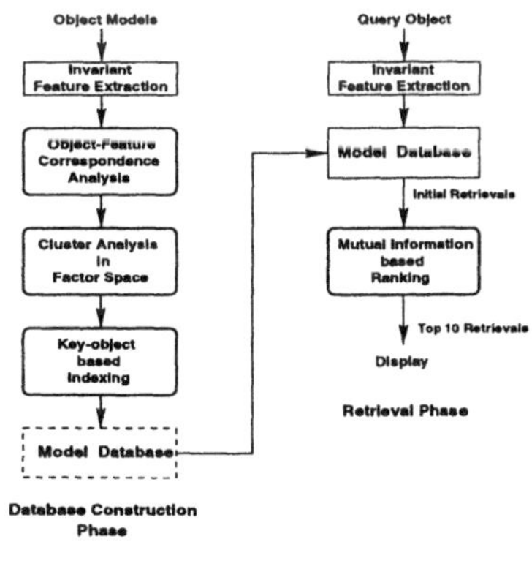

Figure 1: Overview of our database-retrieval oriented approach for object recognition.

tion phase, and (2) Retrieval phase. In the database construction phase, the model objects are processed by an invariant feature extraction module. This represents the model objects in a feature space. It is processed by an object-feature CA module which projects both objects and features in a common reduced-dimension factor space. These projections are further analyzed and clusters of objects are formed in the factor space. For each cluster, a set of *key* objects are computed to enable TI based indexing of the objects in the factor space. Finally, the model information – the model objects, factors, clusters, key objects for each cluster, distances of model objects from key objects in each cluster – is assembled to generate the model database. In the retrieval phase, an unknown (query) object is processed by the invariant feature extraction module to represent it in the feature space. Then its features are input to the model database to index and retrieve a set of candidate models which are further ranked by the mutual information module to output only the top 10 ranked retrievals as the most probable matches to the input query object.

In the following, we briefly describe the key modules in Fig. 1 in the two phases. More details can be found in [10].

3.1 DATABASE CONSTRUCTION PHASE

The first step in this phase is the extraction of a set of invariant features for the model objects to represent them in the feature domain. In our case of SAR target databases, we have used translation invariant features [2]. We present details about these features in Sec. 4. The rest of this subsection assumes that features are already extracted.

3.1.1 Object-feature Correspondence Analysis : The main advantage of feature-based representation of model objects is that the dimension of the feature space is much smaller than dimension of the original model data space. However, there can be *redundancy* in the features for describing the model database. This causes an undesirable *weighting bias* towards a set of redundant features, when any distance is computed between two objects in the feature space. We propose a systematic way of dealing with this using CA of model objects and their invariant features.

Correspondence Analysis (CA) is a type of factor analysis [4, 5]. Like any factor analysis method, it provides a compact representation in a low dimension factor space of large sets of numerical data (which in our case is a matrix $D = [d_{i,j}]$; see below). It shares the linear algebra of finding the *factor axes* with other factor analysis methods. However, in CA, the coordinates of the data points are defined so that the usual Euclidean metric in the factor space corresponds to the χ^2 distance between the points. Thus, the analysis is in terms of the *independence* of the data. Furthermore, unlike other factor analysis methods, CA assigns *symmetric* roles to rows (objects) and columns (features). This permits simultaneous representation of both objects and features in a common factor space which not only helps interpretation of the factor space but also makes clustering of objects easier (see Sec. 3.1.2). We exploit these advantages of CA in our approach. In the following, we describe CA as relevant to the analysis of objects and features.

Let there be M model objects and N features for each object. For large number of model objects, $N \ll M$. The model objects and their features are represented as the matrix $D = [d_{i,j}]$, $1 \leq i \leq M, 1 \leq N$, where, the rows identify the model objects and the columns identify the features. For CA, D is processed using the following sequence of steps [5]: 1: Compute the normalized data matrix $K = [k_{i,j}]$, $1 \leq i \leq M$, $1 \leq j \leq N$ using $k_{i,j} = \frac{d_{i,j}}{\sqrt{d_I\, d_J}}$ where $d_I = \sum_{j=1}^{N} d_{i,j}$ and $d_J = \sum_{i=1}^{M} d_{i,j}$; 2: Compute[3] the χ^2 matrix

[3]This is actually a simplified, computationally less expensive version of the full χ^2 matrix; however, there

$H = K^T K$ where K^T stands for *transpose* of a matrix K. Note that H is a $N \times N$ matrix and its elements in terms of original data matrix D are given by $h_{k,l} = \frac{1}{\sqrt{d_K d_L}} \sum_{i=1}^{M} \frac{d_{i,k} d_{i,l}}{d_I}$; where $d_I = \sum_{j=1}^{N} d_{i,j}$, $d_K = \sum_{i=1}^{M} d_{i,k}$, and $d_L = \sum_{i=1}^{M} d_{i,l}$; 3: Compute Singular Value Decomposition of H to find the eigenvalues $\lambda_i, 1 \leq i \leq N$ and eigenvectors $V_i, 1 \leq i \leq N$ of H. Note that λ_1 is always 1 because of normalization of the data and $\lambda_i \geq \lambda_j$ if $i \leq j$, $2 \leq i, j \leq N$. The eigenvalues λ_2 to λ_N determine the variance of the system and their corresponding eigenvectors (V_2 to V_N) determine the factor space and hence are called *factors*. Let $F_i = V_{i+1}, 1 \leq i \leq N-1$ be the factors; 4: Compute the ratio $r_i, 2 \leq i \leq N$ by using $r_i = \frac{\lambda i}{\sum_{j=2}^{N} \lambda j}$. These ratios indicate the percentage of the total variance of the system that each factor F_i explains. Note that only a few factors can explain up to 90% of the total variance of the system. Let P denote that number, where $P \leq N-1$; 5: Project the model objects $O_i, 1 \leq i \leq M$ along each factor axis $F_k, 1 \leq k \leq P$ using $O_{i,k} = \frac{\sqrt{Z}}{d_I} \sum_{j=1}^{N} \frac{d_{i,j}}{\sqrt{d_J}} f_{k,j}$ where $Z = \sum_{i=1}^{M} \sum_{j=1}^{N} d_{i,j}$, $d_I = \sum_{j=1}^{N} d_{ij}$, $d_J = \sum_{i=1}^{M} d_{ij}$ and $f_{k,j}$ is the jth element of factor F_k. The quantity $O_{i,k}$ represents the scalar coordinate of the object O_i along factor F_k; 6: Project the features $A_j, 1 \leq j \leq N$ along each factor axis $F_k, 1 \leq k \leq P$ using $A_{j,k} = \frac{1}{d_J \sqrt{\lambda_k}} \sum_{i=1}^{M} d_{i,j} O_{i,k}$ where $d_J = \sum_{i=1}^{M} d_{ij}$. The quantity $A_{j,k}$ represents the scalar coordinate of the feature A_j along factor F_k. After these steps, the objects and features are both represented in a common, reduced dimension factor space. Often, only the first two factors determine more than 70% of the total variance (it is so in all the experimental examples reported in this paper). In such a case only the first two *dominant* factors can be considered in the following clustering and indexing phase.

3.1.2 Cluster Analysis in Factor Space : We first identify different "feature-groups" in the factor space and then use their centroids as the *seeds* for generating clusters of model objects. There are two advantages of this: (1) the number of features are far less compared to the number of model objects; thus, determining different groups of features in the factors space is not computationally intensive and can be easily supervised; (2) feature-groups, which act as the seeds around which objects get clustered, also explain automatically why the object cluster was formed; this can be exploited to give a meaningful annotation to a cluster as the set of model objects which are mainly described by their seed feature-group.

3.1.3 Key-object based Indexing : Since the number of feature clusters is usually small (there are just 4 to 6 clusters of features in our experiments), there can be still a large number of model objects inside each cluster. In order to efficiently index objects inside the clusters, we employ the TI based indexing scheme. The TI based indexing schemes rely on comparing a set of key objects to the database objects according to a distance metric, and storing the computed distances. The basic idea is to exploit the TI at the retrieval time to quickly compute the lower bounds on the distance of each database object from the query. The reason behind all these schemes is the fact that the distance between two objects cannot be less than the difference of their distances to any other object. Mathematically, if O is a database object, Q is a query object and K is some *key* object, the inequality $d(O,Q) \geq |d(O,K) - d(Q,K)|$ always holds. Thus, by comparing the database and query

is no difference as far the analysis is concerned since this matrix has the same eigen-structure as the full χ^2 matrix, except that the largest eigenvalue becomes trivial [5].

objects to a third *key* object, a lower bound on the distance between the model and query objects can be obtained. If a threshold T on the distance between a model and query object is known (or given), this lower bound can be compared to T to eliminate from any further consideration all those models whose lower bound is more than T. Note that, if the distances of all the model objects from the key object are stored and hence are readily available, the only distance computation that needs to be done in order to know all the lower bounds is that between the query and key objects. Since the distance computation is often much more expensive compared to simple subtraction involved in the computation of lower bounds, speed-up is achieved in indexing the model objects for each query. In our experiments, for simplicity, we have selected two key objects for each cluster. These two key objects are the two furthest apart ones in a cluster. Thus the total number of keys used to index the model database in our approach is twice the number clusters.

3.1.4 Algorithm for Clustering and Indexing : In the following, we describe the sequential steps for clustering and indexing: 1: Consider the projections of M features along the first $\mathcal{F}$ *dominant* factors. Closely projected features explain the system similarly and are redundant. Group such closely projected features into a "feature-group" representing a single feature class. Let there be C different feature classes. Define the center of feature-group as the centroid of the feature projections of that group; 2: Generate C clusters of model objects using centers of each feature-group as the *seed* and using nearest-neighbor (NN) rule in the factor space; 3: For each cluster, select two model objects k_1 and k_2 which are furthest apart in the cluster. They form two key objects for the cluster; 4: For each cluster, compute the distances of model objects in the factor space with each of the key object; 5: For each cluster, store (*i*) indices of the model objects, (*ii*) indices of the key objects and (*iii*) distances of the model objects to key objects, in the model database.

3.1.5 Building model database : Figure 2 shows in detail the contents of the model

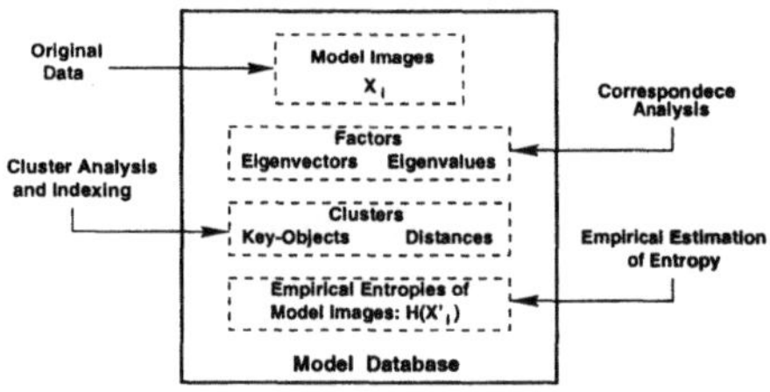

Figure 2: Contents of the Model Database.

database in our approach. The original model data is stored inside the model database. This data is necessary when the mutual information of the query object with each of the candidate model objects needs to be computed. Also, the *factors* computed by the object-feature analysis are stored as part of the model database. These factors will be used in the retrieval phase. The stored clusters contain two main items: key-objects and distances of all the model objects to all the key-objects along with indices to the model objects. Note that these distances are in the factor space. Finally, the empirical entropies of all the model objects are computed *a priori* and stored as part of the model database. This can speed-up the computationally intensive process of empirical estimation of mutual information since model entropies are readily available.

3.2 RETRIEVAL PHASE

In this phase, a new observation is given in the form of a query object. This query object is processed as follows: 1: Compute the same invariant features as done for each model object. Let $Q = [q_1, q_2, \cdots, q_N]$ be the query features; 2: Project the Q along each factor axis $F_k, 1 \leq k \leq P$ using $Q_k = \frac{\sqrt{Z}}{G} \sum_{j=1}^{N} \frac{q_j}{\sqrt{d_J}} f_{k,j}$ where Z, d_J, $f_{k,j}$ come from the stored factor details in the model database and $G = \sum_{j=1}^{N} q_j$. The quantity Q_k represents the scalar coordinate of the query Q along factor F_k; 3: Consider the query projections Q_K in the factor space spanned by the first few *dominant* factors used for clustering and indexing. Classify the query to one of the clusters based on nearest-neighbor classification. Let C_m be the cluster; 4: Consider the two key objects of the cluster C_m. Compute the distance (in factor space) of the query object from each of these two key objects. Using these distances and the stored distances of the other model objects from the two key objects, retrieve the model objects whose TI-based lower bounds are less than a threshold Th[4]. These initial retrievals form candidate matching objects to the query. The candidate models are further ranked using their mutual information (MI) with the query object [9].

4 EXPERIMENTAL RESULTS

In this section, we present the experimental results on several real SAR image databases. The resolution of the real SAR data is 1-foot-per-pixel. Various *model databases* consist of SAR images of (*i*) objects at a particular depression angle, or (*ii*) objects of a particular configuration, or (*iii*) objects at a particular articulation [10]. The corresponding *test data* consists of SAR images of (*i*) objects at a different depression angle, or (*ii*) objects of a different configuration, or (*iii*) objects at a different articulation. In each case, test data is an independently acquired one from which query objects are selected randomly.

The set of features we have used to represent each object in CA are listed in Table 1. The first nine features are computed on the histogram of relative distance between scatterrers (see [10] for more details). Since the relative distances are used, the first nine features are translation invariant. The next three features are computed on the gray level histogram of the SAR image pixels within ROI. While we compute the features 10 to 12 based on histogram of intensity values and use them in CA, we do not consider them in clustering and indexing. This is because they are computed based on gray level values of only the top scatterers which may be unreliable. The last two features are also translation invariant. In all our experiments, we consider only 11 of the 14 features (discounting features 10 to 12) from Table 1, for clustering and indexing.

Figure 3 (left) shows the projections of features in the factor space spanned by the first two dominant factors for *Database* 1 (see Table 2). Note that the *mean*, *std*, *max* and *median* fall closely in factor space and are redundant for describing the target database, whereas, the *mode*, *wdia* and *hdia* fall distant to any other feature and hence form independent descriptors of the database. The other features look smeared in the factor space and so we do not use

[4]This threshold can be *a priori* estimated as the average distance in factor space between pairs of similar objects, by considering a large set of similar object pairs.

Table 1: 14 features used to represent SAR targets in correspondence analysis.

Feature Number	Feature Description	Feature Number	Feature Description	Feature Number	Feature Description
1	mean of HRD	6	skewness of HRD	11	std_{HI}
2	std of HRD	7	kurtosis of HRD	12	max_{HI}
3	max of HRD	8	energy of HRD	13	wdia
4	mode of HRD	9	entropy of HRD	14	hdia
5	median of HRD	10	$mean_{HI}$		

HRD $\Longrightarrow$ Histogram of relative distances between scatterers

HI $\Longrightarrow$ Histogram of intensity values

wdia $\Longrightarrow$ Diameter of the object along width of the image

hdia $\Longrightarrow$ Diameter of the object along height

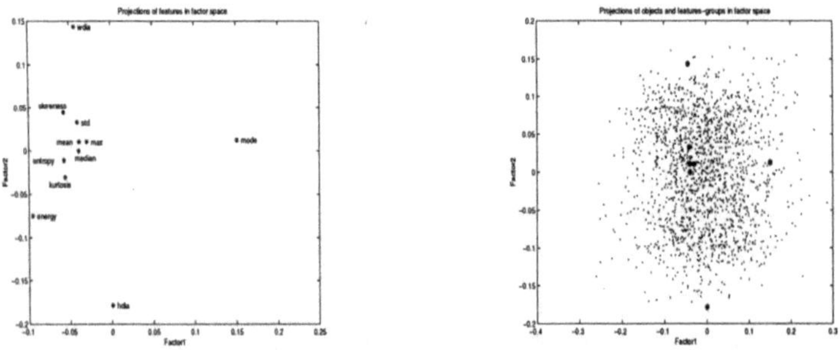

Figure 3: Left: Projection of 11 features (features 10, 11 and 12 are not used; see text for explanation) in factor space spanned by first two dominant factors for the entire *Database* 1 (see Table 2). Right: Projection of both objects and feature-groups in the same factor space for *Database* 1. The features are marked $*$ and the objects (targets) are marked by $+$ in the factor space. Note that the objects appear to be almost randomly spread out in the factor space. The four feature-groups are used as the seeds for forming four clusters of objects using nearest-neighborhood approach.

them in clustering [10]. Based on the observation of feature projections for this database, we form four independent feature-groups: the first consists of (*mean*, *std*, *max* and *median*), and the rest three consist of just one feature each (*mode*, *wdia* and *hdia*, respectively). Figure 3 (right) shows the projections of both objects and the feature-groups in the factor space spanned by the first two dominant factors for the same databases. The centroids of the four feature-groups are used as the seeds for nearest-neighbor clustering of the objects. Table 2 summarizes the details of our experimental databases. Further details are available in [10]. The results of using our approach are summarized in Table 3 and Fig. 4.

5 CONCLUSIONS AND FUTURE RESEARCH

In this paper, we have presented a database-retrieval oriented approach to model-based object recognition, for large model databases. We have presented detailed results on several real SAR target databases to demonstrate our approach. These are difficult databases since feature invariance may be small (20% to 50% [2]). The technique is general and has applica-

Table 2: Model databases of SAR targets.

Model/Test Data Differences	Total no. of model objects in database	Total no. of test objects for database	No. of dominant factors ($\geq$ 90% of total variance)	% of total variance explained by first 2 factors
Depression angle diff.s (*Database* 1)	1621	1351	3	85.31
Configuration diff.s (*Database* 2)	694	1621	4	70.84
Articulation diff.s (*Database* 3)	606	239	3	78.29

Table 3: Results on various model databases of SAR targets.

Model/Test Data Differences	No. of random queries from the test data	Avg. no. of retrievals after indexing in factor space	No. of cases in which a target with correct ID and pose within 10° was present in top 10 retrievals
Depression diff.s	200	84 (5.18%)	185 (92.5%)
Configuration diff.s	200	64 (9.22%)	170 (85%)
Articulation diff.s	200	96 (15.84%)	139 (69.5%)

tions in other interactive object recognition applications involving large model databases. It also helps interactive discovery and acquisition of new models to update database. Currently, mutual information based ranking takes more than 99% of the time during recognition (retrieval) phase. The performance of our approach could be further improved by: (a) efficient computation of mutual information between a query and a candidate model object using a coarse-to-fine strategy, (b) overlapped boundaries in nearest-neighbor clustering method, and (c) efficient methods to adapt factors to dynamically changing databases. We are currently investigating along these directions.

REFERENCES

[1] M. Flickner, H. S. Sawhney, J. Ashley, Q. Huang, B. Dom, M. Gorkani, J. Hafner, D. Lee, D. Petkovic, D. Steele, and P. Yanker. Query by image and video content: The QBIC system. *IEEE Computer*, 28(9), 1995.

[2] B. Bhanu, G. Jones, and J. Ahn. Recognizing articulated objects and object articulation in SAR images. In *SPIE Proceedings: Algorithms for Synthetic Aperture Radar Imagery V*, volume 3370, April, 1998.

[3] T. Pun and D. Squire. Statistical structuring of pictorial databases for content-based image retrieval systems. *Pattern Recognition Letters*, 17:1299–1310, 1996.

[4] J.-P. Benzécri. *Correspondence Analysis Handbook*. Marcel Dekker, New York, 1992.

[5] M. Jambu. *Exploratory & Multivariate Data Analysis*. Academic Press, New York, 1991.

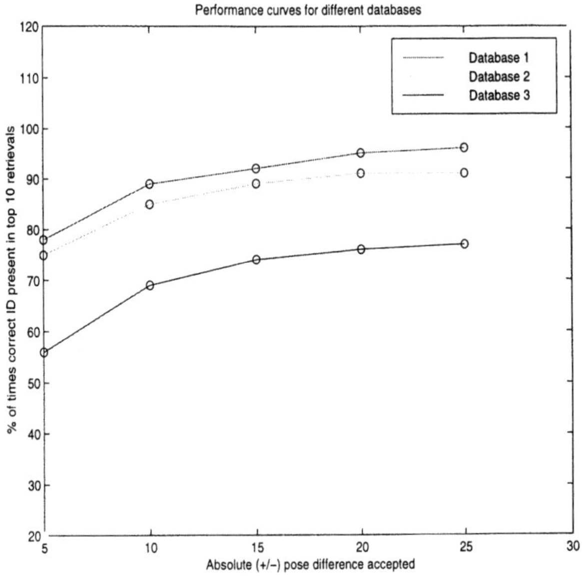

Figure 4: Performance curves for the SAR target databases.

[6] J. F. Barros, W. Martin, P. Kelley, and M. Cannon. Using the triangle inequality to reduce the number of comparisons required for similarity-based retrieval. In *Proc. of IS&T/SPIE - Storage and Retrieval for Still Image and Video Databases*, volume 4, pages 392–403, January, 1996.

[7] A. Berman and L. G. Shapiro. Selecting good keys for triangle-inequality-based pruning algorithms. In *Proc. of IEEE Intl. Workshop on Content-based Access of Image and Video Databases (CAIVD'98)*, pages 12–19, January, 1998.

[8] P. Viola and W. M. Wells III. Alignment by maximization of mutual information. In *Proc. of* 5th *Intl. Conf. on Computer Vision (ICCV'95)*, pages 16–23, 1995.

[9] Y. L. Moon, B. Rajagopalan, and U. Lall. Estimation of mutual information using kernel density estimators. *Physical Review E: Statistical physics, plasmas, fluids, and related interdisciplinary topics*, 52(3):2318–2321, 1995.

[10] G. Sudhir and B. Bhanu. Database-retrieval oriented approach for model-based object recognition. Technical report, Visualization and Intelligent Systems Laboratory, University of California at Riverside, July, 1998.

IMAGE PROCESSING

COMBINED FEATURE SETS FOR TEXTURE CLASSIFICATION

Liang S. Ng, ISIS Research Group, University of Southampton
Mark S. Nixon, ISIS Research Group, University of Southampton
John N. Carter, ISIS Research Group, University of Southampton

ABSTRACT

Many approaches to texture recognition essentially use features derived by single means. We have developed two methods to combine texture descriptions for classification: a composite feature vector which combines data additively, and an extended k-nearest-neighbour (KNN) rule which returns a decision based on the highest confidence in features. Both improve classification capability. Here, we extend the analysis of multiple feature combination by analysing normalised interclass distance to show how multiple feature can improve classification capability. The new techniques have been applied to the whole Brodatz database, with evaluation independent of the number of used test classes by measuring the number of perfect classes. The results of these new methods of combination show that a overall classification rate exceeding 90% can be achieved with 71 perfect classes, improving capabilities above using the measures individually. The analysis of normalised interclass distance is shown to give new insight into how feature combination can be beneficial. As such, this provides a rich avenue for further research which will aim to capitalise on these new developments.

1 INTRODUCTION

Visually and intuitively, textures may be described as replications of one or more elementary images – texture elements or primitives – which may undergo geometrical transformations such as rotation, shift or scaling. Despite the absence of a formal definition of texture, many individual models have been suggested for describing it, such as grey level statistics [1][2][3], spectral [4][5] and morphology [6]. In face recognition [7] and remote sensing [8] applications, authors have shown the advantages of using multiple data sources. Combination of texture features has been suggested by some authors e.g. using Fourier spectrum [9] and morphology [6], but the combination has usually been restricted to derivative measures within the same kind of texture feature.

We have developed two new methods for combining texture features [10]: composite feature vectors and an extended k-nearest-neighbour (KNN) rule. An experimental analysis shows how the new techniques provide promising classification performance using some established and some new texture features, including various spectral, grey-level and statistical features. The whole Brodatz database (112 classes) was used for analysis of classification performance. Also, particular consideration of texture classes for which 'perfect' classification capability was achieved. An analysis based on the normalised interclass distance correlation gives new insight into discriminatory ability and into the Brodatz database.

2 METHODS OF COMBINING TEXTURE FEATURES

A texture feature is a function which transforms the original image into a feature vector. Different features essentially represent different information about the texture image, which we can exploit to improve classification capability through combination. Conventional texture classification systems are usually made up of two stages: feature description and classification. An input image is transformed into a feature vector, then the classifier decides the results by comparing the similarity and difference of the input with the feature vectors in the training set. As such, combination of features could occur at either or both of these two stages. Composite feature vectors seek to combine features at the feature description stage. Various other methods of combining classifiers exist [11]. Here we use an extended k-nearest-neighbour rule that combines the features at the classifier stage.

2.1 COMPOSITE FEATURE VECTORS

Composite feature vectors (c.f. 'stacked-vector' in [8]) are obtained by concatenating two feature vectors of the same texture image, such that

$$F_C(\mathbf{J}) = [F_u(\mathbf{J})|F_v(\mathbf{J})] = [\mathrm{u}|\mathrm{v}] = (u_1\, u_2\, \ldots\, u_R\, v_1\, v_2 \ldots v_S)^T \tag{1}$$

where: F_u and F_v are two different feature functions operating on the original texture image represented by the vector $\mathbf{J}$ resulting in two feature vectors u and v; $u_1, u_2, \ldots$ and $v_1, v_2, \ldots$ are the components of u and v respectively; and R and S are the dimensions of the appropriate feature vectors. For two texture images of different classes $\mathbf{J}_1$ and $\mathbf{J}_2$, the composite Euclidean distance is then given by

$$\begin{aligned} D_C &= \sqrt{\frac{1}{S_u^2}D_u^2 + \frac{1}{S_v^2}D_v^2} \\ &= \sqrt{\frac{1}{\sigma_u^2}|\mathrm{u}_1 - \mathrm{u}_2|^2 + \frac{1}{Sa_v^2}|\mathrm{v}_1 - \mathrm{v}_2|^2} \\ &= \sqrt{\frac{1}{S_u^2}\sum_{i=1}^{R}[u_{(1)i} - u_{(2)i}]^2 + \frac{1}{S_v^2}\sum_{i=1}^{S}[v_{(1)i} - v_{(2)i}]^2}, \end{aligned} \tag{2}$$

where D_u and D_v are Euclidean distances for feature functions F_u and F_v. S_u^2 and S_v^2 are the variance of all the feature vectors of the feature function F_u and F_v respectively, and are used as normalisation factors since they are essentially an estimate of the spread of the distribution of feature vectors in the individual feature space.

2.2 EXTENDED K-NEAREST-NEIGHBOUR RULE

A feature vector can be viewed as one point in the feature space. The k-nearest-neighbour (KNN) rule stipulates that the class of an unknown input image X is determined by the mode class of the k nearest neighbouring feature vectors within the single feature space:

$$X = mode(Y_1, Y_2, \ldots, Y_k) \tag{3}$$

where $(Y_1, \ldots, Y_k)$ are the class of the k nearest neighbours.

For use with multiple features, we consider an extended KNN rule so that that the class of the input is determined by the class of the majority of the nearest neighbours in all feature spaces:

$$X = mode(Y_{11} \ldots Y_{1k}; Y_{21} \ldots Y_{2k}; \ldots; Y_{m1} \ldots Y_{mk}), \tag{4}$$

where we select from m feature spaces with k nearest neighbour in each feature space. The decision is then based on the highest collective confidence over all features.

2.3 ANALYSIS OF NORMALISED INTERCLASS DISTANCE (D/σ)

The normalised interclass distance between two clusters is defined as the ratio of the Euclidean distance between the centroids of two clusters P and Q (D) to the local standard deviation of cluster P (σ). This can be shown to be a direct measure of class separability. Figure 1 shows a typical graph of the number of correct classification for individual classes against the normalised nearest neighbour distance (D_{min}/σ). Here the graph for the functions HG, HD and $HG|HD$ are plotted. In can be seen that the classification rate for individual class becomes nearly perfect (16) if $\frac{D_{min}}{\sigma} > 1$ and when $\frac{D_{min}}{\sigma} < 1$, the number of correct classification is much more likely to be less than perfect (< 16). It is also observed that the graph shows a step-like relation between individual classification rate and D_{min}/σ and this favours the improvement in classification rate instead of degradation, as the likelihood of $D/\sigma > 1$ is higher than otherwise.

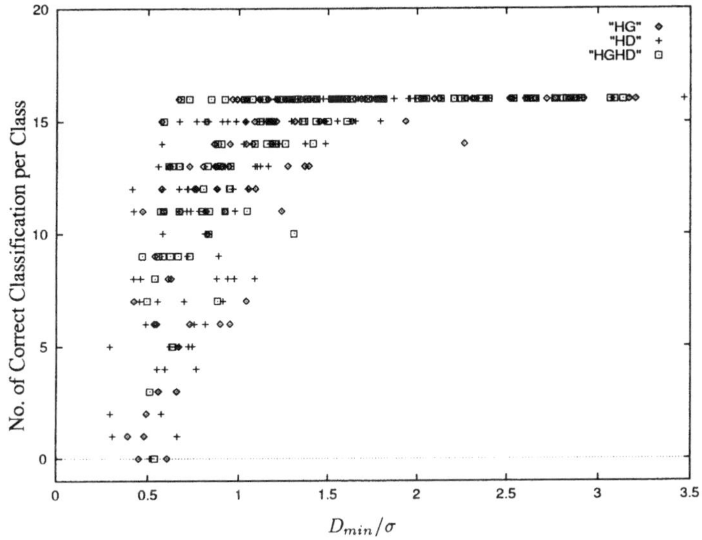

Figure 1: Relation of D_{min}/σ and the number of correct classfication in each class.

It can be shown that, for the composite feature vector,

$$\frac{D_C^2}{\sigma_C^2} = \frac{S_v^2 D_u^2 + S_u^2 D_v^2}{S_v^2 \sigma_u^2 + S_u^2 \sigma_v^2}. \tag{5}$$

where σ_u^2 and σ_v^2 are local cluster variances and S_u^2 and S_v^2 are global variances for feature functions F_u and F_v respectively. This implies that the value of the normalised interclass distance in the composite feature space D_C/σ_C lies between the values of the normalised interclass distance in feature spaces F_u and F_v, D_u/σ_u and D_v/σ_v:

$$\frac{D_u}{\sigma_u} < \frac{D_C}{\sigma_C} < \frac{D_v}{\sigma_v}. \tag{6}$$

For the extended KNN rule, the normalised interclass distance due to the rule is effectively the larger of the individual normalised interclass distance,

$$\frac{D_E}{\sigma_E} = max\left(\frac{D_u}{\sigma_u}, \frac{D_v}{\sigma_v}\right). \tag{7}$$

This also improves the classification rate since the most characteristic properties in each feature space contribute to classification.

For problems involving N classes ($N>2$), such as the classification of the Brodatz texture database ($N = 112$), D_u/σ_u and D_v/σ_v can be viewed as statistical variables each having $N(N-1)$ interclass distances. To analyse difference between two feature sets, we may define the distance correlation r_D as

$$r_D = \frac{\sum_i (x_i - \overline{x})(y_i - \overline{y})}{\sqrt{\sum_i (x_i - \overline{x})^2 \sum_i (y_i - \overline{y})^2}}, \tag{8}$$

using the standard product moment correlation coefficient, where D_u/σ_u and D_v/σ_v are denoted by x and y for convenience. A strong positive correlation between D_u/σ_u and D_v/σ_v ($r_D \simeq 1$) suggests that the differences between D_u/σ_u and D_v/σ_v are generally small, as will be shown in the results in table 3. From equation 5 and 7, it can be seen that the increase, or improvement, due to feature combination depends on the difference between D_u/σ_u and D_v/σ_v. Therefore there is no potential improvement in classification capability by combining the two features if there is a strong positive correlation between D_u/σ_u and D_v/σ_v. Conversely, other values of r_D ($r_D \ll 1$) suggest that classification capability will improve.

3 FEATURE FUNCTIONS

3.1 FOURIER AND WALSH TRANSFORM

For structural texture description, several standard transform functions are used:

(i) The two dimensional Discrete Fourier Transform $H_{m,n}$ and the two dimensional Walsh transform $W_{m,n}$ of an $N \times N$ image **J** are given by:

$$H_{m,n} = \sum_{q=0}^{N-1} \sum_{p=0}^{N-1} J_{pq} e^{2\pi jpm/N} e^{2\pi jqn/N}, \tag{9}$$

$$W_{m,n} = \frac{1}{N^2} \sum_{i=0}^{N-1} \sum_{j=0}^{N-1} J_{ij}\, WAL(n,i)\, WAL(m,j). \tag{10}$$

(ii) One Dimensional Fourier and Walsh transform on Columns and Rows: the one dimensional Fourier transform on columns Hc_n, the one dimensional Fourier transform on rows Hr_n and the average of the column and row transform $\overline{H}_n$ are given by:

$$Hc_{n,m} = \sum_{q=0}^{N-1} J_{pq} e^{2\pi jqn/N}, \tag{11}$$

$$Hr_{n,m} = \sum_{p=0}^{N-1} J_{pq} e^{2\pi jpn/N}, \tag{12}$$

$$\overline{H}_n = \frac{1}{N}\left[\sum_{m=0}^{N-1} |Hc_{n,m}| + \sum_{m=0}^{N-1} |Hr_{n,m}|\right]. \tag{13}$$

Similarly, the one dimensional Walsh transform on columns Wc_n, the one dimensional Walsh transform on rows Wr_n and the average of the column and row transform $\overline{W}_n$ are given by:

$$Wc_{n,i} = \sum_{j=0}^{N-1} J_{ij}\, WAL(n,i), \qquad (14)$$

$$Wr_{n,j} = \sum_{i=0}^{N-1} J_{ij}\, WAL(n,i), \qquad (15)$$

$$\overline{W}_n = \frac{1}{N}\left[\sum_{i=0}^{N-1} |Wc_n(i)| + \sum_{j=0}^{N-1} |Wr_n(j)|\right]. \qquad (16)$$

3.2 GREY LEVEL FUNCTIONS

For statistical texture measures, the grey level distribution is used to give several texture metrics as follow:

(i) Histograms of the Grey Level of Pixels, defined as [2]:

$$HG(\mathbf{J}) = HG(g|\mathbf{J}) = \sum_{i=1}^{N}\sum_{j=1}^{N} \delta(g - J_{ij}), \qquad (17)$$

where $\delta(\cdot)$ is the Kronecker delta function.

(ii) Histograms of the Difference of Grey Level of Adjacent Pixels, defined as [2]:

$$HD(\mathbf{J}) = HD(d|\mathbf{J}) = \sum_{i=1}^{N}\sum_{j=1}^{N} \delta(d - |J_{ij} - J_{i'j'}|), \qquad (18)$$

where (i', j') are the four neighbouring pixels of (i, j).

(iii) Histograms of Grey Level Co-occurrence Lines, whose angle is defined as:

$$HC_d(\mathbf{J}) = HC_d(\theta|\mathbf{J}) = \sum_{\mathbf{z}\in\mathbf{L}} \delta(\theta - \arg(\mathbf{z})), \qquad (19)$$

and the histograms of the length of grey level co-occurrence lines is given by:

$$HC_r(\mathbf{J}) = HC_r(r|\mathbf{J}) = \sum_{\mathbf{z}\in\mathbf{L}} \delta(r - |\mathbf{z}|), \qquad (20)$$

where the set of co-occurrence lines (i.e. lines joining pixels of the same grey level) is defined by:

$$\mathbf{L} = \{\mathbf{z} \mid \mathbf{z}=(i-i', j-j')\ \forall\ J_{ij}=J_{i'j'}\}. \qquad (21)$$

3.3 STATISTICAL GEOMETRIC FEATURES

The statistical geometric features (SGF) [12], are based on two properties of the binary image stacks derived from a grey level image: the number of connected regions and irregularities. The binary image stacks $f_b(x, y; \alpha)$ are generated by thresholding a grey level image $f(x, y)$ by α, so that

$$\begin{aligned} &f_b(x, y; \alpha) = 1\ if\ f(x, y) > \alpha \\ &f_b(x, y) = 0\ otherwise, \\ &\alpha \in \{1, \ldots, n_l - 1\} \end{aligned} \qquad (22)$$

where n_l is the number of grey levels in the image.

(i) Number of Connected Regions. The number of '0'-valued connected regions $NOC_0(\alpha)$ and the number of '1'-valued connected regions $NOC_1(\alpha)$ at successive thresholds α give two complimentary texture features.

(ii) Irregularities: the irregularity of each connected region at a particular threshold α is measured as follows:

$$irgl = \frac{1+\pi^{1/2} max_{i\in I}[(x_i-\overline{x})^2+(y_i-\overline{y})^2]^{1/2}}{|I|^{1/2}} - 1, \tag{23}$$

where

$$\overline{x}=\frac{1}{|I|}\sum_{i\in I} x_i \; and \; \overline{y}=\frac{1}{|I|}\sum_{i\in I} y_i;$$

I is the set of all pixels in the connected region; and $|I|$ is the number of pixels in that connected region. $irgl$ is therefore the ratio of the area of a circle covering the connected region to the actual size of the region. The average irregularity of '0'-valued a binary stack at threshold α is

$$\overline{IRGL_0}(\alpha) = \frac{\sum_{j\in J} |I|_j \cdot irgl_j}{\sum_{j\in J} |I|_j}, \tag{24}$$

where J is the set of all connected region in that binary stack. $\overline{IRGL_1}(\alpha)$ is similarly defined for '1'-valued binary stacks.

4 RESULTS

We tested the feature combination methods with 112 classes/photographs of texture from the whole Brodatz Texture Album. 16 samples were taken from each image and leave-one-out cross-validation tests were performed. Experimental results are based on one conventional measure – classification rate – as well as a new measure – the number of perfect classes (classes where all samples are classified correctly) – which is independent of the selection of test data and the number of test classes. Amongst the Brodatz textures, some appeared to be imperfect (i.e. a mixture of textures) as in figure 2, but we did not omit them.

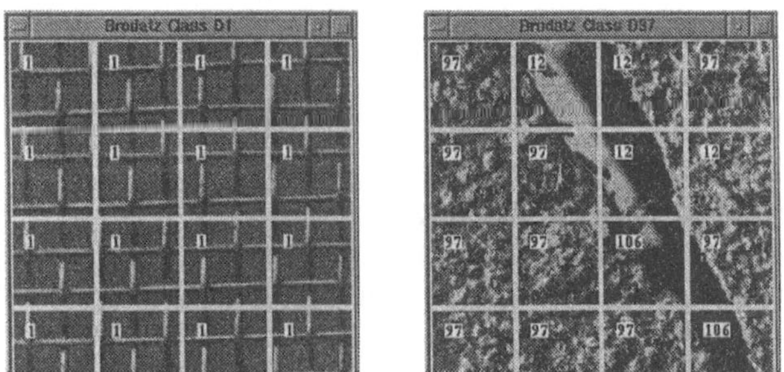

Figure 2: Brodatz textures D1 (homogeneous) and D97 (mixture) with classification results of each class.

Features		Corr'n	Classification Rates (%)				
F_u	F_v	r_D	F_u	F_v	F_C	F_E	$\cap$
CD	CR	0.988	37.7	34.4	38.4	40.1	26.7
F2D	W2D	0.977	57.4	34.7	44.5	50.9	32.8
F1D	W1D	0.962	69.6	62.0	68.0	68.2	59.2
HG	HD	0.800	81.7	75.8	88.7	85.8	69.8
NOC0	NOC1	0.701	66.2	70.0	79.7	77.2	56.2
IRGL0	IRGL1	0.850	42.4	41.7	56.6	49.3	28.2
NOC	IRGL	0.427	79.7	56.6	81.0	79.9	52.4
NOC	HG	0.312	79.7	81.7	89.5	86.9	72.7
NOC	HD	0.330	79.7	75.8	85.0	84.7	68.1
F1D	HG	0.411	69.6	81.7	86.5	86.0	63.6
F1D	HD	0.387	69.6	75.8	83.7	81.8	60.9
F1D	NOC	0.328	69.6	79.7	83.9	82.5	64.4
NOC/HG/HD					89.2	88.3	
F1D/HG/HD			(see above)		89.4	88.3	
F1D/NOC/ /HG/HD					89.2	90.2	

Table 1: Classification rates of individual and combined features. F_C: Composite Vectors; F_E: Extended KNN Rule; $\cap$: percentage of correct classification common to both F_u and F_v.

The results are shown in tables 1 through 3. Table 1 lists the overall classification rates of individual and combined features of all 112 Brodatz classes. The percentage of correct classification common to both individual features is also listed in table 1. The number of perfect classes achieved by individual and combined features are listed in table 2, whereas table 3 shows the analysis of normalised interclass distance. Table 4 lists the acronyms and features used for tests.

It is evident that combination of features with weak correlation ($r_D \ll 1$) results in significant improvement of classification capabilities. In table 1, the basic features such as the two dimensional Walsh and Fourier transforms have only moderate performance, 57% and 35% only. The distance correlation of these features is high ($r_D \simeq 1$) and when combined (F_C), this only achieves 45% classification rate, just better than their average classification capability. By way of contrast, the number of connected regions (NOC) is much less correlated to the histograms of grey level values (HG) and their individual classification rates of 80% and 82% rise to 90% (F_C) when combined. This rise in classification capability is evident in all cases where the distance correlation appears to be low.

Such a rise is also evident in classification based on the extended k-nearest-neighbour (KNN) rule. The rise in classification capability is also reflected in the number of perfect classes achieved by the composite feature vector or the extended KNN rule, as shown in table 2. For the Fourier and Walsh transform approach, the number of perfect classes is 32 and 15 respectively and a intermediate result (22) for the composite feature vector. For NOC and HG, the number of perfect classes rises to 65, a large increase from the individual 48 and 52.

Further combination of more than two features is shown in the bottom section of tables 1 and 2, with classification rates up to 90.2% and 71 perfect classes.

Features		Corr'n	No. Perfect Classes			
F_u	F_v	r_D	F_u	F_v	F_C	F_E
CD	CR	0.988	12	5	8	12
F2D	W2D	0.977	32	15	22	25
F1D	W1D	0.962	31	17	28	27
HG	HD	0.800	52	33	64	61
NOC0	NOC1	0.701	23	26	48	39
IRGL0	IRGL1	0.850	6	5	13	10
NOC	IRGL	0.427	48	13	44	43
NOC	HG	0.312	48	52	65	61
NOC	HD	0.330	48	33	56	58
F1D	HG	0.411	32	52	60	52
F1D	HD	0.387	32	33	49	51
F1D	NOC	0.328	32	48	50	51
NOC/HG/HD					65	68
F1D/HG/HD		N/A			67	64
F1D/NOC//HG/HD					64	71

Table 2: Distance correlation coefficients and the number of perfect classes of individual and combined features. F_C: Composite Vectors; F_E: Extended KNN Rule.

Table 3 shows the mean normalised nearest neighbour distance $\frac{D_{min}}{\sigma}$ for single features F_u and F_v compared with that of the composite feature F_C. It was also found that the mean difference of D_u/σ_u and D_v/σ_v ($\Delta\frac{D}{\sigma}$) and the increment in the normalised nearest neighbour distance $\Delta\frac{D_{min}}{\sigma}$ are in inverse relation to the distance correlation r_D. Significant improvement occurs when the distance correlation $r_D \ll 1$ as shown by a marked increase in the mean $\frac{D_{min}}{\sigma}$ and large mean $\Delta\frac{D_{min}}{\sigma}$. Earlier, the high correlation between the 2D Walsh and 2D Fourier transforms was seen to result in no improvement in classification capability. This is reflected in the difference of their normalised interclass distance which suggests that features derived by each results in similar feature distributions.

The convergence of classification rates and number of perfect classes using different combinations in the regions of 80-90% and 60-70 classes which coincides with the number of homogeneous textures of the Brodatz database suggests that the remaining imperfect textures are potentially unclassifiable by ordinary feature functions. The results (up to 90.2% classification rate using all Brodatz textures with 71 perfect classes) also suggest that combination of simple features provides potent classification capabilities when compared with other current texture models using single feature.

5 CONCLUSIONS

Two methods of combining texture features, composite vectors and extended KNN rule can be used to improved texture classification capability. The distance correlation coefficient is used as a measure of correlation between two features. The combined features yielded potent classification capabilities of classification rates up to 90.2% using all Brodatz textures (112 classes) and the highest number of classes with perfect classification is 71, providing a rich avenue for further research which will aim to capitalise on these new developments. The analysis of the normalised interclass distance correlation is shown to be a promising measure of correlation of different feature functions and a measure for the potential for feature combination.

Features		Corr'n	Mean D_{min}/σ			Mean	
F_u	F_v	r_D	F_u	F_v	F_C	$\Delta\frac{D}{\sigma}$	$\Delta\frac{D_{min}}{\sigma}$
CD	CR	0.999	0.553	0.490	0.558	1.820	0.116
F2D	W2D	0.994	0.901	0.671	0.758	0.807	0.095
F1D	W1D	0.999	1.182	0.872	1.004	0.680	0.134
HG	HD	0.738	1.357	1.126	1.442	1.948	0.456
NOC0	NOC1	0.717	1.016	1.040	1.209	1.246	0.384
IRGL0	IRGL1	0.821	0.664	0.591	0.767	1.223	0.257
NOC	IRGL	0.291	1.209	0.767	1.219	1.941	0.486
NOC	HG	0.038	1.209	1.357	1.500	1.759	0.435
NOC	HD	0.234	1.209	1.126	1.310	2.703	0.353
F1D	HG	0.577	1.182	1.357	1.393	2.928	0.491
F1D	HD	0.401	1.182	1.126	1.417	3.379	0.522
F1D	NOC	0.180	1.182	1.209	1.262	3.200	0.305

Table 3: Mean D_{min}/σ and Mean $\Delta\frac{D_{min}}{\sigma}$ for individual and combined features.

Feature	Acronym
2D Fourier transform	F2D
2D Walsh transform	W2D
1D row/col Fourier transform	F1D
1D row/col Walsh transform	W1D
Histograms of grey level	HG
Hist. of grey level differences	HD
Hist. of angle of co-occur. lines	CD
Hist. of length of co-occur. lines	CR
No. of black connected regions	NOC0
No. of white connected regions	NOC1
Irregularity of black regions	IRGL0
Irregularity of white regions	IRGL1
Composite NOC0/NOC1	NOC
Composite IRGL0/IRGL1	IRGL

Table 4: Feature functions and acronyms used.

References

[1] R. M. Haralick, K. Shanmugam, and I. Dinstein. Textural features for image classification. *IEEE Trans. Systems, Man and Cybernectics*, 3:610–621, 1973.

[2] J. S. Weszka, C. R. Dyer, and A. Rosenfeld. A comparative study of texture measures for terrain classification. *IEEE Trans. Systems, Man and Cybernetics*, SMC-6(4):269–285, April 1976.

[3] G. L. Gimel'farb and A. K. Jain. On retrieving textured images from an image database. *Pattern Recognition*, 29(9):1461–1483, 1996.

[4] A. Laine and J. Fan. Texture classification by wavelet packet signatures. *IEEE Trans. Pattern Analysis and Machine Intelligence*, 15(11):1186–1191, November 1993.

[5] O. Pichler, A. Teuner, and B. J. Hosticka. A comparison of texture feature extraction using adaptive Gabor filtering, pyramidal and tree structured wavelet transforms. *Pattern Recognition*, 29(5):733–742, 1996.

[6] Y. Chen and E. R. Dougherty. Gray-scale morphological granulometric texture classification. *Optical Engineering*, 33(8):2713–2722, August 1995.

[7] X. Jia and M. S. Nixon. Extending the feature vector for automatic face recognition. *IEEE Trans. Pattern Analysis and Machine Intelligence*, 17(12):1167–1176, 1995.

[8] J. A. Benediktsson, J. R. Sveinsson, and P. H. Swaine. Hybrid consensus theoretic classification. *IEEE Trans. Geoscience and Remote Senseing*, 35(4):833–843, 1997.

[9] Song Sheng Liu. Texture analysis and discrimination in additive noise. *Computer Vision, Graphics, and Image Processing*, 49:52–67, 1990.

[10] L. S. Ng, M. S. Nixon, and J. N. Carter. Texture classification using combined feature sets. *In Proceedings of the IEEE Southwest Symposium on Image Analysis and Interpretation*, pages 103–108, April 1998.

[11] K. Woods, W. P. Kegelmeyer Jr., and K. Bowyer. Combination of multiple classifiers using local accuracy estimates. *IEEE Trans. Pattern Analysis and Machine Intelligence*, 19(4):405–410, April 1997.

[12] Y. Q. Chen, M. S. Nixon, and D. W. Thomas. Statistical geometrical features for texture classification. *Pattern Recognition*, 28(4):537–552, 1995.

USING CBR LEARNING FOR THE LOW-LEVEL AND HIGH-LEVEL UNIT OF AN IMAGE INTERPRETATION SYSTEM

Petra Perner, Institute of Computer Vision and Applied Computer Sciences, Leipzig, Germany

ABSTRACT

The existing image interpretation systems lack robustness and accuracy. They cannot adapt to changing environmental conditions and to new objects. The application of machine learning to image interpretation is the next logical step.

Our proposed approach aims at the development of dedicated machine learning techniques at all levels of image interpretation in a systematic fashion.

In the paper we propose a system, which uses Case-Based Reasoning (CBR) to optimize image segmentation at the low level according to changing image acquisition conditions and image quality. The intermediate-level unit extracts the case representation used by the high-level unit for further processing. At the high level, CBR is employed to dynamically adapt image interpretation.

1 INTRODUCTION

The existing image interpretation systems lack robustness and accuracy. They cannot adapt to changing environmental conditions and to new objects. The application of machine learning to image interpretation is the next logical step.

Our proposed approach aims at the development of dedicated machine learning techniques at all levels of image interpretation in a systematic fashion.

The proposed system uses Case-Based Reasoning (CBR) [1] to optimize image segmentation at the low level according to changing image acquisition conditions and image quality [2]. The intermediate-level unit extracts the case representation used by the high-level unit for further processing. At the high level, CBR is employed to dynamically adapt image interpretation [3].

Case-Based Reasoning can be used where generalized knowledge is lacking but a set of cases is available. The CBR unit consists of a case base, which contains formerly processed cases. Each case has an entry in case base. The entry contains the features describing the particular case and the interpretation result. A new case is interpreted by looking up the case base for similar cases and by selecting the closest case with its interpretation result. Learning strategies enable the system to improve it´s system performance over time by learning the similarity or the case base according to different abstraction levels.

This strategy ensures that we can run the system without knowing the general concept description for the objects and without knowing the entire objects that should be interpreted by the system.

In section 2, we describe the proposed system architecture and the fundamental behavior of a CBR learning system. The CBR strategy of the low-level unit is described in Section 3. The feature extraction process and the high-level description of a case image are described in Section 4. In Section 5, we describe the high-level unit and give results to the system performance.

2 BACKGROUND

Learning provides adaptation of algorithms to changes in environment and uses the experience to improve recognition performance over time.
Our work aims at the development of dedicated machine learning techniques at all levels of image interpretation in a systematic fashion as shown in Figure 1.
Case-Based Reasoning is used for image segmentation and the acquisition of object description. This reasoning method is used when generalized knowledge is lacking. The method works on a set of cases formerly processed and stored in a case base. A new case is interpreted by searching for similar cases in the case base. Among this set of similar cases the closest case with it´s associated result is selected and presented to the output.
To point out the differences between a CBR learning system and a symbolic learning system, which represents a learned concept explicitly, e.g. by formulas, rules or decision trees, we follow the notion of Wess et al. [4]: "A case-based reasoning system describes a concept C implicitly by a pair (CB, sim). The relationship between the case base CB and the measure sim used for classification may be characterized by the equation:

Concept = Case Base + Measure of Similarity

This equation indicates in analogy to arithmetic that it is possible to represent a given concept C in multiple ways, i.e. there exist many pairs C= $(CB_1, sim_1), (CB_2, sim_2), ..., (CB_i, sim_i)$ for the same concept C. Furthermore, the equation gives a hint how a case-based learner can improve ist classification ability. There are three possibilities to improve a case-based system. The system can

- store new cases in the case base *CB*,
- change the measure of similarity *sim*,
- or change *CB* and *sim*.

During the learning phase a case-based system gets a sequence of cases $X_1, X_2, ..., X_i$ with $X_i = (x_i, class(x_i))$ and builds a sequence of pairs $(CB_1, sim_1), (CB_2, sim_2), ..., (CB_i, sim_i)$ with $CB_i \subseteq \{X_1, X_2, ..., X_i\}$. The aim is to get in the limit a pair (CB_n, sim_n) that needs no further change, i.e. $\exists n \; \forall m \geq n \; (CB_n, sim_n) = (CB_m, sim_m)$, because it is a correct classifier for the target concept C."
This behavior of the learning approach makes it useful for image segmentation as well as for image interpretation. Most segmentation techniques contain numerous control parameters, which must be adjusted to obtain optimal performance. Learning optimal parameter settings requires search in a large parameter space. The parameters within most segmentation algorithm typically interact in a complex, non-linear fashion, which makes it impossible to model the parameters behavior in an algorithmic or rule-based fashion. The variation between images causes changes in segmentation results. Thus, with fixed parameter settings, the segmentation quality varies from image to image. The technique used to optimize the segmentation quality must be able to adapt to these variations.
At the high-level stage, CBR is useful to dynamically adapt image interpretation to new object and to improve performance results.
As we noted before, the main problems concerned with CBR are [5]:

1. What is an appropriate similartiy measure for the problem?
2. How to organize a large number of cases for efficient retrieval?
3. How to acquire and refine a new case for entry in the case base?
4. How to generalize specific cases to a case that is applicable to a wide range of situations?

All these problems are concerned with learning. Clearly, a chosen organization for case base must be updated with every new stored case. A similarity measure that was chosen based on expert knowledge about the problem domain must not hold when more cases have been seen. In case generalization, specific cases are modified to create cases with more universal applicability and meaning.
In the next section, we will investigate how these problems can be solved for the low-level and the high-level unit of an image interpretation system. For each system, level we have chosen a different approach, which fulfills different requirements.

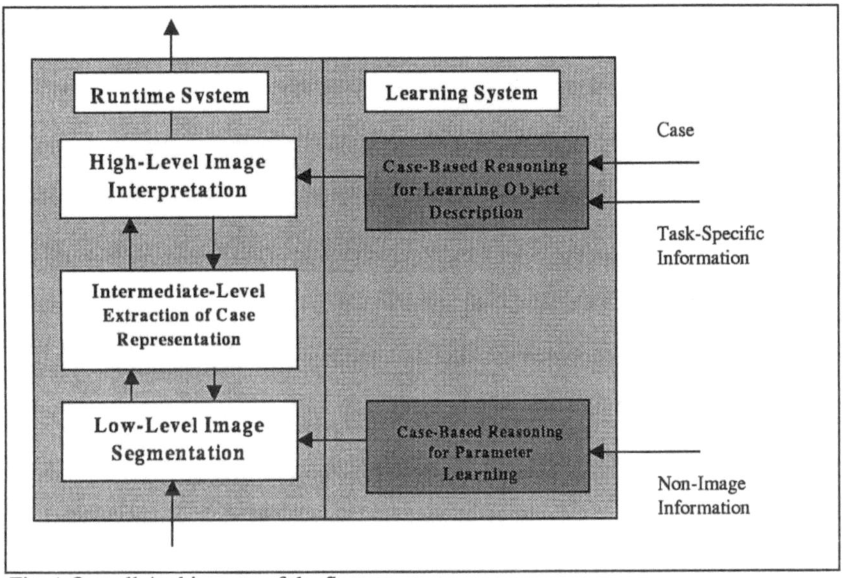

Fig. 1 Overall Architecture of the System

3 CASE-BASED REASONING FOR LOW-LEVEL VISION

Most segmentation techniques contain numerous control parameters, which must be adjusted to obtain optimal performance. The parameter selection is usually done on a large enough test data set, which should represent the entire domain well enough in order to be able to built up a general model for the segmentation. However, often it is not possible to obtain a large enough data set so that the segmentation model doesn't fit well to the data and needs to be adjusted to new data. Besides that, a general model does not guarantee the best segmentation for each image rather it guarantees an average best fit over the entire set of images. Another aspect goes along with changes in image quality caused by variations in environmental conditions, image devices, etc. Then the segmentation performance needs to be adapted to these changes in image quality. All that makes it necessary to equip the segmentation unit with learning capabilities, which can incrementally acquire new knowledge about the model for segmentation.
The case-based reasoning unit for parameter learning of image segmentation consists of a case base, in which formerly processed cases are stored by their original images, their non-image information (e.g. image acquisition parameters, object characteristics and so on), and their image segmentation parameters. The task is now to find the best segmentation for the current image by looking up the case base for similar cases. Similarity determination is done

based on non-image information and image information. The evaluation unit will take the case with the highest similarity score for further processing. In case there are two or more cases with the same similarity score the first appeared case will be taken. After the closest case has been chosen, the image segmentation parameter associated with the selected case will be given to the image segmentation unit and the current image will be segmented, see Fig. 2. It is assumed that images having similar image characteristics will show similar good segmentation results when the same segmentation parameters were applied to these images.

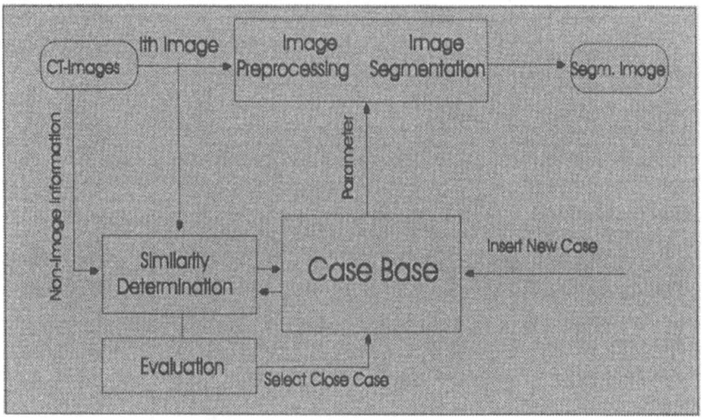

Fig. 2 Similarity-Based Image Segmentation Unit

3.1 SIMILARITY MEASURE FOR NON-IMAGE INFORMATION

We use Tversky's similarity measure [6] for the non-image information. The similarity between a Case C_i and a new case b presented to the system is:

$$S(C_i, b) = \frac{|C_i|}{\alpha|A| + \beta|D| + \gamma|M|} \tag{1}$$

$$\alpha = 1, \beta, \gamma = \frac{1}{2}$$

where $|C_i|$ is the set of attributes in case C_i, A is the set of corresponding attributes in case C_i and b, D is the set of attributes having different values, and M is the set of attributes having missing values.

3.2 SIMILARITY MEASURE FOR IMAGE INFORMATION

Determination of similarity is done with an algorithm proposed by Zamperoni et al. For detailed description of the algorithm, we refer the interested reader to [7]. The input to the algorithm is two images that should be compared. According to the specified distance function, the proximity matrix is calculated for one pixel at position r,s in image A to the pixel at the same position in image B and to surrounding pixel within a predefined window. The same is done for the pixel at position r,s in image B. Then, clustering is performed based on that matrix in order to get the minimum distance among the compared pixel. Afterwards, the average of both values is calculated. This repeats until all pixels of both images are processed. Then from the average minimal pixel distance, the distance value for the whole image is calculated and this value is given to the output. Summarizing this, the similarity is calculated in three steps: point-to-point, point-to-image, and image-to-image. The algorithm considers the distance in gray level as well as the distance in space. Therefore, the algorithm can detect changes in gray level as well as shift in space. Table 1 shows the similarity based on the algorithm of Zamperoni et al. for the images shown in Figure 3.

Image	B1_1	B2_1	B2_3	B2_4	B2_5	B4_1
B1_1	0	0,19748	0,15646	0,15748	0,16216	0,32239
B2_1	0,19748	0	0,13614	0,15844	0,16099	0,30203
B2_3	0,15646	0,13614	0	0,10337	0,10571	0,28891
B2_4	0,15748	0,15844	0,10337	0	0,09431	0,27510
B2_5	0,16216	0,16099	0,10571	0,09431	0	0,28985
B4_1	0,32239	0,30203	0,28891	0,27510	0,28985	0

Tab. 1 Similarity Values for the Images in Fig. 2

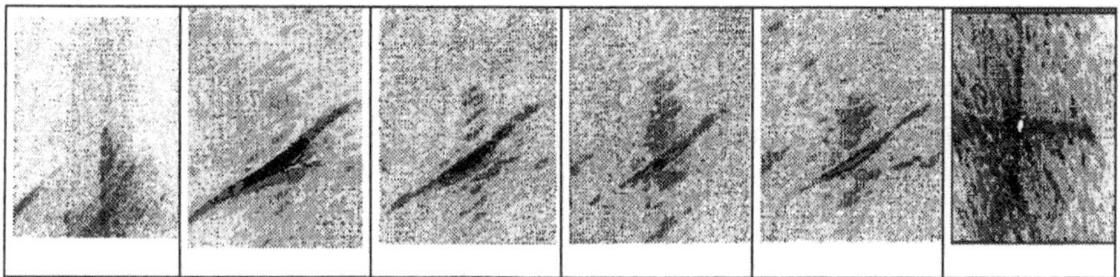

B1_1	B2_1	B2_3	B2_4	B2_5	B4_1

Fig. 3 Images used for Similarity Calculation shown in Tab. 1

3.3 SEGMENTATION PARAMETERS

Segmentation is done by thresholding in this application. The segmentation parameter, which is given to the segmentation unit, is the threshold.

3.4 MONITORING THE SYSTEM PERFORMANCE

There are several approaches for monitoring the segmentation performance possible. The most common strategy in CBR is to let the user evaluate the result of the system. Whereas at the high-level unit such an approach may be adequate since the decision is only `right answer` or `wrong answer`. At the low-level unit, a subjective decision might not be useful although this has widely been done in the past.

To objectify the quality of the segmentation result we calculate the similarity between the gray levels of the original image and the segmented image based on Zamperoni et al. dissimilarity measure [7]. The learning system will be called if the calculated value for similarity exceeds a predefined threshold.

Figure 4 shows the similarity between the original image and the processed image for different thresholds. The subjective chosen threshold gives also the best similarity.

3.5 LEARNING

If the learning system was called by the evaluation unit, the run-time system will give the recent case (the image and the non-image information) to the learning system. In an off-line process, the right threshold will be chosen interactively by the user so that the similarity measure will be less than the predefined threshold. Afterwards, the segmentation parameter, the image and the non-image information is collected to a new case and stored into the case base.

In principal, all case-based management and learning functions for the case base described at the high-level unit are applicable here as well. But we restricted our work at this level to the kind of learning described above since we use a parallel system for the processing, which guaranties us the efficiency in computation time.

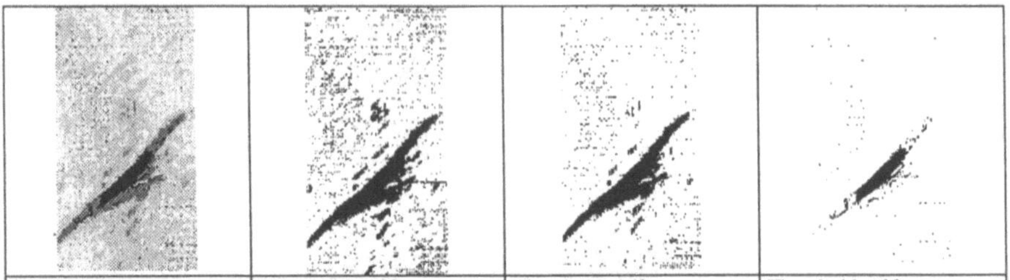

B2_1	Threshold =190	Threshold=169	Threshold=100
	D=0,170983	D=0,161021 Best	D=0,169589

Fig. 4 Different Segmentation Results for Image B2_1 and the Similarity Values

3.6 ORGANIZATION OF CASE BASE AND RETRIEVAL

The case base is organized as a flat structure. The cases are stored one behind the other in the case base. To ensure the efficiency of the retrieval process we implemented the low-level unit on a parallel system (4 node processor based on Power PC 604). The case base is partitioned into three equally portions. Each of these three portions is distributed to one of these three processor nodes. A query is given to each of these three nodes. Each processor calculates the similarity to each of the cases in its case base. The similarity values are given to the fourth processor node to score out the highest similarity. The image segmentation parameters associated to the close case are given to the fourth processor. Afterwards, the original image is processed by the segmentation unit and the result is evaluated. If the segmentation result is not satisfactory, the recent case is interactively processed. The final segmentation parameter together with the original image and the non-image information are stored into one of the three processor node so that the cases are equally distributed.

4 EXTRACTION OF FEATURES AND HIGH-LEVEL DESCRIPTION OF A CASE

After the image is processed by the segmentation unit, the intermediate-level unit calculates the high-level description of the image, which is given as case representation to the CBR unit at the high-level stage [8].

A single image, following called case, is represented by objects, their attributes (e.g. graylevel = light, gray, black; size = large, middle and small) and the spatial relations (e.g. left_behind, right etc.) between the objects. That gives a structural representation for an image represented as an image graph. Images of that kind are for example ultra sonic images for defect classification shown in Figure 5. The images were acquired by the SAFT ultra sonic system [9]. Thresholding technique is used for segmentation (s. Fig. 6), preprocessing is done by using morphological operators like dilation and erosion (s. Fig. 7) and afterwards the objects are labeled by the line coincidence method. Symbolic transformation of the numeric information of an object is done with the help of a functional model for space [10], size and gray level. The symbolic description of the image is used since it is natural to an operator to describe images in these terms. The final representation of a case is shown in Fig. 8.

Fig. 5 Original Image

Fig. 6 Binary Image

Fig. 7 Result

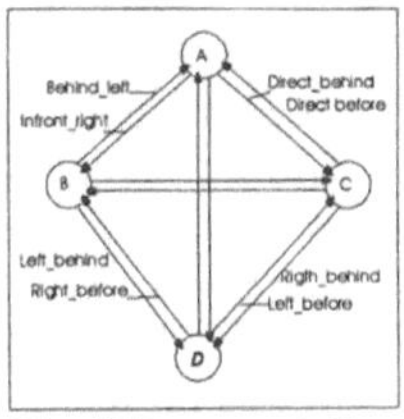

Fig. 8 Representation

5 CASE BASED REASONING FOR IMAGE INTERPRETATION

The basis for the development of our system is a set of cases $CB = \{G_1, G_2, ..., G_i, ..., G_n\}$, each case is a 3-Tupel $G_i = (N, p, q)$, which is a structural symbolic representation of an image, and a similarity measure δ for structural representations. For the current image an image graph is extracted by image analysis. This structure is used for indexing . The interpretation of a current image S is done by case comparison: Given an image $S = (N_s, p_s, q_s)$, find a case G_m in the case base CB which is most similar to the current image. Output the case G_m and the stored solution (e.g. in our case, the defect name)[11][12].

5.1 SIMILARITY DETERMINATION

For similarity determination between our image graphs, we chose part isomorphism [12] :

Definition 1

Two graphs $G_1 = (N_1,p_1,q_1)$ and $G_2 = (N_2,p_2,q_2)$ are in the relation $G_1 \leq G_2$ iff there exists a one-to-one mapping $f: N_1 \rightarrow N_2$ with (1) $p_1(x) = p_2(f(x))$ for all $x \in N_1$

(2) $q_1(x) = q_2(f(x), f(y))$ for all $x,y \in N_1$, $x \neq y$.

Is a graph G_1 included in another graph G_2 then the number of nodes of graph G_1 is not higher than the number of nodes of G_2. In order to handle the unsharp attributes and distortion in a graph representation we relaxed the required correspondence of attribute assignments of nodes and edges in such a way that we introduced ranges of tolerances according to the semantic terms [12].

5.2 ORGANIZATION OF CASE BASE

If we have many cases in case base then it can becomes very time consuming to find the closest case to an actual case. We have seen before that we can speed up the retrieval process by using a parallel platform for our processing unit. Another way to improve the efficiency of our CBR system is to develop an index structure which allows us to find the closest case without examining all existing cases for similarity in case base. On way to impose constraints on retrieval is to index cases using a case base hierarchy [11][12]. Elements in the case base are representations between graphs. As an important relation between this graph we have considered similarity based on part isomorphism. Because of this characteristic, it is possible to organize the case base as directed graph.

In the following, we define the case base as graph that contains the before described image graphs (or only a pointer to this image graphs) in the nodes:

Definition 2

Given is H, the set of all image graphs.

A case base graph is a Tupel CB = (N,E,p), with

(1) $N \subseteq H$ set of nodes and

(2) $E \subseteq N^2$ set of edges.

This set should show the part isomorphism in the set of nodes, meaning it should be valid

$x \leq y \Rightarrow (x,y) \in E$ for all $x,y \in N$.

(3) $p: N \rightarrow B$ mapping of attribute assignments to the image graph (also the attribute values for the description of the defect classes and categories).

Because of the transitivity of part isomorphism, certain edges can be directly derived from other edges and do not need to be separately stored. A relaxation of top (2) in definition 5 can be reduced storage capacity.

5.3 LEARNING

By the development and usage of the case base, it is to consider that the case base may be permanently changing during learning process. The initial case base may be built up by existing cases therefore; a nonincremental learning procedure is required. During the use of the system, new cases may be stored in the case base. They should be integrated in the already existing case base. Therefore, we need an incremental learning procedure.

Now, the task is to build up the graphs of CB in a supergraph by a learning environment. After the expert or operator has done the assignment for the defect category or class, the system is able to find automatically an answer to the given image graph. Formally, this task is to solve permanently:

Input is:

case base Supergraph $CB = (N, E)$ and

image graph $x \in H$.

Output is:

modified case base Supergraph $CB' = (N', E')$

with $N' \subseteq N \cup \{x\}$, $E \subseteq E'$,

At the beginning of the learning process or the process of construction of case base N can be an empty set.

The inclusion $N' \subseteq N \cup \{x\}$ says that the image graph x can be isomorphic to one in the case base contained image graph y, so $x \leq y$ and also $y \leq x$ hold. Then, no new node is created that means the case base is not increased.

The algorithm for the construction of the modified case base CB' can also use the circumstance that no image graph is part isomorphic to another image graph if it has more nodes then the second one.

For technical help for the algorithm there are introduced a set N_i. N_i contains all image graphs of the case base CB with exactly i nodes. The maximal number of nodes of the image graph contained in the case base is k then it is valid:

$$N = \bigcup_{i=1}^{k} N_i$$

The image graph, which has to be included in the case base, has l nodes ($l > 0$). By the comparison of the current image graph with all in the case base contained graphs, we can make use of transitivity of part isomorphism for the reduction of the nodes that has to be compared.

Algorithm

```
E' := E;
Z := N;
for all y∈ N_l
if x ≤ y then [ CB' := CB; return];
N' := N ∪ {x};
for all i with 0 < i < l;
      for all y ∈ N_i\Z;
      for all y ≤ x then [ Z := Z\{u _ u ≤ y, u ∈ Z};
                           E' := E' ∪ { (y,x)}];
for all i with l < i ≤ k
      for all y ∈ N_i\Z
      if x ≤ y then [ Z := Z \{u _ y ≤ u, u ∈ Z };
                      E' := E' ∪ { (x,y)}];
```

If we use the concept of [12] for uncertainty handling, then we can use the algorithm without any changes. However, we should notice that for each group of image graphs that is approximately isomorphic, the first occurred image graph is stored in the case base. Accidentally, this can be a "bad" image graph. Therefore, it is better to calculate of every instance and each new instance of a group a prototype and store this one in the case base. Thus, we can learn the appropriate instance_of.

The described approach allows to learn new cases and store the new case into the case base according to the similarity relation to the already existing cases in case base. If we relax the part isomorphism relation to the concept for uncertainty handling then in each node of the hierarchy is stored a class of cases, which is represented by a prototype. The generalization ability of the algorithm can be described as follows: Given a set of structural relations and two cases x and y, then construct a case g such that $g \succ x$ and $g \succ y$. Then g is the most specific common substructure of the two cases, which gives a generalization of the two cases. In this learning approach, the learned hierarchy depends on the chosen threshold for similarity. An approach were no threshold is necessary is shown in our further work in [13].

5.4 INDEXING AND RETRIEVAL

Retrieval is done as follows: The current case is matched according to the case base hierarchy. The case class with the maximal structural similarity is indexed. Among the members of the indexed case class the closest cases is determined.

6 EVALUATION OF THE SYSTEM

Accuracy (A = (number of right recall / number of samples) * 100) was calculated based on 100 samples [8]. The information „no similar case“ was only taken as an error if there was a similar case in case base but the system could not call it based on the chosen similarity. Among this data set were 5 cases, which are not related to any case in case base. Accuracy was 95%.

7 CONCLUSION

In image interpretation, we are often faced with the problem that it is easier to acquire cases than a compact vision model for reasoning. This makes it interesting to use Case Based Reasoning for an image interpretation system. We have shown how Case-Based Reasoning can be employed for the low-level and high-level unit of an image interpretation system. It can be used for reasoning as well as for learning. At the low-level stage, we can learn incrementally a better system performance of the segmentation unit and at the high-level stage, we can learn a more compact case representation for the objects. The main problem is to find an appropriate measure for similarity. For the low-level unit, we have shown how the similarity measure of Zamperoni et al. works for finding similar cases by comparing the image matrix and for evaluating of the segmentation result. At the high-level unit, the nature of the cases requires a structural representation and because of that, a structural similarity measure is needed. The case base can be organized in different ways. As flat structure if the system platform allows retrieving cases in suitable short time and as hierarchical structure, which speeds up the time since not all cases needs to be matched. The nature of the CBR process allows learning incrementally new cases and/or the case base, which improves the performance of the system over time. Therefore, a CBR can be used for an interpretation task although not all objects have been observed yet, which is the case in large domains like interpretation of technical drawings or in inspection tasks.

REFERENCES

[1] Kolodner, J.L., Case-Based Reasoning, Morgan Kaufmann, 1993.

[2] Perner P. Similarity-Based Image Segmentation. In: T. Lehmann, V. Metzler, K. Spitzner, T. Tolxdorff (eds.). Bildverarbeitung für die Medizin, Springer Verlag, 1998, pp 214-218.

[3] Perner P. Case-Based Reasoning for Image Interpretation in Non-Destructive Testing. In Proceedings EWCBR-93, volume 2, 1993, pages 403-409.

[4] Wess St., Globig Chr. Case-Based and Symbolic Classification. In: Wess St., Althoff K.-D., Richter M.M. (eds.). Topics in Case-Based Reasoning. Springer Verlag 1994, pp 77-91.

[5] Perner P., Anderson P., Summner D., Kyle J. An Application of Case-based Reasoning in Test Process Diagnosis. In Proceedings of the IBM ITL Conference on Expert Systems, Yorktown Heights USA, 1992, pp 73-85.

[6] Tversky A. Feature of Similarity. Psychological Review 1977; 84(4): 111-147.

[7] Zamperoni and V. Starovoitov, „How dissimilar are two gray-scale images", In Proc. of 17. DAGM Symposium 1995,Springer Verlag, pp.448-455

[8] Perner P. Ultra Sonic Image Interpretation for Non-Destructive Testing. In Proceedings of the IAPR Workshop on Machine Vision Applications, 1996, pp 552-554.

[9] Schmitz V. Ultra Sonic Imaging Techniques. In Proceedings of the DGzfP- Annual Conference, 1989.Perner P. Case-Based Reasoning for Image Interpretation in Non-Destructive Testing. In Proceedings EWCBR-93, volume 2, 1993, pages 403 409.

[10] Hernandey D. Relative Representation of Spatial Knowledge: The 2-D Case. Report FKI 135-90, Aug. 1990, TU München

[11] Perner P., Paetzold W. An Incremental Learning System for Interpretation of Images. In: D. Dori and A. Bruckstein (eds.). Shape, Structure, and Pattern Recognition. World Scientific Publishing Co., 1995, pp 311-323.

[12] Perner P., Paetzold W. An Incremental Learning System for Image Interpretation. HTWK Report 5/93.

[13] Perner P. Different Learning Strategies in a Case-Based Reasoning System for Image Interpretation. In: Barry Smith (eds.). EWCBR'98 Dublin. Lncs, Springer Verlag, 1998 to appear.

APPLICATION OF THE TRACE TRANSFORM TO CHANGE DETECTION

A Kadyrov and M Petrou,
University of Surrey,
School of Electronic Engineering,
Information Technology & Mathematics,
Guildford GU2 5XH, UK.
Tel: (01483)259801, Fax: (01483)259554,
email: m.petrou@ee.surrey.ac.uk

ABSTRACT
The Trace transform consists of tracing an image with straight lines along which a functional of the image is computed. Covering the image by all possible lines that could trace it creates the Trace transform of the image. By further computing functionals along the rows and columns of the Trace transform one can compute features that may have pre-specified properties. In this paper we propose the set of functionals that should be computed for monitoring the change in a land use application.

1. INTRODUCTION
In a monitoring problem often the change we are looking for manifests itself as a change in the texture of the object. Examples of such situations arise in remote sensing where the phenomenon we monitor is change of land use, in reconnaissance, where the phenomenon we are looking for is, for example, increased activity in an area, in medical images where various progressive diseases manifest themselves by changes in the texture of the tissue in question, etc.

The purpose of this work is to propose a new method for extracting texture features from images that can reflect the change from one image to the next in a sequence of images of the object, obtained under more or less the same conditions. Our approach is demonstrated with the help of a collection of 20 images of the same car park where we are looking for increased activity, expressed by the number of cars parked in it. These images in order of increasing number of cars they contain are shown in figure 1.

Our approach to the solution of the problem is related to a method of Integral Geometry. The method of Integral Geometry is very simple, and our approach is a generalisation of it. After the theoretical background presented in section 2, we discuss issues concerning the practical application of the method in section 3, some experimental results in section 4 and our conclusions in section 5.

2. THEORETICAL BACKGROUND
Consider many lines crossing an image F. Along every line we can compute a characteristic function T of the image. The characteristic T can be chosen as, for example, the integral of the image function along the line. We have no restrictions on the choice of T. In our simulations we use a large number of options for T.

After computing T along every line, we have a set of numbers. The sum of these numbers $\Pi(T, F)$ is used to characterise image F. The purpose of Integral Geometry is to compute

geometrical characteristics of objects from the sum $\Pi(T, F)$ choosing T appropriately [1]. For example, for some choices of T we can get $\Pi(T, F)$ =*integral* of image F or $\Pi(T, F)$ =*length* of the boundary of the image F (for binary images), etc.
This sum can also be used for image classification in texture analysis. As well as using that in our simulations, we also use some generalisation of the approach that yields "Triple Features".
Our method differs from the Integral Geometry method in one important point: we take into account the position of each line. A position of a line is described by two parameters. Therefore, we can supplement the computation along lines with computations over the other two parameters. These parameters are the angle φ of the position of a line and its distance p from the origin point in the plane [2].
One particular characteristic derived with the help of our method is called "triple feature". This name displays the theoretical way of getting it, involving three functionals.
To get a triple feature, we at first have to choose a triplet of functionals designated with letters T, P and Φ. For example, each of them can be an *integration* of an underlying function or taking *maximum* and so on. Many examples are presented later on.
A line in the plane can be represented by its standard parametrisation. Let $x(t)$ and $y(t)$ be the coordinates of any point on the line, with t being a parameter along the line. Then the line can be represented by

$$x(t) = p\cos(\varphi) + t\sin(\varphi)$$
$$y(t) = p\sin(\varphi) + t\cos(\varphi)$$

Having an image $F(x(t), y(t))$, we can compute functional T along the line, that is along variable t. The result is denoted by $T(F(x(t), y(t)))$
Therefore, we get a function $g(p, \varphi)$ of two variables p and φ:

$$g(p, \varphi) \equiv T(F(p\cos(\varphi) + t\sin(\varphi), p\sin(\varphi) + t\cos(\varphi))), \tag{1}$$

by computing T along t.
Now we can apply the second functional P to $g(p, \varphi)$ along the variable p and get a function

$$h(\varphi) \equiv P(g(p, \varphi)), \tag{2}$$

by computing P along p,
and at the last stage we have

$$\Pi \equiv \Phi h(\varphi), \tag{3}$$

by computing Φ along φ.
Briefly we can write

$$\Pi = \Pi(F, T, P, \Phi) = \Phi(P(T(F(p\cos(\varphi) + t\sin(\varphi), p\sin(\varphi) + t\cos(\varphi))))), \tag{4}$$

obtained by computing T along t, P along p and Φ along φ.

5. FROM THEORY TO PRACTICE

To fix a triple feature is equivalent to selecting a triplet (T, P, Φ) of functionals. After having chosen (T, P, Φ), we have to perform three stages of computation.
At first, we fix angle φ and consider a set of parallel lines indexed by i:

$$x(t) = p_i\cos(\varphi) + t\sin(\varphi)$$

$$y(t) = p_i\sin(\varphi) + t\cos(\varphi)$$

having the same φ but different parameter p. In the computations parameter p takes uniformly distributed discrete values. Every line is represented by a finite number of points $(x(t), y(t))$ where parameter t also takes uniformly distributed discrete values. In the first stage of computation, for each p_i we compute functional T of function $F(x(t), y(t))$ (F is the image function and t ranges over a uniform discrete grid here) and get a number $g(p, \varphi)$ that depends on p_i. Therefore, at the first stage we compute a number for every line in a parallel batch. The result obtained is a vector $g(p_i, \varphi)$, where φ is fixed and p_i ranges in the finite set. (Therefore in the computer $g(p_i, \varphi)$ is a matrix; we call it the "trace matrix".)

Using many lines consumes a lot of computation time. However, by performing some pre-computation we can reduce the time to a reasonable level.

Every line is presented by a sequence of pixels that we want to involve into our computation. Let us suppose that we know beforehand the size of the underlying picture and all the quantisation parameters (number of lines, line quantisation, φ and p sampling) have been chosen. Therefore we can compute the pixel sequences for the lines and then use them in our computations. (Sometimes such pre-computation could reduce the computational time by a factor of 10).

At the second stage we apply the second functional P to the vector $g(p_i, \varphi)$ and get a number $h(\varphi)$.

After performing computations in the first and second stage for every angle φ from a finite uniform grid we have a 2π- periodic function $h(\varphi)$ known for some values of φ.

The third stage consists of applying the third functional Φ to this function $h(\varphi)$ and hence getting the triple feature Π of the underlying image.

The tables that follow list the functionals that were used for T, P and Φ in conjunction of the problem of change detection. These were chosen as the most successful from among a much larger number that were tried. In all three tables the first column gives a code number with which each functional can be identified. The formulae for the Trace function contain parameter N that signifies the number of sample points considered for each line.

Trace functionals

Case	*name*	*formula*
100	*Radon*	$\sum_{i=0}^{N} x_i$
101	*moment1*	$\sum_{i=0}^{N} ix_i$
102	*gravityCenter*	$\sum_{i=0}^{N} ix_i / \sum_{i=0}^{N} x_i$
103	*moment2central*	$\sum_{i=0}^{N} i^2(x_i - gravityCenter)$
104	*standardDeviation*	$moment2central / Radon$
105	*gilbert*	$\sqrt{\sum_{i=0}^{N} x_i^2}$
106	*max*	$\max_{i=0}^{N} x_i$
107	*variation*	$\sum_{i=0}^{N-1} \lvert x_{i+1} - x_i \rvert$
108	*variation2*	$\sqrt{\sum_{i=0}^{N-1} \lvert x_{i+1} - x_i \rvert^2}$
111	*plainSym0*	$\sum_{i=3}^{N-3} \lvert x_{i-3} + x_{i-2} + x_{i-1} - x_{i+3} - x_{i+2} - x_{i+1} \rvert$
112	*plainSymN2*	$\sum_{i=2}^{N-2} \lvert x_{i-2} + x_{i-1} - x_{i+2} - x_{i+1} \rvert$
113	*plainSymN4*	$\sum_{i=4}^{N-4} \lvert x_{i-4} + x_{i-3} + ... + x_{i-1} - x_{i+4} - x_{i+3} - ... - x_{i+1} \rvert$
114	*plainSymN5*	$\sum_{i=5}^{N-5} \lvert x_{i-5} + ... + x_{i-2} + x_{i-1} - x_{i+5} - ... - x_{i+2} - x_{i+1} \rvert$
115	*plainSymN6*	$\sum_{i=6}^{N-6} \lvert x_{i-6} + ... + x_{i-2} + x_{i-1} - x_{i+6} - ... - x_{i+2} - x_{i+1} \rvert$
116	*plainSymN7*	$\sum_{i=7}^{N-7} \lvert x_{i-7} + ... + x_{i-2} + x_{i-1} - x_{i+7} - ... - x_{i+2} - x_{i+1} \rvert$
117	*plainSymN4abs*	$\sum_{i=4}^{N-4} \sum_{k=0}^{4} \lvert x_{i-k} - x_{i+k} \rvert$
118	*plainSymN5abs*	$\sum_{i=5}^{N-5} \sum_{k=0}^{5} \lvert x_{i-k} - x_{i+k} \rvert$
119	*plainSymN6abs*	$\sum_{i=6}^{N-6} \sum_{k=0}^{6} \lvert x_{i-k} - x_{i+k} \rvert$
120	*plainSymN7abs*	$\sum_{i=7}^{N-7} \sum_{k=0}^{7} \lvert x_{i-k} - x_{i+k} \rvert$
121	*plainSymN10abs*	$\sum_{i=10}^{N-10} \sum_{k=0}^{10} \lvert x_{i-k} - x_{i+k} \rvert$
122	*plainSymN15abs*	$\sum_{i=15}^{N-15} \sum_{k=0}^{15} \lvert x_{i-k} - x_{i+k} \rvert$
123	*plainSymN20abs*	$\sum_{i=20}^{N-20} \sum_{k=0}^{20} \lvert x_{i-k} - x_{i+k} \rvert$
124	*plainSymN25abs*	$\sum_{i=25}^{N-25} \sum_{k=0}^{25} \lvert x_{i-k} - x_{i+k} \rvert$
125	*plainSymDivide1*	$\sum_{i=10}^{N-10}((1 + \sum_{k=0}^{10} \lvert x_{i-k} - x_{i+k} \rvert)/(1 + \sum_{k=-10}^{9} \lvert x_{i+k} - x_{i+k+1} \rvert))$
127	*plainSymDivide2*	$\sum_{i=10}^{N-10} \sqrt{(\sum_{k=0}^{10} \lvert x_{i-k} - x_{i+k} \rvert)^2/(1 + \sum_{k=-10}^{9} \lvert x_{i+k} - x_{i+k+1} \rvert)}$
130	*variationId1*	$\sum_{i=0}^{N-2} \lvert x_i - 2x_{i+1} + x_{i+2} \rvert$
131	*variationId2*	$\sum_{i=0}^{N-3} \lvert x_i - 3x_{i+1} + 3x_{i+2} - x_{i+3} \rvert$
132	*variationId3*	$\sum_{i=0}^{N-4} \lvert x_i - 4x_{i+1} + 6x_{i+2} - 4x_{i+3} + x_{i+4} \rvert$
133	*variationId4*	$\sum_{i=0}^{N-5} \lvert x_i - 5x_{i+1} + 10x_{i+2} - 10x_{i+3} + 5x_{i+4} - x_{i+5} \rvert$
134	*variationId1tr*	$\sum_{i=0}^{N-2} \lvert x_i - 2x_{i+1} + x_{i+2} \rvert x_{i+1}$
135	*variationId2tr*	$\sum_{i=0}^{N-3} \lvert x_i - 3x_{i+1} + 3x_{i+2} - x_{i+3} \rvert x_{i+1}$
136	*variationId3tr*	$\sum_{i=0}^{N-4} \lvert x_i - 4x_{i+1} + 6x_{i+2} - 4x_{i+3} + x_{i+4} \rvert x_{i+2}$
137	*variationId4tr*	$\sum_{i=0}^{N-5} \lvert x_i - 5x_{i+1} + 10x_{i+2} - 10x_{i+3} + 5x_{i+4} - x_{i+5} \rvert x_{i+2}$

P functionals

Case	*name*	*formula*
8	*integral*	$\int_{-\infty}^{\infty} f(p)dp$
9	*max*	$\max f(p)$
11	*hilbert*	$\sqrt{\int_{-\infty}^{\infty} f(p)^2 dp}$
12	*gravityCenter*	$\int_{-\infty}^{\infty} pf(p)dp/integral$
13	*moment2central*	$\int_{-\infty}^{\infty} p^2(f(p) - gravityCenter)dp$
14	*standardDeviation*	$moment2central/integral$
16	*mediana*	m such that $\int_{-\infty}^{m} f(p)dp = \int_{m}^{\infty} f(p)dp$
17	*Variation*	$\int_{-\infty}^{\infty} \|f'(p)\|dp$
18	*medianaVar*	m such that $\int_{-\infty}^{m} \|f'(p)\|dp = \int_{m}^{\infty} \|f'(p)\|dp$
18	*medianaVar*	m such that $\int_{-\infty}^{m} \|f'(p)\|dp = \int_{m}^{\infty} \|f'(p)\|dp$
19	*absDer3*	$\int_{-\infty}^{\infty} \|f'''(p)\|dp$

Φ functionals

Case	*name*	*formula*
18	*variationSqr*	$\sqrt{\int_0^{2\pi} \|f(\varphi)'\|^2 d\varphi p}$
19	*variation*	$\int_0^{2\pi} \|f(\varphi)'\|d\varphi$
20	*hilbert*	$\sqrt{\int_0^{2\pi} \|f(\varphi)\|^2 d\varphi}$
21	*integral*	$\int_0^{2\pi} f(\varphi)d\varphi$
22	*max*	$\max f(\varphi)$
23	*max_min*	$\max f(\varphi) - \min f(\varphi)$
24	*argMin*	m such that $f(m) = \min f(\varphi)$
25	*argMax*	m such that $f(m) = \max f(\varphi)$
26	*argMaxMinus1*	$argMax(f(\varphi) - firstHarmonicOf(f(\varphi)))$
27	*max_minMinus1*	$max\_min(f(\varphi) - firstHarmonicOf(f(\varphi)))$
28	*ampl1*	*amplitude of the 1st harmonic of* $f(\varphi)$
29	*phase1*	*phase of the 1st harmonic of* $f(\varphi)$
30	*ampl2*	*amplitude of the 2st harmonic of* $f(\varphi)$
31	*phase2*	*phase of the 2st harmonic of* $f(\varphi)$
32	*ampl3*	*amplitude of the 3st harmonic of* $f(\varphi)$
33	*phase3*	*phase of the 3st harmonic of* $f(\varphi)$
34	*ampl4*	*amplitude of the 4st harmonic of* $f(\varphi)$
35	*phase4*	*phase of the 4st harmonic of* $f(\varphi)$

4. EXPERIMENTAL RESULTS

To be able to detect change we must assume that the images are processed in a random sequence, with no prior knowledge of the classes we expect to see. The first image is used as a reference image, and all subsequent images are compared with it and a single similarity measure is computed for each image. This similarity measure must reflect the amount of change that we can perceive in the image. The triple features that we adopted were chosen so that they have this property. However, in order to have a single similarity measure, we calculated from them a single number for each image, by simply scaling and averaging them. The scaling is necessary because each feature varies within a different range of real numbers. The scaling is done in such a way that the range of each feature is roughly between 0 and 10. It is impossible to predict that the feature of *all* subsequent images will be exactly in this range, as some unexpected changes may happen to the inspected scene. However, this is not important as we are looking for trends and it does not matter if the characterising numbers spill out of the pre-specified range. Figure 2a shows this average "feature" computed for the 20 available images, with the images sorted in ascending order of cars present in them (the same order with which the images are presented in figure 1). Figures 2b–1e show the absolute difference values that are obtained for each image if it is compared with the reference one, which is taken to be image 1b, 1f, 1p and 1t with 6, 9, 19 and 21 cars respectively.

5. CONCLUSIONS

It is worth stressing that the method presented here is not equivalent to counting cars in each image. It is more about characterising the texture present in each image. Indeed, car counting amounts to blob counting and this is haunted by problems of segmentation, blob size thresholds, variable illumination, smoothing etc [3].
The most important step of our method is to develop different useful T- functionals using our intuition and experience. Suppose that we have 10 options for functional T, 10 options for functional P and also 10 options for functional Φ (and note that they may coincide, that is one T functional is allowed to be the same as one of the P- functionals). After these 30 computational procedures have been installed into the computer, we are able to produce $10 \times 10 \times 10 = 1000$ triple features. Definitely, most of them will not be useful; nevertheless we can investigate them and make the appropriate choice for the specific task with the help of experimentation.
Therefore the main advantage of our method is that it helps to increase our options in our search for effective characterisation of images. This method is so versatile that allows us to choose among thousands of features those that exactly reflect the phenomenon we wish to monitor. We consider the presented results very promising. There is a lot of scope in improving the algorithm to make it run even faster. Its performance largely depends on the hardware used, but we could process a single image in 10 secs on a Sparc10 workstation with no effort made to optimise the code.

ACKNOWLEDGEMENTS: We are grateful to Ralf Jackson from DERA for supplying the images which are Crown Copyright and are used by permission

6. REFERENCES

[1] Fedotov N G. Methods of stochastic geometry in pattern recognition. Moscow, Radio and Communications 1990.
[2] Kadyrov A and Petrou M. The Trace transform as a tool to invariant feature construction. Proceedings of 14th ICPR 1998.
[3] Song K Y, Kittler J and Petrou M. Defect detection in random colour textures. Image and vision computing 1996; 14:667–683.

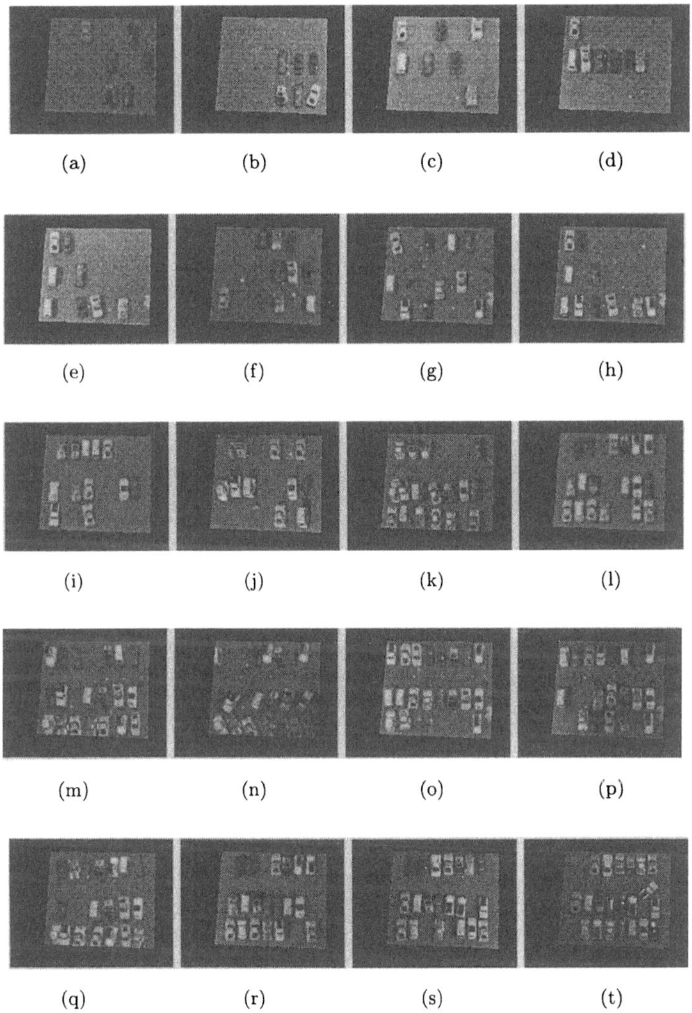

Figure 1: Images of a carpark that have to be characterised in terms of the degree of use of the carpark.

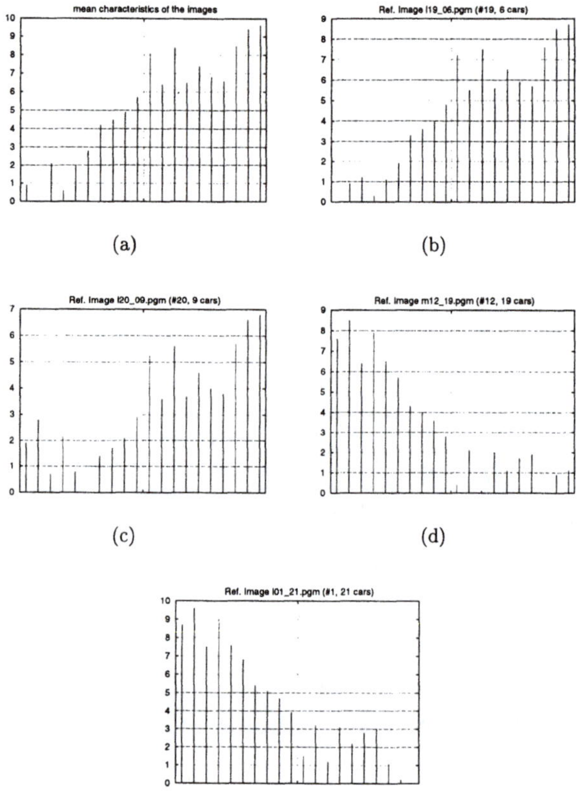

Figure 2: (a) Mean characteristics of the images; (b)-(e) absolute values of differences of mean characteristics: (b) with reference image 1b, containing 6 cars; (c) with reference image 1f, containing 9 cars; (d) with reference image 1p, containing 19 cars; (e) with reference image 1t, containing 21 cars.

USING NATURAL LANGUAGE AND VIDEO DATA TO QUERY AND LEARN AMERICAN FOOTBALL PLAYS

Mihai Lazarescu, Dept. of Comp. Sc., Curtin University of Technology
Svetha Venkatesh, Dept. of Comp. Sc., Curtin University of Technology
Geoff West, Dept. of Comp. Sc., Curtin University of Technology
Terry Caelli, Ohio State University

ABSTRACT

In this paper we describe methods currently under investigation for learning, recognising and representing American Football plays. This is a complex spatio-temporal pattern recognition problem which we propose to solve by integrating image understanding and natural language understanding. Specifically, this paper describes the model representation used at different levels of abstraction incorporating several types of knowledge: expert knowledge, domain knowledge and spatio-temporal knowledge. We also describe a decision tree based incremental learning algorithm which combines context knowledge, attribute selection and the ageing of knowledge to keep the model representation of the plays consistent with the information extracted from the American Football video tapes.

1 INTRODUCTION

Natural language understanding, image understanding and machine learning are three of the main areas of research in artificial intelligence. In this paper we present a system that combines these three areas to *query* and *learn* American Football plays. The main benefit of combining image information from the American Football tapes and natural language commentary is that it allows for information to be fused from both sources. Thus the play classification is not dependent on a single source of information. Furthermore it allows semantic understanding of video at a higher level than would be possible by looking at video images alone.

The VITRA (VIsual TRANslator) [5, 2] is one of the few projects which tries to integrate computer vision and the generation of natural language expressions for the description of image sequences in traffic scenes (CITYTOUR system [8, 4]) and soccer sequences (SOCCER system [8, 12]).

Another project which combines natural language understanding with image processing is Informedia: News-on-Demand [10, 1]. This project creates a digital library of text, images, video and audio data available for full content search and retrieval. News-on-Demand [7] is a fully-automatic system that monitors TV, radio and text news material and allows selective retrieval of news stories based on spoken queries.

The benefits offered by combining natural language processing with video data analysis though significant are still limited. The performance of the system cannot be improved further, once the combined processing of the types of data has been optimised. Furthermore, the system does not have the ability to deal with completely new situations.

These limitations can be removed by using machine learning. If the system has the ability to learn then it is capable of continuously improving its classification performance as well as dealing with new examples. Several methods of learning have been developed but the one that is best suited for real world situations is *incremental learning*.

The objective of our work is to use natural language understanding and image processing to query and learn American Football plays from video tapes. We have developed a model for representing spatio-temporal characteristics of multiple objects in dynamic scenes in this domain and a decision-tree like structure which stores the models. Our representation combines several types of knowledge: expert knowledge, domain knowledge (game rules), spatial knowledge (player relationships) and temporal knowledge (action sequencing in individual plays). The input data consists of both commentary and the video data. The recognition system built around the play data model has the advantage of not being dependent on accurate low level data, and that its search for a match is driven by both sources available.

The incremental learning system combines context knowledge, attribute selection and the ageing of knowledge to keep the model representation of the plays consistent with the information extracted from the video tapes. The algorithm uses short term memory and summary statistics of the data to build, update and when necessary reorganise the decision tree.

2 THE DATA STRUCTURES

American Football plays are complex and can have many variations. The representation of the play therefore has to be detailed in order to handle all the variations that may occur, and robust so it could handle noisy data (the input data come from segmenting video frames of the play) without compromising the recognition and learning process. We refer to the play descriptions that we have designed as *play models* which consist of several types of knowledge: *expert knowledge*, *spatial knowledge*, *temporal knowledge* and *domain knowledge*.

2.1 THE PLAY MODEL

The play model description we use to represent an American Football play has several components which describe the play action in terms of *player significance*, *player relationships*, *player movements*, *player actions*, *player positions* and the *temporal sequencing* of the *player actions* and *movements*. The significant characteristic of the *play model* representation is that it is mainly made up of *symbolic* data. The play model has the following features:

The **play class** - there are three classes of plays in American Football that are defined by the main action that takes place in the play. The play classes are defined by set A where: A = {*offensive*, *defensive*,*special*}.

The **significant players and actions in the play** - each play involves significant players performing predefined tasks. We define as significant the players whose actions are very likely to have a major impact on the main action and outcome of the play. The player significance is defined by set B where: B = {*low, average, high, very-high*}. The possible actions are defined by set C where: C = {*pass, toss, give, hand, catch, get, receive, fake, tackle, block, push, grab, intercept*}.

The **player combination** - each play (offensive/defensive/special) requires a specific combination of players.

The **temporal sequencing** of the actions in the play - in each play certain actions take place at specific times and in a certain order. The temporal representation of the play model is based on a set of simple movements combined with a play action. The *play action* is the main action in the play already defined in the first part of the play model. The *movement* describes the type of movement of a given player *at an instance in time.* A player can either move to a position or make a turn relative to the direction in which the football player is facing. The possible movements of a player are defined by set D where: D = {*move, turn-left, turn-right*}.

The order and timing of the combined movement of the players is described with the help of five of Allen's [6, 3] temporal primitives defined by the set E where: E = {*before, after, during, meets, equals*}. To derive the temporal relationships between the players, the spatial model of a play (all spatial models are extracted from coaching books) is considered and the movement of the players is described as a series of moves and turns.

The **movement of individual players in the play** - players generally have specific movement patterns in specific plays. The movement of the player *over the entire play period* is described in terms of *shape* and *distance*. The shape of the movement indicates whether the movement is **straight** or **contains turns**. The occurrence of a turn is signalled by a change in the direction of the player's movement which is detected over adjacent frames in the video sequence. The distance covered by the player during the play can be either short or long. To determine the type of distance, the system uses the player's starting and finishing positions and the position of the defensive line. If the player started *behind* or *in the same line* with the defensive line and finished *in-front* of the defensive line *then* the distance covered is considered to be *long*. Otherwise the distance is *short*. The possible overall movements are defined by the set *F*: *F* ={*short-and-straight, short-and-turn, short-and-many-turns,long-and-straight, long-and-turn, long-and-many-turns*}. The **relationships between a player and the other teammates** at different instances throughout the duration of play are described symbolically and derived from four reference points which are assumed to be known at all times. These are the left boundary, the right boundary, the opponent's goal and the team's own goal line and they produce the relationships: *in-front, behind, to-the-left and to-the-right.* Two more relationships can be further defined: *in-line-with-horizontal* and *in-line-with-vertical*. The references are dependent on which way the attacking team is *facing*. The possible relationships are defined by the set *G*: *G* = {*in-front, behind, to-the-left, to-the-right, in-line-with-horizontal, in-line-with-vertical*}.

To build the play models we have created a database of play information which includes data about the player combinations, play actions, player significance and player movement over the duration of a "by the book" play. The information about the plays has been gathered from several sources which include Gridiron play manuals, video tapes and Gridiron computer games. The system collects information, forms the database about a specific play requested and generates the play model description.

The system uses a well defined semi-dynamic hierarchical structure to store the models of the American Football plays. We refer to this structure as the *memory of the system*. The structure was designed specifically to enable the system to recognise and learn (when there is evidence that suggests learning from the new data is justified) from the data it receives.

3 THE MEMORY STRUCTURE

The structure has three levels: the class level, the condition level and the model level.

The class level defines the type of the play: offensive, defensive and special. The class of the play is determined from the commentary. If this is not possible (the commentary is too ambiguous or not related to the play), the class of the play is determined (though not as accurately) from the initial setup of the players.

The condition level defines the labels (positions) of the players involved in the play and the relationships between the players in the initial setup. The labels used are very specific. This helps resolve any ambiguity that may occur as shown in Figure 1 and makes the relationships between the players more unique. Figure 1a shows a pass play which involves 3 receivers, 2 corner-backs, 4 blockers, 1 quarterback and 1 guard. The problem with enumerating the types of players is that the resulting description is not specific enough. If we wanted to refer to a receiver we would need a way of specifying precisely which receiver we wanted to refer to. Also when we describe the relationship between a receiver and a corner-back we need to be able to specify the receiver and the corner-back. The simplest way to disambiguate is to refer to the 3 receivers as *receiver1*,*receiver2* and *receiver3*. However, this designation does not accurately describe the position of the players (they are all on the left hand side of the ground). The ambiguity problem is solved by using the spatial properties of the players. The three receivers are positioned on the left hand side of the ground. Therefore the three receivers become *receiverL*. Also the receiver represented by *P1* is the leftmost of the three. Hence he becomes *receiverLLL*. The receiver represented by *P2* is to the right of *P1* and hence his label becomes *receiverLL*. The last receiver remains as *receiverL*. The ambiguity problem for the receivers is solved. The labelling of the corner-backs, the blockers and the guard is handled in a similar way. Figure 1b shows the player labels after the ambiguity problem has been solved.

The relationships between the players in the initial setup are defined along two axes: left-to-

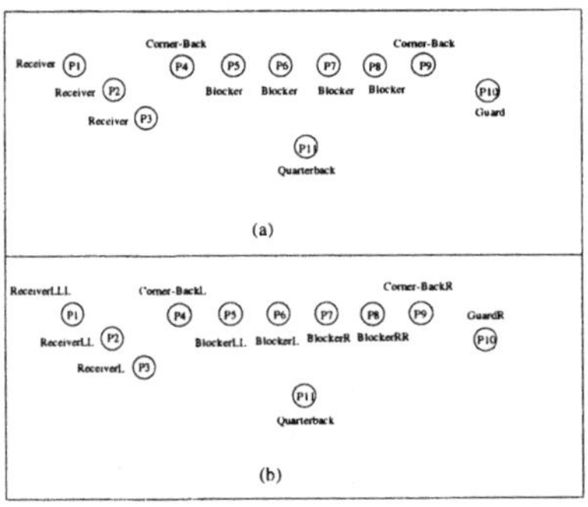

Figure 1: The player labelling problem.

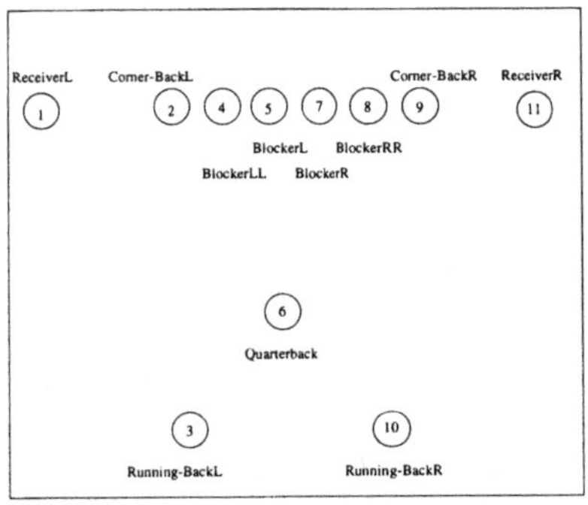

Figure 2: Initial setup for a pass play.

right and back-to-front and are described with the help of two long strings, one for the left-to-right relationships and one for the back-to front relationships. For example the relationships of the players shown in Figure 2 are defined by the strings:

- Left-To-Right: ReceiverL (Left-Of) Corner-BackL (Left-Of) Running-BackL (Left-Of) BlockerLL (Left-Of) BlockerL (Left-Of) Quarterback (Left-Of) BlockerR (Left-Of) BlockerRR (Left-Of) Running-BackR (Left-Of) Corner-BackR (Left-Of) ReceiverR.

- Back-To-Front: Running-BackL (In-Line) Running-BackR (Back-Of) Quarterback (Back-Of) ReceiverL (In-Line) Corner-BackL (In-Line) BlockerLL (In-Line) BlockerL (In-Line) BlockerR (In-Line) BlockerRR (In-Line) Corner-BackR (In-Line) ReceiverR.

The model level in the hierarchy is where the models of the plays are stored.

The structure designed to represent the memory of the system enables the system to learn incrementally. While designing the structure the following issues were considered: memory size, attribute selection, forgetting and context.

3.1 MEMORY SIZE

The trend in the development of systems that learn from the input has been to use *full-memory* or *complete-memory*. This means that the system employs a learning method that modifies known concepts but it does not forget any of the facts it has seen (it stores every example). This offers the advantage that the system is able to consider all the input data when it needs to modify a known example. Full-memory systems generally perform better than partial memory systems but are not suited for real world situations. When considering how humans learn, one can see that humans learn concept descriptions from facts and then incrementally refine those descriptions when new facts or observations become available. Humans do not remember everything they are exposed to. They apparently store only prominent facts and generalisations, and then modify the generalisations when new facts are available [11].

We have therefore chosen to build a system that has partial memory and is capable of remembering only a small set of examples at a time. The partial memory is implemented in the form of a window of fixed size which moves over the input data. As the window moves over the data it discards old examples while it reads in new ones.

3.2 ATTRIBUTE SELECTION

The input data from the video may contain a significant amount of noise. Some of the attributes used in the model descriptions such as player movement over the duration of the play can be severely affected by the noise in the data. When the system attempts to determine which model in the memory (if any exists) best matches the input it performs a recognition routine which uses these attributes. Therefore, the system's processing can be affected by the noise in the data.

The system we have designed handles the noisy data by employing attribute selection. The effect of the noise in the data can be minimised if *only* the attributes (such as player relationships) which are least affected by the noise are to be used in the recognition.

3.3 FORGETTING (AGEING OF KNOWLEDGE)

Due to the very nature of learning the system uses, some of the data acquired previously becomes irrelevant and hence it can be forgotten. Forgetting also offers the following advantages: it helps restructure the acquired knowledge, it shortens the retrieval time and it helps to reduce the memory size required for processing [9].

The system implements ageing at three levels: the *data level*, the *model level* and the *condition level*. The data level refers to the data which is contained in the model. Each attribute in the model has one or more generalised symbolic descriptions and each description has an age value associated with it. Similarly the models and the conditions in the hierarchy have an age value associated with them.

There are three age stages at the data level: *system-seen*, *system-learned*, *expert-learned*. The difference between the three stages is the way in which the age of the data is updated. Any data that has reached the *expert-learned* stage no longer ages and therefore it cannot be forgotten. The difference between *system-seen* and *system-learned* is the amount by which the age of the data increases or decreases.

The age of the data in a given model is updated only when two conditions are satisfied. The first condition is that the system has determined that the given model is the best match for the input data. The second condition is that the model *has* a similarity coefficient which is greater or equal to the set threshold of 0.75 (75% of the attribute values in the *input data* match their corresponding values in the model). The similarity coefficient is computed during the recognition (classification) stage.

If the input data is found to be similar to the model, then the age of each of the attribute values (provided it is at the *computer-seen* or *computer-learned* stage) is reassessed. If there is an attribute value in the model which matches its corresponding value in the input data, then that attribute value is reinforced and its age is decreased. If the attribute value in the model does not match its corresponding value in the input data, then the age of the value is increased.

The system starts with a basic set of models which are expert learned. The data in these models is automatically set to the *expert-learned* stage.

Data which is seen by the system for the first time is given the age of -200. Every time that data is seen again, the age is decreased by 5. Similarly if the data is not seen the age is increased by 5. If the data seen reaches the age of -100, it reaches the stage of *computer-learned*. Each time that data instance is seen, the age is decreased by 10. Otherwise the age of the data is increased by 10. If the data reaches the value of 0, it reaches the stage of *expert-learned*. If the age value falls below -100, it gets to the stage of *system-seen*. Finally, if the age falls below -200 the data is no longer considered to be relevant and it is discarded.

The model age is computed using the age of the data contained in the model. Each time the age of the model reaches the value of -200, the model is removed from the hierarchy.

The condition age is determined by the age of model nodes associated with that condition. If a condition no longer has any nodes associated with it, then it is removed from the hierarchy.

3.4 CONTEXT

American Football has three distinct play classes. The memory structure of the system reflects this through the use of the play class level in the hierarchy. The context plays an important role in the analysis of the input data and in constraining the amount of information which is to be learned. During the analysis of the input data, the system may encounter facts which are not likely to occur in real world situations. For example the system may encounter a pass play in which 6 players are labelled as running-backs. Such a play does not exist and the system through the use of context rules is able to determine that the information is incorrect and therefore it should be ignored.

By ignoring the incorrect information from the input data, the number of facts that have to be learned (the learning process takes place *only* if there is evidence to suggest that learning is required) is reduced. This helps keep the size of the models to a minimum and improves the access time.

The memory structure used by the system has been designed specifically for the context of American Football. The structure however, can be easily modified to be used in the context of other problems that deal with multiple labelled objects in a dynamic scene. By removing the class level in the hierarchy, we obtain a structure with just the condition level and the model level and this structure can be easily used to classify and learn complex spatio-temporal patterns.

4 LEARNING INCREMENTALLY FROM THE INPUT DATA

The system can learn new facts from the input data by either modifying a known concept (model), by building a completely new concept or by filling in the knowledge gaps that may be present in previously built concepts.

When the system examines a new query, it attempts to find the best match for it in the memory. In case the system is successful in finding a model that matches the query, it checks its similarity coefficient.

If the coefficient is greater or equal to 0.75 the system searches for any existing differences between the model and the query. The differences found are then used to build generalised descriptions which include the old facts from the model and new facts from the query.

If the coefficient is smaller than 0.75 then there is not enough evidence to justify the update of the model. The system therefore builds a new model that is based on the query.

Another case in which the system builds a new concept is when the search for a model that matches the query is unsuccessful.

When a new concept is necessary, the system assigns the values and descriptions generated from the input data to the attributes in the model structure described previously. The query data is not complete and in the best case the query will contain information about 5 or 6 players. All American Football plays involve 11 players and hence gaps in the knowledge *will be present* in any newly created concept. These gaps can only be filled in the future when the system *will learn new facts from similar queries.*

In case the model has to be updated to be consistent with the new query, the spatial and temporal attribute descriptions go through a process of generalisation.

4.1 GENERALISING THE SPATIAL INFORMATION

There are two spatial attributes in the play model. The player movement and the player relationship.

Generalising the description of the player movement is simple and involves the union of the player movement description in the model with that of the corresponding player in the query. For example, if the player movement description in the model was *short-and-straight* and the movement of the corresponding player in the query was defined as *short-and-turn*, then the new generalised description of the player becomes *short-and-straight* ***or*** *short-and-turn.*

The process of updating the relationship description requires that the order in which the relationships changes occur is preserved. For example consider the relationships of the *Player1* and *Player2* in Figure 3. Figure 3a shows how the relationships between the two players are evolving over the duration of the play in the case of the model. Figure 3b shows the relationships between the two players in the query while Figure 3c shows the updated description of the relationships between the players (notice that now the relationships that occur both in the query and the model can be extracted - Player2 now has two patterns). The description generated by

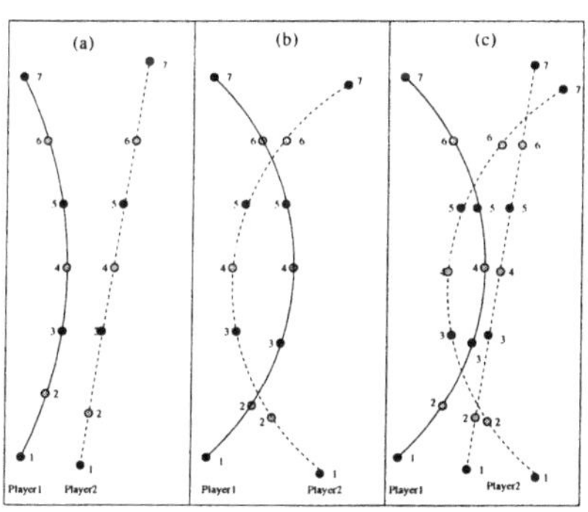

Figure 3: The filled circles indicate the position of the players at different instances in time for the entire duration of the play. To update the model the new facts from the query have to be incorporated into the relationship description. After this is done, Player2 has two patterns in the description.

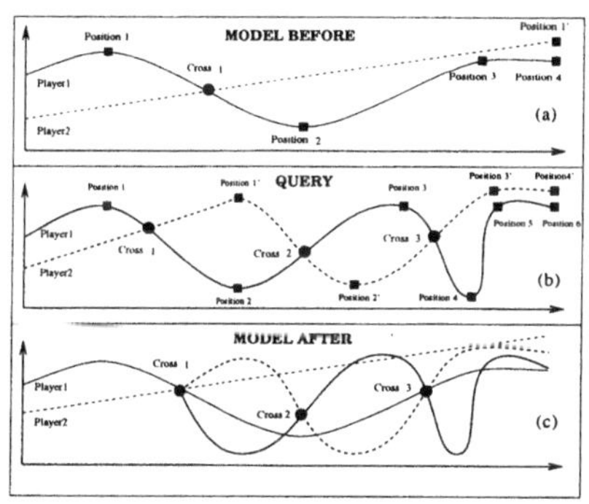

Figure 4: The movement and actions of Player1 and Player2 are similar in both the model and the query up to the instance when they cross each other's path. From that instance on the movement and actions are different in the query. To reflect the new data from the query the system updates the temporal description by adding the different movements and actions from the query (as shown in (c)).

the system for the model and query is:

Model Description ——————— Query Description

Time Index	Player No.	Relationship	Player No.
1	1	Left-Of	2*
2	1	In-Front	2*
3	1	In-Line-Horizontal	2
4	1	Behind	2

Time Index	Player No.	Relationship	Player No.
1	1	Left-Of	2*
2	1	In-Front	2*
3	1	Right-Of	2
4	1	Behind	2
5	1	In-Line-Horizontal	2
6	1	Left-Of	2
7	1	In-Front	2

The relationships marked by with a "*" are common to both the model and the query. However, the query has the same set of relationships occurring twice (at the beginning and at the end of the query). When the generalisation takes place the system attempts to enlarge the description by adding to it those relationships in the query which are different from those in the model, while still keeping the time index at which they took place. The updated description is defined as:

Time Index	Player No.	Relationship	Player No.
1	1	Left-Of	2
2	1	In-Front	2

AND

Time Index	Player No.	Relationship	Player No.
3	1	In-Line-Horizontal	2
4	1	Behind	2

OR

Time Index	Player No.	Relationship	Player No.
3	1	Right-Of	2
4	1	Behind	2
5	1	In-Line-Horizontal	2
6	1	Left-Of	2
7	1	In-Front	2

4.2 GENERALISING THE TEMPORAL INFORMATION

The temporal description is updated in a similar fashion to that in which the relationship description is updated. However, in the case of the temporal description the system deals with actions (movement, turns and path crossing) and the occurrence of the actions is referenced using Allen's temporal primitives. For example consider the movement and actions of the players 1 and 2 in Figure 4 (Figure 4a shows the model, while Figure 4b shows the query).

The description of the actions of the two players in the model is defined as:

Individual Player Actions

Player No.	Action Type	Time Relation	Action Index
1	Moved-To-Position1	BEFORE	Action1*
1	Turn-Right	BEFORE	Action2*
1	Moved-To-Position2	BEFORE	Action3*
1	Turn-Left	BEFORE	Action4
1	Moved-To-Position3	BEFORE	Action5
1	Turn-Right	BEFORE	Action6
1	Moved-To-Position4	BEFORE	Action7
2	Moved-To-Position1'	BEFORE	Action1'**

Player Interaction

Player No.	Action Type	Player No.	Action	Time Relation	Action No.
1	Crossed-Path	2	Cross1	DURING	Action3**

Action Sequencing

Action No.	Time Relation	Action No.
Action 1,2,3,4,5,6,7	DURING	Action1'

In the case of the query the temporal description is defined as:

Individual Player Actions

Player No.	Action Type	Time Relation	Action Index
1	Moved-To-Position1	BEFORE	Action1*
1	Turn-Right	BEFORE	Action2*
1	Moved-To-Position2	BEFORE	Action3*
1	Turn-Left	BEFORE	Action4
1	Moved-To-Position3	BEFORE	Action5
1	Turn-Right	BEFORE	Action6
1	Moved-To-Position4	BEFORE	Action7
1	Turn-Left	BEFORE	Action8
1	Moved-To-Position5	BEFORE	Action9
1	Turn-Right	BEFORE	Action10
1	Moved-To-Position6	BEFORE	Action11
2	Moved-To-Position1'	BEFORE	Action1'**
2	Turn-Right	BEFORE	Action2'
2	Moved-To-Position2'	BEFORE	Action3'
2	Turn-Left	BEFORE	Action4'
2	Moved-To-Position3'	BEFORE	Action5'
2	Turn-Right	BEFORE	Action6'
2	Moved-To-Position4'	BEFORE	Action7'

Player Interaction

Player No.	Action Type	Player No.	Action	Time Relation	Action No.
1	Crossed-Path	2	Cross1	DURING	Action3**
1	Crossed-Path	2	Cross2	DURING	Action5
1	Crossed-Path	2	Cross3	DURING	Action7

Action Sequencing

Action No.	Time Relation	Action No.
Action 1,2,3	DURING	Action1'
Action 4	DURING	Action2'
Action 3',4'	DURING	Action5
Action 6,7,8,9	DURING	Action5'
Action 6'	DURING	Action9
Action 10,11	DURING	Action7'

The temporal information that is marked by "*" and "**" is common to both the model and the query. The system extracts the actions from the query which are different from those in the model (all actions that are not marked) and updates the description while preserving the timing and the duration of the events. The resulting description is shown below (also see Figure 4c):

Individual Player Actions

Player No.	Action Type	Time Relation	Action Index
1	Moved-To-Position1	BEFORE	Action1*
1	Turn-Right	BEFORE	Action2*
1	Moved-To-Position2	BEFORE	Action3*

AND

Player No.	Action Type	Time Relation	Action Index
1	Turn-Left	BEFORE	Action4
1	Moved-To-Position3	BEFORE	Action5
1	Turn-Right	BEFORE	Action6
1	Moved-To-Position4	BEFORE	Action7

OR

Player No.	Action Type	Time Relation	Action Index
1	Turn-Left	BEFORE	Action4
1	Moved-To-Position3	BEFORE	Action5
1	Turn-Right	BEFORE	Action6
1	Moved-To-Position4	BEFORE	Action7
1	Turn-Left	BEFORE	Action8
1	Moved-To-Position5	BEFORE	Action9
1	Turn-Right	BEFORE	Action10
1	Moved-To-Position6	BEFORE	Action11

Individual Player Action

Player No.	Action Type	Time Relation	Action Index
2	Moved-To-Position1'	BEFORE	Action1'**
2	Turn-Right	BEFORE	Action2'
2	Moved-To-Position2'	BEFORE	Action3'
2	Turn-Left	BEFORE	Action4'
2	Moved-To-Position3'	BEFORE	Action5'
2	Turn-Right	BEFORE	Action6'
2	Moved-To-Position4'	BEFORE	Action7'

Player Interaction

Player No.	Action Type	Player No.	Action	Time Relation	Action No.
1	Crossed-Path	2	Cross1	DURING	Action3**

OR

Player No.	Action Type	Player No.	Action	Time Relation	Action No.
1	Crossed-Path	2	Cross1	DURING	Action3**
1	Crossed-Path	2	Cross2	DURING	Action5
1	Crossed-Path	2	Cross3	DURING	Action7

Action Sequencing

Action No.	Time Relation	Action No.
Action 1,2,3,4,5,6,7	DURING	Action1'

OR

Action No.	Time Relation	Action No.
Action 1,2,3	DURING	Action1'
Action 4	DURING	Action2'
Action 3',4'	DURING	Action5
Action 6,7,8,9	DURING	Action5'
Action 6'	DURING	Action9
Action 10,11	DURING	Action7'

Of the 103 tests carried, the system (the system has a starting memory of 50 play models) was able to classify and learn correctly in 82 cases. In 17 of the 21 cases when it failed, the system generated an incomplete (the system was unable to solve the ambiguity in the player position) or incorrect (some players received incorrect labels) hypothesis.

5 CONCLUSIONS

We have developed a model for representing multiple labelled objects in a dynamic scene. We also developed a dynamic hierarchical structure that stores the models and automatically rearranges itself to be consistent with the input data. Depending on the input data, the system creates new models, updates known models or removes known models from the structure.

Our model representation combines several types of knowledge: expert knowledge (game tactics), domain knowledge (game rules), spatial knowledge (player relationships) and temporal knowledge (action sequencing in individual plays). This is used in a system that is able to recognise American Football plays. The recognition system has the advantages that: (1) it is not dependent on accurate low level data, (2) its search for a match for a potential query is driven by expert input and that it cross checks its input from the several sources it has available.

A semi-dynamic hierarchical structure is used in the incremental learning part of the system. The incremental learning method employed in the system uses partial memory and incorporates attribute selection, ageing of knowledge and context knowledge in its processing.

References

[1] The CMU informedia project. http://www.informedia.cs.cmu.edu.

[2] VITRA. http://www.dfki.uni-sb.de/vitra/.

[3] J. F. Allen. Towards a general theory of action and time. *Artificial Intelligence*, (23):123–154, 1984.

[4] Gerd Herzog Elisabeth Andre and Thomas Rist. On the simultaneous interpretation of real world image sequences and their natural language description: The system SOCCER. In *Proceedings of the 8th European Conference on AI*, pages 449–454, 1988.

[5] Gerd Herzog Elisabeth Andre and Thomas Rist. Natural language access to visual data: Dealing with space and movement. 1st Workshop on Logical Semantics of Time, Space and Movement in Natural Language, 1989.

[6] Hans Werner Geusgen. Spatial reasoning based on Allen temporal logic. Technical report, International Computer Science Institute, Berkeley, August 1989.

[7] Alexander Hauptmann and Michael A. Smith. Text, speech and vision for video segmentation. In *AAAI-95 Fall Symposium on Computational Models for Integrating Language and Vision*, November 1995.

[8] Gerd Herzog and Karl Rohr. Integrating vision and language: Towards automatic description of human movements. In *Proceedings of the 19th Annual German Conference on Artificial Intelligence (KI-95)*, June 1995.

[9] Miroslav Kubat and Ivana Krizakova. Forgetting and ageing of knowledge in concept formation. *Applied Artificial Intelligence*, 6:195–206, 1992.

[10] A. Hauptmann Michael Witbrock and M. Cristel. News-on-demand - an application of informedia technology. *D-LIB magazine*, 1995.

[11] R. E. Reinke and R. S. Michalski. Incremental learning of concept descriptions: A method and experimental results. *Machine Learning*, pages 263–289, 1984.

[12] Jorg Schirra and Eva Stopp. Antlima - a listener model with mental images. In *International Joint Conference on AI (IJCAI-93)*, pages 175–180, August 1993.

INVARIANT CONTENT-BASED IMAGE RETRIEVAL USING THE FOURIER-MELLIN TRANSFORM[1]

Ruggero Milanese, University of Geneva, Switzerland
Michel Cherbuliez, Swiss Federal Institute of Technology, Switzerland
Thierry Pun, University of Geneva, Switzerland

ABSTRACT

We describe a method for computing an image signature, suitable for content-based retrieval from image databases. The signature is extracted by computing the Fourier power spectrum, performing a mapping from cartesian to logarithmic-polar coordinates, projecting this mapping onto two 1D signature vectors, and computing their power spectra coefficients. Similar to wavelet-based approaches, this representation is *holistic*, and thus provides a compact description of all image aspects, including shape, texture, and color. Furthermore, it has the advantage of being invariant to 2D rigid transformations, such as any combination of rotation, scaling and translation. Experiments have been conducted on a database of 2082 images extracted from various news video clips. Results confirm invariance to 2D rigid transformations, as well as high resilience to more general affine and projective transformations. Moreover, the signature appears to capture perceptually relevant image features, in that it allows successful database querying using example images which have been subject to arbitrary camera and subject motion.

1 INTRODUCTION

Recent advances in storage, computing and communication technology have created the need for user-friendly access to large and distributed multimedia repositories. Among the most demanding users of this technology are multimedia content providers, such as television studios, which increasingly employ digital media for all production and postproduction phases. Efficient handling of multimedia data also opens new applications in other markets, such as the corporate document management, the distribution of news and accompanying image and video data by press agencies, and the home computing world.

In order to enable efficient and user-friendly access to multimedia archives, database management systems should provide two types of indexes. The first originates from textual descriptions that can be entered either manually by a documentalist, or automatically generated from close-captioning, or data files. The second concerns an automatically-extracted representation of the visual appearance of the image or video document, and should allow search by means of example documents (*content-based search*). By combining the two types of indexes, a user can efficiently explore the database by iteratively specifying the most interesting items retrieved through previous queries. For video material, the extraction of visual indexes requires several processing steps which decompose the

[1]The financial support of the Swiss Federal Government through OFES grant 95.0493, in the framework of the EU ACTS project AC089, is gratefully acknowledged.

clip into a hierarchy of uniform segments, and provide a number of keyframes representing each segment [4] [10]. For images (including video keyframes), the visual appearance that must be indexed is clearly multi-faceted, and may include information about the overall image layout, as well as about individual objects and their properties.

The rest of this paper is structured as follows. Section 2 provides a brief review of state-of-the-art technology in image indexing. Two main approaches are described, and their main weaknesses are outlined. This analysis motivates the need for new techniques that provide an integral, "holistic" representation of an image, that is invariant to various image transformations. In section 3 we describe the main contribution of this article, i.e. a method for representing images invariant to rotation, translation, and scale changes. In section 4 this method is experimentally validated, using a database of images extracted from two TV studio archives.

2 PREVIOUS WORK

Several methods have been proposed to represent image appearance for content-based retrieval (for a more extensive survey, the reader is referred to [4] [1] [2]). Two well-known systems are QBIC [5] and VIRAGE [6], since they have been integrated with commercial database products. Their underlying principle is the extraction of multiple image descriptions, representing various features. These include a representation of the image color distribution by histograms, and the extraction of uniform regions segmented from the image, likely to contain isolated objects. From these regions, various statistical descriptors are computed, as well as a representation of their spatial relationships. Other features include texture descriptors, such as co-occurrence matrices and the overall response of oriented band-pass filters, which can be useful to characterize outdoor images or regular surfaces. Other systems based on similar principles include Photobook [12], VisualSEEK [14], ImageRover [13], the UCSB Alexandria Digital Library Project [9], and Chabot [11].

One problem with the above disjoint multi-feature image descriptions is how to integrate them at query time. Since the average user is not likely to understand the underlying numerical representation of each feature, it is hard to determine the appropriate balance between them through weighting coefficients. Furthermore, features may exhibit different statistical properties from each other, and unless they are correctly equalized, small changes in the relative weights may lead to large variations of the top-ranked retrieved items. The user may thus spend considerable time adjusting weights at query time, and may eventually miss the desired images.

In order to overcome the above problems, alternative approaches have been proposed. These include integral orthogonal image transforms such as wavelet decomposition [8] [7]. The idea is to represent the image by a small number of meaningful coefficients that describe it at various resolution levels, and which also encode spatial relationships between various image components, by virtue of the space-frequency localization property of the wavelet transform. Meaningful coefficients can be extracted through vector quantization procedures, or by selectively picking those with the largest magnitude. Although these methods successfully address the multiple-feature integration problem, they suffer from a major weakness, namely their lack of invariance to translation and rotation, and, to a lesser extent, to scale changes. If a set of images of the same subject contains object motion, or is captured with a moving camera, it will therefore be difficult to retrieve all images of the set, given one sample.

In this paper, we propose a method that is also based on an orthogonal transform (the Fourier transform), but which offers invariance to geometric transformations. In particular, it is designed to be fully invariant to 2D rigid transformations, i.e. a combination of 2D rotation, translation and scaling (RTS). In general, the changes induced by object and camera motion are not restricted to this type of transformation (cf. [3] for an alternative representation that is invariant to affine and projective transformations). However, experimental results from a large database of heterogeneous videos show that it provides a good approximation to invariance under more general, non-rigid transformations.

3 THE PROPOSED METHOD

We propose an image representation invariant to 2D rigid transformations, i.e. to a combination of 2D rotation, translation, and scaling (RTS). Since the representation is non-invertible, it will also be referred to as an image *signature*. The construction process is incremental, and starts with the computation of the discrete Fourier transform (DFT) F of the image I:

$$F(m,n) = \sum_{x=\frac{-M}{2}}^{\frac{M}{2}-1} \sum_{y=\frac{-N}{2}}^{\frac{N}{2}-1} I(x,y) \mathrm{e}^{-2\pi i(\frac{mx}{M}+\frac{ny}{N})} \tag{1}$$

where $m = \frac{-M}{2}, \dots, \frac{M}{2} - 1$, $n = \frac{-N}{2}, \dots, \frac{N}{2} - 1$.

3.1 TRANSLATION INVARIANCE

The DFT can be represented by the phase and power spectra Φ, P:

$$\Phi(m,n) = \mathrm{atan}\frac{\mathrm{Im}[F(m,n)]}{\mathrm{Re}[F(m,n)]} \tag{2}$$

$$P(m,n) = \sqrt{\mathrm{Re}[F(m,n)]^2 + \mathrm{Im}[F(m,n)]^2}. \tag{3}$$

Since the image I is real, $\mathrm{Re}[F]$ is even and $\mathrm{Im}[F]$ is odd symmetric around the origin. In other words, $F(-m,-n) = F^*(m,n)$. If the original image I is circularly translated into $\tilde{I}(x,y) = I(x + x_x, y + y_0)$, its DFT will be given by $\tilde{F}(m,n) = F(m,n) \cdot \mathrm{e}^{-2\pi i(\frac{x_0}{M}+\frac{y_0}{N})}$. Therefore the power spectrum of the translated image will be $\tilde{P} = P$, while the phase spectrum will be altered. In order to build a translation-invariant representation, we retain the power spectrum, and discard the phase spectrum.

By virtue of the power spectrum's even symmetry, one only needs to retain the coefficients $P(m,n)$ in the two quadrants $\{(m,n), m \geq 0, n = \frac{-N}{2}, \dots, \frac{N}{2} - 1\}$, thereby reducing storage needs by half. It should be noted that, albeit shift invariant, this initial representation involves a loss of information and is therefore not invertible.

3.2 ROTATION AND SCALE INVARIANCE

In order to achieve invariance to rotation and scaling transformations also, we perform further non-linear and non-invertible operations on the power spectrum P. The first is a coordinate transformation, from cartesian (m,n) to logarithmic-polar (ρ, ϑ), where $\rho = \log\sqrt{(m - m_0)^2 + (n - n_0)^2}$, $\vartheta = \mathrm{atan}\frac{n-n_0}{m-m_0}$, and (m_0, n_0) is the origin of the new coordinate frame with respect to the cartesian one.

Although such a coordinate change is bijective in the continuous domain, it is not so for the discrete case, where the coordinates of the transformed domain only assume the following values:

$$\rho = \frac{1}{5}r, \frac{2}{5}r^2, \ldots, \frac{64}{5}r^{R-1} \quad (4)$$

$$\vartheta = 0, \frac{\pi}{S}, \frac{2\pi}{S}, \ldots, \frac{(S-1)\pi}{S} \quad (5)$$

In our implementation, we used $r = 10^{\frac{1}{64}}$ for the 64 magnitude bins, and $S = 32$ orientation bins, appropriate for images of size 256×256. The difference between this mapping and the traditional polar one is in the use of the logarithm, which results in an exponential sampling frequency as a function of the distance from the origin (m_0, n_0). In order to remove the aliasing effect introduced by this subsampling process, a low-pass filtering operation is performed. Since the distance between samples varies, the cut-off frequency of the filter should decrease with the distance from the origin. We do so by filtering the domain P with a Gaussian filter before the log-polar mapping, according to the following space-varying convolution:

$$P'(m,n) = \frac{1}{2\pi\sigma^2(m',n')} \sum_{k,l} P(k,l) \cdot \exp[-\frac{(m'-k)^2 + (n'-l)^2}{2\sigma^2(m',n')}] \quad (6)$$

$$\sigma(m',n') = \max(a, b \cdot \log\sqrt{(m')^2 + (n')^2}) \quad (7)$$

$$(m',n') = (m - m_0, n - n_0) \quad (8)$$

where $a = 2.0$ is a constant guaranteeing a finite upper bound for the cut-off frequency to the low-pass filter for points close to the origin (m_0, n_0), and $b = 0.07$ is a scaling coefficient. For efficiency reasons, the convolution is computed by truncating the Gaussian coefficients outside a square window, whose size is a function of $\sigma(m', n')$. Figure 1 shows the log-polar representation, together with the underlying sampling grid, applied to both an input image (for illustration purposes) and its power spectrum. In both cases the origin of the mapping is located at the center of the images.

An important parameter of this transformation is the origin (m_0, n_0), since different values generally produce very different representations. When it is applied to the power spectrum of natural images, the most appropriate choice is to set $(m_0, n_0) = (0, 0)$, since the magnitude of the Fourier coefficients is known to follow an approximately negative exponential distribution, around the DC component. Furthermore, as pointed out above, P is even symmetric for real input images, and this choice of the origin also leads to savings in memory space.

Let $L(\rho, \vartheta)$ denote the log-polar representation of the power spectrum. The advantage of using L instead of P resides in some degree of invariance to rotation and scaling transformations of the input image I, on the top of the translation invariance, already achieved by P. Indeed, it is easy to show that a rotation of the image by an angle ϕ results in a rotation of the Fourier coefficients by the same angle. Therefore, the rotation produces a shift in the ϑ coordinate of L by ϕ. Similarly, a scaling transformation on the input image, i.e. the division of the coordinates (x, y) by a constant α, has the effect of multiplying the coordinates (m, n) of P by the same constant. Due to the logarithmic sampling of L, this multiplication reduces to a shift by $\log \alpha$ in the ρ coordinate of L.

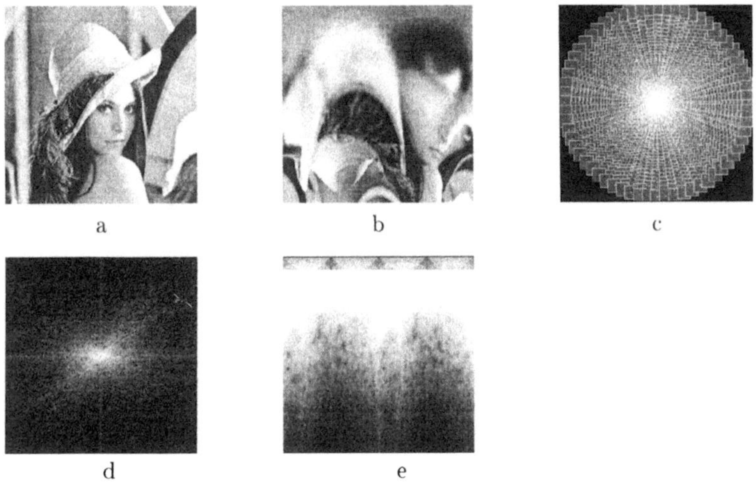

Figure 1: Illustration of the logarithmic-polar mapping. First row: (a) input image; (b) transformed image; (c) log-polar sampling grid. Second row: (d) Fourier power spectrum of image a; (e) transformed image.

To summarize, the proposed log-polar representation of the power spectrum is inherently invariant to image translations, and also provides invariance to rotation and scaling, up to a translation factor.

3.3 APPLICATION TO IMAGE ARCHIVAL AND RETRIEVAL

The representation L introduced above is invariant to translation and, up to a coordinate shift $(\log \alpha, \phi)$, also to scaling and rotation. In order to get rid of the latter shift, one may compute, once again, the power spectrum $\mathcal{L}$ of L, obtaining what is known as the Fourier-Mellin transform. This would make $\mathcal{L}$ completely invariant to the three transformations, and make it a candidate representation for comparing images in a database. The effective size of this representation, due to the symmetry properties described above, would be one half of L's size. For the sampling scheme described above (32×64 matrix L, appropriate for input images of size 256×256), this would produce an invariant signature vector of 1'024 coefficients. One may think of any distance function in this multidimensional feature space, such as the Euclidean distance, in order to assess the visual similarity between two images.

However, this straightforward approach presents some weaknesses. On one hand, the dimensionality of this feature space is clearly too large for efficient indexing. On the other hand, the feature vector is still too close to a global "photographic" representation of the input image, in the transformed space. Ideally, one should be able to assess the perceptual similarity between two images in a more "local" fashion, e.g. by distinguishing between the overall background of an outdoor picture, and its foreground objects. Since the basis functions of the DFT are not spatially localized, and all spatial information has been dropped with the phase spectrum, it is not possible to isolate coefficients which describe spatially-distinct components of an image. However, "foreground" objects are often defined over a limited frequency band (as opposed to the "background"). Therefore one may envisage the use of some robust distance function which discounts occasional band-limited differences between two vectors. Still, the design of such a distance function for the representation $\mathcal{L}$ would be quite complex, since frequency-band and orientation information are merged together.

In order to overcome the above problems, rather than computing the power spectrum of L, we compute two 1-D signature vectors by projecting $L(\cdot,\cdot)$ onto the two axes ρ and ϑ. In other words, we compute the marginals

$$L_\rho(s) = \sum_{\vartheta} L(s,\vartheta) \tag{9}$$

$$L_\vartheta(t) = \sum_{\rho} L(\rho,t) \tag{10}$$

where ρ and ϑ vary as defined in eq. 5. However, the representation L is still RTS-invariant up to a shift, and so are the vectors L_ρ, L_ϑ. In fact, L_ρ is already invariant to rotation (thanks to the projection) but not to scaling, while the opposite holds true for L_ϑ. Both can be made fully RTS-invariant by computing their power spectra $\mathcal{L}_\rho, \mathcal{L}_\vartheta$. Figure 2 shows the signature vectors $\mathcal{L}_\rho, \mathcal{L}_\vartheta$ computed from two images, which have been RTS-transformed with respect to one another. It can be seen that the two vectors are indeed invariant, despite all subsampling and numerical approximation errors.

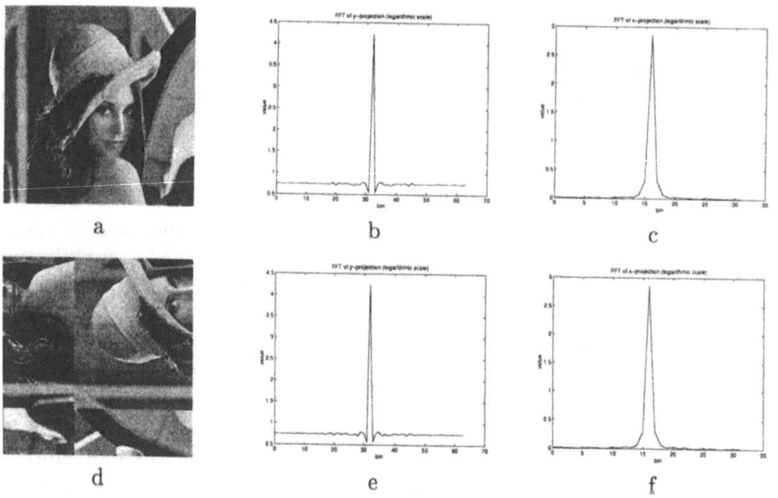

Figure 2. Example of invariant signature vector pairs extracted before (first row) and after (second row) RTS transformation. (a) Input image I; (b) vector $\mathcal{L}_\rho$; (c) vector $\mathcal{L}_\vartheta$; (d) transformed image I'; (e) transformed vector $\mathcal{L}'_\rho$; (f) transformed vector $\mathcal{L}'_\vartheta$.

On one hand, using these vectors as signatures dramatically reduces the dimensionality of the data, thereby facilitating indexing. Also, thanks to the symmetry of the power spectra of the two real-valued vectors, only half of the power spectra coefficients $\mathcal{L}_\rho, \mathcal{L}_\vartheta$ need to be retained. For the sizes used in our current implementation, this amounts to $\frac{1}{2}(32+64)+2 = 50$ coefficients. On the other hand, by separating frequency band magnitude from orientation, it is easier to design a robust distance function on the $\mathcal{L}_\rho$ vector that discounts (or identifies) band-limited objects.

It should be noted that the above signature vectors represent a gray–level image. For color images, three different pairs of vectors should be computed (one for each color plane), which we align into $3 \times 50 = 150$ dimensional vectors. It is appropriate in these cases to first perform a color mapping from RGB to another space, such as YIQ, where the luminance information (Y) is separated from the two chrominance channels.

4 EXPERIMENTAL VALIDATION

In order to validate any image representation for content-based retrieval, it is important to employ an experimental dataset for which a ground-thruth classification is available. However, it is very difficult (except for a few classes, such as faces, buildings, and landscapes) to create a collection of still pictures that can be clustered into disjoint classes without any subjective evaluation.

In order to overcome this problem, we decided to employ still pictures estracted from videoclips. We assumed that the action of uninterrupted recording from a video camera naturally implies a continuity in its visual content, with gradual changes from frame to frame due to camera operations and subject motion, including object appearance and disappearance.

In particular, we employed video clips of various news programs, all compressed in the MPEG-1 format, provided by the Greek television MegaChannel and by the Swiss television TSR. For each clip, we run a program that automatically segments a clip into *shots* by detecting scene cuts [10], and extracts a keyframe right after each cut. In addition to the keyframe, we also manually extracted from some shots a number of other frames in the middle and at the end of the corresponding shot, whenever object or camera motion was causing major changes between their visual appearance. The images classes were thus objectively defined by shot membership. In total, 1405 shots were extracted, providing a total of 2082 still images.

In order to determine the similarity between any two images I^i, I^j in the database, the simple Euclidean distance function between their signatures was used, and their average value was retained as the overall distance:

$$d(i,j) = \frac{1}{2}\left(\sqrt{\sum_s (\mathcal{L}^i_\rho(s) - \mathcal{L}^j_\rho(s))^2} + \sqrt{\sum_s (\mathcal{L}^i_\vartheta(s) - \mathcal{L}^j_\vartheta(s))^2}\right) . \qquad (11)$$

In this way, all images from the database could be compared with any query image (also selected from the database), and ranked by the value of d. A fixed number W of top-ranked images could then be displayed to the user, enabling browsing through the database. Figure 3 shows sample sets of top-ranked images retrieved from two query images belonging to shots that present considerable camera and subject motion (query images correspond to the highest-ranked hits, reported in hte top-left corners). It can be seen that, even though camera and subject motion clearly violate the RTS transformation model underlying the image representation, the target images are always retrieved with high similarity.

Two statistical measures were computed to assess system performance. One is called *recall*, and consists of the proportion of target images (i.e. images from the same class as the query) that have been retrieved among the top W hits. This measure is clearly monotonically increasing with W and attains 100% when W includes the whole dataset. For simplicity we shall only report the value of recall for the number of images that could fit into a display window of size $W = 12$. The other measure is *precision*, and consists of

Figure 3: Results of database retrieval using the query image shown in the top-left corner of each window. Images are ranked from left to right, top to bottom, by decreasing similarity (increasing distance measure d).

the number of target images that are retrieved among the top W hits. However, since the image classes are very small (up to 7 images per class), we employed a slightly different definition of precision, namely the proportion of target images that are retrieved up to the last correct one. A high value of precision therefore indicates that the top-ranked hits *all* contain target images.

The average recall measure computed from 16 queries of this kind, matched against the whole database of 2082 images partitioned into 1405 classes was 66.7%. The average precision at 100% recall was 54.6%. These results confirm the robustness of the invariant signature well beyond rigid 2D transformation, and its applicability to the indexing of real images, captured with a moving camera. Indeed, the shots from which all query images where selected present complex tracking and dollying motion (in addition to pan/tilt/zoom producing RTS transformations) that would in principle require more complex and computationally time-consuming geometric models for signature extraction (cf. [3]). Furthermore, subject motion causes objects to enter and leave the camera field of view, thereby altering the image content.

As far as storage and CPU requirements are concerned, the proposed method refers to color images of size 256×256, for which it computes two 1D feature vectors, for a total of 192 coefficients. At archival time, the extraction of the signature vectors for a new image requires approximately 6 s, including file I/O, FFT calculations and the log-polar mapping. At query time, the search through the database is performed linearly, which requires on average 399 μs per image comparison on a Sun Ultra-2 workstation. The full database of 2082 images is searched in 0.83 s.

5 CONCLUSIONS

In this paper we presented a method for constructing an image signature invariant to 2D rigid transformations, such as rotation, translation, and scaling (RTS), in order to provide a representation suitable for content-based image retrieval. This method requires the computation of the image power spectrum, performs a coordinate mapping from cartesian to logarithmic-polar, projects a 2-D representation onto two 1-D feature vectors, and computes their power spectra.

This signature has been shown to withstand more complex transformations than RTS, such as affine transformations induced by motion around the camera axis, as well as unrestriced camera and subject motion. The proposed representation has been shown to capture the perceptually relevant information of an image, since it provides good retrieval performance for a database of 2082 images extracted from a variety of news video clips. In comparison to methods extracting different representations and matching tools for color, texture, and shape features, it employs a holistic approach, and does not require the user to set appropriate weights to combine their results. With respect to other holistic approaches, such as those based on the wavelet transform, its invariant properties are a clear advantage.

Future work will improve the computational performance at query time, by indexing the feature vector and by using hierarchical search strategies. By virtue of the underlying holistic representation, it is also possible to introduce weights for fine-tuning the matching function, without compromising the interpretability of the search process by the user. These weights may, for instance, describe the relevance of color, or indicate the most relevant frequency band corresponding to an object or an image region selected by the user.

ACKNOWLEDGEMENTS

We would like to thank A. Jacot-Descombes for useful comments and F. Deguillaume for providing the shot segmentation programs used for the experimental validation. D. Squire proof-read the article and helped in evaluating system performance. Images and videos comprising the experimental dataset were kindly provided by the television studios Télévision Suisse Romande (Switzerland) and MegaChannel (Greece).

REFERENCES

[1] F. Idris and S. Panchanathan, Review of image and video indexing techniques. J. Visual Comm. and Image Repres. 1997, 8(2), pp. 146-166.

[2] M. De Marsico, L. Cinque, and S. Levialdi, Indexing pictorial documents by their content: a survey of current techniques. Image and Vision Computing 1997, 15, pp. 119-141.

[3] S. Startchik, R. Milanese and T. Pun, Projective and photometric invariant representation of planar disjoint shapes. Image and Vision Computing Journal, accepted for publication, 1998.

[4] B. Furht, S.W. Smoliar, H. Zhang, Video and image processing in multimedia systems. Kluwer Academic Publishers, 1995.

[5] M. Flickner, H. Sawhney, W. Niblack, J. Ashley, Q. Huang, B. Dom, M. Gorkani, J. Hafner, D. Lee, D. Petkovic, D. Steele and P. Yanker, Query by image and video content: the QBIC system. IEEE Computer, Sept. 1995, pp. 23-32.

[6] A. Gupta and R. Jain, Visual Information Retrieval. Communications of the ACM, Vol. 40, 5, May 1997.

[7] F. Idris and S. Panchanathan, Image indexing using wavelet vector quantization. Proc. SPIE Storage and retrieval of image and video databases III, Vol. 2420, Febr. 1995, pp. 373-380.

[8] C.E. Jacobs, A. Finkelstein, and D.H. Salesin, Fast Multiresolution Image Querying. Proc. Siggraph '95, ACM, New York, 1995.

[9] W. Y. Ma, Y. Deng and B.S. Manjunath, Tools for texture/color based search of images. Proc. SPIE Conference on Human Vision and Electronic Imaging II, 1997, Vol. 3106, San Jose, CA, pp. 496-507.

[10] R. Milanese, F. Deguillaume, and A. Jacot-Descombes, Video segmentation and camera motion characterization using compressed data. Proc. SPIE Conf. on Multimedia Storage and Archiving Systems II, Dallas (TX), Nov. 2-7, 1997.

[11] V.E. Ogle and M. Stonebraker, Chabot: retrieval from a relational database of images. IEEE Computer, Vol. 28, No. 9, Sept. 1995.

[12] A. Pentland, R.W. Picard and S. Sclaroff (1994). Photobook: tools for content-based manipulation of image databases. Proc. SPIE Storage and Retrieval for Image and Video Databases II, San Jose, CA, Feb. 1994. Vol. 2185, pp. 34-37.

[13] S. Sclaroff, L. Taycher and M. La Cascia, ImageRover: a Content-based Browser for the World Wide Web. Proc. IEEE Workshop on Content-Based Access of Image and Video Libraries, June 1997, San Juan, Puerto Rico.

[14] J.R. Smith and S.F. Chang, VisualSEEk: a fully automated content-based image query system. Proc. Fourth ACM International Multimedia Conference, Nov. 1996, Boston, MA, USA.

PERFORMANCE ASSESSMENT OF EDGE-BASED RANGE IMAGE SEGMENTATION

Xiaoyi Jiang, Horst Bunke
Dept. of Computer Science, Univ. of Bern
CH-3012 Bern, Switzerland
Email: {jiang,bunke}@iam.unibe.ch

ABSTRACT

In this paper we present a general experimental framework to characterize the performance of edge-based range image segmentation systems consisting of an edge detector and a grouper. This way we investigate the overall performance of generating complete region representations instead of earlier approaches of comparing edge maps alone. A case study using four segmenters resulting from two edge detectors and two groupers demonstrates the usefulness of the proposed framework to quantitatively characterize their performance and relative merit.

1 INTRODUCTION

The necessity and importance of evaluating computer vision algorithms by *using empirical data* has been recognized in the recent years in order to increase the number of real world applications of vision research and maturate computer vision from both scientific and industrial points of view. Nowadays, sound empirical comparison of vision algorithms is increasingly being accepted as original research, including research aspects such as methods, tools, and databases for performance evaluation, design of experiments, and actual comparison of different algorithms for vision problem, etc [1, 2, 3].

In the range image domain, two recent studies [5, 11] have reported performance assessment of *region-based* image segmentation algorithms. The present paper proposes a framework for performance assessment of *edge-based* complete range image segmentation. An edge-based complete segmentation relies upon an edge detection, followed by a grouping procedure that closes the gaps inherent in an edge map to form a complete region map.

A variety of methods have been proposed for assessing the performance of edge detectors, see [4] for a review. For edge detection in range images, an evaluation approach [7] has been proposed that contains sixteen performance measures related to correct edges, spurious edges, and missing edges in range data using hand specified ground truth. However, vision tasks based on range image analysis have been relying in most cases upon scene representations in terms of surface patches (regions). The measures from [7] are generally not able to provide enough evidence of suitability of a complete segmentation into regions. In this work we take an alternative approach of considering the overall performance of edge-based segmentation systems. Therefore, we don't investigate the performance of edge detectors alone, but instead their performance of generating a complete segmentation in cooperation with groupers.

We first introduce the test image sets used in our study. Then, the framework for performance assessment of edge-based complete segmentation is described in Section 3. As a case study, we consider four concrete edge-based segmentation methods, resulting from a combination of two edge detectors and two groupers. These edge detectors and groupers are briefly described in Section 4. The comparison results are given in Section 5, where we show that with the proposed framework we are able to quantitatively characterize the performance and relative merit of the studied segmenters. Finally, some discussions conclude the paper.

2 TEST IMAGE SETS AND GROUND TRUTH

For the range image segmentation problem we are faced with a large number of factors to be considered in the test imagery design:

- type of range scanners, the associated number of bits per pixel (quantization level) and type and amount of noise (besides quantization);
- number of surfaces in the image, size of surfaces (in pixels);
- jump edges: amount of depth discontinuity between two adjacent surfaces, edge length (in pixels);
- crease edges: angle between two adjacent surfaces, incident angle of edge to viewpoint, edge length (in pixels).

Ideally, an algorithm should be tested on an image set spanning the full range of all these design parameters. However, acquiring, ground-truthing, processing and analyzing the necessary image data, and comparing the results would require a prohibitive amount of effort. Therefore, we have to find some compromise.

For the comparison study described in [5], 40 images from an ABW structured light scanner and 40 images from a PERCEPTRON laser range finder were acquired to reasonably explore the problem dimensions listed above. Both image sets contain only polyhedral objects and were randomly divided into a 10 image training set and a 30 image test set. In the present paper, we use the 30 ABW test images and 30 PERCEPTRON test images. In addition we selected 20 images of the popular image set acquired by a WHITE triangulation scanner at the State University of Michigan which contain both planar and curved surfaces. Totally, the test image sets in our study consist of 80 images. Although numerous methods to acquire range data have been demonstrated, these three types of sensors predominate.

Ground truth was created for each image by a human operator. The ground truth for ABW and PERCEPTRON images is already available from [5]; we only manually ground-truthed the WHITE images. Figure 1 shows one image of medium complexity of each type. There are 457/438/105 total ground truth segmented regions in the ABW/PERCEPTRON/WHITE test image set.

3 EXPERIMENTAL PROTOCOL

Given m edge detectors E_i and n groupers G_j , we have mn segmenters in total. The experimental protocol for evaluating the performance of the segmenters is outlined in

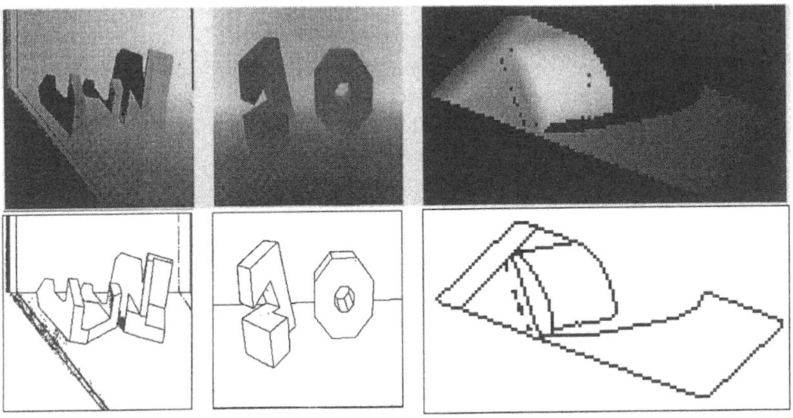

Figure 1: One ABW/PERCEPTRON/WHITE test image and the corresponding ground truth (outlines of borders of regions).

Figure 2. First, we experimentally determine one reasonable value of each parameter of each edge detector and grouper. By considering k values around this reasonable parameter value, a parameter space sampling is defined. This way the segmenter E_iG_j will be evaluated on $k^{\#E_i+\#G_j}$ parameter settings, where the symbol $\#$ denotes the number of parameters. Note that the value of k may vary for different parameters; the use of a constant value here is solely due to the notational simplicity. To gather the performance data we finally run all segmenters on the test images using the defined parameter settings and compute the performance measures.

We use the technique of analysis of variance (ANOVA[1]) to statistically analyze the performance data. For each segmenter we compare the performance between the "optimal" parameter setting fixed for the entire image set and the "optimal" parameter setting adapted on a per image basis. Then, we study the relative performance of the segmenters for fixed and adapted parameters separately.

The experimental performance evaluation is independently performed on the ABW/-PERCEPTRON/WHITE image set so that we can judge the performance of the segmenters for different types of image data.

3.1 PERFORMANCE MEASURES

The performance metrics defined in [5] are adopted to measure the goodness of a machine-generated segmentation. These measures are: number of correct detection, CD*, over-segmentation, OS*, under-segmentation, US*, missed regions, MI*, and noise regions, NO*; see [5] for details. The classification decisions are based upon a threshold $0.5 < T \leq 1.0$ which can be set to reflect the strictness of desired classifications. In our study we set T to the moderate value 0.8. To make the measures of images of different complexity (in terms of number of regions) comparable, we define the percentage measures $\mathrm{M} = \mathrm{M}^*/\mathrm{GT}$, $\mathrm{M} \in \{\mathrm{CD}, \mathrm{OS}, \mathrm{US}, \mathrm{MI}, \mathrm{NO}\}$, where GT represents the number of ground truth regions.

For a particular image and parameter setting we also define the stability of segmentation around the parameter setting. We consider the performance measures CD for all

[1]ANOVA is a general statistical method for analyzing experimental data, see for example [9].

```
/* Gather performance data */
for each edge detector E_i and grouper G_j do
    determine parameter space sampling
for each segmenter E_iG_j do {
    run E_iG_j on all test images
    compute performance measures
}
/* Analyze performance data */
for each segmenter E_iG_j do
    compare fixed and adapted parameter settings
compare relative performance of all segmenters
```

Figure 2: Experimental protocol of performance evaluation.

parameter settings which are at most one step apart in each of the parameter dimensions[2] and compute the standard deviation which will be denoted by ST. The reason for the restriction to the measure CD alone will become clear in Section 3.2. In total we therefore have defined six performance measures.

3.2 FIXED AND ADAPTED PARAMETERS

In our study we investigate the performance of each segmenter with a fixed parameter setting giving the best overall performance and the best adapted parameter setting (out of the sampled parameter space) on each image. Ideally, one would like to adaptively choose the parameters based on a per image basis. However, the present state of art usually precluded such a possibility. Hence, we include the fixed parameter scenario which reflects the current practice. Together they constitute in some sense a best-case and an average-case performance characterization.

The selection of the best parameter setting for a particular image proceeds as follows. The measures CD, OS, US, MI, and NO are not independent: CD is roughly inversely proportional to OS, US, and MI. Generally, CD is the main concern and the use of the segmentation results crucially depends on this factor. Therefore, we define the best parameter setting as the one (out of the sampled parameter space) with the highest CD value. This is also the reason for the restriction of the stability definition to the measure CD alone. The best overall parameter setting for the image set is associated with the highest mean CD over all images.

For each segmenter the performance measures resulting from the fixed and adapted parameters can be tabulated. We apply ANOVA to answer the question whether the performance differences between fixed and adapted parameters are statistically significant. This question is important because a negative finding would imply the highly desirable property that the fixed parameters are able to provide nearly optimal results on a per image basis. In this analysis there are two variations: images and parameter choices (fixed or adapted). Therefore, two-way ANOVA is performed.

[2] This is a generalization of the 8-neighborhood to higher dimensions.

3.3 RELATIVE PERFORMANCE COMPARISON

To evaluate the relative performance of the segmenters, we consider the performance data of all segmenters together, but separately for the fixed and adapted parameters. For each parameter choice, a two-way ANOVA (variations: images and segmenters) is conducted to decide whether the performance differences among the segmenters are statistically significant. If so, then a pairwise two-way ANOVA between all pairs of segmenters is carried out to establish a rank list of segmenters.

4 EDGE DETECTORS AND GROUPERS

In our current experimental study we have used two edge detectors and two groupers, resulting in four segmenters. The first edge detector E_1 is described in [6]. It makes use of the fact that a scan line (row, column or diagonal) of a range image is a curve in 3D space. Each scan line is partitioned into a set of curve segments by a splitting method. All the splitting points represent potential edges. The jump and crease edge strength of the edge candidates are determined by analytically computing the height difference and angle between two adjacent curve segments, respectively. Each pixel can be assigned up to four edge strength values of each type (jump and crease) from the four scan lines passing through the pixel. These edge strength values are combined by taking the maximum to define the overall edge strength of each type.

The second edge detector E_2 is based on the Canny operator. Unit surface normals (n_x, n_y, n_z) are computed by a robust estimation method. Then, the Canny operator is applied to the four channels $z, \cos^{-1} n_x, \cos^{-1} n_y, \cos^{-1} n_z$. The channel z provides the jump edge strengths, while the crease edge strengths are computed by the maximum of the other three channels.

The first grouper G_1 [8] takes a hypothesis generation and verification approach. From a binary edge map regions can be found by a component labeling. Due to the inevitable gaps in the edge chains, however, this initial grouping usually results in an under-segmentation. To recognize the correctly segmented and under-segmented regions, a region test is performed for each region of the initial segmentation. If the region test is successful, the corresponding region is accepted. Otherwise, the edge points within the region are dilated once, potentially closing the gaps. Then, hypothesis generation (component labeling) and verification (region test) are carried out for the region. This process is recursively done until the generated regions have been successfully verified or they are no longer considered because of a too small region size. After the grouping process, a postprocessing step is done in order to merge the pixels not labeled so far.

The second grouper G_2 [10] works with an edge strength map and is basically based on the same hypothesis generation and verification approach. It starts with a high threshold for generating a binary edge map. Region hypotheses are found by a component labeling and verified by the same region test as in G_1. For an unsuccessful region, the binarization threshold is decreased, and the hypothesis generation (component labeling) and verification (region test) are carried out again. This process is recursively done until termination under the same condition as in G_1. Note that in [10] no postprocessing was considered, resulting in unlabeled edge points. To make the two groupers comparable, we have added the postprocessing step of G_1 to G_2 as well.

fixed	CD	ST	OS	US	MI	NO
S_1	0.906	0.017	0.008	0.002	0.082	0.036
S_2	0.876	0.103	0.009	0.002	0.116	0.048
S_3	0.198	0.041	0.004	0.012	0.774	0.074
S_4	0.881	0.073	0.017	0.006	0.089	0.036

adapted	CD	ST	OS	US	MI	NO
S_1	0.913	0.017	0.005	0.002	0.078	0.034
S_2	0.911	0.098	0.008	0.000	0.080	0.047
S_3	0.220	0.043	0.004	0.016	0.733	0.078
S_4	0.891	0.161	0.019	0.006	0.078	0.053

Table 1: Mean performance measures over the entire ABW image set.

fixed vs. adapted	CD	ST	OS	US	MI	NO
S_1	*0.0493*	0.8910	0.1642	1.0000	0.1703	0.5095
S_2	*0.0006*	0.2603	0.8324	0.3256	*0.0121*	0.9218
S_3	*0.0163*	0.4560	1.0000	0.1709	*0.0377*	0.7655
S_4	0.1389	*0.0006*	0.3256	1.0000	0.1124	0.0653

Table 2: ANOVA results: fixed vs. adapted parameters (ABW).

5 EXPERIMENTAL RESULTS

The performance evaluation procedure described in Section 3 has been applied to the four segmenters $S_1(E_1G_1)$, $S_2(E_2G_1)$, $S_3(E_1G_2)$, and $S_4(E_2G_2)$ resulting from the edge detectors E_1 and E_2, and groupers G_1 and G_2. Both E_1 and E_2 have a single parameter that has been sampled by three values, respectively. The grouper G_1 (G_2) needs four (three) parameters that have been sampled by 2, 2, 3, 3 (2, 2, 3) values, leading to a total of 108 (36) parameter settings for S_1 and S_3 (S_2 and S_4). Note that the appropriate parameter values were determined by visual inspection of segmentation and the sampling density was chosen dependent on how critical a parameter is. After the parameter space sampling we run the four segmenters on the test images and compute the performance measures. These measures are fed to the performance data analysis procedure.

The analysis of performance data starts with the determination of the optimal fixed and adapted parameters. For the ABW image set these parameter settings produce the mean performance measures as listed in Table 1. For lack of space we will only give the performance data and their ANOVA results on the ABW image set.

5.1 FIXED AND ADAPTED PARAMETERS

Totally, 24 two-way ANOVA tests are performed (one for each combination of measure and segmenter) and the results for the variable parameter choice are tabulated in Table 2. The value P in each table entry (S_i, M_j) represents the estimated probability that, for segmenter S_i, the difference of the measure M_j of fixed and adapted parameters could have arisen because of pure chance. This significance value should be lower than 0.05, fixed parameters, all segmenters

CD	ST	OS	US	MI	NO
0.0000	*0.0000*	*0.0459*	0.0713	*0.0000*	*0.0222*

fixed parameters, pairwise comparison

	CD	ST	OS	US	MI	NO
S_1 vs. S_2	*0.0114*	*0.0000*	0.7541	1.0000	*0.0074*	0.3051
S_1 vs. S_3	*0.0000*	*0.0019*	0.4059	0.0585	*0.0000*	*0.0239*
S_1 vs. S_4	*0.0220*	*0.0001*	*0.0248*	0.1841	0.3655	0.9982
S_2 vs. S_3	*0.0000*	*0.0000*	0.3286	0.0585	*0.0000*	0.1414
S_2 vs. S_4	0.7270	*0.0182*	0.0260	0.1841	0.0990	0.3763
S_3 vs. S_4	*0.0000*	*0.0198*	0.0402	0.3765	*0.0000*	*0.0150*

Table 3: ANOVA results for fixed parameters (ABW).

indicating a 95% confidence level that the difference is not due to chance. If $P > 0.5$ holds, the factor parameter choice can be considered to have no effect on the measure M_j. A P value between 0.01 and 0.05 signals an appreciable dependence, while $P < 0.01$ reveals a strong dependence. In Table 2 entries with $P < 0.05$ are shown italic. We see that the main performance measure CD is weakly dependent on parameter choice for segmenter S_1, while segmenter S_2 and S_3 demonstrate a strong dependence. The difference in CD between fixed and adapted parameters is not significant only for segmenter S_4. The other five performance measures have mostly no dependence on parameter choice. Note that the ANOVA tests above contain two variables: parameter choice and image, and compute therefore P values for the variable image as well that are not listed in Table 2. Images have turned out to be generally a strong source of variation for all measures and all segmenters.

5.2 RELATIVE PERFORMANCE COMPARISON

For this study we investigate all four segmenters together, but separately for the fixed and adapted parameters. For lack of space we only illustrate this analysis for fixed parameters. First, six two-way ANOVA tests are performed (one for each performance measure) and the results for the factor segmenter are recorded on the top of Table 3. Again, results of the other factor image are omitted. Clearly, all performance measures except US are, partly strongly, dependent on the segmenter. This finding is not surprising if we take a look at Table 1. Segmenter S_3 namely demonstrates a strong performance discrepancy to other segmenters.

We continue the performance data analysis by performing pairwise two-way ANOVA tests between all pairs of segmenters. The results for the variable segmenter are tabulated on the bottom of Table 3. Note that this pairwise comparison is actually not necessary for the measure US since the overall ANOVA test demonstrated the equivalence of all segmenters with respect to this measure. The recording of pairwise comparison on US is given only for completeness.

We must be careful when we interpret P values from the pairwise comparison because we are performing multiple comparisons. For this purpose the significance threshold should be decreased. We use the modified form of the Bonferroni test [9]. The significance threshold α^* for multiple comparisons is related to the overall significance threshold α by $\alpha^* = \alpha \cdot DF/l$, where DF is the degree of freedom and l is the number of comparisons.

In our case DF equals three, the number of segmenters minus one, and l is six. So, to establish an overall significance of $\alpha = 0.05$ (95% confidence) we have to apply the significance threshold $\alpha^* = 0.025$ for the multiple comparisons. In Table 3 entries with $P < \alpha^*$ are shown italic.

We use the measure CD to demonstrate how to make a rank list of segmenters with respect to a particular measure. The mean CD values for fixed parameters in Table 1 lead to an order S_3, S_2, S_4, S_1 in ascending goodness. The column CD in Table 3 shows that only S_2 and S_4 have no significant difference. Therefore, the rank list for CD is:

$$\text{CD:} \quad (S_3) < (S_2, S_4) < (S_1)$$

Similarly, we can establish rank lists for other measures:

$$\begin{array}{ll} \text{ST:} & (S_2) < (S_4) < (S_3) < (S_1) \\ \text{OS:} & (S_4, S_2, S_1, S_3) \\ \text{US:} & (S_3, S_4, S_1, S_2) \\ \text{MI:} & (S_3) < (S_2, S_4, S_1) \\ \text{NO:} & (S_3) < (S_2, S_4, S_1) \end{array}$$

From these comparison results we can make a number of interesting observations. Segmenter S_1 has not only the highest CD measure but also the highest global stability. The latter is an importance issue because it indicates the sensitivity of segmentation quality against non-optimality of fixed parameter choice. The worst segmenter is obviously S_3. The reason lies in the use of edge detector E_1 which computes the edge strengths only for a subset of pixels as edge candidates. If there is an error in the localization of the edge candidates, gaps will be generated that cannot be closed by any binarization threshold and thus cannot be handled by grouper G_2. Segmenter S_2 has a bad stability measure. Currently, we have no explanation for this effect and it needs to be explored in the future.

The ANOVA results for adapted parameters are listed in Table 4. It is easy to verify that we can draw similar conclusions as for fixed parameters.

5.3 RELATIVE ROLE OF EDGE DETECTOR AND GROUPER

Table 5 shows the main measure CD of the four segmenters in a form suitable for the discussion of the relative role of edge detector and grouper. The use of E_1 obviously precludes the use of G_2. On the other hand, both groupers can be combined with E_2 to achieve similar performance. Grouper G_1 works well with both edge detectors, while G_2 cooperates only with E_2.

6 CONCLUSIONS

In this paper we proposed a general experimental framework to characterize the performance of edge-based range image segmentation systems consisting of an edge detector and a grouper. With the proposed framework we are able to quantitatively characterize their performance and relative merit. From recent work [8, 11] it can be concluded that the performance of edge-based approaches is comparable, in some cases even superior, to that of region-based methods. Considering the advantages of the edge-based segmentation paradigm (regular operators, simple control structure, precise boundary localization, adapted parameters, all segmenters

CD	ST	OS	US	MI	NO
0.0000	*0.0000*	*0.0237*	*0.0081*	*0.0000*	0.0530

adapted parameters, pairwise comparison

	CD	ST	OS	US	MI	NO
S_1 vs. S_2	0.8406	*0.0000*	0.4700	0.3256	0.7941	0.0955
S_1 vs. S_3	*0.0000*	*0.0007*	0.7458	*0.0181*	*0.0000*	0.0320
S_1 vs. S_4	0.0895	*0.0000*	*0.0035*	0.1841	0.9500	0.0785
S_2 vs. S_3	*0.0000*	*0.0002*	0.4249	*0.0170*	*0.0000*	0.1315
S_2 vs. S_4	0.0844	*0.0012*	0.0647	0.0993	0.7444	0.5675
S_3 vs. S_4	*0.0000*	*0.0000*	0.0346	0.1679	*0.0000*	0.2590

Table 4: ANOVA results for adapted parameters (ABW).

fixed		
	E_1	E_2
G_1	0.906	0.876
G_2	0.198	0.881

adapted		
	E_1	E_2
G_1	0.913	0.911
G_2	0.220	0.891

Table 5: Mean CD values of the four segmenters (ABW).

etc.), it possesses large potential of practical use that has not been fully exploited in the research so far.

ACKNOWLEDGMENTS

We thank the Pattern Recognition and Image Processing Lab of Michigan State University of making their database of range images for public usage. The ground-truthing of the images from this database was done by D. Grana.

References

[1] Bowyer KW, and Phillips PJ (eds). Empirical evaluation of techniques in computer vision, IEEE Computer Society Press, 1998.

[2] Christensen H, and Förstner W (eds). Special issue on performance evaluation. Machine Vision and Applications 1997; 9(5/6): 215–340.

[3] Firschein O, Fischler M, Kanade T. Creating benchmarking problems in machine vision: scientific challenge problems. In Proceedings of DARPA Image Understanding Workshop, 1993, pp 177–182.

[4] Heath MD, Sarkar S, Sanocki T, Bowyer KW. A robust visual method for assessing the relative performance of edge-detection algorithms. IEEE Transactions on Pattern Analysis and Machine Intelligence 1997; 19(12): 1338–1359.

[5] Hoover A, Jean-Baptiste G, Jiang X, Flynn PJ, Bunke H, Goldgof DB, Bowyer KW, Eggert DW, Fitzgibbon A, Fisher RB. An experimental comparison of range

image segmentation algorithms. IEEE Transactions on Pattern Analysis and Machine Intelligence 1996; 18(7): 673–689.

[6] Jiang X, and Bunke H. Edge detection in range images based on scan line approximation. Computer Vision and Image Understanding. (to appear)

[7] Jiang X, Hoover A, Jean-Baptiste G, Goldgof DB, Bowyer KW, Bunke H. A methodology for evaluating edge detection techniques for range images. In Proceedings of 2nd Asian Conference on Computer Vision, 1995, Vol.II, pp 415–419.

[8] Jiang X, and Bunke H. Range image segmentation: Adaptive grouping of edges into regions. In: Chin R and Pong TC (eds), Computer Vision – ACCV'98, Springer-Verlag, 1998, pp 299–306.

[9] Keppel G, Design of analysis. Prentice Hall, 1991.

[10] Liou SP, Chiu AH, Jain RC. A parallel technique for signal-level perceptual organization. IEEE Transactions on Pattern Analysis and Machine Intelligence 1991; 13(4): 317–325.

[11] Powell MW, Bowyer KW, Jiang X, Bunke H. Comparing curved-surface range image segmenters. In Proceedings of 6th International Conference on Computer Vision, 1998, pp 286–291.

IMAGE VARIABILITY DECOMPOSITION FOR RECOVERING POSE AND ILLUMINATION FROM OBJECT TRACKING

Peter N. Belhumeur* Gregory D. Hager†
Center for Computational Vision and Control
Yale University
P.O. Box 208285
New Haven, CT 06520-8285

ABSTRACT

As an object moves through space, it changes its orientation relative to the viewing camera and relative to light sources which illuminate it. As a consequence, the images of the object produced by the viewing camera may change dramatically. Thus to successfully track a moving object using computer vision, image changes due to varying pose and illumination must be accounted for. In this paper, we develop a method for object tracking that can not only accommodate large changes in object pose and illumination, but can recover these parameters as well. To do this, we separately model the image variation of the object produced by changes in pose and illumination. To track the object through each image in the sequence, we then locally search the models to find the best match, recovering the object's orientation and illumination in the process. Throughout, we present experimental results, achieved in real-time, demonstrating the effectiveness of our methods.

1 INTRODUCTION

The challenge in visual tracking has been to determine the image configuration of an object (or target region of an object) as the object moves through a camera's field of view. Yet as the object moves, the images of the object may change dramatically. This is not simply due to the translation of the object across the image plane. If it were, it would be simple to track the object through the image sequence using image correlation or a rigid contour tracker. Rather, complications arise due to the fact the object undergoes changes in pose relative to viewing camera and changes in appearance as its pose changes relative to the light sources which illuminate it. Thus to successfully determine the object's position, image changes due to varying pose and illumination must be accounted for.

In this paper, we develop a method for object tracking which offers a solution to this problem. To do this, we explicitly model how changes in pose and illumination of an object, or target region on an object, produce changes in the observed images. We call this approach to handling image changes "Image Variability Decomposition" (IVD). By using IVD, *we are able not only to track the object through the image sequence, but we are able to determine its*

*P. N. Belhumeur was supported by a Presidential Early Career Award, an NSF Career Award IRI-9703134, and ARO grant DAAH04-95-1-0494.

†G. Hager was supported by ARO grant DAAG55-98-1-0168, by National Science Foundation grant IRI-9420982, and by funds provided by Yale University.

pose and illumination as well. This is done in real-time on live video images. Near the end of the paper, we present results on tracking a human face, using the pose and illumination estimates of the tracker to drive a computer animated human head.

2 RELATED WORK

Most current tracking systems are feature-based. These systems overcome the deleterious effects of changes due to illumination by concentrating on a sparse set of edges or corners in the images, i.e. discontinuities in the image intensity [3, 11, 20, 4, 15, 6]. Since these methods focus only on image edges or contours, they are impressively effecient and can easily track objects in real-time.

Yet, one might argue that models using only local features throw out a great deal of information present in the original image. As a possible consequence, feature-based tracking methods require good dynamical models and effective search methods to avoid feature matching ambiguity, see again [3, 11, 20, 15]. And, if the objects do not have piecewise constant albedo patterns, the detection and localization of the edge or corner points are sensitive to changes in illumination. Thus, the Image Variability approach can be seen as a way of using *all* of the gray-value structure of images without committing to a particular set of features.

Only recently have "appearance-based" approaches been developed in an effort to use intensity information to model or learn a representation that captures a large set of the possible images of an object under pose and/or illumination variation [18, 19, 14, 25]. These methods have demonstrated the advantages of using appearance-based descriptions for recognition [14, 25, 19] or for tracking [18, 2]. From these methods, it is even possible to recover the pose of the tracked object [18]. Still, a drawback of these approaches is that in order to recognize (or track) an object seen from a particular pose and under a particular illumination, the object must have been previously seen under similar conditions.

The Image Variability Decomposition paradigm differs in that by decomposing image variability into changes due to illumination and changes due to pose, we are able to uncover low-dimensional *generative* structures for the set of images of an object. Thus, unlike appearance-based methods, it is not necessary to have seen the object under all of the seemingly infinite possible permutations of lighting conditions and pose. In the case of illumination variation, we exploit the results in [1] which show that the set of images of an object seen from a fixed viewpoint, under all possible illumination conditions, is a convex cone in the space of images, and, this cone (termed the "illumination cone") can often be constructed from as few as three images. In the case of pose variation, we exploit the results of Ullman and Basri [26], Jacobs [12], and Tomasi and Kanade [24] which show that, under weak perspective, the set of image coordinates of an object lies in low-dimensional linear subspace of the image coordinate space. This differs from earlier work on handling pose variation by ourselves and others [3, 8, 2, 23] in that image coordinate deformations are not restricted to be affine. Rather, the models described in this paper are specific to the target object's 3-D geometry. As a consequence, not only is the tracking of the object's position more reliable, but we are also able to recover the 3-D orientation of the object through the image sequence.

3 IMAGE VARIABILITY DECOMPOSITION

In the two subsections below, we describe how we model the image variation due to pose and illumination variation. In particular, we argue that from as few as three images of a target, it is possible to generate a complete set of images of the target over a range of pose and illumination variation.

3.1 POSE

Let us represent the structure of an object by the positions in space of a collection of n points on the object's surface. Let us choose the n points on the object's surface so that they map to a dense collection of pixels within an image. We call this collection of points the "target region." The pose of the object relative to an arbitrary fixed coordinate system can be represented by a point in $\mathbb{R}^3 \times SO(3)$. For each position and orientation of the object, we can construct a $3n-$dimensional vector describing the positions in space of the n points on the object's surface, i.e. for each orientation and translation, we have a corresponding point in a $3n-$dimensional coordinate space. The set of all possible 3-D object coordinates under 3-D rotation and translation is then a 6-D manifold[1] in this $3n-$dimensional coordinate space.

For each position and orientation of the object, we can likewise construct a $2n-$dimensional vector describing the positions in the image of the n points on the objects surface. The set of all possible 2-D image coordinates under 3-D rotation and translation is likewise a 6-D manifold in this $2n-$dimensional image coordinate space. We call this 6-D manifold the "pose manifold." However, this manifold lies within an 8-D *linear* subspace. As stated in the work of Ullman and Basri [26], because of the symmetry between the x and y image coordinates, both the x and y coordinates lie in the same 4-D linear subspace of an $n-$dimensional coordinate space. This 4-D subspace, which we call the "pose subspace," defines the 8-D linear subspace to which the pose manifold is restricted. Thus, to determine the pose subspace, which in turn determines a superset of all possible $2n-$dimensional image coordinates, we need only x and y coordinates of the n points in two images.

The above is simply a restatement of [26, 24, 21]; no new result is claimed here. However, we will argue that this approach can be used as the foundation for predicting novel images of an image, not simply the new locations of a sparse set of image feature points.

In order to express these ideas in equations, let vectors $\mathbf{x}$ and $\mathbf{y}$ describe the $x-$coordinates and the $y-$coordinates of a dense collection of n pixels in some "model" image. Let us call this collection of pixels the "target region." As discussed above, if the object is viewed orthographically, the resulting vector of $x-$coordinates and the resulting vector of $y-$coordinates are each restricted to lie in the same 4-D linear subspace, i.e. the pose subspace. Let $\hat{\mathbf{x}}, \hat{\mathbf{y}}, \hat{\mathbf{z}}$, and $\mathbf{1}$ (where $\mathbf{1}$ is an n-dimensional vector of ones) be the basis vectors for the 4-D pose subspace. Let the vector function $\mathbf{f}(\mathbf{b})$ represent a new vector of $x-$coordinates and the vector function $\mathbf{g}(\mathbf{c})$ represent a new vector of $y-$coordinates, after a rotation and translation of

[1]Due to possible symmetries in the object, the set of coordinates may not be a manifold, but a stratified set [7] composed of manifolds and singular sets of dimension six or less. For simplicity we will refer to these sets as manifolds.

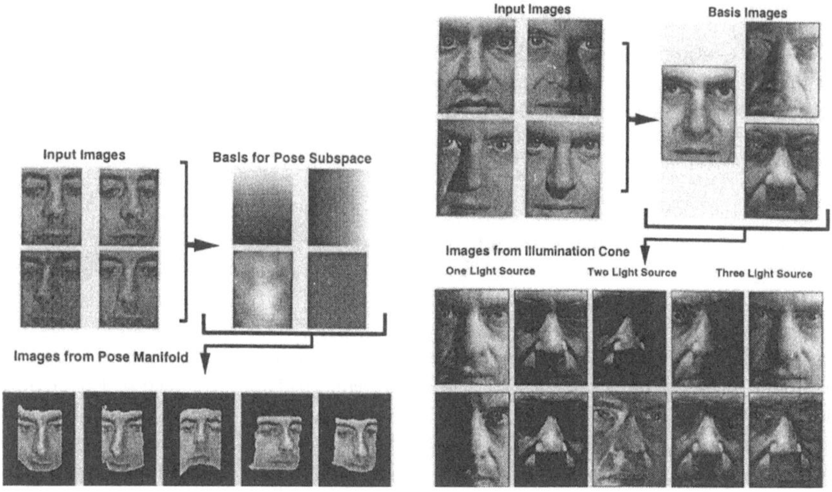

Figure 1: **Left, Pose Decomposition:** In this figure, we have used twenty images, four of which are shown here, to generate the pose subspace in which the pose manifold is embedded. The pictures at the bottom of the figure are artificially generated images of the human face. **Right, Illumination Decomposition:** Six images, of which four are shown, are used to construct the illumination cone of a target region centered on a human face. At the bottom of the figure are artificially generated images of the face that lie in the cone. Note the strong shadow lines and that their locations are consistent with the expected surface normals and light source directions.

the target region. Then we have

$$\begin{aligned} \mathbf{f}(\mathbf{b}) &= b_1\hat{\mathbf{x}} + b_2\hat{\mathbf{y}} + b_3\hat{\mathbf{z}} + b_4\mathbf{1} \\ \mathbf{g}(\mathbf{c}) &= c_1\hat{\mathbf{x}} + c_2\hat{\mathbf{y}} + c_3\hat{\mathbf{z}} + c_4\mathbf{1}. \end{aligned} \tag{1}$$

The eight coefficients in $\mathbf{b}$ and $\mathbf{c}$ together determine a point in the 8-D linear subspace in which the 6-D pose-manifold is embedded. For rigid motions, this point must lie on the pose manifold.

To compute the basis vectors for the pose subspace, let us assume we have chosen n pixels defining the target region of an object. We then acquire a second image of the object after the object undergoes a small rotation (and translation) in space with the proviso that the axis of rotation is not the camera's optical axis. From the correspondences of each pixel in the first image with those in the second image, we can determine the pose subspace [24]. Note that determining the pose subspace only fixes the *affine* structure of the object [13]. To determine the 3-D Euclidean structure of the object or, equivalently, to determine the pose manifold, a third image is needed. (This, of course, was implicit in work of [24], which demonstrated how these subspaces could be computed efficiently and, from them, the 3-D coordinates of the points determined.)

Yet, we stress that the goal of Pose Decomposition is not to necessarily determine the precise 3-D structure of objects. Rather, the goal is to find a pose subspace or pose manifold (if more than two images are available) that can be used to accurately predict images of the object under a range of viewpoints. These objectives are not the same, as points on the objects surface in regions of constant intensity will yield inaccurate structure measurements, but will have little effect on the set of images modeled by pose deformations.

What this all means is that from as few as two images of the object seen from slightly different directions, we can determine the images of the object under a large range of viewing directions. Thus in the case of scaled orthographic projection, there is indeed a simple, generative structure to the set of images of an object under varying pose.

Figure 1 gives a demonstration of an approximation to pose subspace and resulting pose manifold for a human face. Here we have used twenty images, of which four are shown, to generate the pose subspace in which the pose manifold is embedded. The basis vectors spanning the pose subspace were crudely determined by first determining the correspondence using the optical flow techniques of [16]. We then randomly sampled the pose manifold, recreating the images of the object at the new pose. The pictures at the bottom of the figure are artificially generated images of the human face. Note that there is little variation in the original four images shown in the top, left of the figure, yet the artificially generated images demonstrate a wider range of pose variation. Furthermore, while we have shown only five artificially generated images, we can actually generate any image over the continuum of poses.

3.2 ILLUMINATION

Image variability due to illumination has received relatively little attention in the computer vision literature. Yet, the same object seen from the same pose can appear drastically different depending the directions and strengths of the light sources [10, 17]. This fact has profound implications not only for object recognition, but also for object tracking.

The image formation process for a rigid object can be viewed as a function of pose and lighting. Since an object's pose can be represented by a point in $\mathbb{R}^3 \times SO(3)$, the set of n-pixel images of an object under *constant* illumination, but over all possible poses, is at most six dimensional. However, the variability due to illumination may be much larger as the set of possible lighting conditions is infinite dimensional. In particular, in previous work we have shown that the set of $n-$pixel images of the object seen under all possible combinations of light sources can have dimension n [1]. Thus, the set of images of an object seen from a fixed viewpoint, but under varying illumination, in general, spans the image space.

Still, it turns out that while the set of images of an object under varying illumination may be large, it has a great deal of implicit structure. The set of images of an object with arbitrary reflectance functions seen under arbitrary illumination conditions is a convex cone in $\mathbb{R}^n$ where n is the number of pixels in each image, see again [1]. And, if the object has a convex shape and a Lambertian reflectance function, the set of images under an arbitrary number of point light sources at infinity is a convex polyhedral cone in $\mathbb{R}^n$, which can be determined *exactly* from as few as three images.

To express the stated relations through equations, let us assume we have a target object seen from a fixed point, but under varying illumination. Again let vectors $\mathbf{x}$ and $\mathbf{y}$ describe the $x-$coordinates and the $y-$coordinates of a dense collection of n pixels in some image referred to as the "target region." Let $R(\mathbf{x}, \mathbf{y})$ denote the vector of brightness values in the target region. Due to its convexity, the illumination cone of the target region, i.e. the set of images of the object under all lighting conditions, is defined by a collection of extreme rays (images) $R_j(\mathbf{x},\mathbf{y})$ with $j = 1,\ldots,m$. (The number of extreme rays m may be quite large, but we approximate the illumination cone by choosing a small subset.) Any model image of the target region seen from the same viewpoint, but under arbitrary illumination, can then be constructed from a convex combination of the extreme rays:

$$M(\mathbf{x},\mathbf{y},\mathbf{a}) = \sum_{\mathbf{j}=1}^{\mathbf{m}} \mathbf{a_j}\,\mathbf{R_j}(\mathbf{x},\mathbf{y}) \tag{2}$$

where $a_j \geq 0 \quad \forall j$.

The determination of the extreme rays (the R_j) defining the convex cone can be done in two ways. First, we can simply gather a collection of images of the target regions illuminated by point light sources of different directions and use these to define the extreme rays. This method is similar to that of [18], except the illumination cone representation implicitly models multiple light sources since it allows for convex combinations of the extreme rays (images). A drawback of this method (and that of [18]) is that many images are needed to construct the model.

A second method for determining the extreme rays is to gather only a small number of images of the object under varying illumination and use these to generate the complete set of extreme rays. If the object's surface has a Lambertian reflectance function and the shape of the object is roughly convex, then we have shown [1] that the extreme rays defining the illumination cone can be generated from a 3-D linear subspace in the $n-$dimensional image space – we call this subspace the "illumination subspace." Furthermore, the illumination subspace can be generated from as few as three images [22, 5, 1].

Even if the surface reflectance function is more general than Lambertian and the object is non-convex in shape, this method still seems to work quite well. Figure 1 gives a demonstration of such an approximation for varying illumination of a face. Here we have used six images, of which four are shown, to generate what we call the illumination subspace which, in turn, generates the extreme rays which define the illumination cone. We then randomly sampled the illumination cone. The pictures at the bottom of the figure are artificially generated images of the face.

4 THE TRACKING SYSTEM

We pose the tracking problem as one of finding an optimal (according to the criterion stated below) pair of trajectories through the illumination cone and along the pose manifold. Let $I(x,y,t)$ denote the brightness value at the location $(x,y)^T$ in an image acquired at time t. If, as before, $\mathbf{x}$ and $\mathbf{y}$ are the x and y coordinates of n pixels defining the target region, let $I(\mathbf{x},\mathbf{y},t)$ denote an image of the target region. In the absence of noise, and if our pose and illumination models are exact, then it follows that the image of the target region must satisfy the following relation:

$$I(\mathbf{f}(\mathbf{b}),\mathbf{g}(\mathbf{c}),t) = M(\mathbf{x},\mathbf{y},\mathbf{a}) \tag{3}$$

for some $\mathbf{a} \in \mathbb{R}^m$, $\mathbf{b} \in \mathbb{R}^4$ and $\mathbf{c} \in \mathbb{R}^4$. This expression can be interpreted as follows: the observed image is first "warped" by a deformation selected from the pose manifold so that it is in the same configuration as the original image. An image is then synthesized from the extreme rays of the illumination cone (which is also in the same configuration as the original image) so that the result is identical to the distorted copy of the observed image.

It follows that the temporal correspondence of the target region across an image sequence can be determined by finding the pose parameters and the illumination parameters that minimize

$$O(\mathbf{a}, \mathbf{b}, \mathbf{c}) = \|I(\mathbf{f}(\mathbf{b}), \mathbf{g}(\mathbf{c}), t) - M(\mathbf{x}, \mathbf{y}, \mathbf{a})\|^2. \quad (4)$$

As we have recently shown [8], for problems of this form it is possible to efficiently compute both the illumination and pose parameters of a problem of this form. Briefly, the procedure is to linearize the above expression and to solve for the pose and illumination parameters incrementally in each frame. Expressing the problem as one of "warping back" to the original image makes it possible to factor the resulting expressions so that the estimation procedure is efficient enough to compute in real-time. Furthermore, we have shown that this estimation process can be made robust to statistical outliers with little loss in performance.

The result of this process is both a vector of coefficients characterizing the object's pose and a vector of coefficients describing a point in the illumination cone. To determine the actual pose, we simply choose a specific representation for rotations, equate the first two rows of the rotation matrix to the appropriate elements of **b** and **c** and solve the resulting equations for three rotation angles and a scale factor. In addition, once we know these values, we can also enforce consistency constraints on the parameter vectors, increasing the robustness of the tracking process. This can be done continually as the object is being tracked, i.e. we can recover the object's 3-D position and orientation at each instant in time. Likewise, the illumination coefficients each correspond to different light source directions, with the magnitudes of the coefficients proportional to the light source strengths.

5 RESULTS

A tracking algorithm based on these ideas has been implemented in the XVision tracking environment [8, 9]. In this section, we present three runs of the system applied to the problem of human face tracking. We note that the pose and illumination models for the face have been described in Sections 3.1 and 3.2, respectively. All experiments were performed on live video data on an SGI Indy equipped with a VINO digitizing system.

In the first experimental run, we emphasize the use of the pose manifold. In order to demonstrate the accuracy of the pose estimates, we animated a range model of a human head using the pose parameters computed by the algorithm. The results are shown in Figure 2. The first row of images are frames taken from the live sequence; the second row are the corresponding frames from the animation. Note in particular that the algorithm computes accurate pose information even when significant areas of the face become occluded.

In the second run, we vary the illumination dramatically, but keep the pose relatively constant. In Figure 3, we show three frames excerpted from the sequence and below them the corresponding artificial images synthesized using the lighting coefficients computed by the tracking algorithm.

In the third run, we vary both pose and illumination. The results appear in Figure 4. The graph at the upper left shows the pose angles for the face, and the graph at the upper right

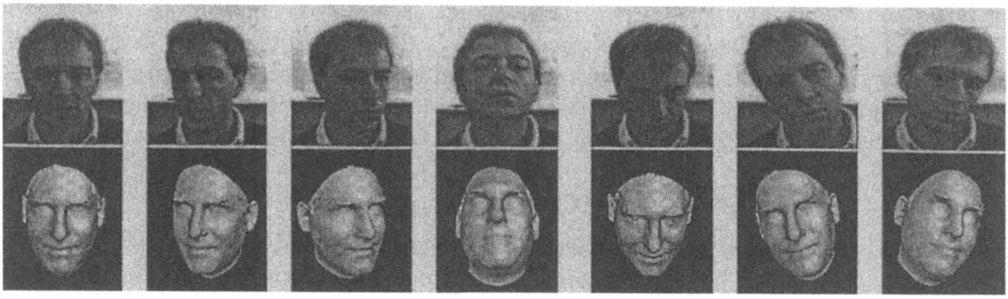

Frame 000 Frame 030 Frame 090 Frame 165 Frame 270 Frame 330 Frame 375

Figure 2: The results of animating a head using the pose coefficients of the tracking algorithm. Above, the live images, and below an image of the range model of a head rotated by the angles computed by the tracking algorithm.

Frame 000 Frame 225 Frame 300

Figure 3: The results of animating a head using the illumination coefficients computed by the tracking algorithm. Above, three frames excerpted from the sequence and below the corresponding artificial images synthesized using the lighting coefficients computed by the tracking algorithm.

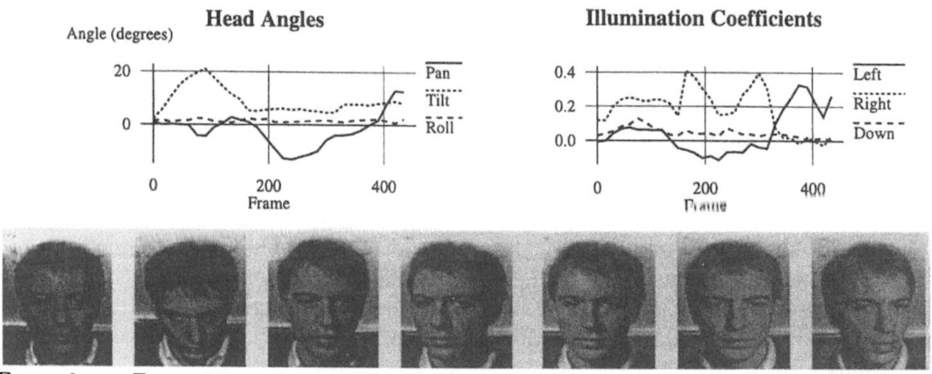

Frame 0 Frame 75 Frame 165 Frame 225 Frame 300 Frame 375 Frame 420

Figure 4: Above left, a graph of the three head orientation angles as a function of frame number. Above right, the corresponding illumination coefficients for the three components corresponding to illumination from the left, right, and above. Below, selected frames from the sequence.

shows the illumination coefficients for three of the rays defining the cone. The coefficients represent the contribution of illumination from the left, illumination from the right, and illumination from above. The lower row of images are frames from the sequence. By comparing the graphs and the images, we see that the parameters vary in exact correspondence to the physical situation.

6 DISCUSSION

In this paper, we have answered the following question: Is there some underlying "generative" structure to the set of images of an object under varying illumination and pose such that to create the set, the object does not have to be viewed under all possible conditions? Through image variability decomposition, we have shown that the answer is yes: from a small set of images it is possible to generate novel views and shadings of a target object accurate enough for object tracking.

As a result, we have shown that it is possible to track objects *and* compute their pose and illumination in a computationally efficient manner. At the moment, this tracking process assumes that the pose manifolds and illumination cone are built in advance. However, we believe it may be possible to estimate one or both during the tracking procedure. All that is needed to build the pose manifolds are images of the target seen under several rotations – rotations small enough for a tracker using only affine deformations to keep a lock on the target. Likewise, in order to determine the illumination cone, the tracking system must be sufficiently robust to tolerate novel deviations in illumination long enough to incorporate these deviations into the cone representation.

In future work, we plan to investigate the online development of pose and illumination models, and also to extend the algorithm to handle multiple views. Incorporating view switching will make it possible to track objects through the complete pose space. By successfully learning views online (each with its own pose and illumination model), we hope to demonstrate completely automated tracking of novel objects in real time.

References

[1] P. Belhumeur and D. Kriegman. What is the set of images of an object under all possible lighting conditions? In *IEEE Proc. Conf. Computer Vision and Pattern Recognition*, 1996.

[2] M. Black and A. Jepson. Eigentracking: Robust matching and tracking of articulated objects using a view-based representation. In *European Conf. on Computer Vision*, pages I:329–342, 1996.

[3] A. Blake, R. Curwen, and A. Zisserman. Affine-invariant contour tracking with automatic control of spatiotemporal scale. In *Proc. Int'l Conference on Computer Vision*, pages 421–430. IEEE Computer Society Press, 1993.

[4] R. Deriche and O. Faugeras. Tracking line segments. In O. Faugeras, editor, *Proc. 1st European Conference on Computer Vision*, pages 259–268. Springer–Verlag, 1990.

[5] R. Epstein, A. Yuille, and P. N. Belhumeur. Learning and recognizing objects using illumination subspaces. In *Proc. of the Int. Workshop on Object Representation for Computer Vision*, 1996.

[6] D. Gavrila and L. Davis. Tracking humans in action: A 3D model-based approach. In *Proc. Image Understanding Workshop*, pages 737–746, 1996.

[7] M. Goresky and R. Macpherson. *Stratified Morse Theory.* Springer-Verlag, New York, 1980.

[8] G. D. Hager and P. N. Belhumeur. Real-time tracking of image regions with changes in geometry and illumination. In *Proc. IEEE Conf. Computer Vision and Pattern Recognition*, pages 403–410. IEEE Computer Society Press, 1996.

[9] G. D. Hager and K. Toyama. XVision: A portable substrate for real-time vision applications. *Computer Vision and Image Understanding*, 69(1), 1998.

[10] P. Hallinan. *A Deformable Model for Face Recognition Under Arbitrary Lighting Conditions.* PhD thesis, Harvard University, 1995.

[11] M. Isard and A. Blake. Contour tracking by stochastic propogation of conditional density. In *Computer Vision-ECCV '96*, volume 1, pages 343–356. Springer Verlag, 1996.

[12] D. W. Jacobs. Space efficient 3D model indexing. In *Proc. IEEE Conf. on Comp. Vision and Patt. Recog.*, pages 439–444, 1992.

[13] J. Koenderink and A. Van Doorn. Affine structure from motion. *J. Opt. Soc. Am.*, 8(2):337–385, 1991.

[14] L. Sirovitch and M. Kirby. Low-dimensional procedure for the characterization of human faces. *J. Optical Soc. of America A*, 2:519–524, 1987.

[15] D. G. Lowe. Robust model-based motion tracking through the integration of search and estimation. *Int'l Journal of Computer Vision*, 8(2):113–122, 1992.

[16] B. Lucas and T. Kanade. An iterative image registration technique with an application to stereo vision. In *Proc. of the 7th International Joint Conference on Artificial Intelligence*, pages 674–679, 1981.

[17] Y. Moses, Y. Adini, and S. Ullman. Face recognition: The problem of compensating for changes in illumination direction. In *European Conf. on Computer Vision*, pages 286–296, 1994.

[18] H. Murase and S. Nayar. Visual learning and recognition of 3-D objects from appearence. *Int. J. Computer Vision*, 14(5–24), 1995.

[19] T. Poggio and K. Sung. Example-based learning for view-based human face detection. In *Proc. Image Understanding Workshop*, pages II:843–850, 1994.

[20] D. Reynard, A. Wildenberg, A. Blake, and J. Marchant. Learning dynamics of complex motions from image sequences. In *Proc. European Conf. on Computer Vision*, pages I:357–368, 1996.

[21] L. Shapiro, A. Zisserman, and M. Brady. 3D motion recovery via affine epipolar geometry. *Int. J. Computer Vision*, 16(2):147–182, October 1995.

[22] A. Shashua. *Geometry and Photometry in 3D Visual Recognition.* PhD thesis, MIT, 1992.

[23] J. Shi and C. Tomasi. Good features to track. In *Computer Vision and Patt. Recog.*, pages 593–600. IEEE Computer Society Press, 1994.

[24] C. Tomasi and T. Kanade. Shape and motion from image streams under orthography: A factorization method. *Int. J. Computer Vision*, 9(2):137–154, 1992.

[25] M. Turk and A. Pentland. Eigenfaces for recognition. *J. of Cognitive Neuroscience*, 3(1), 1991.

[26] S. Ullman and R. Basri. Recognition by linear combinations of models. *IEEE Trans. Pattern Analysis and Machine Intelligence*, 13(10):992–1006, 1991.

ON INCREASING THE OBJECTIVENESS OF SEGMENTATION RESULTS

Primo Zingaretti, Istituto di Informatica - University of Ancona, Italy
Antonella Carbonaro, Istituto di Informatica - University of Ancona, Italy

ABSTRACT. Unsupervised image segmentation is a complicated task due to the lack of appropriate measures for judging the quality of segmentation results. At present, most segmentation results are evaluated visually and qualitatively. In a previous paper [1], we presented a system that performs image segmentation without using neither ground-truth information nor human judgement. A genetic algorithm is used to efficiently search the set of parameters that maximises a segmentation quality criterion based on the integration of information from region boundaries and edge pixels. The performance of that system is degraded by the need of binarizing the edge maps, resulting in an information loss that may even hinder the convergence of the GA. In this paper we describe the solutions adopted to overcome this problem and to increase the objectiveness of segmentation results. Basically, human visual criteria are firstly embodied in an automatic image-contrast enhancement-process. The connectivity-code intermediate representation [2] and saliency-enhancing operations derived from the psychology field are then used to increase the significance of edge-pixels that have a small intensity but a high perceptual importance. Both computer simulated and real images have been used to test the performance of our adaptive segmentation system. The increased objectiveness of the segmentation results is confirmed both perceptually and by higher fitness values than those obtained by the previous system.

1 INTRODUCTION

Image segmentation is the process of classifying an image into a set of disjoint regions whose characteristics such as intensity, colour, texture, etc. are similar. Image segmentation is a very important process because it is typically the first task of any automatic image-understanding process, and all subsequent steps, such as feature extraction and classification, object detection and recognition, depend heavily on its results.

Many different segmentation algorithms have been presented in the literature [3, 4]. Most of them use numerous control parameters that must be adjusted to obtain an optimal performance. In practice, we do not know general automatic systems whose parameters provide an optimal performance for any image. Even the choice of an ad hoc setting, based on the actual algorithm or on *a priori* domain knowledge, may result in an unsatisfactory segmentation. On another side, the segmentation evaluation often relies on human visual criteria that can not be used to uniquely define the quality of segmentation results. Validity criteria vary from image to image depending on image characteristics and, sometimes, do not appear to correlate with human conclusions. As a consequence, a performance evaluation of the different algorithms proposed for a given application is inherently difficult to obtain, and none of the segmentation-quality measures suggested in the literature [3, 5] has achieved widespread acceptance.

The chosen segmentation techniques should be robust and flexible to obtain useful vision systems. Machine-learning may strongly contribute to the development of systems with these two characteristics [6]. In [1] we presented an evolutionary image-segmentation system in which image segmentation is formulated as an optimisation problem. A genetic algorithm (GA) is used to efficiently search, in the hyperspace of segmentation parameters, the set that maximises a segmentation-quality criterion based on edge maps. The goal of our system was not to build a new segmentation algorithm for a certain image class, but, rather, to develop a most general possible technique that uses neither ground-truth information nor human judgement in the evaluation of segmentation results. GAs are a general search technique that can locate an approximate global maximum in a search space, in a way not dependent on the particular application domain and without using detailed knowledge about the selected segmentation algorithm. A genetic system accumulates segmentation experience to reduce the computational cost of successive elaborations. The above flexibility, however, may become a handicap if the search is not properly constrained by a suitable evaluation function. So, if it is possible to define an evaluation criterion, a learning system can be applied. The performance of the system described in [1] is degraded by the need of binarizing the edge maps, resulting in an information loss that may even hinder the convergence of the GA. In this paper we describe the solutions adopted to overcome this problem and to increase the objectiveness of segmentation results, i.e., the performance of our evolutionary image-segmentation system.

The paper is organised as follows. Section 2 reports a brief survey of relevant techniques that have been proposed to face the problem of image segmentation. Section 3 describes the evolutionary image-segmentation system. The new image-processing flow leading to a more objective evaluation of segmentation results is described in Section 4, together with the new perceptual processing routines. Finally, preliminary experimental results are discussed in Section 5, and some conclusions are drawn in Section 6.

2 BRIEF SURVEY OF RELEVANT SEGMENTATION TECHNIQUES

Thresholding [7] is a widely used tool in image segmentation. There exist various classifications of thresholding techniques. A distinction between global and local techniques and a distinction between region and edge based techniques are the most generally adopted.

When an object is posed on a background the global grey-level histogram is bimodal and a threshold may be posed in the valley between the two peaks. In more complex images, such as outdoor scenes, a clear foreground / background distinction does not exist, so a single threshold can not be used to detect the objects of the scene; the global histogram is multimodal and a simple solution could be to consider a set of n thresholds (*multithresholding* [8]), one for each valley. In this approach, the simple extension of the valley/peak method is often not applicable due to the not-evidence of valleys or peaks. A solution is to transform the grey-level histogram by deepening the valleys and sharpening the peaks before applying the multithresholding method. Various techniques may be adopted [9]. For example, the pixels corresponding to edges with smaller or greater intensities could be weighted differently, or the grey-level histogram could be computed only for those pixels that have lower edge values.

Region-based segmentation-techniques are often sensitive to parameter values, while edge-based segmentation-techniques frequently have difficulty in establishing the connectivity of edge segments. The integration of information from region boundaries and edge pixels is a widely used approach in computer vision, which we also used in our system. Pavlidis and Liow [10] showed how combining region growing and edge detection produces much better segmentation results. The basis claim of their approach is that the results can be significantly improved if all region boundaries are checked whether qualify as edges rather than attempting to fine-tune the uniformity criterion. They start their algorithm with a split and merge process where the parameters are set up so that an over-segmented image results; region boundaries are then eliminated or modified on the basis of the boundary smoothness and of the variation of the image gradient along the boundary. These criteria use merit functions which are maximised by optimisation algorithms different from GAs. Haddon and Boyce [11] proposed a two stage method; an analysis of the distributions within a cooccurrence matrix defines an initial pixel classification into interior or boundary designation. Local consistency of pixel classification is then implemented by minimising the entropy of local information, where region information is estimated from the cooccurrence matrices, and boundary information is determined a priori. In fact, they suppose that there is an ideal segmentation in which each pixel corresponds to a unique region according to ground-truth or human interpretation. As in our approach, the application of GAs to image segmentation has been proposed by Bhanu, Lee and Ming [12] to adapt the segmentation process to the variable environmental conditions, such as time of day, rain, clouds, etc. They calculate the overall quality of the segmented image using five measures: two global measures (edge-border coincidence and boundary consistency) and three local measures (pixel classification, object overlap and object contrast). The local measures require the availability of object ground-truth information that may not always be obtained. Recently, Chun and Yang [13] presented a region-based image-segmentation system using a GA with a fuzzy validation-function that measures the degree of separation and compactness between and within segmented regions, and the edge strength along boundaries of all regions. The authors consider the 300th generation as the stopping rule, but the validity of segmentation results of this generation can never be guaranteed.

3 EVOLUTIONARY IMAGE SEGMENTATION SYSTEM

The proposed image-segmentation system is mainly constituted by two layers: the *global segmentation layer* and the *single-region evaluation layer*. In Fig. 1, which shows the system's global architecture and information flow, the above two layers are shaded. The system is executed until a good segmentation is achieved, providing an evolution of previous segmentation results at each execution. Our strategy is based on the hypothesis that, by modifying processing parameters, it is possible to obtain a good segmentation at least for some regions. This strategy extends the search space, but we overcome the difficulty in finding a good solution among many alternatives by adopting a GA.

The global segmentation layer adopts a genetic learning technique to produce a new classification of pixels into regions. The GA analyses the characteristics of the input image and uses this information to select an appropriate parameter combination to segment the image. A fitness is then evaluated and the GA cycles until a segmentation result of acceptable quality is reached: the stopping criterion of the GA is based on a fitness threshold T_I that is independent from the processing parameters adopted. In this way, the choice of the number of thresholds (over-under segmentation) is not a problem any more. The single-region evaluation layer is mainly based on the local evaluation of the fitness for each region resulting from the global segmentation. The aim of this layer is to select those regions that need further optimisation. The set of all these regions will constitute the object-of-interest image (OOI) for the next evolution. The global segmentation layer performs a segmentation of the entire image at the first application of the module and of the generated OOIs at the successive evolutions. The subset of individuals (seed population, SP) that have image features more similar (the similarity measure is based on the Euclidean distance, normalised with respect to the range of actual feature values and weighted on the importance of each feature) to those of the currently processed OOI is extracted from a long term population (LTP). Then, the image segmentation is performed using the processing parameters of these individuals, and, if necessary, the genetic operators are applied on these processing parameters until the global fitness does not

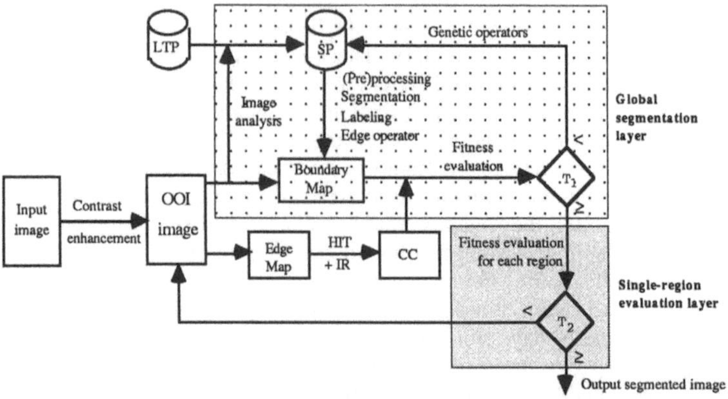

Fig. 1. Architecture and information flow of the system.

exceed T_1 (see Fig. 1). Thus, the aim of the global segmentation layer is to reduce the total computational cost of the system by decreasing the number of fitness evaluations, which are computational expensive. Our approach requires the segmentation evaluation of each region of the segmented image, so the splitting of the system in two layers avoids to compute a high number of fitness evaluations at each segmentation performed by the GA.

Our segmentation approach is based on the multithresholding of the intensity histogram. Histogram-based thresholding is computationally simpler than other existing algorithms and does not need a priori information of the image, even if, using global features, it may be not optimal for all objects of the input image. The parameters of the global segmentation layer include the (pre)processing of the input image, which may be based on global features like histogram transformations, or may concern local operations like spatial filtering and noise removal. Both these operations should be considered as "global processing" because the processing is applied to the whole OOI, even if it enhances some local features of the input image. A real "local processing" is introduced by means of successive evolutions. In fact, at each evolution the second layer should exclude from the input OOI those regions with a fitness value greater than a given threshold T_2. In the next evolution the global processing will be performed on the histogram of a smaller OOI, i.e., in a more local manner. In this sense, we say that our approach uses global techniques in a local context.

3.1 GA'S CODE-STRING

A GA is an iterative, global, stochastic optimisation procedure that evolves in parallel a population of individuals, or solutions. Each individual is represented by a string that codes a set of features. A *fitness function* adds a performance value to the string. The string coding and the choice of a fitness function are the most difficult problems in implementing a GA.

In our system, each individual of the GA population is constituted by three parts: *features*, *segmentation parameters* and *fitness*. The system uses two categories of features to discriminate the input images: global features of the image and features of the image histogram. The segmentation parameter part of each individual of the GA population codes the processing alternatives allowed by the system. More details about these two parts can be found in [1], while the fitness part is described in the next section.

It is important to note that further (pre)processing techniques can be coded in the segmentation parameter part of an individual without requiring substantial modifications of the algorithm's structure. Anyway, from the experimental results we have noticed that the main drawbacks of the system are related to the edge maps and to their binarization. In order to improve the performance and robustness of the system, instead of including more sophisticated processing techniques (e.g., by proposing a new edge detector), we found more effective to modify the architecture of our original segmentation system by inserting three new perceptual processing procedures.

3.2 EVALUATION OF SEGMENTATION RESULTS

The genetic fitness function should direct the system towards an optimal solution, which will correspond to fitness values higher than a given threshold. This threshold, when reached, will represent a stop condition for the iteration of the GA. Usually, a stop condition based on a maximum number of iterations is also set up to detect imperfect evolutions of the GA.

We perform edge detection to assess the performance of region segmentation and then to guide the evolution of the segmentation. In this sense the contribution of our paper may be viewed as a new method for the integration of region-based and edge-based segmentation. Our fitness criterion considers the correspondence between boundaries of regions resulting from the segmentation (*boundary map*) and edges obtained from an edge operator (*edge map*). This correspondence is difficult to find in real images even in presence of a good segmentation, so we have introduced a matching tolerance to overcome errors in the extraction of significant edges. In practice, we compute two types of correspondences: F_1, an exact correspondence between boundaries and edges, and F_2, a fuzzy correspondence, respectively defined as:

$$F_1 = \frac{P_1}{\min(N_1, N_2)} \qquad F_2 = \left(P_1 + \sum_{i=0}^{d-1} \frac{hist(i) \cdot (d-i)}{d} - \frac{E_1 + E_2}{2} \right) \Big/ N_1$$

where: P_1 is the number of pixels resulting from a logical '*and*' between boundary and edge maps; N_1 is the total number of pixels in the boundary map; N_2 is the total number of pixels in the image obtained from the binarization of the edge map at the threshold that minimises the difference between N_1 and the pixels resulting from the binarization itself; d is the tolerance in the matching distance; $hist(i)$ is the number of boundary pixels that have a distance i from the nearest edge pixel in the corresponding edge map; E_1 is the number of boundary pixels that have a distance greater than d from any edge pixel in the corresponding edge map; E_2 is the number of edge pixels that have a distance greater than d from any boundary pixel in the corresponding boundary map.

The fitness function, F, which is also used in the single-region evaluation layer, is obtained by weighting equally the two correspondence measures:

$$F = \frac{1}{2} F_1 + \frac{1}{2} F_2$$

The achievement of a good segmentation is represented by a fitness higher than T_2. For the efficiency of our two-layer approach the threshold T_1, adopted in the global segmentation layer, should be high enough to allow the existence of at least one region exceeding T_2, but also not too high to avoid a great number of GA iterations. In any case $T_1 < T_2$.

A final global fitness F_{tot} is computed for the output segmented image as a weighted average of the area and the fitness value of each resulting region:

$$F_{tot} = \sum_i F_i \cdot \frac{area_i}{area}$$

4 OBJECTIVENESS ENHANCEMENT BY PERCEPTUAL PROCESSING

The computational cost (synthesised by the number of GA's evolutions and of iterations for each evolution) and the segmentation results (in terms of number of regions, percentage of unclassified regions, or *holes*, and global fitness) of our original segmentation system exhibited different behaviours. In particular, some images required a great number of iterations of the first layer, and many holes resulted in some other segmentations. Both the thresholds T_1 and T_2 are critical factors. In some cases, better results were obtained by lowering the T_1 threshold. While a low T_2 impairs the segmentation results, a high T_2 heavily increments the computational cost, because in many evolutions no region resulting from the first layer can be considered well segmented, i.e., no real evolution occurs. Rather than modify thresholds T_1 and T_2, a difficult and not-automatic task because image dependent, we have introduced pre-processing steps that take in great consideration the perceptual weight of each pixel. The architecture of our original segmentation system has been modified by inserting three new perceptual processing procedures before the two layers. In particular, the information flow has been modified by the introduction of an initial image-contrast enhancement, a perceptual spatial-processing (HIT) and the adoption of the connectivity-code (CC) intermediate-representation (IR), as shown in Fig. 1. In this section we explain the role of these new routines and the main motivations that have justified our choices.

4.1 IMAGE-CONTRAST ENHANCEMENT

In consequence of the global operating mode of the first layer, and even if we introduced some locality by the two consecutive layers, in some cases the choice of the thresholds for the binarization of the edge maps, or for the selection of the valleys in the intensity histogram, still remained a problem in our original system. For example, in the case of an object surface not uniformly illuminated any chosen threshold caused the loss of significant edges, or, for isolated objects, problems could arise from the presence of noisy edges. In particular, the global threshold T_1 represented a critical point in the evolution of our system. Instead of decreasing the value of T_1 to overcome the first layer, and execute the second layer for a more local processing, we have opted for increasing the significance of edge-pixels that have a small intensity but a high perceptual importance. To find these edge-pixels and, consequently, to increase the correspondence between the more objective boundaries and edges, the actual system adopts perceptual cues. Among these, the perceived contrast is certainly an important one, so we firstly apply an image-contrast enhancement-process to the input image.

A high-performance contrast-enhancement algorithm should take into account not only local image characteristics but also some basic human visual properties like contrast sensitivity and simultaneous contrast. Our definition of the local contrast value for each pixel is computed according to a function that is based on human visual response and does not take into account the grey-scale and the grey level histogram of the input image. The definition of the contrast value is made according to a piecewise linearization of the Weber function as in Carbonaro and Zingaretti [14]. More rigorously, the contrast C_{xy} associated to the pixel (x,y) is defined as:

$$C_{xy} = \frac{f(x,y) - I(x,y)}{I(x,y)} = \frac{\Delta I(x,y)}{I(x,y)}; \qquad I(x,y) = \sum_{i=x-p}^{x+p} \sum_{j=y-q}^{y+q} w_{ij} f(x-i, y-j)$$

where: p and q are the dimensions of the neighbourhood centred in (x, y), $I(x, y)$ is the mean intensity in this neighbourhood, and the coefficients w_{ij} weight the importance of each pixel according to its location (i, j). We adopt four different functions for each region of the perceived contrast curve: constant, De Vries-Rose, Weber and saturation region. In particular, these functions are, respectively:

$$C_{xy}^{const} = \frac{K_0}{I(x,y)}; \qquad C_{xy}^{DVR} = \frac{K_1}{\sqrt{I(x,y)}}; \qquad C_{xy}^{W} = K_2; \qquad C_{xy}^{sat} = K_3\, I(x,y)$$

The constants K_i are determined by the following formulas:

$$K_0 = K_1\sqrt{I_1}; \qquad K_1 = K_2\sqrt{I_2}; \qquad K_2 = \beta; \qquad K_3 = \frac{K_2}{I_3}$$

where the intensities I_i are computed at the intersection between adjacent regions of the perceived contrast curve and the parameter β can assume a value between 0.02 and 0.06.

4.2 PERCEPTUAL SPATIAL-PROCESSING

Once the image is correctly perceived, it is well known that contours play an important role in the ability of the human beings in segmenting objects. The spatial interactions among edges are another important phenomenon of the focus-of-attention process. The rules that lead this process reinforce the continuity and the separability of salient edges, making the edge-pixels weaker or stronger. Unfortunately, these rules are very complex, not yet well known and, consequently, difficult to implement. On the other hand, in many situations, even an incomplete and naive implementation of these rules yields great improvements in assessing the real perceptual importance of each edge-pixel. Then, further perceptual processing relies on the application of a Helmholtzian transformation that, taking into account the distance among residual edges on binarized edge maps, attenuates or enhances gradient intensities in original multilevel edge maps [15]. In this way, edge intensities are modified depending on their spatial distribution and according to perceptual rules, and, in general, edges belonging to different objects or object parts become more separated. In particular, the Helmholtzian transformation excites the local perceptual power of strong edges and inhibits the weaker edges near them, but, at the same time, leaves unchanged textural patterns far from them. The goal of this processing is to create a perceptual feature map by implementing inhibitory/excitatory mechanisms to outline the perceptual strength of edges. An example of excitatory interaction may be represented by the reconstruction of broken line segments, while an example of inhibitory interaction is represented by the attenuation that strong edges exert on neighbouring weak edges.

4.3 EDGE-BOUNDARY CORRESPONDENCE

From the analysis of the results furnished by our original segmentation system, we have noticed that low fitness values were sometimes obtained even for good region segmentations, as consequence of bad contours resulting from the binarization of the edge maps. In machine vision the extraction of contours from an image is important because it provides useful information for segmenting images into meaningful regions. Unfortunately, problems exist with local edge operators. They are widely known and mainly related to the possibly small spatial extent of the operator relative to the events they are designed to detect, and to the deviation of actual image data from assumed models. Thus, the resulting edge maps cannot always provide perceptually meaningful lines and curves because missing, misplaced, and extraneous edges are often detected. For example, a significant variation in edge contrast along a line due to a changing background behind an occluding surface prevents the extraction of a single line. In addition, the zone of influence of an edge can not be definitively stated, so the problem of the selection of the pixel subset to be considered in the correspondence between boundaries and edges arises, and, in this context, an important cue is represented by the 'direction' of edge-pixels. Puliti, Tascini and Zingaretti [2] presented a system that reduces the transition gap in the flow of information between edge points and contours by the use of the

CC-IR. The IR is constructed by considering both the local gradient magnitude (measured over a small local window) and the local gradient orientation, which will vary relatively little apart from near junctions. We adopt this IR because it offers several advantages. The CC, furnishing information about edge orientations, allows the system to better discriminate the edges to be considered in the correspondence with each boundary part. In addition, the IR avoids the use of domain specific knowledge at the early stages of visual data organisation, allows the focus of attention on perceptually salient elements, and reduces the amount of data to be processed at higher levels.

5 PRELIMINARY EXPERIMENTAL RESULTS

Comparisons with other segmentation algorithms are difficult to perform. In fact, at present, we do not know of the existence of a test bed for image-segmentation results, and it seems very difficult to find an evaluation method different from an ROC analysis. In this paper, we simply analyse the major improvements obtained over the original adaptive image-segmentation system. Experiments have been performed on five computer simulated and five real images. This test bed has also been used to set up the segmentation system. Various perceptual processing alternatives have been checked for the inclusion in the architecture, taking care that neither ground-truth information nor human intervention were required. Each processing adopted exploits some advantages and, in general, they reinforce the goodness of the general framework by improving the objectiveness of the segmentation results.

The initial image-contrast enhancement, differently from the approach described in [14], has been performed always using a value of $\beta = 0.03$ and without optimising the contrast transformation function to avoid a high computational cost. The main advantage of contrast enhancement is not the visual improvement (see Fig. 3), rather, it is the transformation of edge intensities according to the local spatial activity. In particular, not-isolated low-value step-edges (i.e., clear boundary pixels) are increased, making more probable the selection of objective edges by the successive binarization process. This results in the reduction of the number of iterations necessary to overcome T_1, as well as of the number of situations in which the system is not able to overcome T_2 (i.e., it is not able to individuate a region that does not need further elaborations).

The perceptual processing concerning edge interactions and directions allows the system to improve both the F_1 and F_2 values, on the average. The actual implementation of the HIT is

Fig. 2. The grey-level standard image "camera" 256x256x8 pixels.

Fig. 3. The "camera" image after the contrast enhancement.

mainly oriented to reduce the importance of textural patterns near strong edges. The CC allows the system to better discriminate the edges to be considered in the correspondence with each boundary part. For example, in the "camera" image, the ending part of the axis of the tripod (object) was not detected by the old system (see Fig. 4). Even if its boundary was detected correctly, at least visually, the fitness did not exceed T_2 owing to the presence of textural edges in the edge map. On the contrary, the textural edges around this object are partially attenuated by the HIT and their weight is further reduced in the fitness computation by the CC owing to their different orientation with respect to that of the boundary of this object.

We have obtained an increasing performance over the original system for all the images considered. In some cases the improvement is directly observable from the images (for example, on the contrary of the old system, see Fig. 4, the trousers, the glove, the columns and the ending part of the axis of the tripod were correctly segmented by the new system, as shown in Fig. 5), while in other cases the major improvement concerns the saving in the computational cost.

6 CONCLUSIONS

In this paper we have described the solutions adopted for increasing the objectiveness of segmentation results, i.e., the performance of our evolutionary image-segmentation system. The system represents an automatic approach to image segmentation that, using an adaptive methodology, globally searches for a good solution, and then performs subsequent, local segmentation refinements without using neither ground-truth information nor human judgement. Human visual criteria (local perceived contrast, edge interactions and edge directions) have been introduced to increase the significance of edge-pixels that have a high perceptual importance and to introduce further locality in the system. These improvements allow the system to better manage those situations in which the previous system required too much iterations to obtain for the entire OOI-image a fitness value greater than the fixed threshold T_1, or in which the fitness of a region remained always under T_2 due to the poor correspondence between image-edges and region boundaries obtained from the segmentation. In practice, the resulting edges have been made more objective and the correspondence between boundaries and edges, i.e., the GA's fitness value, has been increased. In addition, we have improved the system both from the point of view of efficiency (decreasing the computational cost) and of efficacy (increasing the number of resolved problems).

Fig. 4. Old system's results: region boundaries of Fig. 5 in [1].

Fig. 5. The more objective results of the new adaptive segmentation system.

In conclusion, the main contribution of the paper is the general framework, which allows to autonomously determine the criteria for an objective segmentation, and to embed more advanced perceptual processing procedures without altering the global architecture.
Future works will focus on the detection, or definition, of a statistical model for the quantitative evaluation of segmentation results, with respect to the improvement relative to each perceptual processing procedure as well as to the global framework.

7 REFERENCES

[1] Zingaretti P, Carbonaro A, Puliti P. Evolutionary image segmentation. In: Del Bimbo A (ed.). Image Analysis and Processing. Lecture Notes in Computer Science, Springer-Verlag, vol. 1310, 1997, pp 247-254.

[2] Puliti P, Tascini G, Zingaretti P. Extracting shape elements by perceptual pattern detection. In: Arcelli C, Cordella LP, Sanniti di Baja G (eds). Advances in Visual Form Analysis. World Scientific, 1997, pp 452-461.

[3] Haralick RM, Shapiro LG. Image segmentation techniques. Computer Vision, Graphics, and Image Processing 1985; 29: 100-132.

[4] Pal NR, Pal SK. A review on image segmentation techniques. Pattern Recognition 1993; 26: 1277-1294.

[5] Zhang YJ. A survey on evaluation methods for image segmentation. Pattern Recognition 1996; 29(8): 1335-1346.

[6] Bhanu B, Poggio T. Introduction to Special Section on Learning in Computer Vision. IEEE Transaction on Pattern Analysis and Machine Intelligence 1994; 16(9): 865-868.

[7] Lee SU, Chung SY. A comparative performance study of several global thresholding techniques for segmentation. Computer Vision, Graphics, and Image Processing 1990; 52: 171-190.

[8] Wang S, Haralick RM. Automatic multithreshold selection. Computer Vision, Graphics, and Image Processing 1984; 25: 46-67.

[9] Weszka JS, Rosenfeld A. Histogram modification for threshold selection. IEEE Transaction on System, Man and Cybernetics 1979; 9(1): 38-52.

[10] Pavlidis JT, Liow YT. Integrating region growing and edge detection. IEEE Transaction on Pattern Analysis and Machine Intelligence 1990; 12(3): 225-233.

[11] Haddon JF, Boyce JF. Image Segmentation by unifying region and boundary information. IEEE Transaction on Pattern Analysis and Machine Intelligence 1990; 12(10): 929-948.

[12] Bhanu B, Lee S, Ming J. Adaptive Image Segmentation using a genetic algorithm. IEEE Transaction on System Man and Cybernetics 1995; 25(12): 1543-1567.

[13] Chun DN, Yang HS. Robust image segmentation using genetic algorithm with a fuzzy measure. Pattern Recognition 1996; 29(7): 1195-1211.

[14] Carbonaro A, Zingaretti P. Optimal contrast enhancement based on human visual perception. In: Proceedings of Artificial Intelligence and Pattern Recognition Techniques for Computer Vision. Univ. of Ferrara, Italy, 1998, pp 164-169.

[15] Zingaretti P, Marchegiani F, Puliti P. Perceptually motivated model generation for template matching. In: Tascini G, Esposito F, Roberto V, Zingaretti P (eds). Machine learning and perception. World Scientific, vol. 23, 1996, pp 125-134.

COLOR-BASED MOMENT INVARIANTS FOR VIEWPOINT AND ILLUMINATION INDEPENDENT RECOGNITION OF PLANAR COLOR PATTERNS

Florica Mindru, Theo Moons, and Luc Van Gool
Katholieke Universiteit Leuven, ESAT / PSI, Leuven (BELGIUM)

ABSTRACT

This paper contributes to the viewpoint and illumination independent recognition of planar color patterns such as labels, logos, signs, pictograms, etc. by means of moment invariants. It introduces the idea of using powers of the intensities in the different color bands of a color image and combinations thereof for the construction of the moments. First, a complete classification is made of all functions of such moments which are invariant under both affine deformations of the pattern (thus achieving viewpoint invariance) as well as linear changes of the intensity values in the individual color bands (hence, coping with changes in the irradiance pattern due to different lighting conditions and/or viewpoints). The discriminant power and classification performance of these new invariants for color pattern recognition has been tested on a data set consisting of images of real outdoors advertising panels. Furthermore, a comparison to moment invariants presented in literature ([1] and [2]) that come closest to the aimed type of invariants is made and new approaches to improve their performance are presented.

1. INTRODUCTION

This paper contributes to the viewpoint and illumination invariant recognition of planar color patterns such as labels, logos, signs, pictograms, etc.. It focusses on affine deformations of the shape and linear changes of the color bands.

Much research has been put into invariants for planar shapes under geometrical deformations [3, 4]. Most work has focused on invariants for the shapes' contours. For the patterns considered here, however, the pictorial content usually is too complicated to robustly extract closed object contours from it. On the other hand, they typically have simple outlines such as parallelograms or ellipses. These *can* be found robustly with special shape detectors, but are insufficient for recognition (all parallelograms or ellipses are affinely equivalent). Therefore, moment invariants of the enclosed color patterns are considered.

Color information has proven very useful in pattern recognition, e.g. through the use of color histograms [5, 6, 8] or multiband correlation functions [7]. Another strand of research has focussed on moment invariants under different types of geometric and/or photometric changes [9, 10, 11, 12, 2, 13, 7, 1]. Color histograms do not exploit the spatial layout of the colors, whereas for moment invariants our experiments have shown that in order to increase the recognition performance, one may have to let grow the order of the moments beyond the point where they remain stable. These problems are remedied here, by introducing powers of the color intensities and combinations thereof in the expressions for the moments. In that way, a broad set of moment invariants can be extracted that never call upon high powers of either intensities or spatial coordinates.

In section 2 a complete classification of such moment invariants is presented for affine geometric and linear photometric changes. Such invariants allow a recognition system to cope with both changes in viewpoint and illumination. Section 3 demonstrates their usefulness for the recognition of outdoor advertising panels taken from different viewing angles and under different weather conditions. Moreover, physically different panels representing the same pattern were included.

Apart from assessing the discriminant power of complete bases of these moment invariants, the classification performance of subsets has been tested. It turned out that high recognition rates can already be obtained by using only half of the basis set. Also, the classification results obtained with these new invariants were compared to the classification performances obtained by Van Gool *et al.* [1] and Reiss [2].

2. GEOMETRIC/PHOTOMETRIC MOMENT INVARIANTS FOR COLOR IMAGES

2.1. GENERALIZED COLOR MOMENTS

A color pattern can mathematically be described as a vector-valued function I defined on a region Ω in the plane; i.e. $I : \Omega \subset I\!R^2 \longrightarrow I\!R^3 : (x,y) \longmapsto I(x,y)$ where x and y stand for the row and column coordinates of an image point and $I(x,y) = (\, i_R(x,y)\,,\, i_G(x,y)\,,\, i_B(x,y)\,)$ is the vector containing the RGB-values of the image point (x,y). We define the *generalized color moments* M_{pq}^{abc} by

$$M_{pq}^{abc} = \iint_{\Omega} x^p y^q \; [i_R(x,y)]^a \; [i_G(x,y)]^b \; [i_B(x,y)]^c \; dx dy \ .$$

M_{pq}^{abc} is said to be a generalized color moment of *order* $p+q$ and *degree* $a+b+c$. Observe that generalized color moments M_{pq}^{000} of degree 0 in fact are the (p,q)-shape moments of the image region Ω. Furthermore, the generalized color moments of degree 1, viz. M_{pq}^{100}, M_{pq}^{010}, M_{pq}^{001}, are just the (p,q)-intensity moments of respectively the R-, G- and B-color band. On the other hand, the generalized color moments M_{00}^{abc} of order 0 actually are the non-central (a,b,c)-moments of the (multivariate) color distribution of the RGB-values of the pattern. Hence, these color moments generalize shape moments of planar shapes, intensity moments of greylevel images, and non-central moments of the color distribution in the image. A large number of generalized color moments can be generated with only small values for the order and the degree. In this paper, only generalized color moments up to the first order and the second degree are considered. In the sequel they will be called "moments" for short.

2.2. GEOMETRIC AND PHOTOMETRIC TRANSFORMATIONS

The geometric deformations considered are *affine transformations*:

$$\begin{pmatrix} x' \\ y' \end{pmatrix} = \begin{pmatrix} a_{11} & a_{12} \\ a_{21} & a_{22} \end{pmatrix} \begin{pmatrix} x \\ y \end{pmatrix} + \begin{pmatrix} b_1 \\ b_2 \end{pmatrix} \qquad (1)$$

with $|A| = a_{11}a_{22} - a_{12}a_{21} \neq 0$. This implies that the camera is assumed to be relatively far from the object. This assumption together with the fact that the object is planar can greatly simplify the analysis of the photometric changes. Typically, light sources are far from the objects as well. The geometry of light reflection is the same for all points in that case, i.e. they share the same angles of light incidence and camera viewing direction. Also for the more sophisticated models of diffuse reflection the change in camera or light position will in that case result in an overall scaling of intensity [14]. Furthermore, an offset allows to better model the combined effect of diffuse and specular reflection [15] and has been found to give better performance [2]. Thus the photometric changes to be considered comprise *scaling combined with an offset* for each color band:

$$i'_K(x,y) = s_K\, i_K(x,y) + u_K \qquad \text{with } K \in \{\, R, G, B \,\}.$$

and where $0 \neq s_K, u_K \in I\!R$. The combined effect of the affine and photometric transformations of the moments M_{pq}^{abc} is given by

$$\left(M_{pq}^{abc} \right)' = \iint_\Omega \left[a_{11}x + a_{12}y + b_1 \right]^p \left[a_{21}x + a_{22}y + b_2 \right]^q \left[s_R\, i_R(x,y) + u_R \right]^a \\ \left[s_G\, i_G(x,y) + u_G \right]^b \left[s_B\, i_B(x,y) + u_B \right]^c \text{abs}\left(|A| \right) dx dy$$

which, after expansion, yields a linear combination of moments of order $\leq p+q$ and degree $\leq a+b+c$.

Observe that the actions of the photometric and affine changes on the moments come out to commute. Hence, one might first normalize against one type of transformation and then against the other. Alternatively, one may normalize against one and switch to the use of invariants for the other. To some extent, this latter strategy typically is what has happened in the literature. The photometric offset can e.g. be eliminated through the use of intensity minus average intensity and the photometric scale parameter can be eliminated by normalizing the resulting intensity's variance [2]. After these normalizations one then has to deal with affine deformations exclusively. However, the normalization steps are rather expensive computationally, since they require a pixel-wise modification. So, there is a lot freedom in choosing the point of transition from normalization to invariance, but it is not clear what is computationally the optimal choice. In this paper, only a normalization against photometric offset is performed. The reason being that it is low complexity operation which reduces the photometric transformation to only scaling and yields invariants with a high degree of symmetry in the order and the degree of the moments involved. As these invariants have the 0th order 1st degree moments M_{00}^{100}, M_{00}^{010}, M_{00}^{001} in their denominators, this normalization cannot be performed by subtracting the average intensity from the intensity values in each color band, because this would make these moments zero. Therefore, we take the absolute value of the intensities obtained after subtraction of the average intensity in each color band. In this way, normalization against photometric offset is reached while keeping the 0th order 1st degree moments M_{00}^{100}, M_{00}^{010}, M_{00}^{001} positive.

2.3. CLASSIFICATION OF THE GEOMETRIC/PHOTOMETRIC COLOR INVARIANTS

In order to calculate the combined geometric/photometric color invariants, the effects of the affine and photometric changes on the images is to be determined first. As already mentioned before, only moments up to the first order and the second degree are considered, and the photometric changes only involve intensity scaling of the different color bands. Hence, the resulting invariants are functions of the color moments M_{00}^{abc}, M_{10}^{abc} and M_{01}^{abc} with $(a,b,c) \in \{\, (0,0,0), (1,0,0), (0,1,0), (0,0,1), (2,0,0), (0,2,0), (0,0,2), (1,1,0), (1,0,1), (0,1,1) \,\}$. Under affine image transformations and intensity scaling, these moments transform as

$$\begin{pmatrix} \left(M_{10}^{abc}\right)' \\ \left(M_{01}^{abc}\right)' \\ \left(M_{00}^{abc}\right)' \end{pmatrix} = s_R^a\, s_G^b\, s_B^c\, |A| \begin{pmatrix} a_{11} & a_{12} & b_1 \\ a_{21} & a_{22} & b_2 \\ 0 & 0 & 1 \end{pmatrix} \begin{pmatrix} M_{10}^{abc} \\ M_{01}^{abc} \\ M_{00}^{abc} \end{pmatrix} \qquad \text{for all } a, b, c.$$

As can be seen from the way they transform, the 0th-order moments M_{00}^{abc} can be considered in isolation; and a similar remark holds for the different color bands and for pairs of color bands. Moreover, different powers of the intensity of a single color band can also be taken in isolation. Hence, the invariants can be classified according to 3 degrees of freedom: the order, the degree and the color bands of the moments involved. In order to allow maximal flexibility for the user in the choice of the color bands but also to ensure the highest possible robustness of the invariants in the classification, we have used the following 2 criteria to construct a basis for the moment invariants: (1) Include as much as possible invariants involving fewer color bands; and (2) include as much as possible low-order invariants. This results in the following classification.

1-BAND INVARIANTS

All geometric/photometric invariants involving generalized color moments up to the first order and the second degree in only 1 color band are functions of the following 2 basis invariants:

0th order, 2nd degree:

$$B_{02} = \frac{M_{00}^{2} M_{00}^{0}}{(M_{00}^{1})^2} \,,$$

1st order, 2nd degree:

$$B_{12} = \frac{M_{10}^{1} M_{01}^{2} M_{00}^{0} + M_{10}^{2} M_{01}^{0} M_{00}^{1} + M_{10}^{0} M_{01}^{1} M_{00}^{2} - M_{10}^{0} M_{01}^{2} M_{00}^{1} - M_{10}^{1} M_{01}^{0} M_{00}^{2} - M_{10}^{2} M_{01}^{1} M_{00}^{0}}{M_{00}^{2} M_{00}^{1} M_{00}^{0}} \,,$$

where M_{pq}^{i} stands for either M_{pq}^{i00}, M_{pq}^{0i0} or M_{pq}^{00i}.

2-BAND INVARIANTS

All geometric/photometric invariants involving generalized color moments up to the first order and the second degree in 2 of the 3 color bands are functions of the following 10 basis invariants:

0th order, 2nd degree:

$$B_{02}^{1} \;,\; B_{02}^{2} \;, \text{ and } C_{02} = \frac{M_{00}^{11} M_{00}^{00}}{M_{00}^{10} M_{00}^{01}} \;;$$

1st order, 1st degree:

$$C_{11} = \frac{M_{10}^{10} M_{01}^{01} M_{00}^{00} + M_{10}^{01} M_{01}^{00} M_{00}^{10} + M_{10}^{00} M_{01}^{10} M_{00}^{01} - M_{10}^{00} M_{01}^{01} M_{00}^{10} - M_{10}^{10} M_{01}^{00} M_{00}^{01} - M_{10}^{01} M_{01}^{10} M_{00}^{00}}{M_{00}^{10} M_{00}^{01} M_{00}^{00}}$$

1st order, 2nd degree:

$$B_{12}^{1} \;,\; B_{12}^{2} \;,$$

$$C_{12}^{1} = \frac{M_{10}^{10} M_{01}^{11} M_{00}^{00} + M_{10}^{11} M_{01}^{00} M_{00}^{10} + M_{10}^{00} M_{01}^{10} M_{00}^{11} - M_{10}^{00} M_{01}^{11} M_{00}^{10} - M_{10}^{10} M_{01}^{00} M_{00}^{11} - M_{10}^{11} M_{01}^{10} M_{00}^{00}}{M_{00}^{11} M_{00}^{10} M_{00}^{00}} \,,$$

$$C_{12}^{2} = \frac{M_{10}^{01} M_{01}^{11} M_{00}^{00} + M_{10}^{11} M_{01}^{00} M_{00}^{01} + M_{10}^{00} M_{01}^{01} M_{00}^{11} - M_{10}^{00} M_{01}^{11} M_{00}^{01} - M_{10}^{01} M_{01}^{00} M_{00}^{11} - M_{10}^{11} M_{01}^{01} M_{00}^{00}}{M_{00}^{11} M_{00}^{01} M_{00}^{00}} \,,$$

$$C_{12}^{3} = \frac{M_{10}^{10} M_{01}^{02} M_{00}^{00} + M_{10}^{02} M_{01}^{00} M_{00}^{10} + M_{10}^{00} M_{01}^{10} M_{00}^{02} - M_{10}^{00} M_{01}^{02} M_{00}^{10} - M_{10}^{10} M_{01}^{00} M_{00}^{02} - M_{10}^{02} M_{01}^{10} M_{00}^{00}}{M_{00}^{10} M_{00}^{02} M_{00}^{00}} \,,$$

$$C_{12}^{4} = \frac{M_{10}^{20} M_{01}^{01} M_{00}^{00} + M_{10}^{01} M_{01}^{00} M_{00}^{20} + M_{10}^{00} M_{01}^{20} M_{00}^{01} - M_{10}^{00} M_{01}^{01} M_{00}^{20} - M_{10}^{20} M_{01}^{00} M_{00}^{01} - M_{10}^{01} M_{01}^{20} M_{00}^{00}}{M_{00}^{20} M_{00}^{01} M_{00}^{00}} \,,$$

where B_{pq}^{i} stands for the 1-band invariant B_{pq} defined above but evaluated in the ith (of the 2) color band(s), and where M_{pq}^{ij} stands for either M_{pq}^{ij0}, M_{pq}^{i0j} or M_{pq}^{0ij}, depending on which of the 2 color bands are used.

drink *moulin* *castle1* *mosaic1* *mosaic3* *wheels* *tree*

Figure 1: Examples of images used for discriminant power assessment.

3-BAND INVARIANTS

All geometric/photometric invariants involving generalized color moments up to the first order and the second degree of all 3 color bands are functions of the following 21 basis invariants:

0th order, 2nd degree: B_{02}^{R} , B_{02}^{G} , B_{02}^{B} , C_{02}^{RG} , C_{02}^{RB} , C_{02}^{GB} ;

1st order, 1st degree: C_{11}^{RG} , C_{11}^{RB} , C_{11}^{GB} ;

1st order, 2nd degree: B_{12}^{R} , B_{12}^{G} , B_{12}^{B} , $C_{12}^{1(RG)}$, $C_{12}^{1(RB)}$, $C_{12}^{1(GB)}$,
$C_{12}^{2(RG)}$, $C_{12}^{2(RB)}$, $C_{12}^{2(GB)}$, $C_{12}^{3(RG)}$, $C_{12}^{3(GB)}$, $C_{12}^{4(RB)}$;

where B_{ij}^{K} and C_{pq}^{KL} are the 2-band invariants defined above, but applied to the color bands K and L. As a consequence, it immediately follows that *every invariant involving all 3 color bands can always be written as a function of invariants which involve only 2 of the 3 bands.*

The above classifications are obtained by the techniques explained in [16]. A more detailed discussion and derivation of these results is given in [17].

3. ASSESSMENT OF CLASSIFICATION PERFORMANCE OF THE INVARIANTS

The usefulness of these new invariants for viewpoint and illumination independent recognition of planar color patterns has been tested in a number of experiments on data set of real images. These tests involve both synthetic transformations of real images as well as real changes in viewpoint and illumination conditions. Due to the large number of invariants, the evaluation of the invariants behavior is performed by a statistical analysis of a recognition system built on invariant feature vectors consisting of different numbers and types of invariants. As our image data set is medium size, the classification performance of the system is estimated by means of a jackknifing procedure [18].

3.1. DISCRIMINANT POWER UNDER IDEAL MODEL CONDITIONS

A first test aimed at assessing the discriminant power of the new invariants under ideal model conditions. To this end, parameterized geometric and intensity transformations were applied to a set of 15 real color images, some of which are shown in Figure 1. The images were selected on the basis of their color characteristics in order to evaluate the influence of these characteristics on the invariants behavior. In particular, there are patterns with predominance

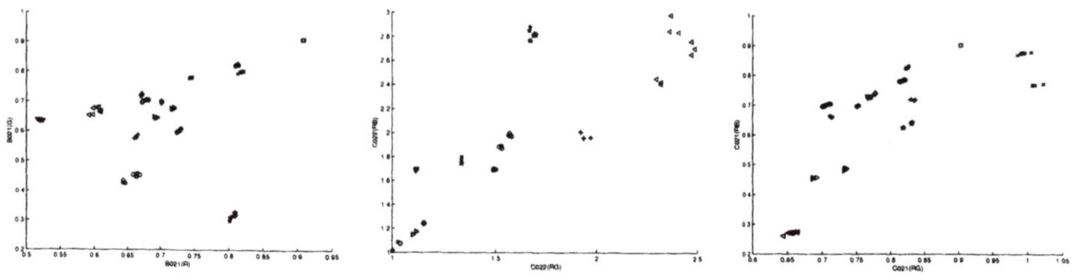

Figure 2: Examples of the clusters formed by different pairs of invariants for the synthetic image transforms.

of a certain color band (e.g. red in *moulin* and *wheels*), with high intensities but different spatial distribution in all 3 bands (e.g. *drink* and *tree*), with highly correlated intensities among the bands (e.g. *castle1*), and similar, fine grained patterns (e.g. *mosaic1* and *mosaic3*). The geometric transformations applied to the images are combinations of (independent) scalings in the x- and y-direction ranging from 0.7 to 1 with 0.1 step size, skewing in the x-direction (i.e. $x' = x + s\,y$) ranging from 0 to 0.3 with 0.1 step size, and rotations ranging from 0° to 45° with 15° intervals. The photometric transformations of the images comprise scalings of the intensity values ranging from 0.65 to 1 with 0.05 step size and offsets ranging from 0 to 30 with 5 unit intervals, both applied independently on each of the color bands.

The 1-band invariants were computed for each band of the transformed images separately and the 2-bands invariants were computed on all 3 combinations of the bands (RG, RB, GB). The average classification performance obtained by a single invariant is between 85.2% and 92% correct assignments. Two invariants suffice for 100% classification performance, but not all couples of invariants yield total discrimination between the patterns. For example, the combinations (B_{02}^{K}, B_{02}^{L}) and $(C_{02}^{KL}, C_{02}^{MN})$ yield clear clusters for many of the patterns, as can be seen in Figure 2. Observe that both B_{02} and C_{02} are 0th order 2nd degree invariants. In particular, they discriminate the patterns on the basis of their color content alone. It should be emphasized, however, that their discriminant power significantly decreases with higher correlation between two of the bands. Therefore, it is advisable to combine invariants from different types.

3.2. Experiments with real changes in viewpoint and illumination

3.2.1. Classification performance of the new invariants

To test the discriminant power of the new invariants under real conditions, color images of different outdoors advertising panels were taken from various viewpoints at different times of the day and under different weather conditions. Physically different panels representing the same pattern were included as well. Figure 3 shows some examples of those images. The panels themselves were manually cut out from the images; and 11 classes of patterns were used for the test, each containing 10 or more images.

When using all the invariants, each class is uniquely recognized by the system. However, since only 11 classes are available, statistically significant conclusions can only be drawn for feature vectors composed of 5 invariants at most. The left side table in table1 shows the classification rates for each of the 11 classes and the mean performance for certain feature

Figure 3: Examples of images in the data set with advertising panels.

vectors mentioned in this paragraph. The performance is expressed in recognition percentages (rounded values). First, feature vectors formed by only one invariant (namely B_{02}, B_{12}, C_{02}, C_{11}, C^i_{12} and

$$\tilde{C}_{02} = \frac{B^1_{02} B^2_{02}}{(C_{02})^2} = \frac{M^{20}_{00} M^{02}_{00}}{\left(M^{11}_{00}\right)^2} ,$$

which is included due to its simple, symmetrical form, respectively) but applied to each combination of the color bands are considered. This allow observing the performance of individual types of invariants and the performance improvement brought by increasing the order and the degree of the moments. The classification performance w.r.t. the individual classes is similar for all of the triplets of first order moment invariants, and their average performance over all classes ranges from 63% to 69% correct matches. On the other hand, an average classification performance of 73.4% is obtained when applying the feature vector $(C^1_{12}, C^2_{12}, C^3_{12})$ to 1 pair of color bands only (see Table1 vector 1). A significant improvement is observed when the feature vector is composed of 3 different invariants, applied to different combinations of 2 of the 3 bands. The average classification range in this case is $78.4\% - 89.1\%$. 2 examples are presented in table1 as vector 2 ($\{\tilde{C}^{(RB)}_{02}, C^{3(RG)}_{12}, C^{4(GB)}_{12}\}$) and vector 3 ($\{\tilde{C}^{(GB)}_{02}, \tilde{C}^{(RG)}_{02}, C^{3(GB)}_{11},\}$). This proves again that the use of color bands is a very important clue in pattern recognition. Vector 4 is obtained by adding a fourth invariant ($C^{4(GB)}_{12}$) to the feature vector 3 and this increases the performance rate by another 4.5%. However, the best classification performance for the given data set with a feature vector of length less than 6, is 96.3% and it is obtained by the invariants in feature vector 5 $\{C^{(RB)}_{02}, \tilde{C}^{(RG)}_{02}, \tilde{C}^{(GB)}_{02}, C^{3(GB)}_{12}, C^{4(RB)}_{12}\}$. Figure 4 shows the clusters obtained by first 2 (left) and the first 3 (right) Fisher's linear discriminant functions [18] for these invariants on the given data set. Fisher's linear discriminant method is applied here for graphical display purposes only.

3.2.2. Conclusions about the new color invariants

Some general observations arise from the classification behavior in the synthetic and real case. Strongly related to the intensity content, all the invariants perform better on patterns with higher intensities. Dark patterns or patterns with bands mainly containing low intensity values tend to be misclassified, especially by the C_{11} invariant, which uses only first degree moments. The second degree moment invariants cope better with low intensity content. Patterns with highly correlated color bands may cause misclassification when using 2 invariants of the same type

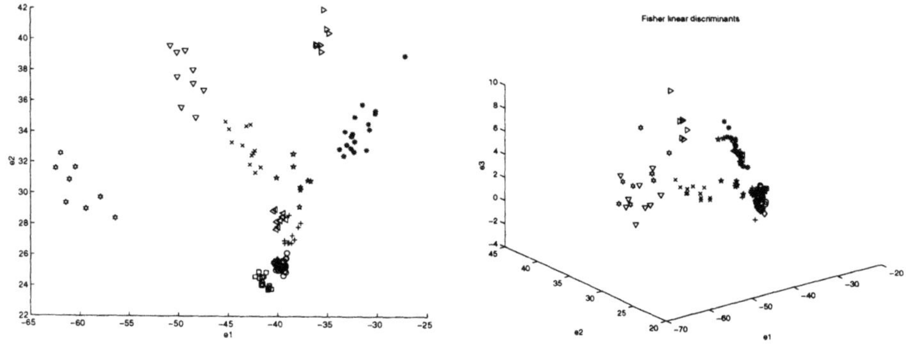

Figure 4: The first 2, respectively 3, Fisher's linear discriminant functions for the invariants $C_{12}^{3(GB)}, C_{12}^{4(RB)}, \tilde{C}_{02}^{(GB)}, \tilde{C}_{02}^{(RG)}, C_{02}^{(RB)}$ on the data set of advertising panels.

applied on different couples of bands. The best way of capturing the information contained in the 3 bands in an uniform manner is to use "symmetric" groups of invariants, which are evaluated on the 3 bands without previous information about their intensity content. Finally, it turns out that the new invariants seem to have enough stability and discriminant power for a reliable use on real data even with an amount of geometrical and/or illuminance distortions not covered by the theoretical model (e.g. perspective deformations, partial shadows, strong light, blurred image), if not too high.

3.2.3. The effect of partial occlusions

It is well known that intensity moments are quite sensitive to partial occlusions of the pattern. Color histograms, on the other hand, are rather robust for partial occlusion, at least if the occlusion is not too severe. Since the new moment invariants derived above combine both approaches, it is natural to investigate how they are affected by partial occlusions. Our data set also contains images in which some of the advertising panels are partially occluded by passing vehicles (see e.g. the lower left image in Figure 3). The occlusions differ by area, intensity and position in the image. Table 1, the righthand side, shows the labels of the 5 best matches that were found for the partially occluded patterns by Fisher's (first) linear discriminant function for the invariants $\{C_{02}^{(RB)}, \tilde{C}_{02}^{(RG)}, \tilde{C}_{02}^{(GB)}, C_{12}^{3(GB)}, C_{12}^{4(RB)}\}$ which have the best average classification performance for the non occluded patterns (cf. section 3.2.1). Depending on the amount of occlusion, the occluded panel is correctly classified or the correct class is found among the two best matches. Hence, as was to be expected, the new color moment invariants are not insensitive to occlusions, but they seem to perform better than their greylevel counterparts. Moreover, the classification result depends on the amount of occlusion and the difference in color of the occluding object.

3.2.4. Comparison to the literature

The classification performances of feature vectors involving the new color invariants defined above were also compared to the classification results obtained on the same data set of real outdoors advertising panels by the geometric/photometric invariants for greylevel images

	1	2	3	4	5	6	7	8	9	10	11	mean
1	46	42	60	83	53	93	89	78	75	100	87	73
2	80	67	80	94	100	78	78	78	62	100	87	82
3	93	100	80	78	100	100	78	89	100	100	62	89
4	93	100	90	83	87	100	89	100	100	100	87	93
5	93	100	100	100	100	93	100	89	87	100	100	96

	5 best matches
5	6, 5, 3, 4, 2
5	5, 3, 4, 2, 6
8	3. 8, 4, 1, 9
8	8, 3, 9, 4, 1
8	3, 8, 9, 4, 1
1	1, 2, 9, 3, 4
1	1, 2, 3, 9, 4
11	4, 11, 9, 2, 8

Table 1: left side: classification performance (in %) for different feature vectors; right side: The 5 best matches found for occluded panels

presented by Van Gool *et al.* in [1] and the geometric invariants of normalized greylevel images as presented by Reiss in [2] for using similar moments computation.

The invariants presented by Reiss are functions of the central intensity moments up to the 4th order, which are invariant under affine transformations of the images. Photometric changes are dealt with by normalization against both intensity scaling and offset. Among the 10 invariants used in [2], J_1, Ψ_5 and Ψ_6 are reported to provide the best performance (see [2] for the notations). When applied to the images in our data set, the feature vector formed by these invariants has an average classification performance of 23.4% correct matches. Extending the feature vector with the 4th and the 5th best invariants, viz. Ψ_1 and Ψ_2, the average performance rate increases to 34.2%. These low recognition rates most probably are caused by the noise in the images and the high order of the moments involved. The overall performance shows to be significantly less than that obtained by the new invariants defined above.

The invariants presented in Van Gool *et al.* can be divided into two classes: Invariants involving both shape and intensity moments up to the 1st order of 2 different parts of the image; and, invariants involving shape and intensity moments up to the 2nd order of the entire image. The first class comprises invariants with a complexity comparable to the color invariants defined above, but the construction of an affine invariant subdivision of the pattern (as put forward in [1]) depends on the shape of the pattern's outline and the intensity content within each part. An alternative is to make a pixel wise division of the pattern by taking one part to consist of all pixels with an intensity value that is lower (resp. higher) than the average intensity. This construction is applied in the tests reported here. The classification rates obtained by an invariant of this class and evaluated in each of the individual color bands are comparable to those obtained by a feature vector consisting of one new invariant and also evaluated at all combinations of the color bands. However, the invariant subdivision needed for this class of invariants in [1] makes it computationally more demanding. The second type of invariants in [1], on the other hand, are much more complex than the new color invariants defined above. Evaluating such an invariant on each color band yields feature vectors whose classification performance ranges from 84.3% to 89.3%. This is clearly better than what is obtained by 1 new invariant applied to all combinations of the color bands. However, combining 3 to 5 of these 2nd order invariants from [1] does not significantly improve the classification performance. When compared to the average of 96.3% correct classifications obtained with the best (new) feature vector of section 3.2.1, the new color invariants perform better both w.r.t. classification results as in view of the complexity of the invariants involved.

References

[1] Van Gool L, Moons T, and Ungureanu D. Geometric/photometric invariants for planar intensity patterns, In Proceedings European Conference on Computer Vision. Springer, 1996, pp. 642 – 651.

[2] Reiss T, Recognizing planar objects using invariant image features. Lecture Notes in Computer Science 676, Springer, 1993.

[3] Mundy JL, and Zisserman A (eds.), Geometric invariance in computer vision, MIT Press, 1992.

[4] Mundy JL, Zisserman A, and Forsyth D (eds.). Applications of invariance in computer vision. Lecture Notes in Computer Science 825, pp. 89 – 106, Springer, 1994.

[5] Gevers T, and Smeulders AWM. A comparative study of several color models for color image invariant retreival. In Proceedings of the First International Workshop on Image Database and Multimedia Search, 1996, pp. 17 – 23.

[6] Healey G, and Slater D. Using illumination invariant color histogram descriptors for recognition. In Proceedings of the IEEE Conference on Computer Vision and Pattern Recognition, IEEE Press, 1994, pp. 355 – 360.

[7] Wang L, Healey G. Using Zernike Moments for the Illumination and Geometry Invariant Classification of Multispectral Texture, In IEEE Transactions on Image Processing, vol.7 , no. 2, 1998, pp. 196 – 203.

[8] Swain M, Ballard D. Color indexing. International Journal of Computer Vision, 1991; 7(1):11–32.

[9] Abo-Zaid A, Hinton O, and Horne E. About moment normalization and complex moment descriptors. In Proceedings of 4th International Conference on Pattern Recognition, 1988, pp. 399 – 407.

[10] Flusser J, and Suk T. Pattern recognition by affine moment invariants. Pattern Recognition, 1993; 26(1):167–174.

[11] Maitra S. Moment invariants, Proceedings of the IEEE conference on Computer Vision and Pattern Recognition, IEEE Press, 1979, pp. 697 – 699.

[12] R. Prokop and A. Reeves, A survey of moment-based techniques for unoccluded object representation and recognition, Computer Vision Graphics and Image Processing: Models and Image Processing, 1992; 54(5):438–460.

[13] H. Schulz-Mirbach, Anwendung von Invarianzprinzipien zur Merkmalgewinnung in der Mustererkennung. VDI Verlag, 1995.

[14] Oren M, and Nayar S. Seeing beyond Lambert's law, In Proceedinge of the European Conference on Computer Vision. Springer, 1994, pp. 269 – 280.

[15] Wolff L. On the relative brightness of specular and diffuse reflection, In Proceedings of the IEEE conference on Computer Vision and Pattern Recognition, IEEE Press, 1994, pp.369 – 376.

[16] Moons T, Pauwels E, Van Gool L, and Oosterlinck A. Foundations of semi-differential invariants, International Journal of Computer Vision, 1995; 14(1):25–47.

[17] Mindru F, Moons T, and Van Gool L. Moment invariants for viewpoint and illumination independent recognition of planar color patterns. Technical Report KUL/ESAT/PSI/9804, Leuven, 1998.

[18] Johnson RA, and Wichern DW, Applied multivariate statistical snalysis. Prentice-Hall, 1992.

MEDICAL ANALYSIS

ERROR AND SHAPE MEASUREMENT TOOLS FOR CARDIAC PROJECTION IMAGES: A CLOSER LOOK

Jasjit S. Suri, Department of Medical Physics, School of Medicine, Health Science Center, University of Wisconsin-Madison, Wisconsin, And Gammex Inc., Middleton, Wisconsin, WI 535652

ABSTRACT

Large number of techniques have emerged as measurement tools for left ventricle analysis in cardiac imaging. Due to the large variabilities in the cardiac data sets, it is not clear which technique is most clinically useful and stable to operate. This paper takes a closer look at existing tools and compares them. Finally the paper presents a general purpose three stage measurement system which incorporates features based on a combination of shape, fitting, and polyline methods.

Key Words: Shape measurements, quantitative tools.

INTRODUCTION

Bookstein [1] defined a shape as the property that is not changed by translation, rotation, and rescaling. These properties including figural shape, inter-figural shape and boundary shape that are very useful for object classification. The measurement of these properties (so called attributes of object) becomes very difficult when the data set has large variability and changes in shape, size, position, and orientation. This is what happens during the left ventricle (LV) motion of the heart in cardiac projection images. Quantification of LV wall motion has been of particular interest to researchers because it relates directly to cardiac disorders [2], [3]. A typical shape of the LV is shown in fig. 1 (extreme right) where the thick contour is hand-drawn by the cardiologist, while the thin contour is estimated by the computer [4]-[6]. Due to large number of quantitative tools, it has become necessary to look at the factors which affect these them. Why is one particular technique good ? What are the drawbacks of a particular technique ? Interestingly, the issue is that one particular quantitative measurement technique may be very good for a particular cardiac data set but may not be good for the other. For this reason, several researchers have explored their techniques (see Suri et al. [4]-[6], Lee [7], Setaredhan et al. [8], Chalana et al. [9], Grattoni et al. [10],[11], Gibson [12], Mancini et al. [13], Staib et al. [14], Bolson et al. [15]). We are interested to find out which technique is most stable, reliable, accurate, robust, noise insensitive, shape free, curvature free, clinically relevant and finally most acceptable. This paper summaries the different quantitative tools And also takes a closer look at the quantitative tools and highlights the necessary factors which a quantitative tool must have to meet the needs of a cardiologist.

CLASSIFICATION OF TOOLS

The earlier techniques has been classified as under: (1) Line-based: Polyline-based (2) Curvature-based: (a) Radical based (b) Centerline-based (c) Circle Fitting (3) Shaped-based: (a) Bending-energy (or Feature based) (b) Active or Deformable Shape Loci Model-based (c) Principal Component Analysis (PCA) (4) Distance-based: (a) Mahanabolis distance method (b) Hamming distance method (c) Hausdorf distance method (d) Bhattacharya distance method (5) Marker-based (6) Intrusion-Protrusion Based (7) Signature-based

LINE OR POINT BASED

Suri et al. [5] developed the *polyline distance* metric that is based on the ratio of the average area between two polygons *to* the average perimeter of the two polygons. Our assumption prior to the *polyline distance* error computation is that the polygons have equal perimeters and the vertices are equal spaced along the perimeter; i.e., the two arc intervals on the two contours is same. Using this assumption, we mathematically show that the ratio of average area between polygons to their perimeters actually is the average *polyline distance* error between the two polygons.

Let the two polygons be B_1 and B_2 consisting of total points P_1 and P_2 having interval lengths of l_1 and l_2 respectively. This is shown in fig. 1. Let the perpendicular distances from each of the vertices (of polygon B_1) to the opposite interval sides of the polygon B_2 be d_n, where, $1 \leq n \leq P_1$. Similarly, let d'_m be the perpendicular distances from each of the vertices (of polygon B_2) to the opposite interval sides of the polygon B_1, where, $1 \leq m \leq P_2$. Thus the areas of the triangle with height d_n and base l_2 is $\frac{1}{2}l_2 d_n$. Similarly the area of the triangle with height d'_m and base l_1 is $\frac{1}{2}l_1 d'_m$. The total area $\bar{A}$ between two polygons is computed by computing the sum of the area of all the triangles whose base lies on the polygon B_1 and the sum of the area of all the triangles whose bases lies on the polygon B_2 and is given as: $\bar{A} = \sum_{n=1}^{P_1} \frac{1}{2}\, l_2\, d_n + \sum_{m=1}^{P_2} \frac{1}{2}\, l_1\, d'_m$ Similarly, we can compute the average perimeter of the two polygons as: $\bar{P} = \frac{l_2 P_1 + l_1 P_2}{2}$ Taking the ratio of $\bar{A}$ and $\bar{P}$,we get:

$$\frac{\bar{A}}{\bar{P}} = \frac{\sum_{n=1}^{P_1} \frac{1}{2}\, l_2\, d_n + \sum_{m=1}^{P_2} \frac{1}{2}\, l_1\, d'_m}{\frac{l_2 P_1 + l_1 P_2}{2}} \tag{1}$$

Using the above assumption, $l_1 \approx .l_2$, Eq. 1 reduces to:

$$\frac{\bar{A}}{\bar{P}} = \frac{\sum_{n=1}^{P_1} d_n + \sum_{m=1}^{P_2} d'_m}{P_1 + P_2} \tag{2}$$

MATHEMATICAL DERIVATION OF POLYLINE DISTANCE ERROR

We show that the *polyline distance* method computes the same measure as derived in Eq. 2 and will be denoted by $D_s(B_1.B_2)$. The *polyline distance* $D_s(B_1 : B_2)$ between two polygons representing boundary B_1 and B_2 is symmetrically defined as the average distance between a vertex of one polygon and the boundary of the other polygon. To define this measure precisely, we first need to define a distance $d(v, s)$ between a point v and a line segment s. The distance $d(v, s)$ between a point v having coordinates (x_o, y_o), and a line segment having end points (x_1, y_1) and (x_2, y_2) is:

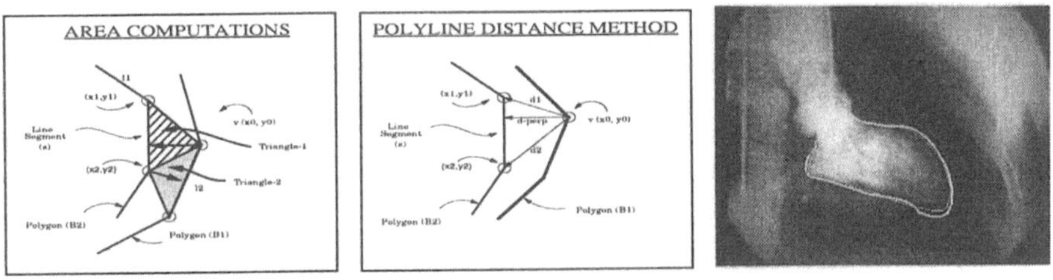

Figure 1: Left: Area of triangles between the two polygons; Middle: Polyline distance computation; Right: Left ventriculogram showing the thick boundary traced by the cardiologist. Thin boundary estimated by computer technique.

$$d(v,s) \quad = \quad \begin{cases} \min\{d_1, d_2\}; & if \;\; \lambda < 0, \lambda > 1 \\ |d^{\perp}|; & if \;\; 0 \leq \lambda \leq 1, \end{cases} \tag{3}$$

where,

$$\begin{aligned} d_1 &= \sqrt{(x_0 - x_1)^2 + (y_0 - y_1)^2} \\ d_2 &= \sqrt{(x_0 - x_2)^2 + (y_0 - y_2)^2} \\ \lambda &= \tfrac{(y_2 - y_1)(y_0 - y_1) + (x_2 - x_1)(x_0 - x_1)}{(x_2 - x_1)^2 + (y_2 - y_1)^2} \\ d^{\perp} &= \tfrac{(y_2 - y_1)(x_1 - x_0) + (x_2 - x_1)(y_0 - y_1)}{\sqrt{(x_2 - x_1)^2 + (y_2 - y_1)^2}} \end{aligned} \tag{4}$$

Note, d_1 and d_2 are the distances from the vertex v to the end points of the segment s. λ is the distance along the vector of the segment s, while $d^{\perp}$ is the perpendicular distance along the vector orthogonal to the segment s. The *polyline distance* $d_b(v, B_2)$ from vertex v to the boundary B_2 is defined by:

$$d_b(v, B_2) \quad = \quad \min_{s \in \, sides \, B_2} \quad d(v, s) \tag{5}$$

This step is a confirmation that we are choosing the closest segment on B_2 from the vertex v. The distance $d_{vb}(B_1, B_2)$ between the vertices of polygon B_1 and the sides of polygon B_2 is defined as the sum of the distances from the vertices of the polygon B_1 to the closest side of B_2.

$$d_{vb}(B_1, B_2) \quad = \quad \sum_{v \in \, vertices \, B_1} \quad d(v, B_2) \tag{6}$$

Reversing the computation from B_2 to B_1, we can similarly compute $d_{vb}(B_2, B_1)$. Using Eq. 6, the *polyline distance* between polygons, $D_s(B_1 : B_2)$ is defined by:

$$D_s(B_1 : B_2) \quad = \quad \frac{d_{vb}(B_1, B_2) + d_{vb}(B_2, B_1)}{(\#vertices \in B_1 + \#vertices \in B_2)} \tag{7}$$

This equation is basically same as Eq. 2 where the numerator is the sum of all the perpendicular distances for both the polygons while the denominator is the sum of total number of vertices on the two polygons. Using the *polyline distance* formulae's, we can compute the error per vertex from one polygon to another polygon. This is defined as the mean error for a vertex v over all the patients and all the frames. The *error per vertex* for a fixed vertex v when computed from B_1 to B_2 and defined as: $e_v^{GC} = \frac{\sum_{t=1}^{F}\sum_{n=1}^{N} d_b(v,G_{nt})}{FN}$ Similarly we can compute the *error per vertex* from B_2 to B_1 using Eq. 5. *Error per arc length* is computed in the following way: For the values e_v^{GC} where v=$1,2,3,\ldots P_1$, we construct a curve f^{GC} defined on the interval [0,1] which takes the value e_v^{GC} at point x which is the *normalized arc length* to vertex v and whose in between values are defined by linear interpolation. We compute the curve f^{CG}, between calibrated boundary and ground truth boundary in a similar way. We then add algebraically these two curves to yield the final *error per arc length*, given as: $f = \frac{f^{GC}+f^{CG}}{2}$.

CURVATURE BASED

Curvature of the LV walls and apex cup is needed due to the inherent nature of the LV contours. Researchers have used curvature measurement for wall motion quantification and bendness measure.

(A) *Curvature Estimation Methods*: There are many ways to compute the curvature of LV. Six ways as discussed by Williams et al. [16] are: (1) Let $u_i = \begin{pmatrix} x_i - x_{i-1} \\ y_i - y_{i-1} \end{pmatrix}$, $u_{i+1} = \begin{pmatrix} x_{i+1} - x_i \\ y_{i+1} - y_i \end{pmatrix}$, and let θ be the angle between the positive x-axis and the tangent vector to the curve. This was a coordinate independent measure whose value was obtained for $\delta\theta = cos^{-1}\left(\frac{\bar{u}_i.\bar{u}_{i+1}}{|u_i||u_{i+1}|}\right)$ when any line was substituted for the x-axis. This measure was invariant under rotation. The curvature was given as: $\kappa = \frac{\delta\theta}{\delta s}$. where, $\delta\theta = cos^{-1}\left(\frac{\bar{u}_i.\bar{u}_{i+1}}{|u_i||u_{i+1}|}\right)$ and δs was given as the central difference of the arc length given as: $\delta s = \frac{\delta s_{i+1}+\delta s_i}{2}$. (2) This definition of the curvature when the parameter was the function of arc lengths and was given as: $\kappa = \left(\frac{|x'y''-x''y'|}{((x')^2+(y')^2)^{3/2}}\right)$. (3)When the parameter is the arc length (s) and the vertices were unit intervals apart, the curvature was given by: $\kappa = |V_{ss}| = |\frac{d^2V_i}{ds^2}|$. (4) If the vertices were evenly spaced unit distances apart and the parameter was arc length (s) and if $u_i = \begin{pmatrix} x_i - x_{i-1} \\ y_i - y_{i-1} \end{pmatrix}$ and $u_{i+1} = \begin{pmatrix} x_{i+1} - x_i \\ y_{i+1} - y_i \end{pmatrix}$ were the vectors; then the curvature κ was given as: $\kappa = |\bar{u}_{i+1} - \bar{u}_i|$. The definition of κ reflected not only the difference between the directions of the two vectors, but also the difference in the lengths. (5) If the above vectors, $\bar{u}_i$ and $\bar{u}_{i+1}$ were normalized to $\frac{\bar{u}_i}{|\bar{u}_i|}$ and $\frac{\bar{u}_{i+1}}{|\bar{u}_{i+1}|}$ then κ was given as: $|\frac{\bar{u}_i}{|\bar{u}_i|} - \frac{\bar{u}_{i+1}}{|\bar{u}_{i+1}|}|$. This measure depended solely upon the direction. The curvature κ was bounded with values in the interval [0,2]. Williams et al. also suggested a method of finding the curvature by fitting a circle of known radius that passes through three points.

(B) *Circle Fitting for LV Curvature Estimation*: Consider a concentric hyperbola as: $Q(x,y) = 0$ and $Q(x,y) = c_i$. where i=1,2,... The rate of change of Q at a particular point "a" is given as the absolute of the gradient of Q at "a". The sum of square distance is given as: $\epsilon^2 = \sum_{n=1}^{n} [\frac{Q(x_i,y_i)}{\nabla Q(x_i,y_i)}]^2$ So, we weight the error Q by the inverse of the norm of its gradient. The above equation is not in a simple quadratic from and cannot be expressed by the solution in analytic form. We thus conclude from Haralick's article [19], page 603, that the error function is given by: $\epsilon^2(w) = \sum_{n=1}^{n} [\frac{f(x_i,y_i,w)}{\nabla Q(x_i,y_i)^2}]^2$. We fit a circle to the given polyline using the above minimization criteria. In the case of a circle, the parameter $w' = (a, b, R)$, where (a, b) is the center of a the circle and R is its radius. The circle is represented by $f(r, c, w)$=0 and is given as: $f(r, c, w) = f(r, c, a, b, R) = (r - a)^2 + (c - b)^2 - R^2$ and the partial differentiation of f with respect to r and c are: $\frac{\partial f}{\partial r} = 2(r - a)$ and $\frac{\partial f}{\partial c} = 2(c - a)$. Thus ϵ is:

$$\epsilon(a, b, R) = \sum_{n=1}^{N} \frac{[(\hat{r}_n - a)^2 + (\hat{c}_n - b)^2 - R^2]^2}{4[(\hat{r}_n - a)^2 + (\hat{c}_n - b)^2]} \tag{8}$$

The initial approximations for a, b and R can be obtained as: $a_0 = \bar{r} = \frac{1}{N}\sum_{n=1}^{N} \hat{r}_n$, $b_0 = \bar{c} = \frac{1}{N}\sum_{n=1}^{N} \hat{c}_n$ and $R_0 = \frac{1}{N}\sum_{n=1}^{N} \sqrt{(\hat{r}_n - a_0)^2 + (\hat{c}_n - b_0)^2}$. The squared distance between a point (r_0, c_0) and a circle centered at (a, b) with radius R is $\sqrt{(\hat{r}\_a_0)^2 + (\hat{c}_n - b_0)^2}$. The error to be minimized over N points is then:

$$\epsilon^2 = \sum_{n=1}^{N} \sqrt{(\hat{r}_n - a_0)^2 + (\hat{c}_n - b_0)^2 - R^2} \tag{9}$$

$$\Delta\epsilon = \begin{pmatrix} \frac{\partial \epsilon^2}{\partial a} \\ \frac{\partial \epsilon^2}{\partial b} \\ \frac{\partial \epsilon^2}{\partial R} \end{pmatrix} = \begin{pmatrix} -2\sum_{n=1}^{N}(1 - \frac{R}{\sqrt{(\hat{r}_n - a_0)^2 + (\hat{c}_n - b_0)^2 - R^2}})(\hat{r}_n - a)) \\ -2\sum_{n=1}^{N}(1 - \frac{R}{\sqrt{(\hat{r}_n - a_0)^2 + (\hat{c}_n - b_0)^2 - R^2}})(\hat{c}_n - b) \\ -2\sum_{n=1}^{N}(\sqrt{(\hat{r}_n - a_0)^2 + (\hat{c}_n - b_0)^2 - R^2}) \end{pmatrix} \tag{10}$$

The value of R can be analytically computed as:

$$\Delta\epsilon = \begin{pmatrix} \frac{\partial \epsilon^2}{\partial a} \\ \frac{\partial \epsilon^2}{\partial b} \end{pmatrix} = -2\sum_{n=1}^{N}(1 - \frac{R}{\sqrt{(\hat{r}_n - a_0)^2 + (\hat{c}_n - b_0)^2 - R^2}}) \begin{pmatrix} (\hat{r}_n - a)(\hat{r}_n - b) \end{pmatrix}$$
$$+[\sqrt{(\hat{r}_n - a_0)^2 + (\hat{c}_n - b_0)^2 - R^2}] \begin{pmatrix} (\frac{\partial R}{\partial a})(\frac{\partial R}{\partial b}) \end{pmatrix} \tag{11}$$

where,
$$\begin{pmatrix} (\frac{\partial R}{\partial a}) \\ (\frac{\partial R}{\partial b}) \end{pmatrix} = \frac{-1}{N}\sum_{n=1}^{N} \frac{1}{\sqrt{(\hat{r}_n - a_0)^2 + (\hat{c}_n - b_0)^2 - R^2}} \begin{pmatrix} (\hat{r}_n - a) \\ (\hat{r}_n - b) \end{pmatrix} \tag{12}$$

We used the gradient descent method for estimating Δw or one can use Newton method as discussed by Haralick [19].

CENTERLINE METHOD

The centerline method developed by Bolson et al. [15] was used to quantify ventricular boundary motion. Their method measured the motion along 100 chords constructed perpendicular to a centerline drawn midway between the end-diastole (ED) and end-systole

(ES) LV contours. The centerline method was developed to find the extent of local LV wall motion. The algorithm consists of the following principle: If the two LV polygons are ED and ES boundaries, ED being having larger number of points on it, then first linearly interpolate the larger contour to get 200 points and then for each tuple of three points on this contour a perpendicular is drawn to the tangent of the circle passing through these three points. Centers of these perpendicular constitute the centerline.

SHAPE BASED

Duncan [17] suggested a bending energy model for comparing the shape change along the LV contour on boundary data as traced by an expert and obtained from contrast ventriculography. Duncan found that bending energy model can be used to study the shape change *along the LV contour* between these study sets. The bending energy model was used for finding the curvature of the LV along the left ventricle contour but it did not compute the extent of the wall motion during the cardiac cycle. Duncan applied the centerline method to find the extent of wall motion from the end diastole to the end systole frame during the systolic heart cycle. Duncan concluded that bending energy and centerline results were computing two different features of the left ventricle function. The bending energy was computing curvature along the left ventricle contour while centerline method was computing the extent of wall motion along the left ventricle contour. The bending energy was based on the following principle. Given an undeformed state (say a straight rod), find out how much energy was required to bend the rod to the deformed state. This energy was expressed using the radius of curvature of the rod or left ventricle contour. The formula is given as:

$$BE(n) = \sum_{k=k_1}^{k_2} [\nu_n(k) - \bar{\nu}(k)]^2 \qquad (13)$$

where, k was the index for angular number along the left ventricle contour. $\nu(k)$ was the curvature for the angular number k. $\bar{\nu}(k)$ was the mean curvature for all the normal patient studies (N) for the angular number k is: $\bar{\nu}(k) = \sum_{n=1}^{N} \nu_n(k)$. For curvature for the angular number (see Duncan et al. [17]).

ACTIVE OR DEFORMABLE SHAPE LOCI MODEL-BASED

Clary [22], [23] used the deformable shape loci (DSL) algorithm to track the LV wall motion in cardiac nuclear images sequence. Clary placed the DSL manually near the LV in the first frame of each sequence and allowed to evolve, which means it is allowed to optimally position itself with respect to the image information. The optimal model position in the first frame is used as the initial position in the second frame. To track the motion over the entire sequence, the final model configuration in one frame was used as the initial configuration ni the next frame ($t+1$ time). Clary et al. defined the term called *endness measure* that measures the degree of circular osculation (curvature) behavior for a circle of a particular radius R_o with a boundary at a distance R_o and is given as:

$$K(r,\theta) = \frac{-(r - R_o)}{(\sigma_r^3)}\ exp(\frac{(r - R_o)^2}{2{\sigma_r}^2})\ exp(\frac{(\theta - \theta_o)^2}{2{\theta_\theta}^2})$$

where, θ_o is the direction tangent to the medial track, σ_r is proportional to R_o and θ_θ is a constant and is the derivative of the Gaussian in polar form, normalized by σ_r to provide zoom invariance, and weighted by a decreasing function of the angle swept by an arc along the circle.

DISTANCE BASED

Using the point model of the LV contours, where each vertex is represented by the pair (x_n, y_n), where n takes the value 1 to N, and N be the number of studies in the population, we can compute the mean x and y positions of the vertex given as: μ_x and μ_y. Similarly, we can also compute the variance of these x and y positions represented by Σ_x and Σ_y. Now using the mahanabolis distance, we can compute the distance between any given point (x, y) to these feature vectors representing the average position of the x and y coordinates of LV represented in this point model. This is given by: $\exp(-\frac{1}{2}(X_x - \mu_x)^T \ \Sigma_x^{-1} \ (X_x - \mu_x))$ and $\exp(-\frac{1}{2}(X_y - \mu_y)^T \ \Sigma_y^{-1} \ (X_y - \mu_y))$. Similarly other popular distance rules like Hamming distance [25], Hausdorf Distance method can be utilized as discussed by Haralick and Shapiro [19].

COMPARATIVE STUDY OF DIFFERENT ERROR MEASUREMENT TOOLS: DISCUSSION AND CONCLUSIONS

Karsch et al. [26], Gelberg et al. [27], have compared different schemes but lacks model-based methods of error measurements, and does not incorporate numerical stability and shape parameter information which are very critical in practical situations. The polyline distance metric has the following advantages over other methods: 1) The method is very stable and computes the error based on the geometry of the triangles and vector calculus. 2) The polyline distance method finds if there are cups or cusps in the polyline. 3) Since prior to the polyline error computation, the curves (LV polygons) undergo the equal arc sampling and interpolation, thus there exists one to one correspondence between two curves. 4) This is a non-iterative computation and thus saves time, unlike Bolson and Sheehan's method [15], where one has to do the computations again to smooth the curves to improve the accuracy. 5) In polyline method, there is no fitting involved. In Bolson et al.'s method, one need to compute the tangents by fitting the circle through three points. The circle fitting algorithm is very sensitive to the number of points taken on either side of the vertex in consideration (see [19]). 6) Another advantage of the polyline algorithm is that it can easily find out whether the distance computed for every vertex is positive or negative, positive when going from one vertex to the opposite polygon and vice versa. 7) The polyline algorithm is in conjunction with the swapping mechanism that make the process symmetric. So the average statistics gives a better estimate of the mean error when computed from one polygon to another and vice-versa. 8) The method has an advantage in that the correct bias errors at every vertex are computable. Since not only the closest perpendicular is computed, but also the coordinate position and its bias relative to the vertex on the opposite polygon, thus we can use this distance to correct the bias errors. 9) One of the major advantages of the polyline distance measure is the coherence with the ejection fraction computation. For example, if the ES left ventricle shape are totally convex and inside the ED left ventricle shape, the ejection fraction number truly reflects the polyline distance error. Since 95% of the ES frames lies inside the ED frames, the polyline distance error will reflect very good approximations for sweeping area between LV shapes for volume computations. Thus the primary advantage of the contour extraction and quantification can be better studied and cardiologist can establish better clinical relevance. Finally, polyline distance method not only computes a similar measure to centerline technique to a third decimal accuracy [6], but has the advantages, superiority and stability compared to other methods. Shape-based method are good if the land marks are correctly identified automatically by computer. A good measurement tool must have the necessary components for convex shape measurement in cardiac projection images and must incorporate the following information's: (i) selection of the land marks for example, the apex of the LV, the extreme interior and/or anterior bulge point, aortic valve plane points. (ii) there should be a fitting or smoothing operation which could take these raw points and generate a smooth curve but constrained by these land marks. The constrained can be introduced by the penalty functions over these land marks. (iii) Lastly, the tools should be able to produce the average curve over the entire database for a particular frame number in the cardiac cycle and then measure the deviation of every contour from this average curve. This can be considered as a bias-estimation for intrusions or extrusions. Besides that the tools should be able to co-relate successive frames for those land mark points so that the shape parameter is not lost. This will allow to measure the error in the periphery of the vertex selected, rather than searching the entire contour as in Pollyanna method as discussed by Suri et al. [6]. In nutshell, the paper presented different methods for LV wall motion quantification and attempted to categorize them in different classes. Issues like stability, clinical usefulness were presented and mathematically explained. These methods however need a validation schemes which is not the scope of this paper.

References

[1] Bookstein, F. L, Morphometric tools for landmark data geometry and biology, Cambridge Press, 1991.

[2] Robert J. Moore, Imaging Principles of Cardiac Angiography, Aspen Publishers, Rockville Maryland, pages pp.1-258, 1990.

[3] Lamberti C., A System to test methods for ventricular wall motion analysis, Computers in cardiology, IEEE computer Society, 89-93, 1984.

[4] Jasjit S. Suri, R. M. Haralick and F. H. Sheehan, Left Ventricle Longitudinal Axis Fitting and LV Apex Estimation using a Robust Algorithm and its Performance: A Parametric Apex Model, Proc. of ICIP, Santa Barbara, 1997.

[5] Jasjit S. Suri, R. M. Haralick and F. H. Sheehan, Greedy Algorithm for error reduction in automatically produced boundaries from Low Contrast Ventriculograms, Proc. of: Int. Conf. in Pattern Recognition, Vienna, Austria, pp.361-365, Vol. IV, Track D, Aug. 25 - 30, 1996.

[6] Jasjit S. Suri, Robert M. Haralick and Florence H. Sheehan, Accurate Left Ventricle Apex Position and Boundary Estimation From Noisy Ventriculograms, Proceedings of the IEEE Computers in Cardiology, Indianapolis, 1996.

[7] C. K. Lee, Automated Boundary Tracing Using Temporal Information, Ph.D Thesis, Department of Electrical Engineering, University of Washington, Seattle, 1994.

[8] S. K. Setaredhan, J. J. Soraghan, Automatic Left Ventricular Feature Extraction and Visualization from Echocardiographic Images, Proceedings of IEEE Computers in Cardiology (CinC), Indianapolis, Sep. 8-11, 1996.

[9] Vikram Chalana, A multiple active contour model for cardiac boundary detection in echocardiographic sequences, IEEE Transactions in Medical Imaging, June 1996.

[10] P. Grattoni and R. Bonamini, Contour detection of the left ventricle cavity from angiographic images, IEEE Transactions on Medical Imaging, Vol. 4, pp 72-78, June 1985.

[11] P. Grattoni, Fabrizio Pollastri and Giorgio Dimino, Detection of moving contours from left-ventricle cineangiograms, Time-Varying Image Processing and Moving Object Recognition, 2 published by Elsevier Science Publishers 1990, V. Cappellini, 3rd international workshop in Florence Italy in May, 1989.

[12] D. G. Gibson, T. A . Prewitt and D. J. Brown, Analysis of left ventricle wall movement during isovolumetric relaxation and its relation to coronary artery disease, Journal of Heart Br., Vol. 38, pp. 1010, 1976.

[13] G. B. John Mancini, M. T. LeFree and R. A. Vogel, Curvature analysis of normal ventriclograms: Fundamental Framework for the assessment of shape changes in man, IEEE Computers in Cardiology, pp. 141-144, 1985.

[14] Lawrence H. Staib and J. S. Duncan, Parametrically Deformable Contour Models, International Conference in Computer Vision, pp. 98-102, 1989.

[15] Bolson EL, Kilman S, Florence H. Sheehan and Harold T. Dodge, Left ventricular segmental wall motion - a new method using local direction information, IEEE Computers in Cardiology, pp. 245, 1980.

[16] Donna J. Williams and Mubarak Shah, A fast algorithm for active contour and curvature estimation, Computer Vision, Graphics and Image Understanding, Vol. 55, No. 1, Jan., pp14-26, 1992.

[17] James. S. Duncan, F. A. Lee, A.W.M. Smeulders, and B. L. Zaret, A Bending Energy Model for Measurement of Cardiac Shape Deformity, IEEE Transactions in Medical Imaging, Vol. 10, No 3, pp. 307-320, 1991.

[18] James. Duncan, R. Owen, P. Anandan, L. Staib, T. McCauley, A. Salazar and F. Lee, Shape-based Tracking of Left Ventricle Wall Motion, Information Processing in Medical Imaging, pp. 41-44, 1991.

[19] Haralick and Shapiro, Computer Vision and Robot Vision, Vol-I, Addison Wesley, 1992, (Vol-II) 1993.

[20] T.F. Cootes, C.J. Taylor, D.H. Cooper and J. Graham, Active Shape models: Their Training and Applications, Computer Vision and Image Understanding, Vol. 61, No. 1, January, pp.38-59, 1995.

[21] Kass, Wikins, Terzapolous, Snakes: Active Contour Models, International Journal of Computer Vision, 1988.

[22] Gregory J. Clary, Stephen M. Pizer, and Daniel S. Fritsch, Left Ventricular Wall Motion Tracking via Deformable Shape Loci, Computers in Radiology (CAR), pp. 271-276, 1997.

[23] Daniel S. Fritsch, Stephen M. Pizer, L. Yu, V. Johnson, and E. L. Chaney, Segmentation of Medical Image Objects Using Deformable Shape Loci, IPMI, pp. 127-140, 1996.

[24] Ehricke et al., Problems and Approaches for Tissue Segmentation in 3D MR Imaging, SPIE Medical Imaging IV, Image Processing, Vol 1233, pp.128-137, 1990.

[25] Chong J C, Jia-JC Assessments of neural network output codings for classification of multispectral images using Hamming distance measure, Vol.2, Piscataway, NJ, USA,94CH3440-5. p 526-528, Conference Information: Proceedings of the 12th IAPR International Conference on Pattern Recognition. Part 2 (of 3). Jerusalem, Isr ISSN: 1051-4651, 1994.

[26] K. R. Karsch, B. Blanke and K. P. Rentrop, Comparison of Nineteen Quantitative Models for Assessment of Localized Left Ventricle Wall Motion Abnormalities, Clinical Cardiology, 3, 123-128, 1980.

[27] Harris J. Gelberg and Bruce H. Brundage, Quantitative Left Ventricular Wall Motion Analysis: A Comparison of Area, Chord, and Radial Methods, CIRCULATION, Vol. 59, No. 5, May 1979.

RECENT ADVANCES TOWARDS A MODEL-BASED PATTERN-RECOGNITION APPROACH FOR THE LEFT VENTRICLE BOUNDARY ESTIMATION

Jasjit S. Suri, † Robert M. Haralick,† †Intelligent Systems Laboratory, Department of Electrical Engineering, Florence H. Sheehan ‡, ‡Cardiovascular Research & Training Center, University of Washington Medical Center, University of Washington, Seattle, WA 98195

ABSTRACT

Large number of computer vision and pattern recognition techniques have lead to recent advancement towards model-based pattern recognition cardiac diagnostics imaging systems. As a result, medical imaging scientists, computer vision and pattern recognition researchers along with cardiologists have started to explore the system which is most clinically useful. Suri et al. [22], [23], [24], [25], [26], [27], [28], [29], [30] showed model-based pattern-recognition system recognizes patterns for segmenting the left ventricle region in temporal and spatial domains. These segmented contours are very vital for the cardiologists to know the behavior of the left ventricle and to quantify the heart parameters like the ejection fraction. We first review the recent model-based pattern-recognition and computer vision approaches for the left ventricle contour estimation by different authors, their success and critiques. Finally, we present a state of the art model-based pattern-recognition system for left ventricle boundary estimation which yields an error as low as **2.5** mm for a data set with **377** patient studies.

Key Words: Motion, Left Ventricle, Model-based, Pattern-Recognition.

INTRODUCTION

Left ventricle (LV) segmentation in X-ray heart images (ventriculograms) began when imaging systems became available for imaging of the heart [1], [2]. In cardiological imaging, the shape of the heart varies considerably between patient studies and through time. The variability in the heart rates, size, position, orientations; gray scale variations in the data sets; noise due to the varying modulation transfer function of the X-ray imaging setup; interference of the other thoraic structures with the LV; and the large number of abnormalities and cardiac disorders have caused different researchers to pursue different paths for segmentation and contouring of the LV. The goal of any LV diagnostic imaging system is to build an accurate, robust, and reliable system for estimating the borders of the LV. It is obvious that one system alone is not enough for accurate or robust border estimation, the main reason being that the designed system has to handle large variability and complex cardiac images in the database. With the current state of the art algorithms, we have divided our model-based review as per different pattern-recognition models proposed for LV border estimation. The layout of this paper is as follows: Section "thresholding and edge based models" presents briefly the edge-based techniques. Section "model-based techniques" concentrates on the model-based LV contouring which is the major part of this paper; its success and critiques. Finally, a state of the art low error model-based pattern-recognition cardiac imaging system is presented.

THRESHOLDING AND EDGE BASED MODELS

In thresholding based methods, a threshold is selected so that all pixels having gray scale intensities greater than the threshold are the cardiac structures and the other pixels are the background pixels (low intensities). These methods consider the dye injected region to be the foreground (brighter region, see fig. 2), but since the catheter and ribs have high gray scale values, they seem to be taken into the foreground after threshold. Several threshold based methods have been developed to separate the data whose distributions can be separated by finding the minimum between the two modes in a histogram of gray scale ventriculograms (LVG's). All these methods are either semi-automatic or are not accurate and robust enough to produce reliable boundaries.

Of the earlier works in thresholding, Chow [3] developed a LV boundary detection algorithm in cardioangiograms using dynamic thresholding. The fundamental assumption of Chow was based on the probability distribution of the intensity for any small region of the picture which consisted solely of the object or the background and was unimodal with Gaussian distribution. Chow's algorithm consisted of the following steps: 1) dividing the image into smaller overlapping regions and then computing its histograms, 2) choosing the histograms which had large variances. Chow et al. showed that the variance of the region was a function of the variance of the contrast agent, mean value of the contrast agent and the fractions of the area of the region by the object, 3) for those selected histograms; Chow et al. then computed the distribution parameters; namely the mean, the variance and the fraction of the area of the object and background in that region. These parameters then underwent the bimodality histogram test, 4) The last step consisted of the estimation of the threshold using the maximum likelihood function by solving the quadratic equation of the form: $Ax^2 + Bx + C = 0$. Chow's algorithm is definitely a statistical procedure to estimate the threshold, but it is not robust enough to handle the gray scale distribution of the cardiac data sets. The histogram of the LVG do not have a Gaussian distribution. Furthermore, Chow assumes only the background and the object, which is not the case when the diaphragm interferes with the LV.

Haralick and Shapiro [5] summarized a set of segmentation techniques. Haralick [6], [7] defined an edge to occur on a pixel if, and only if, there was some point in the pixel's area having a negatively sloped zero crossing of the second directional derivative taken in the direction of a nonzero gradient at the pixel's center. Haralick et al. used a functional form consisting of a linear combination of the tensor products of discrete orthogonal polynomials of up to degree three. Haralick et al. assumed that in each neighborhood of the image the underlying gray tone intensity function f took the parametric form of a polynomial in the row and column coordinates. Haralick et al. also assumed sampling of the digital picture function as a regular equal interval grid sampling of the square plane which was the domain of f. Thus, in each neighborhood, f takes the facet model form:

$$f(r,c) \;=\; K_1 + K_2\, r + K_3\, c + K_4\, r^2 + K_5\, rc + K_6\, c^2 + K_7 r^3 + K_8\, r^2 c + K_9\, rc^2 + K_{10}\, c^3 \quad (1)$$

where the coefficients K_1 to K_{10} changed from one neighborhood to another and were estimated using a least square error surface fit. A pixel was marked as an edge if in the pixel's immediate area there was a zero crossing of the second directional derivative taken in the direction of the gradient and the slope of the zero crossing was negative. The advantage of the cubic fitting model is its low residual error. Also, this edge detector is less sensitive to noise compared to traditional edge detectors like Sobel and Prewitt.

Setarehdan and Soraghan [8], [9] addressed the issue of LV boundary extraction in echocardiogram images using a combination of fuzzy logic [10] and multi-resolution edge detection. Setarehdan's algorithm consisted of two major steps. First, the estimation of a point inside the LV cavity was made using knowledge of the standard echo views and the heart morphology. This point was important as the radical lines were made to originate from this point outwards. It was along these radical lines that an edge was searched using the wavelet transform. The acceptable error for the center point detection was 10%. In second step, Setarehdan et al. searched for a global maxima of the wavelet transform $W(f(s,t))$ in the scale-space domain which corresponded to a positive edge. Eq. 2 shows the wavelet transform of the function $f(s,t)$ where s is the scale and t is the support index. Setarehdan et al. computed the first derivative of a function and took its wavelet transform. If the wavelet transform yielded a maximum, then that position was an edge. This however depended upon the factor s, called the index of the scale. The maximum s value depended on the length of the signal and on the the scales together in the scale-space plane.

$$W(f(s,t)) \;=\; \sqrt{(|s|)} \int \frac{df(x)}{dx}\; \phi(\frac{(t-x)}{x})dx \qquad (2)$$

MODEL-BASED TECHNIQUES

Model-based pattern-recognition boundary extraction is getting more attention these days as it uses information about the imaging modality, anatomical knowledge and any integration of experience. When the data driven approaches like the thresholding techniques and edge-based techniques did not give promising results, new model-based approaches started to emerge. These approaches are faster, more reliable, robust, noise insensitive, accurate. The model-based approaches are classified into the following categories: training-based, fusion-based, active contour based, neural network-based, polar-based and regression time-based. A detailed description can be seen in Chapter 1 by Suri [30].

In LV classification approaches, Lee [12], [13] used a pixel-based Bayesian approach for the LV boundary estimation where the gray scale values of the location throughout the cardiac cycle were taken as a vector. Lee assumed that the distribution was bi-variate normal. For each observed vector, one class was assigned according to the ground truth, which was available by filling the LV region surrounded by the ground truth LV boundary. The ground truth of a pixel through F frames generated 2^F possible classes but, far less than 2^F classes

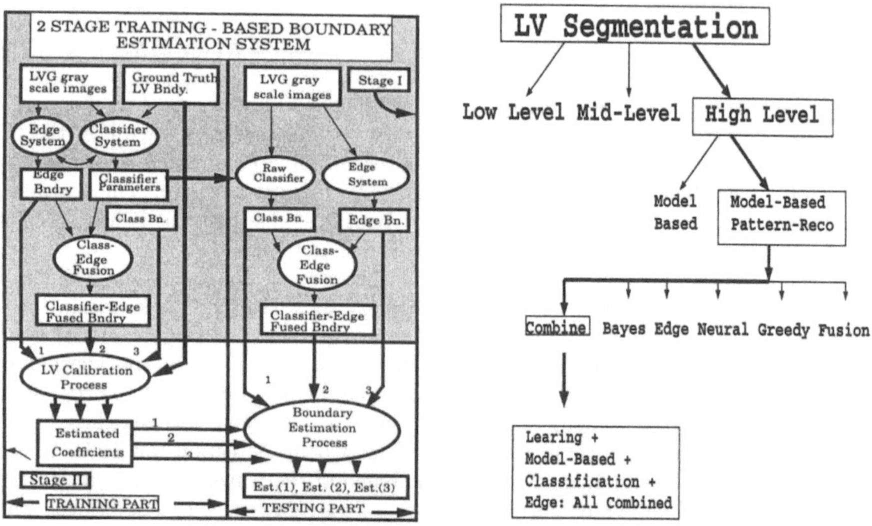

Figure 1: **Left**: Two stage model-based pattern-recognition system for LV boundary estimation. Stage I (upper half, shown black in color) consists of three approaches: Pixel-classification approach, edge detection approach and the classification-edge fusion approach. Stage II (lower half, shown white in color), consists of the calibration stage which smoothes the raw boundaries produced in stage I. **Right:**: Chart showing down the tree the usage of combination of several techniques for accurate model-based pattern recognition system.

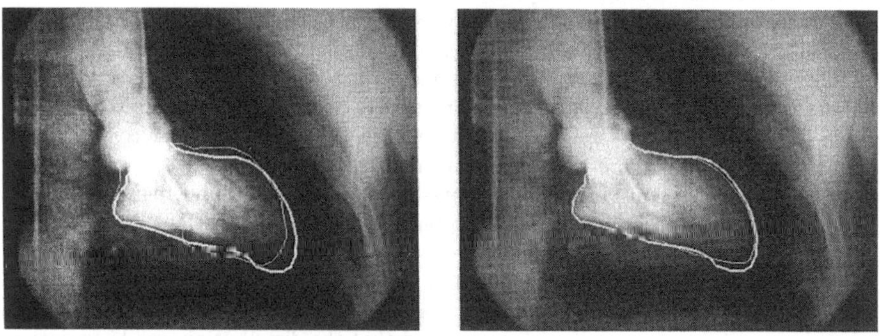

Figure 2: Sample results of the model-based pattern recognition system. Left image is the classification boundary while the right image is the boundary estimation by the entire model based system.

were actually required in order to represent all existent classes. Due to the different heart rates, (i.e. variable number of frames in the cardiac cycle for different studies) Lee allowed different dimensions of the observation vector. Lee simultaneously segmented all the frames from the end diastole through the end systole to the next end diastole instead of separately segmenting each frame separately. Lee assumed that each pixel was statistically independent in the same frame. Lee later modified his assumption by considering the nearest neighbor. For performance and error computation of the detected LV boundary, Lee compared the classifier boundary with the manually traced boundary using the Hausdorf distance measure, and $e(A,B) = max\{max\ i\{d(a_i,B)\}, max\ j\{(b_j,A)\}\}$, where $d(a_i,B) = min\ j||b_j - a_i||$. Because the gray scale contrast in the region of the apex zone was very low, classifier boundaries in that region were not close to ground truth boundaries. Furthermore, the boundaries produced by the classifier did not reflect the true LV shape and sometimes the end diastole and the end systole boundaries could hardly be distinguished. The ACTS model presented by Lee [13] models the heart motion by specifying an inner bound and outer bound of the motion between any two frames in terms of morphological operations. With these motion constraints, ACTS can bound the LV region in one frame of the cardiac cycle based on the detected LV boundary in another frame (see Chapter 4 in [12]). This can be called the time dependent or inter-frame dependent modeling.

Van Bree [14] attempted to find the LV borders using a combination of probability surfaces and dynamic programming. Van Bree's algorithm consisted of three major steps. The first step was building the probability surfaces from a database of hand-drawn boundaries after the LV boundaries were corrected for translation and rotation. The second step consisted of generating the extraction lines (also called search lines) for the design of the search matrix. These search lines originated from the interior of the LV and extended radically outwards to the outer region (background) of the LV. The third step consisted of smoothing the search matrix followed by dynamic programming to search for the optimal path of the LV border. Van Bree's method is an attempt towards a more sophisticated algorithm for boundary estimation. However in Van Bree's approach for third step, the searching of the optimal path depends upon the search lines originating from the LV center, which in turn depends upon the ribbon band generated from the entire database. If the thickness of the ribbon band is large, then the position of the right edge point corresponding to the wall may lead to false alarm. On the contrary if the ribbon band is small, the search is accurate and fast. In other words if the database has very large variabilities, the estimation may not be robust. This is exactly the case in Lee's Bayesian classifier [12], [13]. One way to make it robust is by combing several algorithms beside pixel-classification techniques, such as regularization algorithms, low contrast edge detection algorithms as shown by Suri et al. [26].

Kass et al. [17] presented an energy-minimizing spline guided by external and image forces that pulled the spline towards features such as lines and edges in the image. The energy-minimizing spline was named snakes because the spline softly and quietly moved while minimizing energy. Snakes was an example of a more general technique of matching a deformable model to an image by means of energy minimization. A starting contour was first placed by the user, the snake then deformed itself into conformity with the nearest salient contour. Snakes did not solve the entire problem of finding the salient image contour. Snakes relied on another mechanism to place itself somewhere near the desired contour. The active contour model differed from the traditional approaches of edge detection and edge linking in that the active contour model was based on a variational approach which was dynamic because of the iterative nature of the differential equation on which it was based. The total energy of the snake was given as $E_{snake} = \int E_{int} + \int E_{ext}$ where, $\int E_{int}$ and $\int E_{ext}$ were the internal and external energies of the contour. The internal energy of the contour was defined as the weighted function of the first and second derivative of the contour and was mathematically given as:

$$E_{int} = \frac{\alpha(s)\ |v_s(s)|^2 + \ \beta(s)|v_{ss}(s)|^2}{2} \tag{3}$$

Snakes had the flexibility that it could be dynamically controlled but there was inherent drawbacks when snakes were applied to the low contrast images, images which had lot of noise, or images having objects which had sharp bends and corners like LV apex. The snake's accuracy to minimize the energy depended upon the external energy which also depended upon the image forces or image energy which in turn depended upon the image gradient. In LVG, the image gradient is very poor and not at its right place, and thus this energy contributes little to pushing the snake curve towards the ideal contour drawn by the cardiologist.

Staib [18] suggested a parametrically deformable contour model to represent a closed contour using an elliptic Fourier decomposition method given as:

$$\begin{bmatrix} x(t) \\ y(t) \end{bmatrix} = \begin{bmatrix} a_0 \\ b_0 \end{bmatrix} + \sum_{k=1}^{\infty} \begin{bmatrix} a_k & b_k \\ c_k & d_k \end{bmatrix} \begin{bmatrix} \cos kt \\ \sin kt \end{bmatrix} \tag{4}$$

where a_k, b_k, c_k, d_k were the raw coefficients of the a Fourier expansion. Thus the elliptical properties were expressed using Fourier expansion. Let the elliptical parameters be given by a vector $\mathbf{p}$. The parameters $\mathbf{p}$ were computed from the hand-drawn boundaries of the object from the given population. In step two, Staib did the matching using correlation where the ellipse was the template and search procedure was done on the gradient of the image, ∇I. Staib et al. then found that $\mathbf{p}$ which maximized the probability, $\mathrm{P}(\nabla I|\mathbf{p})$. This method can be considered as a combination of training and fitting, training because the $\mathbf{p}$ was computed from the training population and fitting because the algorithm tried to maximize to obtain the final contour. Staib et al. called this a parametric deformable model because the final contour was estimated after the deformation of the initial contour using the probabilistic approach to maximize the posterior estimate of the parameter vector $\mathbf{p}$.

Chalana [19] modified the original snake model developed by Kass. In Kass's original model, there were two energy components for the total energy of the contour, i.e., $E_{snake} = \int E_{int} + \int E_{ext}$ where $\int E_{int}$ and $\int E_{ext}$ are the internal and external energies of the contour. Internal energy term accounts to: $E_{in} = w_1(s)|V_s(s)|^2 + w_2(s)|V_{ss}(s)|^2$ Chalana et al. modified E_{in} by adding the time domain information; hence, the final internal energy term was given as:

$$E_{in} = \int\!\!\int w_1\,||V_s(s,r)||^2 + w_2\,||V_{ss}(s,r)||^2 + w_3\,||V_r(s,r)||^2 + w_4\,||V_{rr}(s,r)||^2 + w_5\,||V_{sr}(s,r)||^2 ds\,dr \tag{5}$$

where, $V_r(s,r)$, $V_{rr}(s,r)$ and $V_{sr}(s,r)$ are the elastic (stretching) and bending terms in third dimension. V_{sr} was the energy of interaction between in-plane and between planes; s is the normalized contour length and had a value between 0 and 1; r is the plane index and also takes the value in between 0 and 1. The external energy term given by Kass [17] was: $E_{ext} = E_{image} + E_{con}$. Chalana et al. modified these two terms to:

$$E_{ext} = E_{grad} + E_{time} = -w \int\int G_\sigma * ||\delta I(x,y,r)|| dsdr \tag{6}$$

$$E_{time} = \{-w_t \int\int (v(s,r) - v(s,r-\epsilon))\} + \{-w_t \int\int (v(s,r-\epsilon) - v(s,r))\} \, dsdr \tag{7}$$

Note the first term was for the systole (r to $r-\epsilon$) cycle while the second term was for the diastole ($r-\epsilon$ to ϵ). The above equations could be solved using Euler-Lagrange method exactly as solved by Kass. There are certain limitations with this method. Frist, the active contour model assumes that the image sequence be registered with respect to each other, but actually the transducer and patient do move during scanning process. Chalana et al. model does not use the temporal gradient information, so it was okay to use the active contour model for each time frame independently. However, if one uses the time information model then the active contour model requires a pre-registration step. Second, Chalana's first version of the active contour relied only on gradient information derived by Canny's operator. Certainly Canny's operator is a good choice but too simple and non-robust for highly noisy images which requires a reliable LV contouring system. Third, the user interface problem still exits. One solution is Setarehdan and Soraghan's [8] approach of estimating a center point in the LV using fuzzy logic and then computing the raw edges using the wavelet transform. This raw edge boundary can now undergo the regularization term as used by Chalana et al. in fetal development. In other words, an attempt has not been made in ultrasound images, where a combination of several algorithms is the best choice. A Bayesian approach for edge detection is very popular and can be utilized in conjunction with fitting and regularization to approach this problem.

Grattoni [20], [21] addressed the minimum-radical-inertia method for left ventricle contour motion analysis in cineangiographic image sequence. Grattoni et al.'s work could be categorized as model-based work like the snakes. A detailed critique of Grattoni et al. can be found in [30]. Other model-based approaches can be seen in Chapter 1 by Suri [30].

A COMBINATION OF CLASSIFCATION AND LEARNING

Suri et al. [22], [23], [24], [25], [26], [27], [28], [29], [30] presented a system which used a combination of model-based pattern-recognition techniques to estimate the smooth and accurate boundaries of LV. This comes down the tree in fig. 1, right. Pixels can be classified in time or space using the standard quadratic forms like: $\{X - \mu_c)^T \Sigma_c^{-1} (X - \mu_c)\}$, where, X is the feature vector in space or time and Σ_c is the covariance matrix. Such forms are Mahanobolis distance as shown by Ehricke [31] and Lee [12]. Because of the low gray scale contrast in the apical zone of the LV, Bayes classifier boundaries were not close to the ground truth in that region. Furthermore the boundaries produced by the classifier did not reflect the true

LV shape and sometimes the ED and the ES boundaries could hardly be distinguished. The ACTS model presented by Lee [13] models the heart motion by specifying an inner bound and outer bound of the motion between any two frames in terms of morphological operations. With these motion constraints, ACTS can bound the LV region in one frame of the cardiac cycle based on the detected LV boundary in another frame (see Chapter 4 by Lee [12]). This can be called the time dependent or inter-frame dependent modeling. The raw boundaries due pixel classification can be smoothed to a high accuracy using quadratic calibrations as developed by Suri et al. [29]. Fig. 1 shows such a model-based pattern-recognition system while fig. 2 shows the results. The above system was validated by Suri et al. [27].

CONCLUSIONS

The main reason of success of model-based pattern-recognition system its training capability using the prior knowledge of the anatomy, training experience and a combination of image processing techniques. Our low error system has a mean error less than 2.5 mm [29], [30] over a database of 377 patient studies with on-line processing time of one second per patient on a PC.

References

[1] Robert J. Moore, Imaging Principles of Cardiac Angiography, Aspen Publishers, Rockville Maryland, pages pp.1-258, 1990.

[2] Duglas S. Moodi and John Yiannikas, Digial Subtraction Angigraphy of the heart and lungs, Grune and Stratton Inc., Harcourt Brace Jovanovich Publishers, 1986.

[3] C. K. Chow and T. Kaneko, Border Detection based on Local Characteristics, Computers in Biomedicine Research, Vol. 5, p388-p410, Aug, 1972.

[4] L. S. Davis, A survey of edge detection techniques, Computer graphics and Image Processing, Vol. 4, pp.248-270, 1975.

[5] Robert M. Haralick and Linda G. Shapiro, A Survey: Image Segmentation Techniques, Journal of Computer Vision, Graphics, and Image Processing, Vol. 29, pp.100-132, 1985.

[6] Robert M. Haralick, Digital Step Edges from Zero Crossing of Second Directional Derivatives, PAMI-6, No. 1, January, 1984.

[7] Robert M. Haralick, Cubic Facet Model Edge Detector and Ridge Valley Detector: Implementation Details, Elsevier Science Publishers B.V. (North Holland) 1986.

[8] S. K. Setaredhan, J. J. Soraghan, Automatic Left Ventricular Feature Extraction and Visualization from Echocardiographic Images, Proceedings of IEEE Computers in Cardiology (CinC), Indianapolis, Sep. 8-11, 1996.

[9] S. K. Setaredhan, J. J. Soraghan, Fully Automatic Left Ventricular Mayocardial Boundary Detection in Echocardiographic Images, Proceedings of IEEE Engineering in Medicine and Biology, The Netherlands, ISBN 90-9010005-9(CD-ROM) SOE 9609001, Oct 31-Nov. 3, 1996.

[10] L. A. Zadeh, Fuzzy Sets, Information and Control, Vol. 8, pp. 338-353, 1965.

[11] James S. J. Lee and Robert M. Haralick, Morphologic Edge Detection, IEEE Journal of Robotics and Automation, Vol. RA-3, No. 2, April 1987.

[12] C. K. Lee, Automated Boundary Tracing Using Temporal Information, Ph.D Thesis, Department of Electrical Engineering, University of Washington, Seattle, 1994.

[13] Sheehan, Lee and Haralick, Automated Boundary Tracing Using Temporal Information, US Serial Number. 08/251,733, filed May 31, 1994. The University of Washington at Seattle, WA.

[14] van Bree, Improving Left Ventricular Border Recognition Using Probability Surfaces, IEEE Computers in Cardiology, pp.121-p124, 1989.

[15] Donna J. Williams and Mubarak Shah, A fast algorithm for active contour and curvature estimation, Computer Vision, Graphics and Image Understanding, Vol. 55, No. 1, Jan., pp14-26, 1992.

[16] T.F. Cootes, C.J. Taylor, D.H. Cooper and J. Graham, Active Shape models: Their Training and Applications, Computer Vision and Image Understanding, Vol. 61, No. 1, January, pp.38-59, 1995.

[17] Kass, Wikins, Terzapolous, Snakes: Active Contour Models, International Journal of Computer Vision, 1988.

[18] Lawrence H. Staib and J. S. Duncan, Parameterically Deformable Contour Models, International Conference in Computer Vision, pp.98-p102, 1989.

[19] Vikram Chalana, A multiple active contour model for cardiac boundary detection in echocardiographic sequences, IEEE Transactions in Medical Imaging, June 1996.

[20] P. Grattoni and R. Bonamini, Contour detection of the left ventricle cavity from angiographic images, IEEE Trans. on Medical Imaging, Vol. 4, pp 72-78, June 1985.

[21] P. Grattoni, Fabrizio Pollastri and Giorgio Dimino, Detection of moving contours from left-ventricle cineangiograms, Time-Varying Image Processing and Moving Object Recognition, 2 published by Elsevier Science Publishers 1990, V. Cappellini, 3rd international workshop in Florence Italy in May, 1989.

[22] Jasjit S. Suri, R. M. Haralick and F. H. Sheehan, Two Calibration Algorithms for boundary estimation of Left Ventricle in X-ray Images, Published in Proc. of: 18th IEEE International Conference of Engineering in Medicine and Biology (EMBS),

Amsterdam, The Netherlands, ISBN 90-9010005-9(CD-ROM) SOE 9609001, Oct 31-Nov. 3, 1996.

[23] Jasjit S. Suri, R. M. Haralick and F. H. Sheehan, Left Ventricle Longitudinal Axis Fitting and LV Apex Estimation using a Robust Algorithm and its Performance: A Parametric Apex Model, Proc. of ICIP, Santa Barbara, 1997.

[24] Jasjit S. Suri, R. M. Haralick and F. H. Sheehan, Greedy Algorithm for error reduction in automatically produced boundaries from Low Contrast Ventriculograms, Proc. of: Int. Conf. in Pattern Recognition, Vienna, Austria, pp.361-365, Vol. IV, Track D, Aug. 25 - 30, 1996.

[25] Jasjit S. Suri, Robert M. Haralick and Florence H. Sheehan, Accurate Left Ventricle Apex Position and Boundary Estimation From Noisy Ventriculograms, Proceedings of the IEEE Computers in Cardiology, Indianapolis, 1996.

[26] Jasjit S. Suri, R. M. Haralick and F. H. Sheehan, Effect of Edge Detection, Pixel Classification, Classification-Edge Fusion Over LV Calibration: A two Stage Automatic system, Proc. of 10th Scandinavian Conference on Image Analysis, June 9-11, Finland, 1997.

[27] Jasjit S. Suri, R. M. Haralick and F. H. Sheehan, A General technique for automatic Left Ventricle Boundary Validation: Relation Between Cardioangiograms and Observed Boundary Errors, Journal of Digital Imaging, Vol. 10, No.2, May 1997.

[28] Jasjit S. Suri, R. M. Haralick and F. H. Sheehan, Two Automatic Training-Based Forced Calibration Algorithms for Left Ventricle Boundary Estimation in Cardiac Images, EMBS, Oct. 30-Nov. 2, 1997.

[29] Jasjit S. Suri, R. M. Haralick and F. H. Sheehan, Automatic Quadratic Calibration for Correction of Pixel Classifier Boundaries to An Accuracy of 2.5 mm: An Application in X-ray Heart Imaging, 14th ICPR, Brisbane, Australia, 1998.

[30] Jasjit S. Suri, Contour Generation of Motion Objects in Fuzzy and Low Contrast Multiple Image Frames: An Application in Cardiological Imaging, Ph.D Thesis, Department of Electrical Engineering, University of Washington, Seattle, 1997.

[31] Ehricke et al., Problems and Approaches for Tissue Segmentation in 3D MR Imaging, SPIE Medical Imaging IV, Image Processing, Vol 1233, 1990, pp.128-137.

AN APPROACH TO DYNAMIC MODELLING AND TOPOGRAPHIC FEATURE EXTRACTION OF WAKE EEG

David Lowe, Aston University, Aston Triangle, Birmingham B4 7ET, U.K.

ABSTRACT

We consider advanced pattern processing approaches for extracting information from biomedical signals. Signals such as the electroencephalogram are characterised by nonstationarity, a poor signal-to-noise ratio, and a signal which is composed out of many subcomponents. In an application domain such as investigating 'vigilance' we have to develop techniques which are capable of addressing some of these problems. In this paper we develop a singular subspace and an independent components dynamical systems embedding of single channel EEG time series which are then analysed for data clustering by a topographic neural network approach known as NeuroScale.

The work is novel in several respects: the use of unsupervised data (most work in this area is through evoked potential response experiments), the treatment of EEG by short window embeddings directly from the time domain(most work averages 30 second segments of power spectra), the comparison of ICA and PCA embeddings on single channel data (most ICA work so far reported has employed multiple sensor channels) and the use of a 'NeuroScale' architecture for topographic feature extraction.

INTRODUCTION

In this paper we address some pattern processing problems which emerge in the application domain of EEG data. In the long term we are interested in the feasibility of extracting a measure of vigilance from unsupervised wake EEG, without recourse to evoked potential response experiments.

There have been several studies recently, to try and discover whether 'vigilance' (or lack of it) may be recognised from single or multichannel EEG traces. It has long been recognised (since 1938) that the gross level of brain activity is reflected in the frequency structure of the EEG. In states of inactivity such as deep sleep or coma the EEG signal is characterised by larger amplitude and a general lowering of dominant frequency modes (especially α activity in the $8-12$Hz range) and long range spatial coherence. By contrast, wake EEG is a much noisier signal characterised by short range broad band activity [1] where the characteristic frequency bands all tend to be raised in frequency. In part, the assumption of the basic usefulness of a linear Fourier description within the wake state is questioned within this work, essentially because of the nature of the noise sources and complexity of the signal. The gross segregation of overall brain activity by long term power spectrum analysis is insufficient and inadequate to be exploited for more fine-grained inspections of brain state characterisations.

We consider the problem of extracting useful structure from *single channel* EEG which might reflect underlying cognitive brain states, and in particular 'vigilance'. Since we do not yet know how to characterise 'vigilance', we restrict ourselves to examine the emergence of 'interesting' behaviour as indicated in the EEG patterns.

The results are preliminary and demonstrate the usefulness of combining advanced techniques in pattern processing.

To help in this aim, we view the problem as a dynamical system embedding. However it is complicated by noise and intra-signal correlation and coherence. Our approach is to construct models in a *feature space* extracted from the embeddings, rather than attempt to explain the behaviour in terms of the original time series itself - as is almost universal in the clinical diagnostics of EEG.

In particular we use the singular value decomposition and an independent component analysis decomposition to project out the 'interesting' parts in the embeddings from the 'noise'.

The final stage of the paper is to consider the emergence of structure in these feature spaces by constructing a radial basis function network-based version of the techniques of Sammon Mappings and Multidimensional Scaling.

RECENT RELATED WORK

In sleep EEG studies, recent innovative work [2, 3] has demonstrated that a combination of linear signal processing methods and nonlinear neural network based approaches can be successful in elucidating structure in the EEG which may be related to different stages of sleep, and hence may be exploited in an analysis of sleep apnoea.

Explicit studies of alertness [4, 5, 6] have concentrated upon a frequency domain analysis of evoked potential response experiments analysed by a variety of signal processing methods, from multichannel Independent Component Analysis [7] to measuring spectral coherence and classification by feed-forward networks [6].

However no studies of robust unsupervised feature extraction in wake EEG studies have been published apart from [8]. This is not surprising given the complexity of the signal processing task using wake EEG.

FEATURE SPACE EMBEDDINGS:

A basic principle of the approach is that we assume that complexity observed in wake EEG is due to the nonlinear interaction of just a few degrees of freedom (rather than the linear interaction of many degrees of freedom), plus additive noise. This is a dynamical systems perspective which considers the existence of an (unobservable) deterministic generator of observed data. It is the aim of dynamical systems theory to uncover as much as possible about this underlying data generator (or attractor) as possible from just the observations [9].

Even if the assumption of an underlying deterministic system is correct, we do not observe the state $\boldsymbol{s}_t$ of the system directly. Instead we rely upon sensors which provide (scalar) observations on the underlying system states through a measurement function, $X(t) = X[\boldsymbol{s}_t]$. Typically this measurement function is unknown. We cannot invert the measurement function, but we can use a delay reconstruction to construct a vector

$$\boldsymbol{x}(t) = (X(t-\tau), \ldots, X(t-(m-1)\tau) \in \mathbb{R}$$

(where τ is the lag, and m is the number of lags) with the same information content as the original system state (assuming that the measurement function has not introduced its own dynamics into the observations).

It would therefore be possible to reduce the prediction problem for a complex dynamical system (such as EEG signal analysis) to one of evolution on a low dimensional attractor. We 'just' need to uncover this low dimensional attractor.

However a further complication is that this delay vector of observations includes various noise processes, sequential samples are highly correlated and the observations themselves are composed out of underlying correlated phenomena. For EEG we know that the measurements are a consequence of thousands of individual dipole fields generated by macro-cell assemblies. The measured electric field on the surface of the scalp is a sum of many compound brain processed, convolved in both time and space. Hence the apparent complexity of the system is increased as a consequence of these interactions. This is a reason why it has been argued that an independent components analysis would be useful in segregating out the different sources.

As a first step in separating out some of the noise sources we employ a signal–noise subspace decomposition based on the two methods of singular value decomposition, and independent components analysis. Being linear, these projection feature spaces are just as appropriate in which to perform further analysis (such as clustering). The suitability of these spaces are guaranteed since the transformations from the delay vectors to the projected spaces do not introduce any extra dynamics (basically because they are equivalent to a finite impulse response filtering of the data).

Once we have constructed a feature space embedding in this projected domain, we argue that it is more convenient to extract interesting structure from EEG data since confusing correlation structure has been compensated for, and higher order noise processes removed. Note that this approach is intrinsically different to the traditional method of analysing smoothed power spectra. In the embedding approach we are assuming that there exists an inherently nonlinear manifold generating the time series. We use the projected feature spaces as a spanning space in which we can parameterise the nonlinear manifold. This is the job of the neural network topographic feature extraction. In this scheme, the complexity of the observed EEG time series is a consequence of the nonlinearity of the manifold.

PCA AND ICA

In what follows, we employ a singular value decomposition of the delay vectors to construct an appropriate feature space. This performs a projection into the dominant Principal Components as determined by those directions of maximum variance which therefore decorrelates at second order moments. Independent Component Analysis, on the other hand, attempts to produce projections by finding directions (now not necessarily orthogonal) which are as statistically independent as possible (at least, as far as fourth order cumulants are concerned). There has been a major expansion of activity into techniques for ICA, including both batch and on-line (so called 'neural') approaches. We have found some of these approaches to be unsuitable for our problem. In this paper we follow the work of Hyvärinen and Oja [10] in employing an iterative fixed-point algorithm for minimising a cost function of the kurtosis which extracts 'independent' (as far as fourth order cumulants are concerned) components sequentially.

Given a decomposition of the EEG signal into embedding vectors $\boldsymbol{x}(t)$, we are interested in the linear representation, $\boldsymbol{x}(t) = \sum_{i=1}^{n} \alpha_i(t)\boldsymbol{v}_i$. In the singular subspace decomposition, the expansion basis vectors $\boldsymbol{v}_i$ are obtained as the singular vectors from a singular value decomposition of the data matrix — a set of P delay vectors characterising the problem. These basis vectors are mutually orthogonal and are ranked in importance determined by the amount of variance explained in the data matrix. We also only use n of m possible vectors to provide a signal–noise subspace analysis: the embedding vectors are reconstructed in terms of just those singular vectors we believe span the signal subspace. The coefficients $\boldsymbol{\alpha}(t)$ are the m 'source' signals which separate the data into different temporal bands.

Alternatively, in an independent component decomposition, the expansion basis vectors $\boldsymbol{v}_i$ are instead determined as the components of a demixing matrix, by a minimisation of the fourth-order cumulant. Specifically, the delay vectors are first prewhitened and hence decorrelated to second order moments (and so transformed into $\boldsymbol{y}(t) = \boldsymbol{W}\boldsymbol{x}(t)$ where $\boldsymbol{W}$ is determined from the same SVD of the data matrix). We then seek a demixing of $\boldsymbol{y}$ into 'independent sources' $\boldsymbol{\alpha}(t)$ such that $\boldsymbol{y}(t) = \boldsymbol{M}\boldsymbol{\alpha}(t)$. The weight vectors, $\boldsymbol{m}$ constituting the mixing matrix $\boldsymbol{M}$ are determined by minimising the fourth order cumulant of $\boldsymbol{y}(t)$, $\kappa_4 = E[y(t)^4] - 3(E[y(t)^2])^2$ subject to the constraint that $||m|| = 1$ to prevent trivial minimisation. After minimisation, the independent expansion basis vectors are obtained from $\boldsymbol{V} = \boldsymbol{W}^{-1}\boldsymbol{M}$. The independent sources $\boldsymbol{\alpha}(t)$ should represent a separation of the delay vectors into statistically separated com-

ponents. However the basis vectors are no longer orthogonal, and there is no natural method of ordering. In practice, we find that the independent basis vectors (and the independent sources) cluster into groups of similar temporal behaviour. Hence we can reconstruct the delay vectors in terms of a smaller number of independent components. We can also identify artifacts (and noise) in these independent sources which can also be removed in the reconstruction.
Hence, in both approaches we obtain a linear reconstruction of the EEG embedding vectors with a reduced dimensionality. We replace n-dimensional embedding vectors with $m < n$ dimensional 'source' vectors. This provides the dominant noise removal stage. The advantage of ICA over PCA is that the signal space is not constrained to be spanned by orthogonal basis vectors and hence the independent sources obtained from ICA should have a better 'interpretability' in terms of the original EEG problem. The disadvantage is primarily with the lack of an automatic approach to 'source selection' and significance ranking.

DATA

Single channel data from scalp locations T5-Oz sampled at 128Hz and quantised to 1 byte was collected from a study of healthy students over a 1 day period whilst they were performing a set sequence of activities. More detail is presented in [8]. The specific tasks undertaken by the subjects relevant to this study were computer tasks; one was a concentration-demanding visual attention task, and the other was a tedious tracking task. We used data from just one subject and sampled data from the difficult task, and the tedious task. For the 'training' set we used 400 delay vectors, 200 from each of the tasks and also sampled from different times in the day. 400 test vectors were also sampled from different periods in each task session.

THE EEG EMBEDDING BY SINGULAR VECTORS

The first experiment is a study of the singular vector embedding. For this we needed to determine the minimum window size used for the embedding, and the best number of singular vectors to use as a spanning basis for the signal subspace. We have previously [11, 12] discussed these issues in the context of the relevance of matching complexity of data to the complexity of neural networks modelling the generator of the data. For complexity information we need to study the singular spectrum obtained from the data matrix of delay vectors.
From an analysis of the singular spectrum in Figure 1, there is a change in structure around 11 singular vectors. (This is extracted by examining the first significant change in the *curvature* of the curve.) The singular spectrum implies an intrinsic dimensionality of the underlying manifold generating the EEG signal of about 5.

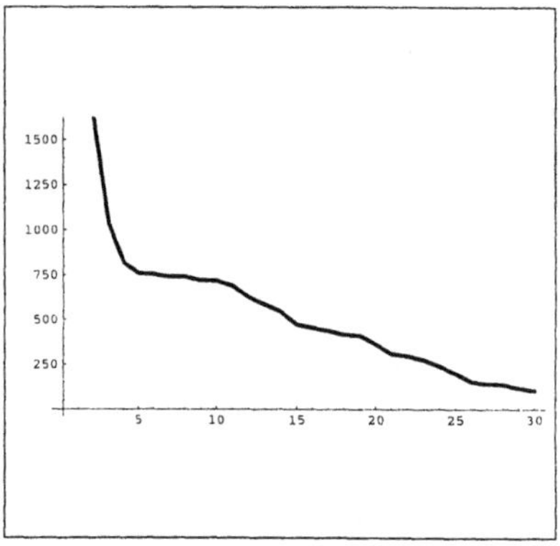

Figure 1: Singular spectrum of the data matrix using 30 samples to construct the delay vectors. Note the change in curvature structure around 11 significant values.

The projection of the original data into a space spanned by the low order singular vectors is a linear projection which is equivalent to a Finite Impulse Response filter. Effectively the signal is smoothed by moderating the high frequency content of the signal presumably due to true random noise. Hence no extra dynamic behaviour

is introduced (unlike the case of an Infinite Impulse Filter which would distort the system manifold as a consequence of injecting influences due to its own dynamics).
Therefore we can use the data-derived singular vector space to effect a reconstruction of the original manifold. Because all transformations up to this point are linear and also do not create additional dynamics of their own, we can still have confidence that a diffeomorphism exists between the reconstructed space and the original (unobservable) space.

THE EEG EMBEDDING BY INDEPENDENT COMPONENTS:

Instead of extracting singular vector projections, we extract the independent sources by the previously discussed technique of kurtosis minimisation. It is interesting to examine some of these extracted 'sources'. Figures 2–5 show the corresponding power amplitudes as a function of frequency for four of the selected independent sources. It can be seen that one extracted source corresponds to background mains hum corrupting the data, and another corresponds to very low frequency signal level deviations. Generally the independent sources correspond to signals with distinct but broad band power spectra. There are several independent sources with approximately the same power spectra, denoting the clustering of the sources. Since we have surmised that there are only really about 5 degrees of freedom in the signal from the embedding techniques, we would expect there to be an equivalent number of independent sources making up the EEG – and hence the clustering effect.

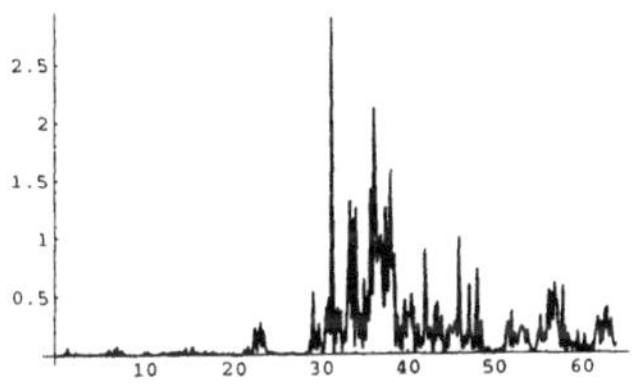

Figure 2: Power spectrum of one of the independent sources

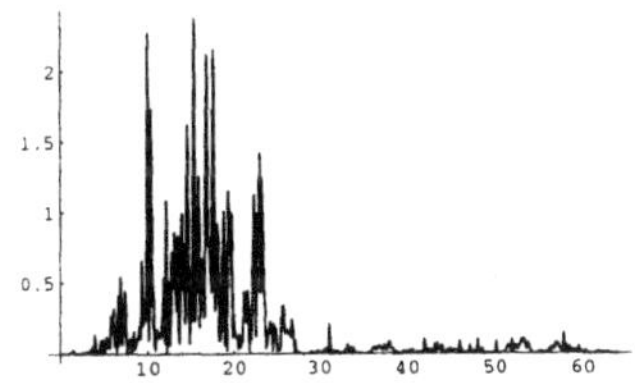

Figure 3: Power spectrum of another source

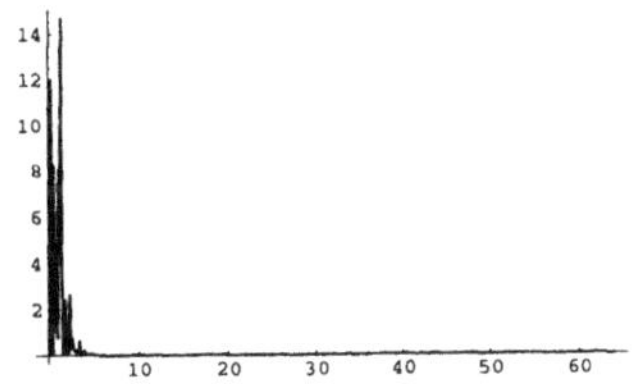

Figure 4: Power spectrum of the low frequency signal level wandering

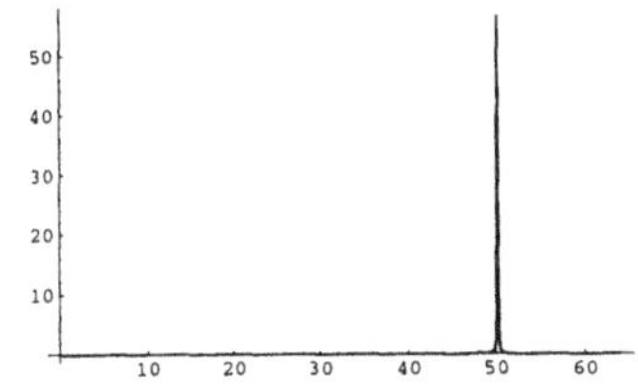

Figure 5: Power spectrum of the mains corruption

This analysis provides a set of nonorthogonal spanning basis vectors which the original EEG signal can be represented by. The original 30 dimensional embedding vectors are reduced to a set of about six independent sources with characteristically distinct power spectra as indicated in the above figures. Hence, instead of analysing the original time series, we could analyse the six independent sources. As we are interested in the emergence of structure in the feature space, we now turn to a nonlinear structure extracting process.

TOPOGRAPHIC CLUSTERING AND NEUROSCALE

We now demonstrate the effect of using a NEUROSCALE approach to perform a nonlinear topographic clustering of the EEG embedding data. To analyse the EEG signals further, we seek a dimension-reducing, *topographic* transformation of data for the purposes of visualisation and clustering. By 'topographic', we imply that the geometric structure of the data be optimally preserved in the transformation, and the embodiment of this constraint is that the inter-point distances in the feature space should correspond as closely as possible to those distances in the data space. The implementation of this principle by a neural network is very simple. A Radial Basis Function network is utilised to predict the coordinates of the data point in the transformed feature space. The locations of the feature points are indirectly determined by adjusting the weights of the network. The transformation is determined by optimising the network parameters in order to minimise a suitable error measure that embodies the topographic principle.

The specific details of this alternative approach are as follows. Given an m-dimensional input space of P data points $\boldsymbol{x}_q$, an n-dimensional feature space of points $\boldsymbol{y}_q$ is generated such that the relative positions of the feature space points minimise the STRESS term:

$$E = \sum_{p<q}^{N} (d^*_{qp} - d_{qp})^2, \tag{1}$$

where d^*_{qp} are inter-point Euclidean distances in the data space: $d^*_{qp} = \sqrt{(\boldsymbol{x}_q - \boldsymbol{x}_p)^T(\boldsymbol{x}_q - \boldsymbol{x}_p)}$, and the d_{qp} are the corresponding distances in the feature space: $d_{qp} = \sqrt{(\boldsymbol{y}_q - \boldsymbol{y}_p)^T(\boldsymbol{y}_q - \boldsymbol{y}_p)}$. The points $\boldsymbol{y}$ are generated by the RBF, given the data points as input. That is, $\boldsymbol{y}_q = \boldsymbol{f}(\boldsymbol{x}_q; \boldsymbol{W})$, where $\boldsymbol{f}$ is the nonlinear transformation effected by the RBF with parameters (weights and any kernel smoothing factors) $\boldsymbol{W}$. The distances in the feature space may thus be given by $d_{qp} = \| \boldsymbol{f}(\boldsymbol{y}_q) - \boldsymbol{f}(\boldsymbol{y}_p) \|$ and so more explicitly by

$$d^2_{qp} = \sum_{l=1}^{n} \left(\sum_{k} w_{lk} \left[\phi_k(\| \boldsymbol{x}_q - \boldsymbol{\mu}_k \|) - \phi_k(\| \boldsymbol{x}_p - \boldsymbol{\mu}_k \|) \right] \right)^2, \tag{2}$$

where $\phi_k()$ are the basis functions, $\boldsymbol{\mu}_k$ are the centres of those functions, which are fixed, and w_{lk} are the weights from the basis functions to the output.

The topographic nature of the transformation is imposed by the STRESS term which attempts to match the inter-point Euclidean distances in the feature space with those in the input space. This mapping is *relatively supervised* because there is no specific target for each $\boldsymbol{y}_i$; only a relative measure of target separation between each $\boldsymbol{y}_i, \boldsymbol{y}_j$ pair is provided. The approach may be extended to incorporate the use of extra 'subjective' information which may be used to influence the transformation. We effect this by allowing the dissimilarity matrix in data space to be modified by an extra inter-point distance function which could embody additional prior preferences on the eventual data distribution. Specifically, the data space distances are composed out of two constituents: the distance between the raw data vectors, d^*_{qp} and a distance between points which reclects our preference δ^*_{qp}. In this case our preference is that for all patterns taken from one specific task should be clustered closely, whilst patterns from the other tasks should be further away. For this study we have chosen the data space distance function to be:

$$\Delta_{qp} = (1 - \eta) d^*_{qp} + \eta \delta^*_{qp}$$

where η denotes our desire for the dominance of one type of distance over the other (and we choose $\eta = 0.5$ here).

Combining the equations and differentiating with respect to the weights in the network allows the partial derivatives of the STRESS $\partial E/\partial w_{lk}$ to be derived for each pattern pair. These may be accumulated over the entire pattern set and the weights adjusted by an iterative procedure to minimise the STRESS term E. Note that the objective function for the RBF is no longer quadratic, and so a standard analytic matrix-inversion method for fixing the final layer weights cannot be employed.

This overall procedure has become known as 'NEUROSCALE' [13]. As a parameterised Sammon mapping this approach offers a generalising topographic visualisation of data, but the exploitation of additional subjective information, via the subjective metric, permits the extraction of 'enhanced', more informative, feature spaces.

Figure 6 depicts the results of applying the NEUROSCALE approach to 400 data vectors extracted from the Singular Vector embedding feature space. The distance metric used as part of this process involved both the distances between the raw data samples, and also some 'supervisorial' knowledge supplied from the class information. The class knowledge was accounted for by defining a uniform distance between classes (i.e. patterns selected from Task 3 were taken to be equidistant from patterns taken from the other tasks, but the 'distance' between patterns within the same class were taken to be zero). In this way, no spurious ordering of patterns by their task was introduced. Any orderings which appear are the result of the relationships between the data points themselves. A final combined distance metric was obtained by taking equal proportions of the objective data space distances and the subjective space class dissimilarities.

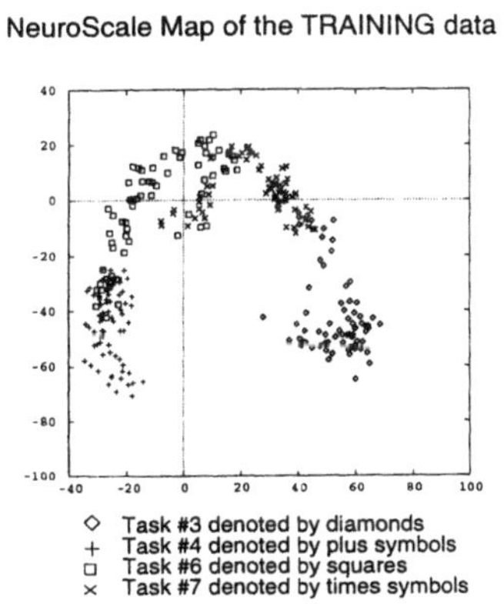

Figure 6: 2 dimensional NEUROSCALE projection of the EEG data (1000 samples taken from each task). Some discriminatory task-specific information has been 'folded' into this transformation. Note the distinct clustering into recognisable groups.

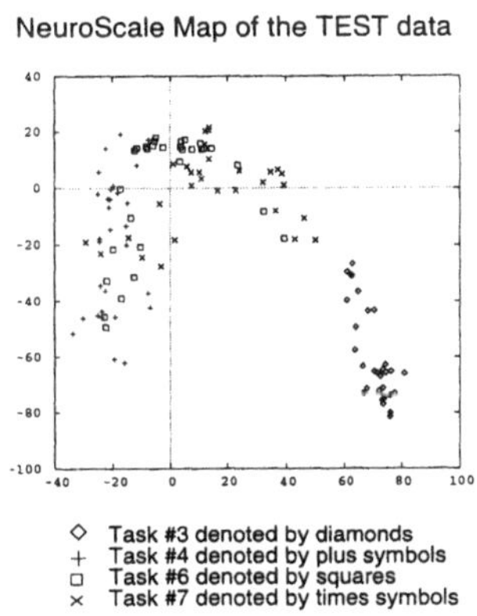

Figure 7: 2 dimensional NEUROSCALE projection of some test EEG data (samples taken from each task - taken from the end of the corresponding files - which were not used as part of the training process to obtain the mapping). Note that the test data conforms to the structure obtained as part of the training process.

As seen in Figure 6, an apparent structure has emerged in this feature space in which there appears to be an ordering along a (noisy) one dimensional string in this two dimensional Euclidean space. However it is important to note that the ordering along this one dimensional string is *not* related to the *type* of task undertaken by the subject, in that Task 3 is adjacent to Task7 which is adjacent to Task 6 which is adjacent to Task 4. Tasks 3 and 6 are monotonous tracking tasks and Tasks 4 and 7 are difficult visual attention tasks. Naïvely one might expect that if there are to be any groupings in a feature space then it would be more likely that there would be clusters arranged according to similar tasks. This is not observed in this experiment. Neither is the ordering a function of the time of day (hence speculation about a daily drift of general EEG activity is not corroborated by this experiment).
Although there does appear to be a broadly linear ordering, it is not the type of task or time of day that is acting as an order parameter. One could speculate that instead perhaps the ordering is related to the *way* in which the task is carried out (and so could reflect in some sense a measure of vigilance). Tasks 6 and 7 were performed after the subject had spent a short amount of time asleep, which could support a change in vigilance. We conclude that the clustering effect is a genuine aspect of the data itself, though the source remains a mystery.

CONCLUSIONS

We have considered a sophisticated signal and pattern processing problem based on wake EEG data. The problem required signal enhancement (achieved by PCA and ICA embeddings) and nonlinear clustering (achieved by a NEUROSCALE approach). Preliminary results are encouraging. From a dynamical systems embedding, we obtained a linear feature space in which the signal components were described by a spanning set of basis functions derived from either a PCA or ICA-based description. A topographic clustering of the projected EEG samples was obtained by using a neural network implementation of the Sammon mapping, where the inputs to the transformation were the projections onto the appropriate spanning basis functions. The PCA and ICA descriptions both returned a decomposition of the EEG signals into broadly distinct frequency bands and with resulting clusterings which are similar, though only results from the PCA embedding are shown in this paper. Currently the ICA approach is limited by having to perform manual clustering and then ranking of the independent sources. However the ICA approach seems to provide an interesting alternative feature space in which the resulting sources have an interpretability. This is also the first time that a single channel EEG analysis has been performed by the ICA approach, by explicitly recognising the embedding approach as a viable description of the time series. We have discussed complexity issues, but as yet can draw no final conclusions as to the link between degrees of freedom as determined by the embedding approach, and the intrinsic number of sources (after clustering) in the ICA approach. The EEG analysis has been unsupervised, and has resulted in some interesting directions. The study examined the possibility of extracting a measure of vigilance/attentiveness/concentration from wake EEG. Again, we can only comment that an interesting quasi-1-dimensional structure emerged which requires further study. This is now continuing. But in addition we would now also speculate that this approach is likely to have some merit in the analysis of *anomalous* brain activity, such as epilepsy, as well.

ACKNOWLEDGEMENTS
This work was supported in part by the EPSRC contract GR/K51815, " *Nonstationary Feature Extraction and Tracking for the Classification of Turning Points in Multivariate Time Series*", and under collaboration with Helen Stone and Andy Wright of British Aerospace plc, UK. I would also like to acknowledge the help and support I received with this work from Mike Tipping and Nathalie Nöel.

* REFERENCES

[1] Nunez PL. *Neocortical Dynamics and Human EEG Rhythms*. Oxford University Press, NY., 1995.

[2] Roberts S and Tarassenko L. The Analysis of the Sleep EEG using a Multilayer Network with Spatial Organisation. *IEE Proceedings F:*, 139(6):420–425, 1992.

[3] Siegwart DK, Tarassenko L, Roberts SJ, Stradling JR, and Partlett J. Sleep Apnoea from Neural Network Post Processing. In *4th IEE International Conference on Artificial Neural Networks*, 1995.

[4] Makeig S and Inlow M. Lapses in alertness: coherence of fluctuations in performance and EEG spectrum. *Electroencephalography and Clinical Neurophysiology*, 86:23–35, 1993.

[5] Makeig S and Jung T-P. Changes in Alertness are a Principal Component of Variance in the EEG spectrum. Technical Report, Naval Health Research Centre, 1995.

[6] Makeig S, Jung T-P, and Sejnowski T. Using Feedforward Neural Networks to Monitor Alertness from Changes in EEG Correlation and Coherence. In *Advances in Neural Information Processing Systems 8.*, 1996.

[7] Comon P. Independent Component Analysis: A new concept. *Signal Processing*, 36:287–314, 1994.

[8] Lowe D. Embedding the EEG. In *SPIE's Aerospace/Defence Sensing and Controls Conference: Applications and Science of Artificial Neural Networks III*, 1997.

[9] Broomhead DS and King GP. Extracting qualitative dynamics from experimental data. *Physica*, 20D:217–236, 1986.

[10] A Hyvärinen and A Oja. A fast fixed-point algorithm for independent component analysis. *Neural Computation*, 9:1483–1492, 1997.

[11] Lowe D. Characterising Complexity by the Degrees of Freedom in a Radial Basis Function Network. *NeuroComputing Journal, Special Issue on Radial Basis Functions*, 1997.

[12] Lowe D and Hazarika N. Complexity modelling and stability characterisation for long term iterated time series prediction. In *5th IEE International Conference on Artificial Neural Networks*, volume Conference Publication number 440, pages 53–58. The Institute of Electrical Engineers, 1997.

[13] Lowe D and Tipping ME. Neuroscale: Novel topographic feature extraction with radial basis function networks. In M.C. Mozer, M.I. Jordan, and T. Petsche, editors, *Advances in Neural Information Processing Systems 9*, pages 543–549. Cambridge, Mass: MIT Press, 1997.

ALGORITHMS FOR FUZZY SEGMENTATION

Bruno M. Carvalho, MIPG, University of Pennsylvania
C. Joe Gau, Graduate School & University Center, City University of New York
Gabor T. Herman, MIPG, University of Pennsylvania
T. Yung Kong, Queens College, City University of New York

ABSTRACT

Segmentation is the process of recognizing an object of interest in a picture. Thresholding is not an appropriate method of segmentation if there is some nonuniform shading in the picture or if what distinguishes the object of interest is not the exact values assigned to the individual pixels but rather some textural property. In such cases one can usefully apply fuzzy segmentation. We call a sequence of pixels in which consecutive pixels are adjacent a chain, and a pair of adjacent pixels a link. In fuzzy segmentation, the strength of any link is automatically defined based on statistical properties of the links within regions identified by the user as belonging to the object of interest. The strength of a chain is the strength of its weakest link. The fuzzy connectedness between any pair of pixels is the strength of the strongest chain between them. The fuzzy object containing a given pixel at a particular threshold is the set of all those pixels whose fuzzy connectedness to the given one exceeds or equals the threshold. A potentially time-consuming step in fuzzy segmentation is the calculation of the fuzzy connectedness of all other pixels to the given one. Previously this was done by a dynamic programming technique. We investigate the usefulness of replacing this by either of two greedy algorithms that have asymptotically better worst-case running times. We experimentally demonstrate that, even on quite small pictures, the greedy algorithms are many times faster than the dynamic programming technique.

1. THE THEORY OF FUZZY SEGMENTATION

The idea of fuzzy connectedness goes back to the seminal work of Rosenfeld[8]. Our approach is based on that advocated in [10], but generalized to arbitrary digital spaces [3].

A digital space is a pair (V, π), where V is a set and π is a symmetric binary relation on V such that V is connected under π. We can obtain a digital space, for example, as follows. Let us consider a tessellation of the plane into identical regular hexagons. We select V as the set of all such hexagons whose centers lie within a much larger closed regular hexagon and we say that two hexagons in V are in the relation π if, and only if, they are distinct and share an edge. In this case V is finite, as it is likely to be in most practical applications. We refer to elements of V as *spels* (short for "spatial elements") and we call two spels which are in the relation π to each other *proto-adjacent*. We observe that for a finite V, (V, π) can be interpreted as a connected graph [2] with V as the set of nodes and π as the set of arcs.

We define a *real-valued picture* over the digital space (V, π) as a triple (V, π, f), where f is a function which maps V into the real numbers R. *Binary pictures* are real-valued pictures in which the range of f is the two-element set $\{0, 1\}$. One way of identifying an object of interest in a real-valued picture is to produce from it a binary picture (over the same digital space), in which the spels of value 1 are exactly the spels that are contained in the object of interest. This is referred to as *segmentation.*

A commonly used method of segmentation is *thresholding*. For any $t \in R$, the *t-level set* of the real-valued picture (V, π, f) is defined as the set of spels $\{c \mid f(c) \geq t\}$. Each such t gives rise to a *thresholded picture*, which is the binary picture (V, π, f_t) with

$$f_t(c) = \begin{cases} 1, & \text{if } f(c) \geq t, \\ 0, & \text{if } f(c) < t. \end{cases} \tag{1}$$

Thresholding is very often not an appropriate method of segmentation. Examples of this are if there is some nonuniform "shading" in the picture (i.e., the interesting information is superimposed on a background whose darkness slowly varies, as is often the case in many physically obtained digital pictures) and if what distinguishes the object of interest is not the exact values assigned to the individual spels but rather some textural property. We illustrate below that in these cases thresholding fails to provide satisfactory segmentation, but an alternative approach, called *fuzzy segmentation*, produces better results.

A *fuzzy spel affinity* on a digital space (V, π) is a function $\psi : V^2 \rightarrow [0, 1]$ (i.e., a function which assigns to each ordered pair of spels a real value not less than 0 and not greater than 1), such that

(i) for all $c \in V$, $\psi(c, c) = 1$, and

(ii) for all c, $d \in V$, $\psi(c, d) = \psi(d, c)$.

The intuitive idea is that the value of the fuzzy spel affinity indicates how close the relationship is (in some sense relevant to the purpose of segmentation) between the spels in question. In other words, it indicates our degree of confidence that after segmentation the two spels should belong to the same class (e.g., they should either both be identified as bone or both be identified as not bone), with the value 1 indicating absolute certainty. The kinds of things that might be considered in defining a fuzzy spel affinity include the nearness of the spels to each other, the similarity of the values assigned to them in the real-valued picture that is to be segmented, and the similarity of the variances of these assigned values in the immediate neighborhoods of the two spels. For the definition to be useful for segmentation in a specific application, it will usually have to take into consideration the overall purpose of performing the segmentation. We will return to this point below and will give a specific example.

The definition of a fuzzy spel affinity is, intentionally, quite general. In particular, there is no requirement of transitivity: it frequently happens that spels c and d have a high fuzzy spel affinity, d and e have a high fuzzy spel affinity, and yet c and e have a low fuzzy spel affinity. For this reason we do not expect a fuzzy spel affinity, by itself, to be immediately useful for segmentation. (It cannot be that both c and d are identified with the same type of tissue and d and e are identified with the same type of tissue, and yet c and e are identified with different types of tissue.) To do segmentation, we first associate with the fuzzy spel affinity ψ a *fuzzy connectedness* function $\mu_\psi : V^2 \rightarrow [0, 1]$, defined by

$$\mu_\psi(c, d) \quad = \quad \max_{\substack{\langle c^{(0)}, \cdots, c^{(k)}, \cdots, c^{(K)} \rangle \in V^{K+1} \\ c^{(0)} = c, \ c^{(K)} = d}} \quad \min_{1 \leq k \leq K} \ \psi(c^{(k-1)}, c^{(k)}) \, . \tag{2}$$

Clearly, $0 \leq \psi(c, d) \leq \mu_\psi(c, d) \leq 1$ (the second inequality follows from the choice $\langle c, d \rangle$ for the sequence from c to d) and so, in particular, $\mu_\psi(c, d) = 1$ if $c = d$. (In the terminology of the fuzzy pattern recognition literature [5, 6] $\mu_\psi(c,d)$ is the *grade of membership* of (c,d) in the fuzzy set of "connected pairs of spels.")

It is worthwhile to give an intuitive discussion of this last definition. In it we use an arbitrary sequence $\langle c^{(0)}, \cdots, c^{(K)} \rangle$ of spels, which we call a *chain*. We think of each pair of consecutive elements $(c^{(k-1)}, c^{(k)})$ as a *link* in the chain and of $\psi(c^{(k-1)}, c^{(k)})$ as the *strength* of the link. We say that the strength of the chain $\langle c^{(0)}, \cdots, c^{(K)} \rangle$ is the strength of its weakest link, i.e., the minimum of $\psi(c^{(k-1)}, c^{(k)})$ over $1 \leq k \leq K$. Then the fuzzy connectedness of the pair of spels (c,d) is the strength of the strongest chain from c to d. The use of this concept in segmentation depends on the following quite general result. (The proofs of the theorems in this section can be found in Section 5.2 of [3] and will not be reproduced here.)

Theorem 1. *For any fuzzy spel affinity ψ on a digital space and for $0 \leq t \leq 1$, the binary relation $K_{\psi,t}$ on V defined by*

$$(c,d) \in K_{\psi,t} \Leftrightarrow \mu_\psi(c,d) \geq t \tag{3}$$

is an equivalence relation.

This theorem says that any fuzzy spel affinity and any threshold t partitions the set of spels into equivalence classes. If the threshold is low, then the equivalence classes will tend to be large. In particular, $t = 0$ results in V being the only equivalence class. Generally speaking, as the threshold increases, so will the number of equivalence classes, and the individual equivalence classes will tend to be smaller. If the fuzzy spel affinity is strictly less than 1 for any two distinct spels, then $t = 1$ will result in each equivalence class being a singleton set. The equivalence classes of $K_{\psi,t}$ are referred to as *ψt-objects* or, in general, as *fuzzy objects*. These objects have some very desirable properties which we now indicate without a precise definition of our terminology. (For the corresponding mathematically precise statements, see Section 5.2 of [3].) First, a fuzzy object is always connected. Second, the boundary between a fuzzy object and a connected subset of its complement is always "Jordan" in the sense that it is always the boundary between its "interior" (a connected set containing the fuzzy object) and its "exterior" (a connected set containing the connected subset of the complement), which partition V and are such that every path from one to the other crosses the boundary.

In practice, we are probably not interested in all the fuzzy objects that arise from a particular choice of fuzzy spel affinity. We are more likely to be concerned with a particular spel and ask which other spels belong to the same fuzzy object as the given one. For example, let us assume that we have found a fuzzy spel affinity appropriate for segmenting bone in CT images. To use this, we may just wish to point at a particular displayed pixel which we are pretty sure is bone-containing (probably because of its lightness) and then ask which other voxels in the three-dimensional array belong to the same piece of bone. This is where the "fuzziness" of the fuzzy segmentation comes into play: the fuzzy object containing the given spel is not uniquely determined by the fuzzy spel affinity (as we decrease the threshold, the same spel is a member of a fuzzy object of increasing size). This reflects the typical state of knowledge in a practical application. From our data alone, it is usually impossible to say with absolute certainty which spels belong to the same object as the selected spel. The larger thresholds give us smaller fuzzy objects, but also greater confidence that we are including few spels which in reality would not be judged to be in the same object.

We formalize the intuitive discussion of the previous paragraph as follows. For any fuzzy spel affinity on a digital space (V, π) and any spel o, we define the *connectedness map for* o as the real-valued picture (V, π, f), where $f(c) = \mu_\psi(o, c)$. The usefulness of this concept is reflected in the following theorem.

Theorem 2. *Let ψ be a fuzzy spel affinity on a digital space (V, π) and t be a real number,* $0 \le t \le 1$.

(i) *The ψt-object that contains a spel o is exactly the t-level set of the connectedness map for o.*

(ii) *If c is in the t-level set of the connectedness map for o, then the t-level set of the connectedness map for c is the same as the t-level set of the connectedness map for o.*

We can restate this result as follows. First, we can find all fuzzy objects that contain a given spel by generating the connectedness map for that spel and then thresholding this map at various levels. Second, this procedure is robust: if, instead of finding the connectedness map for o and thresholding at t to get a fuzzy object, we find the connectedness map for any other element of this fuzzy object and threshold that at t, then we end up with exactly the same fuzzy object. In view of this, it is desirable to find an efficient algorithm which, **given** a fuzzy spel affinity ψ in a digital space (V, π) with a finite V and an $o \in V$, **finds** the connectedness map for o.

2. ALGORITHMS FOR FINDING CONNECTEDNESS MAPS

From now on we assume that V is finite, and that $\psi(c, d) = 0$ if c and d are distinct but not proto-adjacent spels. The first assumption is necessary for our algorithms to terminate. The second assumption allows us to simplify the description of our algorithms, but most of what follows would be true even without it.

The design strategy that has been adopted in the literature on fuzzy segmentation [3, 10, 11] in answer to the need stated at the end of the last section is based on the principle of *Dynamic Programming* [1]. Specifically, the following *Dynamic Program for Fuzzy Objects* has been used.

Dynamic Program for Fuzzy Objects

Auxiliary Data Structures: a spel queue O, and
a real-valued array f with one element $f(c)$ for each spel c.

(1) Initialization:
  a. Put o into O.
  b. Set $f(o) = 1$, and set $f(c) = 0$ if $c \neq o$.
(2) Remove an element d from O. For each spel c that is proto-adjacent to d, do the following:
  a. Set $v = \min\{f(d), \psi(c, d)\}$.
  b. If $v > f(c)$, then
    - Put c into O.
    - Set $f(c) = v$.

(3) Check if O is empty.
If it is, STOP.
If it is not, go back to step (2).

The rationale for step (2)b is that if $v > f(c)$ then we have discovered a chain from o to c that is stronger than any previously discovered chain from o to c; we put c in O so that extensions of the newly discovered chain will be considered. Essentially the same algorithm is implemented in the software system 3DVIEWNIX [9]; the algorithm has successfully segmented a wide variety of medical images [10, 11]. It has been found to be an efficacious, robust and acceptably efficient technique, which can provide high quality segmented pictures in spite of the presence of shading and noise; the practitioners seem to be quite satisfied with its performance. Nevertheless, it occurred to us that there is a possibility of replacing this algorithm by one which is significantly more efficient.

One possibility of improvement is offered by the use of so-called *greedy algorithms* [1]. In particular, the earlier observation that a digital space with a finite V is essentially a connected graph suggests that some known-to-be-efficient graph algorithms may well be applicable here. Observing further that we may consider the cost of the arc (c, d) to be $1 - \psi(c, d)$, we see that there is a possibility of adapting algorithms which find paths of lowest cost to our problem.

One such algorithm which is particular near in its description to the Dynamic Program for Fuzzy Objects is *Dijkstra's algorithm* [1]. To obtain a version of this algorithm that solves our problem we need to make only two changes to the Dynamic Program for Fuzzy Objects: make O a set rather than a queue, and replace the first sentence of step (2) by "Remove an element d from O for which $f(d)$ is maximal." (Since O is now a set, in step (2)b, if c is already in O, then "put c into O" is an empty action; but we still need to update $f(c)$.) An important effect of these changes is that spels that have been removed from O are never put into O again. As opposed to this, the Dynamic Program for Fuzzy Objects may find a stronger chain to d after it has been removed from O (once or repeatedly), in which case subchains starting from d have to be reinvestigated. This is the reason why Dijkstra's algorithm has the potential of being faster than the Dynamic Program for Fuzzy Objects. However, there is a price to be paid: each time we execute step (2) we must find an element d in O for which $f(d)$ is maximal.

In most applications the number of spels proto-adjacent to a given spel is bounded by a small integer (six, in the case of the above example with hexagonal spels). As described on p. 530 of [1], in such a case one can use a binary heap implementation of O to achieve an $O(|V| \lg |V|)$ running time. We have been able to prove that even in such cases the worst-case running time of the Dynamic Program for Fuzzy Objects is $\Theta(|V|^2)$. More importantly from the point of view of practical applications, we demonstrate below that Dijkstra's algorithm performs much faster even on pictures of quite limited size.

Another greedy algorithm that we have investigated is *Prim's algorithm* [1] for finding a minimal spanning tree. This is because it can be shown that, if we consider the cost of each arc (c, d) to be $1 - \psi(c, d)$, then in any minimal spanning tree the unique path between any two spels is a chain of maximal strength. The performance of this algorithm was found to be very similar to that of Dijkstra's algorithm.

3. APPLICATION TO SEGMENTATION

One of the beauties of fuzzy segmentation is that in many applications an appropriate fuzzy spel affinity can be automatically created by a computer program, based on some minimal information supplied by a user. It is easiest to demonstrate this with an example.

Consider Figure 1. The leftmost image in this figure is a real-valued picture defined for a V consisting of regular hexagons which are inside a large hexagon (with 30 spels on each side). The rectangular region in the upper half in which the brightness increases slowly from left to right cannot be segmented by thresholding; no choice of threshold would produce a much better result than the binary picture to the right of it. (We chose to use hexagonal pixels partly because the previous papers reporting on fuzzy segmentation [4, 10, 11] illustrated its use only on pictures with square pixels, and we wished to demonstrate the generality of the underlying concepts by choosing pixels of a different shape. However, there are actually many reasons to prefer hexagonal pixels to square pixels; see Chapter 2 of [3] for a general discussion and [7] for why such pixels are advantageous in pattern analysis.)

The automation of finding an appropriate fuzzy affinity function for segmentation of such pictures depends on the following observation: even though a user may not be able to describe the precise nature of the difference between the region of interest and its background in the leftmost image of Figure 1, it is easy to identify some spels which are definitely in that region. We can compute some statistics of the spels that are identified, and then the fuzzy spel affinity can be automatically defined on the basis of such information.

To demonstrate this on our example, let us assume (as is the case here and as is also the case in many applications) that the important distinguishing characteristics of regions have to do with the real values assigned to spels in them and also with the likely differences of these values between adjacent spels. Given a real-valued picture (V, π, f), we select the fuzzy spel affinity ψ such that, for $c \neq d$,

$$\psi(c,d) = \begin{cases} 0, & \text{if } (c,d) \notin \pi, \\ \frac{1}{2}[g_1(f(c)+f(d)) + g_2(|f(c)-f(d)|)], & \text{otherwise,} \end{cases} \tag{4}$$

where, for $i \in \{1,2\}$,

$$g_i(x) = e^{-\frac{(x-m_i)^2}{2\sigma_i^2}}. \tag{5}$$

It is easy to check that this ψ is indeed a fuzzy spel affinity on (V, π). Appropriate values of the m_i and σ_i can be obtained as follows. The user identifies some regions in the real-valued

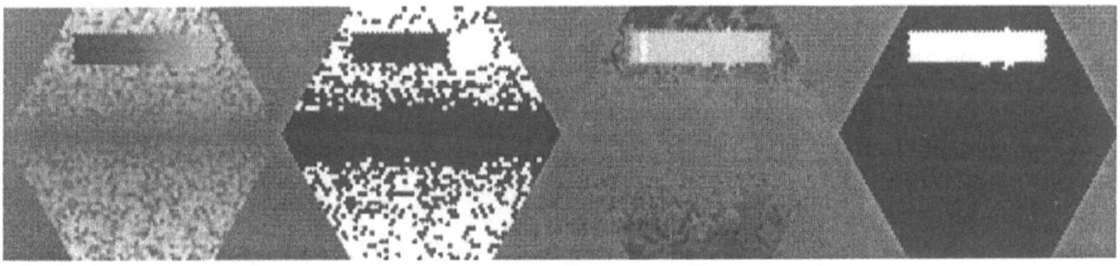

Figure 1. Example of fuzzy segmentation. From left to right: a real-valued picture, a binary picture obtained by thresholding, a connectedness map, a binary picture obtained by fuzzy segmentation.

picture which definitely lie in the object that should be segmented out from its background (such as regions containing only heart muscle in a CT image). Then m_1 and σ_1 can be defined to be the mean and standard deviation, respectively, of $f(c) + f(d)$ over all proto-adjacent spels c and d in the identified regions and m_2 and σ_2 can be defined to be the mean and standard deviation, respectively, of $|f(c) - f(d)|$ over all proto-adjacent spels c and d in the identified regions. This implies that for any pair of proto-adjacent spels c and d, their fuzzy spel affinity will be large if both $f(c) + f(d)$ and $|f(c) - f(d)|$ have values that are typical of the identified regions and will be low if neither $f(c)+f(d)$ nor $|f(c) - f(d)|$ has a value typical of the identified regions. In the programs which produced Figure 1, the regions were defined to consist of a hexagonally-shaped pixel selected by the user and the six pixels adjacent to it. The user was asked to select two such pixels, providing us with a total of 24 pairs of proto-adjacent spels in the identified regions (of seven spels each) to calculate the m_i and σ_i. (This is, of course, only one of many reasonable choices of fuzzy spel affinity; for alternatives see the ideas presented in [5, 6].)

The third image of Figure 1 is the connectedness map produced by Dijkstra's algorithm when the two pixels provided by the user were near the two ends the rectangular region in the upper half. The brightest pixel is the o of the algorithm, which is also one of the two pixels identified by the user. The rightmost binary picture of Figure 1 is obtained by thresholding the connectedness map. It is a fuzzy object that is a much better approximation of the rectangular region than can be obtained by thresholding the original real-valued picture.

4. EXPERIMENTAL COMPARISON

In our experimental comparison we used five basic images, each digitized four different ways. One of the basic images is illustrated in Figure 1; the other four are shown in Figure 2. In these figures the images are digitized so that there are 30 hexagonal pixels on each edge; in the other digitizations the numbers of hexagonal pixels on each edge were 40, 50, and 60. On each of the 20 pictures each of the algorithms was run 49 times using all possible pairs of pixels from a regular sampling of the picture. In Table 1 we report on the timings. Since the major influence on the running time of each algorithm was the number of spels, the numbers for each algorithm in Table 1 are summed times across the five images (digitized in the same way). Since all algorithms find the same connectedness maps, there is no difference in the quality of segmentations obtained by them; this is why they are compared only in terms of their CPU time requirements. (The memory requirements of the Dijkstra's and Prim's algorithms are essentially identical and are never much greater than that of the Dynamic Program for Fuzzy Objects.)

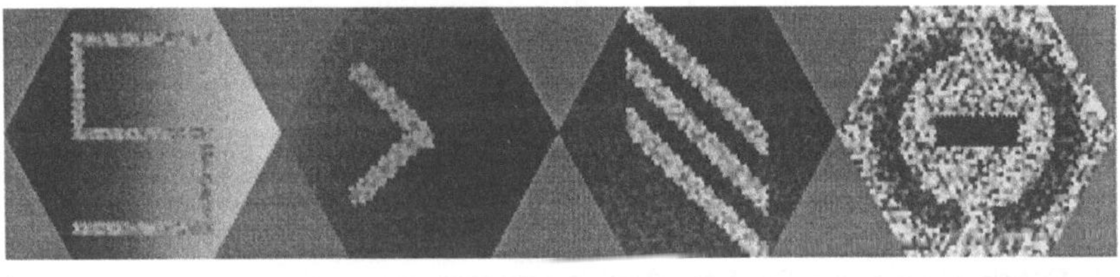

Figure 2. Four real-valued pictures used in the experimental study.

$\|V\|$	**DP**	**DA**	**PA**	**DP / DA**
2,611	247	37	36	6.7
4,681	472	67	65	7.0
7,351	837	110	107	7.6
10,621	1,350	164	163	8.2

Table 1. Total CPU time in seconds of the algorithms on five images (digitized so that the number of spels is as indicated in the left column) with 49 runs on each picture (**DP**: Dynamic Program for Fuzzy Objects, **DA**: Dijkstra's algorithm, **PA**: Prim's algorithm).

We see from the table that for our test images there is no significant difference between Dijkstra's and Prim's algorithms, but they are both several times more efficient than the Dynamic Program for Fuzzy Objects. We also see that the superiority of Dijkstra's and Prim's algorithms increases with the number of spels, but not as quickly as the theoretical worst-case running times might suggest. (If we used an affinity function that was less expensive to compute, then the superiority of Dijkstra's and Prim's algorithms probably would not be as great.) Since in many applications [10, 11] the number of spels can be in the order of millions, we expect the running time to be reduced by more than an order of magnitude when either of the greedy algorithms is used instead of the Dynamic Program for Fuzzy Objects.

We illustrate in Figure 3 the performance of fuzzy segmentation on a real image. We see that the brain can be segmented out more efficaciously in this computed tomography image of a human head by fuzzy segmentation than by thresholding. The timings of the different algorithms on this image are similar to those reported in the table above.

5. DISCUSSION

The examples reported above together with those reported in [10, 11] show that fuzzy segmentation is an effective approach. Nevertheless, just as all other segmentation procedures, it is not universally applicable. For example, if the region of interest is separated from another region of similar characteristics by a narrow wall, then noise in the image may cause a break in this wall and make the two regions "leak" into each other. This is illustrated in the attempt to segment out a cardiac left ventricle in an MRI image in [4]. Nevertheless, it is also shown

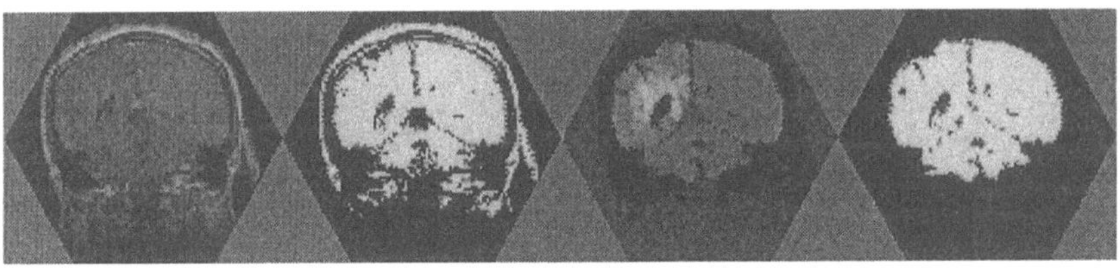

Figure 3. Example of fuzzy segmentation on an image obtained from a computed tomography scan of a patient. From left to right: the real-valued picture (10,621 pixels), a binary picture obtained by thresholding which attempts to identify the brain, a connectedness map obtained by specifying two points in the brain, a binary picture of the brain region obtained by fuzzy segmentation.

there that a correct segmentation can be achieved when a "deformable model" is combined with the fuzzy affinity concepts. In the rest of this discussion we concentrate on the relative capabilities of the various algorithms for fuzzy segmentation.

An advantage of Prim's algorithm over the other two is that once an minimal spanning tree is found, it can be used to calculate the fuzzy connectedness between an arbitrary pair of spels at very little cost. However, since regions other than the one which is our current interest should be defined by their own spel affinities, this observation may be of limited practical use. It may be applicable when there are two or more objects with the same characteristics in the data set (such as the two kidneys). Then the minimal spanning tree can be used to inexpensively recalculate the connectedness maps with respect to a spel in each of the objects.

A simple alteration of any of the algorithms allows us to recover, for any spel c, a chain of maximal strength from c to o. This can have useful applications: it can be used to find a path entirely within a region between two user-selected points in that region; see Figure 4.

Typically there will be many strongest chains between any two specified spels. It may be desirable in this case to select one among these which is optimal with respect to some secondary criterion. For example, we might try to find (among the strongest chains) a chain for which the product of strengths of the links is as large as possible. (Note that if all the links have the same strength and this common strength is less than 1, this secondary criterion aims for the shortest chain.) We do not have an efficient algorithm which is guaranteed to find such a chain, but both the Dynamic Program for Fuzzy Objects and Dijkstra's algorithm can easily be adapted to find an approximation to it. We just keep a record, for each spel c that has been visited, of the product of the strengths of links for the chain from o to c that is "best so far," and we modify step (2) so that when $v = f(c)$ it puts c into O if the new chain to c has a higher link-strength product than the previously best chain to c. (In the case of Dijkstra's algorithm, the heap representation of O also needs to take into consideration the secondary criterion.) We have implemented this option as well; in fact, Figure 4 was produced using it. We have found that the cost of both algorithms goes up, but while for Dijkstra's algorithm the increase is only 50%, the Dynamic Program for Fuzzy Objects becomes three to four times more expensive. Also, the chain output of Dijkstra's

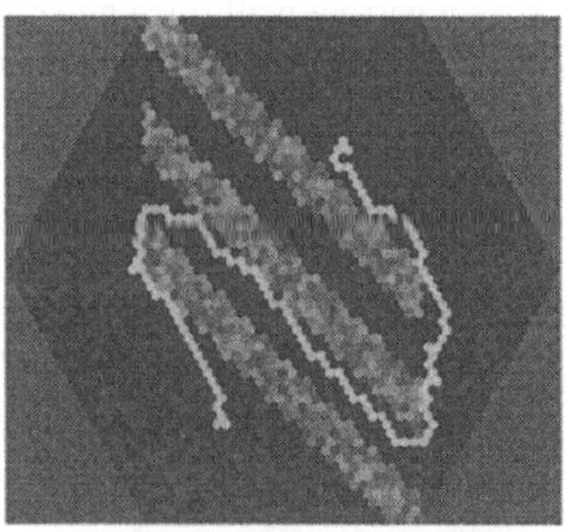

Figure 4. The user points at two hexagonal pixels of the real-valued picture. Based on these, a fuzzy spel affinity is calculated as explained in the text. The indicated chain is a strongest possible chain (for the calculated fuzzy spel affinity) between the two user-selected pixels. It has been generated using a version of Dijkstra's algorithms that also tries to optimize with respect to a secondary criterion, as explained in the text.

algorithm will always be at least as good with respect to the secondary criterion as the chain output by the Dynamic Program for Fuzzy Objects (but will sometimes be better).

Finally, we note that if our aim is not to get a fuzzy segmentation, but only to find the strongest chain between two given spels c and d, then we need not compute a connectedness map for the entire image. We can just interleave two instances of Dijkstra's algorithm which start at c and d respectively, and stop both instances as soon as the two connectedness maps meet at any spel. If s is the spel where the two maps meet, then it is not hard to prove that a strongest chain from c to d is obtained when we combine the chains from each of c and d to s that have been found by the two instances of Dijkstra's algorithm.

In conclusion, the two greedy algorithms are clearly superior to the currently used Dynamic Program for Fuzzy Objects in the fuzzy segmentation process.

ACKNOWLEDGMENTS

This research has been supported by NIH Grant HL28432 (BMC and GTH), NSF Grant DMS96122077 (GTH), and CAPES-BRASILIA-BRAZIL (BMC). The authors are grateful to Eric Tsai and Samuel Matej for programs which were incorporated into the final package used in our experiments and to Michel Habib for suggesting the use of optimal spanning trees.

REFERENCES

[1] T.H. Cormen, C.E. Leiserson, and R.L. Rivest. *Introduction to Algorithms*. MIT Press, Cambridge, MA, 1990.

[2] F. Harary. *Graph Theory*. Addison–Wesley Publ. Co., Reading, MA, 1969.

[3] G.T. Herman. *Geometry of Digital Spaces*. Birkhauser Boston, Cambridge, MA, 1998.

[4] T.N. Jones and D.N. Metaxas. Segmentation using deformable models with affinity-based localization. In J. Troccaz, E. Grimson, and R. Mösges, editors, *Proc. CVRMed/MRCAS'97*, volume 1205 of *Lecture Notes in Computer Science*, pages 53–62. Springer-Verlag, Berlin, 1997.

[5] A. Kandel. *Fuzzy Techniques in Pattern Recognition*. John Wiley & Sons, New York, 1982.

[6] S.K. Pal and D.K.D. Majumder. *Fuzzy Mathematical Approach to Pattern Recognition*. Wiley Eastern Ltd., New Delhi, 1986.

[7] K. Preston, Jr. Multidimensional logical transforms. *IEEE Trans. Pattern Anal. Mach. Intell.*, 5:539–554, 1983.

[8] A. Rosenfeld. Fuzzy digital topology. *Inform. and Control*, 40:76–87, 1979.

[9] J.K. Udupa, D. Odhner, S. Samarasekera, R. Goncalves, K. Iyer, K. Venugopal, and S. Furuie. 3DVIEWNIX: An open, transportable, multidimensional, multimodality, multiparametric imaging software system. *Proc. SPIE*, 2164:58–73, 1994.

[10] J.K. Udupa and S. Samarasekera. Fuzzy connectedness and object definition: Theory, algorithms and applications in image segmentation. *Graph. Models Image Proc.*, 58:246–261, 1996.

[11] J.K. Udupa, L. Wei, S. Samarasekera, Y. Miki, M.A. van Buchem, and R.I. Grossman. Multiple sclerosis lesion quantification using fuzzy-connectedness principles. *IEEE Trans. Med. Imag.*, 16:598–609, 1997.

NEURAL AND EVOLUTIONARY COMPUTING

UNSUPERVISED LEARNING WITHOUT OVERFITTING: EMPIRICAL RISK APPROXIMATION AS AN INDUCTION PRINCIPLE FOR RELIABLE CLUSTERING

Joachim M. Buhmann, Institut für Informatik III, Universität Bonn, Germany
Marcus Held, Institut für Informatik III, Universität Bonn, Germany

ABSTRACT

Unsupervised learning algorithms are designed to extract structure from data samples on the basis of a cost function for structures. For a reliable and robust inference process, the unsupervised learning algorithm has to guarantee that the extracted structures are typical for the data source. In particular, it has to reject all structures where the inference is dominated by the arbitrariness of the sample noise and which, consequently, can be characterized as overfitting in unsupervised learning. This paper summarizes an inference principle called *Empirical Risk Approximation* which allows us to quantitatively measure the overfitting effect and to derive a criterion as a saveguard against it. The crucial condition for learning is met if (i) the empirical risk of learning uniformly converges towards the expected risk and if (ii) the hypothesis class retains a minimal variety for consistent inference. Parameter selection of learnable data structures is demonstrated for the case of k-means clustering and Monte Carlo simulations are presented to support the selection principle.

1 PHILOSOPHY OF UNSUPERVISED LEARNING

Learning algorithms are designed to extract structure from data. Two classes of algorithms have been widely discussed in the literature – **supervised** and **unsupervised learning**. The distinction between the two classes depends on supervision or teacher information which is either available to the learning algorithm or missing in the learning process. This paper describes a statistical learning theory of unsupervised learning. We summarize an induction principle for unsupervised learning which is refered to as *Empirical Risk Approximation* [1]. This principle is based on the optimization of a quality functional for structures in data and, most importantly, it contains a safeguard against overfitting of structure to the noise in a sample set. The extracted structure of the data is encoded by a loss function and it is assumed to produce a learning risk below a predefined risk threshold. This induction principle is summarized by the following two inference steps:

1. *Define a hypothesis class containing loss functions which evaluate candidate structures of the data and which measure their quality. Control the complexity of the hypothesis class by an upper bound on the costs.*

2. *Select an arbitrary loss function from the smallest subset which still guarantees consistent learning (in the sense of Statistical Learning Theory).*

The reader should note that the learning algorithm has to return a structure with costs *bounded* by a preselected cost threshold, but it is not required to return the structure with *minimal empirical risk* as in Vapnik's "Empirical Risk Minimization" induction principle for classification and regression [2]. All structures in the data with risk smaller than the selected risk bound are considered to be equivalent in the approximation process without further distinction. Various cases of unsupervised learning algorithms are discussed in the literature with emphasis on the optimization aspect, i.e., data clustering or vector quantization, self-organizing maps, principal or independent component analysis and principal curves, projection pursuit or algorithms for relational data as multidimensional scaling and pairwise clustering and histogram based clustering methods.

How can we select a loss function from a hypothesis class with desired approximation quality or, equivalently, find a structure with bounded costs? The nested sequence of hypothesis classes suggests a tracking strategy of solutions which are elements of smaller and smaller hypothesis classes in that sequence. The sequential sampling can be implemented by solution tracking, i.e., admissible solutions are incrementally improved by gradient descent if the process samples from a subset with smaller risk bound than in the previous sampling step. Candidate procedure for the sampling of structures from the hypothesis class are stochastic search techniques or continuation methods like simulated or deterministic annealing, although the theory does not refer to any particular learning algorithm.

The general framework of *Empirical Risk Approximation* and its mathematical formulation is presented in Sec. 2, whereas a more detailed discussion can be found in [1]. This theory of unsupervised learning is applied to the case of central clustering in Sec. 3.

2 MATHEMATICAL FRAMEWORK FOR UNSUPERVISED LEARNING

The data samples $\mathcal{X} = \{\mathbf{x}_i \in \Omega : \Omega \subset \mathbf{R}^d,\ 1 \le i \le l\}$ which have to be analysed by the unsupervised learning algorithm are elements of a suitable d-dimensional Euclidian space. The data are distributed according to a measure μ which is assumed to be known for the analysis.

A mathematically precise statement of the *Empirical Risk Approximation* induction principle requires several definitions which formalize the notion of searching for structure in the data. The quality of structures extracted from the data set $\mathcal{X}$ is evaluated by a learning cost function

$$\hat{\mathcal{R}}(\alpha; \mathcal{X}) = \frac{1}{l} \sum_{i=1}^{l} \mathbf{h}(\mathbf{x}_i; \alpha). \tag{1}$$

$\hat{\mathcal{R}}(\alpha; \mathcal{X})$ denotes the **empirical risk** of learning a structure α for an i.i.d. sample set $\mathcal{X}$. The function $\mathbf{h}(\mathbf{x}; \alpha)$ is known as **loss function** in statistics. It measures the costs for processing a generic datum $\mathbf{x}$ and often corresponds to the negative log-likelihood of a stochastic model. For example in vector quantization, the loss function quantifies what the costs are to assign a data point $\mathbf{x}$ to a particular prototype or codebook vector. Each value $\alpha \in \Lambda$ parametrizes an individual loss functions with Λ denoting the parameter set. The parameter α characterizes the different structures of the data set which are hypothetically considered candidate structures in the learning process and which have to be validated. Statistical learning theory distinguishes between different classes of loss functions, i.e., $0-1$ functions in classification problems, bounded functions and unbounded non-negative functions in regression problems. This paper is concerned with the class of *unbounded non-negative functions* since we are particularly interested in polynomially increasing loss function ($\mathcal{O}(\|\mathbf{x}\|^p)$) as they occur in vector quantization. Note that the quality measure $\hat{\mathcal{R}}(\alpha; \mathcal{X})$ depends on the i.i.d. data set $\mathcal{X}$ and, therefore, is itself a random variable. The relevant quality measure for unsupervised learning, however, is the expectation value of this random variable, known as the **expected risk** of learning

$$\mathcal{R}(\alpha) = \int_{\Omega} \mathbf{h}(\mathbf{x}; \alpha)\, d\mu(\mathbf{x}). \tag{2}$$

While minima of $\hat{\mathcal{R}}(\alpha; \mathcal{X})$ or solutions with bounded empirical risk are influenced by fluctuations in the samples, it is the expected risk $\mathcal{R}(\alpha)$ which completely assesses the quality of learning results in a sound probabilistic fashion. The distribution μ is assumed to be known in the following analysis and it has to decay sufficiently fast such that all rth moments ($r > 2$) of the loss function $\mathbf{h}(\mathbf{x};\alpha)$ are bounded by $\mathbf{E}_\mu\{|\mathbf{h}(\mathbf{x};\alpha) - \mathcal{R}(\alpha)|^r\} \leq r!\tau^{r-2}\mathbf{V}_\mu\{\mathbf{h}(\mathbf{x};\alpha)\}$, $\forall\alpha \in \Lambda$. $\mathbf{E}_\mu\{.\}$ and $\mathbf{V}_\mu\{.\}$ denote expectation and variance of a random variable, respectively. τ is a distribution dependent constant. The moment constraint on the distribution μ holds for all distributions with exponentially fast decaying tails which include all distributions with finite support.

Empirical Risk Approximation is an induction principle which requires the learning algorithm to sample from the smallest consistently learnable subset of the hypothesis class. In the following, the hypothesis class $\mathcal{H}$ contains all loss functions $\mathbf{h}(\mathbf{x};\alpha), \alpha \in \Lambda$ and the subsets of risk bounded loss functions $\mathcal{H}_{\mathcal{R}^*}$ are defined as

$$\mathcal{H}_{\mathcal{R}^*} \quad = \quad \{\mathbf{h}(\mathbf{x};\alpha) : \alpha \in \Lambda \ \wedge \ \mathcal{R}(\alpha) \leq \mathcal{R}^*\}. \tag{3}$$

The subsets $\mathcal{H}_{\mathcal{R}^*}$ are obviously nested since $\mathcal{H}_{\mathcal{R}_1^*} \subseteq \mathcal{H}_{\mathcal{R}_2^*} \subseteq \cdots \subseteq \mathcal{H}$ for $\mathcal{R}_1^* \leq \mathcal{R}_2^* \leq \cdots \leq \infty$ and $\mathcal{H} = \lim_{\mathcal{R}^*\to\infty} \mathcal{H}_{\mathcal{R}^*}$. $\mathcal{R}^*$ induces a structure on the hypothesis class in the sense of Vapnik's "Structural Risk" and essentially controls the complexity of the hypothesis class.

The *Empirical Risk Approximation* induction principle requires to define a nested sequence of hypothesis classes with bounded expected risk and to sample from the hypothesis class with the desired approximation quality. Algorithmically, however, we select the loss function according to the bounded empirical risk $\hat{\mathcal{R}}(\alpha;\mathcal{X}) \leq \mathcal{R}^*$. This induction principle is consistent if a bounded empirical risk implies in the asymptotic limit that the loss function has bounded expected risk $\mathcal{R}(\alpha) \leq \mathcal{R}^*$ and, therefore, is an element of the hypothesis class $\mathcal{H}_{\mathcal{R}^*}$, i.e.,

$$\forall\alpha \in \Lambda \ \lim_{l\to\infty} \hat{\mathcal{R}}(\alpha;\mathcal{X}) \leq \mathcal{R}^* \Longrightarrow \mathbf{h}(\mathbf{x};\alpha) \in \mathcal{H}_{\mathcal{R}^*}. \tag{4}$$

This implication essentially states that the expected risk asymptotically does not exceed the risk bound ($\mathcal{R}(\alpha) \leq \mathcal{R}^*$) and, therefore, the inferred structure α is an approximation of the optimal data structure with risk not worse than $\mathcal{R}^*$. The consistency assumption (4) for *Empirical Risk Approximation* holds if the empirical risk uniformly converges towards the expected risk

$$\lim_{l\to\infty} \mathbf{P}\left\{\sup_{\alpha\in\Lambda_\epsilon} \frac{|\mathcal{R}(\alpha) - \hat{\mathcal{R}}(\alpha;\mathcal{X})|}{\sqrt{\mathbf{V}_\mu\{\mathbf{h}(\mathbf{x};\alpha)\}}} > \epsilon\right\} = 0, \quad \forall\epsilon > 0, \tag{5}$$

where Λ_ϵ denotes the hypothesis set of ϵ distinguishable structures. Λ_ϵ defines an ϵ-net $\mathcal{H}_{\epsilon,\mathcal{R}^*}$ on the set of loss functions $\mathcal{H}_{\mathcal{R}^*}$ or coarsens the hypothesis class with an ϵ-separated set if there does not exist a finite ϵ-net for $\mathcal{H}_{\mathcal{R}^*}$. Using results from the theory of empirical processes the probability of an ϵ–deviation of empirical risk from expected risk can be bounded by Bernstein's inequality ([3], Lemma 2.2.11)

$$\mathbf{P}\left\{\sup_{\alpha\in\Lambda_\epsilon} \frac{|\mathcal{R}(\alpha) - \hat{\mathcal{R}}(\alpha;\mathcal{X})|}{\sqrt{\mathbf{V}_\mu\{\mathbf{h}(\mathbf{x};\alpha)\}}} > \epsilon\right\} \ \leq \ 2|\mathcal{H}_\epsilon| \exp\left(-\frac{l\epsilon^2}{2(1+\tau\epsilon/\sigma_{\min})}\right) \equiv \delta. \tag{6}$$

The minimal variance of all loss functions is denoted by $\sigma_{\min}^2 = \inf_{\alpha\in\Lambda_\epsilon} \mathbf{V}_\mu\{\mathbf{h}(\mathbf{x};\alpha)\}$. $|\mathcal{H}_\epsilon|$ denotes the cardinality of an ϵ-net constructed for the hypothesis class $\mathcal{H}_{\mathcal{R}^*}$ under the assumption of the measure μ. The confidence level δ limits the probability of large deviations [1].

The large deviation inequality weighs two competing effects in the learning problem, i.e., the probability of a large deviation exponentially decreases with growing sample size l, whereas a large deviation becomes increasingly likely with growing cardinality of the hypothesis class. A compromise between both effects determines how reliable an estimate actually is for a given data set $\mathcal{X}$. The sample complexity $l_0(\epsilon, \delta)$ is defined as the necessary number of training points to guarantee that ϵ-large deviations of the empirical risk from the expected risk relative to the variance occur with probability not larger than δ. According to Eq. (6) the sample complexity $l_0(\epsilon, \delta)$ is defined by

$$l_0 = \frac{2}{\epsilon^2}\left(1 + \frac{\tau\epsilon}{\sigma_{\min}}\right)\left(\log|\mathcal{H}_\epsilon| + \log\frac{2}{\delta}\right). \tag{7}$$

Equation (7) effectively limits the accuracy of *Empirical Risk Approximation* . A selected accuracy ϵ for the ERA induction principle and a predefined confidence value δ require a minimal size l_0 of the data set. Solving Eq. (7) for ϵ yields a lower bound of the achievable accuracy for a given sample set. An obvious strategy to improve this critical accuracy is to decrease the cardinality of the hypothesis class by lowering the risk bound $\mathcal{R}^*$ and sampling from a smaller subset of loss functions. In the extreme case of zero learning, e.g. if $\mathcal{H}_\epsilon$ is a singleton set with exactly one loss function, the log-cardinality of the hypothesis class $\log|\mathcal{H}_\epsilon|$ vanishes.
Is this extreme case achievable and if not, what is the minimal admissible complexity of the hypothesis class $\mathcal{H}_\epsilon$? The cardinality of the hypothesis class is controlled by the risk bound $\mathcal{R}^*$. A minimal value for the risk bound would ensure a minimal size of the hypothesis class $\mathcal{H}_{\epsilon,\mathcal{R}^*}$ which is equivalent to a minimal variety of structures in the data considered in the unsupervised learning task. The second condition of the *Empirical Risk Approximation* principle ensures that all loss functions with ϵ-typical risk should be included in the hypothesis class. Consequently, the large upper deviation with $\hat{\mathcal{R}}(\alpha; \mathcal{X}) \leq \mathcal{R}(\alpha) + \epsilon\sqrt{\mathbf{V}_\mu\{\mathbf{h}(\mathbf{x}; \alpha)\}}$ provides a lower bound for the risk bound $\mathcal{R}^*$. The ERA-principle requires that we randomly select a loss function with the property $\hat{\mathcal{R}}(\alpha; \mathcal{X}) \leq \mathcal{R}^*$. Inserting this constraint yields a minimal admissible value for the loss bound

$$\mathcal{R}^* > \min_{\alpha\in\Lambda_\epsilon}\left(\mathcal{R}(\alpha) + \epsilon\sqrt{\mathbf{V}_\mu\{\mathbf{h}(\mathbf{x}; \alpha)\}}\right). \tag{8}$$

Violations of this inequality (8) deprive the inference algorithm of possible hypotheses which cannot be ruled out on the basis of the samples and which, therefore, should be considered as candidate structures in the data. In general, $\mathcal{R}^*$ is larger than the minimal expected risk. The lower bound on $\mathcal{R}^*$ protects the unsupervised learning algorithm against attempts of too restricted inference and serves as a built–in self–consistency principle.
The two bounds (7) and (8) are coupled by the considered hypothesis class $\mathcal{H}_\epsilon$. A decrease of ϵ with fixed confidence δ increases the number of required samples. On the other hand, an increasing number of samples allows us to reduce ϵ which, as a consequence, reduces the number of candidate structures in $\mathcal{H}_\epsilon$.

3 A STATISTICAL LEARNING THEORY OF CENTRAL CLUSTERING

As an important example of the general framework for unsupervised learning, a statistical theory is developed in this section for central clustering, i.e., for the problem to partition a data set $\mathcal{X}$ into k different regions. A partition is represented by a mapping $m : \mathbf{R}^d \rightarrow \{1, \ldots, k\}$ which assigns a partition label $\nu \in \{1, \ldots, k\}$ to each data vector $\mathbf{x}_i$, i.e., $m(\mathbf{x}_i) = \nu$. The quality of a partition is measured by the sum of squared distances between data points which are assigned to the same partition, i.e., the empirical cost function $\hat{\mathcal{R}}(m; \mathcal{X})$ is given by

$$\hat{\mathcal{R}}(m; \mathcal{X}) = \frac{1}{l}\sum_{i=1}^{l}\frac{\sum_{j=1}^{l}\Delta_{m(\mathbf{x}_i),m(\mathbf{x}_j)}\|\mathbf{x}_i - \mathbf{x}_j\|^2}{\sum_{j=1}^{l}\Delta_{m(\mathbf{x}_i),m(\mathbf{x}_j)}}. \tag{9}$$

$\Delta_{i,j} = 1\,(0)$, if $i = j\ (i \neq j)$ denotes the Kronecker delta. This criterion favors clusters with high cluster compactness.

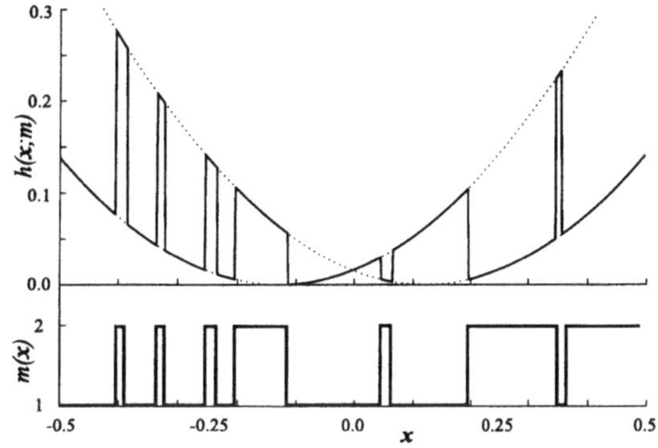

Figure 1: A particular loss function for two means located at $\mathbf{x}_{1,2} = \pm 0.125$ is shown as the bold solid line which is bounded by the two parabolas depicted by dotted lines. The respective assignment mapping jumps between the values 1 and 2.

The expected risk $\mathcal{R}(m)$ and the loss function $\mathbf{h}(\mathbf{x}; m)$ of k-means clustering are defined by (2) and

$$\mathbf{h}(\mathbf{x}; m) = \frac{\int_\Omega \|\mathbf{x}-\mathbf{z}\|^2 \Delta_{m(\mathbf{x}),m(\mathbf{z})}\, d\mu(\mathbf{z})}{\int_\Omega \Delta_{m(\mathbf{x}),m(\mathbf{z})}\, d\mu(\mathbf{z})} \equiv \|\mathbf{x} - \mathbf{y}_{m(\mathbf{x})}\|^2 \tag{10}$$

with the k means

$$\mathbf{y}_\nu = \frac{\int_\Omega \mathbf{z}\, \Delta_{\nu,m(\mathbf{z})}\, d\mu(\mathbf{z})}{\int_\Omega \Delta_{\nu,m(\mathbf{z})}\, d\mu(\mathbf{z})} \qquad \nu \in \{1, \ldots, k\}. \tag{11}$$

A loss function for two means is depicted in Fig. 1. The risk bounded hypothesis class of k–means clustering is defined as $\mathcal{H}_{\mathcal{R}^*} = \{\mathbf{h}(\mathbf{x}; m) : m(\mathbf{x}) \text{ is a } k \text{ partition } \wedge\ \mathcal{R}(m) \leq \mathcal{R}^*\}$. The complexity of the hypothesis class is determined by the μ-measurable k-partitions of Ω. $\mathcal{H}$ cannot be covered by a finite ϵ-cover if μ-measurability is the only restriction on m. We, therefore, have to introduce an appropriate regularization of the function set $\mathcal{H}$. A natural choice is to quantize the data space $\Omega = \cup_{i=1}^{\tilde{n}} \Omega_i$ into $\tilde{n}$ cells Ω_i and to require constant assignments of data to clusters within a cell, i.e., $\forall \mathbf{x} \in \Omega_i\ m(\mathbf{x}) = m_i,\ 1 \leq i \leq \tilde{n}$.

Other learning theoretical approaches to k-means clustering assume that data are always assigned to the closest mean [4, 5, 6]. A clustering algorithm without this constraint on data assignments can be found in [7], i.e., algorithm III with hard assignments selected according to predefined probabilities comes close in spirit to a randomized selection of a loss function from the hypothesis class $\mathcal{H}_{\mathcal{R}^*}$.

How should the cells Ω_i be defined? A natural choice is to quantize the data space in such a way that two loss functions which are identical everywhere except in cell Ω_{i^*} have a $L_1(\mu)$ distance of ϵ if the data are assigned to the two closest clusters, respectively, i.e.,

$$\epsilon \equiv \frac{1}{\sigma_{\min}} \int_{\Omega_{i^*}} \left| \|\mathbf{x} - \mathbf{y}_{i^*}^{\text{2nd}}\|^2 - \|\mathbf{x} - \mathbf{y}_{i^*}^{\text{1st}}\|^2 \right| d\mu(\mathbf{x}). \tag{12}$$

The centroids $\mathbf{y}_i^{\text{1st}}, \mathbf{y}_i^{\text{2nd}}$ are the closest and the second closest centroid of cell Ω_i, being defined by $\int_{\Omega_i} \|\mathbf{x} - \mathbf{y}_i^{\text{1st}}\|^2 \, d\mu(\mathbf{x}) \leq \int_{\Omega_i} \|\mathbf{x} - \mathbf{y}_i^{\text{2nd}}\|^2 \, d\mu(\mathbf{x}) \leq \int_{\Omega_i} \|\mathbf{x} - \mathbf{y}_\nu\|^2 \, d\mu(\mathbf{x}) \;\forall \mathbf{y}_\nu \neq \mathbf{y}_i^{\text{1st}}$. Summation of both sides of (12) yields the number of cells

$$\tilde{n} = \frac{2}{\epsilon \sigma_{\min}} \sum_{i=1}^{\tilde{n}} \int_{\Omega_i} \left| \left(\mathbf{y}_i^{\text{2nd}} - \mathbf{y}_i^{\text{1st}}\right)^{\mathrm{T}} \left(\mathbf{x} - \frac{\mathbf{y}_i^{\text{2nd}} + \mathbf{y}_i^{\text{1st}}}{2}\right) \right| d\mu(\mathbf{x}) \tag{13}$$

Equation (12) quantizes the space in cells analogous to the data partitioning of K-nearest neighbor classifiers. Low data density and small loss lead to large cells, whereas parts of the data space with high density are finely partitioned. The hypothesis class $\mathcal{H}_\epsilon$ which results from the space quantization is finite and can be considered as a regularized version of $\mathcal{H}$. It is defined as $\mathcal{H}_\epsilon = \{\mathbf{h}(\mathbf{x}; m) : \mathcal{R}(m) \leq \mathcal{R}^* \wedge \forall i \, \forall \mathbf{x} \in \Omega_i \; m(\mathbf{x}) = m_i \in \{1, \ldots, k\}\}$.
Other schemes to regularize the hypothesis class $\mathcal{H}$ of all μ-measurable k-partitions of the data space Ω are imaginable, e.g., for distributions with finite support the data space could be uniformly partitioned into cells of size γ yielding the hypothesis class $\mathcal{H}_\gamma$. Loss functions with different assignments in cells with low data density and short distances to the next mean have smaller $L_1(\mu)$ distances than loss functions with high data density and long distances to the next mean. The hypothesis class $\mathcal{H}_\epsilon$ can be considered as an ϵ-net of the class $\mathcal{H}_\gamma$. In this sense $\mathcal{H}_\epsilon$ is the prototypical, coarsened hypothesis class for a variety of different regularization schemes. The probability of large deviations (6) depends on the cardinality of the hypothesis class $|\mathcal{H}_\epsilon|$. This cardinality can be calculated by techniques borrowed from statistical physics. For a large number of cells the following stationary equations are derived [1]

$$\mathbf{y}_\nu = \frac{\sum_{i=1}^{\tilde{n}} \mathbf{P}_{i\nu} \int_{\Omega_i} \mathbf{x} \, d\mu(\mathbf{x})}{\sum_{i=1}^{\tilde{n}} \mathbf{P}_{i\nu} \int_{\Omega_i} d\mu(\mathbf{x})} \quad \text{with } \mathbf{P}_{i\nu} = \frac{\exp\left(-\hat{x}\tilde{n} \int_{\Omega_i} (\mathbf{x} - \mathbf{y}_\nu)^2 \, d\mu(\mathbf{x})\right)}{\sum\limits_{\eta=1}^{k} \exp\left(-\hat{x}\tilde{n} \int_{\Omega_i} (\mathbf{x} - \mathbf{y}_\eta)^2 \, d\mu(\mathbf{x})\right)}, \tag{14}$$

$$\mathcal{R}^* = \sum_{i=1}^{\tilde{n}} \sum_{\nu=1}^{k} \mathbf{P}_{i\nu} \int\limits_{\Omega_i} (\mathbf{x} - \mathbf{y}_\nu)^2 \, d\mu(\mathbf{x}). \tag{15}$$

$\mathbf{P}_{i\nu} = \mathbf{P}\{m_i = \nu\}$ denotes the probability that data in cell i are assigned to cluster ν when a loss function is randomly selected from $\mathcal{H}_\epsilon$. Equation (14) is a probabilistic version of the k-means definition (11). The hard assignment of datum $\mathbf{x}$ to clusters ν encoded by $\Delta_{m(\mathbf{x}),\nu}$ is replaced by the probabilistic assignment $\mathbf{P}_{i\nu}$. It is quite instructive to compare the stationarity equations (14) with the reestimation equations for deterministic annealing of central clustering given a data set $\mathcal{X}$ [8, 9]:

$$\tilde{\mathbf{y}}_\alpha = \frac{\sum_{i=1}^{l} \tilde{\mathbf{P}}_{i\alpha} \mathbf{x}_i}{\sum_{i=1}^{l} \tilde{\mathbf{P}}_{i\alpha}} \quad \text{with } \tilde{\mathbf{P}}_{i\alpha} = \frac{\exp\left(-(\mathbf{x}_i - \mathbf{y}_\alpha)^2 / lT^{\text{comp}}\right)}{\sum_{\nu=1}^{k} \exp\left(-(\mathbf{x}_i - \tilde{\mathbf{y}}_\nu)^2 / lT^{\text{comp}}\right)}. \tag{16}$$

The auxiliary variable $\hat{x} = 1/lT^{\text{comp}}$ corresponds to the inverse computational temperature [8, 9]. $\tilde{\mathbf{P}}_{i\alpha}, \tilde{\mathbf{y}}_\alpha$ are the empirical estimators of the assignment probabilities and the means on the basis of the data set $\mathcal{X}$. Deterministic annealing approaches to probabilistic clustering utilize the inverse temperature as a parameter to control the smoothness of the effective cost function for clustering, i.e., optimization is pursued by gradually reducing the temperature. The relation between the loss bound $\mathcal{R}^*$ and the inverse temperature $\hat{x} = 1/lT^{\text{comp}}$ is established by (15), i.e., $\hat{x}$ can be interpreted as a Lagrange variable to enforce the risk bound. Solutions of (15) are only permitted for $\mathcal{R}^* \leq \int_\Omega \|\mathbf{x}\|^2 \, d\mu(\mathbf{x})$ assigning data all with the same probability $1/k$

to clusters which are all located at the center of mass of the data distribution ($\mathbf{y}_1 = \cdots = \mathbf{y}_k = 0$). Equality in this equation defines a critical point and is related to the phenomenon of phase transition in clustering [8]. Additional phase transitions occur at lower values of $1/\hat{x}$ and indicate that the data set can be partitioned into finer and finer clusters. Figure 2 shows the position of six clusters means for a one-dimensional partitioning problem with a mixture distribution composed of five Gaussians centered at $\mathbf{x}_0 \in \{-2, -1.5, -1, 0, 2\}$. The temperature as a resolution parameter controls the complexity of the partition, e.g., at $T = 0.8$ the clusters $\mathbf{y}_2, \ldots, \mathbf{y}_6$ are all located at $x = -1.1$. For $T < 0.25$ all six clusters are separated.

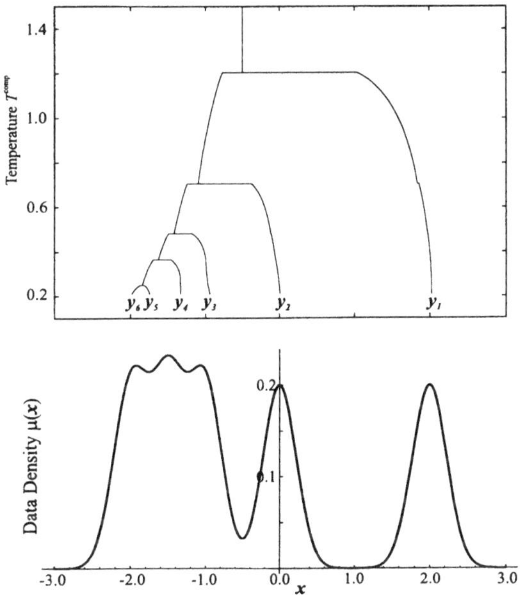

Figure 2: The position of six means $\mathbf{y}_1, \ldots, \mathbf{y}_6$ is shown as a function of the computational temperature. The data distribution μ depicted below is a mixture of five Gaussians with variance 0.05 located at $\mathbf{x}_0 \in \{-2, -1.5, -1, 0, 2\}$.

Neglecting exponentially small terms in $\hat{x}$, the sample complexity l_0 in (7) yields a lower bound for the computational temperature $1/\hat{x}$

$$l_0 T^{\text{comp}} = \frac{1}{\hat{x}} \geq \frac{2\tilde{n}\epsilon\sigma_{\min}}{l_0\, \epsilon^2 - 2\log\frac{2}{\delta}}. \tag{17}$$

The correction $\tau\epsilon/\sigma_{\min}$ has been neglected. Inequality (17) ensures that the hypothesis class $\mathcal{H}_\epsilon$ is not too constraint and that a minimal variety of possible loss functions is considered in the inference process. If we select a too small accuracy value ϵ for a given size of the sample set l then the computational temperature diverges and balances overfitting effects. We like to emphasize the point that *inequality (17) defines a parameter selection criterion for data partitionings*, i.e., it provides a bound on the maximal number of clusters which can be estimated reliably. Lowering the temperature in simulated or deterministic annealing yields more and more clusters by a cascade of phase transitions (see Fig. 2). The ERA induction principle, however, stops this refinement before the extreme of as many clusters as data points is reached

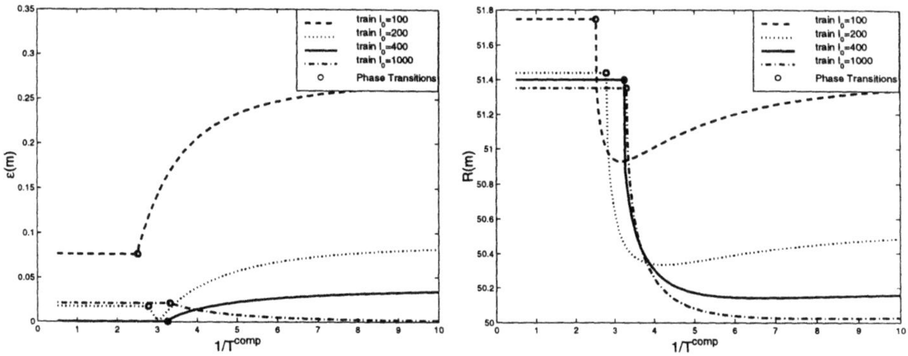

Figure 3: Overfitting effects in four typical learning sequences: $\epsilon(m) = |\mathcal{R}(m) - \hat{\mathcal{R}}(m;\mathcal{X})|/\sqrt{\mathbf{V}_\mu\{\mathbf{h}(\mathbf{x};m)\}}$ (left) and $\mathcal{R}(m)$ of hard partitioning (right) is plotted vs. $1/T^{\mathrm{comp}}$.

since splitting of the data in too small groups is not warranted by the uniform convergence requirement. Too large fluctuations might render unreliable cluster estimates $\mathbf{y}_\alpha$ for small sample sets. The computational temperature acts as a regularization parameter to prevent cluster refinements with overfitting behavior.

Figure 3 demonstrates empirically the predicted small sample size overfitting effect for the central clustering problem. The data source for all experiments is a bimodal mixture of two 50–dimensional Gaussians with unit variance and means $\mu = \pm 1/\sqrt{50}\,(1,\ldots,1)^T$ chosen according to the analysis in [10]. The expected risk $\mathcal{R}(m)$ and its variance $\mathbf{V}_\mu\{\mathbf{h}(\mathbf{x};m)\}$ are approximated by an empirical test set of size 10000. The curves in Figure 3 plot the quantity $\epsilon(m) = |\mathcal{R}(m) - \hat{\mathcal{R}}(m;\mathcal{X})|/\sqrt{\mathbf{V}_\mu\{\mathbf{h}(\mathbf{x};m)\}}$ for a typical assignment function $m(\mathbf{x})$ which has been calculated by deterministic annealing techniques [8]. These curves indicate that the decrease of the computational temperature might yield overfitting, i.e., an increase in the ϵ–deviation between expected risk and empirical risk. In addition, these curves depict cases $l_0 = 100, 400$ where the criterion of large ϵ–deviations discards cluster splits in the case of too small sample size since the two cluster centers are uncorrelated with the means of the source modes [10]. Note that the hard partitioning is defined by the application of the nearest neighbor rule on a set of prototypes given by equation (16). Therefore the inferred hypothesis is indeed a mixture of a set of hypotheses each of which weighted by their plausibility. Or, to turn it the other way around, the result of the deterministic annealing algorithm can be interpreted as an ϵ–typical hypothesis.

Additional experiments are performed to verify the presented theoretical bound for overfitting phenomena in unsupervised learning resp. central clustering by Monte Carlo simulations. For the evaluation of the inferred probabilistic bound (17) extensive simulations of learning on finite sample sizes are necessary. Such Monte Carlo experiments consist of

1. Fix ϵ and the size of the training set l_0.

2. Carry out a number L of experiments with different sample sets each of size l_0.

3. For each inverse temperature $T^{\mathrm{comp}} = 1/\beta$ calculate the fraction of experiments with deviation larger than ϵ.

This fraction will be an estimate for δ and has to be inserted into the (ϵ, δ, l_0)–bound on the critical temperature (17). Note that the unknown values $\tilde{n}$ and $\sigma_{\min}$ always can be estimated via

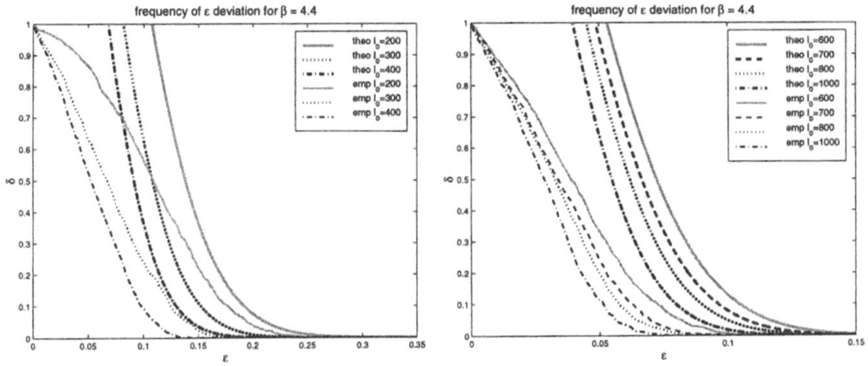

Figure 4: Empirical and theoretical ϵ vs. δ dependencies for different sample sizes and a fixed temperature $\beta = 4.4$ are compared on the basis of 1000 error curves.

Monte Carlo sampling or by analytical means for tractable data distributions. For the generative bimodal distribution utilized in our experiments we estimate $2\tilde{n}\epsilon\sigma_{min} \approx 18.4$ and $\tau \approx 4.3$. Figure 4 indicates that the experiments at least qualitatively support the derived relationship between the overfitting phenomenon and the computational temperature. Note that the estimated empirical values for ϵ are biased towards larger values of $\frac{|\mathcal{R}(m)-\hat{\mathcal{R}}(m;\mathcal{X})|}{\sqrt{\mathbf{V}_{\mu}\{\mathbf{h}(\mathbf{x};m)\}}}$ since we use the mean field solutions in the DA experiments to define the probabilistic partition of the data space.

4 DISCUSSION

The theory of *Empirical Risk Approximation* for unsupervised learning problems extends the highly successful statistical learning theory of supervised learning to a large class of unsupervised learning problems with the respective loss functions. The two conditions that the empirical risk has to uniformly converge towards the expected risk and that all loss functions within an ϵ range of the global risk minimum have to be considered in the inference process limits the complexity of the hypothesis class for a given number of samples. The maximum entropy method which has been widely employed in the deterministic annealing procedure for optimization problems is substantiated by our analysis and it is identified as optimal procedure for large scale problems.

Many unsupervised learning problems are formulated as combinatorial or continuous optimization problems. The presented framework for unsupervised learning also defines a theory of robust algorithm design for noisy combinatorial optimization problems, e.g., minimum flow problems with noisy cost values, process optimization with fluctuating capacities, the traveling salesman problem with fluctuating travel times between cities or scheduling problems with stochastic demands on the process. Robust solutions for all these noisy optimization problems require stability against fluctuations in the problem definition, i.e., solutions have to generalize from one problem instance to an equally likely second instance. Neglecting the noise influence and searching for the global optimum yields inferior solutions with higher expected risk than necessary. Furthermore these inferior solutions are often harder to find for computational complexity reasons than approximations with minimal expected risk.

Structural Risk Minimization (SRM) was introduced by Vapnik as an induction principle for circumstances when the size of the sample set increases. Hypothesis classes are defined as nested structures of sets of functions and the function with minimal empirical risk is selected from the appropriate subset according to the number of samples. *Empirical Risk Approximation* differs from the SRM principles in two respects: (i) the ERA algorithm samples from a subset in the sequence rather than selects the function with minimal empirical risk; (ii) the inference algorithm initially samples from a large subset representing a crude approximation and it proceeds to smaller and smaller subsets in the sequence when additional data permit a refined estimate of the parameters.

The most important consequence from a pattern recognition point of view is the possibility to derive a parameter selection criterion from the *Empirical Risk Approximation* principle. Solutions with too many parameters clearly overfit the problem parameters and do not generalize. The condition that the hypothesis class should contain at least all ϵ-typical loss functions close to the global minimum forces us to stop the stochastic search at the lower bound of the computational temperature. The ERA driven induction process returns a set of indistinguishable hypotheses. The similarity between temperature dependent regularization and structural risk minimization as a scheme for complexity control in supervised learning is apparent and hints at additional, yet still unexplored parallels between supervised and unsupervised learning.

Acknowledgments: It is a pleasure to thank N. Tishby and J. Puzicha for illuminating discussions. This work has been supported by the German Research Foundation (DFG, #BU 914/3–1) and by the German Israel Foundation for Science and Research Development (GIF, #1-0403-001.06/95).

REFERENCES

[1] J. M. Buhmann. Empirical risk approximation. Technical Report IAI-TR 98-3, Institut für Informatik III, Universität Bonn, 1998.

[2] V. N. Vapnik. *The Nature of Statistical Learning Theory*. Springer-Verlag, New York, Berlin, Heidelberg, 1995.

[3] A. W. van der Vaart and J. A. Wellner. *Weak Convergence and Empirical Processes*. Springer-Verlag, New York, Berlin, Heidelberg, 1996.

[4] D. Pollard. Quantization and the method of k-means. *IEEE Transactions on Information Theory*, 28(2):199–205, 1982.

[5] L. Devroye, L. Györfi, and G. Lugosi. *A Probabilistic Theory of Pattern Recognition*. Springer Verlag, New York, Berlin, Heidelberg, 1996.

[6] T. Linder, G. Lugosi, and K. Zeger. Empirical quantizer design in the presence of source noise or channel noise. *IEEE Transactions on Information Theory*, 43(2):612–623, March 1997.

[7] M. Kearns, Y. Mansour, and A. Y. Ng. An information-theoretic analysis of hard and soft assignment methods for clustering. In *Proceedings of Uncertainty in Artificial Intelligence*. AAAI, 1997.

[8] K. Rose, E. Gurewitz, and G. Fox. Statistical mechanics and phase transitions in clustering. *Physical Review Letters*, 65(8):945–948, 1990.

[9] J. M. Buhmann and H. Kühnel. Vector quantization with complexity costs. *IEEE Transactions on Information Theory*, 39(4):1133–1145, July 1993.

[10] N. Barkai and H. Sompolinski. Statistical mechanics of the maximum-likelihood density estimation. *Physical Review A*, 50:1766–1769, September 1994.

APPLICATION OF NEURAL NETWORKS TO VEHICLE RECOGNITION AND TRACKING

P.Dainty, Wheatstone Laboratory, King's College London
J.F.Boyce, Wheatstone Laboratory, King's College London
C.H.Dimitropoulos, Wheatstone Laboratory, King's College London
P.Edmundson, Wheatstone Laboratory, King's College London
D.L.Toulson, Wheatstone Laboratory, King's College London
M.Bernhardt, DERA Farnborough

ABSTRACT

Three aspects of the application of neural networks to object recognition and tracking from a moving camera are evaluated on real data. The combination of a correlator with a Kalman filter and a neural network embedded within the tracking loop is shown to increase true recognitions and decrease false recognitions. Large training sets may be reduced by condensing via a k-nearest-neighbour algorithm without significant loss of network performance. Preprocessing the data using a self-adapting layer of discrete wavelet nodes yields performance that is comparable to a multilayer perceptron net.

INTRODUCTION

The objective is to recognise vehicles in forward-looking infrared image sequences taken from a low-flying aircraft [1]. The input data includes inertial navigation data. The recognition system is based on a set of track-files which correspond to vehicles and clutter of various classes. Their creation, maintenance and elimination are implemented via a continuously-evolving blackboard data-structure. Each track-file contains a list of pixel-locations in successive images at which an object (vehicles or clutter) has either been detected in the image or inferred from previous images, together with associated features and probabilities of classification into different classes. The primary method of classification is via artificial neural nets. The present work is concerned with the integration of the networks within the system together with their training.

Captured images are pre-processed to reduce systematic noise, either swathing or fixed-pattern, and registered relative to a terrain model using the inertial navigation data. A range-value is associated with each pixel, an atmospheric-absorption correction is applied and the images are possibly summed for signal-to-noise enhancement using inter-frame registration.

Potential vehicles are detected using a non-linear, range-adaptive, filter and corresponding region-of-interest sub-images are selected for further processing. The sub-images are supplied as input to a recognition neural-net that is trained to exclude only those signals that are clearly clutter, *i.e.* a relatively high number of false-alarms per image is acceptable, so long as few true vehicles are rejected. The purpose of the net is to act as an initial clutter-rejection classifier. It is important that the output of the net is probabilistic, rather than a hard-classification, so as to permit the possibility of errors being rectified by a succeeding stage of the analysis.

Batch training is employed for the recognition network. Around 2000 frames are used in the training data, leading to data sets of the order of 100,000 patterns. To reduce these data sets, a nearest-neighbour algorithm is employed to replace a number of patterns of the same class, close to each other in the input space, by their average, which is weighted accordingly in the training set. Our results show that a eight-fold reduction in the size of the training set, leading to a similar reduction in the training time, may be achieved without significant degradation of network-performance.

Vehicles are typically detected only intermittently, due to the poor signal-to-noise ratio of infrared images, however, even when undetected, the sub-image including a vehicle may contain sufficient information to permit tracking and confirmation of a previous recognition. The system described incorporates a correlation-tracker based on a Kalman filter and a confirmation net, whose purpose is to identify vehicles with high recognition rate. This second net is trained using only sub-images that have passed the recognition net and been consistently tracked by the correlator. The hypothesis is that this reduced data set will enable the second net to be more specific in its recognition performance. Results using real data confirm the hypothesis: true recognitions are increased by 10%, while the number of false recognitions per frame is decreased by 33%; hence both the specificity and sensitivity of the classifier are improved.

We have investigated a four layer feed forward neural network architecture which implements an adaptive discrete wavelet transform in the first processing layer, followed by a conventional multi-layer perceptron. The positions and scales of the "wavelet nodes" are treated as free parameters of the architecture, together with the conventional adaptive weights in the subsequent layers; the weights between the input nodes and the wavelet nodes are constrained to be a function of the wavelet position and scale. Results using independent test data showed performance comparable to that of a multilayer perceptron.

VEHICLE CONFIRMATION WITHIN THE TRACKING LOOP

The tracking of objects in images frequently depends solely on the basis of the trajectory of the object in the image plane, achieved using a linear Kalman or non-linear Extended Kalman Filter [2]. The observations are assumed to be subject to independent additive Gaussian noise. Difficulties arise if objects are detected only intermittently, false objects are detected or the trajectories of the objects intersect.

Data association techniques have been devised to deal with such problems, but the association is usually performed primarily using object trajectories. Extended objects supply additional radiometric information that should be incorporated into the tracking and data association process. We utilise a joint probabilistic model for the two separate sources of information (intensity and trajectory).

Consider a sequence S of T images of dimension $L \times L$ whose intensity is sampled at $2N \times 2N$ equidistant points.

$$S = \{F_t\ ,\ t = 1, ..., T\}, \quad \text{where} \quad F = \{f(\mathbf{x}) | \mathbf{x} \in \mathbf{P}\} \tag{1}$$

is the set of intensities at pixel locations (the pixel set)

$$P = \{\mathbf{x} \mid -(N-1) \leq l, m \leq N\} \tag{2}$$

with

$$\mathbf{x} = (l - 1/2)\Delta x\ \hat{\mathbf{i}} + (m - 1/2)\Delta y\ \hat{\mathbf{j}}; \qquad \Delta x = \Delta y = L/(2N). \tag{3}$$

Suppose that a number of detections are observed in each frame, classified as possible vehicles by the recognition net and formed as a list,

$$D_t = \{\mathbf{d}_{ti},\ i = 1, ..., N_D(t)\}, \tag{4}$$

where $\mathbf{d}_{ti}$ is the position-vector of the ith detected vehicle and $N_D(t)$ the number of detections in frame t. A trackfile is a set of temporally associated locations hypothesised to correspond to a single physical object in the image plane. It describes the motion of a possible vehicle from when first detected by the system, the initialisation time , until when no longer identifiable. Let the contents of the ith trackfile at time, t, be $T_i(t)$. At time t each trackfile T_i contains a set of observed locations

$$T_i(t) = \{\mathbf{x}_{ti}, t = t_s, ..., t_e\}, \tag{5}$$

where t_s is the initialisation time and t_e is either the current time t or the time of the final observation of the vehicle. (Note that the vehicle locations $\mathbf{x}_{ti}$ are not necessarily the same as the detected locations $\mathbf{d}_{ti}$.)

A common approach to tracking is to update trackfiles at time t on the basis of the latest detections D_t. The detections are first associated with the trackfiles to find which detections correspond to which trackfiles. After association, Kalman filter estimates of the current locations and the one-frame-ahead predictions are updated. Tracks that do not have detections associated with them estimate the current location by using the Kalman filter in closed-loop mode. Detections that do not correspond to any existing trackfile cause a new trackfile to be opened. Trackfiles that consistently fail to attract associated detections are deleted. Instead of using a data-association stage we use the most recent detections to initiate new tracks only in areas where there is not a currently open trackfile. Current locations in open trackfiles are re-estimated by combining the Kalman filter estimates from the previous frame with radiometric information from the current image.

Consider a trackfile $T_i(t)$ that is open at time t and suppose that the (t+1)'th image, F_{t+1} has been observed. We wish to update our estimate of the current position of the vehicle in the light of the new image data. Let $p(\Delta\mathbf{x})$ be the probability that the location of the vehicle has been displaced through a distance $\Delta\mathbf{x}$ in the image plane between frames t and $t+1$. Using Bayes' rule, the probability of displacement may be expressed in terms of the probability of observation of change of intensity ΔF as

$$p(\Delta\mathbf{x}|\Delta F) = \frac{p(\Delta F|\Delta\mathbf{x})p(\Delta\mathbf{x})}{p(\Delta F)} \tag{6}$$

where the prior probability of intensity-change may be expressed as the integral of the product of the conditional and prior probabilities as

$$p(\Delta F) = \int_{\Delta\mathbf{x}} p(\Delta F|\Delta\mathbf{x})\, p(\Delta\mathbf{x}) d\Delta\mathbf{x}. \tag{7}$$

The significant quantity is the probability of displacement conditioned by the change of intensity, $p(\Delta\mathbf{x}|\Delta F)$. It is determined by the probability of the observation of the change of image data given a particular vehicle displacement $p(\Delta F|\Delta\mathbf{x})$, times the prior probability of displacement $p(\Delta\mathbf{x})$. We examine the estimation of these probability densities in turn: the former requires a model of change of image-intensity, the latter a model of displacement propagation.

Consider a patch (sub-image) of size $\Delta N \times \Delta N$ pixels centered about the location $\mathbf{x}$ of a vehicle in frame F_t. The pixel-set corresponding to the patch is, analogously to equation 2,

$$P_{\mathbf{x}} = \{\mathbf{x}' \mid -\Delta N \leq l' - l, m' - m \leq \Delta N\}. \tag{8}$$

The pixel-intensities of the patches may be modeled as the sum of a signal $s(\mathbf{p})$ and additive Gaussian noise of zero mean and variance σ^2

$$f(\mathbf{x}) = s(\mathbf{x}) + N(0, \sigma^2). \tag{9}$$

Consider two such patches which are centered about the locations $\mathbf{x}$ and $\mathbf{x} + \Delta\mathbf{x}$ of the same vehicle in two successive frames, F_t and F_{t+1}. Subject to the assumptions that the overall magnitude of the signal does not alter between frames and there is no spatial distortion of the signal between frames then the intensities of the signal of corresponding pixels in the two patches would be equal. Consequently the differences of the intensities of corresponding pixels may be approximated by a random variable that is normally distributed,

$$\begin{aligned} f_{\Delta\mathbf{x}}(\mathbf{x}) &\equiv f(\mathbf{x} + \Delta\mathbf{x}) - f(\mathbf{x}) \\ &= N(0, 2\sigma^2) \end{aligned} \tag{10}$$

Assuming that the noise is pixel-independent, the likelihood of observing the difference of intensities ΔF between the two patches given an assumed inter-frame motion of $\mathbf{\Delta x}$ between frames, is

$$p(\Delta F|\Delta\mathbf{x}) = \prod_{P_{\mathbf{x}}} p(f_{\Delta\mathbf{x}}(\mathbf{x})|\Delta\mathbf{x}) = \prod_{P_{\mathbf{x}}} \frac{1}{2\sigma\sqrt{\pi}} \exp\left(-\frac{f^2_{\Delta\mathbf{x}}(\mathbf{x})}{4\sigma^2}\right) \tag{11}$$

If a vehicle is tracked using a Kalman filter then, at time t, the filter provides estimates of the vehicle's current location $\mathbf{x}(t|t)$, the vehicle's predicted location in the next frame $\mathbf{x}(t+1|t)$, and of the uncertainty of the predicted state, expressed as a covariance matrix $\Sigma(t+1|t)$. We wish to calculate the probability $p(\Delta\mathbf{x})$ that the image-location of the vehicle is displaced by $\Delta\mathbf{x}$ between frames. We can estimate this by a probability density function constructed from the tracking predictions $\mathbf{x}(t+1|t)$ and $\Sigma(t+1|t)$. Let the estimated inter-frame motion of the vehicle obtained from the Kalman filter be denoted by $\mathbf{x}_k$,

$$\mathbf{x}_k = \mathbf{x}(t+1|t) - \mathbf{x}(t|t). \tag{12}$$

The probability (according to the Kalman prediction) of the vehicle moving by a vector $\Delta\mathbf{x}$ between frames is then

$$p(\Delta\mathbf{x}) = \frac{1}{2\pi|\sigma|^{\frac{1}{2}}} \exp\left(-(\mathbf{x}_k - \Delta\mathbf{x})^T \, \Sigma^{-1} \, (\mathbf{x}_k - \Delta\mathbf{x})\right) \tag{13}$$

where Σ is the covariance of the vehicle location.

Recalling equation 6 we can now write

$$p(\Delta\mathbf{x}|\Delta F) = \frac{1}{2\pi|\Sigma|^{\frac{1}{2}}} \quad \exp\left\{-\left((\mathbf{x}_k - \Delta\mathbf{x})^T \, \Sigma^{-1} \, (\mathbf{x}_k - \Delta\mathbf{x})\right)\right\}$$
$$\prod_{P_\mathbf{x}} \frac{1}{2\sigma\sqrt{\pi}} \exp\left(-\frac{f^2_{\Delta\mathbf{x}}(\mathbf{x})}{4\sigma^2}\right) \tag{14}$$

A method of discrete association is employed. The maximum *a posteriori* inter-frame vehicle displacement

$$\Delta\mathbf{x} = \arg\max p(\Delta\mathbf{x}|\Delta F)_{\mathbf{mp}} \tag{15}$$

is assumed to be the actual displacement of the vehicle. This displacement is then registered with the Kalman filter as the latest observation and the filter updated in the usual way.

The purpose of the confirmation module is to assess the likelihood of potential vehicles located by the initial detection, recognition and tracking stage being actual vehicles. The confirmation net is a homologue of the recognition net, but is trained using the sub-images that have been tracked. The corresponding training set is an order of magnitude smaller, so a condensation stage is unnecessary. The input vector to the net are the intensities of pixels taken from a mask centered about the tracked object. The response from the neuron output layer of the network is then interpreted as being a probability of confirmation.

The performance of the system is expressed using two measures; the percentage of the vehicles that are detected and recognised as vehicles; the number of false recognitions per frame. The system was tested on data from a single flight which was independent of any of the data used to train the neural nets. The changes in the performances between the recognition and confirmation neural nets are displayed in

Number of frames	750
Increase of vehicle recognition rate	10.0 %
Decrease of false recognitions per frame	33.5 %

Table 1: Changes of performance measures due to confirmation network

Table 1. We may conclude that both the specificity and the sensitivity of the system have been enhanced by the inclusion of the confirmation net within the tracking loop.

NET-TRAINING

The main problem of classifier design is to ensure generalisability to other operating environments, due to differing times, seasons, atmospheric conditions, geographical locations. Training data-sets should be as large and representative as possible; the features used for classification should be invariant under changes of average intensity or contrast.

Each track-file contains a sequence of successive locations at which an object has been detected in the current image or inferred from previous images. The input data to the neural net are the intensities of a sub-image of 9×9 pixels surrounding each location. The sub-image is interpolated from the original image by normalising the range to a value for which a vehicle occupies approximately one-quarter of the sub-image, typically one kilometer. Rotating the major axis of the detected object to be horizontal was found to cause only a minor improvement in recognition rate, possibly due to its sensitivity to the noise of the inertial navigation angular data. A greater improvement was obtained by localising the patch about its centroid.

Data were obtained from a number of flights employing the same camera and electronics over different vehicle dispositions and locations. The flights were divided into training/validation and test sets. The recognition-net was a three-layer perceptron having an 81 : 16 : 2 node-structure with sigmoidal hidden and output layer activations, the output-nodes yielding probabilities of vehicle/non-vehicle. The method of training was back-propagation on the training set with early-stopping determined from the validation set: generalisability was estimated from the performance on the independent test data.

The individual intensities of the elements were normalised to zero mean and unit variance. The motivation was to transform the input to the net to be independent of the mean and contrast of the intensity, in order to improve generalisability. Explicit comparison of the above normalisation-by-element with normalisation-by-patch, *i.e.* sub-image, has confirmed the superiority of the former method. The two normalisations were compared by training similar multilayer perceptron nets four times on randomised subsets of the training and validation data, as given in Table 2, and then applying the trained nets to the test data. The training employed class-unbiassing, *i.e.* training starts with the contributions to the total error of the distinct classes weighted inversely by the numbers of examples of the classes in the training set, and the weighting factors tend to unity as training progress, with the result that the final weights correspond to the actual prior class-probabilities.

Normalisation-by-patch trained and validated better than normalisation-by-element, however the performance on the test data was significantly better for the latter, as shown in Table 3, where the changes in recognition rates are shown for a false-alarm rate of 1%. Both forms of normalisation compensate for changes of mean intensity

	Training	Validation	Test
Vehicles	272	133	1311
Non-vehicles	8544	4275	49489

Table 2: Numbers of vehicles and non-vehicles in normalisation comparisons

	Training %	Validation %	Test %
Mean	-5.9	-7.2	17.8
Standard deviation	3.6	3.2	5.1

Table 3: Difference of vehicle recognition rates between normalisations

and contrast ratio. Because clutter dominates vehicles in the data, normalisation-by -element is determined by the characteristics of the clutter. Normalisation-by-patch considers the difference between the patch intensity and the average intensity of the patch, normalisation-by-element the difference between each individual pixel and the average intensity of that pixel in a clutter-patch. The latter is more sensitive to differences between vehicles and clutter, which may explain its superior classification performance.

Batch training is employed for the recognition network, using data composed of sub-images selected by the initial detection stage. Around 2,000 frames are used in the training data, leading to large data sets of the order of 100,000 patterns. To reduce these data sets, the data of the training set is condensed using a nearest-neighbour algorithm to replace any number of patterns of the same class, close to each other in the input space, by their centroid, which is weighted by the condensation number. Our results, shown in Table 5 show that 10-neighbour condensation, which reduces the size of the training set by a factor of about 8 and leads to a similar reduction in the training time, may be achieved without degrading the network performance. Comparative tests have indicated that a single condensation using ten neighbours is near-optimal.

	Training	Condensed Training	Validation	Test
Vehicles	2399	851	1232	1311
Non-vehicles	65903	7475	32920	49489

Table 4: Numbers of vehicles and non-vehicles in condensation comparisons

	Training %	Validation %	Test %
Rate difference	6.2	-10.1	0.3

Table 5: Vehicle recognition rate changes on condensation

DISCRETE WAVELET PRE-PROCESSING

The Discrete Wavelet Transform [3] has been proposed as a technique for the pre-processing of data in applications involving both the compact representation of the original data (i.e. data compression or factor analysis) or as a discriminatory basis for pattern recognition and regression problems such as object recognition. The requirement is to choose a suitable set of child wavelets such that the projection of the original data will enhance the (non-linear) separability of different classes of signal whilst reducing the dimensionality of the data. This may be achieved naturally by implementing the wavelet transform as a set of wavelet neurons contained in the first layer of a multi-layer perceptron net.

The most common activation function used for neurons in the Multi Layer Perceptron architecture is the sigmoidal activation function.

$$\psi(x) = \frac{1}{1 + e^{\frac{-x}{x_0}}} \tag{16}$$

The output of a neuron y_i is dependent on the activations of the nodes in the previous layer x_k, and the weighted connections between the neuron and the previous layer ω_{ki}, i.e.

$$y_i = \psi\left(\sum_{j=1}^{I} x_j \omega_{ji}\right) \tag{17}$$

We can implement the Discrete Wavelet Transform as the first layer of hidden nodes of a Multi Layer Perceptron where the weights connecting each wavelet node to the previous layer ω_{ji} are constrained to be discrete samples of a particular wavelet child $\phi^{\tau_j,\xi_j}(i)$ and the activation function is the identity transformation $\psi(x) = x$. In fact we may ignore the weights connecting the wavelet node to the previous layer and instead characterise the node by the values of scale and translation τ and ξ. The interconnecting weights between the first and second layers are then determined by the parameters of the wavelet node.

The Multi Layer Perceptron is most usually trained using error backpropagation. The error function is defined in terms of desired and required outputs of the samples contained in a training set. For the case of a wavelet neuron however, the weights between the neuron and the input pattern are not free parameters but are constrained to assume the values defined by the parameters of a particular child wavelet. The free parameters for the wavelet nodes are therefore the values of translation and scale τ and ξ. A wavelet-preprocessed network was trained four times on the same

	Training %	Validation %	Test %
Mean	-10.8	-10.3	-0.9
Standard deviation	1.9	2.7	3.0

Table 6: Change in vehicle recognition rates due to wavelet preprocessing

data set used in the condensation experiments, as described in Table 2. The changes in recognition rates between a multilayer perceptron net and a wavelet-preprocessed network, both normalised-by-element, are shown in Table 6 for false-alarm rates of 1%. The average performance of the wavelet-preprocessed network was significantly worse on the training and validation sets, but indistinguishable on the test set. A possible explanation for the equivalence of performance on the test-data is that the multilayer perceptron is approaching the performance of a Bayesian classifier so that no other statistical classifier will perform better.

The effect of normalising the wavelet-preprocessed network by patch rather than by element was examined and found to show a reduction of performance, analogous to that exhibited by the multilayer perceptron.

CONCLUSIONS

The inclusion of a second, confirmation, classification network within the tracking-loop, is a significant improvement.
Class-unbiassing may be used to compensate for differing *a priori* class-probabilities.
Normalisation-by-element is superior to normalisation-by-patch for vehicle recognition in forward-looking infrared images.
Condensation may be used as a preprocessing stage for the training of neural nets thereby shortening the training-times without significantly degrading the classification performance.
Discrete wavelet preprocessed networks, as presently implemented, provide no advantage over multilayer perceptron networks for vehicle/non-vehicle classification in forward-looking infrared image sequences.

ACKNOWLEDGEMENTS

The work described in this paper was supported by the Defence Evaluation Research Agency, Farnborough and the Department of Trade and Industry.

REFERENCES

[1] B. Ernisse, S.R. Rogers, M.P. DeSimio and R.A. Raines. Complete automatic target cuer/recognition system for tactical forward-looking infrared images. Optical Engineering 1997; 36(9): 2593–2603.

[2] F. Amoozegar. Neural-network-based target tracking state-of-the-art survey. Optical Engineering 1998; 37(3): 836–846.

[3] D.P. Casasent and J.S. Smokelin Neural net design of macro Gabor wavelet filters for distortion-invariant object recognition in clutter. Optical Engineering 1994; 33(7): 2264–2270.

AN ARTIFICIAL NEURAL NETWORK BASED ENCODING OF AN INVARIANT SAMMON MAP FOR REAL-TIME PROJECTION OF PATTERNS FROM ODOUR SENSOR ARRAYS

Krishna C. Persaud, Department of Instrumentation and Analytical Science, UMIST, Manchester, M60 1QD, UK
Hyung-Gi Byun, Department of Information and Communication Eng. Samchok National University, Samchok, Kangwondo, 245-080, Korea

ABSTRACT

Odour sensor arrays produce multidimensional patterns of data that may be used as 'fingerprints' to differentiate between different volatile chemicals or mixtures of chemicals. A problem that arises for the human observer, is how to visualise multidimensional data in order to determine whether a certain pattern is similar or different from known patterns. A requirement is to reduce multidimensional data to two or three dimensions, and project unknown patterns on to the resulting map in real time, allowing the observer to make judgements on the incoming data. The SAMMAN network was adopted, but modified by the use of a previously trained neural network encoding principal component analysis to provide weights used to initialise the SAMMAN network. This provided a robust system that was invariant to changes in the order of the data set, and allowed rapid projection of unknown data on to a Sammon map.

INTRODUCTION

There is much interest in the development and application of broad-specificity arrays of sensors of a variety of technologies for volatile chemical detection and discrimination [1,2]. From these sensors, signals can be extracted to characterise a complex gas mixture or odour on the basis of response patterns that can be used as fingerprints. Instruments based on this principle have been designed for laboratory use to analyse samples under highly controlled conditions. At UMIST, we have developed an array of conducting polymer sensors mounted on a ceramic substrate together with associated electronics, that has wide applications for odour measurement and has been commercialised by Aromascan plc, Crewe. The sensors used consist of electrically conducting polymers made up of derivatised pyrroles, thiophenes and other heterocyclic compounds. The sensor arrays contain 32 elements (Figure 1) and were designed so that each sensor element was broadly tuned in terms of chemical selectivity but was different in sensitivity and selectivity from other elements in the array.

Each sensor behaves as a chemiresistor, and after exposure to an odour, the percent change in resistance from a baseline measured in clean air is recorded. This approach has the advantage that the array can respond to many thousands of chemical species due to the broad selectivity of the adsorbent surfaces. Discrimination between adsorbed chemical species or mixtures can be obtained by analysis of the cross-sensitivities between sensor elements. The

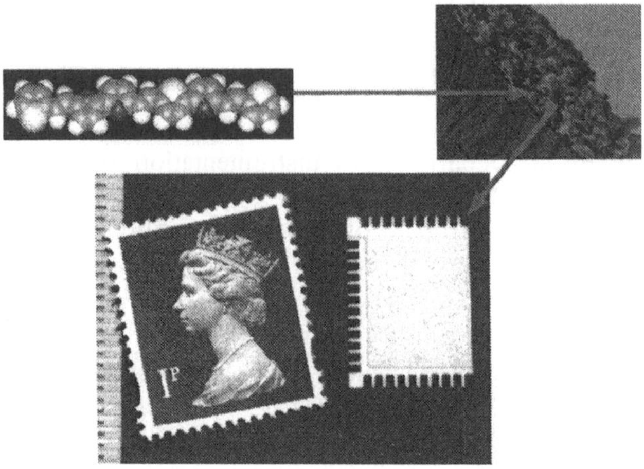

Figure 1. An example of a commercial odour sensing array consisting of 32 conducting polymer sensors. The heterocyclic molecules (top left) are polymerised to form a film (top right), that makes up an individual element of the array. The film is electrically conductive and this is modulated reversibly when volatile chemicals are adsorbed. Each sensor element contributes to a response pattern that allows differentiation between different volatile chemicals.

relative responses between sensor elements produce patterns that can be considered multidimensional 'fingerprints' that may be used as odour descriptors. While many sensor technologies are applicable, the modulation of electrical conductivity of conducting polymers by external physical and chemical interactions make these materials attractive for use in chemical sensing. They are extensively used for quality control of raw materials and finished products in the food industry, detection of off odours in packaging, control of contaminants in plastic materials, malodours in agriculture and in the chemical industry.

For the human observer, visualisation of multidimensional data is difficult, since the eye and brain processes visual information in two or three dimensions. A problem arises when the human observer wishes to examine the multidimensional data produced by an array-based odour sensing system. To devise a simple means of data inspection from the response of sensor arrays, Sammon's nonlinear mapping algorithm [3] or principal component analysis (PCA) [4-11] can be applied to the pattern generated from odour sensor arrays. These techniques are popular for visualising data from 'electronic nose' devices, but suffer from certain defects. The PCA, which is based on the Karhunen-Loeve (K-L) expansion [9], is a well-known statistical method for data projection, and widely used in pattern recognition and data analysis. It is a linear orthogonal transformation from multi-dimensional input space to a two-dimensional space, such that the coordinates of data in the two-dimensional space are uncorrelated and maximal amount of variance from the original data are preserved by only a small number of coordinates. The addition of new patterns into a PCA is a simple matter of using the loading matrix to project the new patterns onto low dimensional space. With the PCA, there is some distortion because not all dimensions can be included. However, PCA projection has disadvantages. These include distortion of the projected data, the axes for plotting the dimensionally reduced data have no physical meaning in terms of how different one cluster is from another, and depending on the method used for calculation, problems with singular matrices when highly correlated data are introduced. On the other hand, Sammon's nonlinear mapping algorithm [3], which reduces multidimensional pattern space by mapping onto two-dimensional or three-dimensional pattern space based on a distance measure such as the Euclidean distance, produces axes that are meaningful in terms of distances of one cluster from another. Nevertheless, it has disadvantages in that changing the order of data, or introducing new patterns into the data set can cause rotation of resulting map, making it difficult for human user to relate one map to another, even if they may be presenting data from the same patterns. It must be noted as well that by rotating the low dimensional space, the same Euclidean distance can be obtained from a different set of axes. The Sammon algorithm does not provide an explicit mapping function governing the relationship between patterns in the sensor array and in the mapping space, hence it is impossible to project previously unseen patterns without recalculation of all input patterns. The true value of these clustering methods may be realized when several methods, including linear and nonlinear mapping techniques, are used in combination as a system [7,9]. In our previous publication [11], we applied the suggestion made by Kowalski [7,8] regarding the use of PCA combined with Sammon mapping, the PCA being used as a starting data grid in low dimensional space. Because the principal eigenvectors produced are invariant, the PCA map will remain constant even if the order of patterns in the database is changed. The initial configuration is also nearly optimal for the Sammon mapping in respect of relative distances. This strategy provided fast convergence and invariant pattern position for the non-linear mapping algorithm.

In order for the user of an 'electronic nose' device to be able to determine visually whether incoming data falls into clusters that are previously known, or whether the incoming data is different, a real-time projection of reduced data onto a map was desired. This would be a marked improvement on previous methods, when normally post-processing of data after acquisition is carried out. The Sammon map approach was preferred because of the direct relationship between one cluster to another on the basis of a distance measure, and also because the technique made no prior assumptions that patterns fall into any particular category. Our requirements for visual data projection presented difficulties with utilising the conventional combination technique of PCA and Sammon nonlinear mapping, because it required a complete recalculation on all input patterns including previously unseen patterns to project a new pattern map.

We adapted an unsupervised backpropagation learning algorithm to train a multilayer feedforward neural network to perform the Sammon's nonlinear mapping, which is called SAMANN (Sammon Artificial Neural Network) [12,13]. This required no category information about patterns, and is an extension of the backpropagation algorithm. A significant advantage of the adapting algorithm, the SAMANN network, is that it is able to project previously unseen patterns after training because of the effect of regularization. We had to address the inherent problems of rotation of the Sammon map when random starting points were used to initialise the calculation.

To avoid problems of local minima during training, and rotation of the clusters projected in the map when the order of data sets were changed, a choice of good initial weights in SAMANN network was needed. We applied the SAMANN algorithm, using a starting point for weights initialisation based on PCA mapping, to produce an invariant Sammon mapping neural network that was applied to odour clustering. To produce initial weights for SAMANN, we first obtain PCA results using the PCA projection method, using only a portion of the training data set. Then, the network is trained using the standard backpropagation algorithm, using all of the training data, to give an output that approximates the PCA. Finally, a SAMANN network is used to refine the project map, using the weights from the PCA network for initialisation. This network is able to project previously unseen patterns in real-time. We have produced a useful tool for routine visual classification of odour patterns measured by an array of conducting polymer sensors (Figure 1).

METHODS

Implementation of the algorithm was carried out in three steps.

STEP 1: PCA PROJECTION

The PCA projection was carried out using established methods [3-11]. The input data sets for PCA projection were scaled between range [0.0, 1.0] by

$$x_k' = (x_k - \min_x) / (\max_x - \min_x)$$

We obtain the PCA components 1 and 2, which are used in the next step.

STEP 2: STANDARD BACKPROPAGATION ALGORITHM COMBINED WITH PCA COMPONENTS

The PCA outputs calculated in step 1 were scaled between ranges [0.0,1.0] and were used to provide target values in a neural network utilising the standard backpropagation algorithm [14]. The input data sets that were used for the PCA, were then utilised as training data sets, and were scaled [10] as

$$x_k' = x_k \Big/ (\max_x - \min_x)\sqrt{d/m}$$

Because the range of each output, which compared with target values, is between 0.0 and 1.0, it is difficult to get the reasonable outputs from stage 2 if the range of input values is large. In this stage, we can obtain the trained weights that are used as initial weights for the next stage.

STEP 3: SAMANN UNSUPERVISED BACKPROPAGATION ALGORITHM WITH MODIFIED STARTING POINTS FOR WEIGHTS INITIALISATION BASED ON STEP 2.

The initial weights for SAMANN neural network were obtained from the previous calculation step. In this step, we have to note that the ranges of each output from SAMANN neural network, which are defined by the maximum valucs of x (1st Dimension)- and y (2nd Dimension)-axis, lics between 0.0 and 1.0. If the range of input values, i.e. each odour pattern for used for learning and recognition using SAMANN, is large, it is impossible for the projection algorithm to preserve the interpattern distances. So, we normalise all input patterns to equalise the maximum interpattern distance in the original space and in the projected space.

The SAMANN algorithm combines the backpropagation algorithm with Sammon nonlinear mapping. The total mapping error for pattern-by pattern based [13] is defined as

$$E_{mu} = \frac{1}{\hat{A}\hat{A}\, d^*(m,u)} \hat{A}\hat{A} \frac{[d^*(m,u) - d(m,u)]^2}{d^*(m,u)}$$

where $d^*(\mu,\upsilon)$ is the distance between pattern μ and the pattern υ in the input space and d

(μ,υ) is also the distance between pattern μ and the pattern υ in the projected space. In addition, the Euclidean distance is commonly used in this projection algorithm. The neural network architecture for the SAMANN starts by calculating the network output y_j where i is the input layer output, and j is the hidden layer output. The $g(h)$ is the sigmoid function, with a range between 0.0 to1.0.

The updating rule of this algorithm is implemented by the backpropagation technique. Hence, the updating rule for the output layer

$$\Delta W^{l}_{jk} = -\eta(\Delta^{l}_{jk}(\mu)\, y^{l-1}_{j}(\mu) - \Delta^{l}_{jk}(\upsilon)\, y^{l-1}_{j}(\upsilon))$$

$$\lambda = \frac{1}{\sum_{\mu=1}^{n-1}\sum_{\upsilon=\mu+1}^{n} d^{*}(\mu,\upsilon)}$$

$$\Delta^{l}_{jk}(\mu) = \delta^{l}_{k}(\mu,\upsilon)[1 - y^{l}_{k}(\mu)]\, y^{l}_{k}(\mu)$$

where η is the learning rate.

Also, the updating rules for hidden layers are

$$\Delta W^{l}_{ij} = -\eta(\Delta^{l}_{ij}(\mu)\, y^{l-1}_{i}(\mu) - \Delta^{l}_{ij}(\upsilon)\, y^{l-1}_{i}(\upsilon))$$

$$\Delta^{l}_{jk}(\upsilon) = \delta^{l}_{k}(\mu,\upsilon)[1 - y^{l}_{k}(\upsilon)]\, y^{l}_{k}(\upsilon)$$

$$\delta^{l}_{k}(\mu,\upsilon) = -2\lambda \frac{d^{*}(\mu,\upsilon) - d(\mu,\upsilon)}{d^{*}(\mu,\upsilon)d(\mu,\upsilon)}[\, y^{l}_{k}(\mu) - y^{l}_{k}(\upsilon)]$$

$$\delta^{l}_{j}(\mu) = \sum_{k=1}^{m} \Delta^{l+1}_{jk}(\mu)\, w^{l+1}_{jk}$$

These steps implement an algorithm that is able to produce a Sammon map that is invariant to the order of patterns used in training. It is capable of projecting previously unseen patterns in real time on to a map to determine whether they match clusters on a previously calculated map.

RESULTS

We tested the performance of the SAMANN algorithm with modified weights initialisation based on the PCA projection. This produced an invariant Sammon mapping neural network. We tested this on a data clustering problem using the response patterns of a twenty sensor array to a series of five volatile chemicals – methanol, ethanol, n-butyl acetate, butanone, and mixture of ethanol in a constant background of 1617 ppm methanol. The normalised responses of individual sensors were applied as input patterns to the SAMANN algorithm described previously.

A three-layer (one hidden layer) network with 10 hidden units was used. The optimum number of hidden units were obtained by a series of trials of the network on different data sets. In typical operation, the network was firstly trained using the standard backpropagation algorithm with a learning rate of 0.7 and momentum rate of 0.3, and this required about 750 iterations to approximate PCA results and to produce initial weights for next procedure. Then, the SAMANN unsupervised backpropagation algorithm was used to train the previous network for 3000 iterations. The learning rate and momentum rate in this algorithm were 0.07 and 0.04, respectively, for the odour data sets.

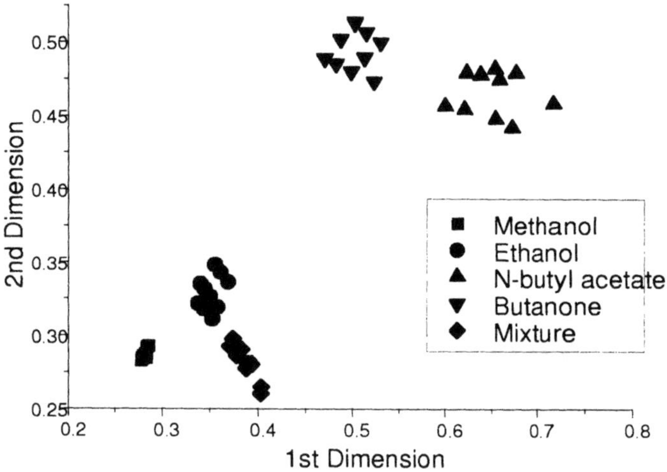

Figure 2. Training of the SAMMAN using a PCA neural network to generate the initial weights. The figure shows the multidimensional data reduced to 2 dimensions. Distinct clusters are observed. The data set labeled 'Mixture' consisted of a range of ethanol concentrations in a constant methanol background.

The plot of the result in Figure 2 shows that five data clusters are visible. The same data were then presented in different order, which normally would cause rotation of the Sammon map with the conventional algorithm, and the networks were again trained to the new data. Figure 3 shows that the results were identical to Figure 2, indicating that the pattern rotation problem of the conventional Sammon map algorithm did not occur. We then tried to project an unknown data set onto the map shown in Figure 3. These were patterns obtained from measurements of volatiles from a popular soft drink labeled as beverage in Figure 3. The trained network was able to project previously unseen patterns in real-time as data was being acquired from the sensor array, on to a map. The neural network has now been incorporated as part of the data acquisition system, and provides a rapid means of multidimensional data reduction, projection of unknown patterns onto a known pattern set, and allows the observer to make rapid decisions about the quality of incoming data from the sensor array. This will be of great use in quality control applications in the food and beverage industries, where very often the quality of the current batch is to be compared to a 'standard'.

CONCLUSION

Display methods are usually the first step in pattern recognition application. We adapted the SAMANN unsupervised backpropagation algorithm, combining a starting point for weights initialization based on PCA projection, to eliminate the rotation of clusters when the order of patterns in a database was changed. This allowed us to rapidly project new input patterns without having to recalculate the entire map.

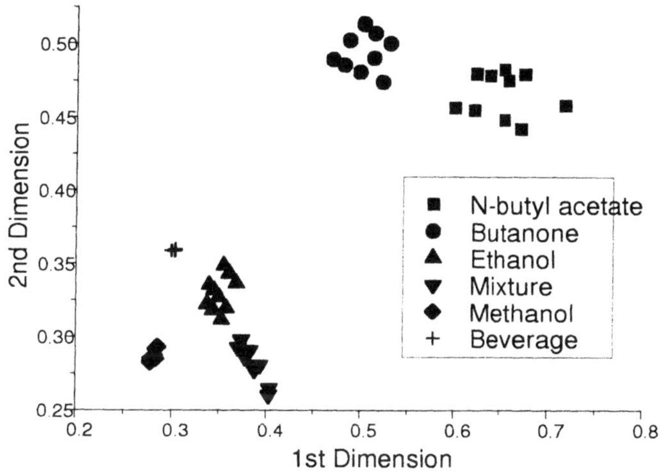

Figure 3. The same data shown in Figure 2, but presented in different order to the SAMANN for training. No rotation of clusters is observed. The data set labeled 'Beverage' is a previously unseen set of data projected in real time through the trained neural network.

The experimental trials confirmed that SAMANN having good initial weights based on a PCA was able to project previously unseen patterns in real time on to a map. This allowed the user to quickly judge whether they matched clusters on a previously calculated invariant map.

We have thus achieved a very flexible, rapid and invariant Sammon mapping system, that allows the user to visualise clusters of multidimensional data without making any assumptions that the data belong to any particular class. This system may thus be used as a pre-screening of data for feature extraction, for testing previously unseen data sets to determine how far away they are from the training patterns, and may form the core of a real-time classification system. In terms of the chemometric and neural network methods currently used for processing data from 'sensor arrays', the method adopted here provides a powerful tool that complements the current methods, and allows the user to further understand the nature of the data that is to be subject to further post-processing.

Furthermore, the system has applications in a wide number of areas, apart from 'electronic noses', where the user is dealing with multidimensional data and needs to make a rapid evaluation of the quality of such data.

ACKNOWLEDGEMENTS

This work was partially supported by a travel grants from Samchok University, Korea, the British Council, and by Aromascan plc, Crewe, UK.

REFERENCES

[1] Pelosi P, Persaud KC. Gas sensors: towards an artificial nose. In: Dario P, ed. Sensors and sensory systems for advanced robots. NATO ASI Series Vol. F43. Berlin, Heidelberg:Springer-Verlag, 1988, pp 49-70

[2] Amrani MEH, Ibrahim MS., Persaud K.C. Synthesis, chemical characterisation and multifrequency measurements of poly N-(2-pyridyl) pyrrole for sensing volatile chemicals. Mat Sci Eng C 1994; 1:17-22

[3] Sammon, Jr, JW. "A nonlinear mapping for data structure analysis", IEEE Trans. Comput., 1969, 5 C-18 : 401-409.

[4] Abe, H. et al. "Extended studies of automated odour-sensing system based on plural semiconductor gas sensors with computerized pattern recognition techniques", Anal. Chem. Acta, 1988, 215: 155-168.

[5] Gardner, JW. "Detection of vapours and odours from a multisensor array using pattern recognition Part 1: Principal component and cluster analysis", Sensors & Actuators B, 1991, 4: 109-115.

[6] Gardner JW. and Bartlett, PN. "Pattern recognition in gas sensing", In: Moseley et al. (Editors), Techniques and Mechanisms, Adam Hilger, Bristol, 1991, pp. 347-384.

[7] Kowalski, B.R. and Bender, C.F. "Pattern recognition a powerful approach to interpreting chemical data", J. Am. Chem. Soc., 1972, 94(16): 5632-5639.

[8] Kowalski, BR. and Bender, CF. "Pattern recognition II. Linear and nonlinear methods for displaying chemical data", 1973, J. Am. Chem. Soc., 95(3): 686-692.

[9] Kittler, J. and Young, PC. "A new approach to feature selection based on the Karhunen-Loeve expansion", Patt. Recog. 5: 335-352

[10] Gardner JW. and Shurmer, HV. "Odour discrimination with electronic noses", Sensors & Actuators B, 1992, 8: 1-11.

[11] Byun, HG. et al. "Application of unsupervised clustering methods to the assessment of malodour in agriculture using an array of conducting polymer odour sensors", Computers and Electronics in Agriculture, 1997, 17: 233-247.

[12] Jain, AK. and Mao, J. "Artificial neural network for nonlinear projection of multivariate data", In Proc. IEEE Int. Joint Conf. Neural Networks, Baltimore, MD, 1992, Vol. 3 : 335-340.

[13] Mao, J. and Jain, AK. "Artificial neural networks for feature extraction and multivariate data projection", IEEE Trans. On Neural Networks, 1995, Vol. 6, No. 2: 296-316.

[14] Rumelhart, D. and McClelland, J. (Eds) "Parallel Distributed Processing (PDP): Exploration in the Microstructure of Cognition", Vol. 1, MIT Press, Cambridge, MA, 1986.

PROBABILISTIC AND OTHER NEURAL NETS IN MULTI-HOLE PROBE CALIBRATION AND FLOW ANGULARITY PATTERN RECOGNITION

Subbiah Baskaran
Raytheon STX/MSFC/NASA and
Institute for Theoretical Chemistry,
University of Vienna, Austria

Narayanan Ramachandran
Universities Space Research Association
NASA, MSFC, Huntsville, AL-35812 USA

David Noever
National Aeronautics and Space Administration
George C. Marshall Space Flight Center
Huntsville, AL-35812 USA

ABSTRACT

The use of probabilistic (PNN) and multilayer feed forward (MLFNN) neural networks are investigated for the calibration of multi-hole pressure probes and the prediction of associated flow angularity patterns in test flow fields. Both types of networks are studied in detail for their calibration and prediction characteristics. The current formalism can be applied to any multi-hole probe, however the test results for the most commonly used five-hole Cone and Prism probe types alone are reported in this article.

PROBLEM STATEMENT

Experimental determination of the flow characteristics is often required in many complex flow fields as in the study of the aerodynamic characteristics of the internal flow of rocket engines. Five hole pressure probes of various types have long been employed in low speed incompressible flows to compute the flow angles and velocity information [3, 4, 5, 6, 7]. Until now calibration charts have been used with regression/spline procedures requiring double interpolation techniques for reading (computing) the flow angles from the chart with varying degrees of success [1, 2].

Neural networks have been successfully applied in many fields [10, 11]. In this, we present our recent results of applying neural networks for the calibration of multi-hole probes. The calibration problem is addressed here as learning of a nonlinear mapping for a given neural network from an input space of normalized pressure coefficients computed from experimentally determined multi-hole pressures to an output space of flow angles. The anticipated advantages are using the probes in non-nulling mode and the ability to do two plane calibration as often as required during the life time of the probe [1].

CALIBRATION DATA

Full and part scale air and water flow test models of Advanced Solid Rocket Motors (ASRM) and Space Shuttle Main Engine (SSME) components have been built and are being tested in Marshall Space Flight Center (MSFC) fluid flow facilities for defining and studying the aerodynamic characteristics of the internal flow of rocket engines. The associated wind tunnel calibration experiments are conducted not only to calibrate multi-hole probes but also to study the characteristics of the probes in flow experiments marked by high velocity and Reynolds number. At MSFC the Calibration Wind Tunnel (CWT) is used for these purposes.

Two main parameters defining flow fields are the flow direction (given by the Pitch and Yaw angles) relative to a reference plane or axis system and the flow magnitude. Five hole Cone and Prism pressure probes have been used for this study in the past. However three, seven and nine hole probes are also available.

For the study we report, the data has been collected in the above open jet calibration facility (CWT) in connection with earlier experimental investigations by one of the authors [1, 2]. The five-hole probes in the study were all used in fixed position or non-nulling mode. Data for three Cone probes labeled as C1,C2,C3 and three Prism probes labeled as P1,P2,P3 are analyzed. In discussions, C1 is also called as, 'Cone Probe 1', and P3 as, 'Prism Probe 3', and so on. Actual experimental data sample consists of the five measured pressures, and the two set up angles. However after the five pressures are reduced to two normalized coefficients, we end up with two coefficients and two angles in a sample for the neural network. The Yaw and Pitch angles are denoted by β and α respectively, while the corresponding pressure coefficients by $C_{P\beta}$ and $C_{P\alpha}$ respectively.

Figure 1 shows a typical calibration chart for the Cone Probe 3 used in our study. The graphical data have been represented by continuous parametric curves passing through the computed pressure coefficients. Through using this chart, the values of α and β are calculated from the grid of $C_{P\beta}$ vs $C_{P\alpha}$. Since the values to be determined are a function of two independent variables, we need a double interpolation procedure to compute the flow angles. The "relatively horizontal" curves are curves of constant α. whereas the "relatively vertical" curves are curves of constant β. Superposed stars on the chart are the test data to be used later in the testing of the trained neural net. However charts of this type are no longer required when neural nets are used for calibration as they directly output the angle pairs.

CHOICE OF NEURAL NET ARCHITECTURES

The network architectures considered include the probabilistic (PNN), and the three and four layer feed forward networks. The PNN neural network is the first general purpose regression network which has one pass learning advantage over back propagation. PNN is modeled upon Bayes decision theory and a novel neural model of estimating continuous system variables [9, 8]. It can be applied on sparse data and also in real time.

The three and four layer feed forward (MLFNN) neural networks are studied because of their robust generalization features and favorable approximation properties. Good generalization and minimal reproduction error of learned input-output pairs are basically the two driving factors in neural network applications nevertheless remaining contradictory objectives.

The four quantities C_β, C_α, β, and α constitute a single training pattern of which C_β and C_α are the inputs and the angles β, and α are the outputs for all the networks considered. In other words each network has two input nodes and two output nodes. An ideal setup would be to use the probes in the non nulling mode and to derive the flow angularity pattern and the velocity information directly from the measured probe pressures. The current neural net formalism is just one step towards accomplishing that goal.

TRAINING AND TEST DATA PARTITIONING

For a successful application of neural networks we need to have appropriate training and testing data suitably drawn from the application. We need the training data to teach the neural net about the application and we need the testing data to verify the network's prediction capability after it has been successfully trained. From any calibration experiment conducted for this study, a total of 49 data samples are collected which are uniformly spread over a $7X7$ grid of Yaw and Pitch angles.

We generated the test data in three possible methods: In the first two methods, we split the total experimental data into test and train subsets. In the first method, we selected one random sample for every seven Pitch angles measured at a fixed Yaw angle. There are 7 setup Yaw angles, so this gave a total of 7 test samples. In the second approach we choose the 7 test samples randomly from the entire 49 samples without any preference in selection. In this kind of random selection, it may happen that two successive Pitch angles will be selected as test data resulting in a gap of as much as 30° in the remaining training set. Please note the calibration samples are 10° apart in the Yaw-Pitch grid. This would make training very difficult and predictions from such training cannot be reliable. But in the former a smaller gap of 20° is obtained. However even such a gap is certainly larger than the experimental uncertainty of three degrees [1].

In the third method we kept all the 49 calibration data intact for training and generated the test data through linear interpolation from the pairs of input pressure coefficients in the training set (see Figure 1). These interpolated coefficients should correspond to intermediate Yaw and Pitch angles in the setup grid. As interpolation between two successive sets of Pitch angles is invalid, we had 42 samples in the testing set. This method is very much realistic and is closer to the purpose for much the calibration neural nets are trained. If the training were satisfactory then the predicted angles should fall on or very close to the set up Yaw Pitch grid occupying intermediate positions. In fact as expected this was found to be the case in all our network predictions.

We could have as well interpolated the experimental pressures directly and then would have computed the test pressure coefficients. We did not do so because that would introduce errors in two successive steps and may be cumulative. In the future study the effect of that will be analyzed.

PROBABILISTIC NEURAL NETS

In the PNN considered for the current study, we have two nodes in the input layer for the C_{P_β} and C_{P_α} coefficients, 49 or 42 nodes in the pattern layer corresponding to the available training samples based on the training/test data partition, three nodes in the summation layer, and finally two nodes in the output layer for the two angles, β and α.

The net learned in one pass of all the training samples through its four layers. The holdout method was used for computing the optimal value of the smoothing parameter, σ in the PNN net. Two models, BASIC and SEPVAR and one kernel, Gaussian are considered in the study.

ONE HIDDEN LAYER NETWORK

Although three layer feed forward networks are universal function approximators, we have no hard rules to decide on the correct number of hidden nodes required for a given application. Since the overall experimental uncertainty in the flow angles was around 3°, we took the total percentage of correctly predicted Yaw-Pitch angles within 3 degrees by the trained net as a probable measure to evaluate the required number of hidden nodes. In order to access the maximum achievable accuracy in learning we also plotted the correctly recognized angles within 2 and 1 degrees as depicted in Figure 10. From the figure we read that 15 hidden nodes are sufficient to provide the maximum percentage of recognition within 3, 2, and 1 degrees corresponding to a reproduction of 99%, 98%, and 81% respectively. Similar results were obtained for all the Cone and Prism probes.

This choice of 15 hidden nodes is used in the rest of our simulations. We discovered that symmetric sigmoidal activation function gave excellent robust training results while the standard unipolar sigmoidal function more are less failed to converge even after 80000 learning iterations with back propagation algorithm in both instances. Only fixed values for learn rate and momentum parameters are used. A forthcoming paper explains other possibilities experimented and the results in detail.

TWO HIDDEN LAYER NETWORK

When test results with the standard sigmoidal activation function did not produce appreciable results for three layer nets, we decided to test four layer nets based on the proposition that the maps might be highly non linear. Also as the training data grid is finite, we needed to have a net that is capable of learning complex maps with few training cases. After the symmetric sigmoidal function was found to yield satisfactory results we still wanted to test the four layer networks for appreciable differences between the Cone and Prism probes in their learning and prediction features.

With two hidden layers, a network acquires additional synaptic connections and the plasticity associated with learning inherently increases. Such networks are suitable in certain complex applications. We considered a choice of 8 nodes in each hidden layer with total hidden nodes approximately equal to the corresponding three layer net so that the results may be easily compared with each other.

CALIBRATION AND PREDICTION RESULTS

The functional connection between the pressure coefficients and the angles is a four dimensional mapping. Neural network based calibration treats them as a mapping between two, 2-dimensional vectors. The network during training learns to construct this map internally in the form of its synaptic weights. We show the results of the network calibration and prediction as four individual function plots.

PROBABILISTIC NEURAL NETS

A set of sample plots corresponding to Cone Probe 1 are given in Figures 2 through 5. Figure 2 depicts the Yaw angle as a function of the $C_{P\alpha}$ coefficient. The horizontal lines show that for a fixed Yaw angle, the changes in the coefficients are related only to the Pitch angle which is under calibration. However in an arbitrary flow setting both coefficients influence both angles. Figure 3 depicts the Yaw angle as function of the $C_{P\beta}$ coefficient. This shows clearly the dependence of the Yaw angle on this variable during calibration. The scattering present at extreme angles is seen as short linear segments, although point like clusters are anticipated (similar to the case at acute angles).

Figure 4 depicts the Pitch angle as function of the $C_{P\alpha}$ coefficient. These monotonically increasing parametric curves have a characteristic sigmoidal like behavior at both ends. This may reflect the pressure saturation effects of the coefficients at both extreme Yaw angles. The Figure 5 shows the Pitch angle as function of the $C_{P\beta}$ coefficient. For smaller absolute values of the coefficient, the parametric curves are near linear and at large values they exhibit concave characteristics. This is comparable to the sigmoidal bends in Figure 4, although the independent variables are different in each plot.

Neural nets are never expected to reproduce the actual input output pairs especially while learning non linear mappings, but are trained to learn the underlying generalized complex functional only. The non linear effects of pressure at the tips of the probe at extreme Yaw and Pitch angles are reflected in this way in the maps. The interesting feature is that the neural net formalism is able to capture the non linear effects and reflect them in its learned mapping as shown in the various figures.

The overall performance of PNN networks for Cone and Prism type probes were satisfactory for the models (BASIC and SEPVAR) and kernel (Gaussian) type considered. Figures 6 through 9 show the results. The figures show the inverted map of the usual calibration chart. In other words they plot the Yaw and Pitch angles against one another. For the experimental values these plots will appear perfect rectangular grids. But the predicted grid from trained nets in general may not be exactly rectangular, and it will be distorted based on the degree of learning accuracy. For figures 6, and 7 all data were used in the training whereas for figures 8, and 9 the calibration data was split into 42 training and 7 testing samples. The latter case has an expected angular gap of 20° in Yaw angles in 7 places on the grid. PNN has performed well in the case of Cone probe but has performed some what less satisfactorily for the Prism probe. It appears that since distortion is present under both types of training data for Prism probe we could reasonably state that PNN type networks are better suited for Cone probes than Prism probes.

Thus PNN appears to favor a particular geometry in this case Cone type. PNNs learn in one pass and we do not have direct control on the learning expect through the values of the sigma parameter. In the holdout method we tried 200 sigma values in the range 0.01 – 5.0 for all our network simulations. Thus the generalization features of PNN over both probe types do not appear to be similar or universal.

ONE HIDDEN LAYER NETWORK

Figures 11, 12, 13, and 14 show the four plots for the Prism Probe 1 using a three layer network with 15 hidden nodes. Notable differences exist between this set for a Prism probe and those for a Cone probe given earlier. The relationship between Yaw and $C_{P\beta}$ show more scattering than the Cone probe, the relationship between Pitch and $C_{P\alpha}$ also shows more spread. Most remarkably the functional relationship between Pitch and $C_{P\beta}$ is now convex inwards for large values of the coefficient and near linear for small values. Finally as in the Cone probe, the relationship between Yaw and $C_{P\alpha}$ exhibits no dependence. The same explanation holds good here also. This empirically reinstates that the calibration is only for the Pitch angle and while that is varied, the associated changes in the Pitch coefficient do not change the setup Yaw angle.

Although each probe will have its own neural net for calibration and prediction, important features like the number of hidden layer nodes, learn rate and momentum parameters were found to be same (universal) in our experiments for both type of probes as well as for different probes within the same type. We initially anticipated that difference in geometry may reflect in the required number of hidden nodes for satisfactory calibration, but our results proved the contrary. The results indicate that the overall structure of the network is same for all probes. However as expected each probe will have its own characteristic set of synaptic weights and bias values after training.

TWO HIDDEN LAYER NETWORK

Figures 15, and 16 show two typical results using the four layer network. The former figure depicts the inverse calibration chart as a grid of calibrated Yaw and Pitch angles for the Cone Probe 1. The calibrated grid is nearly rectilinear with minor deviations. The latter figure shows the results for Prism Probe 3 but in this case the calibrated grid is not as nearly rectilinear as in the former case. For this probe, we have also superposed the predicted angles (marked as stars) from interpolated test pressure coefficients. This is not the usual calibration chart provided by the vendor. Instead this corresponds to an inverse mapping of the vendor calibration chart. Since the trained network can directly map the coefficients into angles we no more require classical type calibration charts.

Unlike PNN, in the case of multilayer nets we do not notice appreciable differences between Cone and Prism probes. Thus MLFNN networks seem to be independent of probe geometry in their calibration and prediction features which is a favorable property. However one difference is indicated by the comparison of the two $C_{P\alpha}$ vs. $C_{P\beta}$ grids, in that the prism probe has a much smaller range of $C_{P\alpha}$ values. This reduced range will result in an increased sensitivity of the prism probe to small flow variations in the Pitch plane. The velocity component in this plane may, therefore exhibit more data scatter [1, 7].

Although the three and four layer nets are very slow in learning, their generalization characteristics are very good. Even with a worst expected gap of 20 degrees in calibration measurement in all random, and grid based methods, the trained nets were able to predict the missing calibration values within $\pm 10°$. Albeit the fact that they are designed to have approximately the same number of hidden nodes, the four layer net has more synaptic weights than the two layer net because of the additional intra hidden layer connections. More connection weights in a two layer net is useful in general to learning very complex and intricate mappings. Since all our simulation results do not indicate significant difference, we can decide upon choosing the one layer net over the two layer net for calibration studies of multi-hole probes in future.

One of the characteristic feature observed in all the calibration using neural nets is that the charts do not pass in most instances through the experimental set up angles. Thus the difference between 1 and 3 degree (corresponding to 81% and 99%) threshold learning reflects the networks characteristic ability to trade off between robust generalization and exact reproduction.

CONCLUSIONS

From our study we conclude that PNN, three and four layer MLFNN all perform considerably well in calibration and prediction of five-hole Cone and Prism probes. However PNN predicted Cone type probes appreciably better than Prism type probes. On the other hand both three and four layer MLFNN networks showed remarkable calibration-prediction features with robust generalization on both probe types. More simulations need to be conducted before deciding between the three layer nets and PNN type networks for probable hardware implementation.

The difficulties associated with complex double interpolation procedures and related data manipulations are all avoided in the neural network based calibration and prediction. The formalism proposed in the current study can be extended to the calibration studies of any multi-hole probe type without loss of generality.

The most direct extension of the current study will address predicting the flow angularity variables from the measured partial pressures without going through the intermediate normalizing pressure coefficients. The second extension of the current study will address the design of novel pressure probes. The testing reported here will form part of a comprehensive study of several neural network formalisms to finally select a model network for such a hardware implementation. In that issues related to installing these networks as neural chips in the hardware of the pressure probe with user selectable learn (calibration) and test (prediction) modes will be addressed.

REFERENCES

[1] Narayanan Ramachandran, "The Calibration Wind Tunnel," NASA Technical Report, MSFC-ED35, NASA, Oct. 1992.

[2] Narayanan Ramachandran, "High Reynolds number Effects on Hot Wire and Multi-hole Probes," NASA Technical Report, USRA/ED-36 NASA MSFC, May 1994.

[3] Janes, C.E., "Instruments and Methods for Measuring the Flow of Water Around Ship Models," David Taylor Model Basin Report 487, March 1978.

[4] Krause, L.N. and Dudzinski, T.J., "Flow-Direction Measurement with Fixed Position Probes in Subsonic Flows over a Range of Reynolds Number," NASA TMX-52576, May 1969.

[5] Treaster, A.L. and A.M. Yocum, "The Calibration and application of Five-hole Probes," ISA Transactions, Vol.18. No.3, pp 23-34, 1979.

[6] Pien, P.C., "Five-Hole Spherical Pilot Tube," David Taylor Model Basin Report 1229, May 1958.

[7] G.G. Zilliac, "Modeling, calibration, and error analysis of seven-hole pressure probes," Experiments in Fluids vol.14, pp 104-120, 1993.

[8] K.S. Narendra and K. Parthasarathy, "Identification and control of dynamical systems using neural networks," IEEE Trans. Neural Networks, Vol. 1, pp. 4-27, Mar.1990.

[9] D.F. Specht, "A General Regression Neural Network," IEEE Trans. Neural Networks, Vol. 2. pp. 568-576, Nov. 1991.

[10] D. Noever, et. al., "Artificial neural network prediction of tetragonal lysozyme face growth rates," Journal of Crystal Growth Vol 167, pp 221-236, 1996.

[11] D. Noever, et. al., "Neural net formulations for organically modified, hydrophobic silica aerogel," J.Mater.Res. Vol 12(7) 1-7, 1997.

FIGURES

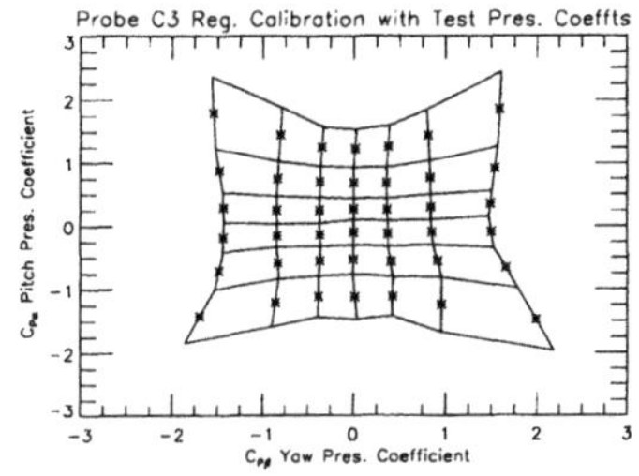

Figure 1: A sample Calibration Chart. Cone Probe 3. Superposed stars are the interpolated pressure coefficients as test data.

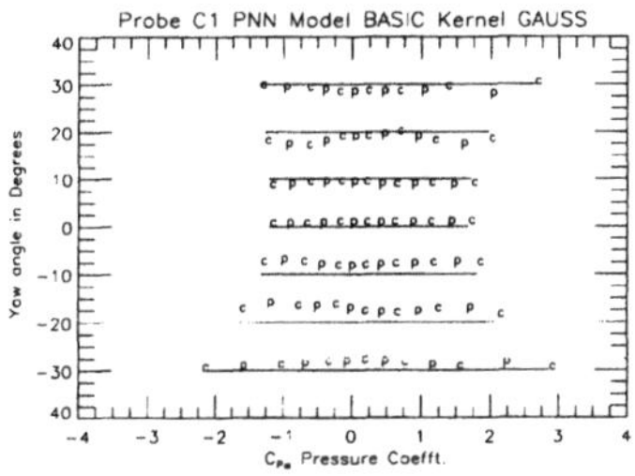

Figure 2: Relationship between β and $C_P\alpha$. Superposed are experimental measurements(full line), network calibrated (c), and network predicted (p) cases.

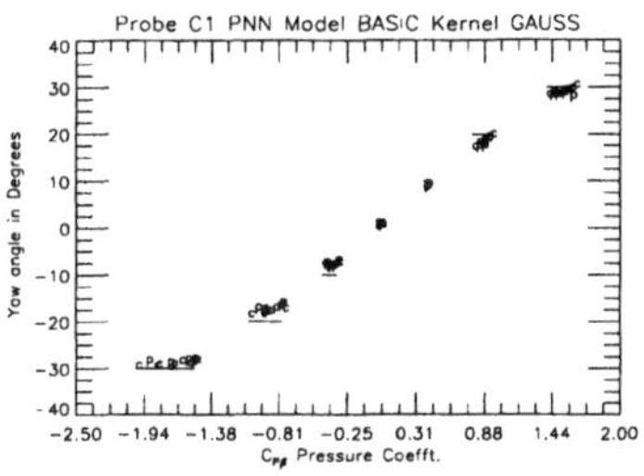

Figure 3: Relationship between β and $C_P\beta$. Superposed are experimental measurements(full line), network calibrated (c), and network predicted (p) cases.

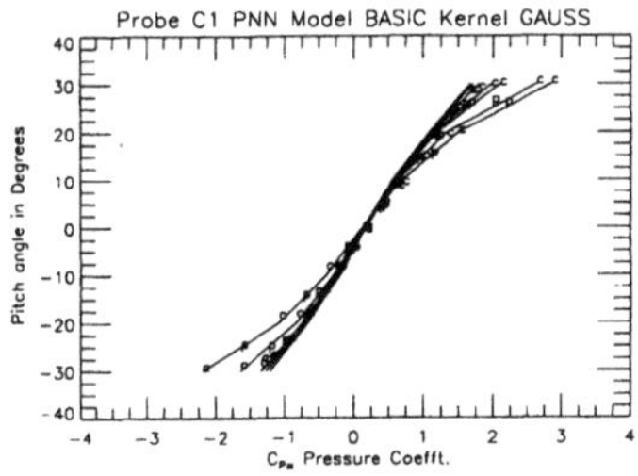

Figure 4: Relationship between α and $C_P\alpha$. Superposed are experimental measurements(full line), network calibrated (c), and network predicted (p) cases.

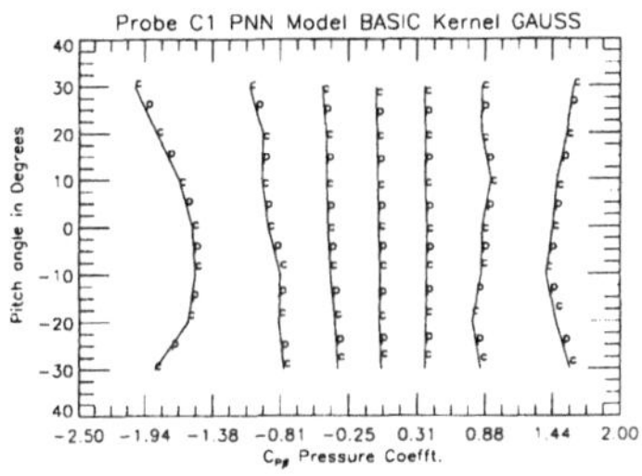

Figure 5: Relationship between α and $C_P\beta$. Superposed are experimental measurements(full line), network calibrated (c), and network predicted (p) cases.

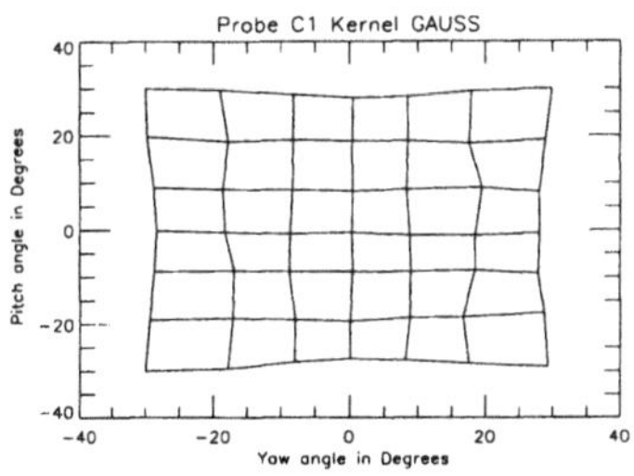

Figure 6: The calibration data for Cone Probe 1. Basic Model. Gaussian Kernel. Calibration with all data points. No training and test set partition.

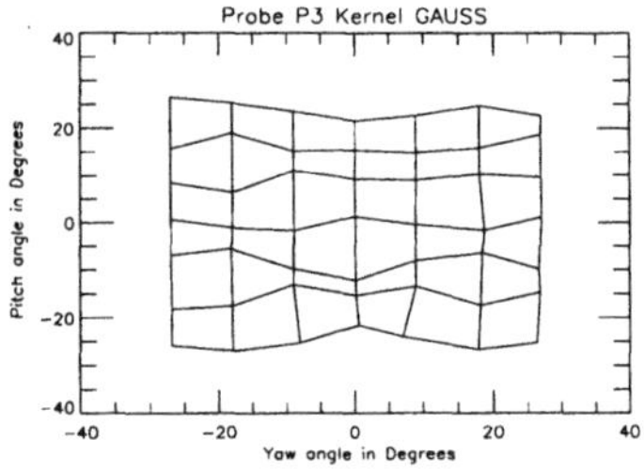

Figure 7: The calibration data for Prism Probe 3. Basic Model. Gaussian Kernel. Calibration with all data points. No training and test set partition.

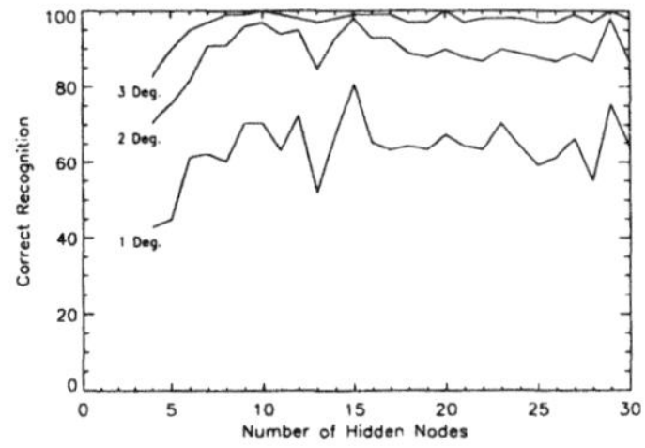

Figure 10: The determination of required number of hidden nodes for a three layer net using the percentage of correctly recognized Yaw and Pitch angles. The plot is for Prism Probe 3.

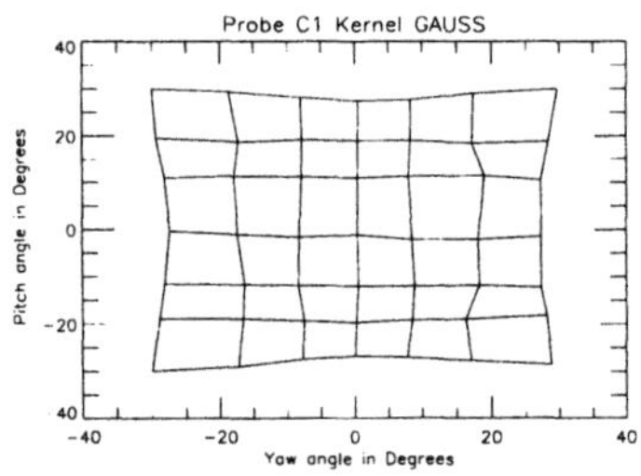

Figure 8: The calibration data for Cone Probe 1. Basic Model. Gaussian Kernel. The training set has 42 points and the test set has 7 points

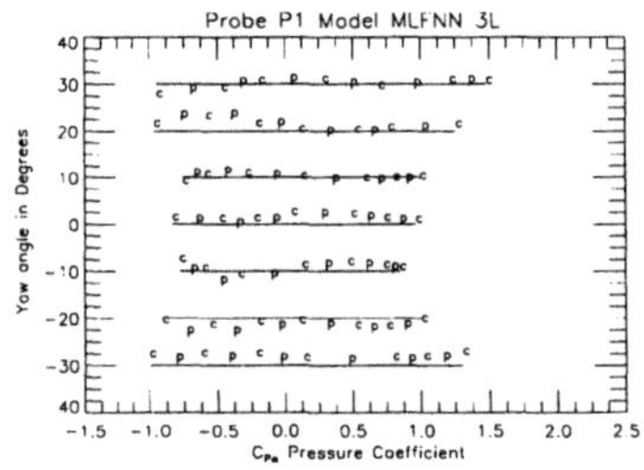

Figure 11: Relationship between β and $C_P\alpha$. Superposed are experimental measurements(full line), network calibrated (c), and network predicted (p) cases. Cone Probe C1, MLFNN 3Layers with 15 hidden nodes.

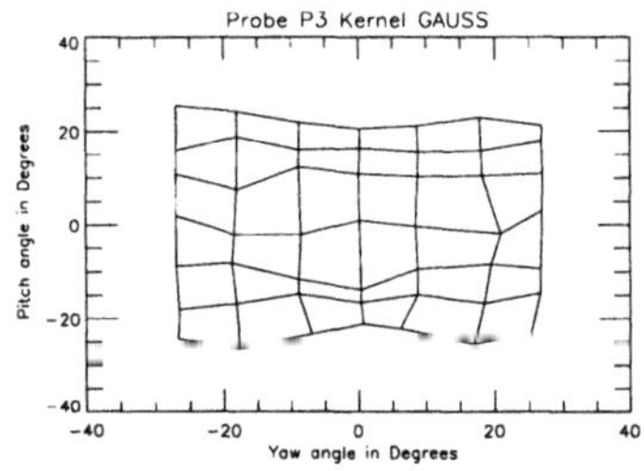

Figure 9: The calibration data for Prism Probe 3. Basic Model. Gaussian Kernel. The training set has 42 points and the test set has 7 points

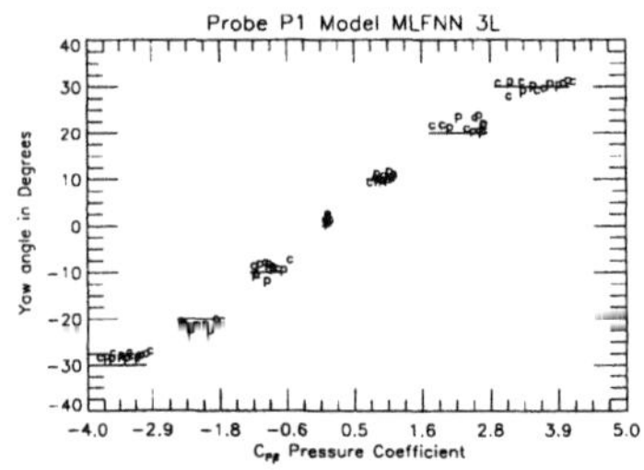

Figure 12: Relationship between β and $C_P\beta$. Superposed are experimental measurements(full line), network calibrated (c), and network predicted (p) cases.

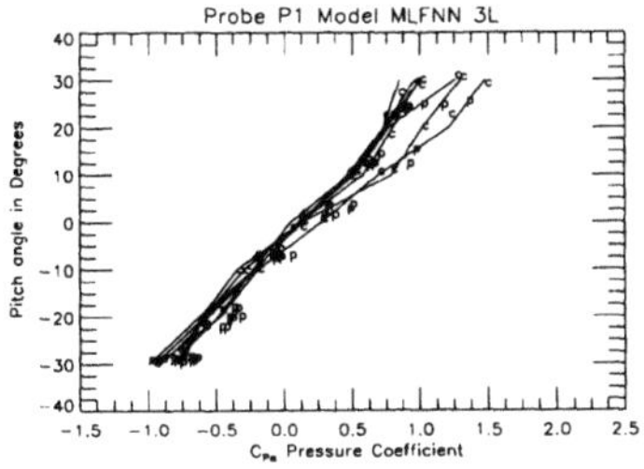

Figure 13: Relationship between α and $C_P\alpha$. Superposed are experimental measurements(full line), network calibrated (c), and network predicted (p) cases.

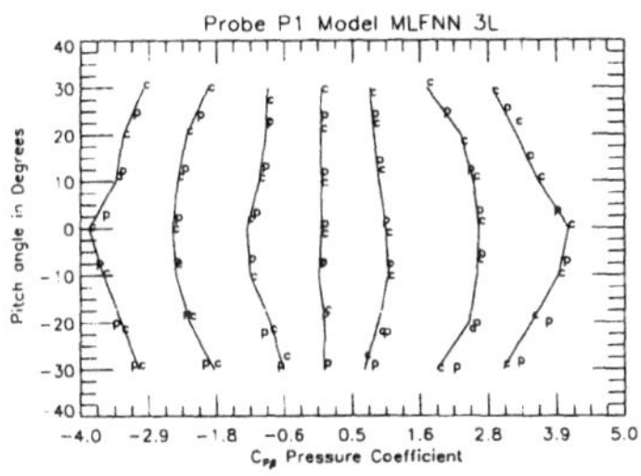

Figure 14: Relationship between α and $C_P\beta$. Superposed are experimental measurements(full line), network calibrated (c), and network predicted (p) cases.

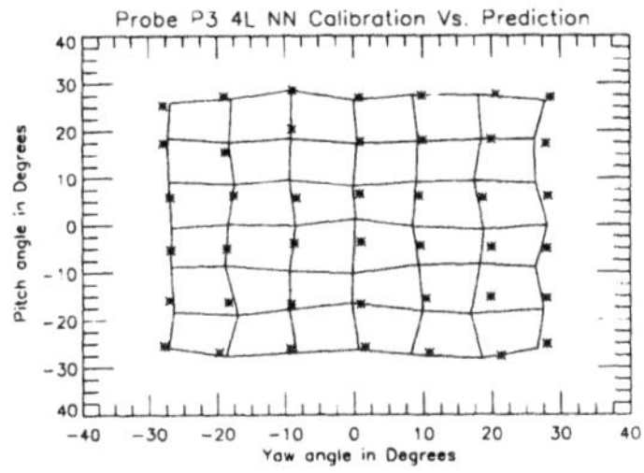

Figure 16: Inverted calibration map for Prism Probe 3. Four layer MLFNN network with 8 nodes in both hidden layers. Fixed rate for Neta and Alpha.

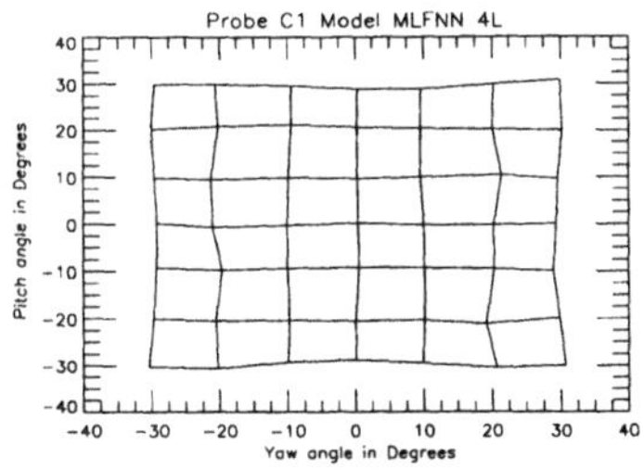

Figure 15: Inverted calibration map for Cone Probe 1. Four layer MLFNN network with 8 nodes in both hidden layers. Fixed rate for Neta and Alpha.

BEYOND PARADISE: EXTENSIONS TO A NEURAL NETWORK FOR VISUAL OBJECT RECOGNITION

I. France, Sch. of Elec. Eng. & Comp. Sys., University of Wales, Bangor,
A.W.G. Duller, University of Wales, Bangor, A.Duller@sees.bangor.ac.uk

ABSTRACT

This paper describes extensions to a self-organising object recognition system called PARADISE[1]. The design provides image recognition with on-line learning and aims to be as generic as possible, requiring a minimum of application specific information to be included to produce a solution. A three layer structure is used which can be described as feature extraction, pattern detection and finally object classification. The first layer currently consists of a set of Gabor filters which are used to extract information at various scales and orientations from the input image. From this information the next layer automatically creates or reuses a series of small pattern detection modules which extract the important features. During recognition these pattern detectors allow some disagreement with those found in the current image so that a degree of deformation invariance is built-in to the network. Once the set of required pattern detectors has been chosen these are linked to a cell in the final layer to provide the classification.

In order to characterise the effect of the proposed extensions a set of test shapes is used. In addition, results from the application of the network to microscopic pollen identification are presented in which correct recognition requires information regarding both the internal structure and the outline shape of the objects.

INTRODUCTION

The PARADISE network [1][2] is a neural network developed for visual object recognition and uses ideas drawn from the Neocognitron [3], Feature Recognition Network [4] and Adaptive Resonance Theory [5].

In the original work which developed the network, the applications (hand gesture recognition and hand written character recognition) [1][2] were such that the outline "shape" of the object could be regarded as their most important attribute. The internal structure of the object was generally assumed to contain little useful information to the recognition process. This led to certain assumptions being made regarding the automatic placement of pattern detection modules which break down when there is considerable internal detail in the object. The original network used the average activation over a large area in order to place the pattern modules and while internal structure is then located, the edges do not produce sufficient average activation to trigger the placement of additional pattern modules. To produce a system which picks up both forms of information the feature placement uses centre weighting which means that the feature can be contained in a small area while the pattern module picks up context information from the surroundings.

Deformation invariance is an important part of the structure of the network. However, in the original design the nature of the deformation was only loosely constrained. This means that random deformations within an object are treated in the same way as rigid body motion,

---

[1] PAttern Recognition Architecture for Deformation Invariant Shape Encoding

contraction or expansion. To overcome this the pattern of deformation is considered rather than just its magnitude.

An overview of the original network is given initially and the limitations of various aspects of the design are detailed. A description is then given of the three new developments of the network and finally results are presented which show the effect of the changes on the categorisation of a series of test shapes and a set of images of microscopic pollen. The recognition of pollen is an important application due to its use in ancient climate reconstruction and the analysis of bore samples by oil companies. Initial results are given in [6].

ORIGINAL PARADISE NETWORK

In this section we provide an overview of the original PARADISE network. The PARADISE network is composed of three major layers, the Feature Extraction Layer, The Pattern Detection Layer and the Classification Layer. These layers will be explained below. The network is self-organising, and can create as many classes as are needed in order to represent the data. In this regard it differs from the Neocognitron which can only represent a fixed number of classes. In the PARADISE network the number of classes created is only indirectly controllable, via a classification threshold which specifies how similar two images must be before they can belong to the same class.

FEATURE EXTRACTION LAYER

The Feature Extraction (FE) Layer contains a number of Feature Extraction planes. Each plane consists of identical non-adaptive neurons which detect a feature in the input image. The output of each FE plane is thus a feature map for whichever feature they are detecting. In addition to a number of FE planes there is also an Activation Map which is simply the sum of the FE planes.

The FE planes are the most application specific part of the network and the exact features to detect should be matched to the type of objects to be recognised. However, it has been found that for many applications the use of zero-integral Gabor filters as FE planes has been successful. In particular, Gabor filters looking for lines which are oriented at 0° and 90° at varying frequencies have been used.

PATTERN DETECTION LAYER

The Pattern Detection layer consists of a number of Pattern Detection Modules (PDMs). These modules are designed to detect local sub-patterns in the image, by combining the responses of the FE planes over a fixed area. In order to provide translational tolerance each PDM looks for its pattern over a square area surrounding the centre of the PDM. This is achieved by using an "invariance plane" consisting of shared weight RBF cells which are all connected to the FE planes at shifted locations. All of the PDMs are connected to all of the FE planes.

CLASSIFICATION LAYER

The classification layer consists of neurons which are connected to subsets of the PDMs. Each classification cell (Ccell) represents a collection of features which may be found in the image in a loosely constrained shape. The output of a Ccell is the average of the outputs of the PDMs to which it is connected.

TRAINING THE NETWORK

When training the network on an unrecognised input the following steps are taken:

1. Calculate the FE planes, and the activation map.
2. Scan the activation map for an area whose average activation is greater than the training threshold.
3. If there is such an area, create a new PDM over that area.
4. Repeat 2 and 3 until no new areas found.
5. If less than the minimum number of PDMs has been found, delete them and discard the image as rubbish. (Not enough activation.)
6. Create a new classification cell and connect it to the new PDMs.

PATTERN RECOGNITION

When attempting to recognise an image the following steps are taken:

1. Calculate the FE planes, and activation map.
2. Calculate the responses of all the PDMs.
3. Calculate the responses of the Classification Cells.
4. Find the highest activated Classification Cell.
5. If activity is less than the classification threshold then the image is not recognised.
6. Otherwise, calculate the result of the hypothesis test (see below).
7. If hypothesis test fails, inhibit the Classification Cell and goto 4.
8. Otherwise, recognise the image as belonging to the Classification Cell.

THE HYPOTHESIS TEST

The hypothesis test runs as follows:

1. All PDMs connected to the Classification Cell blank the area in the activation map corresponding to the areas in the FE planes to which they are responding.
2. Pretend to create new PDMs using the remains of the activation map.
3. $\text{Hypothesis value} = \dfrac{\text{No. of PDMs attached to Ccell}}{\text{No. of PDMs attached to Ccell} + \text{No. of new features in image}}$
4. If the Hypothesis value is greater than the Hypothesis threshold, then the test is passed, otherwise it is failed.

LIMITATIONS OF THE ORIGINAL DESIGN

The concept of PARADISE was to be as generic as possible, requiring only a small amount of application specific information. However, during the design the type of application that was envisaged obviously had an effect on the decisions that were taken. This led to a number of limitations being built-in to the design and perhaps more importantly, the implementation of the network.

The original application images, hands and characters, are essentially binary objects (the grey level variance across the object is low). After filtering with Gabors the majority of the activation is at the object boundaries. In contrast, many types of pollen have a detailed internal structure, resulting in far more complicated feature maps. The method used to find important features meant that the internal features of the pollen were picked up by the network but a large proportion of the boundary was ignored.

PARADISE EXTENDED

There are three basic changes which have been made to the network which produce a better conceptual framework. Again, they have been driven by a specific application, but there has been an attempt to produce sensible general concepts from the limitations highlighted by the application. The three modifications will be detailed and then tests of each in turn are presented.

CENTRE WEIGHTED FEATURE SELECTION

When images of pollen were presented to PARADISE, the network created PDMs within the interior of the image, but left large parts of the periphery unmodelled, see figure 1, where the square outlines indicate the positions of the PDMs used to model the object. This led to many misclassifications when non-pollen objects bearing a superficial resemblance to the inside of pollen were presented.

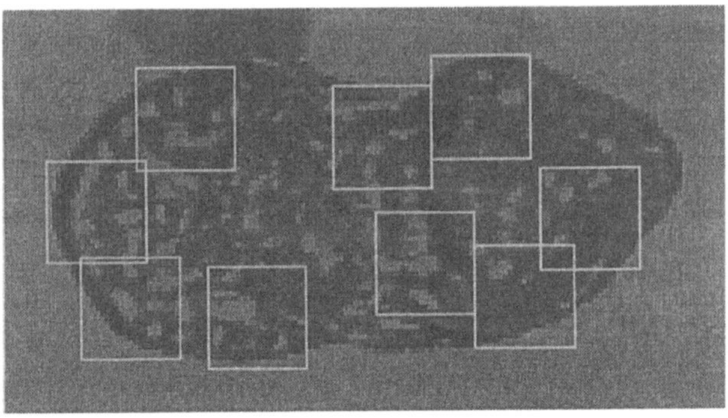

Figure 1: Example of a poorly modelled pollen image.

Using smaller PDMs would ensure that more of the edge was picked up. However, this introduces its own problems, small PDMs are very unspecific and badly constrained; their use tends to lead to a great many misclassifications due to a lack of context for the small features. To reduce this problem, important features are chosen by using a small window (say 5x5) but then a larger area centred around this window (say 11x11) is taken as the PDM feature. This centre weighting places the small features in context.

SHAPE CONSTRAINTS

The original network had very simple shape encoding. Features were searched for in a square area around the position in which they were found during the training phase. The only shape constraint was provided by the finite size of the PDM invariance planes. However, within this constraint any random movement of the PDMs was considered acceptable.

This simple scheme has been extended to provide a tighter constraint on the shape of the objects which accept translation, contraction or expansion, but reject random shape changes. Thus the new shape measure is invariant to translations and scaling but not to large rotations. It is assumed that large rotations will be dealt with by producing rotated versions of the training set (perhaps 8 different angles) which will result in a number of classes being generated for each object type.

Shape training

When a new class is created, the shape of the object is encoded as X given by

$$X = (x_1, y_1, x_2, y_2, \ldots, x_n, y_n),$$

where (x_i, y_i) is the position of the ith PDM, after the normalisation procedures given below. This shape vector is then used to train the weights of the shape cell associated with the new class. The shape cell is implemented using an RBF.

Normalising the shape vectors

In order to give the network translational invariance, the mean of the PDM positions are subtracted from each position. Having subtracted the mean, the shape vector is created and normalised to unit length. This gives the shape vector the required scale invariance.

Shape recall

During the recall phase, when the network is attempting to recognise an object, shape recall is required. When the maximum Ccell has been found, the shape created by its PDMs is converted into a shape vector, Y, using the normalisation procedure given above. Y is then presented to the shape cell associated with the chosen class and the shape measure, S, is calculated, using the normal RBF equation given by

$$S = \exp\left(\frac{-|X - Y|^2}{2\sigma^2}\right).$$

Currently the network uses a fixed value of $\sigma = 0.40$ which was determined empirically from looking at the results from a range of images.

HYPOTHESIS MEASUREMENT

The hypothesis testing implemented by the original PARADISE involved blanking out areas in the original image which were covered by PDMs attached to the Ccell under test. The network then attempted to create new features in the remainder of the image to account for the unmodelled activation in the FE planes. The hypothesis value was given by

$$H = \frac{\text{Number of PDMs attached to Ccell}}{\text{Number of PDMs attached to Ccell} + \text{Number of new features in image}}.$$

However, this definition produced the following undesirable effects,

- PDMs which are hardly activated will still blank the image,
- the ratio is easy to calculate but it is unclear what it means in real terms.

In order to provide a more useful value the level of activation in the image is compared to the activation successfully modelled by the Ccell and its associated PDMs. To provide a comparison, the total sum of the activation in the image is calculated.

The activation modelled by a Ccell is calculated by constructing an image and allowing each PDM to "stamp" its weights into the initially blank image. The amount of activation "stamped" is modified according to the level of recognition registered by the PDM. Thus, a poorly recognised PDM will only indicate a small proportion of the activation as having been modelled.

This reconstructed image is subtracted from the original feature detected image and the remaining activation is summed. The new hypothesis measure is then given by

$$H = 1 - \frac{\sum \text{Activation remaining}}{\sum \text{Original activation}}.$$

TESTING THE NEW CONCEPTS

In order to demonstrate the effect of each of the changes, each is taken in isolation in the following sections and tested using appropriate sets of images.

CENTRE WEIGHTED FEATURE SELECTION

To show the effect of the change in the method of automatic feature selection a test set of images consisting of shapes with a complex internal structure was generated. All of the images are 64x64 pixels. The shapes vary considerably in size and outline and can be seen in figure 2.

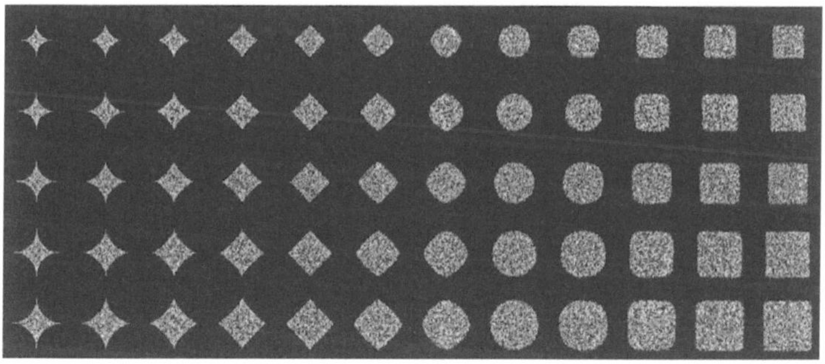

Figure 2: A set of test images for the feature detector

Bearing in mind that the aim of the centre weighting change was to allow the network to pick up more of the activation from the image, the following measure, R, is used to assess the success of the change.

$$R = \frac{\text{Number of active pixels unused}}{\text{Number of active pixels in original image}}.$$

The PDM creation routines were run on all of the images, using feature detection sizes varying between 1 and 15 and a PDM weight width of 15. The results are shown in figure 3, which demonstrates the rise in unmodelled activity with increasing feature size. Thus, if a PDM size of 15 is required the unmodelled activation drops from 24% when using a feature detection size of 15 to 2% when using a feature detection size of 5.

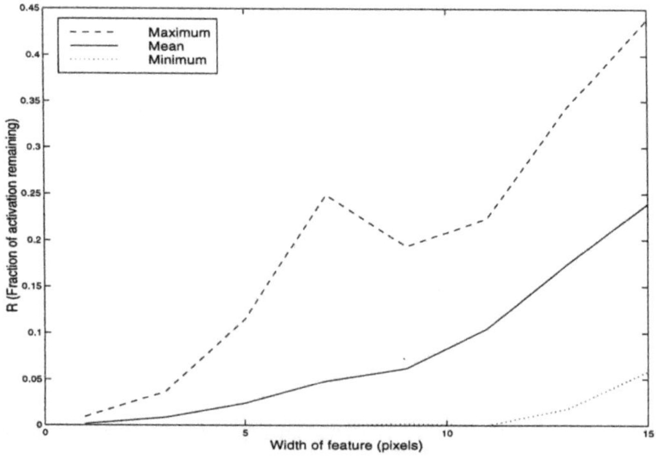

Figure 3: The maximum, mean and minimum proportion of activation remaining after extracting features using a weight width of 15 and feature widths from 1 to 15

The improved coverage can also be seen visually in figure 4, where the features chosen are indicated for a weight width of 15 and feature widths of 15 and 5.

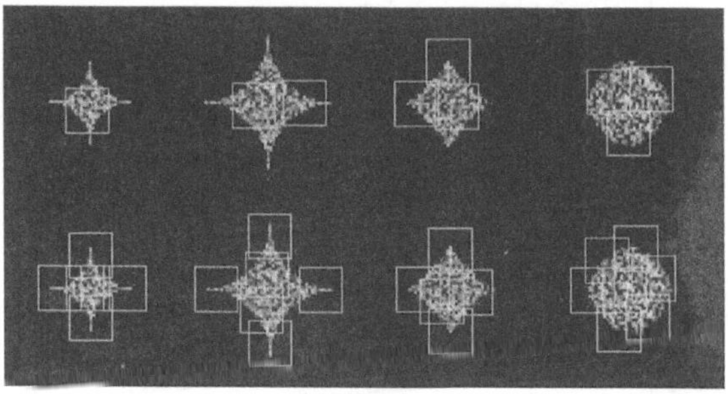

Figure 4: Examples of feature coverage. Feature width of 15 (top), 5 (bottom)

SHAPE TESTING

The limited shape constraints of the original network caused some erroneous classifications when applied to pollen images. In order to evaluate the shape constraints, a selection of pollen images were applied to a network with no shape constraints and a network with the new shape constraint system. The major classes created are shown in figures 5 and 6. The images within a class are arranged in decreasing order of recognition quality, with the class exemplar on the extreme left. For each row the leftmost number indicates the class identity and the value in brackets gives the number of images in the class. Where a class is too large to display in full only the three sections from the beginning, middle and end of the class are shown.

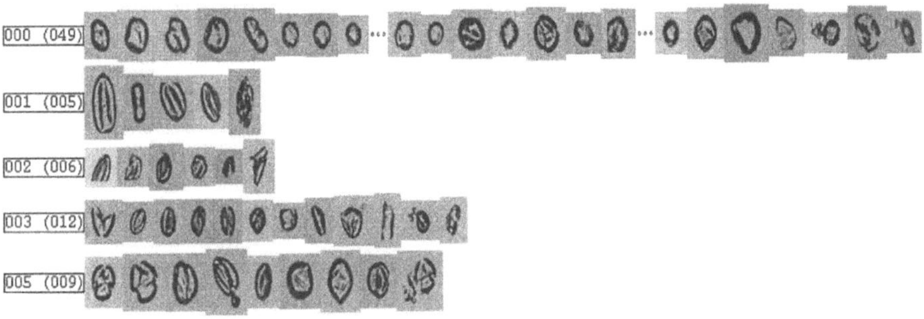

Figure 5: Major classes created by a network with no shape constraints

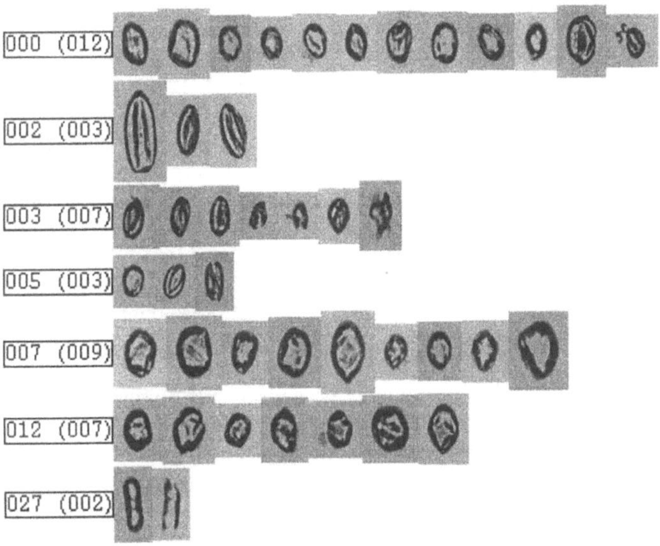

Figure 6: Major classes created by a network with the new shape constraints

The new constraints create classes which are far more consistent and the number of images in each class which can be considered as erroneous is much reduced.

HYPOTHESIS MEASUREMENT

The new hypothesis measure is impossible to isolate from the feature selection changes. The information which is missed by the original PARADISE when training classes, drastically reduces the value given by the new hypothesis test, simply because considerable amounts of activation are not being modelled. However, it is clear that this measure is much more robust than the old measure, which can change drastically when a PDM position moves by one pixel, exposing enough area to form a new PDM.

As an example of the different results given by the new measure compared to the old measure, examine figure 7. The network was trained on the first image and then recognised the next two with hypothesis values 0.83 and 0.625 for the old hypothesis measure and 0.24 and 0.21 for the new measure. In both recognition cases the PDMs have a low activation (maximum value 0.3). This is reflected in the new hypothesis result, but not in the old one.

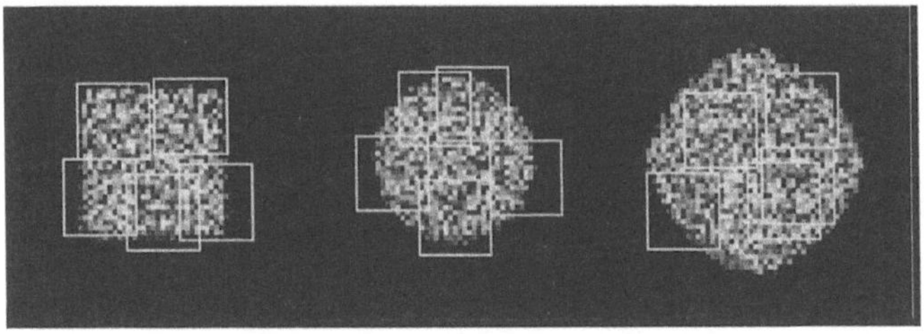

Figure 7: Example shapes from the test set.

RESULTS

In order to assess the effect of the changes on the consistency of the classes for the real application of interest, a set of pollen images was presented to both versions of the network. Firstly, a training set was presented to the networks, this consisted of 753 images automatically collected from the microscope slide. The classes created by the networks were analysed and classified as pollen or non-pollen. These classes were then used to classify the test set which consisted of 818 objects. Within this set were 225 pollen images (although many are poor images, or contain clumps of pollen) and 593 non-pollen images.

One measure used to analyse the results is class purity, which is given by,

$$\text{Class purity} = \frac{1}{\text{No. of classes}} \sum_{\text{All Classes}} \frac{\text{No. of correct matches by this class}}{\text{No. of matches by this class}}.$$

This gives a measure of the specificity of each class. The original PARADISE gives a result of 0.91, whereas the updated PARADISE gives a class purity of 0.93.

The old network created 36 pollen classes and 50 non-pollen classes (classification threshold 0.2, hypothesis threshold 0.6). The classification results obtained are shown in table 1. The new network created 12 pollen classes and 22 non-pollen classes (classification threshold 0.4, hypothesis threshold 0.5, shape threshold 0.75). The classification results are shown in table 1.

Object type	Original: Recognised as			Updated: Recognised as		
	Pollen	Non-pollen	Unclassified	Pollen	Non-pollen	Unclassified
Pollen	79.1%	16%	4.9%	75.1%	3.1%	21.8%
Non-pollen	4.9%	28.7%	66.4%	3.7%	20.1%	76.2%

Table 1: PARADISE classification results. Left: original network, Right: updated network.

The new network had a higher rejection rate of both pollen and non-pollen images. In recall mode we do not allow the network to create new classes if it has not recognised an image; thus objects which have not been modelled by the training set are rejected. This higher rejection rate corresponds to the increased selectivity of the network. Examination of the rejected pollen shows that it is mostly badly deformed, out of focus or in clumps and it is clear that it should not be recognised as pollen in the same sense as good quality pollen.

CONCLUSIONS

The original PARADISE network was envisioned as a general purpose image recognition system, which would need very little application specific information in order to produce a working system. Inevitably the choice of applications had an effect on the design and implementation of the initial network. Testing the network with a very different problem, that of fossilised pollen analysis, produced some odd results and made it clear that the network needed altering. The changes which have been introduced are not specific to the new application and are generally applicable concepts.

The new shape constraint allows improved control over the amount and nature of the deformation allowed in objects. This, together with the improved feature selection and the more intuitive hypothesis test, results in a greatly improved classifier. For the difficult problem of pollen recognition, the classes created by the network are now much more consistent and visually believable. Unfortunately, it is not to perform a meaningful comparison with the results from other researchers methods as there is no standard database of pollen available.

Acknowledgments

The authors would like to thank Dr Henry Lamb and Dr Geoff Duller from the University of Wales, Aberystwyth for providing the pollen samples and for many discussions regarding pollen identification.

REFERENCES

[1] D.S. Banarse and A.W.G. Duller. Deformation invariant visual object recognition: Experiments with a self-organising neural architecture. *Neural Computing and Applications*, 6(2):79–90, 1997.

[2] D.S. Banarse and A.W.G. Duller. Vision Experiments with Neural Deformable Template Matching. *Neural Processing Letters*, 5(2):111–119, 1997.

[3] Kunihiko Fukushima. Analysis of the process of visual pattern recognition by the neocognitron. *Neural Networks*, 2:413–420, 1989.

[4] Basit Hussain and M. R. Kabuka. A novel feature recognition neural network and its application to character recognition. *IEEE Transactions on Pattern Analysis and Machine Intelligence*, 16(1):98–106, 1994.

[5] G. A. Carpenter and S. Grossberg. The ART of adaptive pattern recognition by a self-organizing neural network. *Computer*, 21:77–88, 1988.

[6] I. France, A.W.G. Duller, H.F. Lamb, and G.A.T. Duller. A comparative study of model based and neural network based approaches to automatic pollen identification. In *Proceedings of British Machine Vision Conference*, pages 340–349, 1997.

PARALLEL DECOMPOSITION OF GENERIC MORPHOLOGICAL STRUCTURING ELEMENTS

Alberto Broggi, Alessandra Fascioli
Dipartimento di Ingegneria dell'Informazione
Università di Parma, I-43100 Parma, Italy
E-Mail: {broggi,fascal}@CE.UniPR.IT

ABSTRACT

The decomposition of a binary morphological structuring element is a well-known problem in pattern recognition that has often been addressed in the literature. Generally, only deterministic solutions have been considered, each relying on different assumptions. A different solution, with no such constraints, has been proposed by Anelli, Broggi and Destri: it is based on a stochastic evolutionary technique which is obviously computationally demanding. This work presents its parallel implementation aimed to the improvement of both the qualitative and quantitative performance of this approach.

1 INTRODUCTION

Mathematical Morphology [12, 16, 9] concerns the study of shape using the tools of set theory. Mathematical morphology has been extensively used in low-level image processing and analysis applications, since it allows to filter and/or enhance only some characteristics of objects, depending on their morphological shape. A lot of tutorials [9, 16, 21, 12, 19, 18, 20] can be found in the literature.

Within the mathematical morphology framework, a binary image A is defined as a subset of the two-dimensional Euclidean space E^2 ($Z \times Z$):

$$A = \{a = (a_i, a_j) \mid a_i, a_j \in Z\}. \tag{1}$$

In [9], monadic transforms acting on a generic image A (*complement*, *reflection*, and *translation*) and dyadic operators between sets (*dilation*, *erosion*, *opening*, and *closing*) are defined. In the following only the definitions of operators used throughout this paper are recalled, such as *translation*

$$A_t \triangleq \{x \in E^2 \mid x = a + t, \text{ for some } a \in A\} \quad \text{with } t \in E^2 \tag{2}$$

and *dilation*

$$A \oplus B \triangleq \{x \in E^2 \mid x = a + b, \text{ for some } a \in A, b \in B\} \tag{3}$$

where A represents the image to be processed, and B is called *Structuring Element* (SE), namely another subset of E^2 whose shape parameterizes each operation.

A SE B is said to be *convex with respect to a given set of morphological operations (e.g. dilation) with a given set of SEs (factors)* $\{F_i, i = 1, ..., M\}$ if it can be expressed as a chain of dilations of the F_i elements:

$$B = F_{k_1} \oplus F_{k_2} \oplus F_{k_3} \oplus \ldots \oplus F_{k_m}, \text{ with } k_j \in [1, M], \text{ for } j = 1, ..., m. \tag{4}$$

Otherwise B is said to be *non-convex with respect to the same set of SEs*, and thus it can only be expressed as a chain of boolean operations (e.g. unions and/or intersections) between convex elements (called *partitions*):

$$B = C_1 \odot C_2 \odot C_3 \odot \ldots \odot C_z, \tag{5}$$

where $\odot$ represents any boolean operation (such as unions $\cup$, intersections $\cap$,...) and C_i are convex elements that can be expressed as chains of dilations, as shown in eq. (4).

Hereinafter, a *dilation* between a generic image A and a complex SE B is considered; thanks to the property of union discussed in [9], namely

$$A \oplus (B_1 \cup B_2) = (A \oplus B_1) \cup (A \oplus B_2), \tag{6}$$

in the following non-convex SEs are decomposed using chains of unions of convex SEs (using the equality expressed by relation (6)), instead of using chains of intersections or other boolean operations (where no equality relations hold).

The decomposition of a binary SE into a chain of operations involving only elementary factors is a key problem; it can be related to many different goals, such as:

- the minimization of the number of decomposing sets (to reduce the number of dilations);
- the minimization of the total number of computations (for speed-up reasons);
- the minimization of the total number of elements in the decomposing sets (to reduce the size of the data structures and thus also the memory requirements in serial systems);
- the possibility to implement complex morphological operations on cellular systems whose Instruction Set (IS) is based on simple, elementary operations (to overcome the problem caused by the simple interconnection topology that limits the size of possible SEs);
- or even the determination of factors with a given shape (to aid the recognition of 2D objects).

Generally, only *deterministic* solutions have been considered [14, 15, 3], each relying on different assumptions (such as *convex* SEs, specific sets of elementary operators, etc.). This paper addresses the problem following a *stochastic* approach, based on Genetic Algorithms, proposed by Anelli, Broggi and Destri [1]. Being based on an evolutionary technique, this approach is computationally demanding. This work presents a parallel implementation of the described approach, aimed at the improvement of the algorithm performance both in terms of processing time and in terms of memory requirement.

This work is organized as follows: Section 2 briefly summarizes the Genetic Approach and describes the implementation of the decomposition algorithm; Section 3 discusses the parallel implementation; Section 4 presents the analysis of the results while Section 5 concludes the paper with some remarks and a discussion on future developments.

2 THE STOCHASTIC APPROACH

Genetic Algorithms (GAs), widely used in various fields [6], are optimization algorithms based on a stochastic search [10], operating by means of *genetic operators* on a *population* of potential solutions of the considered problem (*individuals*). The genetic search is driven by a *fitness* function: each individual is evaluated to give some quantitative measure of its fitness, that is the "goodness" of the solution it represents. At each iteration (*generation*) the fitness evaluation is performed on all individuals. Then, at the following iteration, a new population is generated, starting from the individuals with the highest fitness, and replacing, completely or partially, the previous generation.

The study of GAs led to the more general *Evolution Programs* (EPs) [13], or *Generalized GAs*. In EPs, individuals are represented by generalized data structures without the fixed-length constraint of "standard" GAs [2, 5]. In addition, ad-hoc operators are defined to act on these data structures.

EPs perfectly match the requirements of the SE decomposition problem, since the varying number of elementary items forming a solution does not allow to know the size of a generic solution, that is the length of the coding of a generic individual, a priori. In fact, for an efficient implementation, the data structure representing a decomposition must explicitly encode both the number and the shape of each single elementary operation composing the solution. Moreover, this coding must also allow fast and easy processing and evaluation phases. For these reasons it has been necessary to develop an ad-hoc EP with specific genetic rules, exploiting a method similar to the one presented in [4] for the solution of the bin-packing problem. An individual is represented by an arbitrarily long *chain of genes* (*chromosome*), each gene representing a *partition* of the input SE; the *logical union* of all genes produces the individual.

2.1 INITIALIZATION OF THE POPULATION

In order to understand this fundamental step, some definitions are introduced.

Definition 1: The IS is a set of M factors: IS = $\left\{F_i, i = 1, ..., M\right\}$.

Definition 2: Notation $H_{(x,y)}$ stands for $H \oplus \left\{(x,y)\right\}$, namely it represents a translation, as in eq. (2).

Definition 3: For a generic image H, $nH \triangleq H \oplus \cdots \oplus H$ (n terms, $n \geq 0$).

Definition 4: For a generic image H, O_H represents its origin.

In the following, B is the input SE, B_i is a generic subset of B with the same origin, and H represents any generic set, convex with respect to the IS:

$$H = q_1 F_1 \oplus q_2 F_2 \oplus \cdots \oplus q_i F_i \oplus \cdots \oplus q_M F_M. \tag{7}$$

If $O_{F_i} \in F_i$ for every F_i belonging to the IS[1], then $O_H \in H$.

The process starts with the identification of every element of set $C(B)$, which is defined as

$$C(B) \triangleq \left\{H \mid H_{(h,k)} \subseteq B \quad \text{for some} \quad (h,k)\right\} \tag{8}$$

since every element of $C(B)$ may represent a possible gene; this search has to be *deterministic* and *exhaustive*. Since $O_{F_i} \in F_i$, the set of possible pairs (h,k) is given by the set of all elements of B; for a generic image H, if $(h,k) \in B \ominus H$, then $H_{(h,k)} \in C(B)$. Therefore, the algorithm scans all the elements of the SE and determines which factors can form a legal chain of dilations starting from that element. The gene obtained so far needs an additional shift in order to overlap its origin with the origin of B.

Since the length of the best solution is not known a priori and since randomly linking together some genes seldom yields a legal solution, it has been decided to use each element of $C(B)$, which comprises all the workable genes, as constituting an individual with a chromosome composed of a single gene only. It is also possible, as an option, to include in the population multiple copies of each individual so formed. In this way the set of individuals forming the initial population is obtained.

[1] In the current implementation each factor is limited in size to 3×3 and $O_{F_i} \in F_i$.

2.2 THE FITNESS FUNCTION

The *fitness* function $f(I)$ is used to evaluate each individual I in order to drive the algorithm during the search. A cost function $f_C(I)$ has been introduced, which is identical to $f(I)$ iff $\bigcup_{i=1}^{N} B_i = B$, where B_i is the general partition forming the solution I of length N. This function must have several properties:

1. for legal solutions it is equal to $f(I)$;
2. it is defined also for non-legal solutions (i.e. solutions not covering perfectly the original SE), thus widening the search space;
3. it is easily implemented as a penalty function.

Penalty functions are used in highly constrained problems when the need of evaluating non-legal solutions is met by penalizing them with respect to the legal ones. The cost function thus includes a penalty term:

$$f_C(I) = af(I) + bf_P(I) \tag{9}$$

where a is equal to 1 iff $\bigcup_{i=1}^{N} B_i = B$, as stated above, otherwise a is expressed by a term proportional to the ratio between the number of elements present in the solution and the total number of elements in B. The term b is related, via user-defined parameters, to the current population size, and f_P is the *penalty function*, that is still related to the percentage of elements of B covered by the decomposition contained in the considered individual.

Assuming that the goal of the process is to obtain the decomposition that minimizes the number of operations required to compute the dilation of a generic image with SE B, the *fitness* function $f(I)$ is mainly constituted by the sum of the cost of every partition B_i; in addition, it takes into account also the number of logical union operations required, weighted by an appropriate coefficient, and the additional saving obtained with a further optional optimization of the solution (multi-level solution).

2.3 THE GENETIC SEARCH

A single processing cycle of the algorithm is composed of four stages:

- SELECTION OPERATORS: choose two individuals among population for reproduction purpose;
- BINARY GENETIC OPERATORS: combine in various way the parents' chromosomes in order to get offspring (i.e. one child or two children);
- COMPARISON OPERATORS: set up a competition between parents and offspring for inclusion in the next generation;
- UNARY GENETIC OPERATORS: mutate the chromosomes of the individuals winning at the previous stage.

When the list containing the individuals of the current population is exhausted, i.e. every individual has been chosen for reproduction, the population just formed undergoes the same processing in the following iteration. This iterative process stops when a specific termination criterion is met (different termination criteria are currently under evaluation).

The following presents a brief review of the operators; more details can be found in [1].

2.3.1 Selection operators

The operator is based on the *tournament selection scheme* as exposed in [8] with a tournament size of two. The scheme implemented makes use of a slightly modified version of the *genic selective crowding* technique [8] which forces individuals to compete with similar individuals, incrementing in this way the significance of the tournament.

2.3.2 Binary genetic operators

In order to obtain individuals that cover the SE, in the initial phase we need an operator which varies appreciably the length of individuals' chromosomes. Conversely, after this phase, when the average length of individuals is roughly close to the optimal one, we are concerned about the *quality* of the chromosome; for this reason two different operators have been conceived.

- The first one is based upon the *cut and splice* operator [7]. This operator cuts the chromosome randomly in correspondence to one of the possible points. The chromosome segments of two different individuals are either merged, creating in this way a single child, or promoted to a full individual.
- The second operator attempts to improve the fitness of the parents by mixing their chromosomes. A gene composing the first parent is injected into the chromosome of the other parent, replacing one of its genes, thus not changing the length of the chromosome but altering only its content.

2.3.3 Comparison operators

At this stage the operator chooses among parents and offspring the individuals to be inserted in the next generation. The scheme followed is based upon the *Deterministic Crowding* scheme presented in [11].

2.3.4 Unary genetic operators

Mutation has the primary goal of re-inserting genes previously discarded and otherwise definitively lost; typically this is the case of little partitions, whose contribution to the fitness improvement has been underestimated in the previous phases of the execution. This contribution can be essential later to achieve the covering of the whole SE. Two operators have been created:

1. this operator substitutes the gene to be inserted to the most similar one in the chromosome of the individual;

2. this operator forces the gene to be included and suppresses those which overlap with it. It can cause a big fitness worsening but it has the advantage to increase diversity in the chromosomes as a whole.

The complete process is shown in fig. 1 where a simple selection (which does not use a tournament scheme) is added. It is possible to traverse the graph following 2^3 paths and the decisions are made according to the value of the respective probability values p_1, p_2, p_3. These parameters are computed at the beginning of every generation starting from parameters describing the *status* of the current generation; they can be regarded as *adaptive parameters* [17].

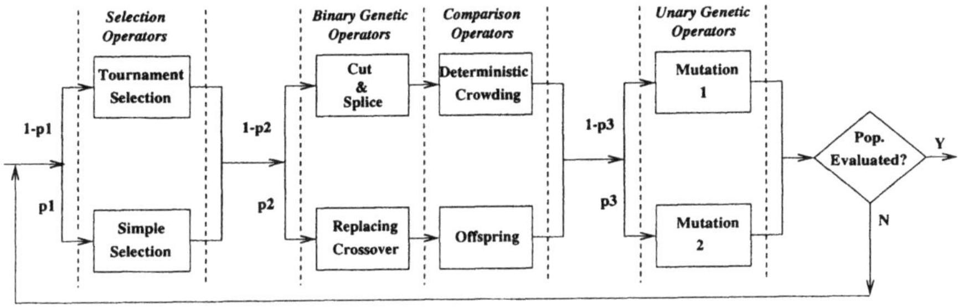

Figure 1: A schematic representation of the generational process

3 THE PARALLEL IMPLEMENTATION

Being based on an evolutionary technique, the discussed stochastic approach is highly computationally demanding: as an example, elements up to 16×16 have been decomposed using ISs composed of 8 basic operations on a two processors HP 9000 with 128 megabytes of RAM; the decompositions took about 6 hours of CPU time and computed 200 generations starting with an average of 2000 individuals; the computations required about 80 megabytes of memory. For this reason a parallel implementation, based on the MPI programming technique, has been developed in order to speed up the decomposition task by exploiting the distribution of the processing among different processors.

The analysis of the algorithm behavior suggested enlarging the search space to achieve convergence in a small number of generations, rather than distributing the computation of the genetic operators which is not computation intensive.

Among the different possible parallel implementations, a *fully connected network* model composed of n independent interacting processes has been prefered with respect to a *master-slave* configuration in which a single process performs the selection and entrusts the application of the genetic operators to the other processes. In fact this second approach would not be efficient because of the relevant interprocess communication time required.

The processing is split among several computing nodes which work independently using different evolution parameters in order to enlarge the search space. The distribution of the parameters on a sufficiently large number of nodes grants the inclusion of the optimal ones, thus making the processing less dependent on the specific set of parameters. Another important benefit gained from the distribution of the processing is the reduction of the number of local resources needed for the decomposition of a given SE.

Each computing node performs a local search based on its evolution parameters. After a given number of iterations the best partial results of the processing (i.e. the best solutions) are sent to the other nodes using an *all to all* communication model. The frequency of this information exchange can be set by the user and remains fixed for the whole run. Each node then continues the evolution toward its optimal solution benefitting by the received injections. At the end of the processing one of the nodes is in charge of the identification of the best solution among all the nodes.

3.1 MEMORY OPTIMIZATION

One of the most critical aspects of the serial version of the algorithm is the extensive memory requirement in case of large SEs decomposition. To cope with this problem, two different strategies, aimed to reduce the resource requirement, have been introduced in the parallel im-

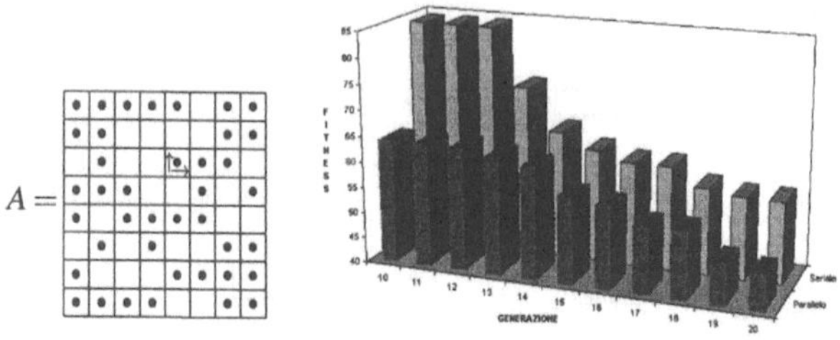

Figure 2: Fitness of the serial and parallel decomposition of the SE A

plementation.

The first parameter available to the user controls the size of the individuals of the initial population. This limitation on the expansion level drastically reduces the memory occupation by shrinking the search space and represents a trade off between the resource requirements and the quality of the solution. In fact, it allows to decompose large SEs even on machines with limited resources, yet granting the algorithm convergence by the presence of the necessary genetic material distributed over different processing nodes. Nevertheless, the accomplished solutions can be quite far from the minimum cost ones since they are likely to be composed of long collections of small genes.

The other coefficient introduced to control the resource use exploits the distribution of the processing. A probability threshold on the genes insertion has been defined: after the initial phase (the creation of the tree formed by all the legal genes), the tree is randomly subsampled and this threshold controls the probability of insertion of the genes in the initial population of each node, which samples a different region of the tree in order to distribute the search areas. During the information exchange phase, the genes which contribute to form the best individuals are sent to the other nodes within the individuals themselves. Each node then receives individuals with a new genetic material. The limitation of the search space is less drastic than in the first strategy and the possibility to accomplish the minimum cost solution is maintained by the different selections of the nodes over the gene tree. The possibility of a multiple selection of the same gene by different nodes has a positive influence on the convergence speed.

4 ANALYSIS OF THE RESULTS

Several different SEs have been processed in order to test the algorithm, to compare the parallel implementation to the serial version and to analyze the influence of the various parameters.

4.1 THE SERIAL AND THE PARALLEL VERSIONS

The comparison between the serial and the parallel versions of the algorithm has been based on the decomposition of a number of different SEs. The tests have been performed without distributing the initial gene tree among the nodes so that the two implementations work in similar conditions. In this case the parallel version shows performance similar to the serial one's, since the time required by the interprocess communications represent a small part of the overall processing time. However, the higher convergence speed of the parallel version demonstrates that the enlargement of the search space has been a successful choice. Fig. 2 shows the results of the tests on a 8×8 SE.

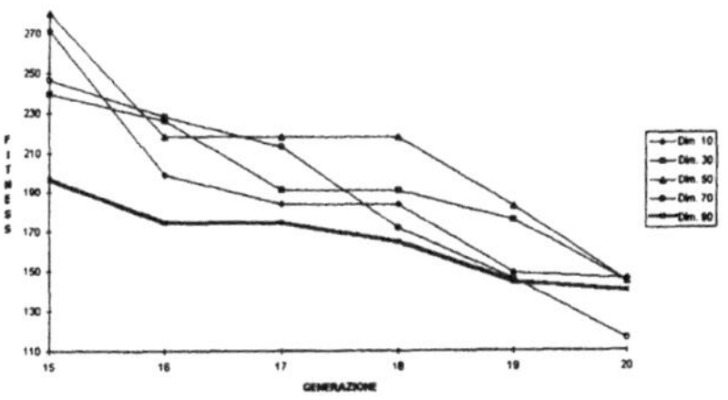

(a) (b)

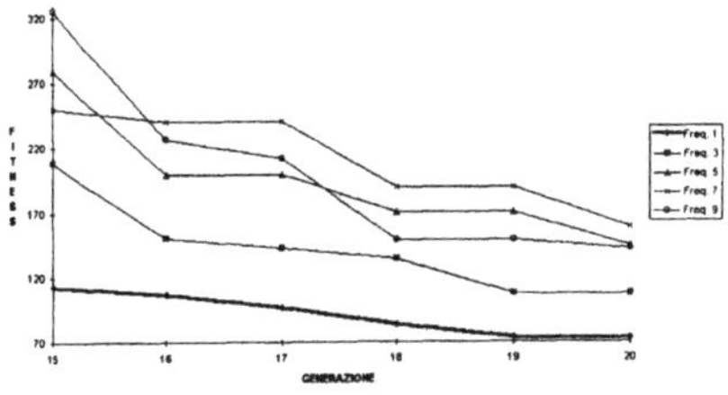

Figure 3: Fitness of the best individual as a function of the number of generations for different values of (a) the size and (b) the frequency of the injections (number of generations between two successive injections)

4.2 SIZE AND FREQUENCY OF THE INJECTIONS

The decomposition of a specific SE has been tested by uniformly distributing the population among the nodes and varying the size and the frequency of the injections in order to estimate the appropriate number of individuals to be exchanged and a convenient value for the frequency of the information exchanges.

The number of injected individuals should generally be inversely proportional to the number of computing nodes in order to avoid the risk for useless exchanges of similar individuals due to the fine distribution of the evolution parameters among many nodes. It has been observed that small injections yield few benefits, while excessively large injections cause a useless expansion of the population which slows the convergence (see fig. 3.a). The optimal value of the number of individuals to be sent is near 10% of the population. Moreover, as the evolution progresses the new received individuals are less likely to be decisive for the future evolution. In fact, a number of tests has shown that large part of the genetic material is distributed by the first injections, while the following ones tend to distribute the best organization found of the same material. For these reasons a decreasing importance has been given to the injections as the evolution proceeds by defining an injection probability coefficient whose value is determined from statistics on the processing state.

Furthermore, the tests have proved that frequent injections are preferable since they speed up the accomplishment of the convergence (see fig. 3.b). In fact, in case the initial population is split among the different nodes, the exchange phases assume a great importance for the local search performed by the single nodes: if a missing gene is necessary to improve the cost of the solution, thanks to a high frequency of the injections the need for that specific gene can be satisfied with few generations.

4.3 NUMBER OF COMPUTING NODES

A different specific SE has been used to study the effect of the distribution of the search on multiple nodes. The distribution of the data among few nodes handling large populations has been compared to the choice of many nodes with a reduced local population (see fig. 4). The tests have shown that the use of many nodes with few individuals improves the algorithm convergence speed because it increases the number of explored paths in the search space and it decreases the processing time since each node has less data to process. Nevertheless, this solution requires a great deal of interprocess communications, hence it does not suit a configuration featured by a slow interconnection network.

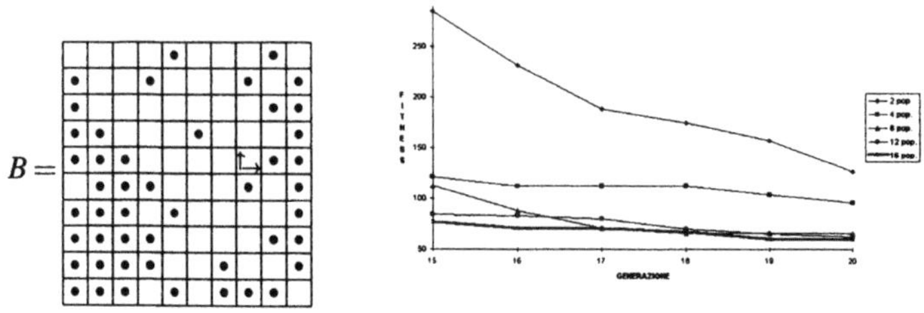

Figure 4: Fitness of the best individual representing the decomposition of the SE B as a function of the number of generations for different values of the number of populations

4.4 DECOMPOSITION OF TYPICAL SES

The results of the tests performed on several typical SEs frequently used in pattern recognition problems have shown that sparse SEs tend to be decomposed as the union of a long chain of elementary genes, while compact SEs are decomposed as the union of few complex genes (made of long chains of factor dilations). This is intuitive, however, since for compact elements a large number of dilations are legal, conversely sparse elements limit the sequence of legal dilations and have to be covered by means of longer chains of genes.

The processing time depends on the SE size, as well as on its morphology as related to that of the IS factors. Obviously, the processing of compact elements is more complex because many different decompositions with similar costs are feasible. On the other hand sparse elements tend to have a faster decomposition. Similarly, the resource requirement increases with the complexity of the SE.

5 CONCLUSION

This paper presented the parallelization of a stochastic evolutionary technique aimed to the decomposition of arbitrarily shaped binary morphological SEs into chains of elementary factors.

The parallel implementation improves both the qualitative and the quantitative performance of the algorithm: the distribution of the search on multiple independent computing nodes has shown to be effective reducing both the number of generations needed for the convergence and the processing time. Moreover, it allows to decompose large-sized SEs that cannot be handled by a single machine because of their extensive memory requirements.

The definition of the IS factors, the decomposing SE, and the evolution parameters is done through a Java-based graphical interface. A further development regards meta-evolution, i.e. the possibility to modify the algorithm behavior at runtime, thoroughly analyzing the influence of the various parameters on the processing.

References

[1] G. Anelli, A. Broggi, and G. Destri. Decomposition of Arbitrarily Shaped Binary Morphological Structuring Elements using Genetic Algorithms. *IEEE Transactions on PAMI*, 20(2):217–224, February 1998.

[2] P. Angeline, G. Saunders, and J. Pollack. An Evolutionary Algorithm That Constructs Recurrent Neural Networks. *IEEE Transactions on Neural Networks*, 5:54–65, January 1994.

[3] A. Broggi. Speeding-up Mathematical Morphology Computations with Special-Purpose Array Processors. In T. N. Mudge and B. D. Shriver, editors, *Proceedings of the 27th Hawaii International Conference on System Sciences*, volume I, pages 321–330, Maui, Hawaii, January 4-7 1994. IEEE Computer Society.

[4] E. Falkenauer. A New Representation and Operators for Genetic Algorithms Applied to Grouping Problems. *Evolutionary Computation*, 2(2), 1994.

[5] D. Fogel. An introduction to Simulated Evolutionary Optimization . *IEEE Transactions on Neural Networks*, 5:3–14, January 1994.

[6] D. Goldberg. *Genetic Algorithms in Search, Optimization and Machine Learning*. Addison Wesley, Readings, MA, 1989.

[7] D. E. Goldberg, B. Korb, and K. Deb. Messy Genetic Algorithms: Motivation, Analysis and First Results. *Complex Systems*, 3:493–530, 1989.

[8] D. E. Goldberg, B. Korb, and K. Deb. Messy Genetic Algorithms Revisited: Studies in Mixed Size and Scale. *Complex Systems*, 4:415–444, 1990.

[9] R. M. Haralick, S. R. Sternberg, and X. Zhuang. Image Analysis Using Mathematical Morphology. *IEEE Transaction on Pattern Analysis and Machine Intelligence*, 9(4):532–550, 1987.

[10] J. Holland. *Adaption in Natural and Artificial Systems*. University of Michigan Press, Ann Arbor, MI, 1975.

[11] S. W. Mahfoud. Crossover Interactions Among Niches. In *Proceedings of the First IEEE Conference on Evolutionary Computation*, pages 188–193, 1994.

[12] G. Matheron. *Random Sets and Integral Geometry*. John Wiley, New York, 1975.

[13] Z. Michalewicz. *Genetic Algorithms + Data Structures = Evolution Programs*. Springer-Verlag, Berlin, 1992.

[14] H. Park and R. T. Chin. Optimal Decomposition of Convex Structuring Elements for a 4-Connected Parallel Array Processor. *IEEE Transaction on Pattern Analysis and Machine Intelligence*, 16(3), March 1994.

[15] H. Park and R. T. Chin. Decomposition of Arbitrarily Shaped Morphological Structuring Elements. *IEEE Transaction on Pattern Analysis and Machine Intelligence*, 17(1), January 1995.

[16] J. Serra. *Image Analysis and Mathematical Morphology*. Academic Press, London, 1982.

[17] M. Srinivas and L. Patnaik. Adaptive Probabilities of Crossover and Mutation in Genetic Algorithm. *IEEE Transactions on System, Man, and Cybernetics*, 24(4), Apr 1994.

[18] R. van den Boomgaard. *Mathematical Morphology: Extensions Towards Computer Vision*. PhD thesis, Universiteit Van Amsterdam, 1992.

[19] R. van den Boomgaard and R. van Balen. Methods for Fast Morphological Image Transforms Using Bitmapped Binary Images. *Computer Vision, Graphics, and Image Processing: Graphical Models and Image Processing*, 54(3):252–258, May 1992.

[20] S. S. Wilson. Theory of Matrix Morphology. *IEEE Transaction on Pattern Analysis and Machine Intelligence*, 14(6):636–652, June 1992.

[21] X. Zhuang and R. M. Haralick. Morphological structuring element decomposition. *Computer Vision, Graphics, and Image Processing*, 35:370–382, September 1986.

NEURAL LEARNING OF SPIRAL STRUCTURES

Sameer Singh, Department of Computer Science, University of Exeter, UK

ABSTRACT

Spiral structures are one of the most difficult patterns to classify. In this paper, some important characteristics of the two-spiral problem are discussed. The paper discusses the reasons why linear and non-linear approaches have difficulties with classifying such data. The paper focusses on how structural information about spirals can be useful in providing critical information to a neural network for their recognition. Results are presented on neural network solutions to the classical two-spiral problem by extracting structural and rotational information from the spiral training data.

1. SPIRAL STRUCTURES

Spiral data is found in several natural and physical domains. The classic double helix DNA, the motion of particles in cyclotrons, and spiral feed in manufacturing are some of the well-known examples. Spirals are particularly intriguing because of their high levels of non-linearity and resistance to shape transformation under rotation, translation or other scalar operations. Spirals structures are also attractive for their temporal properties and are found to be particularly hard to classify. For pattern recognition purposes, spiral recognition problems are specially attractive since we can manipulate their complexity with relative ease and control its size.

The spiral problem is a classic example of non-linear data. It is impossible to separate two spirals coiling around each other with a linear method. The spiral data is considered here in two dimension since previous work exists in this area for comparison. However, spirals can be generated in any number of dimensions. The benchmark spiral program, available from the Carnegie Mellon AI repository, generates two sets of points, each set with 96.density + 1 data points (3 revolutions of 32 times the density plus one end point). If a total of N data points are to be generated, then the spiral shape parameters change as follows, $1 \leq i \leq N$:

$$\text{angle} = (i.\pi) / (16.\text{density}) \qquad \ldots(1)$$

$$\text{radius} = \text{maxRadius}.((104.\text{density}) - i) / (104.\text{density})) \qquad \ldots(2)$$

$$x = \text{radius}.\cos(\text{angle}) \qquad \ldots(3)$$

$$y = \text{radius}.\sin(\text{angle}) \qquad \ldots(4)$$

Here x and y are the spiral data points generated by the program, and $\pi = 3.14$. Since data points are generated in sequence, equations 1-4 are time dependent. The temporal nature of the resultant spiral is shown in Figure 1. Here the angle and radius of the spiral changes as new data is generated in sequence. The spiral is temporal because at a given point in time, the angle of the spiral that determines its position (x, y) is dependent on time (*i* in equation 1).

The two spirals are governed by three parameters: density φ, radius σ, and offset δ[1]. The density variable defines the total number of points generated within an envelope defined by

[1] The original spiral was proposed with $\varphi = 1$, $\sigma = 6{,}5$ and $\delta = .1$ (ref: Carnegie Mellon AI Repository)

the radius. Data belonging to two different classes lie on these two different spirals (represented as a sequence of white and black circles in Figure 1). By manipulating spiral parameters, it is possible to generate different spirals with varying radius and length.

Figure 1. 2D Spiral data scatterplot. Two spirals with a maximum radius of 6.5 coil around each other. The two different classes are highlighted in a hypersphere with their training data (white and black points) and a test pattern is illustrated with a black square.

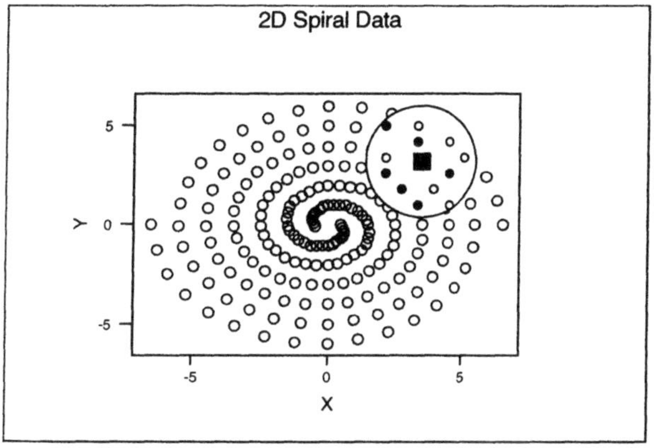

A pattern classifier working on the problem should be able to recognise the training set before making test classifications. The benchmark has a training set, and test sets. The training set is represented by the vector {**x**, **y**}. The test sets may be thought of as noisy spirals, i.e. training set plus a uniform level of noise δ. For the two spiral problem, three test sets are possible: {**x**, **y**+δ}, {**x**+δ, **y**} and {**x**+δ, **y**+δ} where δ is a pre-defined scalar representing noise or offset. This method of offsetting test sets on different variables has been used for historical reasons than personal preference. It is possible to generate several different test sets of noisy spirals with varying δ. Uncertainty in pattern recognition occurs when: the offset δ is large for a small radius σ spiral or when data is dense, i.e. φ is large.

2. PREVIOUS RESEARCH

Recognising the two spiral benchmark is a difficult task for several pattern recognition approaches since spiral data is highly non-linear. The problem has been difficult to solve using neural approaches (see Touretzky and Pomerleau[1] for a discussion). It has been observed that backpropagation and its relatives encounter significant problems when training the neural network. In particular, deriving the optimal architecture is difficult, and furthermore, the training times are large. In addition, the spiral is under-constrained, i.e. data not lying on the spiral is often misclassified. For this reason, the two spiral problem has been particularly popular for testing novel neural and statistical pattern recognition classifiers. Considerable work has been done in the area since mid 1980s and in 1990s and a number of intelligent approaches have been applied to solving the spiral problem; neural networks: Fahlman[2], Fahlman and Lebiere[3], Lang and Witbrock[4], Tay and Evans[5]; neurofuzzy methods: Sun and Jang[6]; and data encoding methods: Chua et al.[7], Jia and Chua[8]. In addition, several other studies have tested their proposed pattern recognition methods on this benchmark problem since this process served as an indicator of their success with real-world problems, e.g. Ulgen et al.'s[9] hypercube separation algorithm's initial success with this benchmark confirmed superior results with hand-written character recognition data. Singh[10] used a single nearest neighbour method to recognise the two spiral data. Singh[11] used a fuzzy classifier to recognise spiral data and Singh[12] studied the effect of noise contamination of various types on the recognition performance. Singh[13] have also extended the fuzzy approach to recognising spirals in three dimensions.

3. LEARNING SPIRALS

The two-spiral problem, and its variants in higher dimension have some very interesting structural and spatial properties. If we are to study each spiral individually (*n* spirals in *n* dimension), we find that spirals are generated from the origin and move outwards in a helical structure. As they move outwards, the distance of the spiral from the origin increases and the distances between two successive points on the spiral also increase. However, these two distances are of little help for classification since they remain the same for both spirals and are not discriminatory.

The spirals have very interesting spatial properties. The overall structure of the spiral remains a spiral under rotation, translation or displacement. One of the methods for solving the problem may be the spiral unfolding such that the two spirals become linearly separable. However, this proposition is more difficult that it seems. The only other method of learning about spirals is to learn functions generating them using a black box type method. Neural networks, often claimed as universal approximators, have found spiral learning difficult. This is for two reasons. Spiral function is non-linear and time-dependent. Neural networks using standard MLP with backpropagation do not have the necessary information on the time-element through feedback loops to learn such a structure. Another reason is that both spirals, candidates in the discrimination process, have nearly the same function, except for some constant displacement scalar that preserves the distance between them. So, what additional tools do we have to enable ordinary neural networks to recognise different spirals?

Figure 2 shows the change in angle of the two spirals as it grows. Figure 3 shows how we may use this information. The angle θ is calculated as the change from (x_i, y_i) to (x_{i+1}, y_{i+1}) on the same spiral, rather than the angle of a given point from the origin with respect to the x axis. A close observation of the two spirals in Figure 1, and Figure 2 will reveal the fact that this change in θ for the two spirals at any given time is different from each other. This is a very important observation. If we are to calculate the sine of θ, then we find that this additional information gives us the power to discriminate between the two spirals.

The procedure now is to divide the training data into two halves; one for the first spiral and two for the second spiral. For each spiral, we compute the change in angle starting from the first point; if we represent spiral points as (x_i, y_i), then we create a new training file for each spiral with the information $(x_i, y_i, \sin\theta)$, where $\sin\theta$ is given by:

$$\sin\theta = (y_i - y_{i+1}) / \sqrt{(y_i - y_{i+1})^2 + (x_i - x_{i+1})^2}$$

The two new training files are now combined by interleaving the patterns from the two spirals. This training file is now fed to the neural network for training.

Figure 2. The two-spiral problem in three dimension. The spirals are separated on the basis of their class (left side of the class axis represents spirals or type1, and the right hand side represents spirals of type 2).

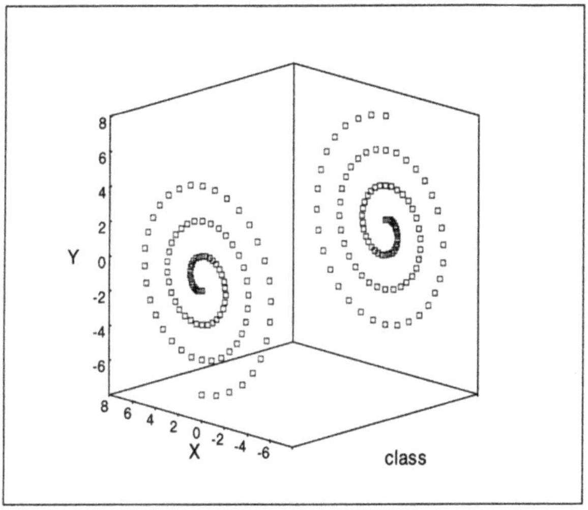

Figure 3. Change in angle with spiral movement

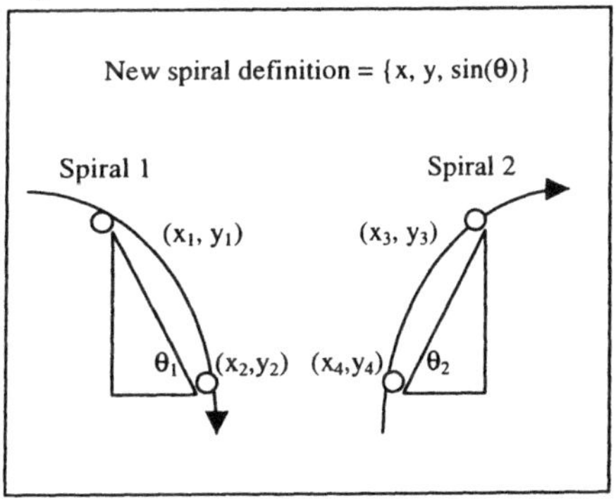

4. EXPERIMENT

The training data now consists of the tuples {**x**, **y**, **sin**(θ)}for spirals. The test data originally formulated as {**x**, **y**+δ}, {**x**+δ, **y**} and {**x**+δ, **y**+δ} is also represented as {**x**, **y**+δ, **sin**(θ) }, {**x**+δ, **y**, **sin**(θ) } and {**x**+δ, **y**+δ, **sin**(θ)}. For the test set, the sine of θ is calculated from the test data.

A simple multi-layer perceptron network using backpropagation with momentum is implemented with a learning rate of η=.1, and momentum of μ=.9. The network has the configuration 3x*h*x1 where *h* is the number of hidden nodes in a single hidden layer. The neural network is randomly initialised before the start of the training. The number of hidden nodes is increased in every trial and the generalisation error is noted. The number of hidden nodes is selected for the model that provides the least complexity and the least generalisation error. This is shown in Figure 3.

Figure 4. The selection of optimal network architecture

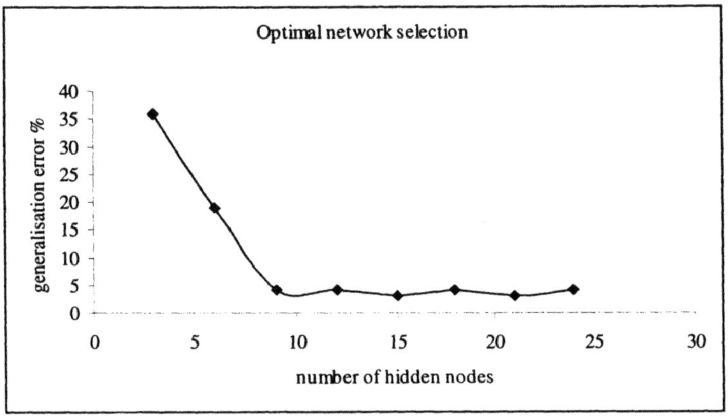

In Figure 4, the generalisation error decreases as the number of hidden nodes is increased. The increase in hidden nodes lead to a larger network that has a better generalisation ability. This performance however saturates after *h*=15. From Figure 4, we select the optimal number of hidden nodes equal to 15. Our experimentation is conducted from now on with a neural network having an architecture of 3x15x1. The three inputs to the network are the coordinates and the sine of the angle. The one output of the network is the class of the spiral, coded as 0 or 1 for spiral type 1 and 2.

5. RESULTS

The neural network was trained with an architecture of 3x15x1 for a total of 5000 epochs. The training and testing was performed using the Stuttgart Neural Network Simulator (SNNS). The training was performed with patterns from different spirals interleaved for a stable change in network weights. The trained network was then given the test data. The test data is produced for the three cases of spiral displacement as described before. For each case, the offset δ is varied from .1 to 1.0; these values are chosen as appropriate since for the spiral envelope of 6.5, each spiral coils roughly three times within this envelope as shown in Figure 1.

The test results are shown in Table 1. The recognition rate on different types of test sets is shown. Considering the combination of test data type and the offset δ, a total of 30 test sets have been used. The test results are very impressive. The neural network performance on classification approaches up to 97% correct recognition, and even with high values of spiral displacement in either one or both dimensions, the recognition rates remain particularly high.

Table 1. Testing on displaced data sets; spiral radius = 6.5

δ	Recognition rate % on $(x+\delta, y)$	Recognition rate % on $(x, y+\delta)$	Recognition rate % on $(x+\delta, y+\delta)$
.1	97	95	95
.2	97	92	92
.3	97	91	92
.4	96	92	91
.5	95	92	92
.6	94	91	91
.7	93	90	87
.8	92	88	86
.9	89	90	86
1.0	89	91	87

The results show that the neural learning of spiral structures is assisted by including training information on change in spiral angle with the generation of each successive point on the spiral.

6. CONCLUSION

In this paper, spiral structures have been recognised using the standard neural network method. The paper discusses why traditionally neural networks find it difficult to learn spiral structures without information on their temporal movement. When this information is available, neural networks are very efficient in their recognition. This work will prompt further work on using the same technique for recognising spirals in higher dimension.

REFERENCES

[1] Touretzky, DS, and Pomerleau, DA. What's hidden in the hidden layers? Byte 1989; August issue:227-233.

[2] Fahlman, SE. Faster-learning variations on back-propagation: An empirical study. In Proceedings of the 1988 Connectionist Models Summer School, Morgan Kaufmann, 1988.

[3] Fahlman, SE and Lebiere, C. The cascade-correlation learning architecture, In Advances in neural information processing systems 2, Touretzky, DS (ed.), Morgan Kaufmann, 1990.

[4] Lang, KJ and Witbrock, MJ. Learning to tell two spirals apart, In Proceedings of the 1988 Connectionist Models Summer School, Morgan Kaufmann, 1988.

[5] Tay, LP and Evans, DJ. Fast learning artificial neural network (FLANN II) using the nearest neighbour recall. Neural, Parallel and Scientific Computations 1994; 2(1):17-27.

[6] Sun, CT and Jang, JS. A neuro-fuzzy classifier and its applications, In Proceedings of the IEEE International conference on fuzzy systems, 1993, vol. 1, pp. 94-98.

[7] Chua, H, Jia, J, Chen, L and Gong, Y. Solving the two-spiral problem through input data encoding, Electronics letters 1995; 31(10):813-14.

[8] Jia, J and Chua, H. Solving two-spiral problem through input data representation, In Proceedings of the IEEE International conference on neural networks, 1995, vol. 1, pp. 132-135.

RANKING PATTERN RECOGNITION FEATURES FOR NEURAL NETWORKS

Wenjia Wang, Phillis Jones and Derek Partridge
Neural Computing Research Group
Department of Computer Science
University of Exeter, UK.

ABSTRACT
In all pattern recognition technologies, a crucial question is what features to extract and use for the basis of a recognition system. There are well-established techniques for ranking features to be used in linear combination, but when non-linear combination technologies, such as neural networks, are contemplated feature significance ranking is more problematic. In this paper we present a practical technique for ranking features in terms of significance for a neural-net pattern recognizer. We provide the results of applying this clamping technique to a small selection of problems, both well-defined abstract problems that permit a precise exploration of the technology, and more realistic data-defined problems that demonstrate its practical worth.

1 INTRODUCTION

When faced with a set of data with a view to data mining using neural networks, one of the important initial problems is what features to use, given that some are likely to be redundant, others are likely to be crucial and efficient and effective use of the technology requires application of as few features as possible. Principal component anaylsis(PCA)[1] is one of commonly used techniques for reducing dimensions of a problem. But it is limited by its linear trsnformations and may be unable to capture non-linear correlations in more complex problems[2], especially in data defined environments where data inevitably contains noise. Other techniques developed based on neural networks, e.g. pruning or optimal brain damage [3], have been used primarily to optimize the structure of a neural network by eliminating either weights or hidden units, even inputs through calculation of second derivative of error function over weights. However, apart from intensive computation, for real problems, due to their non-linearity and noisiness, the pruning results vary as changes of structure of nets, training initial conditions and parameters of learning algorithms, which makes the results inconsistent and therefore very difficult to interpret and extract out the most significant features.

In general, we are faced with the problem of ranking the significance of potential features of real problems with respect to their utility for predicting the correct class for any pattern. In practice, a second factor — the cost of generating the feature — will be significant and must be used together with bare significance. But in this paper we look at the significance issue using a clamping technique in multi-version system of neural networks and rank the significance of features consequently.

After describing the basic hypothesis, we test elements of it on several well-defined problems, i.e. a component of the Launch Intercepter problem (LIC1) and a triangle decision problem, so that the results obtained are uncluttered by concerns of noise, underlying data model, and real significance. We then apply the techniques to real-world problems, i.e. two medical problems - medicine prescription and osteoporosis prediction, where we still find general support for the hypothesis but complicated by further issues, not all of which have yet been resolved.

Finally, a point of nomenclature: our problems are not always typical pattern recognition problems — i.e. not 'visual' patterns. We take the view that any categorization problem that is based on a data set of examples and non-examples is fundamentally a pattern recognition problem.

2 THE CLAMPING HYPOTHESIS

The basic insight concerns redundant features: *if a feature is redundant with respect to classification of patterns, then the clamping of the values (i.e. the systematic fixing of the values independent of what the patterns themselves generate) will have no adverse effect on the generalization performance of a trained neural network in comparison to the same tests with this feature left to assume its 'natural' values.* A generalization of this insight leads to the hypothesis that the relative significance of a feature (with respect to pattern classification) can be assessed by the relative effect that clamping the feature has on generalization performance. If true, this means that a series of preliminary experiments with the pattern features, clamping one at a time and re-running the generalization test, can be used to rank all the features in terms of classification significance. This, in turn, will permit an experimentor to systematically explore the trade-off between minimizing the number of input features and maximizing classification performance.

We defined the significance as:

$$Sig(x_i) = 1 - \frac{g(\overline{x_i})}{g(\mathbf{x})}.$$

Where, $g(\mathbf{x})$ is the generalisation probability without any clamping, $g(\overline{x_i})$ is the generalisation probability when x_i is clamped. The generalisation probability is calculated by the number of patterns correctly prodicted (tested) over the number of patterns in a test set.

3 EXPERIMENTAL STUDIES

A series of experiments were performed, on a number of problems, in order to explore different elements of the clamping hypothesis.

3.1 CLAMPING TRULY REDUNDANT FEATURES

LIC1 is a well-defined boolean problem which we have explored extensively in the past (the detail description of the problem and the data sets can be found in [4]). It is a simple problem but one that is difficult (if not impossible) to implement with 100%

reliability using neural networks. It is defined as follows:

$$LIC1 = \begin{cases} \textbf{true} & \text{if } d((x_1, y_1), (x_2, y_2)) > LENGTH \\ \textbf{false} & \text{otherwise} \end{cases}$$

where $d((x_1, y_1), (x_2, y_2))$ is the euclidean distance between two points specified by cartesian coordinates (x_1, y_1) and (x_2, y_2), and $LENGTH$ is an input parameter. It is a problem of whether the distance between two points is greater than some value -$LENGTH$, or not. Then the problem can be represented by a pattern vector, with five input features: x_1, y_1, x_2, y_2, $LENGTH$ and one output–*decision* (each parameter is normalised to the interval [0,1] with six decimal place), i.e.

$$\mathbf{x} \;=\; [x_1,\, y_1,\, x_2,\, y_2,\, LENGTH,\, decision]$$

The original problem was deliberately modified by adding a sixth feature (with random values) in order to examine the basic hypothesis stated above, by knowing that this extra feature is complete redundant. Then the pattern become

$$\mathbf{x} \;=\; [x_1,\, y_1,\, x_2,\, y_2,\, LENGTH,\, in6,\, decision]$$

A variety of networks, multilayer perceptrons with one hidden layer, were trained using the standard backpropagation algorithm with training sets (containing a 1000 and later 100 patterns) that included this sixth, randomly valued input feature. The experiments were conducted by training a family of 27 nets with different architectures, initial conditions and training methods. The training was repeated 4 times with different partitions of the data set, thus 108 nets were created and then tested by clamping one of the input parameters to a value of zero (we trained a large number of nets in these investigations in order to examinate the consistency of the results. In theory, as described in [4], as few as 3 nets can form an optimal system. But in practice, 5 to 15 nets would be reasonable for constructing a multi-version system). The test results of the generalization of these nets, using 1000 patterns in each case, are shown in Figure 1.

As can be seen, clamping $in6$, the (known) redundant feature has very little adverse effect on performance despite the fact that this feature figured equally with the other five features in network training. In addition, note that the major degradation in performance occurs when the feature $LENGTH$ (denoted by *len* in Figure 1) is clamped, and that clamping of each of the other four features has much the same, quite significant, effect. The same effects are observed if the features are clamped to mean values, to 1 or to other values. This leads to a further hypothesis. i.e. if a feature is completely redundant, it can be clamped to any values in [0,1] without affecting the performance of trained neural networks.

However, with the smaller training sets (perhaps more realistically around 100 patterns), the results were not as clear-cut because the smaller training set may lack some information that a neural network needs to learn from. But the experiments with smaller pattern sets still clearly identified that $LENGTH$ was the most significant input and the sixth (the redundant one) was always portrayed as less significant than the others. It was also found that with a smaller pattern set cleanest results were obtained when each feature was clamped to its mean value within the pattern set.

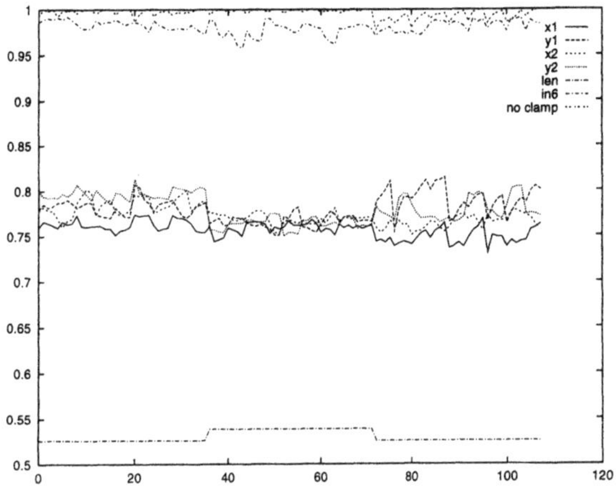

Figure 1: Generalisation performance for a variety of architectures showing effects of feature clamping (Note: in Figure 1-2: x-axis represents Nets, y-axis, the generalisation). The lowest generalisation rate, *len* (i.e. feature $LENGTH$ is clamped), means that $LENGTH$ has the strongest effect on the performance. The generalisation rate of *in6* is almost the same as that of *no clamp*, which indicates that the introduced feature *in6* has no or very little adverse effect on performance. The other 4 features, x_1, y_1, x_2, y_2, are of equally significant because of having the same generalisation rates when they were clamped.

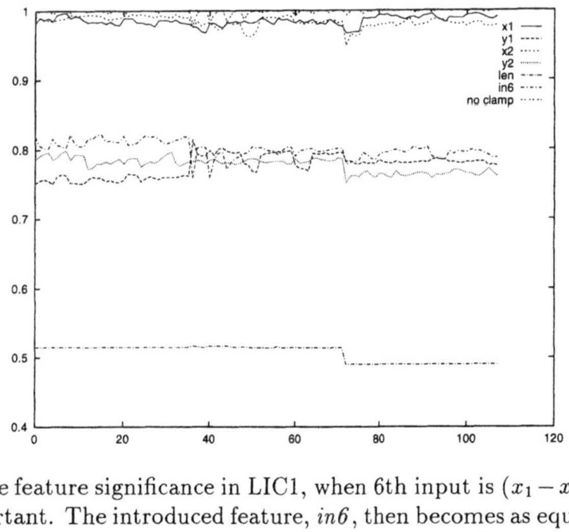

Figure 2: Relative feature significance in LIC1, when 6th input is $(x_1 - x_2)$. Feature *len* is still most important. The introduced feature, *in6*, then becomes as equally significant as y_1 and y_2 while features x_1 and x_2 are constrained to much less significance.

3.2 MANIPULATING FEATURE SIGNIFICANCE

If patterns come from a population where one feature is clustered around a single value then we would expect that feature to hold little significance when training a net. For example if medical data is available about patient treatment and the majority of the patients in the sample are given equal, or near equal, doses of a drug then the dose size will not be significant. The objective was to simulate this with a simple artificial situation where the population distribution of each feature can be easily manipulated and to demonstrate that the clamping technique does identify the reduced significance.

A simple, symmetrical problem was devised in order to permit explicit manipulation of problem-feature significance and thus determine how well various clamping strategies can indicate relative significance. The simple triangle problem has three input features, a, b and c, and a single boolean target, represented by a pattern vector $\mathbf{x}=[a, b, c, target]$. The target is true if a, b and c could be the sides of a triangle, and false otherwise. Each population of feature values is constructed independently. Features b and c are uniformly distributed over [0,1] and various distributions of a are considered. Only models where there are approximately equal numbers of the two target categories are considered. The distribution of a was manipulated to vary its relative significance.

For each population small sets of 500 patterns and a large test set of 10,000 patterns were generated. The small sets of 500 simulate the quantity of data likely to be available in a real problem. The large set of 10,000 patterns are to demonstrate that the clamping technique applied to the small set discloses the correct significance ranking.

Each net was trained to a fixed number of epochs using a complete small set. Then the 4 types of generalisation rates, i.e. g_1, $g_1(\overline{a})$, $g_1(\overline{b})$ and $g_1(\overline{c})$, were calculated based on the training sets without clamping, with a clamped to its mean value, with b clamped to its mean value, and with c clamped to its mean value, respectively. It was hoped that the values of g_1, $g_1(\overline{a})$, $g_1(\overline{b})$ and $g_1(\overline{c})$ considered over a family of 27 nets would disclose the relative significance of a to b and c. These nets were then tested with the large test set and the generalisation, $g_1(test)$, was calculated.

The second set of nets were trained using the same training set but only 2 input features b and c were used. The nets were also tested with the large test set to give a generalisation value $g_2(test)$. Feature a can be considered to be insignificant for net training if $g_2(test)$ is close to $g_1(test)$.

Firstly the experiment was conducted with a uniformly distributed over [0,1]. This population is clearly symmetric in a, b and c and hence a is significant. Indeed in the 27 cases tried g_2 was always greater than 95% while $g_2(\overline{a})$ was slightly below 75%. This was clearly demonstrated by the clamping technique on the small sets. g_1 was always above 97% and $g_1(\overline{a})$, $g_1(\overline{b})$ and $g_1(\overline{c})$ all took values between 65% and 75%.

Secondly various clusterings of the distribution of a were considered.

- 85% of patterns with $a = 0.1$ and the remainder uniform on [0,1] gives $g_2(test) =$ 87% and this is predicted by clamping results of $83\% < g_1(\overline{a}) < 90\%$ while $g_1(\overline{b})$ and $g_1(\overline{c})$ are considerably lower and between 56% and 60%

- 80% of patterns with a uniformly distributed on [0,0.1] and remainder uniform on [0,1] gives $g_2(test) = 82\%$ and this is predicted by clamping results of $77\% <$ $g_1(\overline{a}) < 85\%$ while $g_1(\overline{b})$ and $g_1(\overline{c})$ are between 60% and 65%

- 90% of patterns with $a = 0.3$ and the remainder uniform on [0,1] gives $g_2(test) =$

94% and this is predicted by clamping results of $93\% < g_1(\overline{a}) < 98\%$ while $g_1(\overline{b})$ and $g_1(\overline{c})$ are 58% and 66%

Notice how in each case the widespread values of $g_1(\overline{a})$ obtained by this rather crude clamping technique on a small set of data correctly predicts a range within which the value of $g_2(test)$ will lie.

Patterns often come from a population where features are interdependent. Could clamping reveal this? Again a simple artificial population was probed with the clamping procedure. As the obvious algorithmic solution to $LIC1$ would be based on the differences $(x_1 - x_2)$ and $(y_1 - y_2)$, redefining the sixth feature as, $in6{=}(x_1 - x_2)$, would make it interdependent with the features x_1, x_2 and also make x_1, x_2 unnecessary for network training. An experiment was then conducted to show that clamping technique has demonstrated this. As earlier, 108 nets were trained and tested with the training set clamped. The results are shown in Figure 2. $LENGTH$ is still the most significant feature. Features y_1, y_2 and $in6(=x_1 - x_2)$ are of equal significance with a clamped generalisation of about 80%, while x_1 and x_2 are shown to be extremely insignificant with a clamped generalisation of over 95%.

3.3 A CASE STUDY

Data was obtained from an experimental evaluation of a software and is about prediction of the types of medicines prescribed to patients with a particular disease. There are 5 factors, i.e. Age, Sex, Blood pressure, Cholesterol level and the ratio of Na/K, which are believed to be relevant to the disease and 5 types of drugs that can be used to treat the disease accordingly. The original problem demonstrated in the software is to predict which one of 5 drugs should be prescribed based on these 5 factors. The preliminary experiments had shown that nets trained easily even on a small subsection of the data and gave very good generalisation when tested with another large subset of the data.

This problem was taken in our research in order to demonstrate how clamping could be used to identify redundant features for a real problem when only a small number of patterns from a population are available. In our experiments only a small random set of 50 patterns was used. In the earlier experiments nets had been trained for a fixed number of epochs, the number of epochs being chosen such that almost all nets trained to 100% of generalisation rate on the training set. In this experiment, in order to obtain more meaningful averages over nets and to demonstrate how to proceed if the available pattern set will not train to 100%, nets were tested throughout training at fixed values of training set generalisation. 27 nets were trained and tested with the training set clamped at each feature in turn. Figure 3 shows the ratio of the generalisation of the clamped data to the generalisation of the unclamped data against the generalisation of the unclamped data. It can be clearly seen that the ratios for Age and Sex are close to one, which means these two factors are redundant.

If our hypothesis is correct then training a net without these 2 features should be nearly as successful as using all 5 features. This was shown to be the case by testing nets with a large, 1000, separate set of patterns. Figure 4 shows generalisation of the large test set against generalisation of the small training set for 2 families of 27 nets. It can be clearly seen that the new family trained with the reduced patterns with 3 features perform as satisfactorily as the original nets trained with 5 feature patterns.

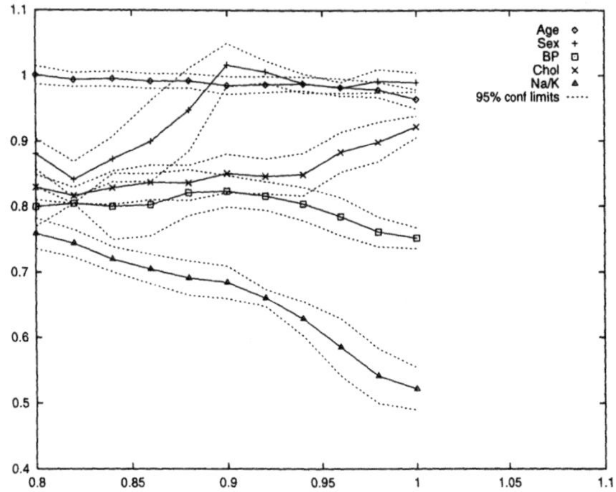

Figure 3: The results of the feature clamping for a small set of 50 patterns. The nets were able to identify that the features Age and Sex are less significant than the other 3 features when the learning performance of the nets reached to about 90% of generalisation rate. (Note: in figure 3 and 4, x-axis represents the learning performance, i.e. generalisation rate; y-axis, the ratio of clamped generalisation to unclamped generalisation)

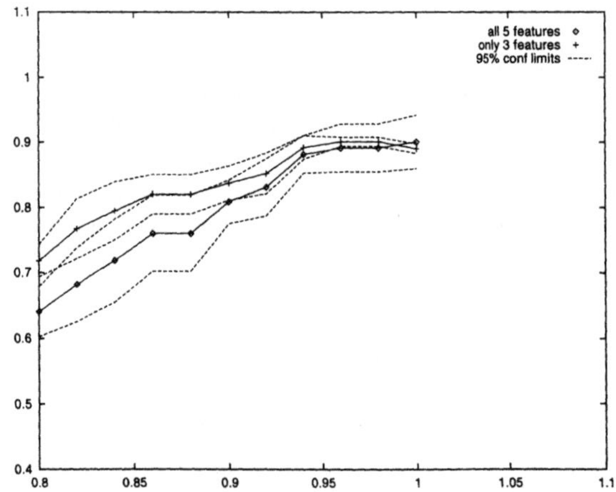

Figure 4: Confirmation of feature ranking and eliminating. The performance of the nets trained with only 3 features (left by eliminating the least significant 2 features identified by clamping) is actually slightly better than that of the nets trained with all 5 features when the nets were tested with a large test set.

3.4 A DIFFICULT REAL PROBLEM

Finally, we have applied these ideas to an ongoing task of predicting the risk of osteoporosis from a minimum of risk factors. This problem and first results have been reported elsewhere [5, 6] The data was collected by ourselves with questionnaire forms designed by the relevant experts, which ask for about 40 items and the diagnosis is made in accordance with the Ultra sound scanning results. 527 cases have been collected so far and computerised. Of more than 40 items, as many as 31 factors were thought to be more or less relevant to the disease occurrence or treatment and therefore they were taken as input variables.

The ultimate goal of the research project is to develop a computer aided system which can predict the risk of osteoporosis disease without using expensive scanning equipment. But, obviously, 31 factors are too many to be used in medical practice. What the doctors want is to pinpoint the few factors which have the most significance to the disease. The fewer factors identified, the better. The other method, e.g. linear correlation analysis, has been used for this purpose and the results will be published in a separate paper in a medical journal. By applying this clamping technique to these 31 risk factors, we hoped to obtain the significance ranking and consequently pick out the most relevant factors. Figure 5 shows the results of our experiments. Because all 31 factors were plotted on a limited space the figure seems a bit difficult to look at the significance of each individual factors. But it clearly shows the categories of the factors in terms of their signifcance, especially for the most significant factors which stand out.

These results suggest that four features (depicted by the thick lines on Figure 5) — Family history(FH), Kyphosis, BackPain and early Oestrogen Deficient(OesDef) — are particularly more significant than the others, with a second category (the thin lines on Figure 5) — Vitamin D(VitD), Exercise, Inactivity, Years since menopause (YrsMo), Calcium, HRT treatment, Steroid treatment, Age — as moderately important. The others with the value of significance between 0.05–0.01 are much less important. 7 factors with significance value less than 0.01 can be claimed redundant. The interpretation was later confirmed by the further experiments in which the least significant 10 factors were eliminated and the performance of the nets was almost the same as the previous ones. However, if only the most significant four factors ranked on the top were selected for training the performance of the nets was bad. This indicates that these 4 features which even appeared clearly on the top of ranking list are still not sufficient to represent the problem since their absolute significance values were small and therefore require further consideration.

As comparison, the data was analysed using PCA method and 12 principal components (eigenvalues>1.0) were extracted out, which cover 69.6% cumulative variance. The relationship between the principal components and the original factors is represented by a component correlation matrix and its interpretation is not simple. The top 4 factors which have the highest correlation coefficients with the first principal component are Age, YrsMo, H_loss and Height (obviously, they are all analogue variables). Of these 4 factors, only YrsMo and Age were ranked within top 12 in the neural network's result. Nevertheless, the comparison seems not really meaningful in this situation.

All the results were then assessed by a group of experts in the osteoporosis field and the factors ranked on the top of neural network's results appeared more reasonable and were adopted for selecting potential patients for further examination with scanning

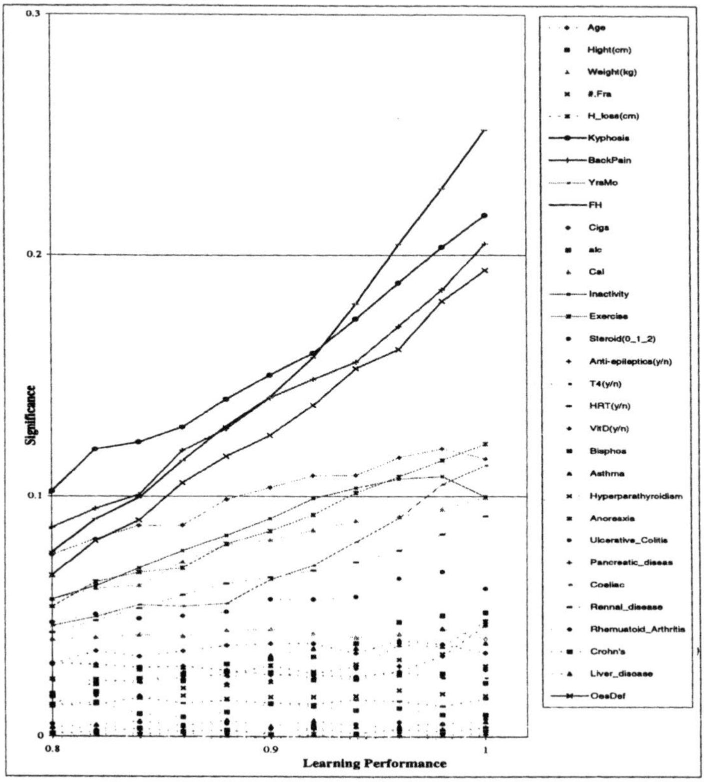

Figure 5: Significance of the risk factors of the osteoporosis problem

equipment.

Further investigations will be carried out to verify these primary results and to pinpoint the factors which can be used to represent the problem without losing too much information.

4 DISCUSSION AND CONCLUSIONS

The experiments described in this paper for a number of problems have revealed that the clamping technique does provide useful information on the relative significance of features with respect to neural-network based pattern recognition. However, the results for real problems are not as simple to interpret as the first two experiments led us to believe. For the first two problems we have prior knowledge about the significance of their variables by analysing their mathematical models. Then we can interpret the results with this knowledge and confirm that the rankings of significance are correct. We also deliberately manipulated the data patterns by introducing an extra input (which is either completely redundant or represents an important feature derived from other existing features) or modifying data distribution in order to verify the performance of the neural network clamping technique. But for each of the last two problems, particularly for the osteoporosis problem, there is no known mathematical model to describe it precisely and also no standard answers to the problem. In this case, although the results obtained from our technique are quite clear in terms of ranking of their significance and interpretation, it is not easy to verify them. The comparison with the other methods (e.g. Linear correlation and PCA) is not straightforward because they either produce correlation matrix or extract principal components instead of factors. Moreover, the results produced by these other techniques are distorted by their linear limitations. At this stage it appeares that the relevant human experts' assessment is reasonable and the result of the neural network clamping method has the least disagreement with experts' experience.

It should be pointed out that because of interdependencies between features, the removal of a feature or a number of features may result in a re-ranking of the remainder. On the other hand, the most significant factors which stand out from the others may not be simply selected in the hope of using them to represent the problem satisfactorily. The notion of a threshold will be set up with respect to not only relative values of significance but also some absolute measure of significance in order to better judge whether a subset of features are significant enough as a whole.

5 ACKNOWLEDGEMENTS

This research is funded by the EPSRC under grant number GR/K78607.

6 REFERENCES

[1] Tabachnick, B. and Fidell, L. "Using Multivariate Statistics" 3rd Edition, HarperCollins College Publishers, New York, 1996.

[2] Bishop, C. "Neural networks for Pattern Recognition" Claredon Press, Oxford, 1995.

[3] Le Cun, Y. et al. "Optimal Brain Damage." in D.S. Touretzky, ed.*Advances in Neural Information Processing Systems*, 1990, Vol.2, pp. 598-605.

[4] Partridge, D. et al. "Engineering multiversion neural net systems." Neural Computation. 1996, Vol. 8, no. 4, pp. 869-893.

[5] Wang, W., Partridge, D. and Rae, S. "Multiversion systems of neural networks for predicting the risk of osteoporosis," *Proc. 11th Internat. Florida AI Research Conference.*, Sanibel Island, 18-20 May, 1998, pp. 317-321.

[6] Partridge, D., Tallis,D. and Wang, W. "Inductive programming and a multiversion approach to data mining," *Proc. IASTED Conf. on AI and Soft Computing*, Cancun, Mexico, 27-30th May, 1998, pp. 19-22.

SPEECH RECOGNITION

A HYBRID APPROACH TO PATTERN MATCHING FOR TEXT-TO-SPEECH CONVERSION

Chew Lim Tan, Yan Rong Chen
School of Computing
National University of Singapore
Kent Ridge
Singapore 119260

Paul Hong Jyh Wu
Kent Ridge Digital Labs
Kent Ridge
Singapore 119597

ABSTRACT

Assignment of phonetic symbols to characters in a text-to-speech conversion system is a pattern analysis and recognition process. This research proposes a hybrid approach to pattern matching for speech synthesis by machine. The problem statement may be reduced as follows: How do we assign a phoneme to a character given its contextual information, i.e. the characters preceding and following the character? In our present study, we use a contextual window of five characters wide allowing up to two characters on either side of each character in question for phoneme assignment. The assignment method is based on a machine learning approach by training the system with a large set of examples. The hybrid approach is to integrate an information gain learning algorithm with a transformation-based error driven learning algorithm. The examples for training and testing in the present work are taken from NETtalk Corpus, containing a list of 20,008 English words along with a phonetic transcription for each word. This hybrid approach has been shown to achieve a final accuracy of 96.86%.

1. INTRODUCTION

Assignment of phonetic symbols to characters in a text-to-speech conversion system is a pattern analysis and recognition process. Grapheme-to-phoneme conversion is an essential module in every *text-to-speech system*. In earlier research, system builders hand-crafted a huge amount of rules which are closely dependent on various *language specific* (e.g. phonological, morphological, etc.) *knowledge*. This type of approach is very language dependent and expensive in the sense that solutions to the problems require considerable manual encoding of phonological and morphological knowledge structures, analysis and synthesis programmes. This is a very labour intensive process. Recently, there has been research interest in *data-oriented approach* which is language independent [1-4]. Therefore the knowledge acquisition bottleneck could be eliminated and the system becomes more flexible and portable so that the conversion engine could be reused among different language environments with few modifications. Data-oriented systems have been shown to achieve a comparable accuracy with earlier rule-based systems in various Natural Language Processing tasks. A hybrid approach is now proposed in this paper to further improve the accuracy.

The hybrid approach combines two data-oriented algorithms, namely, the Information Gain Learning Algorithm and the Transformation-based Error Driven Learning Algorithm, which are described in sections 2 and 3, respectively. The method for training and testing using the NETtalk corpus will be explained in section 4 followed by experimental results in section 5. Section 6 will conclude this paper with a discussion on our future works.

2. INFORMATION GAIN LEARNING ALGORITHM

This is a supervised learning technique proposed by Daelemans for speech synthesis in Dutch [1-4]. The method is based on a corpus of *exemplars* and a weighted *similarity metric* to predict new mappings. In the training stage, all exemplars are first stored in the memory. In the testing stage, if the testing pattern could be matched with an exemplar in the memory, the exemplar's phoneme is taken as the output. However, if there is no exact match, every exemplar in the memory will be examined and compared with the testing pattern by using a similarity metric to find the most similar exemplar to the testing pattern and take its phoneme as the output.

Table 1 shows a 5-character wide window spanning with the centre character in focus. Assignment of a phoneme to the focal character is based on its contexts of up to two characters on either side. Where there is no character present in a contextual position, a hyphen '-' is used to indicate so. Referring to row 1, for instance, the phoneme /@/ is assigned to the letter <*a*>, by virtue of its two succeeding letters <*ba*> and nothing preceding it, based on a chosen exemplar pattern in the memory. (/@/ is the NETtalk's phonetic symbol equivalent to the international phonetic symbol /æ/).

pattern number	Left-2	left-1	focus	right-1	right-2	target phoneme
1	-	-	*a*	*b*	*a*	@
2	-	*a*	*b*	*a*	*c*	*b*
3	*a*	*b*	*a*	*c*	*u*	*x*
4	*b*	*a*	*c*	*u*	*s*	*k*
5	*a*	*c*	*u*	*s*	-	*x*
6	*c*	*u*	*s*	-	-	*s*

Table 1: Assignment of English word <abacus> with the phoneme /@bxkxs/

2.1. COMPUTING SIMILARITY METRIC

The concept of Information Gain [4] is now used to capture the weighted information of the positions in the contextual window in determining phonetic assignments. First, the information entropy E of a database D is defined as the number of bits of information needed to know the decision of the database given a pattern:

$$E(D) = -\sum_i p_i * \log_2 p_i \qquad (1)$$

where p_i is the probability of the occurrence of phoneme i. Thus, p_i is the number of occurrences of phoneme i over the total number of patterns in the database. Equation (1) sums over all the 52 phonemes in the system.

Now for each position in the contextual window, its relative importance in the database can be calculated by computing the average information entropy of the database for specifically position f as follows:

$$E(D_{[f]}) = \sum_{v \in \alpha} E(D_{[f=v]}) * \frac{|D_{[f=v]}|}{|D|} \tag{2}$$

where $D_{[f=v]}$ refers to instances in the database that have value v at position f, v being one of the 26 English alphabets (the set α), and $|D|$ is the number of instances in database D.

Now the information gain G of position f is defined as:

$$G(f) = E(D) - E(D_{[f]}) \tag{3}$$

With the above, the similarity for two patterns X and Y could be obtained as follows:

$$sim(X,Y) = \sum_{i=1}^{n} G(f_i) * \delta(x_i, y_i) \tag{4}$$

where n is the total number of positions in the pattern (here, n=5), and

$$\delta(x_i, y_i) = 1 \quad if \quad x_i = y_i \quad else \quad 0 \tag{5}$$

An example in computing the similarity of two patterns is shown in Table 2 where $sim(X,Y)$ = 0.33 + 0.79 + 0 + 0 + 0 = 1.12. With the similarity measure, two approaches to pattern selection are described below.

position f_i	1	2	3	4	5
pattern x_i	*a*	*c*	*u*	*s*	-
pattern y_i	*a*	*c*	*c*	*o*	*u*
$\delta(x_i, y_i)$	1	1	0	0	0
$G(f_i)$	0.33	0.79	3.35	0.88	0.33

Table 2. Similarity between two patterns at each position

2.2. INSTANCE-BASED LEARNING SIMILARITY MATCHING

The most straightforward way in pattern selection is to scan through all exemplars and select the most similar pattern among all. However, among the most similar patterns selected, there are *conflicting rules*, where two or more identical patterns are assigned to different phonemes in the training exemplars. For instance, *<eface>*➔/*a*/, *<eface>*➔/*e*/ and *<eface>*➔/*x*/ are three such conflicting rules. In this case, a random choice is made to select one phoneme assignment, which may be erroneous. This approach suffers from the long searching time and its inability to coup with conflicting rules. This leads to the next approach by using the IG tree concept.

2.3. INFORMATION GAIN TREE (IG TREE)

In the training stage, the Information Gain value of each position in the contextual window is first computed in the training corpus. Next, the letters within the contextual window are reordered according to the descending order of the above Information Gain values, and at the same time, conflicting cases are resolved by a statistical method. Finally, the selected phoneme is attached to each letter at that particular position. The statistical method is done by computing the distribution of phonemes for each letter at each particular position and picking the one with the highest frequency. After gathering all these information, all the exemplars are inserted in a tree, and hence the Information Gain (IG) Tree is constructed, similar to Quinlan's ID3 [5].

Taking an English word *<abacus>* as an example. With the third *<a>* in focus, the five letters in the contextual windows *<abacu>* is re-ordered according to the descending order of IG values to become *<acbau>*, noting that the first *<a>* here is actually the third *<a>* (the focal letter) in the original word before reordering. With all the five characters in the contextual window, /@/ is assigned to the focal letter <a> from the training corpus. However, for contextual window with less than 5 characters, other phoneme assignments are possible from the training corpus. Thus we have the following pattern matched pronunciation of the focal letter <a> :

- single <a> will be pronounced as /@/ ,
- pattern *<ac>* will be pronounced as */x/* ,
- pattern *<acb>* will be pronounced as /@/ ,
- pattern *<acba>* will be pronounced as /@/ ,
- pattern *<acbau>* will be pronounced as */x/* .

The above phonemes form the labels for the arcs in the IG Tree with the final phoneme forming the leaf node as shown in Figure 1. As the width of the contextual window is 5, each leaf node in the IG Tree is at most five levels deep.

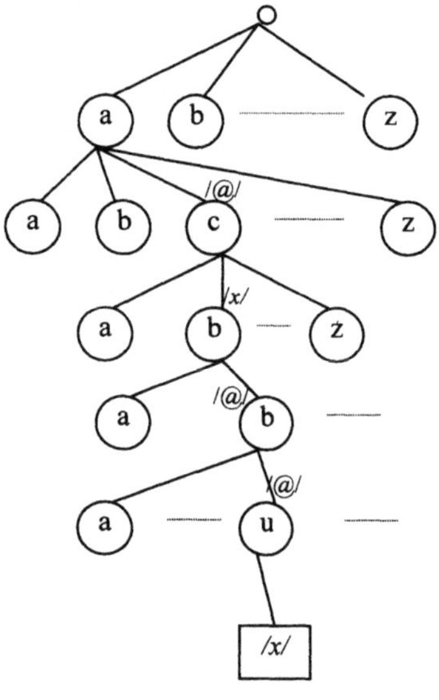

Figure 1. A partial IG Tree with <abacus> example in view.

In the testing stage, for each input word, testing patterns are created by taking each letter in the word as the focal letter together with the contextual information within its contextual window. Each testing pattern is then ordered according to the IG value for each contextual position. The ordered testing pattern is then used to search the tree to see whether we could find an exact match for the testing pattern (if the search ends up at the leaf level). If the searching stops at an internal node in the tree, which implies that no exact match could be found, the phoneme attached to that internal node is taken as the phoneme for the focal letter in that testing pattern.

3. TRANSFORMATION-BASED ERROR-DRIVEN LEARNING ALGORITHM

This is adapted from the work of Brill originally used for part-of-speech tagging [6,7]. The simple idea behind this learning algorithm used here for phoneme assignment is that: once a pair of a wrongly assigned phoneme and its corresponding correct phoneme is obtained, their *contextual information* will be examined. If the window contexts for these two phonemes are matched, then, a *transformation rule* may be proposed: transform from the wrong phoneme to the correct phoneme if the window context is detected. By applying the transformation rules, the errors in the initially tagged data could be reduced and the accuracy is increased accordingly.

For example, an initial tagging gives */@bk--/*, while the correct tags should be */@bx--/*, then using templates, some transformation rules may be created as follows:
/@bk/ ➔ */x/* (i.e. if we see /k/ preceded by /@ b/, then change it to /x/.)
/@-k/ ➔ */x/* (i.e. if we see */k/* preceded by */@/* in the left-2 position, change it to */x/*.)

3.1. GENERATION OF TRANSFORMATION RULES

In the training stage:

1. An *initial annotator* is used to give an initial tagging to the letters in the input word. The output will be the phonemes.
   e.g. *input --- English word: <aback>*
   output --- phoneme in NETtalk phonetic symbol: /xb@k-/
2. The initial annotated text is compared with the correctly tagged word, and a list of transformation rules is generated
3. The above generated rules are applied to the training pattern and their corresponding scores *(number of correct transformations - number of wrong transformations)* are recorded.
4. The highest scoring rule is selected as the winner for the current run (a greedy method). If the winner's score is greater than a predefined threshold, then store it in the ordered best-rule list and use it to update the current training data to get a set of newly tagged data and goto step 2 for the next run; else stop training session.

In the testing stage:

1. Words in the test corpus are tagged by the same initial annotator used above.
2. The rules in the ordered best-rule list (generated in the training stage) are applied on the testing patterns in the order of the rule list. The output will be a set of newly tagged phonemes for the original words which should have a higher accuracy compared to the phonemes generated in step 1 (by the initial annotator).

Figure 2 depicts the above process.

3.2. INTEGRATING WITH INFORMATION GAIN LEARNING APPROACH

The IG tree method is efficient and gives a very high accuracy. However, its accuracy appears to fall within a certain range of values (i.e. within about 88% and 95%), and no matter how we fine-tune the similarity metric, we could not improve the accuracy further beyond around 95%.

The idea of the transformation-based approach, on the other hand, is to focus on the reduction of errors. It is found that the initial accuracy determines the final achievable accuracy. Thus, the IG Tree system may be used as the initial annotator for the Transformation-based approach, allowing the latter to further improve the accuracy of the IG Tree method. A final accuracy of 96.86% is achieved as discussed in section 5.

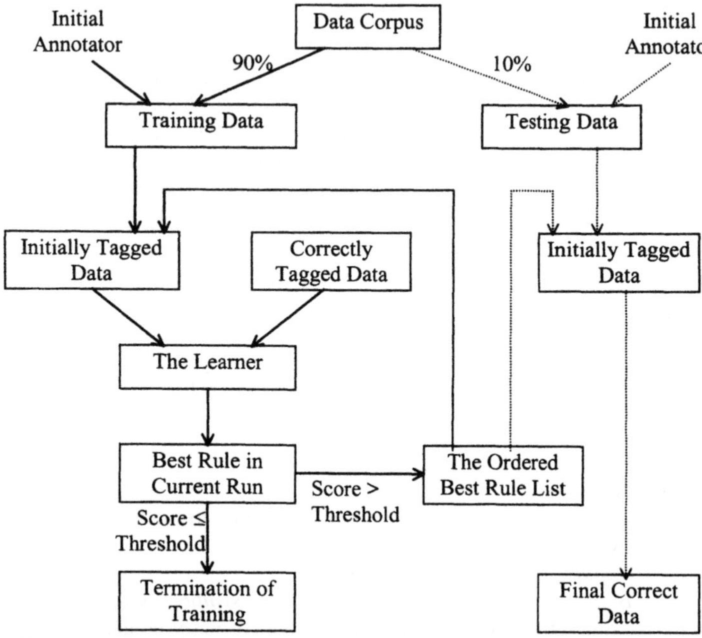

Figure 2. Transformation-based Error-Driven Learning Algorithm (Solid Line denotes Training; Dashed Line denotes Testing

4. TRAINING AND TESTING

The training and testing data are taken from the NETtalk corpus downloaded from the Internet. NETtalk was used by Sejnowski and Rosenberg in their influential study of speech generation using a neural network [8,9]. The downloaded corpus contains a list of 20,008 English words, along with a phonetic transcription for each word. The total number of patterns we could extract out is about 160,000. It could provide us enough data to run experiments and analyse results. It is an example of an input/output mapping task that exhibits strong global regularities, but also a large number of more specialised rules and exceptional cases[8].

4.1. TRAINING AND TESTING METHOD

We use a 10 fold method to divide the whole data corpus into training and testing data, i.e. we randomly pick 10% data as the testing corpus. By removing the testing corpus from the original data corpus, the training data is obtained. Thus the testing data is not inside the training data. We apply the same method 10 times to get 10 different sets of training and testing corpora and use each of them to do the training and testing. We compute the average result among these testing results to obtain the final result.

4.2. PRE-PROCESSING THE TRAINING AND TESTING DATA

After segregating the training and testing data, we need to do "data alignment", as in figure 3 because the original word and its phonetic transcription may differ in length. For phonetic matching, these two representations need to be of equal length so that each individual graphemic symbol can be mapped to a single phonetic symbol.

graphemes	a	b	a	te	graphemes	a	b	a	t	e
	|	|	|	|		|	|	|	|	|
phonemes	x	b	e	t	phonemes	x	b	e	t	-
	(a)					(b)				

Figure 3. Example of word to phoneme correspondence (a) before word alignment and (b) after word alignment

5. EXPERIMENTAL RESULTS

5.1. INFORMATION GAIN LEARNING ALGORITHM

Comparing between the Instance-based Learning approach and the IG Tree approach, as discussed earlier in section 2, the former is very time consuming and has a lower accuracy due to its lack of resolution for conflicting rules. Table 3 compares the accuracy and time taken between the two approaches.

(Training pattern=144,000, Testing pattern=16,000)

	Accuracy	Time(minutes)
Instance-based	92.71%	9580
IGTree	95.25%	148

Table 3. Comparison between Instance-based Approach and IG Tree Approach

5.2. TRANSFORMATION BASED ERROR-DRIVEN LEARNING ALGORITHM

The final accuracy of this algorithm depends on the starting accuracy of the initial annotator. If the accuracy of initial tagging is low, no matter how we decrease threshold, the final accuracy will still be very low; whereas, if the accuracy of initial tagging is high, an even higher accuracy can always be achieved. This indicates that there is a limit to the number of errors that the system could reduce. We could reason this by looking at the winners' score: in each run, the score of the current run's winner is decreasing in a non-linear manner. So eventually, it will reach the threshold and the training stops. Moreover, it has been observed that the lower threshold value will give more increment on the accuracy, and after a certain number of runs, the best score in each run will converge to a small number close to zero. Thus a question arises as to whether the accuracy will continue to increase slowly and eventually reach a very high degree, if the threshold is set to zero? The answer is No. Through our experiments, it has been shown that once the threshold is set to zero, a so-called "*flipping rules*" phenomenon will occur and this prevents the accuracy from increasing further.

Observing the best rules set produced after the training stage, it is found that, when the threshold is set to zero, after a certain number of runs, there will be two rules always at the top of the list in alternate runs. That is, they appear in the best rules list in a flipping manner. The application of each of these two rules creates a triggering condition for each other. Table 4 demonstrates a case in point.

flipping rules	accuracy
/nx/→ /k/ : *if /x/ is proceeded by /n/, change it to /k/, and obtain /nk/.*	*94.5%*
/@nk/→ /x/ : *if /k/ is proceeded by /@n/, change it to /x/, and obtain /@nx/.*	*93.8%*

Table 4. Example of two flipping rules (when threshold = 0)

Flipping rules also lead to a flipping accuracy -- accuracy changes after each run in an oscillating manner. This is the reason why there is a limit to the maximum increment of the accuracy that the Error-driven algorithm can achieve. Thus, the final accuracy has to depend very closely on the initial accuracy. Table 5 shows the effects of the initial accuracy and the threshold values on the final accuracy figures.

Initial accuracy	15.4%	92.3%	97.98%
Threshold value	Final accuracy	Final accuracy	Final accuracy
8	20.52%	96.56%	98.34%
2	24.10%	97.88%	99.13%
0	24.78%	99.49%	99.76%

Table 5. Effects of initial accuracy and threshold value on final accuracy for Transformation-based Error-driven Method

A variant of the above method is also attempted. Instead of picking the top one rule in each run during the training phase, the top two rules are selected. Understandably, it cuts down on operation time. Moreover, the experiment shows that it also improves on the accuracy too. Table 6 compares the results of top-1 and top-2 approaches.

(Initial tagging accuracy=15.4%, number of training pattern=9000)

	Top-1 Approach			Top-2 Approach		
Threshold	Final accuracy	time (minutes)	Number of runs	Final accuracy	time (minutes)	Number of runs
8	20.52%	174	20	20.52%	45.5	13
2	24.10%	1056	76	23.80%	288	50
0	24.78%	2492	200	25.14%	1565	100

Table 6. Comparison between selection of top-one and top-two rules.

5.3. HYBRID APPROACH: COMBINING ERROR-DRIVEN AND IG LEARNING

Using the IG method as an initial tagger, the Transformation-based Error-driven approach could elevate the accuracy further as discussed earlier. In our experiment, we first use the Instance-based Similarity Matching method as the initial tagger with an initial accuracy of 92.71% which is raised to 95.32% by the Error-driven method. With the IG Tree method, the initial accuracy is higher, i.e. 95.25% and the final accuracy achievable at threshold zero is 96.86%.

The above accuracy figures are with respect to individual phoneme patterns. As most words are assigned with multiple phonemes, correct pronunciation of the whole word requires all phonemes for the word be correctly assigned. Thus, accuracy at the word level will be lower than the phoneme level. Table 7 gives accuracy on phonemes as well as on words for the hybrid approach.

(Training pattern=144,000, Testing pattern=16,000)

Initial Annotator	Threshold	Initial accuracy on phonemes	Improvement on accuracy after Error-driven learning	Final accuracy on phonemes	Final accuracy on words
Instance-based	8	92.71%	2.81%	95.32%	70.35%
IG Tree	8	95.25%	1.11%	96.31%	74.71%
IG Tree	2	95.25%	1.36%	96.55%	76.39%
IG Tree	0	95.25%	1.69%	96.86%	78.71%

Table 7. Final Accuracy of the Hybrid Approach

5.4. COMPARISON WITH OTHER WORKS

We will compare our results with two other systems, namely, NETtalk [8] and TABTALK [10]. NETtalk uses a neural network to do speech synthesis. It is interesting to see how our corpus-based hybrid approach compares with a connectionist approach. The NETtalk corpus size available from the internet is 20,008 words of which 18,000 words (90%) are used for training our system. The amount used by Sejnowski and Rosenberg in training their NETtalk system is 50,000 words [8]. Moreover, they use a window size of 7 as opposed to 5 in ours. On the other hand, TABTALK uses table lookup and IG-aided similarity-based reasoning with a window size of 5. In one of the TALBTALK's experiments [10], a subset of an English CELEX-corpus consisting of 10,000 words was used. Table 8 shows that the hybrid approach compares favourably with NETtalk's and TABTALK's results in accuracy both on phonemes and words.

System	Training data size	Window size	Accuracy on phonemes	Accuracy on words
Hybrid Approach	18,000	5	96.86%	78.71%
NETtalk	50,000	7	95%	56%
TABTALK	10,000	5	84.4%	28.2%

Table 8. Comparison with NETtalk's and TABTALK's experimental results.

6. CONCLUSION

We propose a hybrid approach by integrating two pattern matching approaches for automatic text-to-speech conversion. One approach uses the Information Gain Tree proposed by Daelemans. The IG Tree compresses phoneme contextual information through training with the NETtalk corpus to permit efficient assignment of phonemes to characters in the testing phase. The other approach adapts from Brill's work in his part-of-speech tagger to apply to phoneme tagging in our present application. The method requires an initial annotator to start with a set of phoneme assignment and uses a transformation-based error-driven approach to iteratively improve the assignment accuracy. The final accuracy attainable relies on the initial accuracy of the initial annotator. Our hybrid approach thus uses the IG Tree system to serve as the initial annotator and allows the error-driven method to fine tune the accuracy. The IG tree method provides an initial accuracy of 95.25% which is further improved by the error-driven approach to 96.86%. The accuracy also compares well with the NETtalk neural network experimental results.

In our experiments, selecting two best rules in the transformation-based error-driven method has shown promise in improving the accuracy over the top-one approach. Other variations in the number of top rules selected will be attempted to find the optimal number of best rules to be selected.

Another issue to be investigated is in the window size used in both the IG Tree construction and in the transformation rule construction. The current window size is 5. Other window sizes may be experimented in our future work. We may consider the use of multiple window size templates in the construction of transformation rules and allow the system to select the best rules in its error-driven refinement of accuracy.

REFERENCES

[1] Daelemans W. GRAFON-D: A Grapheme-to-phoneme Conversion System for Dutch. AI Memo 88-5, AI-LAB Brussels, 1988.

[2] Daelemans W and van den Bosch A. Data-Oriented methods for Grapheme-to-Phoneme Conversion. In proceeding of the 6th Conference of the European Chapter of the ACL, Utrecht, April 1993, pp 45-53.

[3] Daelemans W and van den Bosch A. Language-independent, data-oriented grapheme-to-phoneme conversion. In: van Santen JPH, Sproat RW, Olive JP and Hirschberg J (eds). Progress in Speech Synthesis, 1997, pp 77 – 89.

[4] Daelemans W and van den Bosch A. Generalisation performance of backpropagation learning on a syllabification task. In M. Drossaers and A. Nijholt (Eds.), Proceedings of the 3rd Twente Workshop on Language Technology. Enschede: Universiteit Twente, 1992, pp 27-37.

[5] Quinlan JR. Induction of Decision Trees. Machine Learning 1, 81-106, 1986.

[6] Brill EA. Corpus-Based Approach to Language Learning. Ph.D. Dissertation, Department of Computer and Information Science, University of Pennsylvania, 1993

[7] Brill EA. Some Advances in Transformation-Based Part of Speech Tagging In proceeding of the 12th National Conference on Artificial Intelligence(AAAI-94), 1994.

[8] Sejnowski TJ and Rosenberg CR. NETtalk: A parallel network that learns to read aloud. Technical Report JHU/EECS-86/1, John Hopkins University Department of Electrical Engineering and Computer Science, 1986.

[9] Sejnowski TJ and Rosenberg CR. Parallel networks that learn to pronounce English text. Complex Systems, 1987; 1:145-168.

[10] Daelemans W and van den Bosch A. TABTALK: reusability in data-oriented grapheme-to-phoneme conversion. In Proceedings of Eurospeech 1993, Berlin, pp 1459-1466.

ROBUST SPEECH RECOGNITION USING FUZZY MATRIX/VECTOR QUANTISATION, NEURAL NETWORKS AND HIDDEN MARKOV MODELS

Lin Cong, Advanced Micro Devices, 5204 E. Ben White Blvd, Mail Stop 622, Austin, TX, 78741, USA.
Saf Asghar, Advanced Micro Devices, 5204 E. Ben White Blvd, Mail Stop 622, Austin, TX, 78741, USA.

ABSTRACT

This paper proposes a new hybrid IWSR system which combines Fuzzy Split Matrix Quantization (FSMQ) and Fuzzy Split Vector Quantization (FSVQ) with a Hidden Markov Model (HMM) to utilize efficiently processing resources and improve speech recognition performance. This FSMQ/HMM_FSVQ/HMM system exploits the "evolution" of the speech short-term spectral envelopes with error compensation from FSVQ/HMM processes. Acoustic noise may affect particular frequency domain subbands. This system exploits localized noise by efficiently allocating enhanced processing technology to target noise-affected input signal parameters and minimize noise influence. The enhanced processing technology employs a weighted LSP distance measure in a LBG algorithm. Computer simulation using gender-dependent HMMs in a speaker-independent mode clearly indicates superiority over conventional FVQ/HMM and FMQ/HMM systems with 96% and 92.1% recognition accuracies at 15 dB and 5 dB SNR levels respectively, in a car noise environment.

1. INTRODUCTION

Today, the art and science of speech recognition has advanced to facilitate oral communication with a computer when speaking in a disciplined manner and using a moderate to large size vocabulary. Speech recognition (SR) software packages are now emerging for the PC market. Speaker-Dependent (SD)/Speaker-Independent (SI) Isolated Word Speech Recognition (IWSR) and continuous speech recognition (CSR) is required for the next generation of voice communication and information systems. Such as hand-free dialing, iteration voice store and forwarding systems, SI/SD, IWSR/CSR is an enabling technology for these next generation systems.

Recent advances in probabilistic and neural network classification have improved the performance of speech recognition systems operating in a car environment ([1] and [2]) and will inspire demand for voice dialling in the near future to improve driving safety. However, some severe noise problems continue to affect adversely hands free dialing applications at SNR levels lower than 10 dB, especially with regard to low cost, uncomplicated computational systems. Discrete HMM processing based on VQ is still a popular method to reduce the computational complexity, although the quantization error is a well-known problem.

In this paper, we investigate two kinds of quantization methodologies, which divide the speech parameters into matrices operating in both time and frequency domains. In this way, robust speech recognition systems can be optimally designed when the noise spectrum is localized in the frequency domain (e.g. car noise) by combining split quantization with a special distance measure. Matrix Quantization (MQ) captures spectral envelope "dynamics", and Vector Quantization (VQ) compensates for MQ time domain errors. The combination of these quantization methodologies can provide the highest recognition accuracy for SI IWSR in the car noise environment.

Within the context of intrinsically robust systems, FMQ and FVQ have been used in conjunction with HMM, or HMM combined with a Multilayer perceptron neural network (MLP) in this paper. In addition, we present a new hybrid robust IWSR system which employs FMQ/FVQ as the spectral labelling process, combined with both the strength of HMM in modelling stochastic sequences and the non-linear classification capability of MLP neural networks. The system employs a FMQ/FVQ codebook and u HMM models, where u is the number of possible input words. Given an input word, the FMQ/FVQ codebook produces effectively an observation sequence O and a Fuzzy distortion measure *FD* and u probability-dependent maximum likelihood probabilities $P(O/\lambda_j)$, which are presented to the MLP network to improve further the performance of the FMQ/HMM_FVQ/HMM SR system.

This paper is structured as follows. The databases used are described first in Section 2. The hard split matrix classification matrix and unifying fuzzy clustering methodology are studied in Section 3. The proposed weighted LSP distance measure in a LBG algorithm is discussed in Section 4. The systems FSMQ/HMM_FSVQ/HMM and FSMQ/HMM/MLP_FSVQ/HMM/MLP are considered in the following Section. Computer simulation results are given in Section 6, and Conclusions are presented in Section 7.

2. THE DATABASES

Three speech databases are used in this paper. The database1 used here for speaker-independent speech recognition was TIDIGITS. In the training part, there were 60 males and 60 females who repeated each English digit from zero to nine twice. 2210 utterances from 52 males and 54 females which were not used in training were used for recognition. The database2, consisting of our separate recordings of 11 speakers, was used only for recognition. The database3 NOSEX_92 was used for designing/testing the systems in SD mode [5].

Two kinds of car noise database were also used. One was from NOISEX_92, for a car travelling at 120 km/h. The other noise database consisted of our separate recordings of a 1995 Mazda travelling at 30 and 60 mph, respectively. Approximately 5 minutes of car noise samples from NOSEX_92 were recycled through the complete training database.

3. SMQ AND SFMQ CLASSIFICATION MATRIX

3.1 CONVENTIONAL SMQ CLASSIFICATION MATRIX

Consider that a training set X TO speech spectral vectors, results in a set $X = \{x_1, x_2, \ldots, x_T\}$ of T, $P \times N$ matrices, where $T = \text{int}(TO/N)$ (N is the number of consecutive speech frames) and each matrix x_k, $k = 1, 2, ..., T$ is split into a fixed S of sub-matrices, $s = 1, 2, ..., S$, $S \leq P$:

$$X_k = \begin{bmatrix} x_{11}^k & x_{12}^k & \cdots & x_{1N}^k \\ x_{21}^k & x_{22}^k & \cdots & x_{2N}^k \\ \cdots & \cdots & \cdots & \cdots \\ x_{P1}^k & x_{P2}^k & \cdots & x_{PN}^k \end{bmatrix} = [\hat{x}_{1k}(m_1) \ \ \hat{x}_{2k}(m_2) \ \ \cdots \ \ \hat{x}_{Sk}(m_S)] \tag{3.1}$$

where $\sum_{j=1}^{S} m_j = P$. Each set X_S of T $\hat{x}_{sk}(m_s)$ submatrices is processed to produce a C_s-matrix entries MQ codebook containing C_s v_i^s, $i = 1, 2, ..., C_s$, $m_s \times N$ submatrices

$$v_i^s = \begin{bmatrix} v_{\rho+1,1}^j & v_{\rho+1,2}^j & \cdots & v_{\rho+1,N}^k \\ v_{\rho+2,1}^j & v_{\rho+2,2}^j & \cdots & v_{\rho+2,N}^k \\ \cdots & \cdots & \cdots & \cdots \\ v_{\rho+m_s,1}^j & v_{\rho+m_s,2}^j & \cdots & v_{\rho+m_s,N}^j \end{bmatrix} = [\bar{v}_{s1}^i, \ \bar{v}_{s2}^i, \ \ldots, \ \bar{v}_{sN}^i] \tag{3.2}$$

where $\rho = \sum_{j=0}^{s-1} m_j$. The resulting quantization of X_S can be described by a $C_s \times T$ classification matrix U_s with elements $u_{iks} \in \{0, 1\}$. The columns O_{js} of the classification matrix U_s "map" effectively an input matrix $\hat{x}_{sj}(m_s)$ into a vector $O_{js} = \{u_{1js}, \ u_{2js}, \ \ldots, \ u_{C_s js}\}$ with all zero values except one element $u_{ijs} = 1$ so that the distortion $J(O_{js}, V_s) = \sum_{i=1}^{C_s} u_{ijs} d(\hat{x}_{sj}, v_i^s)$ is minimized. $d(\hat{x}_{sj}, v_i^s)$ is a distance measure. An optimum sth sub-MQ codebook ensures that

$$J(U_s, V_s) = \sum_{j=1}^{T} \sum_{i=1}^{C_s} u_{ijs} d(\hat{x}_{sj}, v_i^s) \tag{3.3}$$

is minimized. This kind of matrix quantization classification is a conventional hard decision.

3.2 FUZZY SPLIT MATRIX CLASSIFICATION MATRIX

Following similar arguments and definition as with SMQ discussed in section 3.1, the FSMQ of X_s is described by a $C_s \times T$ fuzzy classification matrix U_{sF} with elements $u_{iks} \in [0, 1]$, $i = 1, 2, ..., C_s$, $k = 1, 2, ..., T$. The value of u_{iks}, $0 \leq u_{iks} \leq 1$, indicates the degree of fuzziness of the k-th input matrix $\hat{x}_{sk}$ to the i-th partitioning cell which is represented by the centroid v_i^s. In this case, u_{iks} is derived from:

$$u_{iks} = \frac{1}{\sum_{j=1}^{C_s} \left(\frac{d(\hat{x}_{sk}, v_i^s)}{d(\hat{x}_{sk}, v_j^s} \right)^{\frac{1}{(F-1)}}} \tag{3.4}$$

where the constant F influences the degree of fuzziness. $d(\hat{x}_{sk}, v_i^s)$ is a distance measure.

3.3 THE FUZZY SPLIT MQ CLUSTERING CRITERION

The columns O_{js} of the classification matrix U_{sF} "map" an input matrix $\hat{x}_{sj}(m_s)$ into a vector $o_{js} = \{u_{1js}, \ u_{2js}, \ \ldots, \ u_{C_s js}\}$ which results in the distortion $J(O_{js}, V_s) = \sum_{i=1}^{C_s} u_{ijs}^F \, d(\hat{x}_{sj}, \, v_i^s)$. Furthermore, the overall distortion of the c_s entries fuzzy matrix quantizer operating on the X_s matrix set is

$$J(U_s, V_s) = \sum_{j=1}^{T} \sum_{i=1}^{C_s} u_{ijs}^F \, d(\hat{x}_{sj}, v_i^s) \tag{3.5}$$

Note that the largest component is the one which corresponds to the cell (centroid) with the smallest $d(\hat{x}_{sj}, v_i^s)$ value. O_{sj} can be interpreted as a probability mass relating the input matrix $\hat{x}_{sj}$ to all v_i^s, $i = 1, 2, \ldots, C_s$. Equations (3.3) and (3.6) provide the SMQ and Fuzzy SMQ distortion and can also be represented by the general distortion equation:

$$J(W, V) = \sum_{j=1}^{T} \sum_{i=1}^{C_s} w_{ijs} \, d(\hat{x}_{sj}, v_i^s) \tag{3.6}$$

where $w_{ijs} = \begin{cases} u_{ijs} & u_{ijs} \in \{0,1\} \\ u_{ijs}^F & u_{ijs} \in [0,1] \end{cases}$

FSVQ can also be formed by the Fuzzy LBG algorithms as discussed in [2], in the special case where N equals one.

Furthermore, the overall distortion of the C entries ($C = C_1 + C_2 + \ldots + C_s$) in the S codebooks of the fuzzy matrix quantizer operating on the X matrix set in the recognition process is:

$$J(U_f, V) = \sum_{j=1}^{T} \sum_{s=1}^{S} \sum_{i=1}^{C_s} u_{ijs}^F \, d(\hat{x}_{sj}, v_i^s) \tag{3.7}$$

4. WEIGHTED LSP DISTANCE MEASURE IN A LBG ALGORITHM

A new robust distance measure is proposed for the systems based on the LSP parameters. The information provided by speech signals corrupted by car noise was used to change the

Euclidean measure in the original LBG algorithm. It is known that the peaks of all the car noise spectra are located at low frequencies and affect low-order LSP parameters more than the high-order LSP parameters. Therefore, a 15-dimension speech parameter matrix consisting of 12 LSP parameters and the normalized log frame energy, together with the 1st and 2nd order time derivatives of the frame energy (e_t, Δe_t and $\Delta^2 e_t$) are experimentally divided into two parts, according to the distribution of the car noise spectrum. Each part is sub-matrix quantized separately using MQ. The first part has the first 6 order LSP parameters in the low frequency band, and the second part has the remaining 6 LSP coefficients and the 3 energy parameters. The robust LSP distance measure $d(f_{sj}, \hat{f}_j^s)$ between the test LSP sub-matrix f_{sj} and the reference sub-matrix $\hat{f}_j^s$ proposed in the split LBG algorithm is given by:

$$d(f_{sj}, \hat{f}_j^s) = \frac{1}{N}\sum_{n=1}^{N} d(\bar{f}_{sn}^j, \hat{f}_{sn}^j) \tag{4.1}$$

when s=1: $d(\bar{f}_{sn}^j, \hat{f}_{sn}^j) = \sum_{i=1}^{N_1}[(f_{i,n}^j - \hat{f}_{i,n}^j)e_i^{\beta_1}]^2$ and when s=2: $d(\bar{f}_{sn}^j, \hat{f}_{sn}^j) = \sum_{i=N_1+1}^{P}[(f_{i,n}^j - \hat{f}_{i,n}^j)]^2$

where P = 15. e_i is the weighting for the i-th LSP only at the first six LSP parameter part, i.e, i = 1, 2, ..., 6 and is given by the LPC error power spectrum based on different speech frames at the different test LSP frequencies. β_1 is experimentally determined and is set to 0.1. The weighting factors e_i enhance noise immunity while FSMQ and FSVQ allows targeting noise affected parameters without incurring an unnecessarily high processing overhead for the high-order LSP parameters. It is clear that when noise is large, the prediction error is large.

5. SYSTEMS DESCRIPTION

The new system FSMQ/HMM_FSVQ/HMM, or FMQ/HMM_FVQ/HMM in their recognition process configuration are shown in Figure 1. The speech parameter analysis is performed every 20 msecs, allowing for a 10 msecs overlap between analysis frames which makes the neighbor matrices overlap. System training consists of two parts: the SMQ/MQ/HMM part and the SVQ/VQ/HMM part. Notice that SVQ/VQ is a special case of the SMQ/MQ when N = 1 and MQ/VQ is the special case of the SMQ/SVQ when S = 1.

SMQ/MQ is used as the front end of the HMM classifier [2], since the feature matrices contain not only the short-term spectral features, but also the temporal information embedded in the speech signal. The system splits the spectral parameters into sub-matrices according to the distribution of the car noise spectrum so that a higher identification rate can be achieved, compared with the VQ scheme. For IWSR, a speaker is generally not able to speak at precisely the same rate for different repetitions of the word, which can cause difficulty for MQ if a speaker speaks a word very quickly. The solution to this difficulty has been to use SVQ, or VQ to compensate for MQ error by obtaining the best knowledge for the training system and the best recognition accuracy in the recognition process.

SMQ/MQ or SVQ/VQ Codebook Design Processes

Both processes of designing the SMQ/MQ and SVQ/VQ codebook parts involve the following two steps:

1. The training part of the input database (TIDIGITS) is sub-divided into seven sections D1 to D7 based on signals obtained at seven different car noise (NOISEX_92) SNRs levels (∞dB, 35dB, 25dB, 20dB, 15dB, 10dB, 5dB).
2. Each database section D_i, $i = 1, 2, ..., 7$, provides an assembly of vectors containing 15 speech parameters based on LSP spectral coefficients and e_t, Δe_t and $\Delta^2 e_t$ called data stream 1. It also provides 12-dimension LSP mean normalization vectors called data stream 2. The two data streams are used to design four codebooks for each word separately. The resulting codebooks contains $C \times u$ codewords. (u is the size of the vocabulary). Notice that each entry is a m_s by N matrix for SMQ, P by N matrix for MQ [2], and m_s by 1 matrix for SVQ.

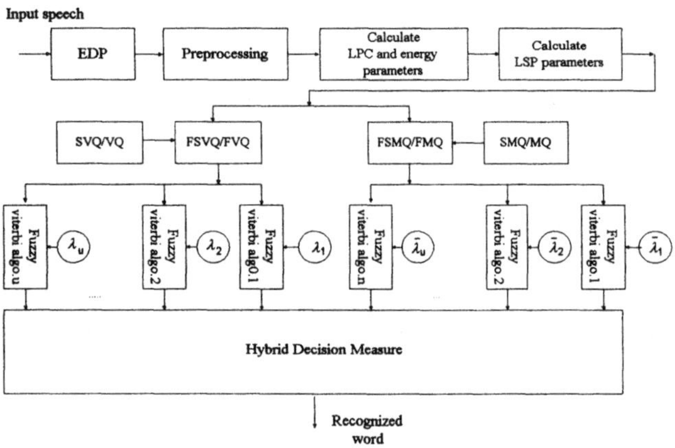

Fig. 1 The FSMQ/HMM_FSVQ/HMM recognition system

HMM Design Process

Following the completion of designing the robust codebooks, we build gender-dependent HMMs λ_j, $j = 1, 2, ..., u$ for each input word based on the two data streams. However, in this case, the observation sequences $O = \{o_1, o_2, ..., o_{T_i}\}$ are now obtained from a given word at different car SNR levels, which are quantized with SMQ/MQ and SVQ/VQ separately by the corresponding and previously designed robust codebooks.

FSMQ/HMM_FSVQ/HMM Recognition Process

When the system operates in a recognition mode, an input word W_j represented by a series $\{x_1, x_2, ..., x_{T_j}\}$ of T_j LSP, energies and LSP mean normalization speech parameters, is computed by the Fuzzy Viterbi algorithm in parallel by u different probability measures $\Pr_1(O_j \mid \lambda_i)$ from the FSVQ/HMM (or FVQ/HMM) part and u probability measures $\Pr_2(O_j \mid \lambda_i)$ from the FSMQ/HMM (or FMQ/HMM) part, which are combined to form:

$$D_h(i) = \Pr_1(O_j \mid \lambda_i) + \alpha \Pr_2(O_j \mid \lambda_i), \quad i = 1,\ 2, \ldots, u \tag{5.1}$$

where α is a scaling constant, which is experimentally determined. The system associates an unknown input word W_j to W_i if $D_h(i) = \min(abs(D_h(i)))$, $i = 1,\ 2, \ldots, u$ (Note that the Viterbi algorithm internally computes the logarithm of outcome probabilities). Meanwhile, in the Fuzzy Viterbi algorithm, the proposed $B_t(i)$ ($\Pr ob\{o_t \mid q_i\ at\ t\}$) for $1 \le t \le T$ and $1 \le i \le N_q$ (where N_q is the number of states in HMM) based on the M data streams is:

$$B_t(i) = \prod_{s=1}^{M} \sum_{j=1}^{C} [u_s(j,t)\, b_{si}(j)] \tag{5.2}$$

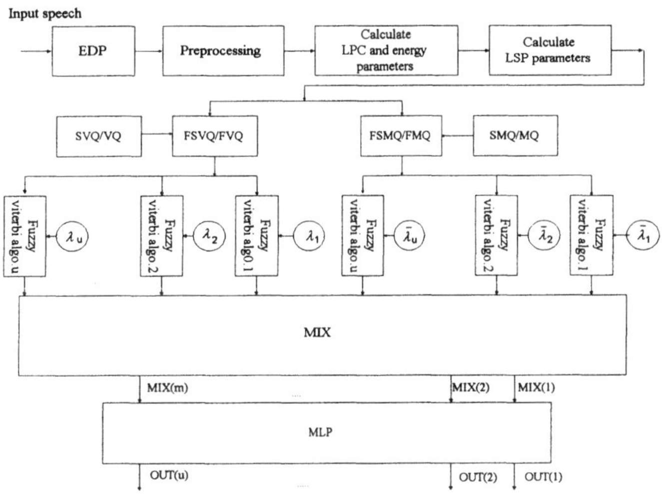

Fig. 2 The FSMQ/HMM/MLP_FSVQ/HMM/MLP recognition system

The System FMQ/HMM/MLP_FVQ/HMM/MLP

The FMQ/HMM/MLP_FVQ/HMM/MLP system in recognition process configuration is shown in Figure 2 [6]. In the train/recognition processes, u-dimensional probability-dependent maximum likelihood probability vector from $D_h(i) = \Pr_1(O_j \mid \lambda_i) + \alpha \Pr_2(O_j \mid \lambda_i)$:

$$\overline{MIX} = [D_h(1),\ \ D_h(2),\ \ \ldots,\ \ D_h(u)] \tag{5.3}$$

or the 2u-dimensional probability-dependent maximum likelihood probability vector separately from $\Pr_1(O_j \mid \lambda_i)$ and $\Pr_2(O_j \mid \lambda_i)$:

$$\overline{MIX} = [\Pr_1(1),\ \Pr_1(2),\ \ldots,\ \Pr_1(u),\ \Pr_2(1),\ \Pr_2(2),\ \ldots,\ \Pr_2(u)\,] \tag{5.4}$$

is presented to the MLP classification process and the system classifies the input word W_j to the i-th vocabulary word if :

$$OUT(i) = \max\{OUT(1),\quad OUT(2),\quad \ldots,\quad OUT(u)\} \tag{5.5}$$

6. EXPERIMENTS AND RESULTS

The systems FSMQ/HMM_FSVQ/HMM, FSMQ/HMM/MLP_FSVQ/HMM/MLP, FMQ/HMM_FVQ/HMM and FMQ/HMM have been tested by using the TIDIGITS and car noises in computer simulation experiments in both match and mismatched noise conditions [5] in the SI mode. In these experiments, the matrix quantization length is chosen as N = 2, F is set to 1.2 and α is set to 2. Two data streams were used in the computer simulation experiments. We have found that increasing the order of the LSP parameter does not improve the recognition performance (when changing P from 12 to 14 or 16).

6.1 TESTING SYSTEMS IN THE MACHED NOISE CONDITION

Figure 3 shows the performances of the systems FSMQ/HMM/MLP_FSVQ/HMM/MLP, FSMQ/HMM_FSVQ/HMM and FMQ/HMM_FVQ/HMM when trained and tested with the same kind of car noise (NOISEX_92). In order to see if the LSP mean normalization speech parameter could increase the robustness of the proposed systems, we tested the system FMQ/HMM_FVQ/HMM, called FMQ/HMM_FVQ/HMM1 based on the data stream 1 and FMQ/HMM_FVQ/HMM2 based on the data stream 1 and 2 and results are shown in Figure 4. The performances of the FMQ/HMM/MLP and FMQ/HMM systems are shown in Figure 6 in the SD mode based on the database NOISEX_92 [5]. 'Old' means by using conventional LSP distance measure and 'new' means by using the proposed distance measure.

It is clear that i) the MLP classifier with the non-linear pattern discrimination combined with FMQ and HMM technology can further enhance the robustness of the proposed systems FSMQ/HMM_FSVQ/HMM, or FMQ/HMM, ii) the system FSMQ/HMM_FSVQ/HMM has better performance than the other two. When the algorithm FMQ/HMM or FSMQ/HMM is combined with the algorithm FSVQ/HMM, FVQ/HMM, or a neural network classifier, the performance of the SR systems can suppress the impact of noise especially in low SNR conditions, iii) the systems can be more robust by adding LSP mean normalization speech parameters, and iv) the performance of systems based on the proposed LSP distance measure are increased from 1% to 4% when SNRs are below 10dB, compared with the systems based on the conventional LSP distance measure as shown in Figure 6.

Futhermore, the proposed system FSMQ/HMM was compared with the system MQ/HMM based on semi-discrect [7] HMMs when SNR is 35 dB and results are shown in Table 1

FSMQ/HMM based on discrete HMM	MQ/HMM based on Semidiscrete HMM	MQ/HMM based on discrete HMM
95.83	95.74	94.81

Table 1. Comparison of recognition accuracy of the systems MQ/HMM and FSMQ/HMM

6.2 TESTING THE SYSTEM IN THE MISMATCHED NOISE CONDITION

We investigated the performance of the simplest system MQ/HMM_VQ/HMM in the different types and speeds of car noise (discussed in Section 2) and results are shown in Figure 5. In this mismatched noise condition, it is experimentally observed that the new system has comparable performance in either matched or mismatched noise conditions when SNR levels are above 5 dB. Also, we tested the system MQ/HMM_VQ/HMM in an office environment with the 11 speakers from the database2 for recognition. In this case, the recognition accuracy reached 99.8%.

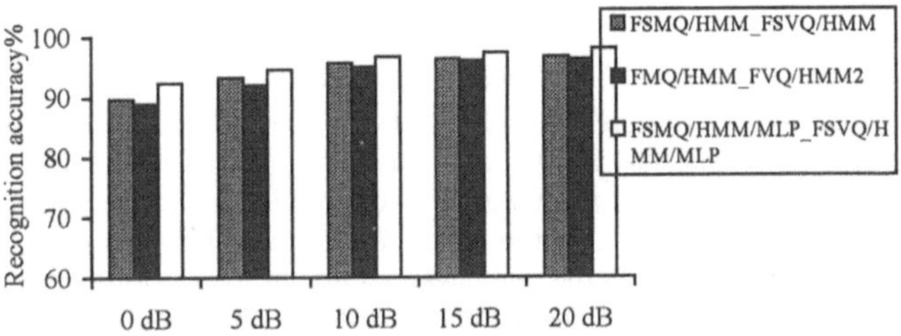

Fig. 3 The performance of the systems

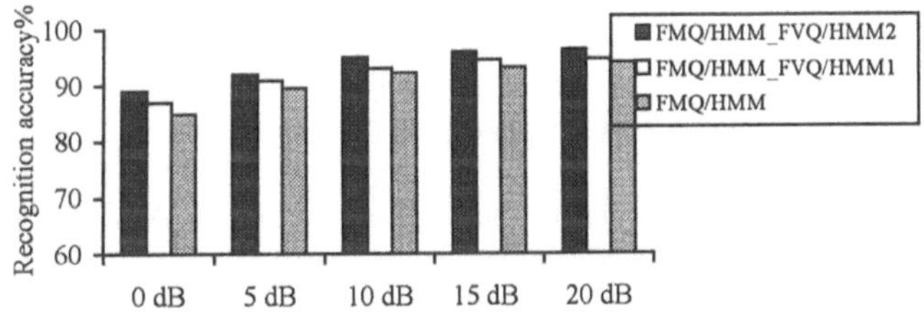

Fig. 4 The performance of the systems

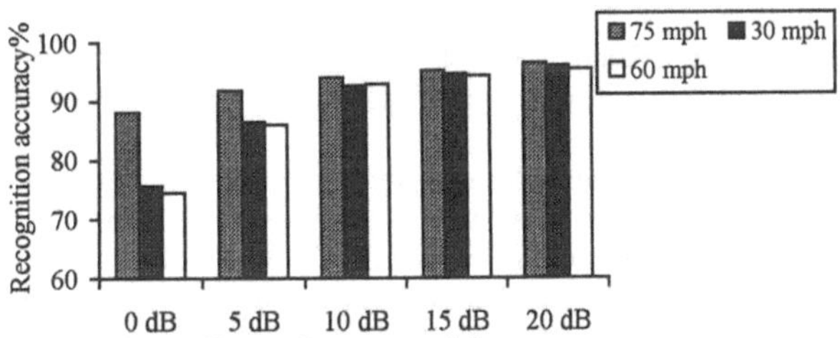

Fig. 5 The performance of the system MQ/HMM_VQ/HMM at different car speeds

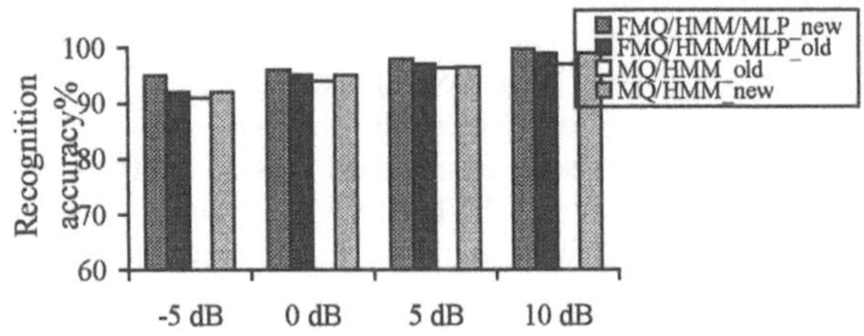

Fig.6 The performance of the systems

7. CONCLUSIONS

The robust isolated word FSMQ/HMM_FSVQ/HMM speech recognizer proposed in this paper combines Fuzzy Split Matrix Quantization and HMM with Fuzzy Split Vector Quantization in a very simple and elegant way. In the car noise environment, split quantization methods were used to enhance further the robustness of the SR systems for localised noise spectra. Also, the NN classifier with the non-linear pattern discrimination combined with FMQ and HMM technology can further enhance the robustness of the proposed speech recognition system. The systems we present provide high accuracy and robustness for speaker-independent IWSR in a car noise environment and efficient use of processing resources.

REFERENCES

[1] L. Cong. A Study of Robust ISWR Systems. Ph.D thesis, University Of Manchester, UK, May, 1996.

[2] C. Xydeas and L. Cong. Robust Speech Recognition in A Car Environment. In proceedings of the Intern. Conference on Digital Signal Processing, Vol. 1. 1995 pp84-89.

[3] S. Furui and M. M. Sondhi. Advances in Speech Signal Processing. Marcel Dekker, Inc. New York, 1992.

[4] L. R. Rabiner. A Tutorial on Hidden Markov Models and Selected Application Speech Recognition. Proc. IEEE Vol. 77, 1989, pp 257-286.

[5] L. Cong and Saf Asghar. Robust Speech Recognition Algorithms in A Car Noise Environment. To be published in proceedings of the European Signal Processing Conference, 1998.

[6] C. Xydeas and L. Cong. Combining Neural Network Classification with Fuzzy Vector Quantization and HMMs for Robust Isolated Word Speech Recognition. In Proceedings of the IEEE International Symposium on Information Theory, IEEE Press, 1995, pp 174.

[7] X. D. Huang and M. A. Jack. Hidden Morkov Modelling of Speech Based on A Semicontinuous Model, Electronics Letters 1988; 24 (1): 6-7.

AN EXPERIMENTAL STUDY ON CONFIDENCE MEASURES FOR ROBUST SPEECH RECOGNITION

Li Jiang and Xuedong Huang
Microsoft Research
One Microsoft Way
Redmond, WA 98052, USA
{lij, xueh}@microsoft.com

ABSTRACT

One of the most critical components in a practical speech recognition system is a reliable confidence measure. In this paper, we report a number of experiments we conducted to improve confidence measures for large-vocabulary speaker-independent speech recognition. We first studied the behavior of confidence measures for mispronounced words during the user enrollment phase. Acoustic features at word, phoneme and senone level were examined. We developed a transformation function based system using sub-word features for high performance confidence estimation. Discriminative training was used to optimize the parameters of the transformation function. In comparison to the baseline system, our experiments show that the proposed system reduced the equal error rate by 15% and the false acceptance error by 40% at a number of fixed false rejection rates. Secondly, we augmented our feature vectors for speech recognition error detection. With multi-dimensional features and a linear classifier, our experiments show that the false acceptance error can be reduced by 80% in comparison with our single feature baseline system. Finally, we investigated how we could use confidence measures to reject noise. With our explicit noise modeling and a secondary classifier, we have reduced the noise rejection error down to 7% - a 68% error reduction over our baseline system.

1. INTRODUCTION

An accurate confidence measure is critical for practical spoken language conversational systems. With an accurate confidence measure for each recognized word, the conversational back-end can repair potential speech recognition errors to improve user's conversational experience. In a speaker-dependent or speaker-adaptive system, the confidence measure can help user enrollment (to eliminate mispronounced words). It is also critical for unsupervised speaker adaptation so that recognition results can be selectively used to further improve adaptation.

The problem of computing the confidence measure can be regarded as a statistical hypothesis testing problem or two-class pattern classification problem. Traditionally, there are two kinds of likelihood used for alternative hypothesis in hypothesis testing. One is the likelihood derived from filler models [1,2], which have been proven to be simple and effective for many spoken language applications. Another is the likelihood derived from so-called anti-keyword models [3,4], which can be built with anti-class samples. Recently some researchers reported that the information of the decoding process is very useful for the confidence measure [5,6,7,8]. In these systems, features such as N-best hypotheses, the number of active hypotheses during decoding, language model scores, acoustic scores are combined to produce the most reliable confidence measure. These features are typically fed to a sophisticated classifier [6,7,8,9] to obtain the classification result.

The confidence measure can be applied to detection of mispronounced words in user enrollment or detection of speech recognition errors in decoding. Transcriptions are given in user enrollment ("supervised"). Therefore, the confidence measure can take advantage of that for better accuracy. We used relatively simple features and focused on using discriminative training with sub-word units. For recognition error detection ("unsupervised"), as correct transcription is unavailable, we need to have more reliable confidence measures. We studied how multiple features can be effectively used to improve the robustness of confidence measures. In particular, we paid special attention to noise rejection, as the approach works well for training does not yield satisfactory results. We proposed a two-level approach to handle the problem. We first used a noise acoustic model in the same way as other conventional phonetic acoustic models. As noise models typically are conservative in detecting noise, we introduced an additional classifier to catch up the remaining noise that could be potentially misrecognized as regular words.

As the problem of confidence measures is essentially a two-class pattern classification problem, we need to use appropriate objective function to optimize our classifier. Discriminative training has been explicitly used in a number of systems [3,4,10]. They are particularly effective in small-vocabulary applications for tasks such as keyword spotting. Most of them have been directly applied to word-level features. It has been reported that phone-level features can improve confidence estimation performance [6,11]. We believe it is important to have a finer granularity in order to distinguish confusable words. In most conventional systems, when a decision is made at the word level with sub-word level features, each sub-word unit is typically weighted equally. In fact, different sub-word units clearly should have different contributions to the overall decision. We proposed a framework of transformation function based system using sub-word features. The transformation function can be optimized by discriminative objective functions so that different sub-words can make different contributions according to their overall discrimination capability. Our experiments indicated that performance could be significantly improved with our linear transformation function.

This paper is organized as follows. In Section 2, we briefly describe *Whisper* speech recognition system and the data we used in our experiments. In section 3, we review some basic approaches used for confidence measures and compare the performance of using features at word, phone, or senone levels. In Section 4 we discuss the framework of transformation of sub-word feature to achieve better word-level performance and how to use discriminative training to optimize parameters. For section 3 and 4, experiments are carried on misspoken error detection task. In section 5, we explore the feature selection for recognition error detection. Section 6 is dedicated to noise rejection, where two-level approach is described. Finally we summarize our major findings and outline our future work.

2. WHISPER SPEECH RECOGNITION SYSTEM

Microsoft's *Whisper* speech recognition system [2,13] is a general purpose speaker-independent continuous speech recognizer. *Whisper* can be used for command and control, dictation and conversational applications by loading different grammars. *Whisper* offers many features such as continuous speech recognition, speaker-independence with adaptation and dynamic vocabulary.

Whisper has a unified architecture that can be scaled to meet different application and platform requirements.

The technology enhancements of *Whisper* system include normalized feature representations for improved robustness, senone models derived from inter- and intra-word context-dependent phonemes, semi-continuous or continuous density hidden Markov models implemented with the generic shared density function architecture, and efficient decoder algorithms. We recently benchmarked *Whisper* with the widely used DARPA SI-284 training set and the 1994 H1 development test set. *Whisper*'s word recognition error rate was 7.7% using the trigram for the H1 DEV94 test set. A simplified version of *Whisper* can be downloaded from http://research.microsoft.com/stg.

The following is a short description of *Whisper* system. A more complete description of the *Whisper* system can be found in [2,13].

- FRONT-END

Whisper processes 16kHz PCM data into MEL-scale cepstrum. A multi-demensional feature vector is formed with the cepstrum and its dynamics. An improved two-mean normalization is employed to smooth out the inter-speaker and channel variation.

- ACOUSTIC MODELING

Whisper is modeling context-dependent triphone or quinphones based on senone [12]. The senone mapping is derived using decision tree from the training data. *Whisper* can use either semi-continuous or continuous density HMMs. The acoustic model we used here is a simplified version – a set of HMMs with continuous-density output probabilities consisting of 3000 senones. A mixture of 4 Gaussian densities with diagonal covariances was used for each senone. The phonetic modeling in the system consists of position and context dependent within-word and crossword triphones.

- LANGUAGE MODELING

Whisper system can work with different language models including statistical N-gram and context-free grammars. For dictation, typically trigram derived from very large text corpora is used. For command-and-control, context-free grammar is often used. In our experiment, a compact trigram was used.

- DECODING

Pronunciation prefix tree is used in *Whisper* for a very efficient single pass decoder [13]. The sharing in the tree can eliminate the redundant computation for different words with the same prefix in pronunciation. Look ahead is also used for efficient pruning of search space.

We have three tasks discussed in this paper. Each task involves different scenario thus requires different setup and data set. We describe the experimental setup as the following.

1) MISSPOKEN ERROR DETECTION

In this task, the transcription is given and detection is done on word-level. The speaker-independent portion of the North America Business News (NAB) was used for this confidence measure experiment. About half the data were used to train the acoustic model. The rest were reserved as development and test sets (no speaker overlap between training, development and test set). The development and test set contains 4251 and 1082 sentences respectively. Two test cases are formed:

- *Random Test:* Every sentence was used twice in the test set; one with correct transcription and another with totally random transcription.
- *Confusable Test:* The recognition results by a simple recognizer with context-independent models using 5000-word lexicon and bigram language model were used as transcription.

The *Confusable Test* was used for most of the experiments in section 3 and 4, which is far more difficult than the *Random Test.* Unless specified explicitly, *Confusable Test* was used there.

2) RECOGNITION ERROR DETECTION

The training data was the same as above. The test set consists of 2330 utterances which is larger than in enrollment. Recognition was performed by *Whisper* using detailed context-dependent acoustic model with 60,000-word lexicon and trigram language model. Confidence measure was computed for each word in the recognition results. Though the test set is similar to *Confusable Test* set mentioned above, it is considerably more difficult. That is because recognition and confidence computation used exactly the same configuration – including large size lexicon and detailed acoustic model, which makes misrecognized words even more "confusing".

3) NOISE REJECTION

In this task, we only consider non-overlapping noise and speech scenario for speech recognition systems, especially the common noises in office environment. We want to reject the noise portion in the signal and keep all speech recognized. Noise data were collected for training and testing purpose. In addition, some noise samples from ATIS spontaneous speech database were also used for training. There was no overlap between training and test data. The test set consists of about 100 noise samples, 150 single-phone words, 300 continuous speech utterances and 300 isolated speech utterances. All of them were collected in-house except that continuous speech utterances were from NAB database.

3. SUBWORD FEATUTURES

1. WORD AND PHONE BASED FILLER MODEL

The filler-model is a fully connected all-phone network [1,2]. It can be evaluated using a Viterbi beam search with its own beam width. Transitions between phones can be weighted by phonetic bigram probabilities that could be trained using a typical lexicon and language model. The best path determined by the evaluation of the all-phone network can be considered as alternative hypothesis. The ratio between the length-normalized score obtained from Viterbi alignment based on given transcription and the length-normalized score obtained from all-phone network was the feature used for confidence measure.

Both context-independent (CI) and context-dependent all-phone (CD) network had been considered in our experiments. Surprisingly, the CD all-phone network did not provide any extra help except the fact that the interpolation of CI and CD all-phone network scores demonstrated modest improvement.

The filler-model can be applied in the word-level or phone-level. In the word-level, the feature is directly compared to a threshold and the decision can be made as CORRECT/INCORRECT. In the phone-level experiment, the features are accumulated for all the phones in the word and then normalized over the number of the phones in the word. Fig. 1 illustrates the performance curve of both phone-level and word-level results.

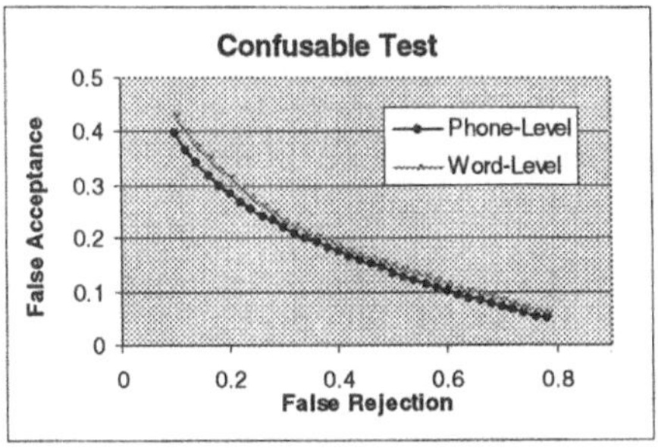

Fig. 1: Comparison of filler-model performance at word and phone level

2. PHONE AND SENONE BASED ANTI-MODEL

The anti-model [3,4] for a class is typically trained with all the data that are not associated with the class. It is often used with a set of specific model trained for confidence measure. In this experiment the confidence model was trained on segmental features for every sub-word unit, which consists of cepstrum feature, its dynamics and segment duration. A Gaussian was built for each sub-word unit. For anti-model, instead building the model with all the data of anti-classes, we used the best Gaussian selected from the context-independent sub-word units which do not belong to the class. The ratio of length normalized likelihood between sub-word unit model and anti-model was used as the feature to compute the confidence score.

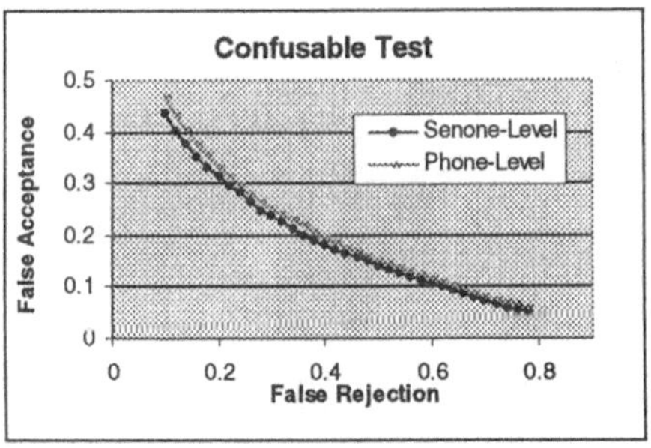

Fig. 2: Comparison of anti-model performance at phone and senone level.

The anti-model can be applied either at the triphone level or at the senone level. Since the number of triphones is generally large, we grouped the triphones to clustered-triphones based on senones – each clustered triphone has a unique HMM in terms of senones. For 3000 senones, we had about 15000 clustered triphones. Some of the triphone models were untrained, but they were not frequently used and can be backed off to context-independent models. Fig. 1 and Fig. 2 shows that finer granularity feature offers slightly better performance. In these experiments, we found that anti-model performs worse than the baseline filler-model.

4. FEATURE TRANSFORMATION

It is clear that sub-word level features are better than word-level features in above experiments. In these experiments, when a decision was made at the word level with sub-word level features, each sub-word unit was weighted equally. In fact, different phones clearly have different impacts on our perception of words. The simplest modification would be assigning each sub-word unit a different weight. The weights can be optimized from the training and development set. In general, we can use a transformation function *f(x)* to map features at sub-word level.

$$CS(w) = \frac{1}{N}\sum_{i=1}^{N} f_{class(U_i)}(x_i)$$

Where *CS(w)* is the confidence score for word *w*, *xi* is the feature (e.g., log likelihood) for *ith* sub-word unit in word *w* and *N* is the number of units in word *w*. *Ui* is the id of the *ith* sub-word unit and the mapping function *class(Ui)* will allow us to determine how many transformation functions we want to use. As in the baseline, typically function *f(x)* is defined as:

$$f(x) = x$$

Here we propose to have a linear transformation function:

$$f(x) = ax + b$$

In this case, we can use discriminative training to optimize the parameters *a* and *b* [3,4]. A cost function can be defined as a sigmoid function on top of *CS(w)*. Then gradient descent algorithm can be used to optimize parameters in function *f(x)* to minimize the expectation of cost function over all the samples used in optimization. In our experiments development set data were used to train the transformation parameters.

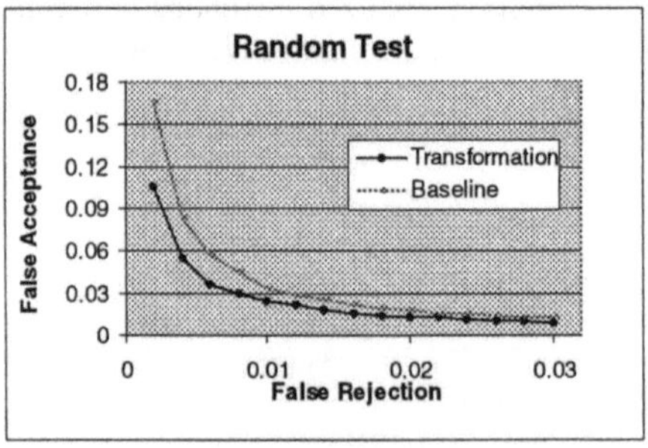

Fig. 3: Comparison of performance on *Random Test* case with and without linear transformation (CI class).

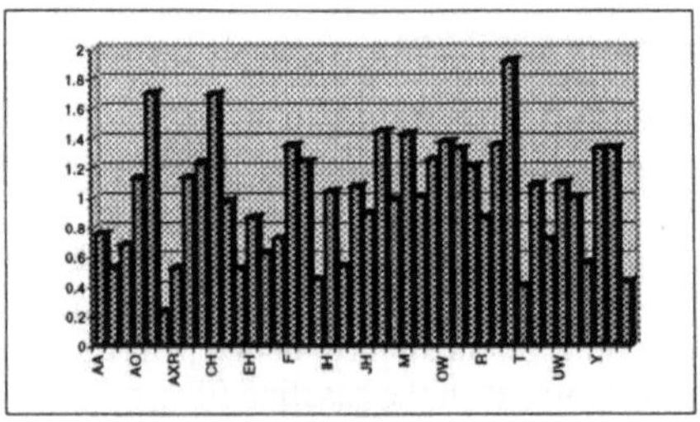

Fig. 4: Transformation parameter *a* for each phone class

1. CONTEXT-INDEPENDENT TRANSFORMATION

Starting with the *Random Test* case, we had a linear transformation function for each context-independent phone class. Filler-model was used to generate feature in this experiment as it performed better than anti-model. From Fig. 3 we can clear see that the linear transformation of the feature helps greatly.

To illustrate the effects of transformation, the transformation parameters of a are illustrated in Fig. 4 (due to resolution, only some of the phone labels are plotted in the figure). We notice that on average the weight for consonants is greater than the weight for vowels.

2. CONTEXT-DEPENDENT TRANSFORMATION

As the *Confusable Test* set is much more difficult than the *Random Test* set, we suspected that we might need more parameters in transformation functions. Experiment shows that using context-independent transformation functions on the *Confusable Test* set only yielded some marginal improvement. That seems to validate our hypothesis. Therefore we extended the transformation function from context-independent class to context-dependent class. In our experiments we had one function for each clustered triphone. The added parameters worked extremely well to model the context-dependencies. In Fig. 5 we can clearly see the significant performance gain by using context-dependent transformation functions. In comparison to the baseline, it shows that the feature transformation based system reduced the equal error rate by 15% with up to 40% false acceptance error reduction at various fixed false rejection rate.

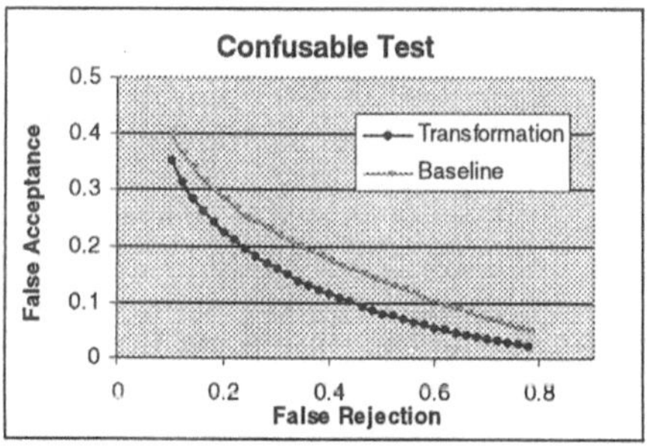

Fig. 5: Comparison of performance on *Confusable Test* case with and without linear transformation (CD class)

5. RECOGNITION ERROR DETECTION

For applications such as dictation, it is extremely useful to highlight potentially misrecognized words. In order to use the confidence measure to mark these erroneous words reliably, we need to further improve the performance of our confidence measure. The task is more difficult than what is needed for misspoken word detection in user enrollment. Several recent papers indicated that multiple features could improve the performance significantly [6,7,8,9]. Our experiments also confirmed the importance of multiple features. We considered the following features:

- Word stability ratio from N (N = 12 in our experiments) different language model weights (*WrdStabRatio*).

- LOG average number of active words around the ending frame of the word (*WrdCntEnd*).
- Acoustic score per frame within the word normalized by the corresponding active senone scores (*AscoreSen*).
- LOG average number of active words within the word (*WrdCntW*).
- Acoustic score per frame within the word normalized by the phonetic filler model (*AscoreFiller*).
- Language model score (*LMScore*).
- Language model back-off (trigram, bigram or unigram hit) for the word (*LMBackOff*).
- LOG average number of active states within the word (*StateCnt*).
- Number of phones in the word (*Nphones*).
- LOG average number of active words around the beginning frame of the word (*WrdCntBeg*).
- If the word has multiple pronunciations (*Mpron*).
- Word duration (*WordDur*).

To understand the relative importance of each feature, we computed the linear correlation coefficient of each feature against the correct/incorrect tag for each word in the training set, as illustrated in Table 1. Not surprisingly, word stability ratio (*WrdStabRatio*) had the largest correlation value, which was also reported previously in [7].

Table 1. The linear correlation coefficients for each feature against correct/incorrect tag

Feature	*Correlation*	*Feature*	*Correlation*	*Feature*	*Correlation*
WrdStabRatio	0.590	*WrdCntEnd*	-0.321	*AscoreSen*	0.250
WrdCntW	-0.223	*AscoreFiller*	0.219	*LMScore*	0.175
LMBackOff	0.171	*StateCnt*	-0.155	*Nphones*	0.091
WrdCntBeg	-0.067	*Mpron*	0.057	*WordDur*	0.012

There are several kinds of classifier that can be used to compute the confidence scores. Previous research has shown that that the difference between classifiers such as linear classifiers, generalized linear models, decision trees and neural networks is insignificant [6,7]. Therefore we just used the simplest linear classifier for our experiments. Linear discriminat analysis was used as the optimization criteria for our linear classifier.

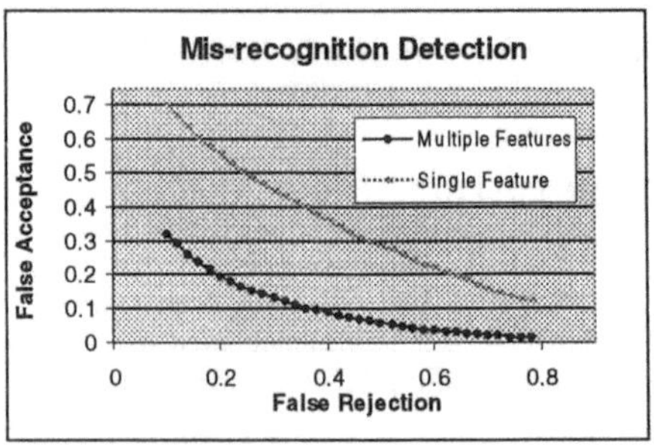

Fig. 6: Multiple features vs. single feature in recognition error detection

Some features are highly correlated to each other and these features are typically related to the same knowledge source. We have experimented iteratively removing features to combat the curse of dimensionality. We have found that *WrdCntBeg* and *WordDur* can be safely discarded. Fig. 6 illustrates the difference between multiple feature and single feature systems (*AscoreFiller* -- filler model based likelihood score). It shows that up to 80% false acceptance error reduction at fixed false rejection rate can be achieved by using multi-dimensional features in comparison to the baseline system using single feature.

6. NOISE REJECTION

Noise immunity is an important feature for practical speech recognition systems. If a recognizer picks up noise and produces some garbage outputs, the benefit of using speech recognition will vanish quickly. In theory, the confidence measure we discussed above could be easily applied to noise rejection. Due to the unique characteristics of noise rejection, we need to further augment our confidence measures. We found that the most typical noises for desktop dictation applications can be classified into following categories:

- Mouth noises: lip smack, throat clearing, cough, nasal clearing, heavy breath etc.
- Computer noises: keyboard typing, microphone adjustment, computer fan, disk head seeking etc.
- Office noises: phone ring, paper rustles, door closing etc.

Traditional approach is to model noises explicitly in a similar way as other phonetic acoustic models. With noise models derived from our noise database, we were able to get 22% noise rejection error rate without any false alarm.

As the noise training data is often limited in terms of coverage, some noises can be easily matched to short word models such as "if", "two". To further improve the baseline performance, we used an additional classifier to provide more detailed discrimination between speech and noise. The feature we used in the second-level noise classifier was the ratio between the score generated by *all-speech model* (fully connected context-independent phone models) and by *all-noise model* (fully connected silence and noise phone models). The ratio was computed for all the word segments. By using second-level classifier on top of noise model, we had significantly improved our noise rejection capability to 7% rejection error rate without any false alarm, which represents a 68% error reduction. Here, the false alarm rate was evaluated on single-phone word set plus continuous and isolated speech data set.

7. SUMMARY

In this paper we have demonstrated the effectiveness of our effort to significantly improve confidence measures for robust speech recognition. In particular, we have shown that the linear transformation of features works significantly better than the widely used all-phone baseline system. By using linear feature transformation, we have achieved 15% equal-error rate reduction, with up to 40% false acceptance error reduction at various fixed false rejection rate. When our confidence measure is used to detect recognition errors, multiple features outperformed single feature significantly. Up to 80% false acceptance error reduction at fixed false rejection rate can be achieved in comparison to the baseline using single feature. Not surprisingly, selection of features is critical to achieve reliable performance. Finally, we have achieved a very low noise rejection error rate (7%) by explicitly modeling noise in acoustic model with our secondary classifier, which represents a 68% error reduction over the baseline system.

8. ACKNOWLEDGEMENTS

The authors would like to thank Milind Mahajan and Hsiao-Wuen Hon for useful discussions.

REFERENCES

[1] Asadi A., Schwartz R. and Makhoul J., "Automatic Modeling of Adding New Words to a Large-Vocabulary Continuous Speech Recognition System", in proc. of the *IEEE International Conference on Acoustics, Speech and Signal Processing,* 1991, pp 305-308.

[2] Huang X., Acero A., Alleva F., Hwang M.Y., Jiang L. and Mahajan M. "Microsoft Windows Highly Intelligent Speech Recognizer: Whisper". In proc. of the *IEEE International Conference on Acoustics, Speech, and Signal Processing*, Detroit, May 1995, pp 93-96.

[3] Sukkar R., Setlur A.R., Rahim M.G. and Lee C.H., "Utterance Verification of Keyword Strings using Word-Based Minimum Verification Error (WB-MVE) Training", in proc. of the *IEEE International Conference on Acoustics, Speech, and Signal Processing*, Atlanta, GA, May, 1996, pp 518-521.

[4] Rahim M.G., Lee C.H., Juang B.H. and Chou W., "Discriminative Utterance Verification using Minimum String Verification Error (MSVE) Training", in proc. of the *IEEE International Conference on Acoustics, Speech, and Signal Processing*, Atlanta, GA, May, 1996, pp 3585-3588.

[5] Eide E., Gish H., Jeanrenaud P. and Mielke A., "Understanding and Improving Speech Recognition Performance through the Use of Diagnostic Tools", in proc. of the *IEEE International Conference on Acoustics, Speech, and Signal Processing*, Detroit, May 1995, pp 221-224.

[6] Chase L., "Word and Acoustic Confidence Annotation for Large Vocabulary Speech Recognition", in proc. of the *European Conference on Speech Communication and Technology,* Rhodes, Greece, September, 1997, pp 815-818.

[7] Schaaf T. and Kemp T., "Confidence Measures for Spontaneous Speech Recognition", in proc. of the *IEEE International Conference on Acoustics, Speech and Signal Processing,* Munich, Germany, May, 1997, pp 875-878.

[8] Siu M., Gish, H and Richardson F., "Improved Estimation, Evaluation and Applications of Confidence Measures for Speech Recognition", in proc. of the *European Conference on Speech Communication and Technology,* Rhodes, Greece, September, 1997, pp 831-834

[9] Weintraub M, Beaufays F., Rivlin Z., Konig Y. and Stolcke A., "Neural Network Based Measures of Confidence for Word Recognition", in proc. of the *IEEE International Conference on Acoustics, Speech and Signal Processing,* Munich, Germany, May, 1997, pp 887-890.

[10] Modi P. and Rahim M. "Discriminative Utterance Verification using Multiple Confidence Measures", in proc. of the *European Conference on Speech Communication and Technology,* Rhodes, Greece, September, 1997, pp 103-106.

[11] Rivlin Z., Cohen M., Abrash V. and Chung T., "A Phone-Dependent Confidence Measure for Utterance Rejection", in proc. of the *IEEE International Conference on Acoustics, Speech, and Signal Processing*, Atlanta, GA, May, 1996, pp 515-518.

[12] Hwang, M.Y. and Huang, X. and Alleva, F. "Predicting Unseen Triphone with Senones", in proc. of the *IEEE International Conference on Acoustics, Speech, and Signal Processing*, Minneapolis, MN, pages 311-314. April, 1993, pp 311-314.

[13] Alleva F., Huang X. and Hwang M., "Improvements on the Pronunciation Prefix Tree Search Organization", in proc. of the *IEEE International Conference on Acoustics, Speech, and Signal Processing*, Atlanta, GA, May, 1996, pp 133-136.

REFINEMENT OF A STRUCTURED LANGUAGE MODEL†

Ciprian Chelba, CLSP, The Johns Hopkins University
Frederick Jelinek, CLSP, The Johns Hopkins University

ABSTRACT

A new language model for speech recognition inspired by linguistic analysis is presented. The model develops hidden hierarchical structure incrementally and uses it to extract meaningful information from the word history — thus enabling the use of extended distance dependencies — in an attempt to complement the locality of currently used n-gram Markov models. The model, its probabilistic parametrization, a reestimation algorithm for the model parameters and a set of experiments meant to evaluate its potential for speech recognition are presented.

1 INTRODUCTION

The task of a speech recognizer is to automatically transcribe speech into text. The most successful approach to speech recognition so far is a statistical one [1]: given the observed string of acoustic features A, find the most likely word string $\hat{W}$ among those that could have generated A:

$$\hat{W} = argmax_W P(W|A) = argmax_W P(A|W) \cdot P(W) \tag{1}$$

This paper is concerned with the estimation of the language model probability $P(W)$. We will first describe current modeling approaches to the problem, followed by a detailed explanation of our model. A few preliminary experiments that show the potential of our approach for language modeling will then be presented.

2 BASIC LANGUAGE MODELING

The language modeling problem is to estimate the source probability $P(W)$ where $W = w_1, w_2, \ldots, w_n$ is a sequence of words. This probability is estimated from a text training corpus. Usually the model is parameterized: $P_\theta(W), \theta \in \Theta$ where Θ is referred to as the parameter space. Due to the sequential nature of an efficient search algorithm, the model operates left-to-right, allowing the computation

$$P(w_1, w_2, \ldots, w_n) = P(w_1) \cdot \prod_{i=2}^{n} P(w_i/w_1 \ldots w_{i-1}) \tag{2}$$

†This work was funded by the NSF IRI-19618874 grant STIMULATE

We thus seek to develop parametric conditional models:

$$P_\theta(w_i/w_1 \ldots w_{i-1}), \theta \in \Theta, w_i \in \mathcal{V} \tag{3}$$

where $\mathcal{V}$ is the vocabulary chosen by the modeler. Currently most successful is the *n-gram language model*:

$$P_\theta(w_i/w_1 \ldots w_{i-1}) = P_\theta(w_i/w_{i-n+1} \ldots w_{i-1}) \tag{4}$$

2.1 LANGUAGE MODEL QUALITY

All attempts to derive an algorithm that would estimate the model parameters so as to minimize the word error rate have failed. As an alternative, a statistical model is evaluated by how well it predicts a string of symbols W_t — commonly named *test data* — generated by the source to be modeled.

2.1.1 Perplexity

Assume we compare two models M_1 and M_2; they assign probability $P_{M_1}(W_t)$ and $P_{M_2}(W_t)$, respectively, to the sample test string W_t. "Naturally", we consider M_1 to be a better model than M_2 if $P_{M_1}(W_t) > P_{M_2}(W_t)$. The test data is not seen during the model estimation process.

A commonly used quality measure for a given model M is related to the entropy of the underlying source and was introduced under the name of perplexity (PPL) [6]:

$$PPL(M) = exp(-1/|W_t| \sum_{i=1}^{N} \ln [P_M(W_t)]) \tag{5}$$

2.2 SMOOTHING

Assume that our model M is faced with the prediction $w_i|w_1 \ldots w_{i-1}$ and that w_i has not been seen in the training corpus in context $w_1 \ldots w_{i-1}$ which itself has possibly not been encountered in the training corpus. If $P_M(w_i|w_1 \ldots w_{i-1}) = 0$ then $P_M(w_1 \ldots w_N) = 0$ thus forcing a recognition error; good models are smooth, in the sense that $\exists \epsilon(M) > 0$ s.t. $P_M(w_i|w_1 \ldots w_{i-1}) > \epsilon, \forall w_i \in \mathcal{V}, (w_1 \ldots w_{i-1}) \in \mathcal{V}^{i-1}$.

One standard approach that ensures smoothing is the deleted interpolation method [7]. It interpolates linearly among contexts of different order h_n:

$$P_\theta(w_i|w_{i-n+1} \ldots w_{i-1}) = \sum_{k=0}^{k=n} \lambda_k \cdot f(w_i/h_k) \tag{6}$$

where: $h_k = w_{i-k+1} \ldots w_{i-1}$ is the context of order k when predicting w_i; $f(w_i/h_k)$ is the relative frequency estimate for the conditional probability $P(w_i/h_k)$; $\lambda_k, k = 0 \ldots n$ are the interpolation coefficients satisfying $\lambda_k > 0, k = 0 \ldots n$ and $\sum_{k=0}^{k=n} \lambda_k = 1$.

The model parameters θ then are: the counts $C(h_n, w_i)$ — lower order counts are inferred recursively by: $C(h_k, w_i) = \sum_{w_{i-k} \in \mathcal{V}} C(w_{i-k}, h_k, w_i)$ — and the interpolation coefficients $\lambda_k, k = 0 \ldots n$.

A simple way to estimate the model parameters involves a two stage process:

1. gather counts from *development data* — about 90% of training data;

2. estimate interpolation coefficients to minimize the perplexity of *check data* — the remaining 10% of the training data.

Different smoothing techniques are also used e.g., maximum entropy [2] or back-off [8].

3 DESCRIPTION OF THE STRUCTURED LANGUAGE MODEL

The model we present is closely related to the one investigated in [3], however different in a few important aspects:

- our model operates in a left-to-right manner, thus allowing its use directly in the hypothesis search for $\hat{W}$ in (1);
- our model is a factored version of the one in [3], thus enabling the calculation of the joint probability of words and parse structure; this was not possible in the previous case due to the huge computational complexity of the model.

3.1 THE BASIC IDEA AND TERMINOLOGY

Consider predicting the word `after` in the sentence:
`the contract ended with a loss of 7 cents after trading as low as 89 cents.`
A 3-gram approach would predict `after` from `(7, cents)` whereas it is intuitively clear that the strongest word-pair predictor would be `contract ended` which is outside the reach of even 7-grams. Our assumption is that what enables humans to make a good prediction of `after` is the syntactic structure of its sentence prefix. The linguistically correct *partial parse* of this prefix is shown in Figure 1.

A binary branching parse for a string of words is a binary tree whose leaves are the words. The headword annotation makes the tree an oriented graph: at each node we have two children; the current node receives a *headword* from either child; one arrow suffices to describe which of the children — left or right — is percolated to become the headword of the parent. It was found that better parse trees are generated when using tags: part-of-speech(POS) tags for the leaves and non-terminal(NT) tags for the intermediate nodes in the parse tree. Any subtree identifies a *constituent*. The word `ended` is called the *headword* of the *constituent* `(ended (with (...)))` and `ended` is an *exposed headword* when predicting `after` — topmost headword in the largest constituent that contains it. The syntactic structure in the past filters out irrelevant words and points to the important ones, thus enabling the use of long distance information when predicting the next word.

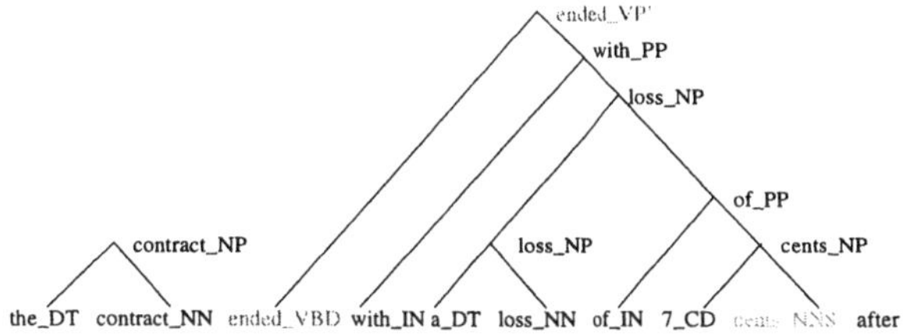

Figure 1: Partial parse

Our model will attempt to build the syntactic structure incrementally while traversing the sentence left-to-right; it will assign a probability $P(W, T)$ to every sentence W with every possible POStag assignment, binary branching parse, non-terminal tag and headword annotation for every constituent of the parse tree T.

Let W be a sentence of length n words to which we have prepended `<s>` and appended `</s>` so that w_0 =`<s>` and w_{n+1} =`</s>`. Let W_k be the word k-prefix $w_0 \dots w_k$ of the sentence and $W_k T_k$ the *word-parse k-prefix*. A word-parse k-prefix contains — for a given parse — only those binary subtrees whose span is completely included in the word k-prefix, excluding w_0 =`<s>`. Single words along with their POStag can be regarded as root-only subtrees. Figure 2 shows a word-parse k-prefix; `h_0 .. h_{-m}` are the *exposed heads*, each head being a pair (headword, non-terminal tag), or (word, POStag) in the case of a root-only tree.

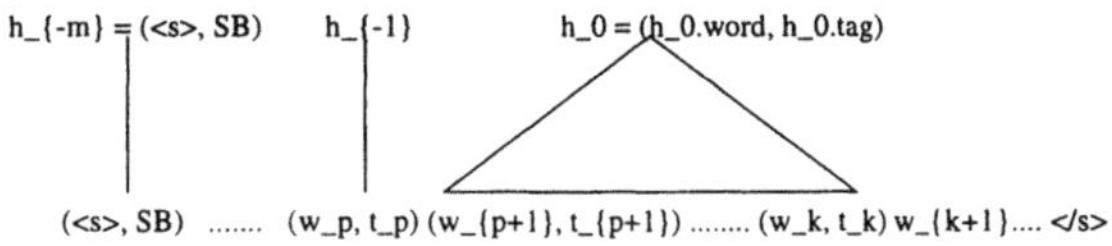

Figure 2: A word-parse k-prefix

A *complete parse* — Figure 3 — is a binary parse of the `(<s>, SB)` $(w_1, t_1) \dots (w_n, t_n)$ `(</s>, SE)` sequence with the following two restrictions:

1. $(w_1, t_1) \dots (w_n, t_n)$ `(</s>, SE)` is a constituent, headed by `(</s>, TOP')`;
2. `(</s>, TOP)` is the only allowed head. Note that $((w_1, t_1) \dots (w_n, t_n))$ *needn't* be a constituent, but for the parses where it is, there is no restriction on which of its words is the headword or what is the non-terminal tag that accompanies the headword.

Our model can generate all and only the complete parses for a string `(<s>, SB)` $(w_1, t_1) \dots (w_n, t_n)$ `(</s>, SE)`.

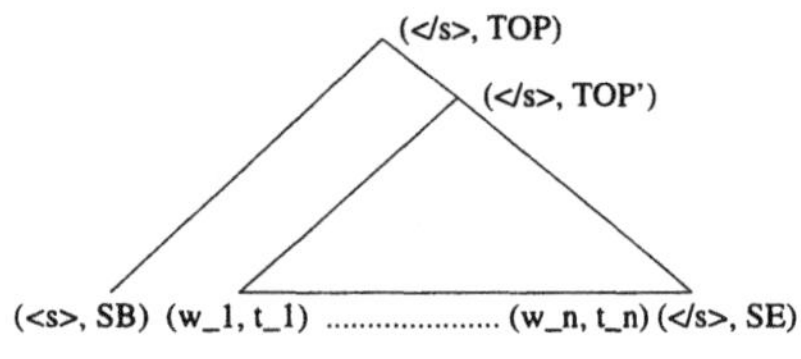

Figure 3: Complete parse

The model will operate by means of three modules:

- WORD-PREDICTOR predicts the next word w_{k+1} given the word-parse k-prefix $W_k T_k$ and then passes control to the TAGGER;
- TAGGER predicts the POStag t_{k+1} of the next word given the word-parse k-prefix and the newly predicted word w_{k+1} and then passes control to the PARSER;

- PARSER grows the already existing binary branching structure by repeatedly generating the transitions: `(adjoin-left, NTtag)` or `(adjoin-right, NTtag)` until it passes control to the PREDICTOR by taking a `null` transition. `NTtag` is the non-terminal tag assigned to each newly built constituent and `{left,right}` specifies from where the new headword is inherited. The parser operates always on the two rightmost exposed heads, starting with the newly tagged word w_{k+1}.

The operations performed by the PARSER are illustrated in Figures 4-6 and they ensure that all possible binary branching parses with all possible headword and non-terminal tag assignments for the $w_1 \ldots w_k$ word sequence can be generated. It is easy

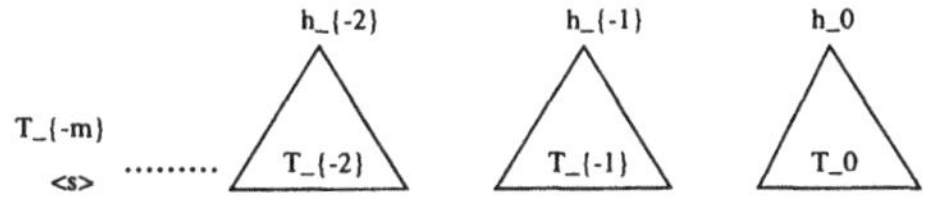

Figure 4: Before an adjoin operation

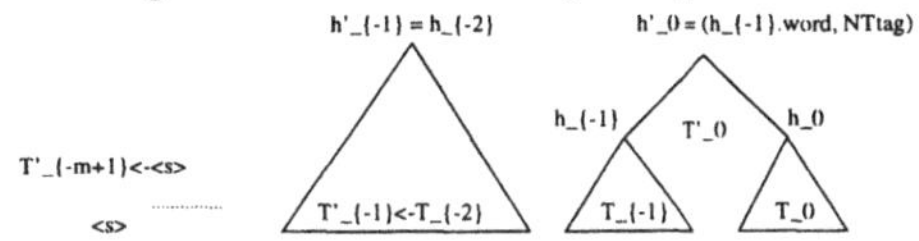

Figure 5: Result of adjoin-left under NTtag

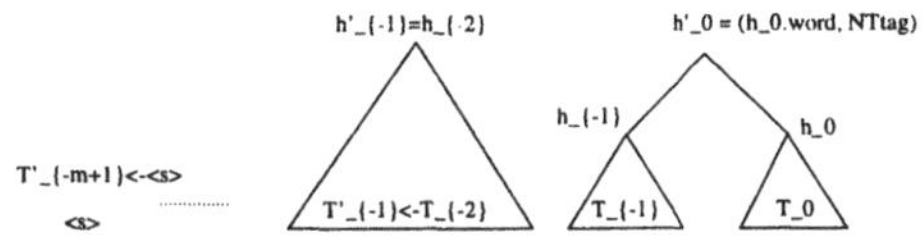

Figure 6: Result of adjoin-right under NTtag

to see that any given word sequence with a possible parse and headword annotation is generated by a unique sequence of model actions.

3.2 PROBABILISTIC MODEL

The probability $P(W,T)$ of a word sequence W and a complete parse T can be broken into:

$$P(W,T) = \prod_{k=1}^{n+1}[P(w_k/W_{k-1}T_{k-1}) \cdot P(t_k/W_{k-1}T_{k-1},w_k) \cdot \prod_{i=1}^{N_k} P(p_i^k/W_{k-1}T_{k-1},w_k,t_k,p_1^k \ldots p_{i-1}^k)] \tag{7}$$

where:

- $W_{k-1}T_{k-1}$ is the word-parse $(k-1)$-prefix
- w_k is the word predicted by WORD-PREDICTOR
- t_k is the tag assigned to w_k by the TAGGER

- $N_k - 1$ is the number of operations the PARSER executes at position k of the input string before passing control to the WORD-PREDICTOR (the N_k-th operation at position k is the null transition); N_k is a function of T

- p_i^k denotes the i-th PARSER operation carried out at position k in the word string; $p_i^k \in$ { (adjoin-left, NTtag), (adjoin-right, NTtag)}, $1 \leq i < N_k$, p_i^k =null, $i = N_k$

Each $(W_{k-1}T_{k-1}, w_k, t_k, p_1^k \dots p_{i-1}^k)$ is a valid word-parse k-prefix W_kT_k at position k in the sentence, $i = \overline{1, N_k}$.

To ensure a proper probabilistic model certain PARSER and WORD-PREDICTOR probabilities must be given specific values:

- $P(\texttt{null}/W_kT_k) = 1$, if h_{-1}.word = <s> and h_{0} $\neq$ (</s>, TOP') — that is, before predicting </s> — ensures that (<s>, SB) is adjoined in the last step of the parsing process;

- $P(\texttt{(adjoin-right, TOP)}/W_kT_k) = 1$, if h_0 = (</s>, TOP') and h_{-1}.word = <s> and $P(\texttt{(adjoin-right, TOP')}/W_kT_k) = 1$, if h_0 = (</s>, TOP') and h_{-1}.word $\neq$ <s> ensure that the parse generated by our model is consistent with the definition of a complete parse;

- $\exists \epsilon > 0, \forall W_{k-1}T_{k-1}, P(w_k{=}\texttt{</s>}/W_{k-1}T_{k-1}) \geq \epsilon$ ensures that the model halts with probability one.

In order to be able to estimate the model components we need to make appropriate equivalence classifications of the conditioning part for each component, respectively.

The equivalence classification should identify the strong predictors in the context and allow reliable estimates from a treebank. Our choice is inspired by [4]:

$$\begin{aligned} P(w_k/W_{k-1}T_{k-1}) &= P(w_k/[W_{k-1}T_{k-1}]) &&= P(w_k/h_0, h_{-1}) && (8) \\ P(t_k/w_k, W_{k-1}T_{k-1}) &= P(t_k/w_k, [W_{k-1}T_{k-1}]) &&= P(t_k/w_k, h_0.tag, h_{-1}.tag) && (9) \\ P(p_i^k/W_kT_k) &= P(p_i^k/[W_kT_k]) &&= P(p_i^k/h_0, h_{-1}) && (10) \end{aligned}$$

It is worth noting that if the binary branching structure developed by the parser were always right-branching and we mapped the POStag and non-terminal tag vocabularies to a single type then our model would be equivalent to a trigram language model.

3.3 SMOOTHING

All model components — WORD-PREDICTOR, TAGGER, PARSER — are conditional probabilistic models of the type $P(y/x_1, x_2, \dots, x_n)$ where $y, x_1, x_2, \dots, x_n$ belong to a mixed bag of words, POStags, non-terminal tags and parser operations (y only). For simplicity, the smoothing method we chose was deleted interpolation among relative frequency estimates of different orders $f_n(\cdot)$ using a recursive mixing scheme:

$$\begin{aligned} &P(y/x_1, \dots, x_n) = \\ &\quad \lambda(x_1, \dots, x_n) \cdot P(y/x_1, \dots, x_{n-1}) + (1 - \lambda(x_1, \dots, x_n)) \cdot f_n(y/x_1, \dots, x_n), \qquad (11) \\ &f_{-1}(y) = uniform(vocabulary(y)) \qquad (12) \end{aligned}$$

The λ coefficients are tied based on the range into which the count $C(x_1, \ldots, x_n)$ falls. The approach is a standard one [7].

3.4 PRUNING STRATEGY

Since the number of parses for a given word prefix W_k grows exponentially with k, $|\{T_k\}| \sim O(2^k)$, the state space of our model is huge even for relatively short sentences. We thus have to prune most parses without discarding the most likely ones for a given sentence W. Our pruning strategy is a synchronous multi-stack search algorithm.

Each stack contains hypotheses — partial parses — that have been constructed by *the same number of predictor and the same number of parser operations*. The hypotheses in each stack are ranked according to the $\ln(P(W_k, T_k))$ score, highest on top. The width of the search is controlled by two parameters:

- the maximum stack depth — the maximum number of hypotheses the stack can contain at any given time;
- log-probability threshold — the difference between the log-probability score of the top-most hypothesis and the bottom-most hypothesis at any given state of the stack cannot be larger than a given threshold.

3.5 WORD LEVEL PERPLEXITY

Attempting to calculate the conditional perplexity by assigning to a whole sentence the probability:

$$P(W/T^*) = \prod_{k=0}^{n} P(w_{k+1}/W_k T_k^*), \tag{13}$$

where $T^* = argmax_T P(W, T)$ — the search for T^* being carried according to our pruning strategy — is not valid because it is not causal: when predicting w_{k+1} we would be using T^* which was determined by looking at the entire sentence. To be able to compare the perplexity of our model with that resulting from the standard trigram approach, we need to factor in the entropy of guessing the prefix of the final best parse T_k^* *before predicting* w_{k+1}, based solely on the word prefix W_k.

To maintain a left-to-right operation of the language model, the probability assignment for the word at position $k+1$ in the input sentence was made using:

$$P(w_{k+1}/W_k) = \sum_{T_k \in S_k} P(w_{k+1}/W_k T_k) \cdot \rho(W_k, T_k), \tag{14}$$

$$\rho(W_k, T_k) = P(W_k T_k) / \sum_{T_k \in S_k} P(W_k T_k) \tag{15}$$

where S_k is the set of all parses present in our stacks at the current stage k.

Note that if we set $\rho(W_k, T_k) = \delta(T_k, T_k^* | W_k)$ — 0-entropy guess for the prefix of the parse T_k to equal that of the final best parse T_k^*— the two probability assignments (13) and (14) would be the same, yielding a lower bound on the perplexity achievable by our model when using a given pruning strategy.

A second important observation is that the next-word predictor probability $P(w_{k+1}/W_k T_k)$ in (14) *need not be the same* as the WORD-PREDICTOR probability (8) used to extract the structure T_k, thus leaving open the possibility to estimate it separately.

3.6 PARAMETER REESTIMATION

3.6.1 *First Model Reestimation*

Our parameter re-estimation is inspired by the usual EM approach. Let $(W, T^{(k)}), k = 1, 2, \ldots, N$ denote the set of parses of W that survived our pruning strategy. Each parse was produced by a unique sequence of model actions: predictor, tagger, and parser moves. The collection of these moves will be called a *derivation*. Each of the N members of the set is produced by exactly the same number of moves of each type. Each move is uniquely specified by identifiers $(y^{(m)}, \underline{x}^{(m)})$, where $m \in$ {WORD-PREDICTOR, TAGGER, PARSER} denotes the particular model, $y^{(m)}$ is the specification of the particular move taken (e.g., for m =PARSER, the quantity $y^{(m)}$ specifies a choice from $\{left, right, null\}$ and the exact tag attached), and $\underline{x}^{(m)}$ specifies the move's context (e.g., for m =PARSER, the two heads).

For each possible value $(y^{(m)}, \underline{x}^{(m)})$ we will establish a counter which at the beginning of any particular iteration will be empty. For each move $(y^{(m)}, \underline{x}^{(m)})$ present in the derivation of $(W, T^{(j)})$ we add to the counter specified by $(y^{(m)}, \underline{x}^{(m)})$ the amount

$$\rho(W, T^{(k)}) = \frac{P(W, T^{(k)})}{\sum_{j=1}^{N} P(W, T^{(j)})}$$

where $P(W, T^{(j)})$ are evaluated on the basis of the model's parameter values established at the end of the preceding iteration. We do that for all $(W, T^{(j)}), j = 1, 2, \ldots, N$ and for all sentences W in the training data. Let $C^{(m)}(y^{(m)}, \underline{x}^{(m)})$ be the counter contents at the end of this process. The corresponding relative frequency estimate will be

$$f(y^{(m)}|\underline{x}^{(m)}) = \frac{C^{(m)}(y^{(m)}, \underline{x}^{(m)})}{\sum_{z^{(m)}} C^{(m)}(z^{(m)}, \underline{x}^{(m)})}$$

The lower order frequencies needed for the deleted interpolation of probabilities in the next iteration are derived in the obvious way from the same counters.

It is worth noting that because of pruning (which is a function of the statistical parameters in use), the sets of surviving parses $(W, T^{(k)}), k = 1, 2, \ldots, N$ for the same sentence W may be completely different for different iterations.

3.6.2 *First Pass Initial Parameters*

Each model component — WORD-PREDICTOR, TAGGER, PARSER — is initialised from a set of hand-parsed sentences, after each parse tree (W, T) is decomposed into its $derivation(W, T)$. Separately for each m model component, we:

- gather joint counts $C^{(m)}(y^{(m)}, \underline{x}^{(m)})$ from the derivations that make up the "development data" using $\rho(W, T) = 1$;
- estimate the deleted interpolation coefficients on joint counts gathered from "check data" using the EM algorithm [5]. These are the initial parameters used with the reestimation procedure described in the previous section.

3.6.3 *Language Model Refinement*

In order to improve performance, we develop a model to be used in (14), different from the WORD-PREDICTOR model (8). We will call this new component the L2R-WORD-PREDICTOR.

The key step is to recognize in (14) a hidden Markov model (HMM) with fixed transition probabilities — although dependent on the position in the input sentence k — specified by the $\rho(W_k, T_k)$ values.

The Expectation-step of the EM algorithm [5] for gathering joint counts $C^{(m)}(y^{(m)}, \underline{x}^{(m)})$, $m =$ L2R-WORD-PREDICTOR-MODEL, is the standard one whereas the Maximization-step uses the same count smoothing technique as that descibed in section 3.6.1.

The second reestimation pass is seeded with the $m =$ WORD-PREDICTOR model joint counts $C^{(m)}(y^{(m)}, \underline{x}^{(m)})$ resulting from the first parameter reestimation pass (see section 3.6.1).

4 EXPERIMENTS

We have carried out the reestimation technique described in section 3.6 on 1 Mwds of "development" data. For convenience we chose to work on the UPenn Treebank corpus [9] — a subset of the WSJ (Wall Stree Journal) corpus. The vocabulary sizes were:
word vocabulary: 10k, open — all words outside the vocabulary are mapped to the <unk> token; POS tag vocabulary: 40, closed; non-terminal tag vocabulary: 52, closed; parser operation vocabulary: 107, closed. The development set size was 929,564wds (sections 00-20), check set size 73,760wds (sections 21-22), test set size 82,430wds (sections 23-24).

Table 1 shows the results of the reestimation techniques presented in section 3.6; E? and L2R? denote iterations of the reestimation procedure described in sections 3.6.1 and 3.6.3, respectively. A deleted interpolation trigram model had perplexity 167.14 on the same training-test data.

iteration number	DEV set L2R-PPL	TEST set L2R-PPL
E0	24.70	167.47
E1	22.34	160.76
E2	21.69	158.97
E3 = L2R0	21.26	158.28
L2R5	17.44	153.76

Table 1: Parameter reestimation results

Simple linear interpolation between our model and the trigram model:

$$Q(w_{k+1}/W_k) = \lambda \cdot P(w_{k+1}/w_{k-1}, w_k) + (1 - \lambda) \cdot P(w_{k+1}/W_k)$$

yielded a further improvement in PPL, as shown in Table 2. The interpolation weight was estimated on check data to be $\lambda = 0.36$. An overall relative reduction of 11% over the trigram model has been achieved.

As outlined in section 3.5, the perplexity value calculated using (13) is a lower bound for the achievable perplexity of our model; for the above search parameters and E3 model statistics this bound was 99.60, corresponding to a relative reduction of 41% over the trigram model.

iteration number	TEST set L2R-PPL	TEST set 3-gram interpolated PPL
E0	167.47	152.25
E3	158.28	148.90
L2R5	153.76	147.70

Table 2: Interpolation with trigram results

5 CONCLUSIONS AND FUTURE DIRECTIONS

A new source model that organizes the prefix hierarchically in order to predict the next symbol is developed. As a case study we applied the source model to natural language, thus developing a new language model with applicability in speech recognition.

We believe that the above experiments show the potential of our approach for improved language modeling for speech recognition. Our future plans include:

- experiment with other parameterizations for the word predictor and parser models;
- evaluate model performance as part of an automatic speech recognizer (measure word error rate improvement).

REFERENCES

[1] L. R. Bahl, F. Jelinek, and R. L. Mercer. A maximum likelihood approach to continuous speech recognition. In *IEEE Transactions on Pattern Analysis and Machine Intelligence*, volume PAMI-5, pages 179–90, March 1983.

[2] A. L. Berger, S. A. Della Pietra, and V. J. Della Pietra. A maximum entropy approach to natural language processing. *Computational Linguistics*, 22(1):39–72, March 1996.

[3] C. Chelba, D. Engle, F. Jelinek, V. Jimenez, S. Khudanpur, L. Mangu, H. Printz, E. S. Ristad, R. Rosenfeld, A. Stolcke, and D. Wu. Structure and performance of a dependency language model. In *Proceedings of Eurospeech*, volume 5, pages 2775–2778. Rhodes, Greece, 1997.

[4] M. J. Collins. A new statistical parser based on bigram lexical dependencies. In *Proceedings of the 34th Annual Meeting of the Association for Computational Linguistics*, pages 184–191. Santa Cruz, CA, 1996.

[5] A. P. Dempster, N. M. Laird, and D. B. Rubin. Maximum likelihood from incomplete data via the EM algorithm. In *Journal of the Royal Statistical Society*, volume 39 of *B*, pages 1–38. 1977.

[6] F. Jelinek. *Information Extraction From Speech And Text.* MIT Press, 1997.

[7] F. Jelinek and R. Mercer. Interpolated estimation of markov source parameters from sparse data. In E. Gelsema and L. Kanal, editors, *Pattern Recognition in Practice*, pages 381–397. 1980.

[8] S. Katz. Estimation of probabilities from sparse data for the language model component of a speech recognizer. In *IEEE Transactions on Acoustics, Speech and Signal Processing*, volume 35, pages 400–01, March 1987.

[9] M. Marcus, B. Santorini, and M. Marcinkiewicz. Building a large annotated corpus of English: the Penn Treebank. *Computational Linguistics*, 19(2):313–330, 1995.

DOCUMENT AND CHARACTER ANALYSIS

AN ADAPTATIVE PRE-PROCESSING FOR ON-LINE HAND-WRITTEN CHARACTER RECOGNITION BY BLIND PEOPLE

R. de Saint Moulin, J.-D. Legat, Y. Deville
Research Centre in Information Technology
Université Catholique de Louvain
Place du Levant, 3
B-1348 Louvain-la-Neuve
Tel. : +32.10.47.25.68
Fax : +32.10.47.25.98
Email : Legat@dice.ucl.ac.be

ABSTRACT

On-line character recognition is an interesting alternative to the use of a standard keyboard by blind people in applications such as Personal Digital Assistant (PDA) where the keyboard size is small. By using a speech synthesiser, a complete dedicated PDA system can be developed for blind people. This approach is of course only valid for those who were not born blind and learned to write. However, the writing quality of blind people is very poor, mainly due to the lack of visual feedback.

This paper presents an adaptative pre-processing method to restore the global shape of written words. Such pre-processing does not perform any recognition process; it is however coupled with a standard on-line recognition system. The main objective of the method is to obtain a linear baseline. This is achieved by modifying the relative vertical position of the different strokes that make up a word. To deal with erroneous stroke displacement, the pre-processing method includes a stroke classification algorithm. It allows to distinguish normal strokes from small strokes, which have to be processed in a specific way. The pre-processing algorithm has been successfully implemented (on a Newton 130 Apple) and tested on a dedicated database created by blind people. We observed that all strokes were duly presented for the recognition process of the Newton 130 Apple.

1. INTRODUCTION

Much research has been done over the past 10 years to improve the performance of on-line hand-written recognition systems. The renewed interest in on-line handwriting recognition stems from a number of factors. First, the availability of hardware combining tablet and flat display allows input and output into the same surface. This combination creates the *electronic ink*, providing immediate feedback to the author of the digitised writing. Second, efforts in automating office work have increased interest in more natural methods of entering data into machines. Third, we know more about the issues of usability and user-friendliness. Finally, we more clearly understand the applications appropriate to handwriting recognition.

So, it became clear that handwriting recognition can be useful for preparing a first draft and concentrating on content creation, but that for editing or copying a text into computer, a keyboard is a more natural way of entering data [1]. The performance obtained with the new systems allows us to imagine new applications for on-line hand-written recognition. We think these systems could be used to the benefit of blind people at the cost of some adaptations to be taken into account (e.g. specific problems encountered in dealing with those people's handwriting). The ultimate goal of our current research is to develop a full on-line recognition system dedicated to blind people, using the results acquired by handwriting research over the last 3 years. This system would couple a high quality text to speech synthesiser to allow exploitation of the stored information. It would then be operated on a Personal Digital Assistant (PDA) to offer the flexibility needed in daily use. This approach is of course only valid for those who were not born blind and learned to write. As we learned from our experiments, such a system would be appreciated as a notepad (e.g. to pick up phone messages) and for planning. Today, these functions are mainly fulfilled by cassette recorders. The main advantage of our new approach is to offer store and search facilities which are non-existent with the more classical Dictaphone.

In this paper, we present a new pre-processing method that has to perform some reconstruction of handwriting, before a signal is transmitted to the recognition stage. Indeed, the writing quality of blind people is very poor mainly due to the lack of visual feedback and the lack of structured commands given to their writing hand. Intensive tests have been performed on a Newton by people who have gone blind. These tests pointed out very poor recognition results using the standard recognition module. The tests also illustrated typical deformations such as non-linear and multiple baselines, as well as overwritten characters.

The pre-processing tool is in charge of restoring the global shape of the written words and does not perform any recognition process. Its basic information is a stroke (a set of sampling points between a pen down and a pen-up) and the method is based on the hypothesis that the stroke is correct. The main task consists in hanging together the different strokes which make up a word, taking into consideration the creation of a global linear baseline. Strict application of this method leads to erroneous stroke displacement. These problems result from the incorrect processing of « special » strokes, such as the accents, the horizontal bar of the 't' letter or the vertical bar of a 'd', which are treated as simple components of the word and shifted to the height of the new created baseline. This can result in an erroneous interpretation of some strokes at the recognition stage, which in turn leads to a false post-processing decision.

To deal with this complication, an additional module has been developed, based on an analysis of the handwriting considered, using fuzzy logic to detect strokes which have to be processed in a specific way. The pre-processing algorithm has been successfully implemented on a Newton 130 Apple and tested on a database created by blind people.

In section 2, we rapidly present the main contributions of others researches in this field. These are the major advances in handwriting recognition of these latest years and allow us to know what is vital to be improved in signal quality to ensure a maximum probability of proper recognition. In section 3, we present our pre-processing method as a tool for matching the signal presentation with the actual characteristics extraction performed at the recognition stage. The performance is discussed in section 4 and conclusions are given in section 5.

2. RELATED WORK

For designing efficient writer-independent on-line or off-line recognition systems able to deal with a large vocabulary, i.e. some thousands of words, it is needed to move from a holistic word recognition approach to an analytical approach based on primitives (e.g. strokes, pseudo-letters, letters, etc.). In such an approach, the problem of the segmentation of the handwriting immediately arises. It is a very hard problem and, to date, not entirely solved. The classical approach for segmentation consists in a detection of some particular points, based on heuristics which are often difficult to justify. Such points are X and Y extrema, sharp corners, loops and, for on-line recognition, Vx and Vy extrema. In fact, these classical systems try to overcome the complex segmentation problem by a direct detection of the segmentation points. According new studies [2], it seems that right segmentation points that separate letters in a word do not merely coincidence with dominant points of the drawing. The global strategy leading to word recognition apparently needs a complete rethink. One of the renewed trends in cursive script recognition is to get inspiration from reading models. These models offer the opportunity to improve the segmentation by taking advantage of contextual information (« *Word Superiority Effect* »). The recognition process can be based [3] on a 3-level structure, hierarchically organised with feature, character and word levels.

The main problem remains the detection of pertinent features for each character model. Classical methods try to extract from the word drawing some physical primitives which will be used for matching with logical character models. The primitive segmentation is performed at classical dominant points (e.g. Y extrema, cusps, multiple points, ...). However, several possible segmentations into primitives can occur according to the type of these points. New methods model each character class by following the robust and basic strokes common to the different allographs of a same character. In [4], the modelling process is based on an automatic fuzzy rules generation to formalise in an explicit manner the pertinent knowledge. After a learning phase, each character class has its own model able to drive a logical segmentation for its class. Contrary to classical approaches based on singularities modelling, the basic principle is to automatically extract and model the stable stroke segments of each character according to the regular portions of the drawing. For a defined allograph, those segments would contain all the signal information, while the rest of the drawing could be considered as within character ligature. Following [4], the morphological differences between two allographs are only to be found in these ligatures.

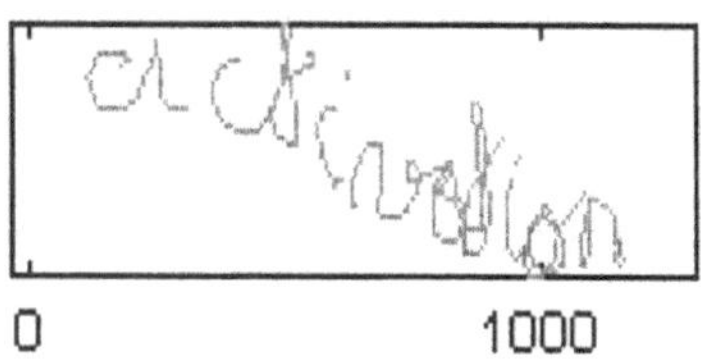

Figure 1(a)
Typical example of poor quality handwriting encountered with blind people word « activation »

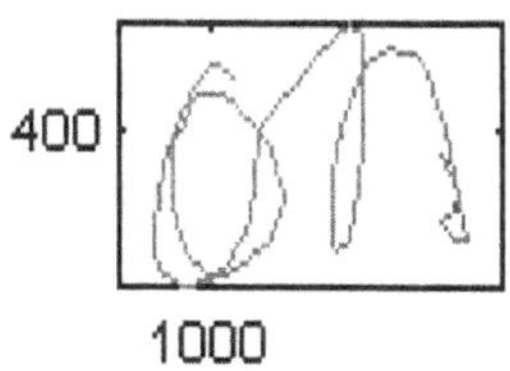

Figure 1(b)
Detail of the last stroke: cusp in the 'n' letter degenerated in a small loop

Based on these new modelling concepts, it must be possible to perform recognition on very poor quality handwriting where the usually chosen recognition criteria are not stable. Blind people's handwriting recognition seems hopeless with such classical schemes, based on crisp detection of well-formed loops, cusps and multiple points of k order. Nevertheless, regular portions of word images as previously defined, seem to be spared by the deformation process due to the lack of feedback. This is illustrated in Figure 1 (a) and (b).

We would like to develop a system based on the above-presented concepts. The system is intended to perform a reasonably good extraction of the stable parts of the word drawing. Before any recognition, the written words have to be « prepared » to ensure a presentation maximising recognition probability. Most currently available systems deal with the intensively used technique of linear baseline extraction before any processing on the input signal. A first real problem with the collected samples of blind people's handwriting is the great degradation of the baseline (see figure 1(a) for example). Secondly, due to the lack of spatial representation of the digitising tablet, the strokes which make up a word are rarely in a valid relative position. The studied subjects were very concerned with this second problem and they took great attention to avoid pen-up which could lead to such stroke displacement. This special care make writing very tiring and can lead to other characters deformations which could have been avoided (see the 'o' letter in Figures 1(b) and 2).

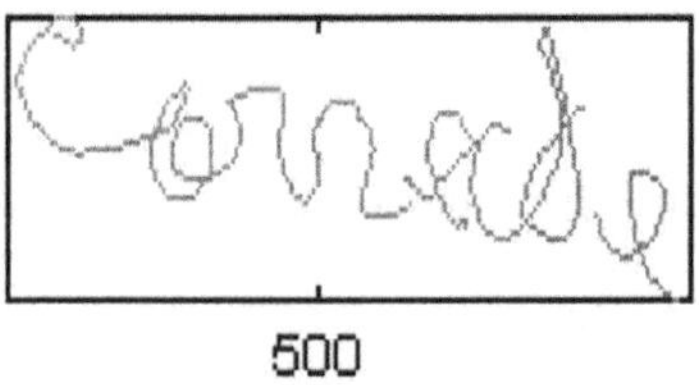

Figure 2: word « correcte »
Remark the missing pen-up at the level of the 'o' and 't' letters
and the cross-over at the level of the intersection of the 'c' and 't' letters

3. A PRE-PROCESSING METHOD DEDICATED TO BLIND PEOPLE

The tasks of the proposed pre-processing method are the following. First, a global linear baseline must be restored to allow correct feature extraction at the recognition stage. Second, the different strokes making up a word must be hanged up. The goal of this second function is to allow the writer to pay more attention to individual character drawing than to keep in mind a virtual spatial representation of the word drawing. We assume this will lead the user to dare to place his pen up where necessary and then, in turn, will improve the general quality of his handwriting. Both utilities are performed by spatial stroke shifting. The main idea is to move each stroke independently so that they form a reconstructed word. As we will see, the strict application of this principle can lead to some erroneous decisions. We thus refined the proposed method by including the detection of special strokes which have to be considered apart.

3.1 STROKE SHIFTING.

Stroke shifting, based on gravity centre calculation is an adaptive process which ensures the creation of a global baseline. The shift is defined as a two-dimensional vector which is determined using a set of variables calculated from geometrical features extracted from the word drawing.

The main idea is to shift each stroke vertically so that the gravity centre of each word describes a horizontal line. This basic strategy must be adapted for ascending and descending strokes which would be moved too low or too high. For each writer, the average slope $\Delta y/\Delta x$ between 2 points in the sampled words is progressively learned and the points which belong to segments with a great slope with regard to this calculated average slope will not be taken into account for the gravity centre calculation.

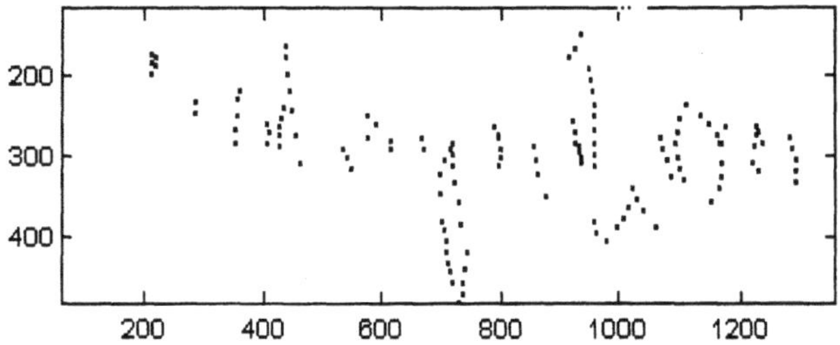

Figure 3: word « interpretation »
Detection of the ascending and descending strokes.

The dark parts on the drawing on figure 3 are the detected « *vertical* » segments which are not to be taken into account for the gravity centre calculation. The pre-processing method is not intended to do any analysis at the letter stage. This explains why we chose for a relatively simple method to implement detection of the ascending and descending parts. The detection is by far not perfect but allows to avoid misinterpretation at the recognition stage of a 't' letter as an 'f', for example.

The horizontal shift is calculated to avoid any horizontal overlap between 2 adjacent strokes. Application of this method gives the following result, as presented on figure 4.

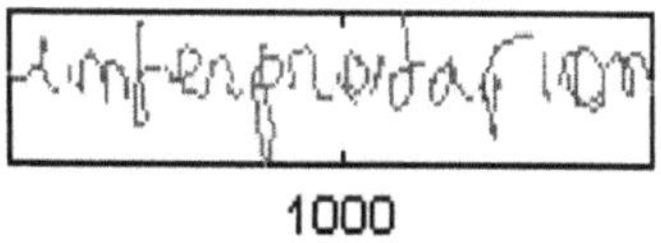

Figure 4(a): word « interpretation »

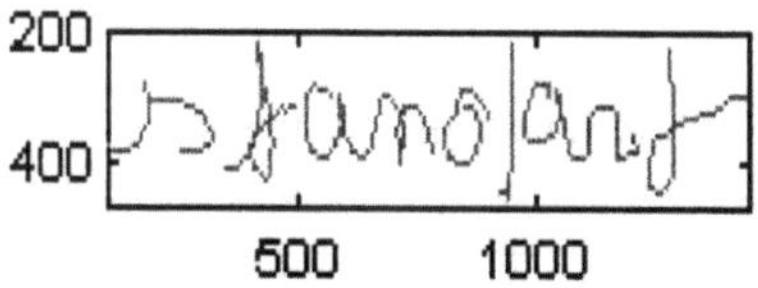

Figure 4(b): word « standard »

Recognition performed with such signals would lead to false decisions due to the independent processing performed for each stroke. So, the dot of the first 'i' letter and the accent on the 'e' letter in Figure 4(a) are erroneously moved. The 'd' letter in Figure 4(b) is now separated in two well defined entities, which is not desired. To deal with this complication, a detection method of such « special strokes » is now presented.

3.2 DETECTION OF SPECIAL STROKES.

Prior to any treatment of original signal, strokes, which are not intended to be moved to the height of the created baseline, are marked off. This mainly applies to the horizontal bar of a 't', the vertical bar of a 'd', dots on a 'i' or a 'j' and accents.

In order to detect these special « delayed » strokes, we assume they are drawn just after the stroke which contains the letter they are attributed to. One may observe that the strokes to be marked out are small, and their horizontal extension is near-integrated in the horizontal extension of the immediately preceding stroke. Both concepts (« small » and « near-integrated ») cannot be easily formulated. This is why we chose for a merged fuzzy representation of both concepts [5].

The length of each stroke is compared with the average length of the 50 former written strokes, the length of which is not greater than 1.75 the updated average length, and not shorter than 0.25 the same average length. This ensures that no parasitic strokes are taken into account in this adaptive part of our method. This yields the relative persistence of the behaviour of the developed system. The process is then slowly but constantly self-adaptive to the writer and leads to a first 'm' value which gives the typical standard for the length of each stroke. The formal definition for the 'm' parameter is fixed during the modelisation process (see below).

The horizontal overlap between a stroke and its predecessor is normalised with regard to its horizontal extension, which in turn gives a 'n' value which forms a good typical standard of the overlap. If x_{curmin} and x_{curmax} are the two bounding abscissa for the current stroke and $x_{prevmin}$ and $x_{prevmax}$ are the bounding abscissa for the previous stroke, then

$$x_{\min} = \max(x_{prev\min}, x_{cur\min})$$
$$x_{\max} = \min(x_{prev\max}, x_{cur\max})$$
$$n = \frac{10 - 10 \cdot (x_{\max} - x_{\min})}{(x_{cur\max} - x_{cur\min})}$$

If the x-extension of the current stroke is fully integrated into the x-extension of the previous stroke, then 'n' is zero. From this point, the value of 'n' becomes linearly greater and greater to a value of 10 for two strokes which are perfectly adjacent.

Note that precautions must be taken to ensure $x_{max} \geq x_{min}$, otherwise 'n' would become negative, which was not intended in this particular case. Indeed x_{min} becomes greater than x_{max} if the two considered strokes are completely disjointed. This situation must correspond to a great value for 'n' (limited to 10 here). Note that a special treatment must be reserved for the purely vertical strokes ($x_{curmax} = x_{curmin}$) too. We have considered these strokes as « fully integrated » (n = 0) as they virtually always correspond to a part of a previously formed character (they can be an accent or the « dot » on a 'i' or a 'j').

Both concepts can be merged on the basis of a classical fuzzification function with as formal form [6,7]:

$$z = \exp(-\beta^2 \cdot (m^x + n^y)), \quad \text{where } \beta, x \text{ and } y \text{ are parameters.}$$

Then, a decision can be taken on the basis of the 'z' value whether or not a particular stroke has to be moved to the height of the created baseline. The decision, or defuzzification, is a function of a threshold value. For 'z' greater than the selected defuzzification threshold, current stroke will be considered as « special » and will be moved according the same two dimensional vector as the previous stroke.

3.3 MODELISATION PROCESS.

The graphical representation of the fuzzification function is a « bell » (see figure 5 below), the sharpness of which is determined by the 'x' in the 'm' direction value, by the 'y' value in the 'n' direction and where 'β' fixes the global shape of the function. Together with the defuzzification threshold value, these 3 parameters must be fixed during the modelisation process.

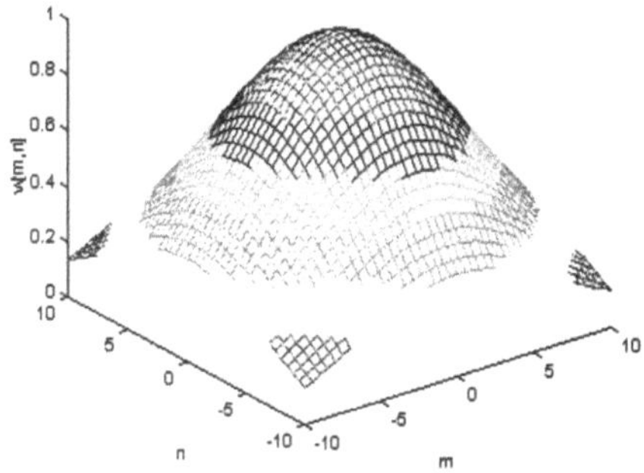

Figure 5: fuzzification function
β= 0.1, x=y=2

The fuzzification function is represented for a range of -10 to 10 for both 'm' and 'n'. This range was selected only for graphic convenience. Indeed, the actual range for both 'm' and 'n' is from 0 to 10.

To keep the fuzzification function in a simple form, we chose to take identical values for 'x' and 'y', and to possibly modify the definition of the 'm' value in order to take into account the sensibility differences which could overcome between both modelled concepts. Furthermore, this allows to maintain feedback on how each concept is eventually modelled. The actual expression for 'z' becomes of the form:

$$z = \exp(-\beta^2 \cdot (m(\alpha)^x + n^y)), \quad \text{where } \alpha \text{ is an additional parameter}$$

The α parameter has a physical meaning in terms of definition of the introduced concept « short ». As learned from our experiments on real samples, the length of true « short » strokes can vary between a « dot » and something larger (for the horizontal bar of the 't' letter for example). Inside these boundaries, the considered stroke is most likely a « short » stroke which has to be moved according to the same translation vector as the immediately preceding stroke.

Greater strokes belong to the « short » concept, the membership of which decreases more or less constantly with their length. For a learned average number of points per stroke '*nbr_pts_moy*' and a number '*nbr_pts_cur*' of points for the current stroke, the modelisation of this behaviour was included in the formal definition of the 'm' parameter:

$$ratio = \frac{nbr\_pts\_curr}{nbr\_pots\_moy}$$

$$m = \begin{cases} \frac{10}{1-\alpha} \cdot ratio - \frac{10}{1-\alpha} \cdot \alpha & for\ ratio > \alpha \\ 0 & for\ ratio \leq \alpha \end{cases}$$

Graphically, the result of this operation is shown on the Figure 6 below. The presented value of the α parameter is equal to 0.25.

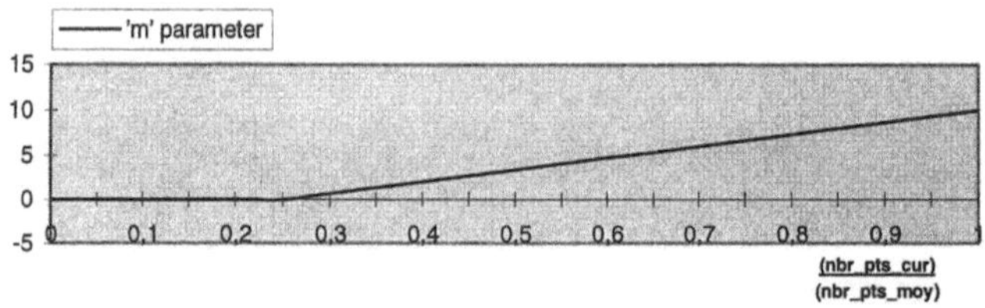

Figure 6 : graphical presentation of the 'm' parameter definition

The development of the fuzzy rule base followed the usual path of rule based systems: an iteration cycle of rule definition, testing and rule refinement. The parameters were iteratively refined on the basis of performance analysis, errors localisation and parameters adjustments. Although this could have lead to a too specific method, we skirted that problem by using various signal sources. Furthermore, we learned from the modelisation process that the developed method shows very little sensitivity to parameters values and that the variation effect of a parameter on the global decision can, for a large part, be compensated by a correction on another one. So, we dispose of a system where each parameter can be easily tuned and which offers a global gain control.

The selection of a defuzzification threshold was merged with other parameter definitions, but was held as « last refinement parameter ». The value that presented the best performances on experimental sample sets was ultimately chosen as threshold. The actual parameters values which are obtained from the modelisation process are summarised in table 1.

	α	β	x	y	**defuzzification threshold**
value	0.25	0.1	2	2	0.6

Table 1 : parameters values found by application of the described modelisation process

4. PERFORMANCES

The recognition rate, which has become the most common way of quantifying the performances of a newly developed system, does not seem to be the best adapted criterion for our approach. Indeed, the developed pre-processing method does not perform any treatment at the letter stage, so the recognition rate becomes more an efficiency measure at the subsequent recognition stage than a estimation of the pre-processing worth. Globally, our system allows for recognition attempts on signals which would not have any chance to be correctly recognised due to the structural problems encountered in the writing samples. On the following figures, we present a set of typical words which illustrate the quality enhancement our system performs.

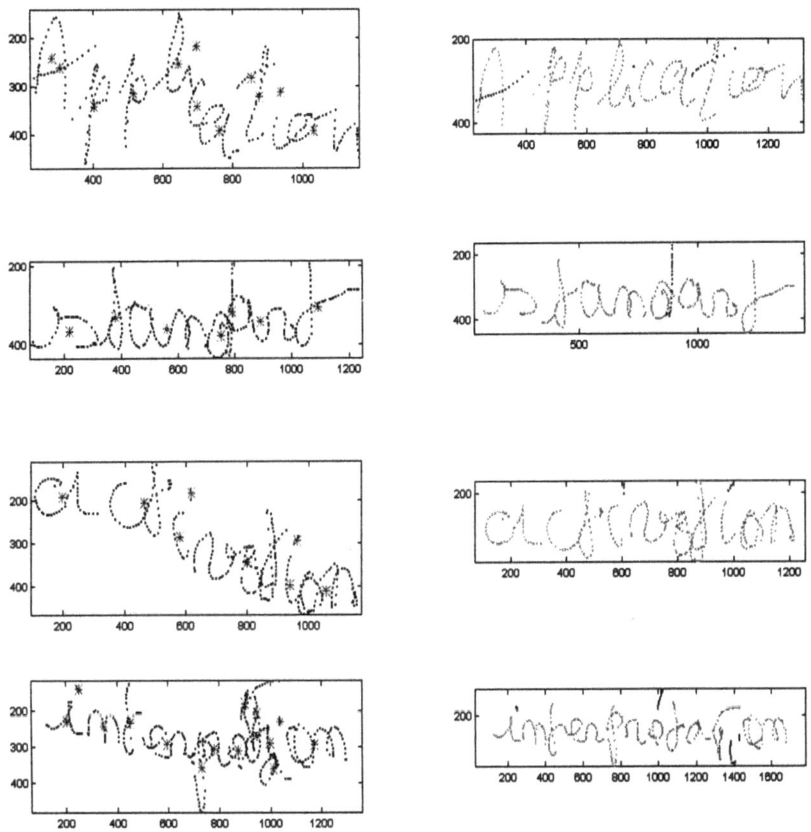

Table 2 : typical words samples with '' indicating gravity center calculations (left) and the same words after application of the described pre-processing method (right). The dark parts on drawings presented on the right are the detected « special strokes »*

The presented method has been successfully implemented on a Newton 130 Apple and tested on a new database. The obtained results indicate the relevance of our assumptions. These tests provide evidence for the feasibility of this approach. The words are now processed as a whole and the only remaining errors are due to misinterpretations of poorly formed characters. Before upgrading our system by adding a complete newly developed recognition stage, we intend to test it extensively with new blind subjects. The main goal of these tests is to see if an adaptation to the less restricting writing conditions at word level provided by our system could lead to a local enhancement of the writing quality at letter level.

5. CONCLUSION

In this paper, we have extended the use of on-line character recognition to blind people. Tests have highlighted typical writing deformations due to the lack of visual control. An adaptative pre-processing method has been proposed to overcome these deformations. The processing is performed at stroke level and consists in stroke shifting. To avoid parasitic stroke displacement, a stroke classifier based on fuzzy logic has been developed.

The tests performed on a Personal Digital Assistant (PDA) with a dedicated database showed that these deformations can be greatly attenuated by the proposed pre-processing method and demonstrated the feasibility of a full on-line recognition system adapted to blind people. They have also confirmed the interest of blind people in such a system.

REFERENCES

[1] Charles C. Tappert, Ching Y. Suen and Toru Wakahara. "The State of the Art in On-line Handwriting Recognition". IEEE Trans. Patt. Anal. and Mach. Intell. 1990,12(8):787-808.

[2] M. Côté, M. Cheriet, E. Lecolinet and C. Suen. "Automatic Reading of Cursive Script Using Human Knowledge". 4th. Int. Conf. on Document Analysis and Recognition, 1997, vol.1, pp.97-101.

[3] E. Anquetil and G. Lorette. "Perceptual Model of Handwriting Drawing Application to the Handwriting Segmentation Problem". 4th. Int. Conf. on Document Analysis and Recognition, 1997, vol.1, pp.112-117.

[4] E. Anquetil and G. Lorette." On-line Handwriting Character Recognition System Based on Hierarchical Qualitative Fuzzy Modeling" Progress in Handwriting Recognition, World Scientific, 1997.

[5] J. Bezdek, "Fuzzy Models - What are they and why?", IEEE Trans. Fuzzy Systems, 1993, 1(1): 1-5.

[6] H. Kwan, Y. Cai, "A Fuzzy Neural Network and its Application to Pattern Recognition", IEEE Trans. Fuzzy Systems, 1994, 2(3).

[7] P. Gader, M. Mohamed, J. Keller, "Fusion of Handwrittten Word Classifiers", Pattern Recognition Letters, 1996, 17(6):577-584.

CATEGORIZING DOCUMENT IMAGES INTO SCRIPT AND LANGUAGE CLASSES

C. Y. Suen, S. Bergler, N. Nobile, B. Waked, C. P. Nadal, and A. Bloch

CENPARMI, Concordia University, 1455 de Maisonneuve Blvd West, Montréal, Québec H3G 1M8, Canada
Email contact: bergler@cs.concordia.ca

ABSTRACT

In order to properly archive and index large numbers of international documents, several challenging processing steps must be completed even before optical character recognition (OCR) can be applied. We present a system that preclassifies documents for further processing and OCR. The system operates in four phases: preprocessing (including skew detection, segmentation, and noise removal), script (Latin, Arabic, Ideographic, or Cyrillic) classification, shape coding, and language classification for seven European languages.

We present a set of statistical techniques, based fundamentally on connected component analysis and horizontal projections, for the first two phases. Even with little training, the system predicts the correct script category in 91% of the cases, when tested on real-life documents of varying kinds, diverse formats and qualities from many sources. The third and fourth phase are based on expert systems approaches. Language identification combines several heuristics based on a statistical analysis of our training corpus. It currently has a 95% success rate on real-life documents of moderate quality. We will discuss the techniques and their combination and the process of improving performance.

1 Introduction

The need to archive paper documents electronically and to process information contained in them has led to the development of sophisticated commercial optical character recognition (OCR) software for different scripts, which is usually also optimized for the language used. In a multilingual environment, neither script nor language can be assumed prior to processing the documents. Our efforts are intended to provide a preprocessing stage that transforms the image of the scanned page into several low-level representations which can be exploited to determine the script (Arabic, Ideographic, or Latin), and in the case of Latin script also whether the document is written in one of seven languages: English, French, German, Spanish, Portuguese, Italian, or Russian[1]. This categorization can then be used to select the proper Latin or Arabic OCR modules for any given document.

This paper describes a system that performs both tasks, but focuses mainly on the language classification task. The script classification will be sketched only briefly; a more extensive account can be found in [1].

Before the script classification task can actually begin, several preprocessing steps must be performed[2]. Thus the scanned image is segmented into text regions and other

[1]Cyrillic script has characteristics very similar to the Latin script, and for ease of processing and describing the systems we pretend that it is a Latin script.

[2]see Hochberg *et al.* [2], Ratner [3], and Lee *et al.* [4] for approaches that do not require preprocessing.

regions, then the text is deskewed and segmented into paragraphs, lines, words, and characters. During this process, noise is filtered out and some distracting text segments (such as very oversized headlines) are removed as well.

For robustness in the face of poor quality data from a variety of sources, we use very low-level statistics throughout the process. One core characteristic is the structure of *bounding boxes*, that is the smallest rectangle that encloses a set of touching pixels (*connected component*). Bounding boxes are used for all preprocessing steps, including deskewing.

The script classification module SCRIPTID relies also on the notion of *horizontal projections*, that is a histogram plotting the number of black pixels for each scan line (see Wood *et al.* [5] for a different use of projection profiles). It turns out that the three script types we aim to distinguish have quite different characteristics in the height distribution of the bounding boxes, in density[3], and in the horizontal projections of a text line. Based mainly on these three aspects we obtain a 91% recognition rate.

Subsequent language identification, in the case of Latin script, is based on the notion of character shapes. Because the final system works from scanned documents without the benefit of OCR, we cannot rely on the shape of the characters, but at best on shape characteristics of the characters, which can be inferred from our low-level data. Based on Sibun and Spitz [7] we developed a new set of character shape codes that map characters with similar characteristics into the same class. Shape codes are determined based on the bounding boxes compiled in the preprocessing phase, taking ascenders, descenders, special diacritics (umlaut, dots, accents), and the size of the character into account.

The language identification module IDDOC computes selected statistics for a given test document, and compares them to the averages extracted in the training phase for all languages. A ranking of each language hypothesis for the given document is produced first, based on the statistics, then an expert system prioritizes certain heuristics or combinations of heuristics with respect to the others. A language hypothesis results from this process, unless a pre-set certainty threshold cannot be met.

The heuristics for IDDOC are based on the occurrence of unique word shapes (strings of character shape codes), character n-grams, and word n-grams. Together these characteristics perform very well. Character n-grams are well-known tools (see Sibun and Spitz [7] and Lee *et al.* [4] for the use of word unigrams on document images; Cavnar and Trenkle [8] for the use of n-grams in determining newsgroup membership; and Gokcay and Gokcay [9] for use of n-gram statistics on text); we have introduced word n-grams and our expert system approach for improved performance. An earlier version of IDDOC has been presented in [10]. The accuracy of IDDOC in combination with SCRIPTID on scanned real-world documents of moderately good quality is 95%.

2 Preprocessing

Figure 1 presents a typical scanned input image. Preprocessing consists of a connected component analysis, filtering of large areas and noise, deskewing, and segmentation.

Creating Bounding Boxes

The bounding box is used in every phase of our SCRIPTID system, starting from deskewing and segmentation to script identification. The bounding box is simply a

[3] We use density information only as an auxiliary function and in particular do not compute reading order distribution of optical density as reported in Spitz [6].

Missa do
5.º Aniversário

Por ocasião do 5.º aniversário de sua morte, informamos os amigos que no próximo dia 27-09-97, celebrar-se-á missa por sua intenção a Celina de Lurdes. Pelas 11h30, a vós que dignarem a comparecer a tal acto, os nossos agradecimentos, marido, filhas, genros e netos.

Descanse em Paz
querida.

Jovens fugitivas viviam num pinhal

Três raparigas adolescentes que fugiram de casa há um mês, em Coimbra, foram encontradas ontem de madrugada, no pinhal onde viveram desde a fuga, por uma patrulha da BT da GNR. As fugitivas, de 13, 14 e 17 anos, residem no bairro da Rosa, na zona norte da cidade de Coimbra, e despareceram de casa no dia 12 de Agosto.

O pinhal onde foram encontradas, às 5 horas e 30 da madrugada, por uma patrulha da BT da GNR de Coimbra, situa-se numa zona isolada da povoação de Ademia, a cerca de quatro quilómetros das residências. A primeira adolescente, de 13 anos, foi descoberta na berma da estrada da Ademia, o que suscitou algumas interrogações, dada a sua pouca idade e a hora, pois era de madrugada.

A rapariga pôs-se em fuga, juntando-se às outras duas, vindo a ser interceptadas pelos militares da BT. As adolescentes confessaram que haviam fugido de casa no dia 12 de Agosto e desde então dormiam no pinhal e alimentavam-se de frutos que colhiam nas propriedades agrícolas das redondezas.

As três raparigas encontravam-se bem de saúde, apenas a de 14 anos parecia "um pouco debilitada". Transportadas para o quartel da corporação até à chegada dos pais, as adolescentes "devoraram todo o pequeno-almoço". A fuga, participada à PSP de Coimbra no dia 12, pelos pais, foi justificada com "problemas familiares" que se escusaram a especificar.

Durante a sua estada no pinhal, deitavam-se no chão sem qualquer aconchego, pois apenas dispunham da roupa que vestiam quando saíram de casa. As duas raparigas mais novas são irmãs e a de 17 anos é amiga de ambas.

Figure 1: Image of a scanned Portuguese document

rectangular box which circumscribes the connected components of black pixels; each box can be represented by two coordinate points, the upper-left and the lower-right corners.

Large Area Filtering
Bounding boxes with more than five times the average area for bounding boxes for a document are removed, as well as bounding boxes with a disproportionate height to width ratio (vertical or horizontal lines). These components are unlikely to contain text, and can be ignored for both script and language identification.

Noise Filtering Bounding boxes with dimensions smaller than the text font stroke width (most frequently occurring black run) are considered noise, and are removed.

Deskewing the Document
Using a Hough transform (see Duda and Hart [11], Le *et al.* [12]) we deskew to an angle of accuracy of 0.5 degrees, limited to a range of ±25 degrees.

Segmentation
The page is segmented into paragraphs, lines, and words. Following Ha *et al.* [13], we rely mainly on white space deduced from horizontal and vertical projections.

3 Script Classification

SCRIPTID classifies the text into 3 types of script: Arabic, Ideographic, and Latin. The identification process is based on the bounding box size distribution and horizontal projections.

First, we extract information from the height distribution of the bounding boxes before the preprocessing phase. Figure 2 shows three typical height distributions for an Arabic, an Ideographic, and a Latin document. The position of the two largest peaks in relation to each other and to the minor peaks determines the relative position of the most frequent bounding box size. Since Latin script has predominantly characters that span from the baseline to the x-height (the size of the letter x), its major peaks lie above the average box size, the same as for Ideographic scripts, whereas Arabic scripts usually have at least one major peak below the average bounding box size.

A second distinguishing feature is character density. Ideographic scripts include very

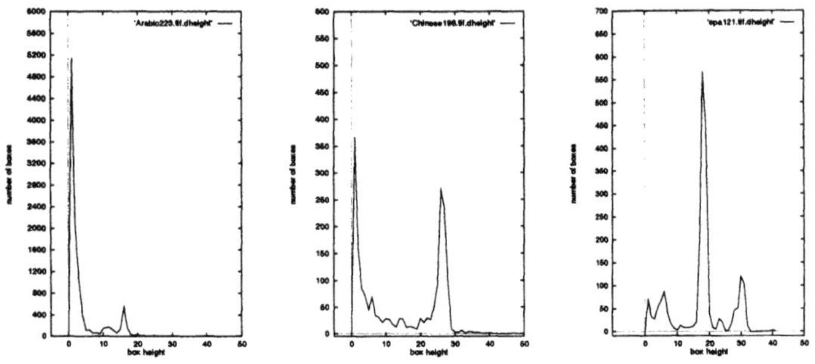

Figure 2: Bounding box height distribution for Arabic, Ideographic, and Latin scripts.

dense characters, whereas Arabic scripts are characterized by low density.

The third and most prominent feature we use to distinguish the three script classes is the horizontal projection of a line. As Figure 3 illustrates, Arabic script is characterized by one prominent peak, Latin scripts by two prominent peaks (at the base line and the x-height), and ideographic scripts have differing patterns, each characterized by more than two peaks.

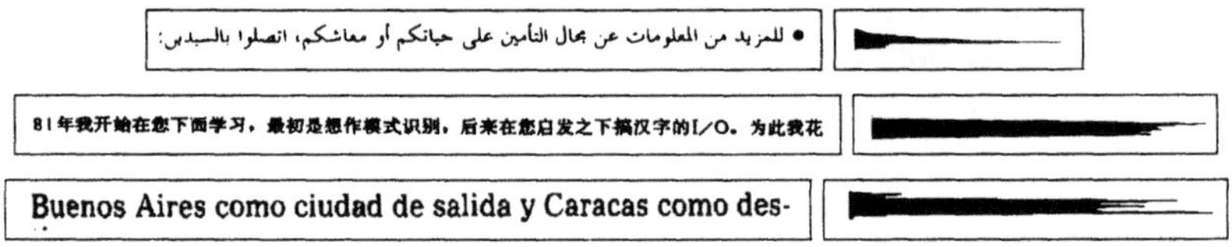

Figure 3: Horizontal projections for Arabic, Ideographic, and Latin scripts.

Script classification is thus a procedure that uses very basic document features, which are largely insensitive to bad data quality (a large percentage of touching lines from smearing or extremely noisy data poses a problem, as does the presence of a large percentage of horizontally broken characters). In fact, testing on 220 documents supplied by a client, ranging in quality from good to extremely poor (photocopies of faxes scanned at 200 DPI) results in 91% accuracy, 7% error, and 2% rejection. A more detailed discussion of the procedures can be found in [1].

Lee *et al.* [4] report an interesting approach based on position of concavities, bounding box height and position, and density. They distinguish Ideographic (Chinese and Japanese) from Latin (English, French, German, Italian, and Spanish) scripts with 98% accuracy on degraded and unoriented pages. While the emphasis of our approach is very different, we feel that our results are comparable given that we include more Asian languages in our testing for Ideographic script and our input includes four scripts, Arabic and Cyrillic in addition to Ideographic and Latin.

4 Shape Coding

Shape coding is a process which converts the bounding boxes contained in each extracted word into one of 13 character shape codes. The following steps describe the conversion process:

1. Determine baseline and x-height line.
2. For each word, correct the position of the baseline and the x-height as required by residual skew or bad alignment of characters to the baseline.
3. Convert the bounding boxes to character shape codes, using the heuristics outlined in Figure 4.

	Simplified calculation	**Samples**
x	A single small box.	a o x
A	A single large box on the baseline.	A T k l
i	A box with one very small box above it.	i é Ñ
ü	A box with two very small boxes above it.	ü ä ë Ö
g	A single large box that descends the baseline.	g p q
j	A single large box which descends the baseline with a very small box above	j ¡ ¿
.	A single small box near the baseline.	. _
!	A larger box above a very small box with a height ratio of at least 3:1.	! ?
:	Two small boxes above each other; the bottom box is near the baseline. : ;	
-	A long box located between the x-height line and the base line.	= ×
,	A small box that crosses the baseline.	,
'	A small box above the x-height line.	" ' 1
?	Any unrecognized character.	

Figure 4: Computation of character shape codes

This procedure is very sensitive to skew angle, noise, and document quality. The number of broken or touching characters in a document affects the shape and position of bounding boxes. But character shape coding is an accurate indicator for the underlying language only when bounding boxes correspond to individual characters. Figure 5 shows the character shape coding for the last two paragraphs of the document shown in Figure 1; this segment has 16 shape coding errors and 2 codes "unknown" ("?"). The system is trained on real world data, which compensates somewhat for these errors (assuming that the training set has an average number of broken or touching characters).

To evaluate the performance of this function, we tested it on different test sets. The first consisted of documents from the WorldWideWeb which were electronically converted from ASCII to image, thus avoiding any skew, noise, or quality problems. The second test set consisted of 298 scanned images. Because proofreading the shape coding output must be done manually, we have evaluated the shape coding procedure indirectly by comparing the language classification results. The test sets performed at 96% and 95%, which is strong indication that our preprocessing phase is very accurate, and that training on scanned documents adequately enhances the system.

5 Language Classification

The language classification module is called IDDOC. It exploits statistics gathered from a training set to match the statistical profile of a test document. It discriminates

```
Ax AxAx xxgxxigxx xxxxxAxxxxx-xx Axx Ax xxiAx, xgxxxx x Ax
xx xxxx gxxxix xx gxxxx AxAiAiAxAx'. AxxxxgxAxAxx gxxx x gxxx-
AxA Ax xxgxxxgix xAi i xAxgxAx Axx gxix, xx xAxAxxxxxAxx Axxx-
xxxxx AxAx x gxgxxxx-xAxxgx'. A Axgx, gxAixigxAx A AAA Ax
AxixAxx xx Aix AA, gxAxx gxix. Axi jxxAiAixxAx xxx gxxAAxxxx Axxi-
Aixxxx' gxx xx xxxxxxxxx x xxgxxiAixxx.
AxxxxAx x xxx xxAxAx xx gixAxA, Axi?xxxx-xx xx xAix xxx gxxA-
gxxx xxxxxAxgx, gxix xgxxx?x Aixgxxxixx Ax xxxgx gxx xxxAixx
gxxxAx xxxxxx Ax xxxx. Ax Axxx xxgxxigxx xxix xxxxx xix ixxix x
x Ax AA xxx i xxigx Ax xxAxx.
```

Figure 5: Shape codes for a fragment of Figure 1.

between seven languages, English, French, German, Spanish, Portuguese, Italian, and Russian. The challenge in this set of languages was to distinguish between Spanish and Portuguese based on the statistics and in the absence of full character recognition.[4]

The languages have been chosen because commercial OCR software has specialized language modules for these languages plus a set of Scandinavian languages. We experimented with several of the Scandinavian languages at the beginning of our project, but found it very hard to compile enough documents for training and testing. Indeed, even at the Dutch embassy we were told that we could get flyers and brochures in Dutch, but that they did not have correspondence, business letters, or memos in Dutch. The same was true for colleagues we contacted in the appropriate countries. It is therefore very unlikely that correspondence in any of these Scandinavian languages will be sent to Canada, and we have excluded them from this system for the moment.

5.1 Training

The training of IDDOC begins with scanning documents into TIFF images. The scanned documents include magazine articles, books, faxes, and newspaper articles. These images are processed by SCRIPTID in order to obtain a character-coded file for each of the images. These files form the basis for the statistics we compile for word shape 1, 2, and 3-grams, character shape classes, character shape 2, 3, and 4-grams. The training set contains about 10500 words (roughly 20 documents) for each language. The training program stores all the frequencies of word and character n-grams for each character-coded file. All those word shapes or n-grams that contain any of the following character classes are filtered out: {. , : ! ?}. Shapes that begin or end with a {-} or a {'} or that contain two consecutive {-} or {'} are also omitted.

Language models for unique word shapes must be compiled semi-automatically. To create models for character classes, the thirteen character classes for a language are sorted in decreasing order of frequency. To create a model for any one of the remaining characteristics requires storing the top T n-grams, where T is the number of n-grams for the language containing the least number of distinct n-grams.

Adding a new language to our models requires computing the statistics for that lan-

[4] Russian is included in this set because Cyrillic cannot be reliably distinguished from Latin scripts with the procedures we use for SCRIPTID. While we have developed a special procedure to identify Russian at the time of character shape coding, we still include Russian in IDDOC to catch documents that are not correctly classified by that special procedure.

guage and to redo the unique word shape computation for all languages. Removing a language from our models just requires that we recompute the unique word shapes.

As has already been discussed in connection with the shape coding function, the ability to quickly retrain on a more appropriate training set is a major strength of this system, and adds to its portability.

5.2 Testing

IDDOC can be described in five steps: Loading the language models, reading the input, generating statistics for each heuristic, computing language probabilities for each heuristic, and running the expert system. Each is described in sequence below.

Loading the language models

The first step reads in the information obtained from the training session. Each heuristic (word shape 1, 2, and 3-grams, character shape classes, character shape 2, 3, and 4-grams) contains a ranked list of the most frequent occurrences for each of the seven languages.

A *shape percentage array* contains, for each language, the probability that each of the following shapes {x, A, i, g, j, ü, ', -} occurs in the training set.

Reading the input

This step reads in the first K words of character coded text from the test document. Longer texts give better results. Figure 6 shows the relationship between length of input and performance. Note that in an application there is no need to artificially shorten a document, as long as processing time is adequate. Our system takes roughly 120 seconds for 1000 words (see Section 6 for values for different cutoff points.)

Generating statistics for each heuristic

Compile statistics for the test document (word shape 1-grams, word shape 2-grams, word shape 3-grams, character shape classes, character shape 2-grams, character shape 3-grams, and character shape 4-grams).

Compute language probabilities for each heuristic

We compare the frequency of occurrence of instances of each heuristic in the document with the ranking of that instance for each language. For example, if the word shape 1-gram instance "AAx" occurred ten times in the document, and that same instance is ranked as the seventh most frequent word shape 1-gram for the English training set, then the *Word 1-gram* heuristic will add a value based on the frequency and rank values (ten and seven respectively) to the strength value $strength[Word\_1gram, English]$ cell. These values are normalized from zero to 100 to counteract the influence of long documents. The following formula is used to compute the values to be added to the heuristic strengths.

For each particular instance of a $Heuristic$, we compute its frequency in the test document, $Freq$, and its rank $Rank$ in the Language Model L. We increase the vector cell $strength[Heuristic, L]$ by the value H as follows

$$H = (MaxRank_{Heuristic} - Rank)^2 * Freq$$

where $MaxRank_{Heuristic}$ is the rank of the most frequent shape in the $Heuristic$ model. This is performed for all $Heuristic$ instances that occurred in the document, and for all languages.

Normalization of heuristic strength values

At this point, each heuristic will have seven strength values (one for each language). These values are nonnegative and have no upper limit[5]. We normalize these values from zero to 100 for display purposes, and to determine whether the difference between the first and second highest strengths is greater than a predetermined threshold (0.1%). If so, this heuristic will conclude that the document is written in the language with the highest strength. Otherwise, this heuristic will REJECT the document because it cannot come to a conclusion with sufficient confidence.

Calling the expert system

The expert system identifies the language of a document based on the normalized strength vector. The expert system is a multi-rule system containing eleven rules. Once a rule fires (succeeds), the expert system exits with its solution to the language identification problem. All results provide a confidence value between zero and 100. The following rule is an example from our rule base:

Rule 12: If Word 1-gram and Word 2-gram heuristics agree on the same language L, then return L with a confidence of $min(50 + max(SF\_1A, SF\_1B), 99.99) * RuleConfidence$ (%) where SF_1A is the probability for L obtained from the Word 1-gram heuristic, and SF_1B is the probability obtained from the Word 2-gram heuristic for the language L and $RuleConfidence = 0.75$.

6 Experimental Results

The different modules have been tested on different test sets throughout their development. We have a large database of text samples from different scripts; most of these are paragraphs copied from library holdings, which were used during development. The performance of SCRIPTID reported here is, however, on a client test set. It consists of 220 documents (66 Arabic, 91 Ideographic, and 63 Latin), which cover a wide range of style and quality (photocopies of faxes scanned at 200 DPI, for instance). SCRIPTID has 91% correct and 7% incorrect classifications; the remaining 2% are rejected.

IDDOC, too, has been tested on several test sets. The expert system approach was originally developed on ASCII data taken from the WorldWideWeb and shape coded-directly (see [10]). In order to assess performance of the shape coding function and the preprocessing steps, we used two in-house test sets. The first consists of 69 documents taken from the WorldWideWeb which are converted to PostScript images (thus there is neither skew nor deterioration). These images are processed by SCRIPTID before IDDOC begins language identification. The system correctly identifies the language for 96% of the documents; 4% are incorrect, with no rejections.

The second test set consists of 319 documents, which include scanned magazine articles, newspaper clippings, foreign correspondence, and brochures. For the second test set, the system showed a 95% correct identification rate, 5% are incorrectly identified, and there is one rejection. We have not been able to conclude a run of this latest system on client data, which has in the past proven to be of poorer quality than our in-house data (which were scanned at 300 DPI.)

We have also experimented with artificially limiting the number of words of each document. The performance degrades, as expected. Figure 6 shows, however, that the

[5]The values are bounded by the maximum value that the compiler can handle.

results are still viable for shorter documents. The results reported above are for a cutoff of 1000 words per document (usually documents are shorter than this, and are processed in their entirety). For a limit of 50 words per document, we still get over 75% correctness with 20% error (this corresponds to roughly 5 lines of text). For a limit of 20 and 10 words the error rate goes up to roughly one third and the recognition rate drops to 60% and 44% respectively. Thus one and two lines are not sufficient for reliable language identification with the current system. We are working on improving the accuracy for lower limits.

Words:	1000	500	100	80	50	20	10
Cor:	95.65%	94.20%	91.30%	89.86%	75.36%	59.42%	43.48%
Inc:	4.35%	5.80%	5.80%	4.35%	20.29%	30.43%	34.78%
Rej:	0.00%	0.00%	2.90%	5.80%	4.35%	10.14%	21.74%

Figure 6: Relationship between text length and accuracy of language classification.

Sample timing results are an average of 120 seconds for the 1000 word cutoff, 63 seconds for the 500 word cutoff, 14 seconds for the 100 word cutoff and 8 seconds for the 50 word cutoff. A cutoff of 2000 words results in 208 seconds runtime with the same accuracy obtained from the 1000 word cutoff.

7 Conclusion

We have presented a robust system that classifies scanned images into four script types (Arabic, Ideographic, Latin, and Cyrillic). Documents identified as Latin script are then shape coded and classified into seven European languages.

The system uses very basic statistics of the document images, mainly bounding box statistics and horizontal projections to derive the classifications. These statistics have proven to be robust. While most of the basic techniques we employ can be found in the literature, we have refined and complemented them, and combined them into a large, coherent system. We have then tested the system on several large test sets. Thus the reported system is a very good indication of the state of the art.

The language classification relies on a training phase which is not very time-consuming (a specialist can retrain the system in an afternoon), and mostly automatic. Thus the system is portable, and can be used and adapted easily.

We believe that this technology is not only useful on its own, but can be employed for other tasks as well. We will extend the number of classes distinguished (i.e. more scripts and languages), and also investigate how to improve results on sparse data (very short documents) and noisy data (very poor quality). Incorporation of OCR techniques will be another investigation to correct some errors introduced by incorrect bounding box determination.

References

[1] B. Waked, S. Bergler, S. Khoury, and C.Y. Suen. Skew detection, page segmentation, and script classification of document images. In *Proceedings of the 1998*

IEEE International Conference on Systems, Man, and Cybernetics, San Diego, CA, October 1998. forthcoming.

[2] J. Hochberg, P. Kelly, T. Thomas, and L. Kerns. Automatic script identification from document images using cluster-based templates. *IEEE Transactions on Pattern Analysis and Machine Intelligence*, 19(2):176–181, 1997.

[3] A.S. Ratner. Simultaneous identification of script and orientation. In *Proceedings of the Symposium on Document Image Understanding*, April-May 1997.

[4] D.-S. Lee, C.R. Nohl, and H.S. Baird. Language identification in complex, unoriented, and degraded document images. In *Proceedings for the International Association for Pattern Recognition Workshop on Document Analysis Systems, Malvern, PA*, pages 76–98, October 1996.

[5] S. Wood, X. Yao, K. Krishnamurthi, and L. Dang. Language identification for printed text independent of segmentation. In *Proceedings of the International Conference on Image Processing*, pages 428–431, 1995.

[6] A.L. Spitz. Determination of the script and language content of document images. *IEEE Transactions on Pattern Analysis and Machine Intelligence*, 19(3):235–245, 1997.

[7] P. Sibun and A.L. Spitz. Language determination: Natural language processing from scanned document images. In *Proceedings of the Fourth Conference on Applied Natural Language Processing, Stuttgart, Germany, 1994*, pages 15–21, 1994.

[8] W.B. Cavnar and J.M. Trenkle. N-gram based text categorization. In *Proceedings of the Third Annual Symposium on Document Analysis and Information Retrieval*, pages 161–169, April 1994.

[9] E. Gokcay and D. Gokcay. Combining statistics and heuristics for language identification. In *Proceedings of the Fourth Annual Symposium on Document Analysis and Information Retrieval*, pages 423–433, Las Vegas, April 1995.

[10] N. Nobile, S. Bergler, C.Y. Suen, and S. Khoury. Language identification of on-line documents using word shapes. In *Proceedings of the Fourth International Conference on Document Analysis and Recognition, Ulm, Germany, August 1997*, pages 258–262, 1997.

[11] R. O. Duda and P. E. Hart. Use of the Hough transform to detect lines and curves in pictures. *Communications of the Association for Computing Machinery*, 15:11–15, 1975.

[12] D.S. Le, G.R. Thoma, and H. Wechsler. Automated page orientation and skew angle detection for binary document images. *Pattern Recognition*, 27(10):1325–1344, 1994.

[13] J. Ha, I.T. Phillips, and R.M. Haralick. Document page decomposition by the bounding-box projection technique. In *Proceedings of the Third International Conference on Document Analysis and Recognition, Montréal, August 1995*, pages 1119–1122, 1995.

TABLE RECOGNITION AND LABELING USING INTRINSIC LAYOUT FEATURES

Thomas Kieninger, German Research Center for AI (DFKI)
Andreas Dengel, German Research Center for AI (DFKI)
P.O. Box 20 80, 67608 Kaiserslautern, Germany
email: <first name>.<last name>@dfki.de

ABSTRACT

Document organization may be described in different ways. The physical presentation on one hand by means of a nested layout structure representing a "part-of"-relationship, e.g. of text blocks, text line segments, words, and characters. The composition of meaningful entities, such as title, author, address, or abstract, on the other, in terms of a logical structure. Both views to the contents of a document are complementary. They relate to each other as being explicitely given by publication guidelines where the position and dimensions of logical objects are precisely described. Moreover such "publication guidelines" more or less hold for various types of documents. Although they are intuitively understandable for human beings, they are hard to formalize explicitly because of the freedom originators and authors of documents have in order to incorporate their own creativity. However, humans use these intrinsic layout features to get first hints towards the logical meaning of document information. This is even obvious when considering the very difficult document examples in Figure 1 where no text is given but it is nevertheless possible to generate hypothesis for logical meaning.

This paper deals with the problem of how to make use of such relationships between the layout structure and logical objects in documents. In particular, we describe an approach for layout based labeling of documents and for recognizing the structure of tables.

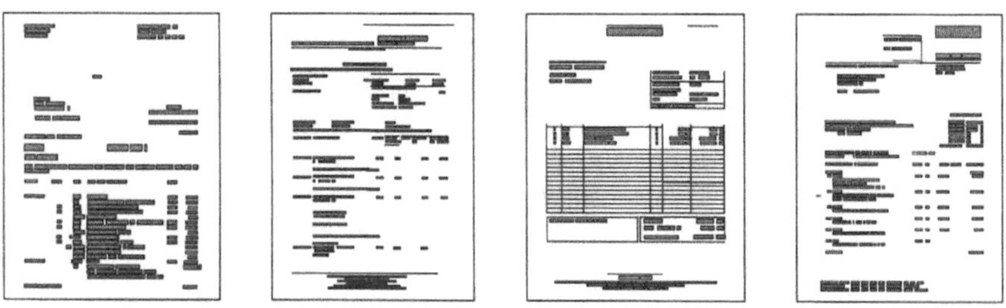

Figure 1: Examples for Relationship between Layout Structure and Logical Meaning.

1 INTRODUCTION

Document structure analysis is emerging as a key technology for enabling the intelligent treatment of information. Page decomposition into areas of text and graphics as well as the recognition of logical structures in the document provide the key for efficient information archiving and retrieval.

But only little number of recent systems have concentrated on tabular structures and their characteristics in order to treat them correctly. To close this gap, we recently developed the *T-Recs* system which is applicable to mixed-mode documents (containing tables and non-tables) and perfoms a bottom-up clustering of word segments with the goal to detect tabular structures, isolate their components and analyze the topology. The approach is independent of textual information and document specific layout rules and thus applicable in a large variety of domains.

Nontheless *T-Recs* has its weakpoints when applied to conventional business letters, i.e. when analyzing the letter head: here we typically find different logical objects in a relative *left-of* or *right-of* relation, which triggers *T-Recs* to interpret these objects as parts of a table. An example would be the *recipient* and the *delivery address* field in Figure 2.

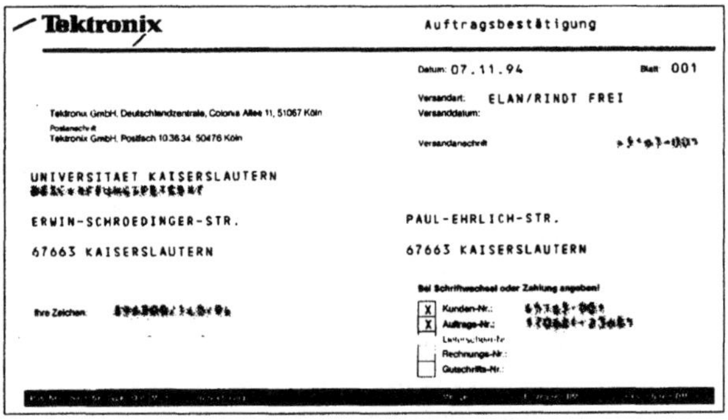
Tektronix
Auftragsbestätigung
Datum: 07.11.94 Blatt 001
Versandart: ELAN/RINDT FREI
Versanddatum:
Tektronix GmbH, Deutschlandzentrale, Colonia Allee 11, 51067 Köln
Postanschrift
Tektronix GmbH, Postfach 10 36 34, 50476 Köln
Versandanschrift
UNIVERSITAET KAISERSLAUTERN
ERWIN-SCHROEDINGER-STR.
PAUL-EHRLICH-STR.
67663 KAISERSLAUTERN
67663 KAISERSLAUTERN
Bei Schriftwechsel oder Zahlung angeben!
Ihre Zeichen
[X] Kunden-Nr.:
[X] Auftrags-Nr.:
Lieferschein-Nr.
[ ] Rechnungs-Nr.:
[ ] Gutschrifts-Nr.:

Figure 2: A typical letterhead.

Obviously, in this specific case, *T-Recs* makes a wrong assumption. To achieve a more reasonable interpretation of the occuring layout objects, a knowledge driven analysis expert needs to be involved. The *Anastasil* system [4] provides a suitable technology to solve this problem.

Anastasil can be classified as a top-down approach based on successive layout cuts in alternating (horizontal and vertical) directions to build a characteristic so called *GTree* [2] representing the overall layout. The leaves point to the appropriate layout entities.

To adapt *Anastasil* to its domain, it needs to be teached with a training set of documents. It thus learns characteristic features of the different layout constellations and the appropriate logical objects which will be assigned to the leaves. On runtime the GTree of an analyzed document is evaluated and the nearest neighbor of the knowledge base is computed. The labels of its leaves will be assigned to the appropriate layout objects accordingly.

In our proposed combination, *Anastasil* will be used to identify regions of interest and discriminate the body from the irritating letter head. *T-Recs* will then be applied to the remaining body with its pontentially occuring tables.

The paper discusses the two systems in detail. It points out their pros and cons and the advantages of applying both systems sequencially to purchasing department documents which are characterized by the presence of typical business letter elements as well as numerous tables in the letter body.

2 THE *T-RECS* SYSTEM

Remarkably, existing table recognition systems disclose an interesting similarity: They all represent top-down approaches, being driven by the detection of separators. Examples are Rus and Summers [14] who present a system for the segmentation and labeling of general structures as well as for tables. They also detect narrow column gaps using so-called *White Space Density Graphs.* Another approache relying on sufficiently large white spaces is described by Rahgozar et. al. [13] who operate on word segments rather than on the bitmap and Tupaj et. al. [15] who takes plain text output of OCR systems as input. Others are explicitly looking for ruling lines to determine the table structure: Representants of this class are Green and Krishnamoorthy [5], who match the set of occuring lines with a given grammar to analyze the table layout, Itonoti [8], who only considers the labeling aspects and expects well segmented blocks as input, or Hirayama [6] with his interesting *DP matching method.* Chandran and Kasturi [1] consider both (ruled lines and so-called *white streams*) to determine the layout structure.

In contrast to these conventional systems, the central idea of *T-Recs* is a *bottom-up* block clustering of previously determined word segments - the input to the system. While other bottom-up approaches (e.g. [7]) determine lines from horizontally adjacent words and blocks from vertically adjacent lines, *T-Recs* rather directly evaluates textblock structures from word segments. Textlines only have an auxiliary function. This also has its effect upon the document model which is shown in Figure 3.

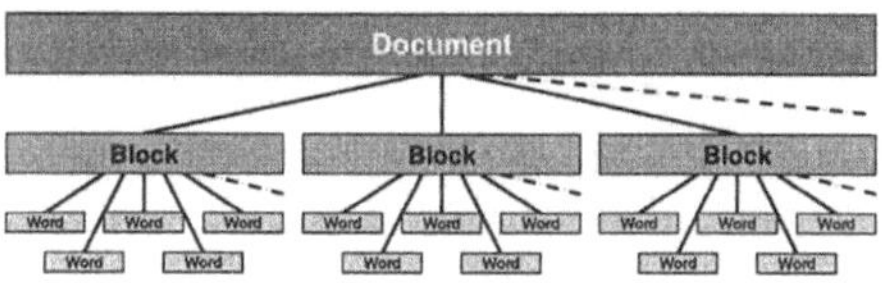

Figure 3: Document model of the *T-Recs* System

The clustering itself does not locate adjacent elements to arbitrary directions as in nearest neighbor based approaches (e.g. Gorman [12]), but is rather restricted to horizontally overlapping words in directly adjacent lines. Two words w_1 and w_2 are thus bound together if the following overlapping relation is given:

$$\begin{array}{rclcl} ovl(w_1, w_2) & \Longleftrightarrow & x_1[w_1] \geq x_0[w_2] & \wedge & x_0[w_1] \leq x_1[w_2] \quad \wedge \\ & & (\, line(w_1) & = & succ_{doc}(line(w_2) \quad \vee \\ & & line(w_2) & = & succ_{doc}(line(w_1))\,) \end{array}$$

In our notation, $x_0[w_i]$ and $x_1[w_i]$ denote the x-values of the upper left and lower right corner of a word bounding box respectively. While $line(w)$ denotes the line to which word w belongs, the function $succ_{doc}(l)$ specifies the successor of a given line l. (At this point, the auxiliary character of the text line structures is visible.) Based on this relation, the clustering works as follows:

1. Find an *unexpanded* word $w_x := w_0$ (the *seed*) and create block b_i;
2. Mark *current word* w_x as *expanded* and add it to b_i;
3. Evaluate all *unexpanded* words w_j in $ovl(w_x, w_j)$;
4. For all w_j, make it the *current word* w_x and perform steps 2, 3 and 4;

5. If no more matching words are found, increment i and go to step 1;

6. Stop, if all words are marked as *expanded*.

Blocks are thus constructed "around" the *block seed* w_0 and can be described as transitive hull ovl^* of the overlapping relation. Due to the symmetrical character of the ovl relation the choice of a different seed has no effect to the clustering result.

Figure 4 visualizes this procedure using a sample block: first we draw a virtual stripe over the bounding box of the block *seed* w_0 (the word "consists") that is to be expanded. This stripe has the width of the bounding box itself and vertically reaches to the directly adjacent lines. All words w_x that touch that stripe ($\equiv ovl(w_0, w_x)$) will be bound to the same block as the initial seed. Thus the block consists of all words that are linked with the *segmentation graph* seen on the right of Figure 4. The edges of this graph represent the ovl relation between the connected words.

Figure 4: Vertical neighbors of the word "consists".

2.1 STRENGTHS OF THE APPROACH

Figure 5: Segmentation of a tabular environment.

In the example of Figure 4 the strengths of *T-Recs* are not very obvious. The system rather proves its advantages when applied to tabular structures as shown in Figure 5: Here we see part of a directory listing with very narrow gaps. Since there are no overlapping words between adjacent columns (as indicated by the segmentation graph), the individual column blocks are clearly isolated. The right part of Figure 5 shows each block painted in a different gray shade to visualize the word to block mapping. Besides the above mentioned strengths, the algorithm is characterized by the following features: It ...

- neglects grid lines and thus allows a faster image preprocessing.
- disregards textual contents and can thus be applied to low quality documents.
- detects very narrow columns gaps.
- accepts *non-Manhattan* layout[1] documents.
- does not depend on characteristic table headers.
- detects table cells that span more than one document line (as in Figure 6).
- is universally applicable (no fixed table classes; no rules; no learning phase).

[1] Kise et al.[11] use the term *"non-Manhattan"* to refer to a page layout that consists of non-overlapping components that are separated by white space and are not limited to rectangular shapes.

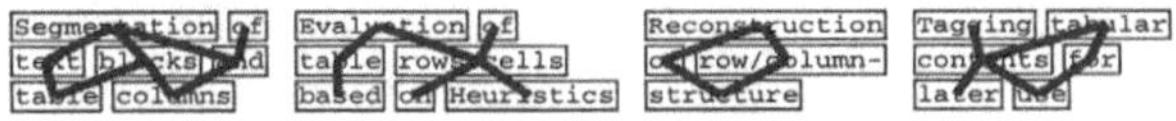

Figure 6: Table cells spanning more than one document line.

2.2 INHERENT ERRORS AND CORRECTION STEPS

The nature of this clustering algorithm also points out some inherent errors.

- Regular paragraphs (typically of only a few lines height) with a space at the same x position throughout all lines cause the first type of errors. Such a paragraph would hence not be clustered as one coherent block and would rather be divided into two parts at the x position of that gap.
- A second class of errors occurs on columns whose top- or bottommost elements overlap with the words of an adjacent block (e.g. a column spanning header). In this case the individual columns would be melted together with that block to one unit.
- Finally it would not be able to cluster single lines as in headers since they do not have any vertical neighbors. Such lines would be interpreted as a table with one row height, with each word representing one column. The same problem occurs with words at the end of a non justified block as there are no overlapping neighbors in the adjacent lines.

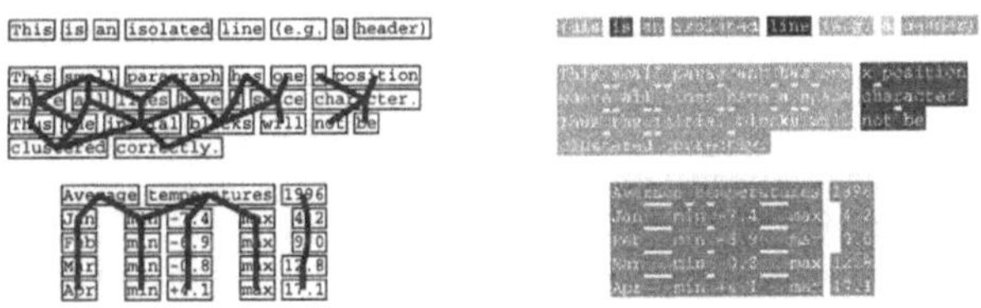

Figure 7: A collection of inherent problems.

Figure 7 illustrates all these situations together with the initial block assignment indicated by different colors of the segments. To correct these errors a set of postprocessing procedures has been developed:

Most mentionable here is the distinction of blocks between *type 1* and *type 2*: blocks with one word (or *token*) in each line are classified as *type 1* (see Figure 5); all others are of *type 2* (Figure 6 shows a some type 2 table cells). Obviously, type 1 blocks are those of *typical* simple *table columns*. This classification allows to selectively merge adjacent type 2 blocks together and thus repairs the first class of errors as described above without loosing typical columns that are separated by only a small gap.

The second problem that we are facing are table columns which are melted together by e.g. a common header. While looking for a simple feature to identify those columns, we realized the *one-to-one relation* one can observe in between the words of typical table columns to be a valuable criterion. This relation is given if word W_a has exactly one lower neighbor W_b and W_b has only that one upper neighbor W_a.

The segmentation graph of the adhered columns shown in the example of Figure 7 also points out a relatively little number of nodes with more than 2 edges in contrast to regular type 2 blocks – a visual indicator for the discussed relation between words.

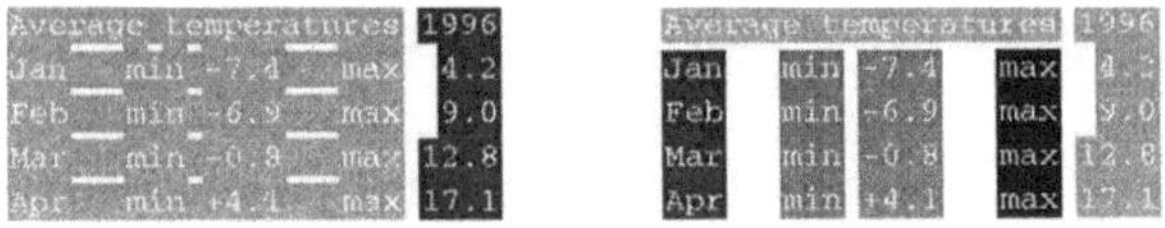

Figure 8: Isolation of merged columns.

Our next step is straightforward: we separate all sequences of words that stand in such a one-to-one relation into new blocks which we further call *splitted son* blocks. Thereby we do not consider any other constraints such as resulting block height or word contents. The result of this splitting procedure when applied to the above mentioned example is seen in Figure 8.

Since this procedure is applied to *all* type 2 blocks, it is obvious that there might be numerous words standing in such a one-to-one relation but nevertheless they do not establish a table column. However, we did not apply any more conditions to the above isolation process, because the real value of this separation can best be rated afterwards.

Figure 9: Remerging of splitted son blocks

The most important heuristics used at this point is the common fact that columns always occurs in the context of other columns. Starting from the current intermediate result, *T-Recs* inspects the neighborhood of the newly separated blocks. The number of surrounding type 1 or splitted son blocks, their height, the isolating space to the left and right and optionally the similarity of the words within a column candidate are taken to evaluate an overall evidence. If this value does not reach a given threshold, the blocks are merged with their father block again. Figure 9 shows an example of a type 2 block with three *splitted sons* and the result after they have been remerged to their *father block*.

We finally need to face the third class of errors: Words that do not have an upper nor a lower neighbor might belong to an isolated line (e.g. a header), stick out of the end of a non justified block or represent the content of a table cell. For all except the last case the initial clustering algorithm keeps these words isolated by fault.

We thus first have to decide whether such an isolated word matches with a table cell or not before we try to merge such a word with a left or right neighbor block.

To gain a global view over all potential columns, we inspect all blocks and record potential table columns which are triggered by the left and right block boundaries. The main structures used to keep the derived information are the so called *margin points* (MP). The represent potential ranges for column gaps and count the number of lines that either end or start within their specified range in a so called *reference counter* (RC).

Figure 10: Evaluation of margin points to identify isolated words.

We now simply need to inspect all isolated words (now representing blocks) and check the reference counters of their left and right margin points. If the RC-value of the appropriate MPs does not reach a theshold value, the word is to be merged with potentially occuring close neighbors to the corresponding side.

Figure 10 shows an example with some isolated words matching with a column as well as some words sticking out of a line together with the evaluated margin points(left). The corrected situation is seen on the right: isolated words that do not fit into a surrounding table column are bound to their neigbor block.

2.3 ADAPTION OF METALEVEL BLOCKS

At this point of processing, *T-Recs* has corrected all inherent segmentation errors. But there is still a conceptual adapbtion to be done: All blocks currently classified as type 1 blocks represent typical table columns and can thus be seen as an aggregation of cells. In contrast, all type 2 blocks already represent atomic information cells. To adapt this abstraction level, we simply decompose all type 1 blocks into their individual linesegments.

Figure 11: Unification of block abstraction level.

While this is sufficient for type 1 blocks - the typical tables column blocks, type 2 blocks in the neighborhood of such type 1 columns still remain as a solid unit. Figure 11 (left) shows such a situation. To deal with this problem, we construct so called *row borders*. These are triggered by the top edge of the blocks and are visualized as horizontal lines. The adjacent type 2 block is now split up into parts, using the row borders a fracture lines.

After this final postprocessing, *T-Recs* has finished its segmentation a passes the blocks over to the layout analysis subsystem. More information about the clustering and its postprocessing can be found in [10]; detailed information about the clustering plus the sequencing layout analysis process is found in [9].

3 APPLYING *T-RECS* TO BUSINESS LETTERS

As mentioned in Section 1, *T-Recs* gets confused on business letter heads, since there are layout objects in a horizontal neighborhood. We will have a look at the results of *T-Recs* when applied to business letters. We take the document whose header was show in Figure 2 as example.

Figure 12 shows (from left to right): the original bitmap, the word segments and detected delineation (generated from XIS OCR), the final block clustering after all postprocessing steps and the regions, where *T-Recs* assumes to have tables.

It is obvious, that only one of the assumed tables really contains tabular informations in the usual sense. This is the table located in the letter body. In the context of automated document processing and information retrieval it is not only of importance to to locate and analyze occuring tables but rather also to avoid misinterpretations of non-tables. To prevent this potential confusion of *T-Recs*, we need an extra instance which is able to point *T-Recs* to the regions of interest.

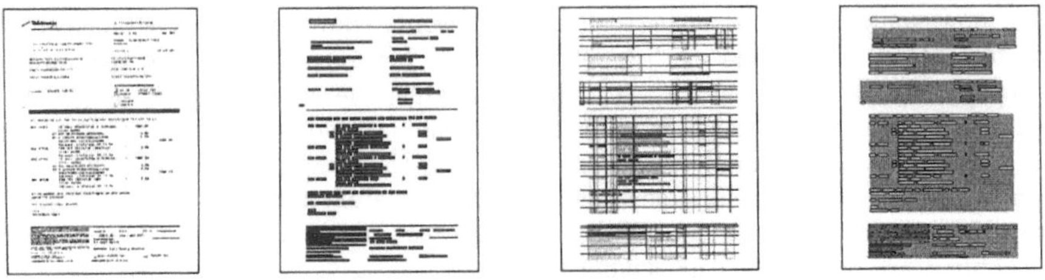

Figure 12: The demoletter and clustering results.

4 THE *ANASTASIL* SYSTEM

The central idea of *Anastasil* is based on the fact that logical objects within a document page typically occur in *relative positions* to others and thus influence each others location. This individual arrangement defines a *characteristic style*.

To analyze a page bitmap, it will successively be divided into subareas that are separated by significant white spaces, the so called *cuts*. In *Anastasil* styles are characterized by the arrangement of logical objects in a document space and are specified in terms of a *Relational Pattern* [3] which in turn defines order, position and orientation of the cuts as well as the corresponding logical labels. The top-down page decomposition procedure leads to a so called *GTree* [2], an internal structure that stores the appropriate information about geometric features and thus represents the knowledge base.

To adapt *Anastasil* to its domain, a set of manually labeled documents is used to establish the corresponing GTree. The system thus learns significant features to distinguish the different layout styles plus the according logical labels and builds a *library of known styles*. On runtime the edges of this GTree are traversed based on the potential cuts on the current document. The finally reached tree node represents the style of the analyzed document which in turn inherits the according labels.

Amongst the different logical objects such as *sender*, *recipient*, *date*, *subject*, *salutation*, *body*, *closure* and *company specific printing* recognized by *Anastasil* in the intended combination with the *T-Recs* system only the correct identification of the *body* area is of importance. Experimental results with 12 layout classes and 82 unknown letters as test set exposed a *recall* of 94% and a *precision* of 94% for the *letter body* [2].

5 APPLYING *ANASTASIL* AND *T-RECS* TO BUSINESS LETTERS

Figure 13 finally shows the results of applying *Anastasil* and *T-Recs* sequentially to the example of Figure 12: the left hand side shows the horizontal and vertical cuts as they are applied to the image bitmap, followed by the tagged layout objects as recognized by *Anastasil*, the block clustering of *T-Recs* being focused to the letter body and the accordingly detected tabular structure.

Comparing these results to those of Figure 12 impressively demonstrates the improvement of the quality (i.e. the precision): only structures that should be treated as tables in the context of automated information extraction are tagged accordingly. In this extreme example the precision increases from 16.6% to 100%.

[2]The measures used for the message understanding conferences (MUC) express the ratio between the *correctly delivered answers* and the correct (*recall*) or delivered (*precision*) answers.

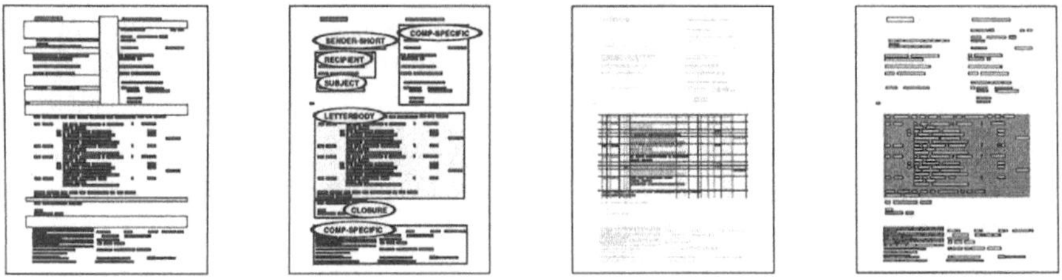

Figure 13: Using *Anastasil* as filter to focus *T-Recs* on letter body.

6 CONCLUSION AND OUTLOOK

A combination of *Anastasil* and *T-Recs* as discussed here has not yet been realized. The results presented here are generated by hand using isolated runs of each system and a manual filtering of the areas of interest.

A real implementation of the two systems has not yet been realized, because both systems rely on different input: while *T-Recs* expects word segments and their geometry as input[3], *Anastasil* operates on the image bitmap using its own skew-correction and top-down block segmentation.

A possible ad-hoc interlinking of those systems requires a twofold image processing - the most time consuming part. Nontheless, the improved precision emphasizes the advantages of making use of a knowledge driven domain specific specialist such as *Anastasil* to cooperate with *T-Recs* and hence justifies the extra effort.

But instead of a fast implementation we rather focus on a new design which considers the already given input and thus operates on the word segments instead of the bitmap.

References

[1] Surekha Chandran and Rangachar Kasturi. Structural recognition of tabulated data. In *Proc. of International Conference on Document Analysis and Recognition - ICDAR 93*, 1993.

[2] A. Dengel. ANASTASIL: a system for low-level and high-level geometric analysis of printed documents. In H. Baird, H. Bunke, and K. Yamamoto, editors, *Structured Document Image Analysis*, pages 70–98. Springer-Verlag, Okt. 1992.

[3] A. Dengel. Initial learning of document structure. In *Proceedings ICDAR-93, Second Int'l Conference on Document Analysis and Recognition, Tokyo, Japan*, pages 86–90, Oct. 1993.

[4] A. Dengel. About the logical partitioning of document images. In *Proceedings SDAIR-94, Int'l Symposium on Document Analysis and Information Retrieval, Las Vegas, NV*, pages 209–218, April 1994.

[5] E. Green and M. Krishnamoorthy. Recognition of tables using table grammars. In *Proc. of the 4-th Symposium on Document Analysis and Information Retrieval - SDAIR95, Las Vegas, Nevada*, 1995.

[3] *T-Recs* is able to read plain text files which are interpreted as if they were printed with a fixed pitch font. Besides our custom format it also reads Xerox XDOC files [16].

[6] Yuki Hirayama. A method for table structure analysis using dp matching. In *Proc. of International Conference on Document Analysis and Recognition - ICDAR 95, Montreal, Canada*, 1995.

[7] F. Hönes and J. Lichter. Text string extraction within mixed-mode documents. In *Proceedings ICDAR-93, Second Int'l Conference on Document Analysis and Recognition, Tokyo, Japan*, pages 655–659, Oct 1993.

[8] Katsuhiko Itonori. Table structure recognition based on textblock arrangement and ruled line position. In *Proc. of International Conference on Document Analysis and Recognition - ICDAR 93*, 1993.

[9] Thomas G. Kieninger. A paper-to-html table converting system. available at http://131.246.242.102:8000/~tables/htmldoc/trecs.ps.gz, April 1998.

[10] Thomas G. Kieninger. Table structure recognition based on robust block segmentation. In *Proc. of the fifth SPIE Conference on Document Recognition, San Jose, California*, January 1998.

[11] Koich Kise, Akinori Sato, and Keinosuke Matsumoto. Document image segmentation as selection of voronoi edges. In *Proc. of IEEE Computer Society Conference on Computer Vision and Pattern Recognition CVPR 97*, June 1997.

[12] Lawrence O'Gorman. The document spectrum for bottom-up page layout analysis. In H. Bunke, editor, *Advances in Structural and Syntactic Pattern Recognition*, pages 270 – 279. World Scientific, 1992.

[13] M. Armon Rahgozar, Zhigang Fan, and Emil V. Rainero. Tabular document recognition. In *Proc. of the SPIE Conference on Document Recognition*, 1994.

[14] Daniela Rus and Kristen Summers. Using white space for automated document structuring. Technical Report TR 94 - 1452, Department of Computer Science, Cornell University, 1994.

[15] Scott Tupaj, Zhongwen Shi, and Dr. C. Hwa Chang. Extracting tabular information from text files. Available at http://www.ee.tufts.edu/~hchang/paper1.ps, 1996.

[16] Xerox Corp., Peabody, MA, USA. *XDOC Data Format: Technical Specification, Version 3.0*, March 1995.

RECOGNITION OF PRINTED ARABIC TEXT VIA MACHINE LEARNING

Adnan Amin
School of Computer Science & Engineering
University of New South Wales
2052 Sydney, Australia

ABSTRACT

The main theme of this paper is the automatic recognition of Arabic printed text using machine learning C4.5. The technique can be divided into three major steps: The first step is pre-processing in which the original image is transformed into a binary image utilizing a 300 dpi scanner and then forming the connected component. At the moment we extract seven types of global features: number of subwords, number of peaks of each subwords, number of loops of each peak, number and position of complementary characters,. Second, global features of the input Arabic word are then extracted such as number subwords, number of peaks within the subword, number of loops of each peak, number the height and width of each peak and position of the complementary character, etc.. Finally, Machine learning C4.5 is used for character classification to generate a decision tree.

The system was tested with a set of 500 different classes of Arabic words (each class has fifteen different fonts) using Cross validation algorithm and the average recognition rate obtained was 96.52%. This is a very promising result and clearly shows that machine learning techniques are well suited to these types of application.

1. INTRODUCTION

For the past three decades, there has been increasing interest among researchers in problems related to the machine simulation of the human reading process. Intensive research has been carried out in this area with a large number of technical papers and reports in the literature devoted to character recognition. This subject has attracted immense research interest not only because of the very challenging nature of the problem, but also because it provides the means for automatic processing of large volumes of data in postal code reading [1, 2], office automation [3, 4], and other business and scientific applications [5–7].

Different approaches covered under the general term "character recognition" fall into either the on-line or the off-line category, each having its own hardware and recognition algorithms.

Many papers have been concerned with the recognition of Latin, Chinese and Japanese characters. However, although almost a third of a billion people worldwide, in several different languages, use Arabic characters for writing, little research progress, in both on-line and off-line has been achieved towards the automatic recognition of Arabic characters. This is a result of the lack of adequate support in term of funding, and other utilities such as Arabic text database, dictionaries, etc.. and of course of the cursive nature of its writing rules. Surveys on Arabic characters recognition can be found in [8-11].

This work describes the design and implementation of a new technique to recognize Arabic words. To recognize an input word, the system does not segment the word in advance into characters, rather, it recognize the input word by detecting a set of primitives on the word.

Symbolic machine learning algorithms are designed to accept example descriptions in the form of feature vectors which include a label that identifies the class to which an example belongs. The output of the algorithm is a set of rules that classifies unseen examples based on generalizations from the training set. This ability to generalize is the main attraction of machine learning for handwriting recognition. Samples of a character can be preprocessed into a feature vector representation for presentation to a machine learning algorithm that creates rules for recognizing characters of the same class. symbolic machine learning has several advantages over other learning methods. It is fast in training and in recognition, generalizes well, is noise tolerant and the symbolic representation is east to understand.

This paper proposes the use of global methods to extract features for classifying and recognizing Arabic words using machine learning C4.5 [12, 13] to generate a decision tree. This decision tree can then be used to predict the class of an unseen character.

2. DIGITIZATION AND PREPROCESSING

The first phase in our character recognition system is digitization. Document to be processed are first scanned and digitized. The algorithm adopted in this paper is similar to that which appears in [14]. A 300 dpi scanner is used to digitize the image in this phase and the output is a standard binary formatted image (PBM format).

2. 1. CONNECTED COMPONENT ANALYSIS

After the digitization is completed, the connected components must be determined. Connected components are rectangular boxes bounding together regions of connected black pixels. The objective of the connected component stage is to form rectangles around distinct components on the page, whether they be characters or images. These bounding rectangles then form the skeleton for all future analysis on the page.

The algorithm used to obtain the connected components is a simple iterative procedure which compares successive scanlines of an image to determine whether black pixels in any pair of scanlines are connected together. Bounding rectangles are extended to enclose any groupings of connected black pixels between successive scanlines [15]. Figure 1 demonstrates this procedure.

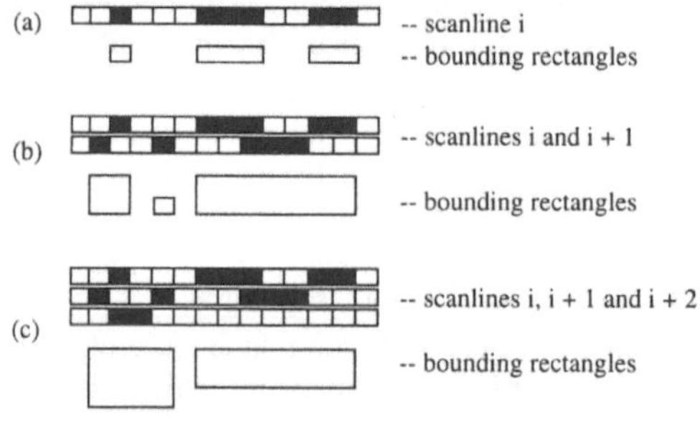

Figure 1: The process of building connected components from image scanlines.

Each scanline in Figure 1 is 14 pixels in width (note that a pixel is represented by a small rectangular block), the bounding rectangles in Figure 1(a) just enclose the black pixel of that scanline, but for each successive scanline the bounding boxes increase to include the black pixels connected to the previous scanline. Figure 1(c) also points out that a bounding box stops growing in size only when there are no more black pixels on the current scanline joined onto black pixels of the previous scanline.

Figure 2: An example of an Arabic text with connected components.

2. 2. *DETECTING A LOOP*

One common phenomenon that occurs in both printed and handwritten Arabic text is blotting. For a human, the blobs can be easily recognized as loop from the context. However, these loops are difficult to deal with and cause problems in automatic recognition system.

The basic idea of detecting a loop in a binary image is to move a widow through the image from right to left, and top to bottom. If certain conditions are satisfied, then the pixels in the center of the window are whitened. The size of the window is determined by the width of the baseline of the word. The algorithm for detecting a loop can be summarized as follows:

- *Locate the baseline of the image*: A horizontal projection for the image can be performed. The rows which have the maximum number of pixels are taken as part of the baseline of the word. Any other adjacent lines with at least 85% of the pixels of these rows are also taken as part of the baseline. The horizontal projection of the Arabic word is shown in Figure 3 (b).

- *Scan the binary image:* A window of size 2H x 2H is used to scan the image sequentially from right to left and top to bottom. The value of the integer H is determined by the width of the baseline of the word. Furthermore, the window is even; hence, the center of the window consists of four pixels. These pixels are whitened if all of the following conditions are satisfied:

  (a) All of the white pixels within the window are located on the first two outermost layers of the window;

  (b) No group of the white pixels is surrounded by black pixels within the window, i.e., no hole exists in the 2H x 2H window;

  (c) The number of the black pixels within the window are at least equal to 2H -2 pixels.

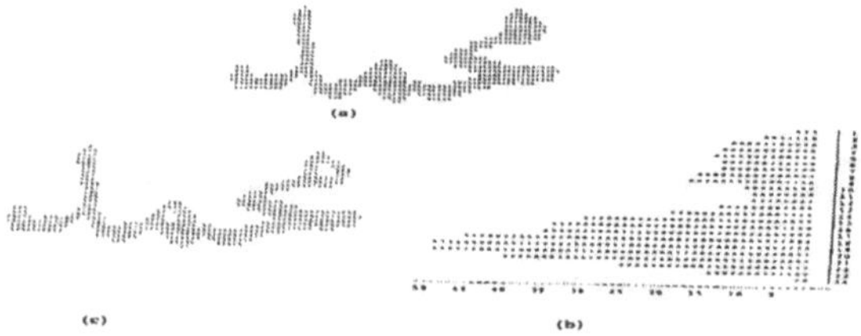

Figure 3: (a) The input image (b) Horizontal projection of the input word (c) Result of the algorithm.

3. GLOBAL WORD FEATURES

In this project, we have used the second approach to exact the proper characteristic of Arabic characters. Seven types of global features have been extracted such as: number of subwords, number of peaks of each subwords, number of loops of each peak, number and position of complementary characters, the height and width of each peak. Feature extraction algorithm can be summarized into the following steps:

Step 1: Loop detection: Loops are detected simply as being the inner contours (as shown in Figure 4) obtained by running the contour tracing algorithm. The tracing algorithm traces outer contour of an object and then it traces the inner contours of the object.

Figure 4: The inner and outer contour of an Arabic word.

Step 2: Determine the number of peaks within the subword: In all printed Arabic characters, the width at a connection point is much less than the width of the beginning character. Therefore, the baseline is a medium line in the Arabic word in which all the connections between the successive characters take place. If a vertical projection of bi-level pixels is performed on the word (Eq.1),

$$v(j) = \sum_{i} w(i, j) \quad (1)$$

where $w(i, j)$ is either zero or one and i, j index the rows and columns, respectively, the peak point will have a sum greater than the average value (AV) (Eq. 2)

$$AV = (1 / Nc)\sum_{j=1}^{Nc} Xj \quad (2)$$

and where Nc is the number of columns and X_j is the number of black pixels of the jth column.

Figure 5, illustrates the segmentation of an Arabic word into peaks.

Step 3: Smooth the histogram by using the averaging scheme where each point in the histogram is replaced by the average of itself and the two points on either side of it

$$X_i = (X_{i-1} + X_i + X_{i-2}) / 3 \quad (3)$$

Step 4: Complementary characters: This feature plays very important role to distinguish between characters having the same shape. The complementary characters could be either a zigzag or a a group of dots (1, 2 or 3). These can be above or below the baseline. Similar characters or subwords with dots have different meaning and pronunciation if the a group of dots below or above the base line.

Step5: Computer the height and width of each peak whether large of small.

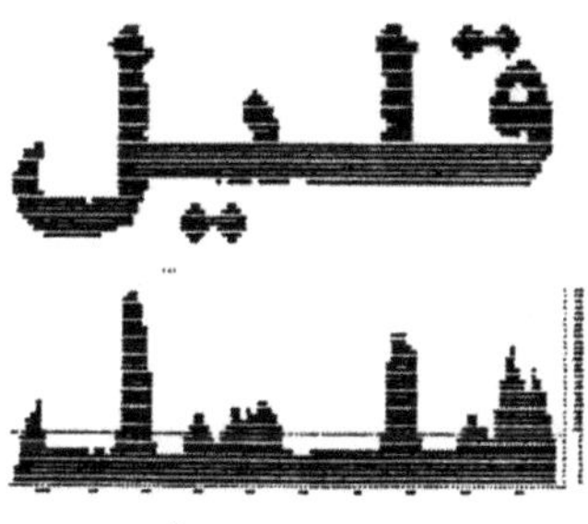

Figure 5: An of segmentation of the word into peaks (a) Arabic word (b) histogram after smoothing

4. MACHINE LEARNING C4.5

C4.5 [12, 13] is an efficient learning algorithm that creates decision trees to represent classification rules. The data input to C4.5 forms a set of examples, each labeled according to the class to which it belongs. The description of the example is a list of attribute/value pairs. A node in a decision tree represents a test on a particular attribute. Suppose an object is described by its colour, size and shape where colour may have values red, green or blue; size may be large or small and shape may be circle or square. If the root node of the tree is labeled *colour* then it may have three branches for each colour value. Thus if we wish to test an object's colour and it is red, the object descends the red branch. Leaf nodes are labeled with class names. Thus when an object reaches a leaf nodes, it is classified according to the name of the leaf node.

Building a decision tree proceeds as follows. The set of all examples forms an initial population. An attribute is chosen to split the population according to the attribute's values. Thus, if colour is chosen then all red objects descend the red branch, all green objects descend the green branch, etc. Now the population has been divided into sub-populations by colour. For each sub-population, another attribute value is chosen to split the sub-population. This continues as long as each population contains a mix of examples belonging to different classes. Once a uniform population has been obtained, a leaf node is created and labeled with the name of the class of the population.

The key to the success of a decision tree learning algorithm depends on the criterion used to select the attribute to use for splitting. If attribute is a strong indicator of an example's class value, it should appear as early in the tree as possible. Most decision tree learning algorithms use a heuristic for estimating the best attribute. In C4.5, Quinlan uses a modified version of the entropy measure from information theory. For our purposes, it is sufficient to say that this measure yields a number between 0 and 1 where 0 indicates a uniform population and 1 indicates a population where there is equal likelihood of all classes being present. The splitting criterion seeks to minimize the entropy.

A further refinement is required to handle noisy data. Real data sets often contain examples that are misclassified or which have incorrect attribute values. Suppose decision tree building has constructed a node which contains 99 examples from class 1 and only one example from class 2. According to the algorithm presented above, a further split would be required to separate the 99 from the one. However, the one exception may be misclassified, causing an unnecessary split. Decision tree learning algorithms have a variety of methods for "pruning" unwanted subtrees. C4.5 grows a complete tree, including nodes created as a result of noise. Following initial tree building, the program proceeds to select suspect subtrees and prunes then, testing the new tree on a data set which is separate from the initial training data. Pruning continues as long as the pruned trees yield more accurate classifications on the test data

The C4.5 system requires two input files, the *names* and the *data* files. The *names* file contains the names of all the attributes used to describe the training examples and their allowed values. This file also contains the names of the possible classes. The classes are the Arabic words.

The C4.5 data files contains the attributes values for example objects in the format specified by the name file, where each example is completed by including the class to which it belongs.

Every word will be classified in terms of features such as: number of subwords (up to five), number of peaks of each subwords (up to seven), number of loops, number and position of complementary characters within the peak (up to three), height and width of each peak (Small or Large) as illustrated in Figure 6.

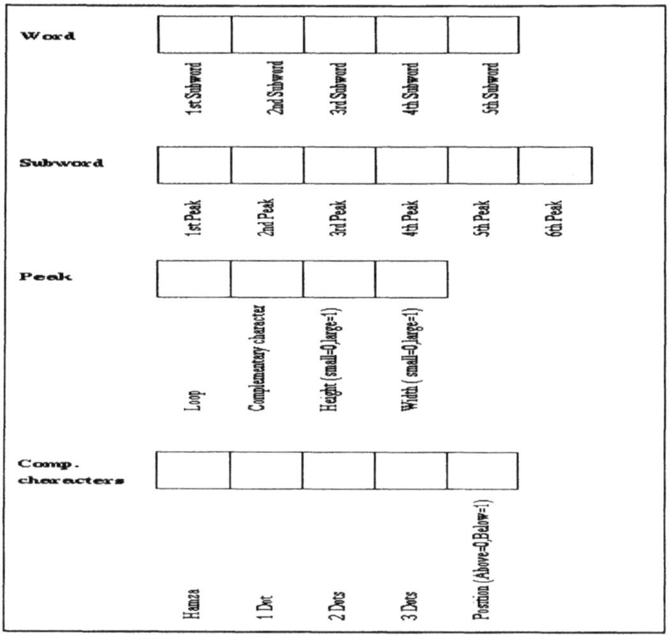

Figure 6: Segment encoding for the C4.5 machine learning.

Figure 7 depicts the complete representation to the Arabic word shown in Figure 5. The word contains only one subword and four peaks.

Word:	1 0 0 0 0 (contains only one subword)
Subword:	1 1 1 1 0 0 (subword contains four peaks)
1st peak :	1 1 0 1 (loop, complementary characters, small height, and large width)
2nd Peak:	0 0 1 1 (no loop, no complementary characters, large height, and large width).
3rd Peak :	0 1 0 1 (no loop, complementary characters: (00101), small height, and large width).
4th Peak :	0 0 1 1 (no loop, no complementary characters, Large height, and large width)

Figure 7: The complete representation of word shown in Figure 5 for the C4.5 machine learning

5. EXPERIMENTAL RESULTS

The first decision required in setting up a machine learning experiment is how the accuracy of the decision tree will be measured. The most reliable procedure is *cross-validation*. N-fold cross-validation refers to a testing strategy where the training data are randomly divided into *N* subsets. One of the *N* subsets is withheld as a *test* set and the

decision tree is trained on the remaining *N-1,* subsets. After the decision tree has been built, its accuracy is measured by attempting to classify the examples in the test set. Accuracy simply refers to the percentage of examples whose class is correctly predicted by the decision tree. The error rate is the accuracy subtracted from 100%. To compensate for sampling bias, the whole process is repeated *N* times, where, in each iteration, a new test set is withheld and the overall accuracy is determined by averaging the accuracies found at each iteration.
In brief, the cross-validation procedure for our purposes involves the following:

begin

1. For a total of 500 classes and 7500 patterns, interleave the patterns so that the pattern of class *j* is followed by a pattern of class *j*+1.
2. Segment data into K sets (k_1, k_2, ... k_K) of equal size, e.g. in our case for K = 10, we have 750 pattern in each set..
3. Train the C.4.5 with K-1 sets and test the system on the remaining one data set. Repeat this cycle K times, each time with a training set which is distinct from the test set.

For i = 1 to K do

{

Train with data from all partitions k_n where $1 \le n \le K$, and $i \ne n$.

Test with data from partition k_i.

}

5. Determine the recognition performance each time and take the average over a total of K performances.

end.

Table 1 shows the recognition success rates performance using ten-fold cross-validation. It is important to note here that the system performs extremely well with recognition rates ranging between 95.09% and 97.61% on different folds and the overall recognition is 96.52%. This is a very good performance taking into account the fact that we have a limited number of samples in each class.

Fold	Recognition Rate % Testing
1	96.87
2	97.22
3	97.05
4	97.61
5	97.57
6	95.88
7	96.16
8	95.09
9	96.23
10	95.45
Average	***96.52***

Table 1. Recognition success rates performance using ten fold cross validation.

Figure 8, shows a sample of the Arabic words used in the experiments.

Figure 8: Sample of Arabic words used in experiments.

6. CONCLUSION

This paper presents a new technique for recognizing printed Arabic text and as indicated by the experiments performed, the algorithm resulted in a 96.5% recognition rate using the C4.5 machine learning system.

Moreover, the system used a global approach which is inexpensive for feature extraction and also to avoid the difficulty of segmentation stage. The computation theory is based on the model of fast reader.

The study also shows that machine learning algorithms such as C4.5 are capable of learning the necessary features needed to recognize printed Arabic text achieving a best average recognition rate of 92% using ten fold cross-validation. The use of machine learning has removed the tedious task of manually forming rule-based dictionaries for classification of unseen characters and replaced it with an automated process which can cope with the high degree of variability which exists in printed and handwritten characters. This is very attractive feature and, therefore, further exploration of this application of machine learning is well worthwhile.

References

[1] Harmon L. D, Automatic recognition of printed and script, Proc. IEEE, 60, 10, 1165–1177, (1972).

[2] Spanjersberg A. A, Experiments with automatic input of handwritten numerical data into a large administration system, IEEE Trans. Man Cybern. 8, 4, 286–288, 1978.

[3] Focht L. R and Burger A, A numeric script recognition processor for postal zip code application, Int. Conf. Cybernetics and Society, 486–492, 1976.

[4] Schuermann J, Reading Machines, 6th Int. Conf. on Pattern Recognition, 741–745, 1982.

[5] Plamondon R and Baron R, On-line recognition of handprinted schematic pseudocode for automatic Fortran code generator, 8th Int. Conf. on Pattern Recognition, 741–745, 1986.

[6] Amin A and Al-Fedaghi S, Machine recognition of printed Arabic text utilizing a natural language morphology, Int. Journal of Man-Machine Studies 35, 6, 769–788, 1991.

[7] Guillevic D and Suen C. Y, Cursive script recognition:A fast reader, 2nd Int. Conference on Document Analysis and Recognition, 311–314, 1993.

[8] P. Ahmed and M. Khan, Computer recognition of Arabic scripts based text- the state of the art. In proceedings of the 4th International Conference and Exhibition on Multilingual Computing (Arabic and Roman Script), pp. 221-215, U.K. 1994.

[9] B. Al-Badr and S. Mahmoud, Survey and bibliography of Arabic optical text recognition, Signal Processing 41 , 49-77,1995.

[10] A. Amin, Arabic Character Recognition. Handbook of Character Recognition and Document Image Analysis edited by H Bunke and P S P Wang, Chapter 15, pp.397-420, 1997.

[11] A. Amin, Off-line Arabic character recognition: The State of the art, to appear in Pattern Recognition 1998.

[12] Quilan J. R., Discovering rules for a large collection of examples, Edinburgh University Press, 1979.

[13] Quilan J. R., C4.5 : programs for machine learning, San Mateo CA, Morgan Kauffman, 1993.

[14] A. Amin and H. B. Al-Sadoun, A new structural technique for recognizing printed Arabic text, *Int. J. of Pattern Recognition and Artif. Intell.* **9**, 1 (1995) 101–125.

[15] D. Drivas and A. Amin, Page segmentation and classification utilising bottom-up approach, 3rd International Conference on Document Analysis and Recognition (ICDAR'95), Canada, pp. 610-614, 1995.

A DETERMINISTIC ALGORITHM FOR RECONSTRUCTING OFF-LINE CALLIGRAPHICAL STROKES WITH PRIORITY RULES

D. C. Douglas Hung, CIS, New Jersey Inst. of Tech., Newark, New Jersey
Jane H. C. Cheng, CIS, Bloomfield College, Bloomfield, New Jersey

ABSTRACT

A new scheme for reinforcing the skeletons of handwritten cursive scripts is proposed in this paper. The goal of this study is to generate off-line calligraphic strokes (c-strokes) from images of handwritten documents without a specific pen-pad hardware that is necessary for on-line handwritten processing. Our algorithm not only solves the problem of edge overlapping, but also provides the engineering for preventing race conditions when more than one edge is considered overlapped in a local area when only one is actually affected. Theoretically and practically, c-strokes established from similar cursive words are topologically consistent.

1. INTRODUCTION

Consider a scenario where a computer user feeds a handwritten note to an optical scanner or a video camera which converts this information in hard copy into an electronic digital form that allows the computer software to process the digitized information, study and understand the content, and finally perform whatever tasks requested by the original handwritten note. The major issue here commanding study is the off-line handwritten processing. Handwritten scripts as the result of the human act are subject to intra-personal variations. A computerized system for handwriting recognition is feasible only if the computer representation of the handwritten image is insensitive to intra-personal variations.

Over the years, a large number of algorithms using a structural pattern have been presented in the literature. By structural pattern, we mean a scheme describing complex structures in terms of simple structural primitives, as well as the assembling grammar [1]. Kaneko [2] developed a line structure extraction method from a line drawing image base on tracing and thresholding. This method is useful in line drawing applications; and for less cursive handwriting, it leads to a good result. Another method proposed by Nishida and Mori [3] classifies curves into 4 types of primitives based on its direction, then represents the whole sequence of strokes by different kinds of concatenation. A number of other structural descriptions were also developed, such as a histogram-based representation by Yousefi and Upda [4], polygon approximation and connection graph by Sirjani and Cross [5]. The connection graph, an image-based general pattern which permits hierarchical redescription of the input image in terms of the significant elements and developed the elementary phrase-structure grammars by Stringa [6] the stroke-based method which uses a divide-and-conquer strategy based on selected critical points by Pan and Lee [7] and Brault and Plamondon [8] are also noted.

Since the local variations have severe impact on syntactical and grammar representations, neither of them are suitable for our purpose. A generalized pseudo on-line stroke sequence is therefore proposed to model a handwriting image. The major challenges of this study are:

1) how to retrieve edges vanished by edge overlapping without causing a race condition;
2) how to reconstruct decomposed stroke pieces into a pseudo on-line stroke sequence—a parametric stroke presentation.

In this study, the former is solved by using priority rule scheduling, and the latter is already solved as it appears in Ref. [11].

2. THE PRELIMINARIES

The problem of reconstructing off-line calligraphic strokes is the problem of dividing and merging skeletonized graphs of handwritten words. Consider a connected graph $\boldsymbol{G}$ consisting of M vertices v_i, $i = 1, \cdots, M$, and N edges e_j, $j = 1, \cdots, N$. Let $\psi_E(e)$ be the endpoint function of an edge e. The *degree* of a vertex $\gamma(\cdot)$ is defined as the number of edges incidenting with it.

Let e_i be an edge with $\psi_E(e_i) = (v_j, v_k)$. e_i is called a *loop* if $v_j = v_k$. Without lose of generality, v_k is called the *secondary* vertex of e_i w. r. t. v_j or vice versa. Let $\kappa_i(v)$ be the unit vector of a tangent along e_i at v and β_i be the smallest contained-angle made by $\kappa_i(v_j)$ and $\kappa_i(v_k)$. The *linearity* of e_i is then defined as:

$$A_0 - A_1 \, \boldsymbol{ln} \left[\boldsymbol{tan} \, \beta_i \right] + A_2 \left[\left[\hat{\kappa}_i(v_j) - \hat{\kappa}_i(v_k) \right] \bullet \hat{u}_i \right]^{-1} \tag{1}$$

where A_0, A_1 and A_2 are constants, and $\hat{u}_i$ is the unit vector of $[v_j - v_k]$. An edge is considered curvilinear if its linearity is less than a pre-determined threshold. Let e_p and e_q be two edges incidenting with the same vertex v. The *smoothness* for joining e_p and e_q at v is defined as:

$$A_0 - A_1 \, \boldsymbol{ln} \left[\boldsymbol{tan} \, \beta_{ij} \right] \tag{2}$$

where $cos \, \beta_{ij} = \hat{\kappa}_p(v) \bullet \hat{\kappa}_q(v)$. The *most prominent edge pair* of v, denoted as *mpp*(v), is an edge pair having the highest smoothness among all the possible edge pairs of v. Similarly, the *least prominent edge pair* of v is an edge pair having the lowest smoothness; denoted as *lpp*(v).

Let v be a vertex and $I(v)$ be its indexing function which returns 1 if $\gamma(v)$ is odd; otherwise it returns 0. Let $\boldsymbol{E}(v)$ be a subset of the incidenting edges of v with $I(v) = 1$ and $\| \boldsymbol{E}(v) \| = m < \gamma(v)$. $\boldsymbol{E}(v)$ is called a *m-macro,* denoted as $\boldsymbol{X}^m(v)$, if every member has an odd degree vertex as its secondary vertex. $\boldsymbol{E}(v)$ is called a *m-minor* if every member has an even degree vertex as its secondary vertex. The remindering edges of v which are not parts of $\boldsymbol{X}^m(v)$ are called the *leftovers.* A macro $X^m(\cdot)$ has to degrade to $X^k(\cdot)$ if $(m-k)$ of its defining member are curvilinear edges. This degradation is denoted as $X^m(\cdot) \rightsquigarrow X^{m-k}(\cdot)$.

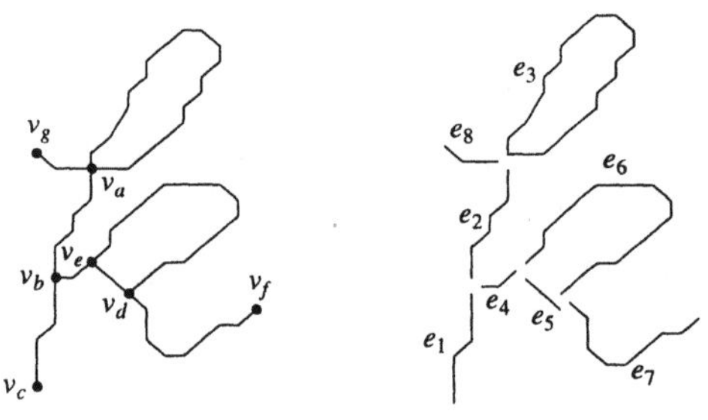

Fig. 1. Cursive script of '*k*.' (a) vertex set $\boldsymbol{V}$ and (b) edge set $\boldsymbol{E}$.

Example 1. Given a cursive letter k, as depicted in Fig. 1, with a vertex set of $\boldsymbol{V} = \{v_a, \cdots, v_g\}$ and an edge set of $\boldsymbol{E} = \{e_1, \cdots, e_8\}$. The following m-macros are identified:

- 3-macros: $\{X^3(v_d) \rightsquigarrow X^1(v_d), X^3(v_e) \rightsquigarrow X^2(v_e)\}$.
- 2-macro: $\{X^2(v_b)\}$
- 1-macros: $\{X^1(v_c), X^1(v_f) \rightsquigarrow X^0(v_f)\}$.

In addition, e_2 is a leftover of $X^2(v_b)$. ■

3. MACRO TRANSFIGURATING LES

A macro is a result of missing edges caused by edge overlapping. It can be restored by duplicating properly selected edges. As a result of edge duplication, the degrees of relevant vertices are changed. This means that a macro may be reconfigurated, added, or even disqualified. A macro-based method is proposed to guide the transfiguration. Initially, both loops and curvilinear edges are assigned a priority of $-\infty$, while the remindering edges get priorities of zeros. Then, their priorities are modified by three heuristically-defined rules. Let e be an edge with $\psi_E(e) = (\nu, u)$ and ΔP be the priority enhancement.

Rule R1. Set $\Delta P = 1$, if $e \in X^1(\nu)$.

Rule R2. Set $\Delta P = 3$, if $e \in X^2(\nu)$ and $e \in mpp(u)$.

Rule R3. Set $\Delta P = 5$, if $e \in X^3(\nu)$ with $e \in mpp(\nu)$ and e is not a part of $lpp(\nu)$.

Rule R4. Set $\Delta P = 7$, if $e \in X^3(\nu)$ and $e \in X^3(u)$ and e is less curvilinear.

In practice, several rules with different priority enhancements may apply to an edge, which is shared by several macros. To avoid a race condition in applying different rules, transfigurating rules are ranked in according to the size of an affecting macro. A proper precedence order of these rules is: R4, R3, R2, and R1.

4. RULE SCHEDULING ALGORITHM (RSA)

Let $I(\nu)$ be a vertex indexing function which returns 1 if $\gamma(\nu)$ is odd; otherwise it returns 0. For a graph consists of n vertices $\nu_j, j = 1, \cdots, n$, a state vector Ψ is defined as:

$$\Psi = [\,I(\nu_1),\ I(\nu_2),\ \cdots,\ I(\nu_n)\,]. \tag{3}$$

An entropy function Φ is also defined as:

$$\Phi = \sum_{\forall\, \nu_j \in V} I(\nu_j). \tag{4}$$

A cursive word is a collective set of single-stroke line-drawings, each of which can be completely decompsed as proposed by Hung [11]. There are two termini for each decomposed single-stroke and each vertex should have an even degree. This implies that the lowest entropy for an ideal graph is $\Phi_\infty = 2$. Thus, the objective of macro transfiguration is to minimize the entropy by applying transfigurating rules recursively until Φ_∞ is achieved.

Let $\pi_k = \Gamma|\nu$ be a *proposal* to which a rule Γ is applying to a macro $X^m(\nu)$. Let $\Phi(\pi_k)$ be an estimated entropy and $\Psi(\pi_k)$ be a *transfiguration state vector* after π_k is applied:

$$\begin{aligned}\Psi(\pi_k) &= \Psi(\pi_{k-1}) \boxplus \pi_n \\ &= \Psi_0 \boxplus \pi_1 \boxplus \cdots \boxplus \pi_{n-1} \boxplus \pi_n\end{aligned} \tag{5}$$

where $\boxplus$ is a *transfiguring operator* and Ψ_0 is an initial state. A proposal $\Gamma|\nu$ is accepted if it results in a lower entropy than that of without it.

Even though transfigurating rules are applied in according with their precedences, there may exist more than one proposal that leads to a new state of lower entropy. However, it is not necessary that a proposal with a high precedence is a proper and correct selection. A backtracking method is hereby proposed to correct malpracticed proposals.

Let H_s and H_a be two time-tables for scheduled proposals and their pending alternatives, respectively. Each table entry consists of two fields: a scheduling-index $Sid(\cdot)$ and a proposal $Pr(\cdot)$. A *rule scheduling algorithm* (*RSA*) is then proposed as follows:

Step 1: Initiate Ψ_0 and Φ_0. Set both H_s and H_a to $\{\varnothing\}$. Set $i = 1$ and $p = 0$.

Step 2: Search for ith level proposals $\pi_i(k)$, $k = 1, \cdots, n_i$, and sort them with their priorities in a decreasing order. If $n_i = 0$ then go to *Step 5*.

Step 3: Set $\boldsymbol{\pi}_i = \boldsymbol{\pi}_i(1)$ and $\boldsymbol{H}_a[p+k] = \{i, \boldsymbol{\pi}_i(k)\}$ for $k = 2, \cdots, n_i$. Set $p = p + n_i - 1$.

Step 4: Set $\boldsymbol{H}_s[i] = \{i, \boldsymbol{\pi}_i\}$. If $\boldsymbol{\Phi}(\boldsymbol{\pi}_i) > 2$, then set $i = i+1$ and go to *Step 2*; otherwise stop.

Step 5: Set $\boldsymbol{H}_s[i] = \{\varnothing\}$. Set $i = Sid(\boldsymbol{H}_a[p])$ and $\boldsymbol{\pi}_i = Pr(\boldsymbol{H}_a[p])$.

Step 6: Set $p = p - 1$. If $p > 0$ then go to *Step 4*; otherwise stop.

(a)

(b)

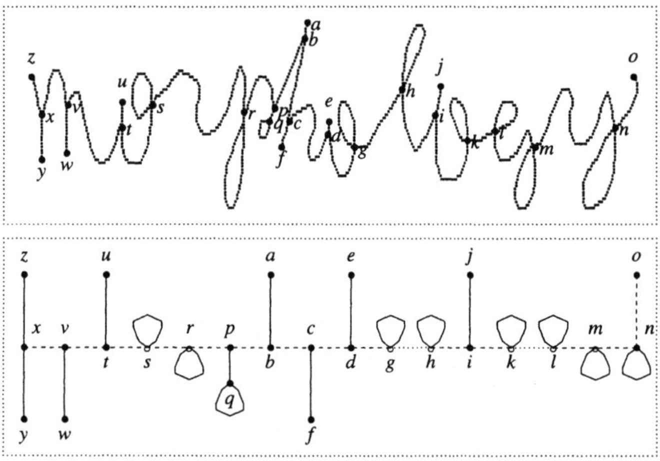

Fig. 2. Cursive word "*morphology.*" (a) The skeleton and (b) the established graph where curvilinear edges and leftovers of macros are drawn as dashed lines and dotted lines.

Example 2: Given a script word shown as Fig. 2(a). Its initial state is:

$$\boldsymbol{\Psi}_0 = [I(a)\ I(b) \cdots I(z)] = [1\,1\,1\,1\,1\,1\,0\,0\,1\,1\,0\,0\,0\,0\,1\,1\,1\,0\,0\,1\,1\,1\,1\,1\,1\,1]$$

and its initial entropy $\boldsymbol{\Phi}_0 = 18$. The following m-macros are detected:

- 3-macros: $\{X^3(b), X^3(c) \sim> X^2(c), X^3(v) \sim> X^1(v), X^3(x) \sim> X^2(x)\}$.
- 2-macros: $\{X^2(p), X^2(d) \sim> X^1(d), X^2(t) \sim> X^1(t)\}$.
- 1-macros: $\{X^1(a), X^1(e), X^1(f), X^1(i), X^1(j), X^1(q), X^1(u), X^1(w), X^1(y), X^1(z)\}$

Let $\prod(X^m) = [X\ m]^T$ be the vector form of a macro X^m and $[X\ k^m]^T$ be a degradation of $X^m \sim> X^k$. Detected m-macros, as a set, can then be represented as a matrix:

$$\Pi_0 = \begin{bmatrix} d & d & d & d & d & d & - & - & d & d & - & - & - & - & s & d & d & - & - & d & d & d & d & d & d & d \\ 1 & 3 & 2^3 & 1^2 & 1 & 1 & 0 & 0 & 1 & 1 & 0 & 0 & 0 & 0 & 1 & 2 & 1 & 0 & 0 & 1^2 & 1 & 1^3 & 1 & 2^3 & 1 & 1 \end{bmatrix}$$

where 'd's and 's's indicate macros and minors, respectively, and '-'s indicate vertices with even degrees. The proposal with the highest priority enhancement for the first iteration is R3|b and

$$\boldsymbol{\Psi}_1 = \boldsymbol{\Psi}(\mathrm{R3|b}) = [0\,0\,1\,1\,1\,1\,0\,0\,1\,1\,0\,0\,0\,0\,1\,1\,1\,0\,0\,1\,1\,1\,1\,1\,1\,1]$$

with $\boldsymbol{\Phi}_1 = 16$ and

$$\Pi_1 = \begin{bmatrix} - & - & d & d & d & d & - & - & d & d & - & - & - & - & s & d & d & - & - & d & d & d & d & d & d & d \\ 0 & 0 & 1^2 & 1^2 & 1 & 1 & 0 & 0 & 1 & 1 & 0 & 0 & 0 & 0 & 1 & 1 & 1 & 0 & 0 & 1^2 & 1 & 1^3 & 1 & 2^3 & 1 & 1 \end{bmatrix}.$$

The rest of the proposals can be listed as: R2|x, R2|c, R1|v, R1|p, R1|t, R1|i, and R1|d. This leads to a goal state $\boldsymbol{\Phi}_\infty$ with

$$\boldsymbol{\Psi}_8 = [0\,0\,0\,0\,0\,0\,0\,0\,0\,0\,0\,0\,0\,0\,1\,0\,0\,0\,0\,0\,0\,0\,0\,0\,0\,1].$$

■

5. EXPERIMENTAL STUDIES, ANALYSES AND FUTURE WORKS

Two dozens handwritten envelops written by different persons, as well as tens handwritten notes, are collected from daily life. Each sample is first digitized by an optical scanner with 300 dpi resolution, and is then processed by the following steps:

a. A skeleton is obtained by a thinning algorithm proposed by [10].
b. Recognized spurious edges are pruned.
c. For each 8-connected word, a vertex-edge graph is established. Furthermore, for each vertex of odd degree, a *m*-macro is tabulated.
d. The RSA-algorithm is applied to schedule hypotheses for edge duplications.
e. For each refined skeleton, a c-stroke is reconstructed by the contour composition algorithms proposed by Hung [11].

To inspect the resultant c-strokes in a quantitative fashion, a *k-tangent* function is defined. Let C be a c-stroke consisting of n connected points $c_t = (x_t, y_t)$, $t = 1, \cdots, n$. The *k-tangent* of C is defined as:

$$\Delta_k c_t = \kappa_c (c_{t+l} - c_{t-l}) \tag{6}$$

with $l = \lfloor k/2 \rfloor$ and κ a scaler. Then, a phase angle θ_k is defined as:

$$tan^{-1}\left(\frac{\Delta_k y_t}{\Delta_k x_t}\right) \tag{7}$$

As an example, k-slopes $\Delta_{25} y$ and θ_k of Fig. 2(a) are shown as Fig. 3.

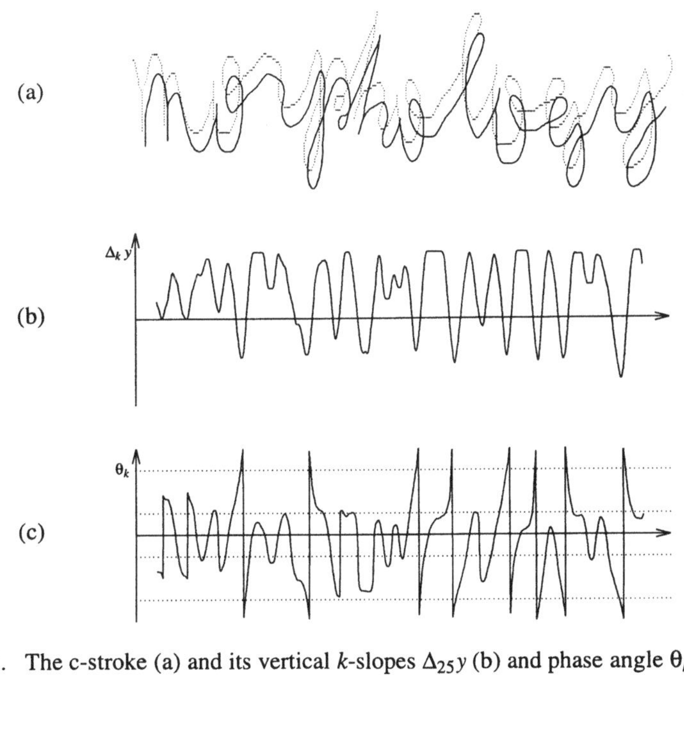

Fig. 3. The c-stroke (a) and its vertical k-slopes $\Delta_{25} y$ (b) and phase angle θ_k (c).

Regarding intra-personal variations, Figures 4 and 5 show two sets of diversified samples of cursive words of "hung" and "push," respectively. By visual inspection, it is noticed that the similarities among these samples are high and their dissimilarities are occurred at the beginnings and the ending of cursive letters. Thus, our future studies will be focused on separating cursive letters and syntacitcally patternize them.

We have presented a new scheme to reinforce skeletons of handwritten cursive scripts and to reconstruct c-strokes off-line. In this paper we address the issue of edge overlapping. Our approach uses structure-dependent priority rules to schedule prospect hypotheses and a backtracking technique to correct the results if a goal state can not be achieved. The proposed technique is robust to the local intra-personal variation. Experimental results have demonstrated that the proposed algorithm provides stable descriptions for various templates of similar cursive and connected words.

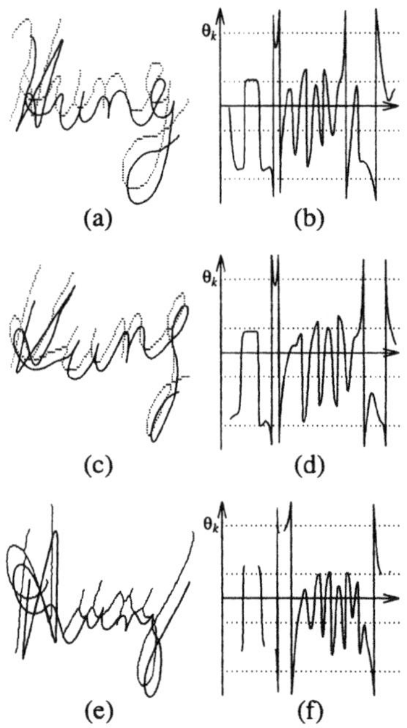

Fig. 4. The original and smoothed c-strokes and the phase angle θ_k for samples "*Hung-1*," "*Hung-2*," and "*Hung-3*."

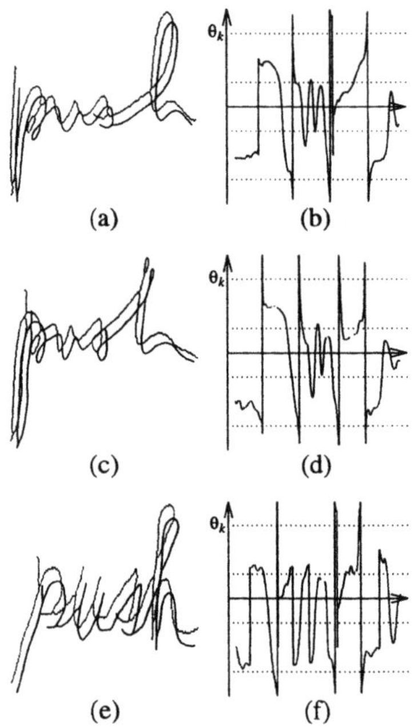

Fig. 5. The original and smoothed c-strokes and the phase angle θ_k for scripts "*push-1*", "*push-2*", and "*push-3*."

REFERENCES

[1] Fu KS and Booth TL. Grammatical inference: Introduction and survey–Part 1 and 2, IEEE Transaction on Pattern Analysis and Machine Intelligence, 1986; 8: 343-375.

[2] Kaneko T. Line structure extraction from line-drawing images. Pattern Recognition, 1992; 25(9): 963-973.

[3] Nishida H and Mori S. Algebraic description of curve structure: application to character recognition. IEEE Transaction on Pattern Analysis and Machine Intelligence, 1992; 14(5): 516-533.

[4] Al-Yousefi H and Upda SS. Recognition of Arabic characters. IEEE Transaction on Pattern Analysis and Machine Intelligence, 1992; 14(8): 853-857.

[5] Sirjani A and Cross GR. On representation of a shape's skeleton. Pattern Recognition Letters, 1991; 12: 149-154.

[6] Stringa L. A New set of constraint-free character recognition grammars. IEEE Transaction on Pattern Analysis and Machine Intelligence, 1990; 12(12): 1210-1217.

[7] Pan JC and Lee S. Off-line tracing and representation of signatures. In Proceedings of the International conference in computer vision and pattern recognition, 1991, pp. 679-680.

[8] Brault JJ and Plamodon R. Segmenting handwritten signatures at their perceptually important points. IEEE Transaction on Pattern Analysis and Machine Intelligence, 1993; 15(9): 953-957.

[9] Singer Y and Tishby N. Dynamical encoding of cursive handwriting. In Proceedings of the IEEE conference on computer vision and pattern recognition, 1993, pp. 341-346.

[10] Hung DC. Enhancement and feature purification of fingerprint images. Pattern Recognition, 1993; 26(11): 1660-1671.

[11] Hung DC. Shape disassembly using generating merging probability. Journal of Systems Integration, 1995; 5(2): 107-121.

OFF-LINE HANDWRITTEN CHINESE CHARACTER RECOGNITION BASED ON STRUCTURAL FEATURES AND FUZZY ARTMAP

Nabeel Murshed[1], Lab. of Document Image Analysis and Neural Networks (LADIANN), Pontifícia Universidade Católica do Paraná (PUC-PR), Brasil, murshed@lambda.pucpr.br.
Adnan Amin, School of Computer Science & Engineering, University of New South Wales, Australia, amin@cse.unsw.edu.au.
Sameer Singh, School of Computing, University of Plymouth, United Kingdom, s1singh@soc.plym.ac.uk.

ABSTRACT

Recognition of printed and handwritten text (characters and digits) has been a challenge for many researchers in the field of Document Image Analysis for almost thirty years. Many existing pattern recognition methods have been used and new ones have been proposed. Despite the satisfactory results obtained in recognizing printed text, recognition of handwritten text is still an open research. This paper presents a method for off-line recognition of handwritten Chinese characters. Each character is described by six structural features extracted using the *dominant point* method. The goodness of each feature is determined by a method called *stroke probability*. The classification was performed by the Fuzzy ARTMAP neural network within the context of the *one-class problem approach*. Evaluation of the proposed method was determined using database of 900 characters (an average of 40 samples/character). The average mean recognition rate was approximately 94%.

KEYWORDS

Chinese Characters, One-class Problem, Dominant Point, Stroke Probability, Fuzzy ARTMAP.

1. INTRODUCTION

Compared to Arabic and Latin characters, Chinese characters are distinct and ideographic, large in size, and a lot of structurally similar characters exist in the character set (more than 50000 characters, of which 6000 are commonly used). Thus, classification criteria are difficult to generate. Moreover, both the writing style and intra-variability make handwriting Chinese character recognition a complex and challenging research problem.

Different approaches within the context of character recognition fall into either *on-line* or *offline* recognition. In on-line recognition, characters are recognized as they are written, whereas in off-line they are recognized after the writing or printing process is completed. This work is concerned with off-line recognition.

Over the past three decades, many existing methods have been explored and new ones have been proposed to solve the problem of Chinese character recognition. For example, Augi and Nagahashi [1] have used concatenation-relation, cross-relation and near relation to analyze Chinese characters. Yamamoto et al [2] have used stroke direction, stroke domain

---

[1] Corresponding Author. Supported by a Research Grant from Itec, S.A. (A Company of Itautec and IBM-Brazil).

and stroke density to classify characters. Hsieh and Lee [3] have used one-dimensional string consisting of stroke sequence interleaved with relationships between two consecutive strokes to represent a character. For all of these methods, an accurate stroke extraction algorithm and a good classifier is essential to achieve high recognition rates. Moreover, adopting rigorous experimental procedures is necessary in order to estimate the classification error. Amin, Kim and Sammut [4] have proposed the use of *dominant point* technique to extract structural features and machine learning algorithm C4.5 for off-line handwritten Chinese character recognition. In this work we propose to use the fuzzy ARTMAP neural network, as the classifier network, and perform the training based on the *one-class-problem* approach [5].

In order to make this paper self-contained, section 2 describes the one-class problem approach. Overview of the fuzzy ARTMAP is given in section 3. Sections 4 and 5 describe, respectively, the feature sets and the experimental results. Discussions and conclusions are given in section 6.

2. THE ONE-CLASS PROBLEM APPROACH [5]

The one-class problem approach was proposed by Murshed et al [5] and applied successfully in various pattern recognition problems [6-10]. In this section we will give a brief description of this approach.

Consider a classifier Z (classical or neural network) and two pattern classes w_1 and w_2, such that Z is required to recognize patterns from class w_1 only. Call the patterns in w_1 *positive patterns* and those in w_2 *negative patterns*. If Z is trained with positive patterns only and tested with positive and negative patterns, then this approach is called *One-Class Problem Approach* [5]. This is similar to how humans perform *Visual Pattern Recognition*. We all know that, children and adult alike are able to recognize the shape of certain objects, such as squares, without learning to recognize the shapes of other disjoint objects. However, one may argue that when solving technological problems one need not follow biological intelligence. This is true, but not in all applications. It is our believe that problems in visual pattern recognition are best solved by adopting *some aspects* from the biological counterpart. In this context, one may raise the following simple question: if a classifier Z is required to recognize patterns from class w_1, then why Z must know about the patterns in class w_2, for example?

There are two main advantages to using the one-class problem approach. First, the measured error (rejection of negative samples), as demonstrated in [8] reflects the true performance of the classifier. Second, training is simplified in terms of both computational complexity and preparation. To illustrate this, consider a classifier Z (traditional or neural network) trained with samples $\mathbf{X}^1$ (positive patterns) and $\mathbf{Y}^1$ (negative patterns) from class w_1 and w_2 respectively. The superscript indicates the data set label and not the class label. Traditionally, this approach is called *two-class problem approach*. Let the parameter set of Z be denoted by Ψ, and the statistical features describing the whole populations of class w_1 and w_2, be denoted by Γ and $\mathbf{\Phi}$, respectively. Also, let the statistical features present in $\mathbf{X}^1$ and $\mathbf{Y}^1$ be denoted by γ^1 ($\gamma^1 \in \Gamma$) and ϕ^1 ($\phi^1 \in \mathbf{\Phi}$), respectively, and the error in terms of correct rejection of w_2 patterns (negative patterns) be denoted by λ^1. When Z is trained with $\mathbf{X}^1$ and $\mathbf{Y}^1$, Ψ is estimated from γ^1 and ϕ^1. That is $\Psi = f(\gamma^1, \phi^1)$. From the viewpoint of cognition, Ψ represents the knowledge (experience) that Z acquired during the training phase. Therefore, the ability of Z to reject similar patterns of $\mathbf{Y}^1$, but distinct, will depend, among other factors, on how much Z knows about the whole population of w_2. If ϕ^1 is representative of w_2, then Z will have enough knowledge of the whole population of w_2. It is known in pattern recognition that different training samples yield different error measures with respect to λ^1, i.e., $\lambda^1 = f(\phi^1)$. This was observed in signature verification [5]. Therefore, one may claim that the ability of Z to reject patterns from w_2 is biased with ϕ^1. In order to improve λ^1, one must develop/adopt special procedures for selecting $\mathbf{Y}^1$. This *may* require extensive computation time. On the other hand, if one adopt the one-class problem approach one need to concentrate only on selecting $\mathbf{X}^1$. If λ^1 is not acceptable, then one must develop more discriminative features, which is more interesting and challenging. Consequently, λ^1 becomes a function of the discriminative power of the feature set.

3. OVERVIEW OF THE FUZZY ARTMAP NEURAL NETWORK [11]

The fuzzy ARTMAP is a system of neural networks that learns to *classify* inputs by pattern of fuzzy membership values between *zero* and *one*. Its structure (Fig. 1) consists of two fuzzy ART modules, ART_a and ART_b, each of which creates stable recognition class exemplars in response to arbitrary sequence of input patterns. The two modules are linked together by an associative network, E^{ab}, called map-field and an internal controller that allows the fuzzy ARTMAP to operate in real time.

Each fuzzy ART module is an *unsupervised clustering network* composed of an input field F_0, representing the input vector $\mathbf{I}$, an activation field F_l and an exemplar field E (Fig. 1). F_l field receives both bottom-up input vector $\mathbf{I}_c$ from F_0 and top-down weight vector $\mathbf{w}_j$ from the exemplar field E. The number of neurons in each field is equal to *M*, *2M* and *N*, respectively. Where *M* is the size of the input vector and *N* is the number of class exemplars (or memory capacity). Each class exemplar is represented by the top-down weight vector $\mathbf{w}_j$. The vectors $\mathbf{x}$ and $\mathbf{y}$ represent, respectively, the activities of the fields F_l and E. The input vector $\mathbf{I}_c$ is a normalization form of $\mathbf{I}$, defined as

$$\begin{aligned} \mathbf{I}_c &= (\mathbf{a}\,.\,\mathbf{a}^c) \equiv (a_1, \ldots, a_M, a_1^c, \ldots, a_M^c) \\ a_i^c &\equiv 1 - a_i,\; i = 1, \ldots, M \end{aligned} \tag{1}$$

where *M* is the size of the input vector. The purpose of this normalization (also called complement coding) is to prevent category proliferation [12].

As mentioned above, the fuzzy ARTMAP is a classification network capable of associating a set of pattern pairs$\{(\mathbf{I}_1^a,\mathbf{I}_1^b),(\mathbf{I}_2^a,\mathbf{I}_2^b),\ldots(\mathbf{I}_k^a,\mathbf{I}_k^b)\}$. Such association is performed at the map-field (Fig. 1) by a set of neurons (called predictive neurons), the number of which is equal to the number of exemplar neurons in ART_b. Each predictive neuron is connected, through non-adaptive connections, to one exemplar neuron in ART_b and, through adaptive connections, to every exemplar neuron in ART_a. With such structure, when a pattern $(\mathbf{I}_i^a,\mathbf{I}_i^b), i = 1,\ldots,k$ is represented to the network, two exemplar neurons, say *J* and *K*, are activated at ART_a and ART_b, respectively. If these neurons activate the same predictive neuron at E^{ab}, then the network resonates and stores this information at the weight vector $\mathbf{w}_J^{ab}$ by locking the value of the weight connection w_J^{ab}, between the neuron *J* in ART_a and the predictive neuron in E^{ab}, at its current value, i.e., $w_J^{ab} = 1$. All other weight connections from neuron *J* to other predictive neurons are set to 0. If on the other hand, the exemplar neurons *J* and *K* activate two distinct prediction neurons, then prediction is disconfirmed. Such error is detected by the map-field vigilance parameter, ρ^{ab} [11]. To correct the error made by ART_a, the match tracking increases the vigilance parameter ρ^a by an amount necessary to trigger a search process for another previously learned exemplar neuron. If no such neuron exists, then another uncommitted neuron is assigned to represent the new pattern. The output, x^{ab}, of the map-field obeys

$$x^{ab} = \begin{cases} y^b \wedge w_J^{ab}, & \text{if the } J\text{th } E^a \text{ exemplar neuron is active and } E^b \text{ is active} \\ w_J^{ab}, & \text{if the } J\text{th } E^a \text{ exmplar neuron is active and } E^b \text{ is inactive} \\ y^b, & \text{if } E^a \text{ is inactive and } E^b \text{ is active} \\ 0, & \text{if } E^a \text{ is inactive and } E^b \text{ is inactive} \end{cases} \quad (2)$$

It can be observed from equation 2 that if the Fuzzy ARTMAP is trained with patterns from one class only, along with the respective association, 1 for example, then the network will learn this association for each presented pattern pairs. During test, or normal operation, when an unknown pattern is presented to the network, the output, $\mathbf{x}^{ab}$, of the map field would be either equal to the weight vector, $\mathbf{w}_J^{ab}$, if the unknown input had activated a previously learned exemplar neuron in the ART_a module, or equal to 0, otherwise. This feature of the Fuzzy ARTMAP allows it to perform pattern classification according to the one-class problem approach mentioned previously.

4. DEFINITION OF THE FEATURE SETS [4]

The image of each character is digitized and binarized with *300-dpi* scanner. For the purpose of classification, each handwritten character is described by two feature sets. The first set consisted of six structural features (Table. 1) extracted from the binary image by applying thinning, line-segment extraction, smoothing, and dominant-point detection processes. The thinning process provides one-pixel-wide skeleton of the character image, which is used as the input to the line-segment extraction process. This process produces a set of line segments from which the structural features are extracted. Example of the results of each process is shown in figure 2. We define line segment as one that is composed of one or more connected structural features. A detailed description of the feature extraction processes is given in [4]. The second feature set, called *stroke probability*, describes the likelihood of each extracted structural feature to be one of the six feature types defined in table 1.

4.1. STROKE PROBABILITY

After segmenting each line segment into a set of structural features, it is necessary to determine the type of each feature. There are many cases where an extracted feature can be considered as one of two feature types. To illustrate this, consider the coordinate system shown in figure 3 where each coordinate axes is called a perfect feature type (horizontal, slash, vertical and backslash). Let C_i, $i = 1, 2, ..., 4$ denotes the *ith* perfect feature type. An unknown line segment L (Fig. 3) located between C_1 and C_2, for example, could be considered as either a feature-type C_1 or C_2. To eliminate such uncertainty we defined a criterion called *stroke probability* that determine the likelihood of a line being one of perfect feature types. In this work we consider the stroke probability of a given line being a perfect feature type is equal to one. This probability decreases as the line is located away from a given perfect feature type, and is equal to 0.5 when the line is located half-way between two adjacent feature types. In handwriting, this is undesirable because of the variation of the writing style. For example, we should not exclude the possibility of 23° inclined line as being horizontal. Based on the above, the likelihood of an extracted structural feature being one of the pre-defined feature type is determined according to the equations shown bellow. Note that in the case of the feature-type 'corner' its stroke probability is approximated by that of a backslash.

Feature 1 (Horizontal)

$$P_s(\theta) = 1 - \frac{\theta}{45^\circ} \qquad \text{for } 0 \le \theta \le 45^\circ$$

$$P_s(\theta) = 1 - \frac{360^\circ - \theta}{45^\circ} \qquad \text{for } 315^\circ \le \theta \le 360^\circ$$

$$P_s(\theta) = 1 - \frac{|180^\circ - \theta|}{45^\circ} \qquad \text{for } 135^\circ \le \theta \le 225^\circ$$

$$P_s(\theta) = 0 \qquad \text{otherwise}$$

Feature 2 (Slash)

$$P_s(\theta) = 1 - \frac{|45^\circ - \theta|}{45^\circ} \qquad \text{for } 0^\circ \le \theta \le 90^\circ$$

$$P_s(\theta) = 1 - \frac{|225^\circ - \theta|}{45^\circ} \qquad \text{for } 180^\circ \le \theta \le 270^\circ$$

$$P_s(\theta) = 0 \qquad \text{otherwise}$$

Feature 3 (Vertical)

$$P_s(\theta) = 1 - \frac{|90^\circ - \theta|}{45^\circ} \qquad \text{for } 45^\circ \le \theta \le 135^\circ$$

$$P_s(\theta) = 1 - \frac{|270^\circ - \theta|}{45^\circ} \qquad \text{for } 225^\circ \le \theta \le 315^\circ$$

$$P_s(\theta) = 0 \qquad \text{otherwise}$$

Feature 4 (Backslash)

$$P_s(\theta) = 1 - \frac{|135^\circ - \;|}{45^\circ} \qquad \text{for } 90^\circ \le \theta \le 180^\circ$$

$$P_s(\theta) = 1 - \frac{|315^\circ - \theta|}{45^\circ} \qquad \text{for } 270^\circ \le \theta \le 360^\circ$$

$$P_s(\theta) = 0 \qquad \text{otherwise}$$

Feature 5 (Corner)

Uses the same probability as that of a backslash

Feature 6 (Dot)

$$P_s(\theta) = 1 - \frac{L}{Tp} \qquad \text{for } L \le Tp$$

$$P_s(\theta) = 0 \qquad \text{for } L > Tp$$

where L is the length of the segment, T_p is a threshold the value of which is determined empirically.

5. EXPERIMENTAL RESULTS

The recognition process is performed by training and testing three fuzzy ARTMAPs for each character, each with a data set, called ***evaluation set*** defined with respect to one feature vector *only*. The definitions of the overall data set, the feature vectors and the evaluation set are given bellow.

5.1 THE OVERALL FEATURE DATA SET

The database [4] contains about 36,000.00 images of 900 characters (an average of 40samples/character). Based on the feature sets defined in section 3, three numerical feature-vectors (s_1, s_2, and s_3) were generated from the image of each character. Feature-vectors s_1 and s_2 describe, respectively, the number of primitives (defined in table 1) that are present in a character and their stroke probabilities. The third feature-vector, s_3, is the concatenation of vectors s_1 and s_2. Note that each of s_1 and s_2 is a 6-bit vector. Based on this scheme, the overall feature data set, D, used for training and test is composed of three feature data sets defined by:

$$D = D_{s_1} + D_{s_2} + D_{s_3} \qquad (3)$$

where the subscript s_k, $k = 1, 2$ and 3 denotes the *kth* type of feature-vector. From each feature data set, an evaluation set (Fig. 4) composed of training and test sets is formed for each character. These two sets were used to evaluate the performance of each fuzzy ARTMAP.

5.1.1 The Evaluation Set

Let X_i, $i=1, 2, \ldots, 900$ denotes the *ith* character in the data set. The *kth* feature data subset, $(D_{s_k})_i$, for the *ith* character, is divided into two disjoint sets one for training and another for test, as shown bellow:

$$\left|(D_{s_k})_i\right| = \left|(D_{s_k})_i^{tr}\right| + \left|(D_{s_k})_i^{te}\right| \tag{4}$$

where $\left|(D_{s_k})\right|$ denotes the number of samples in (D_{s_k}) and the superscripts tr and te denote, respectively, training and test. The number of samples, n, in $(D_{s_k})_i^{tr}$, is not fixed and is equal to *5, 10, 15, 20, 25* **or** *30*. Since the total number of samples in $(D_{s_k})_i$ is 40, therefore, for each n samples in $(D_{s_k})_i^{tr}$, the corresponding number of samples in $(D_{s_k})_i^{te}$ is given by:

$$\left|(D_{s_k})_i^{te}\right| = \left|(D_{s_k})_i\right| - \left|(D_{s_k})_i^{tr}\right| \tag{5}$$

The evaluation set $(D_{s_k})_i^{Ev}$ for the *ith* character is defined by:

$$\left|(D_{s_k})_i^{Ev}\right| = \left|(D_{s_k})_i^{tr}\right| + \left|(D_{s_k})_i^{Te}\right| \tag{6}$$

where $(D_{s_k})_i^{Te}$ denotes the total test set for the *ith* character and is given by:

$$\left|(D_{s_k})_i^{Te}\right| = \left|(D_{s_k})_i^{te}\right| + \left|\sum_{j=1,\, j\neq i}^{900} (D_{s_k})_j\right| \tag{7}$$

From the above it should be noted that, for each character, the training set is composed of positive samples only, and the total test set is composed of positive and negative samples. To illustrate the above terminology, consider the following example. If the training set for the *ith* character contains 5 samples (positive samples) , then, from equations 5 and 7 the total test set will contain 35 samples of this character (positive samples) and 35960 samples of the other charcaters (negative samples).

5.2 ESTIMATION OF CLASSIFICATION ERRORS

The classification error of each fuzzy ARTMAP was measured according to a modified versions of the holdout, or *H* method, and cross-validation, or *Π* method [13]. In the *H* method the data set is divided into two disjoint subsets: one for training and another for test. Traditionally, the number of samples in the training subset is selected to be equal to or higher than that of the test subset. Based on this, the classifier is trained with the training subset and tested with the test subset. The classification errors are calculated based on one trial *only*.

In the *Π* method a small subset of *P* samples is taken for test, such that $1 \leq P << N$, N/P is an integer, and $P/N \leq 1/2$, where *N* is the total number of samples in the data set. The number of training samples is equal to $(N - P)$. Based on this division, the classifier is trained with $(N - P)$ samples and tested with *P* samples. The process is repeated *k* times, $k = 1, 2, \ldots N/P$. Each time with different *P* samples. The classification errors are averaged over N/P trials.

In our present work we adopted a modified versions of the *H* and *Π* methods, in which different number of training samples were used. In addition, in the *Π* method the classification error, for each number of training samples, was averaged over thirty trials. We found, from experience, that thirty trials give a good error estimate. The purpose of adopting such rigorous procedures is to compare the performance of each fuzzy ARTMAP, first, with respect to the number of training samples only, and, second, with respect to different samples. Both of these criteria are necessary in order to measure the robustness of the classifier. The experimental procedures, based on the modified *H* and *Π* methods, are described in the following subsections the.

5.2.1 The modified H method

start;

```
    for each feature vector s_k, k = 1, 2, 3;
        for each character X_i, i = 1, 2, ..., 900;
            for each training samples n, n = 5, 10, 15, 20, 25, 30;
                select randomly n samples from (D_{s_k})_i that have not been selected previously;
                train the fuzzy ARTMAP (FMAP_{s_k})_i with the n samples;
                test (FMAP_{s_k})_i with (D_{s_k})_i^{te};
                record and accumulate the classification errors;
            end for;
        end for;
    end for;
end.
```

5.2.1 *The modified Π method*

```
start;
    for each feature vector s_k, k = 1, 2, 3;
        for each character X_i, i = 1, 2, ..., 900;
            for each training samples n, n = 5, 10, 15, 20, 25, 30;
                for each trial t = 1, 2, ..., 30;
                    select randomly n samples from (D_{s_k})_i that have not been selected previously;
                    train the fuzzy ARTMAP (FMAP_{s_k})_i with the n samples;
                    test (FMAP_{s_k})_i with (D_{s_k})_i^{te};
                    record and accumulate the classification errors;
                end for;
                calculate and accumulate the mean errors and standard deviations;
            end for;
        end for;
            calculate the average mean errors and standard deviations;
    end for;
end.
```

It should be noted that each fuzzy ARTMAP is initialized prior to every training step. The parameters of each Fuzzy ARTMAP were: $\rho = 0.92$, $\beta = 0.5$, and $\alpha = 0.01$. The epoch size and training iteration were, respectively, 16 and 2000. These parameters were determined using a small subset of the evaluation set.

The classification errors, for each character, were measured according to the Correct Classification Rate (CCR) and False Classification Rate (CRR). The CCR measures the ability of a given Fuzzy ARTMAP to recognize the samples of its respective character, whereas, the FCR measures the ability of the same Fuzzy ARTMAP to reject all other characters. Both errors, with respect to each character, are defined by the following equations:

$$CCR_i = \frac{\omega_i}{\eta_i} * 100, \; i = 1, 2, ..., 900 \tag{8}$$

where ω_i and η_i denote, respectively, the number of correctly classified samples of the *ith* character and the total number of test samples defined by equation 5. The CRR is given by:

$$CRR_i = \frac{\omega_j}{\lambda_j} * 100, \; j \neq i, \; j, i = 1, 2, ..., 900 \tag{9}$$

where ω_j and λ_j denote, respectively, the number of rejected samples of all other characters and the total number of test samples defined by the second term in equation 7. The classification errors based on the modified H and Π methods are given in tables 2, 3, 4 and 5.

6. DISCUSSION AND CONCLUSIONS

In this work we have presented a method for off-line handwritten Chinese character recognition, based on structural features and fuzzy ARTMAP neural network. From the database, three feature vectors were generated to perform the classification. The classification stage is based on modular structure, i.e., one fuzzy ARTMAP for each character. This modular structure reduces computational complexity, since there are 900 different characters, and allows the evaluation of each module separately without altering the structure of the whole system.

A close analysis of the results reveals that the *CCR* errors, based on the *H* method, are better than those based on the *Π* method. The reason for such difference is that in the *H* method, we made one selection only and, coincidentally, this selection was optimum. However, in practice this coincidence is not guaranteed to occur every time. In order to get a precise estimation of the classifier error, one must change the evaluation set several time and average the results. Therefore, the *CCR* errors based on the *H* method gives a better measure of the performance of the system. Another observation is that the performance of the Fuzzy ARTMAP increased by approximately 48% as the number of training samples increased from 5 to 15, and it remained almost constant with further increase of the training sample. This indicates that a training set of about 15 samples is sufficient to obtain good results as far as *CCR* errors are concerned. A third observation is that the *CRR* errors are very promising, which indicates that the fuzzy ARTMAP is capable of performing pattern recognition based on the one-class problem approach with satisfactorily results, if good features were used. In terms of the overall system errors, we have observed that they are approximately equivalent to those shown in tables 2-5.

With respect to the descriptive power of the feature vectors, it can be seen that s_1 and s_3 provided the best *CCR* and *CRR* results, as compared to those obtained with s_2. The reason for such difference is that the definition of s_2 as given in section 4 is not very precise. There are some cases where two different features could be considered as being one of a given feature type and, thus, introducing noise to the data.

Compared to the results of 84% obtained by Amin et al [4] with the C4.5 algorithm, the results presented here with the Fuzzy ARTMAP are approximately 9% higher. This was due, first, to the descriptive power of the feature vectors and, second, to the recognition ability of the Fuzzy ARTMAP. However, we are aware that further studies are needed to improve the *CCR* errors and the discriminative power of the feature vector s_2.

7. REFERENCES

[1] Augi T, Nagahashi H. A description method of hand printed Chinese characters. IEEE Transaction on Pattern Analysis and Machine Intelligence 1979; (1): 20-24.

[2] Yamamoto E, Fujii N, Fujita T, Ito C, and Tanahashi J. Handwritten Kanji character recognition using the features extracted from multiple standpoints. In Proceedings of the IEEE Conference of Pattern Recognition and Image Processing, IEEE Press 1981, pp 131-136.

[3] Hsieh CC, Lee HJ. Off-line recognition of handwritten Chinese characters by on-line model-guided matching. Pattern Recognition 1992; 25(11): 1337-1352.

[4] Amin A, Kim SG, and Sammut C. Handprinted Chinese Character Recognition via Machine Learning. In Proceedings of the Fourth International Conference on Document Analysis and Recognition, Vol. 1. IEEE Press, 1997, pp 190-193.

[5] Murshed NA, Bortolozzi F, and Sabourin R. Off-line signature verification without a priori knowledge of class. A new approach. In Proceedings of the Third International Conference on Document Analysis and Recognition, Vol. 1. IEEE Press, 1995, pp 191-196.
[6] _____ A Fuzzy ARTMAP-Based Classification System for Detecting Cancerous Cells Based on the One-Class Problem Approach. In Proceedings of 13th International Conference on Pattern Recognition,Vol. 4, IEEE Press, 1996, pp 478-482.
[7] _____ The use of neural networks for classification of cancerous cells based on the one-class problem approach. In Proceedings of the International Congress on Neuronal Information Processing, Vol. 2, Springer Verlag 1996, pp 1146-1151.
[8] _____ A Cognitive Approach to Off-line Signature verification. In Automatic Bankcheck Processing, Sebastiano I, Patrick SPW and Horst B (Eds.), Vol. 28, World Scientific, 1997, pp 339 363.
[9] Murshed NA, and Bortolozzi F. A Fuzzy ARTMAP Module for Graphics Symbol Recognition. In Proceedings of the International Joint Conference on Neural Networks, Vol. 3, IEEE Press, 1998, pp 1700-1705.
[10] Murshed NA, de Carvalho AC, Aires RF, and Oishii S. Detection of Carcinoma with the Fuzzy ARTMAP NN. To appear in the Proceedings of the Second International Conference on Cognitive and Neural Systems, Boston University Press 1998.
[11] Carpenter G, Grossberg S, Markuzon N, Reynolds J, Rosen D. Fuzzy ARTMAP: A neural network architecture for incremental supervised learning of analog multidimensional maps. IEEE Transaction on Neural Networks 1992; 3(5): 698-713.
[12] Moore B. ART 1 and pattern clustering. In Proceedings of the Connectionist Models Summer School, 1988, pp 174-185.
[13] Toussaint G. Bibliography on Estimation of Misclassification. IEEE Transaction on Information Theory 1974; IT-20(4): 472-479.

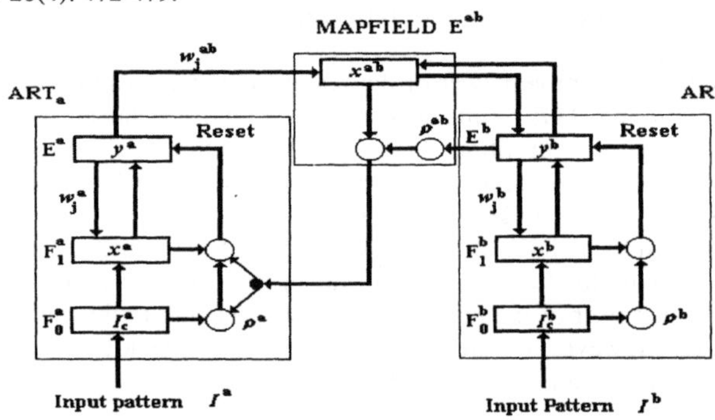

Figure 1. Architecture of the Fuzzy ARTMAP neural network [8].

Primitive	—	/	❚	\	┐	●
Name (*symbol*)	Horizontal (C_1)	Slash (C_2)	Vertical (C_3)	Backslash (C_4)	Corner (C_5)	Dot (C_6)

Table 1. Structural features.

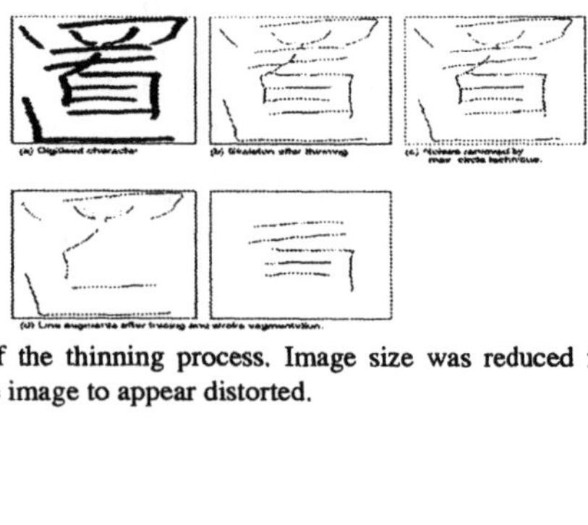

Figure 2. Results of the thinning process. Image size was reduced for space constraint. This has caused the image to appear distorted.

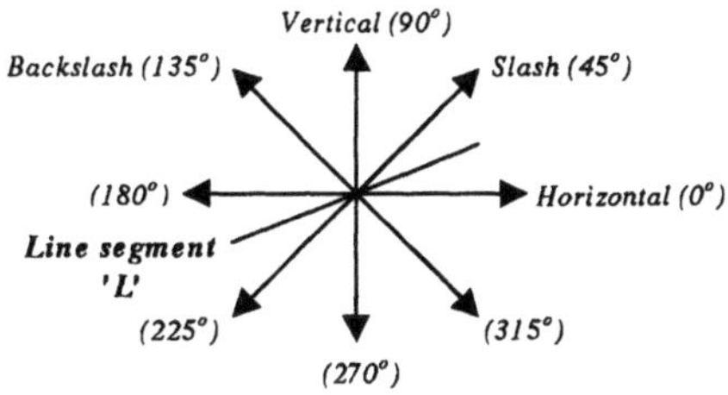

Figure 3. An example of a line that can be considered *horizontal* or a *slash*.

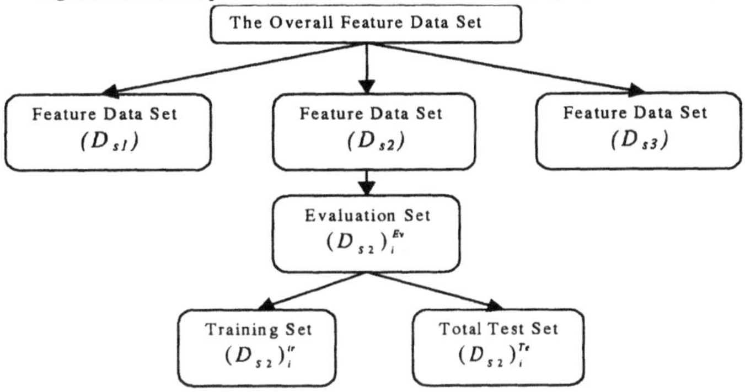

Figure 4. Devision of the ovearll feature data set. The overall feature data set is divided into three feature data subsets according to the type of the feature vector. For each character i, $i=1, 2, \ldots, 900$, an evaluation set is generated from each feature database. The evaluation set is composed of two disjoint sets: one for training and one for test. The definitions of these two sets are given in section 5.1.1.

	# of Training Samples					
	5	10	15	20	25	30
S1	55.48	91.34	99.34	99.26	99.28	99.64
S2	48.16	90.14	99.20	99.22	99.23	99.26
S3	50.02	90.17	99.12	99.21	99.21	99.24

Table 2. Average classification erros, in terms of CCR, based on the H method. S1, S2 and S3 are the feature vectors described in section 4. All CCR values are in percentage.

	# of Training Samples					
	5	10	15	20	25	30
S1	98.87	98.76	97.72	97.75	97.84	98.12
S2	97.26	95.69	96.19	96.16	96.31	96.93
S3	99.37	99.4	99.4	99.4	99.4	99.4

Table 3. Average classification erros, in terms of CRR, based on the H method. S1, S2 and S3 are the feature vectors described in section 4. All CRR values are in percentage.

	# of Training Samples					
Feature Vectors	5	10	15	20	25	30
S1	46.23 ± 2.3	82.13 ± 1.99	93.34 ± 0.83	93.45 ± 0.55	93.67 ± 0.21	93.88 ± 0.03
S2	38.76 ± 3.10	80.95 ± 2.86	85.28 ± 1.05	88.85 ± 1.17	90.67 ± 1.01	90.17 ± 1.12
S3	44.57 ± 2.99	81.13 ± 1.99	92.29 ± 0.79	92.30 ± 0.42	92.33 ± 0.18	92.19 ± 0.08

Table 4. Average mean classification erros with convidence interval, in terms of CCR, based on the Π method. All values are in percent.

	# of Training Samples					
Feature Vectors	5	10	15	20	25	30
S1	96.23 ± 0.23	97.78 ± 0.87	98.22 ± 0.51	98.32 ± 0.50	98.56 ± 0.52	98.23 ± 0.15
S2	96.01 ± 0.45	96.65 ± 1.1	97.38 ± 0.99	97.87 ± 1.04	98.01 ± 0.44	98.1 ± 0.83
S3	97.85 ± 0.03	98.65 ± 0.67	98.78 ± 0.11	99.11 ± 0.27	99.37 ± 0.62	99.49 ± 0.25

Table 5. Average mean classification erros with convidence interval, in terms of CRR, based on the Π method. All values are in percent.

AGENT-BASED TEXT EXTRACTION FROM PYRAMID IMAGES

Chew Lim Tan, Bo Yuan, Chuan Heng Ang
School of Computing
National University of Singapore
Kent Ridge
Singapore 119260

ABSTRACT

A system using multiple agents working on a pyramid structure to do text extraction is described in this paper. The method is based on the observation that text strings appear as different groupings of connected components at appropriate resolutions. The pyramid structure, which is a multi-resolution image representation, is amenable to parallel processing for detection of text strings. Agents in the system individually and concurrently look for groups of connected components at appropriate levels. They may in turn spawn new agents when connected components become disjointed at finer resolution levels. The agent-based pyramidal operations do not require expensive feature analysis among different connected components to detect text strings as found in other existing works.

1. INTRODUCTION

An old adage that "A picture is worth a thousand words" is true to the human eyes but is unfortunately far from the reality to the computer. Today, computer vision research is still facing great challenges in understanding graphical images. Any words that can be found in an image by the computer will certainly assist in the understanding of the image or at least in allowing some kind of image classification. Text string extraction thus will find applications in fax routing, map understanding, news article search from microfilms, etc.

Existing techniques used in text string extraction generally fall into two categories: run-length smoothing [1, 2] and connected component analysis [3-5]. The work reported in [1] assumes that at an appropriate low resolution, a text line looks like a long linear component and at the same time at the next higher resolution, it looks like a more or less regular sequence of transitions. A multi-resolution image structure is used to extract linear sequences of address lines from flat mail pieces. Reference [2], on the other hand, describes a block segmentation algorithm, which subdivides and classifies an image into sub-regions called blocks. Ideally, each block should contain only one type of object, that is either text or graphics. Unfortunately, this broad classification causes text characters which are in a predominantly graphics region to be wrongly labeled as graphics.

The other category of text strings extraction methods relies on the analysis of features of eight-connected components and mutual relationships between adjacent components. Reference [3] uses Hough Transform to detect the set of connected components that lie along a given straight line. Thereafter, properties such as inter-character gap and inter-word gap are used to segment the text block into logical words and phrases. Reference [4], on the other hand, requires some form of pre-processing to build a data structure to allow computation of an Euclidean radius of each connected component. Thereafter, the minimum radius of a group of components must be determined before a way to cluster characters and words can be performed. A multi-stage relaxation technique is used in reference [5] to iteratively go through a labeling process to finally fix the labels of all connected components based on their mutual relationship with neighboring components. The labels further allow grouping of coherently labeled neighboring components. The groupings of these components then go through a new stage of relaxation process, and hence it is called multi-stage relaxation.

Existing methods suffer from either or both of the following problems: (1) The necessity to assume some linear arrangement of characters, which may fail in cases where characters are clustered in some ways rather than just linear sequencing. (2) The computational cost in dealing with individual characters at the full resolution level to find inter-character relationships.

The present method makes use of a pyramid structure similar to the multi-resolution strategy used in [1]. However, instead of detecting linear sequences of text strings, the pyramid is used here to facilitate connected component analysis. Also, the use of pyramid eliminates the need to do expensive process of analyzing inter-component relationship. The present work reported in this paper is an extension of an earlier attempt to use pyramid for text extraction [6]. The present work adopts a different approach to pyramid operations, namely, the use of multiple agents. Furthermore, the previous work requires manual determination of an appropriate pyramid level to proceed with the connected component analysis for the entire image. In the new system, agents can individually determine their own levels to work with.

The next section will first introduce the pyramid structure used in the present work. Section 3 will then describe how multiple agents work among different levels of the pyramid to opportunistically look for connected components. Section 4 will present experimental results of two examples. Section 5 discusses the results in comparison with the earlier work and other existing methods. The final section will conclude the paper with a discussion on future enhancements.

2. THE PYRAMID

A pyramid can be visualized as a sequence of two-dimensional arrays, representing the same image in less and less detail from the base to the top of the pyramid. While various kinds of pyramids have been proposed including their irregular variants [7], a traditional pyramid such as that is used in the present work entails basically a reduction of the dimensions of the arrays by half at each step of progression from the base of the pyramid to its top. Mathematically, such a pyramid may be defined as a set P of cells together with a function F that assigns a value v to each cell. Thus

$$P = ((v, k, i, j) \mid 0 \leq k \leq L ; 0 \leq i, j \leq 2^k - 1 ; v = F(k, i, j)) \qquad (1)$$

is a pyramid of $L + 1$ levels, whose pixel (v, k, i, j) at level k contains the value $v = F(k, i, j)$. The function F determines how a pyramid level is formed from the level immediately below. In the present work, a so-called *binary-pyramid* or *bit-pyramid* [8] is constructed where the value in each cell is either 0 or 1. The function F at level k is the maximum cell value the four descendant cells at level $k + 1$, i.e. except for the base level (level L) whose cells' values are the same as the original binary image, a cell at level k will have a value 1 if any of its four descendant cells at level $K+1$ has a value 1. Otherwise, the cell will have value 0.

$$F(k,i,j) = \begin{cases} \max\limits_{p=0}^{p=1} \max\limits_{q=0}^{q=1} F(k+1, 2i+p, 2j+q) & \mathit{if} \quad 0 \le k \le L \\ \mathit{binary\_value}(L,i,j) & \mathit{if} \quad k = L \end{cases} \tag{2}$$

The beauty of the multi-resolution structure of the pyramid lies in its natural capability in grouping characters and words in the text strings at appropriate resolution levels to permit extraction as a whole without the expensive computation in finding inter-character and inter-word relations. Furthermore, just as the human vision is able to simultaneously examine text strings of different sizes at different locations in an image, multiple agents in the system can individually and concurrently analyze different text regions of various sizes in the image by independently navigating the different resolution levels in the pyramid.

3. AGENT-BASED PYRAMID OPERATIONS

Before the pyramid is constructed, the digitized and thresholded image is first pre-processed to remove big graphics objects from the image. This is necessary as big and obvious graphics object will ultimately touch and join textual objects during the pyramid construction, thereby making it impossible for text extraction. An effective filter to exclude the graphics connected components is given by the area versus frequency of occurrence histogram [3]. This histogram is built as each connected component is analyzed. The connected component area that is most common then becomes the area filter. This is reasonable since the text characters are almost similarly sized. Connected components whose sizes lie outside the permissible range of the area filter are then removed. This process will not only remove large graphics objects but also tiny patches including noise. The filter also rejects long and big objects that are usually not text characters. With the removal of big graphics objects, the system computes the average values of height, width and area of the remaining connected graphics. These values serve as appropriate filter values for subsequent text extraction. Furthermore, as each higher level is created, connected components in that level are formed at the same time such that each level maintains a data structure containing information of the set of connected components in that level (e.g. locations, areas, bounding boxes, etc.).

After the pre-processing, a 10-level pyramid is constructed from the base, i.e. level 9 (512×512) to the top, i.e. level 0 (1×1). The only one pixel at the top will always contain the value 1 by virtue of the construction process given in equations 1 and 2 (unless the whole image contains nothing after the removal big graphics, in which case no agent operation will be initiated). This only pixel thus represents the connected component formed through compression of all objects in the levels below.

Agents in the system are basically an image processing routine that looks for clusters of connected components that are potentially text strings. Each agent works on a particular pyramid resolution level but may spawn child agents to proceed to descend to lower pyramid levels. At the beginning, there is only one agent which starts working on this one and only connected component at level 0 (1×1) and proceeds to descend to lower levels. In each descent, the agent examines whether the connected component in the earlier level has now become disjointed through expansion of resolution. If so, a clustering process is done based on the nearest neighbors and areas of components to cluster components that are in close proximity into clusters [4]. Some components may have no close neighbor and will become the only component in its own cluster. The single component cluster will be subjected to further agent processing at the level below to see if the component will split at next finer resolution. On the other hand, for multiple component clusters, each component is deemed is to be a logical grouping of possible text elements. Such components will be individually subjected to a test operation.

The test operation is done on a connected component by examining the component's image at full resolution to determine whether any part of the image should be considered a graphics object or a text object. The test entails the application of a set of filters (area and dimensions filters). Any parts that are deemed graphics objects will be removed. The remainder portion of the component's image then constitute the logical grouping of characters which form the words and phrases to be extracted as a whole. Figure 1 shows the pseudo-code of the agent-based pyramid operations on component n at pyramid level k. Note also that the agent and the test operations initiated within the **parallel-do** can run on their own in parallel.

4. EXPERIMENTAL RESULTS

Figures 2 and 3 show two full resolution images, respectively. After pre-processing to remove big graphics objects, two pyramid image structures are formed as shown in figures 4 and 5. Only 5 levels including the base are shown in both figures as higher levels will be too small to visualize.

Agent-based pyramid operations then proceed to work on the pyramid images and extract text strings accordingly as shown in figures 6 and 7. In figure 6, a numeric symbol 1 is erroneously treated as a graphics object and hence not extracted. In figure 7, on the other hand, one graphics object below the phrase "Hua Yi Pr. Sch." escapes detection as a graphics object and is treated as part of the text string.

Figure 8 shows the generation of agents during the pyramid operations on the two images. For image 1, the initial agent traverses down to level 4 and spawns five new agents to work on five connected components at level 5. Four of the five agents stop their descent at level 5, and the fifth agent turns itself into six new agents to work on level 6. While four of the six agents stop at level 6, the remaining two agents generate two and three new agents, respectively, to descend to level 7. Altogether 13 agents are produced in the process, identifying 13 logical groupings of text strings at levels between levels 5 and 7. Similar process occurs for image 2 resulting in also 13 agents which stop at either level 5 or level 6.

```
Agent (level k, component n);
begin
        if k = L
        then Test (level k, component n)
        else begin
                descend to level k+1;
                if component remains as one whole component
                    at level k+1
                    then Agent (level k+1, component n)
                    else begin
                            Cluster all components to m clusters, some
                            of which may contain only one component
                            for i = 1 to m parallel-do
                                if cluster i contains only one component j
                                    then Agent (level k+1, component j)
                                    else for each component j in cluster i
                                        Test (level k+1, component j)
                        end;
            end;
end.
```

Figure 1. Pseudo-code of agent-based pyramid operations.

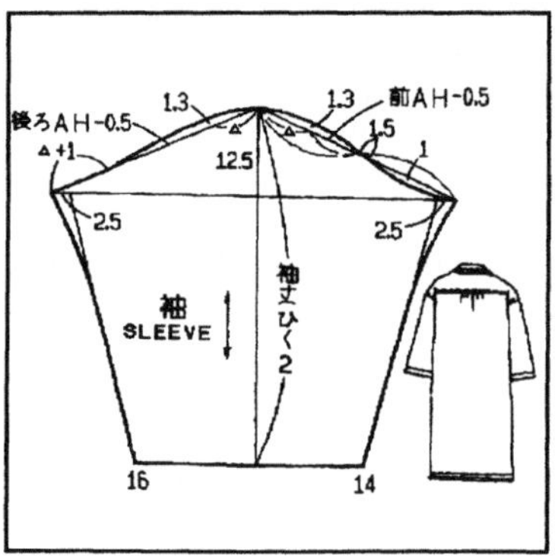

Figure 2. Input image 1 (512 × 512)

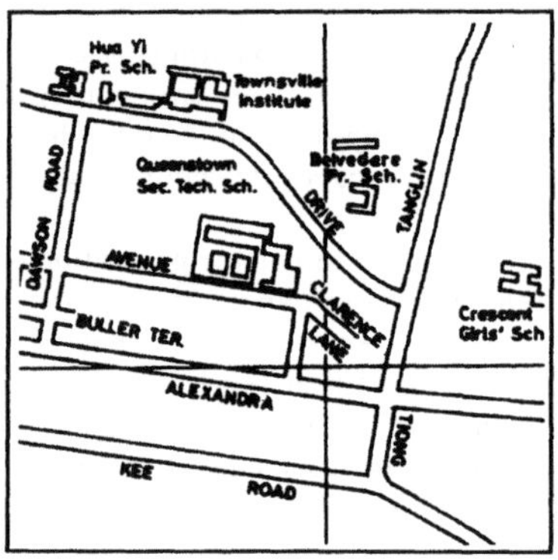

Figure 3. Input image 2 (512 × 512)

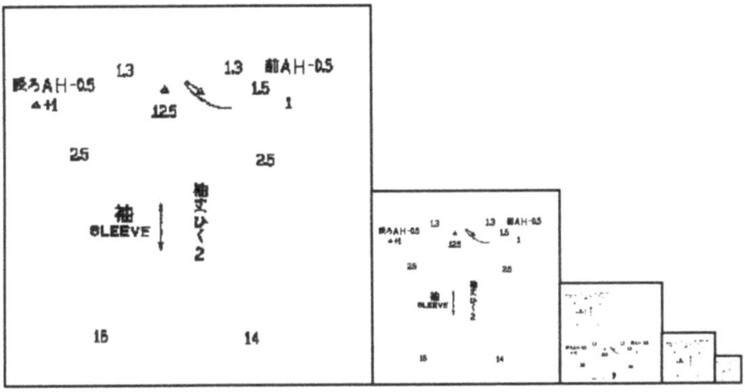

Figure 4. Pyramid for input image 1 after removal of large graphics objects

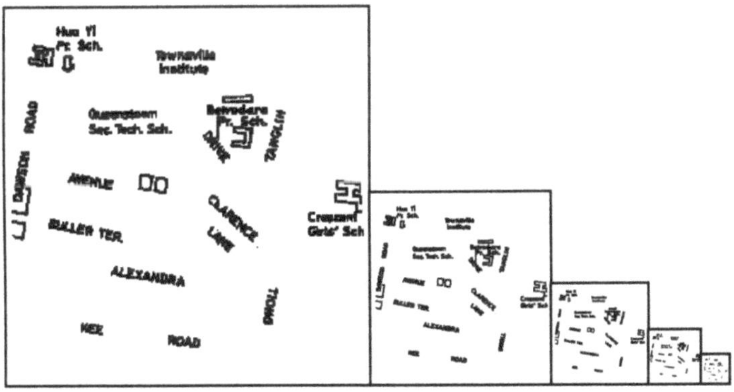

Figure 5. Pyramid for input image 2 after removal of large graphics objects

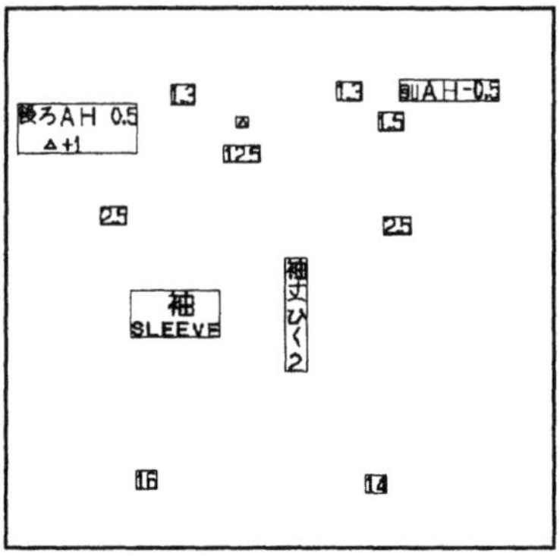

Figure 6. Text extracted from image 1.

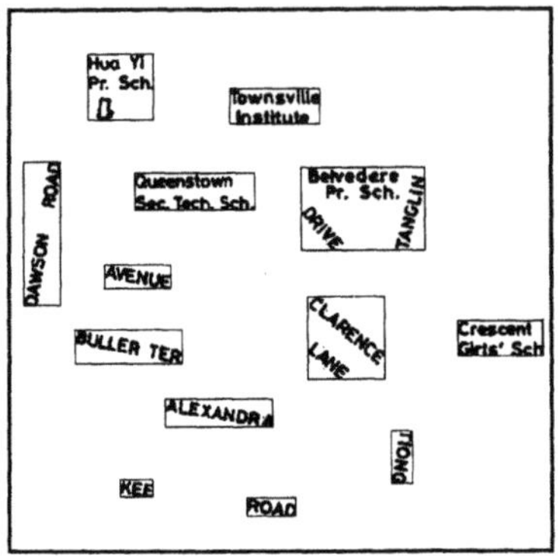

Figure 7. Text extracted from image 2.

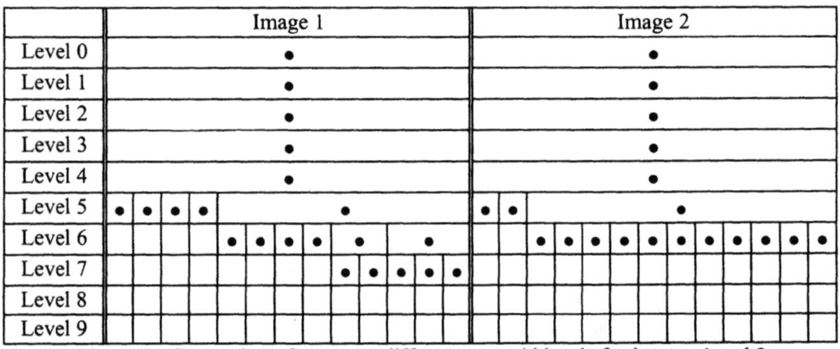

Figure 8. Generation of agents at different pyramid levels for images 1 and 2

5. DISCUSSION

Table 1 shows the number of connected components at full resolution and the number of connected components actually processed by the agents for images 1 and 2. It shows that through the pyramid structure, the number of inter-component processing has been reduced.

	Image 1	Image 2
No. of connected components at full resolution	159	58
No. of connected components processed by the agents	13	13

Table 1. No. of connected components processed

In comparison with the earlier work without the use of agents where the entire pyramid operation was handled by a single process. With the agents implemented in the present work, the processing is now distributed. Assuming parallel implementation is possible, the actual processing time will be reduced with agents running concurrently. Table 2 shows the processing time in terms of CPU ticks for various processes. The connected component generation and pyramid construction is part of the preprocessing needed. The time for text string extraction (which includes time needed for the analysis of connected components) taken by a typical agent is compared with that by the earlier work with a single central process that handles all the text strings in the pyramid.

	Image 1	Image 2
Connected components generation	1150	610
Pyramid construction	330	330
Text string extraction in earlier system (central processing)	1710	720
Text string extraction by an agent in present system (distributed processing)	310	270

Table 2. Performance measure in CPU ticks

The present agent-based pyramid approach has the following strengths: (1) It works at a reduced resolution image and hence lesser numbers of connected components , and (2) the agents adopt a divide-conquer strategy to distribute work load as necessary. The only extra cost needed over the other methods is the pyramid construction which, however, does not constitute a major cost as shown in Table 2. This process is only a one-time cost as part of the preprocessing of the image and will be needed in subsequent pyramid traversal by the agents.

6. CONCLUSION

A system based on the concept of concurrent multiple agents working on a pyramid structure for text extraction from graphical images is proposed. The system does not require expensive computation of inter-component relationship as found in existing works which are based on single process and single resolution. The groupings of text strings need not be in linear sequences as required in some previous works. The agents in the system are autonomous and are able to extract groups of text strings on their own as they navigate the pyramid levels.

A current limitation with the system is that it requires text strings not to be in contact with graphics objects, which is the same assumption adopted in other works based on connected component analysis. However, the pyramid structure holds promise to resolve this problem in our future work. This is based on the observation that text strings appear as regular sequences of transition at a certain resolution as opposed to large graphics objects that remain uniform with changes of resolution. A two-pass pyramid process will be adopted to identify and eliminate large graphics objects before the present agent-based operations proceed.

REFERENCES

[1] Olivier D and Dominique B. A robust and multiscale document image segmentation for block line/text line structures extraction. Twelfth International Conference on Pattern Recognition, Jerusalem, 1994, pp 306-309.

[2] Wahl FM, Wong KY and Casey RG. Block segmentation and text extraction in mixed text/image documents. Computer Graphics and Image Processing, 1982; 20: 375-390.

[3] Fletcher LA and Kasturi R. A robust algorithm for text string separation from mixed text/graphics images. IEEE Transactions on Pattern Analysis Machine Intelligence, 1998; 10(6): 910-918.

[4] He S, Abe N and Tan CL. A clustering-based approach to the separation of text strings from mixed text/graphics documents. Thirteenth International Conference on Pattern Recognition, Austria, 25-29, August 1996, pp 706-710.

[5] Hase H, Shinokawa T, Yoneda M, Sakai M and Maruyama H. Character string extraction by multi-stage relaxation. Fourth International Conference on Document Analysis and Recognition, 18-20 August 1997, pp 298-302.

[6] Tan CL and Ng PO. Text extraction using pyramid. Pattern Recognition, 1998; 31(1): 63-72.

[7] Kropatsch WG. Properties of pyramidal representations. Computing Suppl., 1996; 11: 99-111.

[8] Tanimoto SL. Pictorial feature distortion in a pyramid. Computer Graphics and Image Procesing, 1976; 5: 333-352.

PATTERN RECOGNITION

VECTOR QUANTIZATION AND MINIMUM DESCRIPTION LENGTH*

Horst Bischof, Pattern Recognition & Image Processing Group,
Vienna University of Technology, A-1040 Vienna, Austria

Aleš Leonardis, Faculty of Computer & Information Science,
University of Ljubljana, SI-1001 Ljubljana, Slovenia

In this paper we address the problem of finding the optimal number of reference vectors in vector quantization from the point of view of the Minimum Description Length (MDL) principle. We formulate the VQ in terms of the MDL principle, and then derive depending on the coding procedure different instantiations of the algorithm. Moreover, we develop an efficient algorithm (similar to EM-type algorithms) for optimizing the MDL criterion. In addition we can use the MDL principle to increase the robustness of the training algorithm. In order to visualize the behavior of the algorithm, we illustrate our approach on 2D clustering problems and present applications on image coding. Finally we outline various ways to extend the algorithm.

1 INTRODUCTION

A common goal of unsupervised learning algorithms is to distribute a certain number of reference (weight) vectors in a possibly high dimensional space according to some quality criteria. This is also called Vector Quantization. In this paper we consider the following problem: Given a finite data set $S = \{\mathbf{x}_1, \ldots, \mathbf{x}_n\}, \mathbf{x}_i \in \mathbb{R}^d$, where $\mathbf{x}_i$ are independently and identically distributed (iid) according to some probability distribution $p(\mathbf{x})$, find a set of reference vectors $A = \{\mathbf{c}_1, \ldots, \mathbf{c}_m\}, \mathbf{c}_i \in \mathbb{R}^d$ such that a given distortion measure $E(p(\mathbf{x}), A)$ is minimized. A typical application is, for example, to compress a set of vectors for transmission purpose. This can be achieved by minimizing the expected quantization error

$$E(S, A) = \sum_{i=1}^{m} \sum_{\mathbf{x} \in S_i} ||\mathbf{x} - \mathbf{c}_i||^2, \tag{1}$$

where $S_i = \{\mathbf{x} \in S | i = \arg\min_{j \in \{1,\ldots,m\}} ||\mathbf{x} - \mathbf{c}_j||\}$ is the Voronoi region of a vector $\mathbf{c}_i$.

Many different algorithms have been proposed to find the reference vectors $\mathbf{c}_i$ for the case when their number m is given, e.g., the well-known K-means and Linde-Buzo-Gray (LBG) algorithms [2]. Also, various neural network models have been proposed which can be used for vector quantization, e.g., hard-, soft-competitive learning, neural

*This work was supported by a grant from the Austrian National Fonds zur Förderung der wissenschaftlichen Forschung (No. S7002MAT). A. L. also acknowledges the support from the Ministry of Science and Technology of Republic of Slovenia (Projects J2-8829 and J2-0414).

gas networks, and networks with topological connectivity like Kohonen's self organizing feature maps (see [3] for a recent review on this topic). All these methods assume that the number of reference vectors is *a priori* given. However, finding the "right" number of clusters m remains an important open question. Depending on the complexity of the data distribution, a very different number of clusters may be appropriate. The methods mentioned above require a decision on the number of clusters in advance, and if the result is not satisfying, new simulations have to be performed from scratch. Various heuristics have been proposed to deal with this problem; e.g. ISODATA [2] and scale space clustering [11] are examples from pattern recognition literature. Some neural network algorithms have also been extended to include a mechanism for adding reference vectors during training, e.g., growing cells structures, growing neural gas, etc. (see [3] for an overview). In these methods, the stopping criterion (i.e., when to stop adding units) is crucial for finding the right number of reference vectors. Usually, the growing of the network is stopped when a prespecified performance bound is reached, which is difficult to set a priori, especially if the clusters have unequal distributions. In order to find the right number of reference vectors, an interesting approach was recently proposed by Xu [12]. Xu developed the Ying-Yang machine, which can be seen as a pruning method (i.e., units are removed from an overly complex network). As a pruning criterion he trades-off the error versus the number of reference vectors.

Another problem closely related to finding the optimal number of reference vectors is the problem of outliers. Suppose that in the training set S there are additional data points not belonging to the distribution $p(\mathbf{x})$ (the so called outliers). Ideally one would reject these outliers such that they have no effect on the result of the vector quantization. However, all of the above mentioned algorithms can not deal with this issue. Especially the incremental algorithms tend to add additional reference vectors for the outliers.

In this paper we address the problem of finding the optimal number of reference vectors in vector quantization and the problem of outliers from the point of view of the Minimum Description Length (MDL) principle [10, 9]. MDL has already been applied in the area of neural networks, see e.g. [13, 4, 6, 8]. In most cases, MDL has been used for supervised networks as a penalty term on the error function or as a criterion for network selection. One exception is the work of Hinton and Zemel [5] who applied the MDL principle to autoassociative networks using stochastic binary units. However, the main goal of this work was not to find the size of the network but to determine a suitable encoding of the data.

Our approach has the following distinctive features: We use the MDL principle to reject outliers and as a pruning criterion in an integral scheme: We start with an overly complex network, and while training the network, we gradually reduce its size, arriving at a network which balances the error versus the number of reference vectors. By combining the reduction of complexity and the training phase, we achieve a computationally efficient procedure.

We organize the paper as follows. In the next section we derive the MDL formulation for vector quantization. From this formulation we derive the pruning criterion, which is used together with a training phase to design the complete algorithm. Section 3 shows the experimental results; we illustrate our approach on 2D clustering problems and present applications on image coding. Section 4 presents conclusions and outlines venues of further research.

2 ROBUST VECTOR QUANTIZATION IN AN MDL FRAMEWORK

We approach the problem of vector quantization as the minimization of the length of the description of the training data S (S is, in fact, the only information available to us). A convenient way to derive the MDL formulation is via a communication game. Assume that our goal is to transfer the data S without error to a receiver, and that we have agreed beforehand on a communication protocol. Let us further assume that we have already identified which vectors are outliers, and are therefore not coded by the reference vectors, i.e., $I = S - O$, where O are the outliers and I are the inliers. Using the reference vectors A, the length of encoding S is then given by:

1. The length of encoding the reference vectors A, denoted by $L(A)$.
2. The length of encoding I using A, which can be subdivided into the following two costs:
   (a) The length of encoding the index of A to which the vectors in I have been assigned, denoted by $L(I(A))$, and
   (b) the length of encoding the residual errors, denoted by $L(\epsilon(I_A))$.
3. The length of encoding the outliers, denoted by $L(O)$.

Therefore, the cost of encoding S using A is given by

$$L(S(A)) = L(A) + L(I(A)) + L(\epsilon(I_A)) + L(O). \tag{2}$$

Our goal is to minimize $L(S)$, i.e., determine O, m, and $\mathbf{c}_i, 1 \leq i \leq m$, such that $L(S(A))$ is minimal.

In order to simplify the subsequent derivation and notation we make the following assumptions:

1. All quantities are specified with a finite precision η, in particular we assume that the vectors in the training set and the reference vectors are represented by K bits[1].
2. The samples in S are independently and identically (iid) distributed, which means that $p(\mathbf{x}, \mathbf{y}) = p(\mathbf{x})p(\mathbf{y}), \mathbf{x}, \mathbf{y} \in S$.

Using these assumptions we can rewrite Eq. (2) in the following form:

$$L(S(A)) = mK + L(I(A)) + \sum_{i=1}^{m} \sum_{\mathbf{x} \in S_i} L(||\mathbf{x} - \mathbf{c}_i||) + |O|K. \tag{3}$$

Let us first consider the outliers O: Given a reference vector set A, those data points from S are considered as outliers, according to the MDL principle, which can be encoded with less bits directly, i.e., without having a vector quantizing them. More precisely, a data point is an outlier if the encoding of this data point by the index of a reference

[1]Note that this parameter η can be used as a scale parameter. At a fine scale, each data point in S is in a separate cluster, at a coarser scale (corresponding to a low precision η), all data points might fall into a single cluster.

vector and the error yields a higher number of bits, than coding the data point as it is. Therefore, a data point $\mathbf{x} \in S_i$ assigned to reference vector i is an outlier if

$$K < L(i(A)) + L(||\mathbf{x} - \mathbf{c}_i||) + \mathcal{I}_{|S_i|=1}K \ , \tag{4}$$

where $\mathcal{I}_{|S_i|=1} = \begin{cases} 1 & : \ |S_i| = 1 \\ 0 & : \ \text{otherwise} \end{cases}$ is the indicator function, indicating that $\mathbf{x}$ is the only data point assigned to cluster i.

Our next step is to calculate the change in $L(S(A))$ when we remove a reference vector $\mathbf{c}_j$ from A, i.e.,

$$\Delta L_{\mathbf{c}_j} = L(S(A)) - L(S(A - \{\mathbf{c}_j\})) \ .$$

Our goal is to remove those reference vectors which decrease the description length, i.e., $\Delta L_{\mathbf{c}_j} > 0$. We can estimate $\Delta L_{\mathbf{c}_j}$, according to

$$\Delta \hat{L}_{\mathbf{c}_j} = K + L(I(A)) - L(I(A - \{\mathbf{c}_j\})) + \sum_{\mathbf{x} \in S_j} (L(||\mathbf{x} - \mathbf{c}_j||) - L(\epsilon_{(-j)}(\mathbf{x}))) \ , \tag{5}$$

where $\epsilon_{(-j)}(\mathbf{x})$ is the error caused by the data point $\mathbf{x}$ when the reference vector $\mathbf{c}_j$ is removed from A, i.e. $\epsilon_{(-j)}(\mathbf{x}) = ||\mathbf{x} - \mathbf{c}_k||$, $k = \arg\min_{i=\{1,\ldots j-1, j+1,\ldots,m\}} ||\mathbf{x} - \mathbf{c}_i||$. $\Delta \hat{L}_{\mathbf{c}_j}$ is only an estimate of $\Delta L_{\mathbf{c}_j}$ because Eq. (5) does not take into account the possibility that by removing a reference vector some points may become outliers. However, it can easily be shown (by the definition of an outlier Eq. (4)) that $\Delta \hat{L}_{\mathbf{c}_j} \leq \Delta L_{\mathbf{c}_j}$, therefore we can guarantee that the reference vectors that are removed at this stage definitely decrease the description length. The condition that all reference vectors with $\Delta L_{\mathbf{c}_j} > 0$ are removed can be guaranteed by the iterative nature of the complete algorithm (see section 2.2).

The above derivation holds for the removal of a single reference vector. However, we can prove that all non-neighboring reference vectors with $\Delta \hat{L}_{\mathbf{c}_j} > 0$ can be removed in parallel[2]. The argument goes as follows: Let us consider two non-neighboring reference vectors $\mathbf{c}_i$, $\mathbf{c}_j$ for which holds that $\Delta \hat{L}_{\mathbf{c}_i} > 0$, $\Delta \hat{L}_{\mathbf{c}_j} > 0$. Without loss of generality we have to show that by removal of $\mathbf{c}_i$, $\Delta \hat{L}_{\mathbf{c}_i,\mathbf{c}_j} > 0$, which guarantees that the reference vectors that are removed at this stage definitely decrease the description length. Since the reference vectors $\mathbf{c}_i$, $\mathbf{c}_j$ are non-neighbors, the error term in Eq. (5) does not change, nor does the first term of the same equation. Therefore, it is sufficient to show that $L(I(A-\{\mathbf{c}_j\})) > L(I(A-\{\mathbf{c}_i, \mathbf{c}_j\}))$. This condition can easily be verified for the encodings of the index terms as specified in the next section. In fact, we can not think of any reasonable encoding for which this condition would not be satisfied. Therefore, we can conjecture that all non-neighboring reference vectors with $\Delta \hat{L}_{\mathbf{c}_j} > 0$ can be removed in parallel. In particular we use a greedy algorithm to select the reference vectors for removal. More specifically, under the condition that the neighborhood constrained is not violated, we always select the reference vector with the largest gain first.

2.1 INSTANTIATIONS OF THE MDL-ALGORITHM

Until now we presented the problem of vector quantization in an MDL framework on a general level without specifying the actual coding procedure for the indices and the errors.

[2]Two reference vectors are defined as neighbors when at least for one sample $\mathbf{x}$, one of the reference vectors is closest and the other one is second closest.

Depending on the particular type of encoding, we can calculate various instantiations of the algorithm.

We consider for the index term $L(I(A))$ and for the error term $L(||\mathbf{x}-\mathbf{c}_i||)$ two different types of practically relevant encodings:

$L(I(A))$:

1. A simple type of encoding is to use a fixed length code for each reference vector index; therefore $L(I(A)) = n\log_2(m)$. The decrease in coding length for the index term is then $n(\log_2(m) - \log_2(m-1))$.
2. We code the indices with the optimal variable length code according to their probability of occurrence, i.e., $p_i = n_i/n$. Then $L(I(A)) = -\sum_{i=1}^{m} n_i \log_2 p_i$, and the change in the length of encoding when $\mathbf{c}_j$ is removed can be approximated[3] as, $-n_j \log_2 n_j + \sum_{k=1,k\neq j}^{m} n_{jk} \log_2(\frac{n_k+n_{jk}}{n})$, where n_{jk} is the number of vectors which have the reference vector j as their nearest and k as their second nearest reference vector.

$L(||\mathbf{x}-\mathbf{c}_i||)$:

1. Assuming no prior knowledge on the error distribution and a required accuracy (i.e., quantization) of η, the error $\epsilon(\mathbf{x}) = ||\mathbf{x}-\mathbf{c}_i||$ has to be encoded for each component separately, i.e., $L(\epsilon(\mathbf{x})) = \sum_{j=1}^{d} \max(\log_2(\frac{|x_j - c_{i_j}|}{\eta}), 1)$. Assuming that on the average the error is the same in each dimension, we can simplify the above expression and calculate the change in the error for the removal of the reference vector $\mathbf{c}_j$ as $d\sum_{\mathbf{x}\in S_j} \log_2(\frac{\epsilon(\mathbf{x})}{\epsilon_{(-j)}(\mathbf{x})})$.
2. If we assume a particular distribution $p(\epsilon(\mathbf{x}))$ for the error, we can encode the error using this distribution, i.e., $L(\epsilon(\mathbf{x})) = \log_2(p(\epsilon(\mathbf{x})))$. For example, if we assume a Gaussian distribution with zero mean and a fixed variance of σ^2 in each dimension, the length of encoding the error term is then given by $L(\epsilon(\mathbf{x})) = \sum_{i=1}^{d} \frac{\epsilon(x_i)^2}{2\ln(2)\sigma^2} + d\log_2(\sqrt{2\pi}\sigma) - d\log_2(\eta)$. The change in the error term is then given by $\sum_{\mathbf{x}\in S_j} \sum_{i=1}^{d} \frac{(x_i-c_{ij})^2-(x_i-c_{ik})^2}{2\ln(2)\sigma^2}$. Here we have assumed that the variance σ^2 is constant and known to the sender and receiver. However we could also estimate the variance for each reference vector and include it in the transmission as part of the description of the reference vector. In this case the cost of coding a reference vector will be increased (first term in Eq. (5)).

We can now specify different instantiations of the outlier condition (Eq. (4)) and the conditions for the removal of a reference vector according to Eq. (5)), by replacing the appropriate terms with the above derived equations.

2.2 Complete Algorithm

Having derived the conditions for the removal of superfluous reference vectors and for identifying the outliers, we now formulate the complete algorithm, which is schematically shown in Fig. 1.

[3] In order to calculate this quantity, we made the following approximation $\log_2(n_k) \approx \log_2(n_k + n_{jk})$.

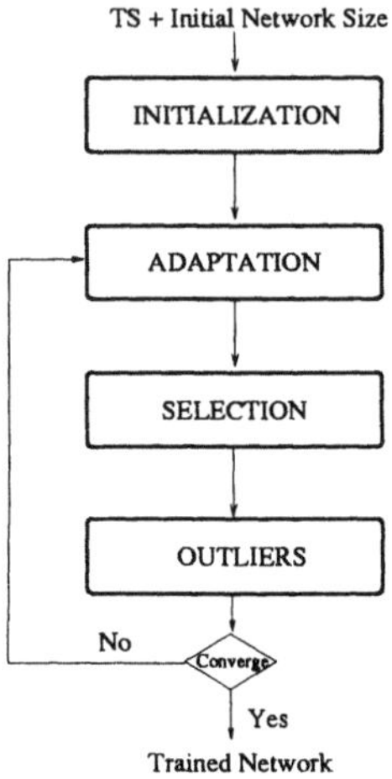

Figure 1: Complete Algorithm.

Step 1 *Initialization:* Initialize the vector quantization network with a large number of reference vectors, e.g., by randomly drawing samples from S, and using them as reference vectors. Initially $I = S$.

Step 2 *Adaptation:* Use an unsupervised algorithm to adapt the reference vectors using the inliers I. In principle, any clustering algorithm can be used [3]. It is also important to note that we do not need to train the network to convergence because we compare the reference vectors on a relative basis (see discussion below).

Step 3 *Selection:* Remove the superfluous reference vectors (in the MDL sense) according to the procedure described in the previous subsection.

Step 4 *Outliers:* Detect outliers according to the MDL outlier condition (Eq. (4)). It is important to note that all vectors S have to be checked because it might happen that a vector classified as an outlier in the previous iteration becomes again an inlier.

Step 5 *Convergence:* If no additional outliers were detected, the selection step has not removed any reference vectors, and the changes in the adaptation step are small, then stop, otherwise goto step 2 (adaptation).

This iterative approach is a very controlled and efficient way of removing reference vectors, and as such shares similarities to EM-type algorithms [1]. In step 2, having m fixed, we estimate the positions of the $\mathbf{c}_j$, which decreases the error term $(L(||\mathbf{x} - \mathbf{c}_i||))$ of the description length. In step 3, we re-calculate the number of reference vectors, keeping the $\mathbf{c}_j$ fixed. In step 4, vectors are classified as outliers if this results in decreased description length. Since we reduce the description length of the network in each of the three steps, and we iterate these steps until no further improvement is possible, we are guaranteed to find at least a local minimum of the description length. Of course, convergence to a global minimum can not be assured. However, starting from an initially high number of reference vectors, we reduce the likelihood of being trapped in a poor local minimum due to initialization problems.

It is also important to note that in order to achieve a proper selection, it is not necessary to train the network to convergence at each step. This is because the selection removes only those reference vectors that cause a decrease in the description length (i.e., other reference vectors can compensate for their omission). Since this is independent on the stage of the training, it is not critical *when* we evoke the selection. One should also note that the quantities needed for the selection can be computed at almost no additional computational cost because they are needed already at the learning stage. Therefore, the costs of the algorithm are dominated by the vector quantizer used, which is typically on the order of $O(n)$.

3 EXPERIMENTAL RESULTS

To test the proposed method, we applied it to various clustering problems of 2-D data (also easy to visualize), and to vector quantization of images. As for the training procedures, we have experimented with two algorithms: K-means clustering algorithm [2] and the unsupervised learning vector quantization (LVQ) algorithm [7]. The results are in terms of the number of clusters found independent of the training algorithm, therefore we show only the results obtained by K-means. In these experiments we have used the instantiation with fixed length of the indices (case 1) and we assume no knowledge of error distributions (case 1).

3.1 2-D CLUSTERING

The clusters were generated according to a Gaussian distribution (different variance) with random placement of the centers in $[0\ldots1] \times [0\ldots1]$. Fig. 2 shows a data set and the reference vectors at different stages of the algorithm. One can see that the algorithm gradually reduces the number of reference vectors and finally ends up with the same number of clusters as were originally generated. Also, the outliers in the dataset have been correctly detected. Fig. 3 shows four results obtained on a set of data with increasing variance and different number of clusters. We have initialized the network with 50 reference vectors, randomly selected from the data set. Usually after 3 ± 1 selection steps the network converged (5 ± 2 in the case of LVQ). One can see that in the cases (a)(b)(d), the algorithm has found the originally generated number of clusters. In the case of (c), one cluster is highly overlapped with the three others (lower left corner); therefore the algorithm did not generate a separate center for it, since according to the MDL principle it is more economically to let the other centers encode also these data points.

In the next experiment we tested the noise sensitivity of the method. We generated 6 Gaussian clusters with $\sigma^2 = 0.05$. Then we added zero mean uncorrelated Gaussian noise with increasing variance ($\sigma^2 = [0.005, 0.085]$, i.e., 10%-170% of the variance of the clusters) to each data point. All parameters were kept the same as in the previous experiment. Fig. 4(a) shows the positions of cluster centers and Fig. 4(b) shows a plot of the mean squared error of the distance between the true centers and the centers resulting from the application of our algorithm. This shows that our method is very tolerant to noise. It is also important to note that the algorithm consistently found 6 clusters in all cases. If we increase the noise further, eventually, more cluster centers will be formed.

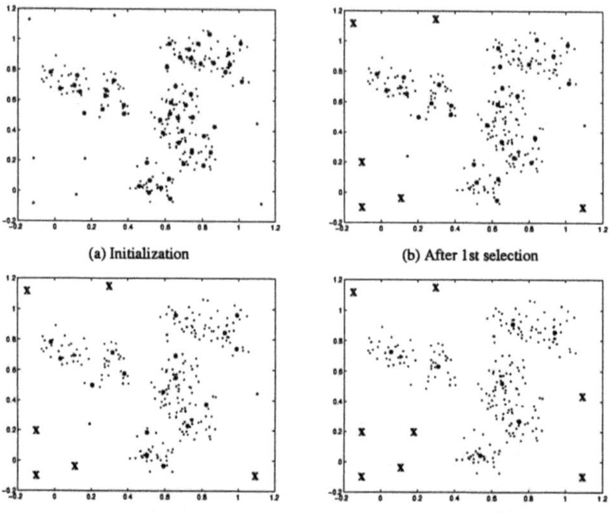

(a) Initialization (b) After 1st selection (c) After 2nd selection (d) After 3rd selection

Figure 2: Different stages of Vector Quantization of 2-D data; dots denote data points, circles denote cluster centers, and "x" denotes outliers.

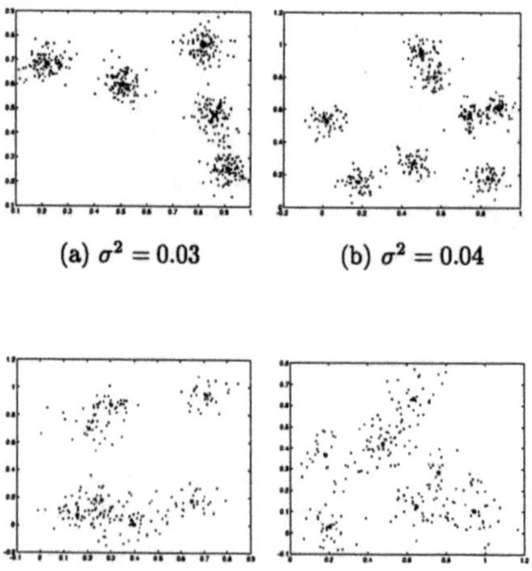

(a) $\sigma^2 = 0.03$ (b) $\sigma^2 = 0.04$ (c) $\sigma^2 = 0.06$ (d) $\sigma^2 = 0.08$

Figure 3: Vector Quantization of 2-D data; dots denote data points and circles denote cluster centers.(a) 5 clusters, (b) 8 clusters, (c) 8 clusters, (d) 7 clusters.

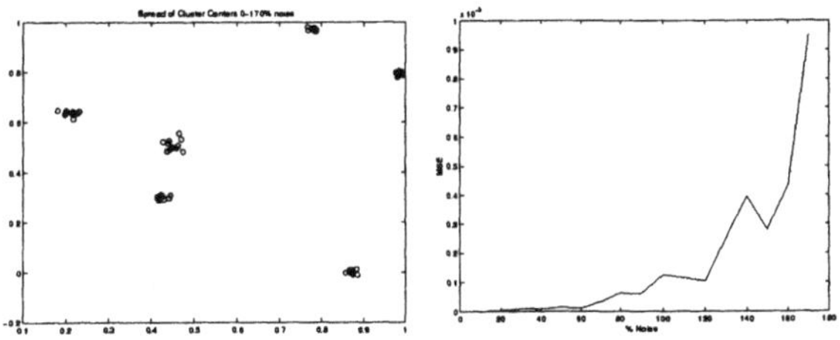

(a) Cluster centers (b) MSE of cluster centers

Figure 4: Error sensitivity of the method

3.2 IMAGE QUANTIZATION

We also performed several experiments on image vector quantization; Fig. 5(a) shows a typical example (size 768×512). We divided the image into non-overlapping 8×8 blocks and use them to form data vectors. Then, we randomly selected half of them for training the network. The network was initialized with 256 reference vectors. After 7 selection steps the network converged at 34 vectors. Fig. 5(b) shows the reconstruction of the image from the reference vectors[4]. Fig. 5(c) shows the error between the original and the reconstructed image (gray represents zero-error). The compression obtained (after run-length encoding of the vector quantized image) is by a factor of 50, i.e., 0.16 bits/pixel as compared to 8 bits/pixel of the original image (run-length encoding of the original image yields a compression factor of 1.26 or 6.35 bits/pixel). The visible errors are mainly due to the blocking effects of taking 8×8 windows, and could easily be removed by a proper smoothing.

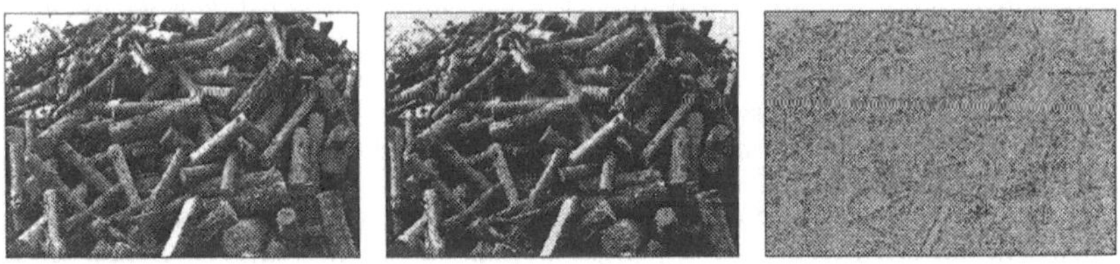

(a) Original Image (b) Reconstructed Image (c) Error Image

Figure 5: Vector Quantization of logs-image.

4 CONCLUSIONS

In this paper we presented an MDL framework for vector quantization networks. This framework was used to derive a computationally efficient algorithm for finding the optimal

[4]One may notice that the printout of the reconstruction is visually more pleasing than the original image due to a reduction in the number of different gray values causing a reduction of the halftoning effect of the printer.

number of reference vectors as well as their positions. This was possible by a systematic approach of removing superfluous reference vectors and identifying outliers. We have demonstrated the algorithm on several examples.

There are various ways to extend the algorithm: For networks which also have topological connectivity, like the Kohonen network, one must add special mechanisms to preserve this connectivity when a unit is removed. Another natural extension is to modify the algorithm to find the number of components in a Gaussian mixture model. It is also interesting to note that the algorithm is very similar to our recently proposed scheme for optimizing RBF networks [8]. One of our future goals is thus to find a common formulation for optimizing the complexity of neural networks which includes both the unsupervised and the supervised networks.

REFERENCES

[1] A.P. Dempster, N.M. Laird, and D.B. Rubin. Maximum likelihood from incomplete data via the EM algorithm. *J.R. Statist. Soc. B*, 39:1–38, 1977.

[2] R. O. Duda and P. E. Hart. *Pattern Classification and Scene Analysis*. Wiley, 1973.

[3] B. Fritzke. Some competitive learning methods (draft). Technical report, Inst. for Neural Computation, Ruhr-University Bochum, 1997.

[4] G. E. Hinton and R. S. Zemel. Autoencoders, minimum description length and Helmholtz free energy. In J. D. Cowan, G. Tesauro, and J. Alspector, editors, *Advances in Neural Information Proc. Systems*, volume 6, pages 3–10. Morgan Kaufmann, 1994.

[5] G. E. Hinton and R. S. Zemel. Minimizing description length in an unsupervised neural network (submitted). *Neural Networks*, 1997.

[6] S. Hochreiter and J. Schmidhuber. Flat minima. *Neural Computation*, 9(1):1–43, 1997.

[7] T. Kohonen. *Self-Organization and Associative Memory*. Berlin: Springer–Verlag, 1989.

[8] Aleš Leonardis and Horst Bischof. An efficient MDL-Based construction of RBF networks. *Neural Networks (in press)*, 1998.

[9] M. Li and P. Vitanyi. *An Introduction to Kolmogorov Complexity and its Applications*. Springer, 2nd edition, 1997.

[10] J. Rissanen. *Stochastic Complexity in Statistical Inquiry*, volume 15 of *Series in Computer Science*. World Scientific, 1989.

[11] S. Roberts. Parametric and non-parametric unsupervised cluster analysis. *Pattern Recognition*, 30(2):261–272, 1997.

[12] L. Xu. How many clusters?: A YING-YANG Machine based theory for a classical open problem in pattern recognition. In *Proc. of 1996 IEEE Int. Conf. on Neural Networks*, volume 3, pages 1546–1551, Washington, DC, June 2-6, 1996. IEEE Computer Society.

[13] R. S. Zemel and G.E Hinton. Learning population codes by minimum description length. *Neural Computation*, 7(3):549–564, 1995.

LOCALIZED SOFT SUBSPACE PATTERN CLASSIFICATION

Thiagarajan Balachander, and Ravi Kothari
Artificial Neural Systems Laboratory
Department of Electrical & Computer Engineering and Computer Science
University of Cincinnati
Cincinnati, OH 45221-0030, USA

ABSTRACT

Subspace classifiers assume that different output classes primarily lie in different subspaces of the original feature space. Hence, associated with each output class is a projection subspace. The class discriminant function is then the projected distance of a given input vector onto these subspaces (each subspace can be uniquely specified by a projection matrix), the input vector being assigned to the class on whose subspace it has the maximal projection. Earlier, we had proposed the Regional Subspace Classifier (RSC) which allows different sub manifolds to be associated with a single class [1]. The design process in the RSC involved minimizing a cost function which allowed determination of these sub manifolds for different clusters by a supervised clustering of the training patterns. In this paper we extend the RSC and allow the training patterns to be shared in a soft fashion between the different clusters and develop the Soft Regional Subspace Classifier (S-RSC). Simulation results show that the proposed method allows for better classification accuracy.

INTRODUCTION

Subspace methods of pattern recognition classify a pattern based on its distance from different vector subspaces. The presumption of course being that each class is linearly spanned by a unique set of basis vectors. Thus the subspace classifier design reduces to the determination of projection subspaces for each class. One of the first subspace classifiers was introduced by Watanabe and Pakvasa [2] called the CLass Featuring Information Compression (CLAFIC). The subspace corresponding to each output class is determined by a principal component analysis of patterns belonging to that class. However, the drawback of CLAFIC is that the subspaces corresponding to each class are determined without taking into account the features of the other class(es). Many improvements over CLAFIC have been proposed and they can be grouped under the following categories (i) those that directly determine the subspaces given the training data set [3], and (ii) those which involve a learning process by which the projection matrices (and hence the subspaces) are calculated (the LSM and its modifications [3],[4]). All these subspace methods of pattern recognition are however global in nature. For each class there exists only one projection subspace over the entirety of the input space.

Local subspace methods of pattern recognition are based on a more general data model and allow patterns of the same class to be associated with more than one sub manifold. Each pattern is thus associated with a distinct sub manifold depending on its location in the feature space. The local subspace classifier thus is a piecewise linear classifier and is more powerful when compared to the linear classification performed by global subspace methods.

Laaksonen [5] introduced locality by combining the subspace projection methods with nearest neighbor classification techniques. For each input vector to be classified, subspaces are formed for each output class from the training data set by identifying patterns from that class which are close to the input pattern. As in any nearest neighbor technique the entire training data has to be stored and prototype vectors for calculating the local subspaces have to be identified every time a new vector is to be classified. This might be a disadvantage when training data set size is large.

Oja and Parkkinen [6] and Prakash and Murty [7] have also suggested the use of local subspace pattern recognition techniques. They apply a dynamic clustering method to partition the data, and associate a projection subspace for clusters in each class. However they strictly use local subspaces rather than local linear manifolds to model the data, which constrains the generality of the data model (although the latter do mention that local linear manifold is a better way to model the data).

Kohonen, Kaski and Lappalainen [8] introduced the Adaptive Subspace SOM (ASSOM) in which each cluster learns a specific low dimensional representation of different temporal events from a stream of consecutive input patterns (like speech inputs). The units (clusters) get tuned to different features in the inputs but ASSOM also imposes a spatial ordering in the clusters through self organization.

Recently, we introduced the Regional Subspace Classifier (RSC) [1] which allowed the modeling of each class in the data set by multiple linear manifolds. Although the RSC, like the ASSOM, can also be looked upon as creating a set of invariant feature banks, it differs from the latter in that no specific attempt was made to introduce spatial ordering in the evolution of the clusters.

In this paper, we consider a modification of the data model (cost function) that was considered for the RSC. Each training pattern is allowed to be shared softly by the many clusters. Also, training patterns that show greater memberships to a cluster are allowed to influence the projection matrices for that cluster to a larger extent. Thus whereas in RSC we allowed the training patterns to be assigned in a hard fashion to the clusters, in the the Soft Regional Subspace Classifier (S-RSC), we allow the patterns to be shared by more than one cluster in a soft fashion.

The rest of the paper has been organized as follows. We first review one of the basic subspace classifiers - The CLass Featuring Information Compression (CLAFIC). We then outline the modification of CLAFIC to allow the data to be modeled by multiple linear manifolds and relate the S-RSC to the earlier proposed RSC. An algorithm is then derived for the S-RSC design followed by simulation results. We conclude the paper with results and discussion.

SUBSPACE CLASSIFIERS

Our idea of introducing a sense of locality into the subspace classifier is very general in that it does not depend on the specific type of subspace classifier used. We however study this change by bringing it about into one of the simpler subspace classifiers, the CLAFIC - CLass Featuring Information Compression, introduced by Watanabe and Pakvasa [2]. The presentation of this classifier and the subsequent notation closely follows Oja's presentation of CLAFIC in [3].

Let the feature vectors be represented by $x \in R^n$ or $x = [x_1\, x_2\, \dots\, x_n]^T$ and come from K classes $\omega^{(1)}, \dots, \omega^{(K)}$. Each class $\omega^{(i)}$ is represented by a $p^{(i)}$ dimensional subspace $\mathcal{L}^{(i)}$ and the goal in CLAFIC is to maximize the average projection of the vectors of a given class $\omega^{(i)}$ on their own subspace $\mathcal{L}^{(i)}$. Thus we seek to[1]:

$$J \uparrow = \sum_{i=1}^{K} E[x^T P^{(i)} x \mid x \in \omega^{(i)}] \tag{1}$$

by finding a set of orthonormal basis vectors $\{u_i^{(1)}, \ldots, u_i^{(p^{(i)})}\}$ and hence a unique projection matrix for the subspace $\mathcal{L}^{(i)}$ is computed as $P^{(i)} = \sum_{j=1}^{p^{(i)}} u_i^{(j)} u_i^{(j)^T}$. Then for any given input vector the classification rule is

$$\text{Classify } x \in \omega^{(i)} \quad \textbf{if} \quad x^T P^{(i)} x \; > \; x^T P^{(j)} x \quad \forall\, j \neq i,$$

The basis vectors for the ith class subspace of CLAFIC can be shown to be (see for *e.g.* [3]) the eigenvectors corresponding to the $p^{(i)}$ largest eigenvalues of the *class correlation* matrix given by

$$Q^{(i)} = E[xx^T | x \in \omega^{(i)}] \tag{2}$$

However if the value of $p^{(i)}$ is larger than half the dimensionality of the input space $(n/2)$, the problem can be restated as a minimization problem whereby we seek to minimize the projection of the feature vectors on their orthogonal subspaces $\tilde{\mathcal{L}}^{(i)}$. Thus,

$$J \downarrow = \sum_{i=1}^{K} E[x^T \tilde{P}^{(i)} x \mid x \in \omega^{(i)}] \tag{3}$$

where $\tilde{P}^{(i)} = \sum_{j=1}^{\tilde{p}^{(i)}} \tilde{u}_i^{(j)} \tilde{u}_i^{(j)T}$, and the tildes in the notation correspond to the *orthogonal subspace* $\tilde{\mathcal{L}}^{(i)}$ where $\tilde{\mathcal{L}}^{(i)} \perp \mathcal{L}^{(i)}$. Then for any given input vector the classification rule is that

$$\text{Classify } x \in \omega^{(i)} \quad \textbf{if} \quad x^T \tilde{P}^{(i)} x \; < \; x^T \tilde{P}^{(j)} x \quad \forall\, j \neq i,$$

The basis vectors for the ith class orthogonal subspace of CLAFIC are then the eigenvectors corresponding to the $\tilde{p}^{(i)}$ smallest eigenvalues of the class correlation matrix given above.

SOFT REGIONAL SUBSPACE CLASSIFIERS

We modify CLAFIC by introducing locality thus allowing more than one cluster (i.e. there is a sub manifold associated with each class within each cluster), and soft sharing by allowing each input pattern to be associated with more than one cluster in varying amounts.

Within this framework, we seek to minimize the total projection of all patterns onto their orthogonal subspaces. As each pattern belongs to more than one cluster, the total projection of a given pattern is computed as the sum of the projections on individual orthogonal subspaces, the projections being weighted by the 'amount' by which the pattern belongs to that cluster.

$$J \downarrow \; = \; \sum_{c=1}^{L} \sum_{i=1}^{K} E[\alpha_c(x)(x - r_c)^T \tilde{P}_c^{(i)} (x - r_c) \mid x \in \omega^{(i)}] \tag{4}$$

[1] $J \uparrow$ ($J \downarrow$) would imply we seek to maximize (minimize) the cost function J

where, $\alpha_c(x)$ denotes the 'amount' by which a given pattern belongs to a cluster with center r_c.

Note that $\alpha_c(x) \in \{0,1\}$ subject to the constraint that $\sum_c \alpha_c(x) = 1$ corresponds to hard clustering which is the case when a given pattern is associated with only one cluster. RSC was developed under this constraint [1]. When $\alpha_c(x) \in [0,1]$ subject to the constraint that $\sum_c \alpha_c(x) = 1$, we allow a pattern to be associated with more than one cluster. We enforce both of these constraints in S-RSC by using a softmax function given by:

$$\alpha_i(x) = \frac{e^{-\gamma d(x,r_i)}}{\sum_{c=1}^{L} e^{-\gamma d(x,r_c)}} \tag{5}$$

where $d(x,r_c) = (x - r_c)^T \tilde{P}_c^{(i)}(x - r_c)$ for $x \in \omega^{(i)}$, and γ is a constant (which controls the membership degree). A smaller γ implies that there is a greater chance for a specific training pattern vector to be softly assigned equally to more than one cluster. A higher γ introduces a lesser degree of softness in clustering.

Thus additionally over CLAFIC, even within the same class the feature vectors are assigned to different clusters in a soft fashion leading to a projection matrix $\tilde{P}$ for each class $\omega^{(i)}$ **and** for each cluster $C^{(c)}$. The decision rule under these modifications can then be defined as,

$$\text{Classify } x \in \omega^{(i)} \quad \textbf{if } (x - r_c)^T \tilde{P}_c^{(i)}(x - r_c) \; < \; (x - r_{c'})^T \tilde{P}_{c'}^{(j)}(x - r_{c'})$$
$$\forall\, j \neq i, \quad c, c' \in \{1, 2, ...L\}$$

The basis vectors of the cth cluster i^{th} class orthogonal subspace are then given by the eigenvectors corresponding to the $\tilde{p}_c^{(i)}$ minimum eigenvalues of the *weighted class cluster covariance matrix* (where $\tilde{p}_c^{(i)}$ is the dimensionality of the subspace) given by:

$$Q_c^{(i)} = E[\alpha_c(x)(x - r_c)(x - r_c)^T \mid x \in \omega^{(i)}] \tag{6}$$

To calculate $Q_c^{(i)}$ it is first necessary to cluster the training data. Thus we could (soft) cluster the training data and calculate the cluster centers using a standard unsupervised clustering algorithm (like C-means). However such an unsupervised clustering scheme is likely to produce sub-optimal clusters (sub-optimal in the sense of the minimization of the classification error). Hence we present an iterative scheme which at each step tries to directly minimize the classification error in the clustering procedure.

The iterative scheme we use is based on the Generalized Lloyd's Algorithm (GLA) [9] in the batch mode to iteratively cluster the patterns in the input space. The distortion measure that is necessary for the clustering, or Vector Quantization, is then the classification error defined in equation (4). This modification is distinct from methods that use annealing for performing vector quantization where in the initial stages of the vector quantization process more cooperation is encouraged among the clusters and as training proceeds the competition is increased to avoid local minima problem.

ALGORITHM FOR S-RSC DESIGN

Let $X = \{(x^1, y^1), (x^2, y^2), \ldots, (x^N, y^N)\}$ represent the N training patterns and their associated class labels, where $x_j \in R^n$ and $y_j \in \{1, 2, \ldots, K\}$. Then we would like to come up with the following (i) the cluster associations, $\mathbf{A}$ which is a NxL matrix and each row vector of the matrix α_j corresponds to the associations of the jth training vector with each of the L clusters, (ii) the cluster centers r_c and (iii) the orthogonal space projection matrix $\tilde{P}_c^{(i)}$ corresponding to all classes and clusters such that J is minimized. This is now in the Soft Vector Quantization framework. Thus adapting the GLA for VQ to S-RSC (*i.e.* to iteratively refine the cluster associations α hence the projection matrices $\tilde{P}_c^{(i)}$ and the cluster centers r_c to minimize J we have the following :

1. Initialize the L cluster centers r_c to L randomly chosen patterns from the training set and initialize the **A** matrix by using equation (5). However since the $\tilde{P}_c^{(i)}$ matrices are not initialized we could just use the Euclidean distance of each training pattern from the cluster centers in equation (5) for initialization of memberships.

2. The above memberships are then used in 6 using which the projection matrices are initialized.

3. Deriving the update rule for r_c (cluster center's) :

   We have the overall cost function from equation (4)

$$J \downarrow = \sum_{c=1}^{L}\sum_{i=1}^{K} E[\alpha_c(x)(x - r_c)^T \tilde{P}_c^{(i)}(x - r_c) \mid x \in \omega^{(i)}]$$

   Now at this point we have the current cluster associations and would like to update each of the cluster centers r_c. The total error corresponding to each cluster $C^{(c)}$ can be expressed as,

$$J_c \downarrow = \sum_{i=1}^{K} E[\alpha_c(x)(x - r_c)^T \tilde{P}_c^{(i)}(x - r_c)|x \in \omega^{(i)}] \tag{7}$$

   which we would like to minimize at this step by proper update of r_c's. Thus finding the partial of J_c wrt r_c, we have

$$\frac{\partial J_c}{\partial r_c} = \sum_{i-1}^{K} E[2\alpha_c(x)\tilde{P}_c^{(i)}(x - r_c) \mid x \in \omega^{(i)}] \tag{8}$$

   Setting the above to zero we can write,

$$\sum_{i=1}^{K} \tilde{P}_c^{(i)}[E[x\alpha_c(x)|x \in \omega^{(i)}] - r_c E[\alpha_c(x)|x \in \omega^{(i)}]] = 0 \tag{9}$$

   and hence we express r_c as

$$r_c = [\sum_{i=1}^{K} E[\alpha_c(x)|x \in \omega^{(i)}]\tilde{P}_c^{(i)}]^- \sum_{i=1}^{K} E[x\alpha_c(x)|x \in \omega^{(i)}]\tilde{P}_c^{(i)} \tag{10}$$

   where $[\cdot]^-$ is the generalized inverse and is equal to the normal inverse if the latter exists [2].

[2]Also if the objective function in equation (4) were to be stated as a maximization problem in terms of $P_{c'}^{(y_i)}$ (as would be the case if we use the 'own' subspace instead of the orthogonal subspace) then we can convert it into a minimization problem by replacing, $P_{c'}^{(y_i)}$ with $I - \tilde{P}_{c'}^{(y_i)}$ in the computations outlined previously.

4. Calculate the *weighted class cluster covariance matrix* $Q_c^{(i)}$ and hence the updated projection matrices $\tilde{P}_c^{(i)}$ (The local subspace dimension is assumed to be the same for all clusters and all classes).

5. We again update the cluster associations α_c of individual training patterns x_j using eq. (5)

6. Iterate steps 3-5 until the cluster centers stabilize or stop after a maximum number of iterations.

SIMULATIONS

The efficacy of the proposed methodology is evaluated with three different data sets as described below. In each of the simulations, we divided a data set into three parts. In each case 5 independent runs were simulated based on different initialization of clusters. These 5 independent trials were each done for varying number of clusters and varying dimensionality of the subspace. The number of clusters and the dimensionality of the subspace giving the best performance on the cross validation dataset were retained and these parameters were then used with the testing data (5 runs) to provide the average accuracy obtained with S-RSC for the three datasets considered.

- *Sonar data*: This is a two class, identification problem of undersea targets (rock or cylinder) [10]. The inputs are in R^{60}. There are 111 cylinder patterns and 97 rock patterns. The training data set size was 104 patterns, and the cross validation and testing data set comprised 52 patterns each.

- *Vowel Data*: This is a speaker identification problem of 11 steady state vowels (classes) uttered by 15 speakers [10]. The inputs are in R^{10}. The training set comprised of 495 patterns equally chosen from all 11 classes. The cross validation and testing data sets were comprised of 253 and 242 patterns respectively.

- *Lymphoma Data*: This is a two class (malignant or benign) identification problem. The inputs are in R^9 and represent textural, tonal and boundary features extracted from segmented cytological preparations of lymph node cells. There are a total of 439 patterns, 145 benign cases and 234 malignant cases. One-tenth of each class was reserved for cross validation and another one-tenth was used for testing. Extraction of features and a comparative performance analysis of various classifiers is described in [11],[12].

Figures 1, 2, and 3 show the testing accuracy obtained for the three datasets as a function of the number of clusters and the number of subspace dimensions used. Each data point is the average obtained over 5 individual runs. Table I summarizes the average testing accuracy with the number of clusters and the number of dimensions in each of the clusters which gave the best performance over the cross validation dataset. Table II compares results obtained with some other standard classifiers. Note that this table should not be interpreted at face value since the condition under which some of the other results are obtained are not fully known. We only provide it to give a sense of the accuracies obtained with different classifiers and to put S-RSC in context.

Figure 4 shows plots of varying membership degrees of the training patterns for each cluster. The memberships are compared with those obtained through the RSC. While

RSC gives crisp memberships and hence the (a) and (c) subplots in Figure 4 are binary, S-RSC gives soft memberships and hence the (b) and (d) subplots in both these Figures are grayscale.

DATA SET	% Accuracy	σ	# Clusters	# Dimensions
SONAR	92.3	1.54	9	3
VOWEL	55.7	3.77	7	2
LYMPHOMA	76.3	3.05	10	6

Table 1: Results obtained with the S-RSC. All numbers are obtained based on averaging over 5 independent trials and the accuracy shown above is obtained over test data based on using cross validation data to choose the number of clusters and number of dimensions.

DATA SET	Classifier	% Accuracy	Reference
SONAR	EALSM	92.0†	[7]
	MLP	90.4	[13]
	RSC	90.0	[1]
	S-RSC	92.3	This paper
VOWEL	k-NN	56.0	[10]
	EALSM	45.9†	[7]
	RSC	50.1	[1]
	S-RSC	55.7	This paper
LYMPHOMA	MLP	83.6	[11]
	RSC	73.9	[1]
	S-RSC	76.3	This paper

Table 2: Comparative performance of different classifiers (†BestCase; other numbers are average accuracies) for a *qualitative* assessment of the performance of different classifiers. In some cases the conditions under which the performance of other classifiers are obtained are not fully known, a direct comparison of the numbers is less meaningful.

DISCUSSION AND CONCLUSION

From the simulation results it can be observed that, on the benchmark problems using some standard classifiers, S-RSC gives a definite improvement in classification. The standard deviations in the accuracies obtained was probably due to the fact that the GLA that was applied for the minimization procedure did not converge to the global minima. Global optimization strategies may be employed to improve performance.

S-RSC represents a modification in the cost function itself rather than just a better way of optimizing the original cost function for the RSC. We have used the simple GLA which does suffer from local minima. Better optimization strategies can of course be used in RSC as well as S-RSC to possibly yield better results.

S-RSC is also distinct from soft competitive Vector Quantization algorithm [14] in which memberships start out to be soft and then are annealed to become crisp. In S-

RSC the memberships determine how much each of the training patterns influence the projection subspaces and even the final memberships could remain soft (as seen from Figure 4) as opposed to crisp final memberships in soft competitive Vector Quantization strategies.

The S-RSC outperforms the classifiers that are close in spirit (the EASLM and the RSC). This improvement does come at a slightly increased computational cost. However, once the class cluster subspaces are formed then time involved for testing a new point would be the same. Since an iterative algorithm was employed for the minimization of the cost function a convergence criterion could be specified. In all of our simulations we found it convenient to run the iteration for a fixed number of times (30). The changes in the cluster centers usually stabilized by then.

Our continued efforts are focussed towards determining the projection subspaces not by simply maximizing the expected projection of patterns of a given class, but by maximizing the ratios in projection distances of patterns belonging to different classes using Oriented Principal Component Analysis (OPCA). Our preliminary results obtained with OPCA indicate a large improvement in performance as compared to RSC, S-RSC, and other variations of subspace classifiers. A bias-variance framework for the general case of subspace classifiers is also under development.

REFERENCES

[1] Balachander T, Kothari R. Localized Subspace Pattern Classification. In Proceedings of IEEE World Congress on Computational Intelligence (IJCNN), 1998, pp 1804-1809.

[2] Watanabe S, Pakvasa N. Subspace Method of Pattern Recognition. In Proceedings of the First International Joint Conference on Pattern Recognition, 1973, pp 25-32.

[3] Oja E, Subspace Methods of Pattern Recognition, Research Studies Press, Letchworth and J. Wiley, New York, 1983.

[4] Oja E, Kohonen T. The Subspace Learning Method as a Formalism for Pattern Recognition and Neural Networks. In Proceedings of the IEEE International Conference on Neural Networks, 1988, pp 277-284.

[5] Laaksonen J. Subspace Methods in Recognition of Handwritten Digits. Ph. D. Thesis Helsinki University of Technology, 1997.

[6] Oja E, Parkkinen J. On Subspace Clustering. In Proceedings of the 7th International Conference on Pattern Recognition, 1984, pp 692-695.

[7] Prakash M, Murty MN. Extended Subspace Methods of Pattern Recognition. Pattern Recognition Letters 1996; 17(11):1131-1139.

[8] Kohonen T, Kaski S, Lappalainen H. Self-Organized Formation of Various Invariant-Feature Filters in the Adaptive-Subspace SOM. Neural Computation 1997; 9(6):1321-1344.

[9] Gersho A, Gray RM, Vector Quantization and Signal Compression. Kluwer Academic Publishers, 1992.

[10] The dataset and results reported are electronically available from *ftp://ftp.cs.cmu.edu /afs/cs/project/connect/bench/* - The Carnegie Mellon University AI Repository.

[11] Balachander T, Kothari R, Cualing H. An Empirical Comparison of Dimensionality Reduction Techniques for Pattern Classification. In Gerstner W, Germond A, Hasler M, Nicoud J-D (eds). Lecture Notes in Computer Science Vol. 1327. Springer-Verlag, 1997, pp 589-594.

[12] Kothari R, Balachander T, Lotlikar R, Cualing H. On the Separability of Grades of

Lymphoma Using Higher Order Cytological Features. Submitted to the IEEE Transactions on Biomedical Engineering.

[13] Gorman RP, Sejnowski TJ. Analysis of Hidden Units in a Layered Network Trained to Classify Sonar Targets. Neural Networks 1988; 1:75-89.

[14] Rose K, Gurewitz E, Fox GC. Vector Quantization by Deterministic Annealing. IEEE Transactions on Information Theory 1992; 38(4):1249-1257.

ACKNOWLEDGEMENTS

Part of this research was supported by a grant from The Whitaker Foundation. The authors also acknowledge Dr. H. Cualing for providing the images of Lymphnode cytological preparations.

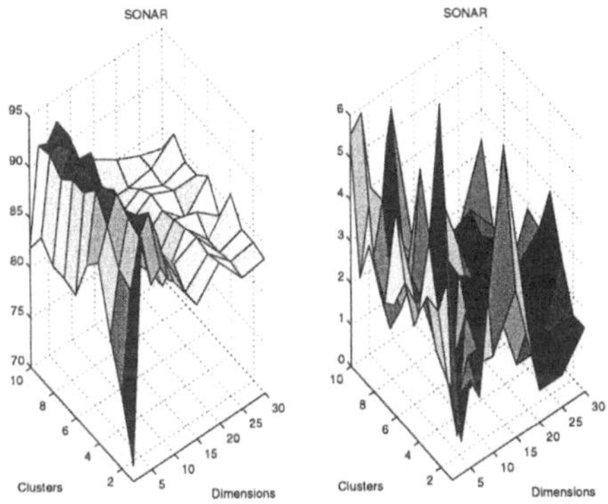

Figure 1: Left: Generalization Accuracy in % for Sonar Data Set, Right: Standard Deviation of Generalization Accuracy

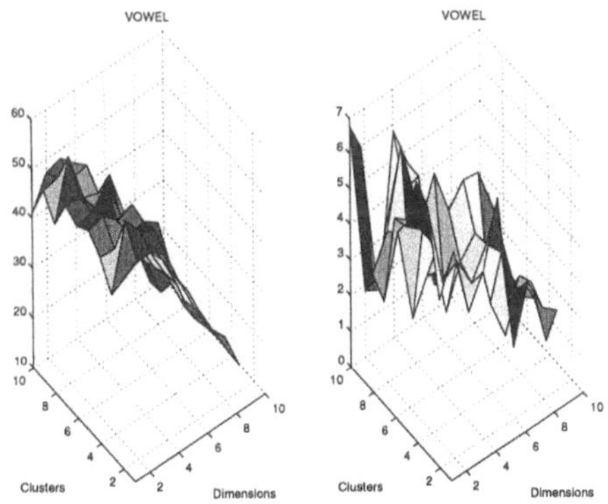

Figure 2: Left: Generalization Accuracy in % for Vowel Data Set, Right: Standard Deviation of Generalization Accuracy

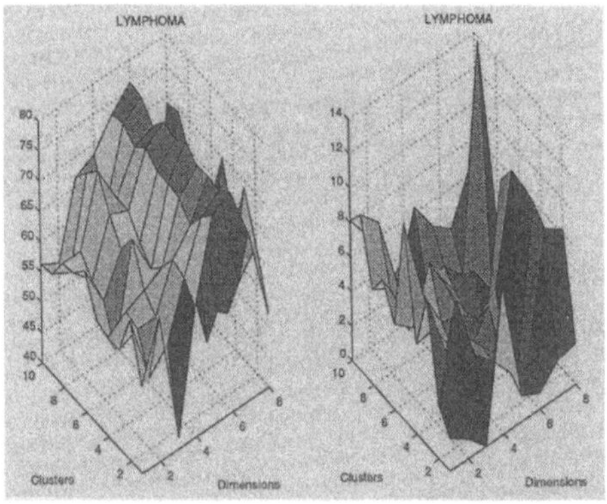

Figure 3: Left: Generalization Accuracy in % for Lymphoma Data Set, Right: Standard Deviation of Generalization Accuracy

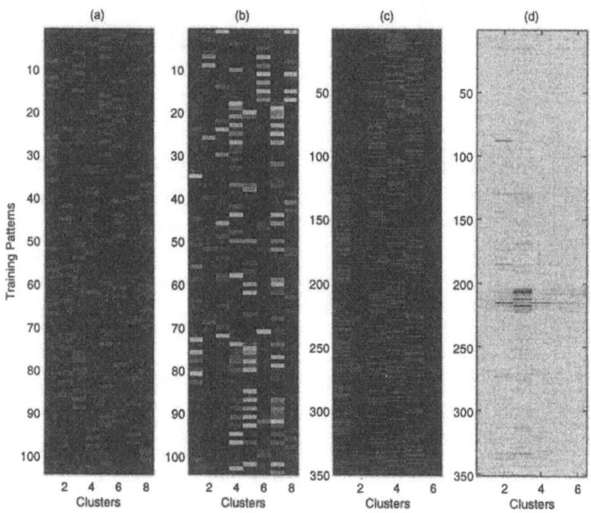

Figure 4: Plot of varying membership degrees of training patterns for different clusters. Plots (a) and (b) were generated for the SONAR dataset and (c) and (d) were generated for the LYMPHOMA dataset. (a) and (c) correspond to the RSC and (b) and (d) correspond to the S-RSC. The varying shades of gray correspond to the degree of membership - lighter shades implying greater memberships.

A QUANTUM LEAP TO ADVANCES IN PATTERN RECOGNITION.

Peter Marcer, European Institute for Quantum Computing, Bristol, UK

ABSTRACT

No discussion of advances in pattern recognition, robotics, etc. in the new millennium can be divorced from the quantum future of computing. The central problem is the ever increasing appetite(of real time pattern recognition, computer vision and image processing, robotics etc) for real time processing of real complexity in the three dimensional real world. This is pushing current technology ever smaller to where the classical modes of computation break down ; due to cross-talk for example. Here the silicon superhighway ends in the apparently alien quantum world and a new millennium crisis begins!

By starting now, however, this impending crisis can be turned into a great opportunity. An understanding of what is quantum computationally possible! Of how the appetite for real time processing of real complexity in the three dimensional real world can be achieved. A practical achievement for which we are ourselves, in the case of pattern recognition, a living existence proof. Is this quantum computational future, therefore, one where the brain/organism is the role model for the computer/robot and not vice versa? Where, intelligence is real and not artificial? A future with an understanding from nature of what information -meaning- truly is? Where, at last, knowledge is directly captured and processed? A future where, mankind has access to all the keys to the computational kingdom? A pattern processing theory, quantum holography, describing existing magnetic resonance imaging (MRI) machines and a valid premise, for which evidence is already accumulating, are advanced that it is!

INTRODUCTION

The continual upgrading of silicon CMOS technology means that by around 2010, current processor speeds will have increased 256 fold, but by that time,

a) the investment in a single manufacturing plant will run into tens of billions of dollars at today's prices, and

b) each chip gate would switch on the basis of the statistics of just 10 electrons and so be unreliable!

The required world financing of the plant could not therefore be technologically nor economically justified, and quantum co-processors will most likely be the only type of devices found in computers later in the next century [1].

WHAT IS QUANTUM INFORMATION PROCESSING?

In 1980 in their book 'The Introduction to VLSI Systems'(Addison Wesley,1980) seminal to the Silicon Revolution, the authors Mead and Conway state in Chapter 9-The Physics of Computational Systems:-

"Classical physics does not provide a sufficient basis for representing the fundamental behaviour of information storage devices. We must instead examine the properties of quantum mechanical systems as they apply to devices with two stable states and develop the basic physical principles underlying the representation and manipulation of information. .... The quantum theory forces us to think about nature in an entirely new way .... The best way to develop one's intuitions here is to view all matter as waves of various types .... Since we are dealing with waves that have both amplitude and phase, it is convenient to represent the wave function as a complex number represented by a point in the complex plane"

In this prophetic vision of quantum information processing, information is no longer seen to consist simply of bits as in Turing's seminal idealization of the now ubiquitous digital computer, but also as the phase between the bits as in a quantum linear superposition or entanglement. Entanglement is the essential feature of quantum physics which distinguishes it from classical physics. It describes correlations between quantum systems much stronger than any classical correlation could be; since quantum correlations do not decline with distance. It is also an intuition that does much to demystify quantum mechanics by explaining its use of complex quantities. It suggests that quantum information processing will generalize computing as it is practiced today. How is this possible?

HOW DO QUANTUM AND DIGITAL COMPUTERS DIFFER?

Digital computation ultimately concerns the notions of true and false represented by the symbols 1 and 0 materialized in physical states $|\uparrow>$ up and $|\downarrow>$ down. However it is known that matter has more generalized physical states than these, that, in quantum theory, are described by the quantum linear superposition $a|\uparrow> + b|\downarrow>$ where a and b are complex quantities. Thus there exist intermediate/ entangled states so called, between up and down, and a digital computer is, ultimately, a quantum machine where the computational operations are restricted to up and down, such that $|\uparrow>$ represents 1 and $|\downarrow>$ represents 0. However if a machine can be constructed such that the more generalized entangled states are the basis of its computational operations, this will be a true quantum computer. How to control such superpositions both in theory and in practice is, therefore, the key to this new technology.

WHAT THEREFORE WOULD BE THE BENEFITS?

In encryption, for example, no one has developed an algorithm for a digital computer that avoids the exponential increase in computer time that results with key bit size, although it remains unproven that such an algorithm cannot be found. Brute force attacks for a 128bit key therefore would take many trillions of years even on a $100m computer system. However in 1994, Shor[2] published a quantum algorithm using the more generalized states, that shows a linear rather than an exponential increase with key size, provided that a suitable quantum computer could be built. This showed that if such generalized states could be harnessed, parallel computers would exist that ' do all their calculations at the same time' as Wooters, a physicist in Massachusetts recently put it.

The potential for real time pattern recognition, robotics, etc. of such quantum parallel computers could therefore be enormous, and since the end of the silicon super-highway is already in sight-a little over ten years away-the incentive to investigate and invest in this new field is now, I would maintain, both essential and imperative!

Early experimental progress[3] is now such that elementary qubit computations demonstrating quantum algorithms have been carried out, for example, utilizing nuclear magnetic resonance(NMR). This indicates that quantum analogue information processing/simulation[4] has already existed unrecognized in advanced medical diagnostic MRI systems for brain and body scan imaging for years. These utilize functional NMR tomography[5], where image computation and extraction is described by quantum holography[6]. Here a resonant coupling of electro-magnetic fields with the nuclear spin populations of soft tissues produce the required high resolution image as a diffraction pattern. This is then converted by fast symplectic Fourier transform (FFT) action into the actual image on a conventional computer screen.

But quantum information processing rests on the ability to control and manipulate quantum superpositions i.e. $a|\uparrow\rangle+b|\downarrow\rangle$ of such nuclear spin states through the appropriate quantum mechanical coherent unitary transformation(s). An ability guaranteed in quantum holography in accordance with well defined signal metrics defined by the Heisenberg group[7], and described, for example, in terms of the creation/ annihilation operators of the quantum emitter/absorber model. Here the different alternatives that can co-exist at the photon level, realise the required quantum superpositions by phase conjugation, through the unique infinite dimensional representations U_v of the Schrodinger type in the Hilbert space $L^2(R)$[6]. This maximises quantum parallelism. Quantum holography, described in later sections, is therefore, an experimentally validated quantum signal processing paradigm for the encoding and decoding of three dimensional information in the form of holographic interference patterns, potentially well suited to advanced real time pattern recognition, computer vision and imaging, robotic systems and to explaining how brains work.

WHAT ARE THE BASES OF THESE CLAIMS?

Firstly in functional MRI, the complex, high resolution body slice image necessary for medical diagnosis, achieved via spin echo, is output as a diffraction pattern, which can be demonstrated to be a hologram. Following page/body slice selection and nuclear spin choreography to be able to compute the appropriate image, the machine functions during repeated spin echo as a resonant cavity, where the pattern slice /hologram, ie memory image closest to that re-input, is amplified, while all other pattern slice/holograms are simultaneously attenuated. Elementary quantum holo -graphic pattern recognition is therefore already in production use in functional MRI, where the body introduced into the machine constitutes its paged memory, see VII(A). These production MRI techniques, where the diffraction pattern holograms output are converted to body slice images on a conventional computer screen by FFT, are those recently used to spin choreograph elementary NMR qubit computations!

Secondly the brain, postulated as such a resonant cavity, is a chemical computer and control mechanism capable of real time processing of real complexity in the three dimensional real world. This serves as an existence proof that carbon based analogue chemical computation and control, does work. Moreover how the brain works (its morphology and dynamics) has never been fully explained. The theory of quantum holography, however, relates to both quantum signal induced chemical reactions (as distinct from thermodynamically induced) see below, and, inversely, chemical reaction induced quantum signal processing. It explains how the quantum holographic signal processing, necessary for cognition and perception, can work conveying such evolutionary advantages as quantum parallelism, a frequency organised paged holographic associative memory with no cross talk between the pages, etc so that the brain is a fully distributed, synchronously partitioned massively parallel processor[8]. It predicts the morphology and dynamics necessary to such processing on various scales, such as the whole human brain, the neurons, the axons, the synapses, the dendrites, and the axonal micro-tubules[8,9], explaining how these ought to account for the brain's neurophysiology. These predictions are not only in good accord with neuro-physiological and psychological fact, but in particular, with the truly remarkable workings of the synapse[10], where an interface of signal induced chemical reactions and, conversely, the chemical reaction induced signal processing exists.

QUANTUM SIGNAL INDUCED CHEMISTRY

Quantum signal induced chemical reactions have already been demonstrated in the laboratory[11]. The goal is, say, to maximize the amount of product in a reaction, by coupling it to an external field. The design of this external field is then an inverse problem; given the goal and the quantum mechanical equations of motion, calculate the guiding field. The now proven methodology used in these calculations[12] is optimal control theory by which it is found that the optimum field has a complicated spectral and temporal structure. This, in the examples, so far studied, can increase the product yield by many orders of magnitude. Quantum correlation determining the efficiency of the guiding field is the underlying physical principle. One experimental apparatus consists of a laser, a sample of molecules, and a control computer equipped with a genetic algorithm[13]. This measuring device, learning laser pulse sequences to excite specific molecular states, acts as an analogue computer that solves the Schrodinger equation for the desired chemistry exactly in real time. It teaches the laser the optimal control for the desired chemical reactions, previously only approximately possible by bulk thermodynamic procedures - the current basis for the whole of industrial chemistry, commercial pharmacology and it is currently thought biological systems.

In principle therefore such quantum signal induced chemistry offers a revolution in the way industrial chemistry and pharmacology will be carried out, in an optimally controlled way in the future so as to minimize energy use and waste. These features are also properties of the internal chemistry of biological systems, and of brains.

QUANTUM HOLOGRAPHY

In holography, phase is the essential quantity of physical significance. It concerns whether signals in the form of waves are in phase or out of phase so as to reinforce or attenuate each other, where

a)wave inference patterns constitute holograms encoding the three dimensional shape and properties of objects, and

b) holograms are not the optically formed image of an object as in photography, but records of the object (image bearing) wave itself. The hologram is produced by mixing the wave with a separate coherent (non-object image bearing) wave or beam. Illumination of this hologram with the corresponding coherent non-object bearing ‘anti-wave or beam’ reconstructs the original object wave yielding the optical object image. This image is practically indiscernible from the original optically formed image including three dimensional parallax effects.

Of particular interest is phase conjugation, the condition whereby the object wave is returned in real or virtual form along its path, so the object image and the original object coincide. In quantum holography these two wavelet mixing processes for the encoding and decoding of three dimensional images, are described mathematically via the usual quantum mechanical formalism[6]. This provides a generic quantum specification of holography so that the optical process described above applies to any form of physical wave, electromagnetic, acoustic, chemical etc, and the condition of phase conjugation results in adaptive resonance. In particular, where wavelet mixing concerns a common source of waves to provide both the object illumination (and thus the object image bearing beam) and the (non-object image bearing) reference beam, quantum holography concerns non local quantum coherence effects.

Thus, the phased two-time average of the holographic transform

$$|H(\psi, \varphi; x, y)|$$

provides the probability of detecting the wave quantum within the unit area attached to the point (x,y) of $R\oplus R$, the hologram plane, where the coherent two wavelet mixing $\psi(t')dt'\otimes\varphi(t)dt$ takes place and ψ and φ are the wave functions. Similarly
$H(\psi, \psi ; x, y)$ defines the holographic trace transform, which models the classic quantum self interference experiment.
That is, the methodology is applicable to all forms of wave (i.e. optical, acoustic, etc where the wave quanta are photons, air molecules, etc, respectively) provided the wavelets are coherent enough so that H exists, H_v concerns the probability of detecting a quantum frequency v, i is $\sqrt{-1}$, and

$$\Psi \otimes \varphi \rightarrow H_v(\Psi, \varphi; x, y) = \int_R \Psi(t-x)\overline{\varphi}(t)\exp(2\pi i v y t)dt$$

where $\rightarrow$ means 'maps onto' describes the first step in the angle-image encoding procedure taking place. In this first processing step, each object to be globally stored, is encoded in the hologram prior to its recording by mixing the coherent object signal beam with an unfocused linearly polarized coherent non-object reference signal beam having a particular angle between its wave vector and the normal vector of the hologram plane $R\oplus R$.
The second stage of encoding and the inverse process of holographic decoding, is described by the filtered back propagation formulae of phase conjugate degenerate coherent four wavelet mixing, where

$$\iint_{R\oplus R} H(\Psi, \varphi; x, y)\exp(-2\pi i y t)\overline{\Psi}(t-x)dxdy = \overline{\varphi}(t)$$

and,

$$\iint_{R\oplus R} H(\Psi, \varphi; -y, x)\exp(-2\pi i y t)F\overline{\Psi}(t-x)dxdy = F\overline{\varphi}(t)$$

hold and describe the harmonic analysis of the Fourier transform action F.

That is, the expanded conjugate reference signal beam acts as a scanner for the readout so that the holographic decoding procedure reconstructs the complete wavefront (including the object image). This is as a consequence of the Fourier transform action F on the Schwarz space S(R) of complex-valued C^∞ wavelet packet amplitude densities on the real line R, which specifies the multiplexed signal energies. Here S(R) is a dense vector subspace of the complex Hilbert space *H* of square integrable complex-valued densities $L^2(R)$ with respect to Lebesque measure $dt \in R$ under its natural isometric embedding.
In the case where non-degenerate four wavelet mixing, called super-resolution imaging, occurs, the second stage of encoding/decoding, described above, generalises to the orthogonality or sharp frequency adaptive coupling conditions

$$\text{(A)} \qquad \langle H_v(\psi, \varphi; ..) | H_{v'}(\psi', \varphi'; ..)\rangle = 0 \text{ if } v \neq v' \quad \text{or} = \langle \psi \otimes \varphi | \psi' \otimes \varphi' \rangle \text{ if } v = v'$$

in the hologram plane $R\oplus R$ for all $\psi, \psi', \varphi, \varphi'$.

That is, these adaptive coupling conditions specify very narrow spectral windows or "pages" with no cross talk, so that the encoding of data for a demultiplexing reference beam "write" and the decoding of data for a corresponding multiplexing reference beam "read", produces a frequency organised page oriented memory, the co-ordinates of which are given by the reference beam angle to $dx_\wedge dy$ at (x,y) of the hologram plane $R \oplus R$, in the case of non-degeneracy produced by non-homogeneity.

A further examination of quantum holography shows that it specifies an emitter/absorber model equivalent to an incremental Feynman sum of histories approach, incorporating signal theory for generic three dimensional image processing and communication into quantum physics in accordance with the symmetries of the nilpotent Heisenberg Lie group G, algebra g and nilmanifold[14]. These symmetries avoid the non-coherence that intuitively in quantum mechanics is expected in other circumstances to prevent the quantum interference, self-interference/ entanglement necessary for the holography. Even so the Lie algebra g of G continues to model Heisenberg uncertainty as was realised by Weyl in 1928. The three dimensional representation of G below

$$\begin{pmatrix} 1 & x & z \\ 0 & 1 & y \\ 0 & 0 & 1 \end{pmatrix}$$

written as (x,y,z) for convenience shows, for example, that with reference to (x,y) in the hologram plane, that x encodes the path difference, and y the phase difference between the two signals ψ and φ having the same frequency centre $v \neq 0$. Thus (x,y) constitute a Fourier duality pair embedding the complex plane in G, so that the hologram contains all the information necessary for full wavefront reconstruction. Any attempt, however, to detect where this information is located, will result in the failure of the quantum interference taking place (and therefore the quantum holography) as a consequence of the uncertainty principle, which g represents.

G shows that signals normal to the hologram plane correspond to the group of symmetries

$$X_v : C_G(0,0,z) \rightarrow \exp(2\pi i v z)$$

which define the centre character X_v frequency $v \neq 0$ of the Heisenberg group G's one dimensional centre C_G of unipotent matrices (0,0,z) where (x,y,z) stands for the three dimensional representation of G, $i = \sqrt{-1}$, and x,y,z have their usual meaning as spatial measures. For any phase conjugate resonant frequency $v \neq 0$, X_v determines up to a unitary isomorphism, a unique infinite dimensional irreducible unitary linear representation of the Schrodinger type U_v of G in the Hilbert space $H = L^2(R)$ of square-integrable complex-valued densities on the real line R. $\bar{U}_v$ the contragredient representation of U_v , is then the feedback or back propagation representation of G such that $U_v/C_G = X_v$ and $\bar{U}_v/C_G = X_{-v}$ are the centre character representations modulo C_G. Thus, this form of holographic pattern processing, for which memory, encoding/ decoding, filtering and transmission of signals is defined:

a) is analogue - utilizing actual physical signals in the form of holograms. These capture a whole sensory 'vista' with respect to both amplitude and phase - be it visual, acoustic, tactile, etc, in phase conjugate form coincident with reality i.e. as knowledge .

b) is both top down and bottom up, allowing optimally efficient i) cognition by filtering a whole into parts or ii) perception, by the assembly of a whole from parts,

c) employs adaption/learning rather an algorithms. No form of logical or mathematical representation is thus required, only a physical morphology and dynamics which the theory prescribes, and
d) allows the treatment of arbitrary or exponential towers of complexity. This is because the Lie group structure exhibits the natural Lie diffeomorphism or differentiable exponential mapping with a differentiable inverse.
Quantum holography combines the advantages of holography such as associative memory, redundancy/fault tolerance , etc with those of quantum computation.
Quantum signal induced chemistry and quantum holography already show that a basis for the control of quantum linear superpositions -the key to the new technology- is already sufficiently advanced in both theory and in laboratory practice, to hold out the promise that quantum computers and information processing can soon be a reality. They allow the citing of extensive evidence in support of the premise below, that this new field could, at the beginning of the new millenium, produce advances across the area of science and technology, far more exciting than any science fiction.

THE EVIDENCE

The following facts, emergent from the new interdisciplinery area of quantum information processing[15], preview a major paradigm change in science :-
a) in computer science, a physical theory - the quantum theory of computation - is now to be regarded as the theory of computation, replacing the mathematical/Turing theory as the correct one,
b) the nature of information has been extended by the concept of quantum information, beyond what, until now, has been accepted in science to be the case,
c) information therefore becomes a new concept on a par with the accepted concept of energy. needing incorporation in understanding physics, and
d) as already experimentally validated and cited, this incorporation radically changes the scientific understanding of how chemistry may be be performed - specifying new designs for chemical systems employing optimally controlled quantum signal induced, rather than approximately thermodynamically induced, chemical reactions.
The new paradigm, implies that we live in a wholly quantum world, where both classical models of physics and computation are at best approximations to physical reality, and where, for example, the recent experimental validation of quantum teleportation[16] is a striking affirmation of the holistic nature of physical reality revealed by quantum mechanics.
Thus, current understanding of all derived disciplines where the concept of information processing plays a leading role - such as molecular biology, biology, neurophysiology, cognitive science, medicine, etc warrant re-assessment and maybe radical revision in the light of this paradigm change. For example, a valid hypothesis is that the 1952-3 experiments of Miller and Urey into the origins of life (where, within a closed flask, electric discharges through a 'primordial Earth atmosphere' for many days produced an amino acid base containing chemical soup) were essentially correct; except that the possibility of optimally controlled quantum signal induced chemical reactions[12] was then unknown and lie at the heart of life's further evolution.
From a programme of investigations already in progress, which concerns DNA, the prokaryote cell, the brain, and its essential sub-unit - the neuron -providing a new model of cognition, and the validatable premise proposed, it becomes clear that no area of science may be immune from this revised understanding of information processing that quantum physics provides, and that the solution to many of the major unsolved problems in science, could now be within reach.

In the new paradigm, the only valid proofs are "engineered solutions" i.e. physical apparatus, be they manmade or biological evolved, which demonstrate the process in question, as theoretically described. Thus brains as "chemically based computer design", have some information processing operations that are astounding from the engineering, technical viewpoint; operations which serve as an existence proof that carbon-based analogue chemical computation does work. The investigations concern quantum holography for which functional magnetic resonance imaging furnishes an engineered solution[5]. They provide existence proofs; ie descriptions of why the morphology and dynamics of the following chemically based computer designs, i.e. "engineered solutions" are the way they are:
i) DNA-describing how its morphology and dynamics can incrementally encode the three dimensional morphology and dynamics of the embryo of its organism[17],
ii) the prokaryote cell - describing how such cells function in an environmental niche, for the purposes of survival, as self-organising, self replicating, self adaptive units, in accordance with an evolving record within the cell of the cell's history[18],
iii) the brain as a cognitive system - describing how it works as a fully distributed, massively parallel, synchronously partitioned processor, filter, memory, and multiple input/output system, which optimizes itself by self adaption/learning [9], and
iv) the neuron of such a brain - describing how it contributes to the brain's capabilities and massively parallel operation and why this is quantum parallelism, such that, in relation to simultaneous activity in geometrically separate brain segments and to affecting of a change of functionality (i.e. the shutting down of activity in one set of segments and replacing this by that in another set), these can be done instantaneously, rather than requiring the use of coordinating signals from a central control or switching centre as in a classical machine[8].
Other engineered or claimed engineered solutions, described by quantum holography are are Mach-Zehner interferometry, NMR qubit quantum computation[19,20] and teleportation as performed by Zeilinger et al. and di Martini et al.[16]

THE VALIDATABLE PREMISE

Biological systems are now simply "engineered solutions" for which DNA - itself an "engineered solution" - provides descriptions. Central to this description to quote de Duve, a Nobel Laureate for cell biology [21] ".... the function of base-pairing is not simply a structural one. Its main role is communication. Amazingly these elementary relationships, the chemical base pairings (where A, U, T, G and C are adenine, uracil, thymine, guanine and cytosine respectively)

$$A = U \text{ or } A = T \text{ and } G \equiv C$$

govern, through the two relatively fragile structures they embody, the whole of information transfer throughout the biosphere. They are truly the cipher of life."
That is, base-pairing, the basis of the genetic code, provides an "engineered solution" or basic machinery of communication fundamental to living systems on Earth. Thus, the hypothesis that biological systems are quantum information processing based chemical computer designs, is reduced to experimentally validating that the machinery of base-pairing corresponds to four operations, a quaternary code, for the maintenance of entanglement or unitarity, namely:
a)the unitary operation that simply does nothing or
b)either one of the three unitary transformations transferring one Bell state to another.
For these four unitary operations, the identity operation, the phase flip, the bit flip and the phase/bit flip, which are central to quantum error correction, and fault tolerance[15], describe an ability -quantum dense coding- to send twice as much information as can be sent classically

with a two-state particle/system. This, it is argued, would result in inevitable evolutionary advantage. It implies that information with respect to both amplitude (bits) and phase is being transmitted. A case, exactly analogous to the condition of 'quadrature' in holography[22], which allows full wavefront reconstruction, restoring the original 3 dimensional image carrying wave in both amplitude and phase; the same condition, which in quantum holography is guaranteed by the symmetries of the three dimensional representation G of the Heisenberg group and where these symmetries imply avoidance of non-coherence.

That is to say, quantum holography extends the classical model of holography for full wavefront reconstruction with complex amplitudes into the quantum domain. Thus the full holographic information needed to reconstruct the relative location and state of an object consists of two parts, one quantum which can be transmitted instantaneously, but cannot be used without the other, the classical part which can only be transmitted by conventional means at the speed of light or slower[16]. This quantum ability alone combined with the other undoubted advantages of holographic information processing such as associate memory, redundancy, etc, could account for the observation that biological systems/brains have some operations that are astounding from the engineering, technical viewpoint. Implicit in the premise, this duality of communication capabilities implies that information processing in biological systems occurs in tandem at both the traditional classical and quantum levels. By this means, for example, when living cells replicate, each cell would be fully aware of its sister cells relative locations and states, explaining how such replication is able to construct the morphology and dynamics of an embryo subject to the master blueprint of their DNA[17], and how, possibly, when the embryo is complete, the immune system maybe brought into play to restore such locations and states.

A description of the physics underlying the origin and functioning of living systems, would constitute a quantum leap in mankind's understanding of the origin of life, and understanding of biological evolved engineered solutions would lead to more rapid technological development of manmade ones.

REFERENCES

[1] Williams RS. Computing in the 21st Century: nanocircuitry, defect tolerence, and quantum logic, Proceedings Royal Society London ; discussion meeting 5/6 November, 1997; in press

[2] Shor PW. Algorithms for quantum computation: Discrete log and factoring, Proc. 35th IEEE Symposium on Foundations of Computer Science, S. Goldwasser, editor, IEEE Computer Society Press, 1994; 124.

[3] Spiller TP. Quantum Information Processing; Cryptography, Computation, and Teleportation, Proceedings IEEE, December 1996; 84(12): 1719-1746.

[4] Lloyd S. Universal Quantum Simulators, Science, 23rd August 1996; 273: 1073-1078.

[5] Schempp W. Resonance Imaging: Mathematical Foundations and Applications, John Wiley, New York, 1998.

[6] Schempp W. Quantum holography and neurocomputer architectures, Journal of Mathematical Imaging and Vision, 1992; 2: 279-326.

[7] Schempp W, Harmonic Analysis on the Heisenberg group with applications in signal theory. Pitman Notes in Mathematics Series 14. Longman Scientific and Technical, London, 1986.

[8] Marcer PJ. and Schempp W. Model of the Neuron Working by Quantum Holography, Informatica 1997; 21(3): 519-534.

[9] Marcer PJ. and Schempp W. The Brain as a Conscious System, International Journal General Systems, 1998; in press.

[10] Eccles J. Do mental events cause neural events analogously to the probability fields of

quantum mechanics? Proceedings Royal Society of London 1986; B227: 411-428.
[11] Rice SA. New Ideas for Guiding the Evolution of a Quantum System. Science, 16th October 1992 ; 258: 412-413.
[12] Dahleh M, Peirce AP, and Rabitz H, Optimal control of uncertain quantum systems, Physical Review A lst August 1990, ; 42(3): 1065-1079.
[13] Judson RS. and Rabitz H. Teaching Lasers to Control Molecules, Physical Review Letters 9th March, 1992; 68(10): 1500-1503.
[14] Schempp W. Bohr's indeterminacy principle in quantum holography, self-adaptive neural network architectures, cortical self-organization, magnetic resonance imaging and solitonic nanotechnology. Nanobiology 1993; 2: 109-164.
[15] Various Authors, Quantum information, New forms of computation and communication. Physics World (special issue) 1998; 11(3); 33-57.
[16] Bouwmeester D. et al. Experimental quantum teleportation, Nature 11th December, 1997; 390: 575-579.
[17] Marcer PJ. and Schempp W. A mathematically specified template for DNA and the genetic code in terms of the physically realisable processes of quantum holography. Proceedings, the Greenwich symposium on Living Computers, editors Fedorec A.M., Marcer P.J. March 9th, 1996; 45-62.
[18] Marcer PJ. and Schempp W. The model of the prokaryote cell as an anticipatory system working by quantum holography. Proceedings 1st International Conference of Computing Anticipatory Systems, Belgium, August 11-15, 1997, ed. Dubois D.,(in press).
[19] Gershenfeld N. and Chuang IL. Quantum Computing with Molecules, Scientific American, June 1998; 50-55.
[20] Jones AJ, Mosca M, Hansen RH, Implementation of a quantum search algorithm on a quantum computer, Nature 28th May, 1998; 393; 344-346.
[21] de Duve C, A Guided Tour of the Living Cell, vol. 2. Scientific American Library, W. H. Freeman, New York 1984, pp 257.
[22] Gabor D. and Goss WP. Interference Microscope with Total Wavefront Reconstruction, Journal Optical Society of America 1966; 56(7): 849-858.

A COMPARATIVE STUDY OF STRING DISSIMILARITY MEASURES IN STRUCTURAL CLUSTERING

Ana L. N. Fred, Instituto Superior Técnico, Lisbon, Portugal
José M. N. Leitão, Instituto Superior Técnico, Lisbon, Portugal

ABSTRACT

This paper addresses structural clustering by stressing the distinction between string matching and structural resemblance. The hierarchical agglomerative clustering concept and a partitional approach are explored in a comparative study of several dissimilarity measures: minimum code length based measures; dissimilarity based on the concept of reduction in grammatical complexity; string matching and error-correcting parsing. Test examples include: synthetic data, with variable length strings; text analysis; and contour images.

INTRODUCTION

Clustering is a powerful tool in revealing the intrinsic organization of data. Concerning structural patterns, it consists of an unsupervised association of data based on the similarity of their structures and primitives. Potential applications of structural clustering are: unsupervised grammatical inference; text analysis; contour image categorisation.

Clustering algorithms for structural pattern analysis based on string descriptions are extensions of conventional clustering methods [1] by introducing dissimilarity measures between strings. Distances and dissimilarity measures commonly found in the literature are based on string matching [2, 3], assuming string edit operations: insertion, substitution and deletion of symbols, to which costs are associated; typically, they are variations of the Levenshtein distance, of which the probabilistic modeling is a particular instance. These measures are applied, for instance, in error correction of noisy sentences [4, 5] and in recognition tasks [6, 7, 8, 9, 10]. Recently we have proposed similarity measures based on the search of common subpatterns [11] or composition rules [12], exploring the concept of minimum description. The basic idea is that, if strings are structurally similar, then the description of the ensemble should be more compact than the description of the strings when considered individually. Reference [11] concerns the search of common subpatterns based on Solomonoff's coding [13, 14], the similarity between strings being defined as a ratio of decrease in code length. In [12] strings structure is modelled by grammars; similar rules of composition lead to a reduction in the global grammar complexity, which is the basis of the proposed similarity measure between strings. The later measures are then extended to sets of strings, constituting the cluster formation rules used in hierarchical agglomerative clustering algorithms. Other clustering strategies found in the literature include: *sentence to sentence clustering*, described in [16, 17], based on the comparison of a candidate string with sentences in previously formed clusters (clustering based on a nearest-neighbor rule) or with cluster centre strings (cluster centre technique); grammatical inference and error-correcting parsing are combined in a procedure described in [15, 17], where grammars characterize the structural identity of the formed clusters and the distance between an input sequence and a language is computed by error-correcting parsing.

This paper addresses structural clustering by stressing the distinction between string matching and structural resemblance. The similarity measures proposed by the authors are analyzed and compared with string matching and error-correcting parsing techniques in the context of structural clustering. Hierarchical agglomerative clustering algorithms using these proximity measures and Fu's algorithm [15] are used in the analysis.

The paper is organized as follows. In a first section the set of dissimilarity measures is defined and analyzed in light of a short example. The second section presents the clustering algorithms; in the next section their performance is evaluated in several test examples in terms of the correctness of the associations made. A final section summarizes the conclusions.

STRINGS, DISTANCES AND DISSIMILARITY MEASURES

A distance between strings s_i and s_j is some function $d(s_i, s_j)$ measuring the dissimilarity between the two strings that obey the following properties:

1. Symmetry: $d(s_i, s_j) = d(s_j, s_i)$.
2. Triangle inequality: $d(s_i, s_l) \leq d(s_i, s_j) + d(s_j, s_l)$.

This paper will focus on four approaches to measure string dissimilarity: (i)- string matching based on error transformations; (ii) - structure modeling by grammars, resemblance being measured by grammatical complexity; (iii) - searching for common subpatterns in a minimum code length framework; (iv) - distances between a string and a language described by a grammar, by means of error-correcting parsing.

DISSIMILARITY BASED ON STRING EDIT OPERATIONS

This approach is based on the definition of string editing operations or error transformations, namely substitution, deletion and insertion of symbols. The well known ***Levensthein distance*** between two strings s_1 and s_2 , $d_L(s_1, s_2)$, is defined as the minimum number of editing operations needed to transform s_1 into s_2. An extension of the Levensthein distance by associating different costs to the several editing operations is known as the ***weighted Levensthein distance***, defined as

$$d_W(s_1, s_2) = min\,\{\gamma(T) | T \text{ is an edit transformation of } s_1 \text{ into } s_2\}$$

where $\gamma(T) = \sum_{i=1} \gamma(T_i)$, T_i is the ith editing operation performed in the transformation T, and $\gamma(T_i)$ is the cost associated with that operation.

In order to preserve the symmetry property, weights can not be assigned arbitrarily. The costs of inserting or deleting a given symbol must be equal, as for the substitution of symbols: $\gamma(T_S(b|a)) = \gamma(T_S(a|b))$. It can be shown that the triangle inequality is verified (see for instance [8] and the references therein); thus it is a metric.

For simplicity, and under the assumption of no ***a priori*** knowledge about the penalizing mechanisms of the error transformations, in the remaining of the paper all edit operations will be assigned unitary costs, except for the operation of maintenance of a symbol, which will be assigned a null weight - d_L.

Normalization of the previous distances with respect to string lengths are obtained by post-normalization ($d_{NW}(s_1, s_2) = d_W(s_1, s_2)/max\{|s_1|, |s_2|\}$) - normalized weighted Levensthein distance, and by optimal minimization of the distance normalized by the length of the editing path - normalized edit distance [6]:

$$d_{NE}(s_1, s_2) = min \left\{ \frac{\gamma(T)}{|T|} \;\middle|\; T \text{ is an editing path between } s_1 \text{ and } s_2 \right\}$$

where $|T|$ is the length of the editing path. Vidal [6] has shown that the latter performs better in many situations. It should be emphasized that normalization leads to dissimilarity measures that are not metrics due to failure of the triangle inequality [8].

DISSIMILARITY BASED ON ERROR-CORRECTING PARSING

Fu [15, 17] defined a distance between strings based on the modeling of string structure by means of grammars and on the concept of error-correcting parsing (ECP). According to this model, the distance between a string and a reference string is given by the error-correcting parser as the weighted Levensthein distance between the string and the nearest (in terms of edit operations) string generated by the grammar inferred from the reference string (thus exhibiting a similar structure):

$$d_{ECP_f}(s_1, s_2) = \overset{min}{y} \{d_W(s_1, y) | y \in L(G_2) \text{ and } G_2 := \text{ Grammar inferred from } s_2\}$$

The computation of the dissimilarity between strings requires two steps: 1- modeling of strings with grammars; 2- computation of the dissimilarity by error-correcting parsing. The grammatical inference procedure is responsible for the identification of regular patterns of composition that lead to the definition of rules. Different inference algorithms will produce distinct results both quantitatively and qualitatively, depending on how far apart are the underlying heuristics or criteria supporting the methods. It is not possible to define the "optimal" grammatical inference algorithm. Several methods can be tested or the election of a specific algorithm has to be based on some assumption or hint about the underlying structure.

It is important to notice that, even with adequate definition of the editing weights, the symmetry property cannot be ensured ***a priori***. In fact, $d_{ECP_f}(s_1, s_2) = min\{d_L(s_1, L(G_{s_2})\}$ which, in general, will be different from $d_{ECP_f}(s_2, s_1) = min\{d_L(s_2, L(G_{s_1})\}$. For instance, using Crespi-Reghizzi's method [19, 20] for grammatical inference one obtains: $d_{ECP_f}(dfg, (abc)^2) = 3$ and $d_{ECP_f}((abc)^2, dfg) = 6$. In order to preserve the symmetry property we will therefore use the new definition:

$$d_{ECP}(s_1, s_2) = min\{d_{ECP_f}(s_1, s_2), d_{ECP_f}(s_2, s_1)\}$$

In this paper we will consider another variation of the previous measure by using the normalized edit distance, which we designate by d_{NECP}. Neither d_{ECP} or d_{NECP} constitute a metric because they do not obey the triangle inequality (for instance, $d_{ECP}((dfg)^8, (abc)^2) = 24, d_{ECP}((abc)^2, dfg) = 3$ and $d_{ECP}(dfg, (dfg)^8) = 0$).

GRAMMAR COMPLEXITY-BASED DISSIMILARITY

In [12] we have proposed a new measure of similarity between strings according to which patterns are described by grammars, and exploring the concept of grammar complexity. The basic idea is that, if two sentences are structurally similar, than their joint description will be more compact than their isolated description due to sharing on common rules of symbol composition; the compactness of representation is quantified by the grammar complexity and the similarity is measured by the ***ratio of decrease in grammar complexity***, as follows:

$$RDGC(s_1, s_2) = \frac{C(G_{s_1}) + C(G_{s_2}) - C(G_{s_1,s_2})}{min\,\{C(G_{s_1}), C(G_{s_2})\}}$$

where $C(G_{s_i})$ denotes grammar complexity.

The complexity of a grammar G, $C(G)$, is defined as [12]

$$C(G) = \sum_{i=1}^{r} \sum_{j=1}^{l_i} C(\alpha_{ij})$$

where α_{ij} represents the right side of the jth production for the ith non-terminal symbol of the grammar, and

$$C(\alpha) = (n+1)log(n+1) - \sum_{i=1}^{m} k_i log k_i$$

with k_i being the number of times that the symbol a_i appears in α, and n is the length of the grammatical sentence α.

Results obtained for the similarity measure, as for the preceding case, depend on the grammatical inference strategies adopted. However, the following characteristics are independent of the method adopted:

$$\begin{aligned} RDGC(s_1, s_2) &\geq 0 \\ &\leq 1 \\ &= 1 \text{ if } s_1 \equiv s_2 \\ &= 0 \text{ if } s_1 \text{ and } s_2 \text{ have non overlaping alphabets} \\ RDGC(s_1, s_2) &= RDGC(s_2, s_1) \end{aligned}$$

As indicated above, the symmetry property is verified; the triangle inequality, however, is not always preserved.

MINIMUM CODE LENGTH-BASED SIMILARITY

In [11] we proposed another measure of structural similarity exploring the notion of compressibility of sequences and algorithmic complexity. Solomonoff's code is there used for the search of pattern regularities and sequence compression. According to this coding scheme a sequence s_i is represented by the triplet: $alphabet$, $symbol\_definition$, s_i_coded, where a coded string is obtained in an iterative procedure where, in each step, intermediate codes are produced by defining sequences of two symbols, which are represented by special single symbols, and rewriting the sequences using them [11, 13]. Compact codes are produced when sequences exhibit local or distant inter symbol interactions. Strings sharing subpattern regularities will therefore produce more compact codes than the gathering of the codes for the individual sequences. The quantification of this reduction in code length forms the basis of the similarity measure which we designate by NRDCL:

$$NRDCL(s_1, s_2) = \frac{code\_len(s_1) + code\_len(s_2) - code\_len(s_1, s_2)}{(as)/2 + abs(|s_1\_coded| - |s_2\_coded|)}$$

with

$$as = |alphabet\_s_1| + |symbol\_definition\_s_1| + |alphabet\_s_2| + |symbol\_definition\_s_2|$$

This similarity measure is symmetric but the triangle inequality does not hold in general.

EXAMPLE

Table 1 illustrates the previous proximity measures. As shown, d_L and d_{NE} are typically conditioned by the similarity of strings lengths, higher similarity being found between $(abc)^8$ and $(cba)^8$ than with $(abc)^{48}$. They serve the purpose of string matching rather than structural similarity. This effect is compensated in the remaining measures with true independence in the strings lengths being obtained with the ECP and RDGC measures - grammatical models. The RDGC similarity gives higher penalization to the situation of distinct alphabets; the ECP method enables the establishment of differentiated costs, but criteria must be defined for the construction of these weights.

ID	String	d_L	d_{NE}	d_{ECP}	d_{NECP}	$RDGC$	$NRDCL$
1	$(dfg)^8$	24	1	24	1	0	0
2	$(dfg)^{18}$	54	1	24	1	0	0
3	$(abc)^8$	0	0	0	0	1	1
4	$(abc)^{18}$	30	0.556	0	0	1	0.878
5	$(abc)^{48}$	120	0.833	0	0	1	0.818
6	$(cba)^8$	16	0.667	13	0.542	0	0
7	$(cba)^{18}$	30	0.556	13	0.519	0	0.146
8	$(abc)^8(cba)^8$	24	0.500	1	0.042	0.586	0.591
9	$(abc)^2(cba)^{14}$	24	0.500	1	0.042	0.586	0.210
10	$(abcf)^7$	16	0.400	8	0.250	0	0.429

Table 1: Dissimilarity and similarity values between string $(abc)^8$ and the strings on the left column.

CLUSTERING

The clustering algorithms proposed by the authors in [11, 12] integrate the RDGC and the NRDCL similarity measures into the hierarchical agglomerative clustering framework. This clustering paradigm can be summarized as follows: begin by assigning each sample to a single cluster and continue by merging clusters based on the similarity between clusters until a one-cluster solution is produced. The algorithm uses a proximity matrix measuring the similarity / dissimilarity between all pairs of clusters at a given step. It produces a sequence of partitions of the original data. A particular clustering is obtained by either fixating the number of clusters desired or by comparing the proximity values between clusters with a threshold; in this case the number of classes obtained is not known *a priori*. A schematic description of the algorithm can be expressed as:

- *Algorithm:* Hierarchical Agglomerative Clustering.
- *Input:* A set of strings $X = \{s_1, s_2, \ldots, s_n\}$; a threshold th or the desired number of clusters N_c.
- *Output:* A partition of X into m clusters ($m = N_c$ if the latter is specified), $C_1, C_2, \ldots, C_m$.
- *Steps:*
  1. Set each pattern into a single cluster. Set $N_a = n$.
  2. compute the proximity matrix between all pairs of strings.
  3. If $N_a = N_c$ go to step 6.

4. Select from the proximity matrix the pair of clusters C_i, C_j most similar and let $simil$ be that value of similarity. If $simil$ is less than th (greater than th if it is a dissimilarity measure) than go to step 6.
5. Merge the two clusters and update the proximity matrix accordingly. Set $N_a = N_a - 1$ and continue in step 3.
6. End the computation by returning the data partition encountered.

Let C_i be a cluster represented by a set of n_i sentences $X_i = \{s_1^i, s_2^i \ldots, s_{ni}^i\}$. Distinct clustering algorithms are obtained by appropriate definition of the dissimilarity between strings and the rule of cluster formation - proximity function between clusters.

For the definition of the proximity matrix, the dissimilarity between pairs of strings are extrapolated for sets of strings. Table 2 (a) summarizes the characteristics of the algorithms analyzed. In the first one, distances are based on string editing operations and the nearest-neighbor (NN) rule is applied in cluster formation; it can be viewed as a hierarchical version of the sentence-to-sentence clustering procedure proposed in [16] by considering both the Levensthein and normalized edit distances. It may be shown that it has the same time complexity, being less sensitive to the order of presentation of the patterns.

a) Hierarchical Agglomerative Schemes			
Philosophy of the method	Proximity between clusters	String similarity	Acronym
String edit operations	Nearest-neighbor rule: $d(C_i, C_j) = min\{d(s_k, s_l) \| s_k \in C_i, s_l \in C_j\}$	d_L d_{NE}	NN-SEO-DL NN-SEO-NED
Grammar complexity	Ratio of decrease in grammar complexity: $RDGC(C_i, C_j) = \frac{C(G_{C_i})+C(G_{C_j})-C(G_{C_i,C_j})}{min\{C(G_{C_i}),C(G_{C_j})\}}$	$RDGC$	MGC
Minimum code length	Normalized decrease in code length: $NRDCL(C_i, C_j) =$ $= \frac{code\_len(C_i)+code\_len(C_j)-code\_len(C_i,C_j)}{(as)/2+abs(\|C_i\_coded\|-\|C_j\_coded\|)}$ $as = \sum_{k=i,j} \|alph\_C_k\| + \|symb\_def\_C_k\|$	$NRDCL$	MCL
b) Sentence to Sentence Clustering			
Error correcting parsing	Nearest-neighbor rule: $d(s_i, C_j) = min\{d(s_i, s_l) \| s_l \in C_j\}$	d_{ECP} d_{NECP}	ECP-DL ECP-NED

Table 2: Clustering algorithms.

Finally, as shown in table 2(b), the study will also include the partitional clustering algorithm based on error-correcting parsing described in [15, 17]. This algorithm assumes grammars to model cluster identity, starting with a single cluster with a first sample; the remaining data is classified by computing the distance defined in the previous section between the candidate string and the grammars describing the clusters formed so far; if the minimal distance found is less than a given threshold, th, the string is included in the corresponding cluster and its grammar is updated; otherwise, a new cluster is formed with this sample.

TEST EXAMPLES

The above measures are evaluated and compared in the clustering of test cases and real data. Concerning grammatical inference, Crespi-Reghizzi's [19, 20] method is used. Evaluation of the methods is based on the *classification error*, which measures the ability of the classifier to correctly associate patterns in clusters.

TEST STRINGS

Figure 1 presents the results of clustering of the test strings defined in section . As shown, grammar based methods (MGC and ECP) perfectly associate patterns at very high similarity (low dissimilarity) values. The MCL method also achieves the perceptual intuitive clusters. Concerning the string matching algorithms, neither the normalized or the unnormalized versions were able to perform reasonable associations, which are mostly dictated by string length proximity.

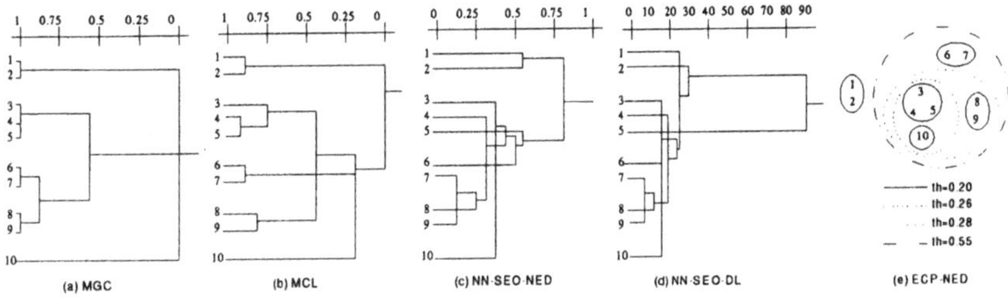

Figure 1: (a) to (d) - Dendrograms for the hierarchical methods. (e) - Clusters obtained with the ECP-NED method for increasing values of the parameter th. Results obtained with ECP-DL are similar, with the particularity that, by increasing the threshold th, a jump from four to two clusters is observed.

CLUSTERING OF CONTOUR IMAGES

In this section we illustrate the capacity of the several clustering algorithms described previously in the partitioning of images of objects of hardware tools based on a differential 8-directional chain code (a more detailed description of the contour definition process and the images database can be found in [18]). Three tools are analyzed, 10 samples per tool. Table 3 illustrates the typical patterns.

Class	Tool	Samples
1		61072620026270163702620026207261072601627026200262
		71172620026200162701637026207261073610726116370262
		71172620026270262002620737016370262002620026200162
2		00000000660000001710000060000010000000075000000003
		00000000500000000000000076000001610000000660000000003
		000000005000000017100000500000161000000076000000003
3		1000000005000000000720700070170000000000500000000012
		100000000500000000000107000702700000000000500000000012
		1000000005700000000710700770270000000000500000000012

Table 3: Sample string contour descriptions of hardware tools.

As the length of the strings is constant, the normalized and not normalized versions of the algorithms based on string edit operations provide the same cluster associations. As shown in figure 2(a) the MGC method completely separates the three classes of patterns. The NN rules are good in associating the patterns of classes 2 and 3 and in distinguishing between pattern

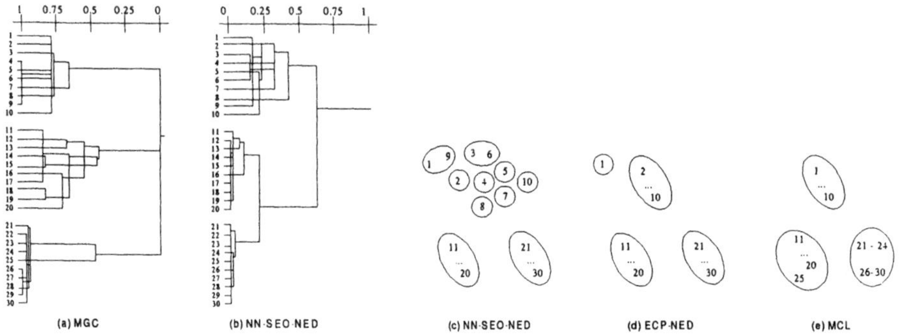

Figure 2: Dendrograms for the MGC method (a) and NN-SEO-NED (b). Clusters obtained with NN-SEO-NED ($th = 0.2$) (c), ECP-NED ($th = 0.1$) (d) and MCL ($th = 0.48$) (e) methods.

1 and the remaining; however, separation between classes 2 and 3 is not possible without fragmentation of class 1 into several (mostly single) clusters, as illustrated in figure 2(c). Error-correcting parsing refines this result by grouping all but one pattern from class 1 into one cluster; the inclusion of sample number 1 into cluster 1 implies the union of samples 11 to 30. The MCL method failed to associate pattern 25 in the correct class.

ORGANIZING EMAIL

The next example consists of the first lines of text extracted from email messages, as shown in table 4, by removing space characters. Variable length samples using the English and the Portuguese language were included.

ID	Mail Type	Cl.	Lang.	# chars	Sample Text
1	call for papers	1	Eng.	142	ISSS'98 FINAL CALL FOR PAPERS (SUBMISSION ...
2	call for papers	1	Eng.	106	CALL FOR PAPERS WORLD MULTICONFERENCE ...
3	call for papers	1	Eng.	160	CALL FOR PAPERS RENSSELAER'S INTERNAT ...
4	call for papers	1	Eng.	87	CALL FOR PAPERS THE PRAGUE STRINGOLOGY ...
5	personal letter	2	Eng.	161	DEAR ANA, THANKS FOR THE EMAIL. PLEASE ...
6	personal letter	2	Eng.	129	DEAR ANA, IN THE BACKUP DIRECTORY THERE ...
7	journal advert.	4	Eng.	137	CONTENTS DIRECT FROM ELSEVIER SCIENCE ...
8	MSc advertisement	3	Port.	153	PROVAS DE MESTRADO EM ENGENHARIA ...
9	MSc advertisement	3	Port.	280	PROVAS DE MESTRADO EM ENGENHARIA ...
10	MSc advertisement	3	Port.	168	PROVAS DE MESTRADO EM ENGENHARIA ...

Table 4: Text from email messages.

In this case, only the MCL method was able to provide meaningful associations, correctly forming the classes 1 to 3; sample 7 (class 4) was assigned to class 1 due to the existence of a common theme in the conference and journal advertisements. Low similarity values (below 10e-2)were found by the MGC method at the character level, no significant associations being made. Methods based on error transformations failed to discover common patterns in the data. The normalized dissimilarity values of the NN method were high and in narrow ranges, resulting in no associations for threshold values above 0.73; when a fixed number of

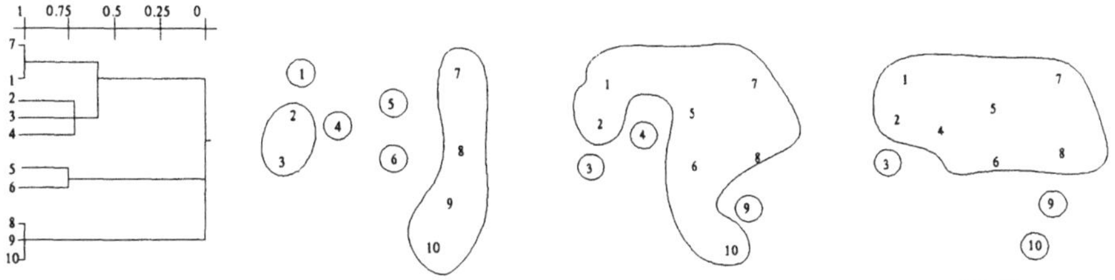

Figure 3: (a) Dendrogram for the MCL method. (b) Associations obtained with the ECP-NED method for $th = 0.5$. (c) - (d) Examples of associations provided by the NN rule when setting the number of clusters to 4. The dissimilarities ranges are, respectively, 0.73-0.76 and 90-214.

classes was imposed, regardless of the dissimilarity measures values, arbitrary associations were provided by the several methods (see a few examples in figure 3). Although several of the sentences have common sequences, resemblance cannot be measured in terms of string matching as the order of the narrative is arbitrary.

CONCLUSIONS

In this paper structural clustering of patterns described in the string format was addressed in a comparative study of four classes of dissimilarity measures. These included distances based on string editing operations, namely the Levensthein distance, d_L, between two strings and its normalization by the length of the editing path, d_{NE}. The dissimilarity measures d_{ECP} and d_{NECP} considered the minimum (normalized) Levensthein distance between one string and the language generated by the grammar inferred from the second string, computed by error-correcting parsing. Finally, the similarity measures $RDGC$ and $NRDCL$ addressed the concepts of grammatical complexity and minimum description length, exploring, respectively, the structural resemblance between strings expressed in terms of common rules of description and common patterns of statistical dependencies between symbols manifesting as similar subsequences.

The above measures were evaluated in the categorisation of synthetic and real data, integrated in hierarchical agglomerative and partitional clustering algorithms. Test examples included the analysis of email messages and clustering of contour images.

The major conclusions are summarized as follows:

- Minimum description-based methods are best suited for context analysis, where the appearance of certain sequences rather than the particular order of their appearance is of major importance.
- String matching techniques are best suited for exact recognition of patterns.
- Grammatical inference-based methods are more reliable in grouping of variable length patterns with regular structures. Additionally, they have the ability to reduce large collections of data into lower dimension models that preserve the underlying structure of the original collection, thus providing a means for data reduction.

ACKNOWLEDGEMENTS

This work was partially supported by the projects PECS/C/SAU/212/95 and PRAXIS 2/2.1/TIT/1580/95.

REFERENCES

[1] Jain AK, Dubes RC. Algorithms for Clustering Data. Prentice Hall, Englewood Cliffs, 1988.

[2] Bunke H. String matching for structural pattern recognition. In: Bunke H, Sanfeliu A (eds). Syntactic and Structural Pattern Recognition, Theory and Applications. World Scientific, 1990, pp 119–144.

[3] Bunke H. Recent advance in string matching. In: Bunke H (eds). Advances in Structural and Syntactic Pattern Recognition. World Scientific, 1992, pp 107–116.

[4] Kashiap RL, Oommen BJ. String correction using probabilistic models. Pattern Recog. Letters 1984; 147–154.

[5] Oommen BJ. Recognition of noisy subsequences using constrained edit distances. IEEE Trans. Pattern Anal. and Machine Intelligence 1987; PAMI-9(5): 676–685.

[6] Marzal A, Vidal E. Computation of normalized edit distance and applications. IEEE Trans. Pattern Anal. and Machine Intelligence 1993; PAMI-2(15): 926–932.

[7] Bunke H, Buhler U. 2-D Invariant shape recognition using string matching. In Proc. 2nd Int. Conf. on Automation, Robotics and Computer Vision, 1992.

[8] Cortelazzo G, Deretta D, Mian GA, Zamperoni P. Normalized weighted Levensthein distance and triangle inequality in the context of similarity discrimination of bilevel images. Pattern Recognition Letters 1996; 17: 431–436.

[9] Cortelazzo G, Mian GA, Vezzi G, Zamperoni P. Trademark shapes description by string-matching techniques. Pattern Recognition 1994; 27(8): 1005–1018.

[10] Peng HL, Chen SY. Trademark shape recognition using closed contours. Pattern Recognition Letters 1997; 18: 791–803.

[11] Fred ALN, Leitão JMN. A minimum code length technique for clustering of syntactic patterns. In Proc. of the 13th IAPR Int'l Conference on Pattern Recognition, vol 2. IEEE Press, 1996, pp 680–684.

[12] Fred ALN. Clustering of sequences using a minimum grammar complexity criterion. In: Miclet L, Higuera C (eds). Grammatical Inference: Learning Syntax from Sentences. Springer-Verlag, 1996, pp 107–116.

[13] Solomonoff RJ. A formal theory of inductive inference (part I and II). Information and Control 1964; 7:1-22, 224–254.

[14] Fred ALN, Leitão JMN. Solomonoff coding as a means of introducing prior information in Syntactic Pattern Recognition. In Proc. of the 12th IAPR Int'l Conference on Pattern Recognition, vol 2. IEEE Press, 1994, pp 14–18.

[15] Fu KS, Lu SY. A clustering procedure for syntactic patterns. IEEE Trans. Systems Man Cybernetics 1977; SMC-7(7):537–541.

[16] Lu SY, Fu KS. A sentence-to-sentence clustering procedure for pattern analysis. IEEE Trans. Systems Man Cybernetics 1978; SMC-8(5):381–389.

[17] Fu KS. Syntactic pattern recognition. In Handbook of Pattern Recognition and Image Processing. Academic Press, 1986, pp 85–117.

[18] Fred ALN, Marques JS, Jorge PM. Hidden Markov models vs syntactic modeling in object recognition. In Proc. 1997 International Conference on Image Processing, IEEE Press, 1997, pp 893–896.

[19] Fu KS, Lu SY. Grammatical inference: introduction and survey -part I and II. IEEE Trans. Pattern Anal. and Machine Intelligence 1986; PAMI-8(5): 343–359.

[20] L. Miclet. Grammatical inference. In: Bunke H, Sanfeliu A (eds). Syntactic and Structural Pattern Recognition - Theory and Applications. Scientific Publishing, 1990, pp 237–290.

SUPPORT VECTOR MACHINES AND LINEAR SPECTRAL UNMIXING FOR REMOTE SENSING

Martin Brown and Hugh Lewis,
Department of Electronics and Computer Science,
University of Southampton, Highfield, Southampton, UK

ABSTRACT

Mixture modelling is becoming an increasing important tool in the remote sensing community as researchers attempt to resolve sub-pixel, mixture information. This paper compares a well-established technique, linear spectral mixture models, with a much newer idea based on data selection, support vector machines. In the simplest case, both algorithms form linear mixture models between "pure" class prototypes, and it is shown that they are equivalent. Support vector machines however, have the ability to perform automatic data selection for non-separable, non-linear data.

1 MIXED-PIXEL CLASSIFICATION

Traditionally, the production of maps from satellite imagery assumes that each pixel of the image can be assigned to a single land cover class. A crisp classification process then aims to attach one of a number of mutually exclusive labels, within a closed world environment. In this context, the algorithms are formulated for **discrimination** which is the practice of dividing up the feature space into a number of non-overlapping regions, and **statistical pattern recognition** which is the practice of modelling the posterior (or prior) distributions for a pre-defined number of discrete objects. In such problems, it is typically assumed that the process of generating observable data may be decomposed into a number of independent classes, each of which is a sub-process generating data according to a particular class-conditional density for that class. When the class conditional densities do not overlap a discrimination approach is appropriate, but when they do overlap, a statistical pattern recognition approach which models the posterior probabilities, $p(C_j|\mathbf{x})$ is more appropriate. This is generally necessary, as the chosen feature vector does not contain enough information to completely separate all the classes.

Implicit in the traditional classification process is the concept that each feature vector should be mapped into one of the classes of interest. However, the spatial characteristics of satellite sensors are such that a significant amount of confusion can arise from variable land cover in the Instantaneous Field Of View (IFOV). In addition, energy transfer into and from neighbouring IFOVs leads to further pixel ambiguity. In order to meet the accuracy requirements imposed upon the production of land cover maps, it is necessary to resolve these ambiguities. The process of mixed-pixel classification is therefore to **model** the class mixing proportions, [9], (percentage ground cover area), rather than estimate the probability that the signature corresponds to a particular class label. In practice, it is often found that the posterior probabilities are correlated with the area predictions, but they represent orthogonal information: errors due to statistical uncertainty and measurements based on area mixing, respectively [11].

Implicit in the traditional classification process is the concept that each feature vector should be mapped into one of the classes of interest. In remote sensing however, this is unrealistic as the classes represented by a pixel's spectral features depend on the sensor's instantaneous field of view. This spectral mixing can originate from both overlap between different land cover classes, and clouds partially obscuring a single pure pixel. Hence, the process of mixed-pixel classification is to **model** the class mixing proportions, [9], (percentage ground cover area), rather than estimate the probability that the signature corresponds to a particular class label. This mixture **cannot** be resolved into either of the two classes, even when the input information is perfect [5], yet the estimate of the mixing proportions may be regarded as a statistical quantity, due to missing features and lack of training data.

This paper compares the Linear Spectral Mixture Modelling techniques which have been developed in the remote sensing community with the recently developed Support Vector Machines (SVM). In the simplest case, both approaches can be shown to be equivalent, although the SVMs are derived using "optimal concepts" which appear to hold the most promise for future research and development.

2 LINEAR SPECTRAL MIXTURE MODELS

Spectral unmixing has been used as a technique for analysing the mixture of components in remotely sensed images for almost 30 years, [9]. During that time, it has been used to study the rock and soil components collected on the Viking Mars missions [1], and to estimate ground and vegetation cover, [6,12,13]. The technique is based on the assumption that the class mixing is performed in a linear manner between so-called end-members (single instances of each class which represent the "pure components"). Two techniques have been proposed for selecting the spectral signatures of the classes of interest: to measure the spectral signature at ground level and then make atmospheric and satellite specific corrections and to identify an exemplar pure pixel in the satellite imagery and use its spectral components. The first technique suffers when the corrections are inappropriate whereas it is sometimes difficult to identify exemplar pure pixels within a satellite image. In addition, both techniques suffer when the class core has more than a single member.

2.1 ALGORITHMIC IMPLEMENTATION

Assuming there exist m classes of interest and n spectral features which are used to model the class mixture, the user must specify an $(n+1) \times m$ matrix **R** which contains the spectral values of the "pure pixels", one from each class. In addition to the n spectral values within each feature vector, it is also assumed that a constant, bias value of +1 has been appended to the start of each input. Note that the selection of these pure pixels is very subjective and is often a compromise between several factors, especially when $m > 2$. Hence, it is often a process of trial and error to obtain satisfactory results.

The assumed linear model is of the form:

$$\mathbf{x} = \mathbf{R}\mathbf{y} \tag{1}$$

where **R** is the matrix of pure pixels, **x** is the vector of spectral inputs and **y** is the vector of mixing proportions. It is assumed that **R** is **full-rank**, ie. all the pure pixels are linearly independent. This represents a forwards model of the satellite, but we are interested in formulating an inverse model for area estimation.

Letting **V** denote the covariance error matrix of the observations **x**, then the goal of predicting the class mixtures can be formulated as minimising the weighted sum squared error:

$$J = (\hat{\mathbf{x}} - \mathbf{x})\, \mathbf{V}^{-1}\, (\hat{\mathbf{x}} - \mathbf{x}) \tag{2}$$

In addition, to ensure that estimated mixtures sum to unity, an additional linear constraint is introduced into the optimisation goal, namely:

$$\sum_{j=1}^{m} y_j = 1 \tag{3}$$

This linear constraint can be combined with the quadratic error loss criteria to produce a closed-form estimate, [7], of the mixing proportions:

$$\mathbf{y} = \mathbf{C}^{-1}\mathbf{e} - \mathbf{C}^{-1}\mathbf{b}^T \left(\mathbf{b}\mathbf{C}^{-1}\mathbf{b}^T\right)^{-1} \left(\mathbf{b}\mathbf{C}^{-1}\mathbf{e} - 1\right) \tag{4}$$

where $\mathbf{C} = \mathbf{R}^T\mathbf{V}^{-1}\mathbf{R}$ is the weighted autocorrelation matrix, $\mathbf{e} = \mathbf{R}^T\mathbf{V}^{-1}\mathbf{x}$ is the weighted cross correlation vector and $\mathbf{b}$ is a unity row vector. Note that the first term on the right hand side of this equation is simply a weighted **least squares estimator**, and the second ensures that the estimates sum to unity. In addition, the output can be expressed as:

$$\mathbf{y} = \mathbf{W}\mathbf{x} \tag{5}$$

for a suitably defined linear gain matrix, $\mathbf{W}$.

The partition of unity constraint in equation 4 doesn't ensure that the estimates lie in the unit interval however, and in order to explicitly impose this on the solution, a common practice is to set $y_j = 0$ when $y_j < 0$ and then normalise the remaining estimates. This produces the Constrained Least Squares LSMM (CLS), [6,12]. Note however, that it may be useful to threshold the outputs when they are greater than 1 as well, prior to normalising the remaining values, and this will be further discussed in section 3.

2.2 INTERPRETATION

The seemingly complex routines for implementing the LSMM algorithm often obscure their basic properties, some of which are briefly described below.

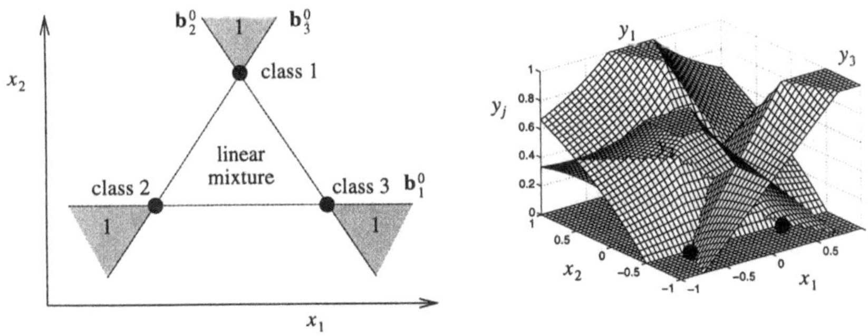

Figure 1: A linear spectral mixture model for two inputs and three classes, where the pure pixels occur at (0,0.5), (-0.5,-0.5), (0.5,-0.5).

At most $m = n + 1$ classes can be linearly mixed, as illustrated in figure 1. There are $n + 1$ linear parameters associated with each linear mixture model. The response must be 1 for the associated pure class pixel and 0 for the $m - 1$ remaining pure class pixels, therefore there can be at most $n + 1$ classes used. For each class C_j and pure pixel $\mathbf{x}_j$, there exists a hyperplane of dimension $n-1$, which passes through the remaining points; this is termed the **linear margin boundary,** $\mathbf{b}_j^{01}$.

Linear mixture domains are determined region enclosed by the linear margin boundaries. When the inner product between all the class boundaries and an input vector produce a non-negative response, the mixture model is linear and is formed from a **convex hull** whose exterior is formed from the pure pixels. When the inner product is negative for some of the pure pixels, the non-negative mixture constraint re-sets the value to zero and explicitly normalises the remaining pixel values. Hence the resulting mixture model is non-linear in these domains. This is illustrated in figure 1.

The selection of the pure pixels prototypes may prove to be problematic. Often the class cores consist of more than a single pixel either due to natural, deterministic class variation for which an area of 1 should always be predicted, or due to random spectral confusion where the aim is to minimise this effect. These two effects should be treated differently, although the vast majority of the LSMM literature has been concerned with the latter. Modelling natural class variation is very different from considering a single pure pixel, and it is argued in the next section that the concepts used to derive the SVM algorithms may be appropriate. In particular, they simplify to the normal LSMM algorithms when the classes can be modelled as single pure pixels.

The CLS LSMM maximises the size of the margin when $m < n+1$. This result shows that the weight vectors calculated by the LSMM algorithm are minimum norm solutions (without the bias term) and a full proof can be found in [3]. It also illustrates how the optimality constraints, given by equation 2 and 3, can be re-posed to explicitly represent this property. It could be argued that the two LSMM constraints are not unique in that they state that the linear margin boundaries should pass through the pure pixels (equation 2) and the linear one and zero boundaries should be parallel (equation 3). This is not enough information to generate a unique solution, although when a pseudo inverse solution is calculated, this implicitly selects a minimum weight vector norm solution.

In summary, LSMM algorithm has some interesting properties but it places severe restrictions on the type of problems to which it can be applied by the assumptions of the existence of a single pure pixel and the fact that the mixing is linear.

3 SUPPORT VECTOR MACHINES

Support Vector Machines (SVMs) attempt to select a subset of the data in order to build a model or discriminate between classes, [4,8,14]. In the simplest case, a linear discriminant is used which maximises the minimum margin between two classes. Inherent in this approach is the idea that only the data points which lie on the class boundary are necessary for discrimination, and the others can be discarded. In its basic form SVMs are used to discriminate between two class types, but multiple classes can be supported via a 1-of-m encoding of the data and the use of m, single output SVMs. Using a discriminant classification algorithm may initially seem quite different from the mixture model approach, where the aim is to model the continuous transition in class membership, but discrimination can be viewed as an extra process which simply thresholds the output of a continuous model, and this is the view taken in this paper. The simplest SVMs use linear discrimination (models), and it is shown that these are equivalent (under certain circumstances) to LSMM. However, it is not essential to simply use a linear discriminant, and other higher-order, non-linear kernel-based classifiers can be used both for non-linear

[1] A boundary $\mathbf{b}_j^\theta$ can be defined as $\mathbf{b}_j^\theta = \{\mathbf{x} : y_j(\mathbf{x}) = \theta\}$, ie. it represents the input points for which the jth model's output is θ.

discrimination and for modelling, although the regression algorithms are not discussed in this paper. The SVM framework thus provides algorithms for automatic pure pixel selection, for both linear and non-linear, modelling and discrimination problems and generalises the basic LSMM.

The concept behind SVMs is best illustrated by considering a simple two class problem which is linearly separable, as shown in figure 2. Here, there are an infinite number of potential linear discriminators which can separate the data, but there exists a unique separator which:

maximises the minimal distance from each class.

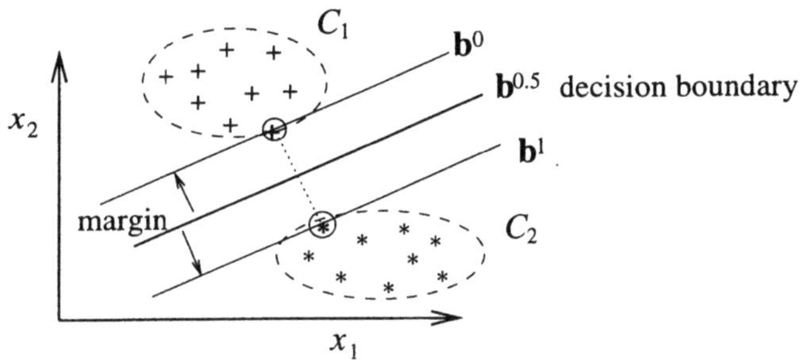

Figure 2: A linear SVM for two inputs and two classes. The stars and crosses represent the labelled training data given to the algorithm and the circles denote the selected support vectors which determine the linear margin's boundaries.

The distance between the discriminant and the edge of the class is known as the **margin**, and the aim is to maximise the margin's size. This is done by using only those **support vectors** which lie on boundary of both class conditional distribution and the discriminant's margin in the calculation of the optimal discriminant, as illustrated in figure 2. Much of the data can therefore be discarded.

It is interesting to compare this simple model with the one implicitly assumed to exist for the LSMM algorithm. In figure 1, there exists a convex, simplex (triangular) region where the mixture model is linear. It is also constant in the simplex (triangular) region "behind" each prototype feature vector. Assuming that the LSMM is a true model of the mixture, that the training set contains vectors from the class' cores and that it also contains the 3 prototype vectors, the following result can be established.

3.1 LINEAR SVM AND LSMM

Theorem 1 The models formed by a linear SVM and the LSMM are equivalent when the same "pure pixel" data set is used for both algorithms and the same thresholding and normalising operations are applied to both models.

Proof. This proof will only consider when $m = n + 1$. There are two cases to consider here, when the data point lies in the margin of all classes and when it lies outside the margin of at least one class.

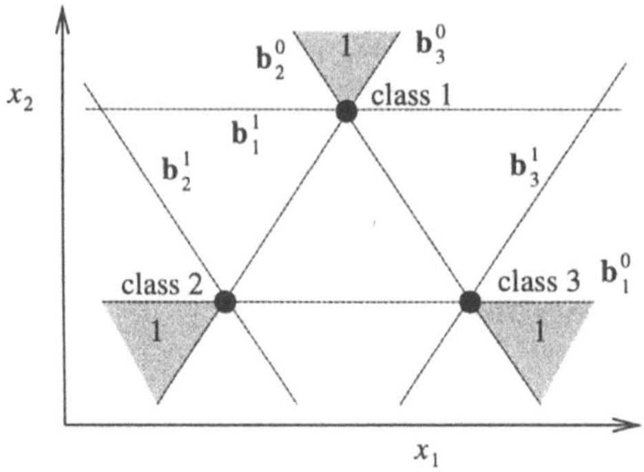

Figure 3: Three linear SVMs and their margins which are denoted by the margins' boundaries $\mathbf{b}_j^0$ and $\mathbf{b}_j^1$, for a two input problem.

When the data point lies within the margin of all the classes, all the unthresholded mixture estimates lie in the unit interval and both models are equivalent. This is easy to establish as both models contain $(n+1)$ linear planes which pass through the same $(n+1)$ data points, hence the outputs must be identical.

When the query point lies outside the margin of at least one class, this class estimate is thresholded at 0 or 1, and the resulting thresholded outputs are explicitly normalised to sum to unity. The motivation for thresholding the outputs of the LSMM are debatable, although it has been reported that thresholding at 0 and normalising the resulting values is a simple and quick way to ensure that the mixtures lie in the unit interval. Thresholding the output at 1 as well is natural when the mixture estimation problem is viewed as a margin maximisation process, and in practice it gives similar results, [3] □

When the number of classes is less than $n+1$, it has recently been shown that the two algorithms are the same [3]. This relies on showing that the output of a single LSMM can be derived from the constraints:

$$\begin{aligned} \text{minimise} \quad & \mathbf{w}^T\mathbf{V}\mathbf{w} \\ \text{subject to} \quad & \mathbf{R}^T\mathbf{w} + b\mathbf{1} = \mathbf{t} \end{aligned} \tag{6}$$

where $\mathbf{w}$ is the linear model's parameter vector, b is the bias term and $\mathbf{t}$ is a 1-of-m target vector. This set of constraints is well-posed in the sense that a unique solution always exists. It also explicitly represents the constraints in terms of maximising the margin (minimising the weight vector) and satisfying the "pure pixel" equations.

3.2 LINEAR SVM: AUTOMATIC DATA SELECTION

In the previous section, it was assumed that the output of an SVM lay in the unity interval, [0,1]. However, for the purposes of deriving the algorithms, it is more convenient to assume the output lies in the bi-polar interval [-1,1]. This can be done without loss of generality.

The linear SVM algorithm is derived from the concepts of optimal separation and support vector (data) selection. The optimality criteria in equation 6, are modified to require that the data should be optimally separated (minimum norm solution), and also that:

$$(\mathbf{w}^T\mathbf{x}^i + b)t^i \geq 1 \qquad i = 1, 2, \ldots, l \tag{7}$$

The solution to these criteria is given by calculating the saddle point of the Lagrange function:

$$L(\mathbf{w}, b, \alpha) = \frac{1}{2}\|\mathbf{w}\|_2^2 - \sum_{i=1}^{l} \alpha^i \left(\left((\mathbf{x}^i.\mathbf{w}) + b \right) t^i - 1 \right) \tag{8}$$

where $\mathbf{w} = (w_1, w_2, \ldots, w_n)$ is the parameter vector associated with the linear decision boundary, b is the corresponding bias term and $\{\mathbf{x}^i, t^i\}_{i=1}^{l}$ is the labelled data set. This can be re-expressed as the *dual problem*:

$$\max_{\alpha} W(\alpha) = \max_{\alpha} -\frac{1}{2}\sum_{i=1}^{l}\sum_{j=1}^{l} \alpha^i \alpha^j t^i t^j (\mathbf{x}^i.\mathbf{x}^j) + \sum_{i=1}^{l} \alpha^i \tag{9}$$

subject to the constraints $\alpha^i \geq 0$ and $\sum_{i=1}^{l} \alpha^i t^i = 0$ for $i = 1, 2, \ldots, l$. Solving this Quadratic Programming (QP) problem for the Lagrange multipliers, α^i, gives a linear discriminant of the form:

$$\mathbf{w} = \sum_{i=1}^{l} \alpha^i \mathbf{x}^i \mathbf{t}^i \tag{10}$$

$$b = -\frac{1}{2}\mathbf{w}.(\mathbf{x}^1 + \mathbf{x}^2) \tag{11}$$

where $\mathbf{x}^1$ and $\mathbf{x}^2$ are any two vectors from C_1 and C_2, respectively, which have non-zero Lagrange multipliers.

The Lagrange multipliers, α^i measure the sensitivity of the solution to a particular constraint (data pair), and for the linearly separable, two class problem just described, only those data points which lie on the margin have a non-zero Lagrange multiplier. Hence solving the QP problem is equivalent to performing data selection. Typically, in large classification problems, about 3 or 5% of the data has been found to be useful (lies in the margin or on the boundary), and the remaining data is considered to be irrelevant for making a decision.

3.3 LINEARLY NON-SEPARABLE MIXTURE MODELLING

When the data is non-separable, as typically occurs in remote sensing, the above quadratic programming problem can be modified by including a set of extra, non-negative variables $\xi_i \geq 0$, [14], which introduce a tolerance to miss-classification:

$$t^i \left(\mathbf{w}.\mathbf{x}^i + b \right) \geq 1 - \xi_i \tag{12}$$

The modified optimisation problem becomes:

$$\min \Phi(\mathbf{w}, \xi) = \frac{1}{2}\|\mathbf{w}\|_2^2 + C\sum_{i=1}^{l} \xi_i \tag{13}$$

where C is a given **smoothness constraint**. Therefore, the cost function is composed of a term which tries to maximise the size of the margin, $\|\mathbf{w}\|_2^2$, and a term which tries to minimise it by tolerating classification errors. The parameter C weights these two competing goals, and can be optimised using cross validation.

3.4 NON-LINEAR MIXTURE MODELLING

Kernel-based mappings can also be used to construct more flexible, non-linear decision boundaries. In pursuing this approach, all of the previous analysis holds for forming the decision boundary, and the only change that needs to be made is to substitute a Kernel function instead of the inner product between two training vectors. Common choices for Kernel functions include:

Polynomial Kernel $K(\mathbf{x}^i, \mathbf{x}^j) = (\mathbf{x}^i.\mathbf{x}^j + 1)^d$ where $d = 1, 2, \ldots$

Gaussian RBF $K(\mathbf{x}^i, \mathbf{x}^j) = \exp\left(\frac{-\|\mathbf{x}^i - \mathbf{x}^j\|_2^2}{2\sigma^2}\right)$

Ridge functions $K(\mathbf{x}^i, \mathbf{x}^j) = \tanh\left(b(\mathbf{x}^i.\mathbf{x}^j) - c\right)$

as well as various spline functions. Therefore, the non-linear Kernels can be used to produce a wide range of decision boundaries, and the data selection procedure is equivalent to the selection of the Kernel functions in the network, ie. only those Kernels with a non-zero Lagrange multiplier, α^i, will contribute to the network's decision.

Non-linear, polynomial transformations of the measured spectral signatures have been proposed within the LSMM framework [2], and the SVM Kernels appear to provide a wider range. However, for all non-linear Kernels, care must be taken not to overfit the data set and a lot more data is required to minimise the variance associated with non-linear modelling.

4 APPLICATION

In this section, the linear, non-separable SVM algorithm is applied to a remote sensing dataset, [10]. The data is split into two base classes:

- Developed & Other; including slate, Tarmac, concrete, tennis court, etc.
- Undeveloped & Vegetation; including sand, water, soil, grass, shrubs, etc.

hence the composite classes have a broad core region which proves problematic for conventional LSMM algorithms. The data is taken from a Landsat TM image of the Leicester suburbs, see figure 4, and data with a membership of greater than 0.95 of these two classes was consid-

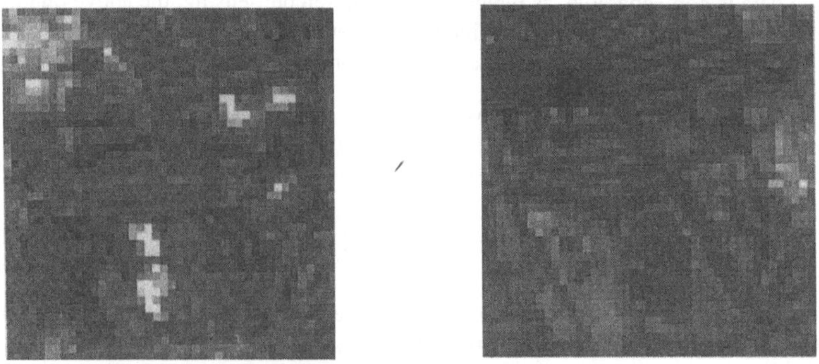

Figure 4: Bands 1 and 4 of the Landsat TM image used to evaluate the linear SVM mixture model.

ered as a potential "pure pixel". This produced a reduced data set of 313 training pairs (76 from the Developed and Other class and 237 from the Undeveloped and Vegetation class) compared to the original 1,000 data points which describe the mixture between these two classes on the tile.

Figure 5 shows the result of applying a linear SVM to this data set. The margins are shown as well as the support vectors (pure pixels) used in the calculation. 25 support vectors (8%) were used in calculating the margin associated with the linear SVM, and it can be seen that these lie within the mixing region or within the other class core. Points correctly classified/identified are not support vectors. In this case, the classification problem cannot be treated solely as a discrimination problem (ie. an element of spectral confusion exists), however the calculated margin, which denotes the region of linear mixing, is sensible and further comparisons between this solution and the "true", estimated mixture quantities will be presented at the conference. In addition, linearly separable data with no spectral confusion and non-linear mixture regions are described in [3].

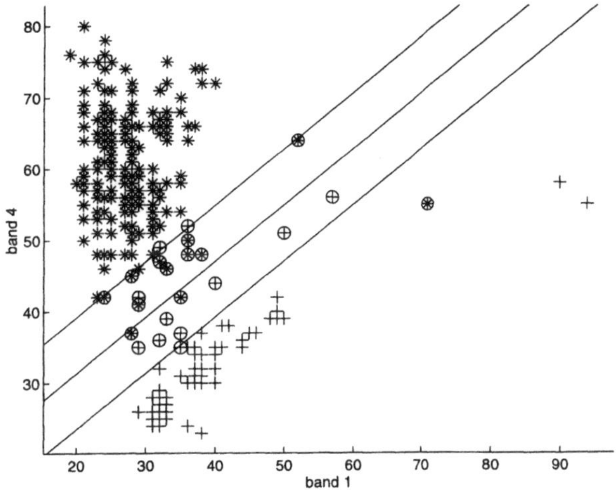

Figure 5: Linear SVM mixture predictions and selected support vectors for Landsat bands 1 and 4. Crosses are used to represent the Developed & Other class data and Stars represent the Undeveloped & Vegetation class data. The 25 data points selected as support vectors are circled.

Note that the *a priori* selection of a set of pure pixels for the classes cores would be extremely problematic, and in this example, this simply reduces to estimating a single bound parameter, C, which determines the width of the margin (in this case $C = 0.01$). Also, for more complex problems, a linear margin may not be appropriate and the non-linear margins which get produced by the kernel-based SVMs could be more appropriate. This is expected to become significant for the broad, composite classes used in this study.

5 CONCLUSIONS

It has been shown that LSMM are related to the basic, linear SVM and under certain circumstances, both algorithms are identical. This is an important observation for the LSMM algorithms as they possess the "maximum margin" property, which always maximises the minimum distance from other classes. However, the observation is probably more important as the quadratic programming algorithms associated with the SVMs perform automatic pure pixel selection, and the associated non-linear techniques mean that non-linear mixture models can be formed from both pure pixel, binary target values and continuous mixture data. The type of non-linear mixtures which can be formed have been demonstrated on some real, remote sensing data, although it still remains to quantify the performance of these algorithms.

ACKNOWLEDGMENTS

The authors gratefully acknowledge the help provided by Dr Steve Gunn during the preparation of this paper, and the financial assistance of the EU Framework IV FLIERS project ENV4-CT96-0305.

References

[1] J.B. Adams, M.O. Smith, and P.E. Johnson. Spectral mixture modeling: A new analysis of rock and soil types at the Viking lander 1 site. *J. Geophysical Research*, 91(B8):8098–8112, 1986.

[2] P. Bosdogianni, M. Petrou, and J. Kittler. Mixture models with higher order moments. *IEEE Trans Geoscience and Remote Sensing*, 35(2):341–353, 1997.

[3] M. Brown, H.G. Lewis, and S.R. Gunn. Linear spectral mixture models and support vector machines for remote sensing. *IEEE Trans Geoscience and Remote Sensing*, 1998. Submitted for publication.

[4] C.J.C. Burges. A tutorial on support vector machines for pattern recognition. In U. Fayyad, editor, *Data Mining and Knowledge Discovery*, pages 1–43, Boston, The Netherlands, 1998. Kluwer Academic Publishers.

[5] G.M. Foody and D.P. Cox. Sub-pixel land cover composition estimation using a linear mixture model and fuzzy membership functions. *Int. J. Remote Sensing*, 15:619–631, 1994.

[6] F.J. Garcia-Haro, M.A. Gilabert, and J. Melia. Linear spectral mixture modelling to estimate vegetation amount from optical spectral data. *Int. J. Remote Sensing*, 17(17):3373–3400, 1996.

[7] P.E. Gill, W. Murray, and M.H. Wright. *Practical Optimisation*, volume 2nd Edition. Academic Press, London, 1981.

[8] S.R. Gunn. Support vector machines for classification and regression. Technical Report ISIS-1-98, Department of Electronics and Computer Science, University of Southampton, 1998.

[9] H.M. Horwitz, R.F. Nalepka, P.D. Hyde, and J.P. Morganstern. Estimating the proportion of objects within a single resolution element of a multispectral scanner. Technical Report NASA Contract NAS-9-9784, University of Michigan, Ann Arbor, Michigan, 1971.

[10] H.G. Lewis, M. Brown, A.R.L. Tatnall, M.S. Nixon, and J. Manslow. Data analysis and empirical classification in FLIERS. FLIERS project report, Department of Electronics and Computer Science, University of Southampton, 1998.

[11] J.F. Manslow, M. Brown, and H.G. Lewis. On the probabilistic interpretation of fuzzy land cover mixing proportions. *Int. J. Remote Sensing*, 1998. Submitted for publication.

[12] J.J. Settle and N.A. Drake. Linear mixing and the estimation of ground cover proportions. *Int. J. Remote Sensing*, 14(6):1159–1177, 1993.

[13] E.J. van Koowijk, H. van der Voet, and J.J.M. Berdowski. Estimation of ground cover composition per pixel after matching image and ground data with subpixel accuracy. *Int. J. Remote Sensing*, 16(1):97–111, 1995.

[14] V. Vapnik. *The Nature of Statistical Learning Theory*. Springer-Verlag, New York, 1995.

WHY CLASSICAL MODELS FOR PATTERN RECOGNITION ARE NOT PATTERN RECOGNITION MODELS

Lev Goldfarb and Jaroslav Hook

Faculty of Computer Science
University of New Brunswick
P.O. Box 4400
Fredericton, N.B., E3B 5A3
Canada
goldfarb@unb.ca
http://wwwos2.cs.unb.ca/profs/goldfarb.htm

ABSTRACT. In this paper we outline a simple explanation of why, we think, the classical, or vector-space-based (including the artificial neural net) models for pattern recognition are *fundamentally* inadequate as such. The present simple explanation of this inadequacy is *based on a radically new understanding of the nature of inductive learning processes.* The latter became possible only after a careful analysis of the axiomatic foundations of a new inductive learning model proposed by the first author in 1990 which overcomes the above limitations. The new model—evolving transformation system—has emerged as a result of a 13-year long attempt to find a mathematical framework that would unify the two main and structurally different approaches to pattern recognition: the vector-space-based and the syntactic approaches. The decisive deficiency of the classical vector-space-based pattern recognition models, as it turns out, relates to the intrinsic inability of the underlying mathematical model, i.e. the normed vector space, to accommodate, during the learning process in a realistic environment, the discovery of the corresponding *class distance function* under more general than numeric, symbolic, pattern representation. Typically, such *symbolic* distance functions have *very* little to do with a *very* restricted, *"Euclidean", class of distance functions*, which due to the underlying algebraic structure of the vector space are *unavoidably associated with this form of pattern representation*. In other words, the more general class of *symbolic* distance functions is incomparably larger than that consistent with the vector space structure, and so the discovery and construction of the appropriate *class distance function* during the learning process simply cannot proceed in the vector space setting.

1. INTRODUCTION

The area of pattern recognition is almost half a century old, but today, as in 1974, one can repeat with Vapnik and Chervonenkis that "the problem of pattern recognition still has not acquired the formal formulation that would satisfy all the researchers" [1, p.9]. In the same preface to their book they further suggest:

"In essence, the different points of view on the statement of pattern recognition problem are determined by the answer to the question: Is there a single construction principle for adequate description of patterns of various nature or in each case the construction of the description language is the problem for the specialists in the concrete area?

If the answer is 'yes', then the discovery of this principle must form the main research direction in pattern recognition. It should form the main direction since it would be a general and principally new direction.

If the answer is 'no', then the pattern recognition is reduced to the problem of the average risk minimization for a special class of decision rules and can be considered as one of the direction in applied statistics.

The answer to this question has not been found and that is why the choice of the problem statement has been so far a question of faith" [1, p.11].

Indeed, since the late 70's early 80's the field of pattern recognition has basically been dominated by two *fundamentally different* formal frameworks: the original vector-space-based framework and the syntactic framework. In spite of the optimistic hopes, the integration of the two approaches into a single one has proved to be much more difficult than was anticipated. It is important to stress that each of the two approaches has some desirable *complementary* features arising from the two corresponding axiomatic structures: the normed vector space structure and the Chomsky's formal grammar structure. To simplify, one can say that the critical relevant feature of the former structure is the existence of the metric-based decision surfaces, while that of the latter is the presence of the generative class representation, however rigid that representation is.

The first author has been working on the unification of the above two frameworks for more than twenty years. During that time, it has gradually become clear that a very closely related problem, the problem of inductive learning (formulated in a radically new form), absorbs the main difficulties associated with a satisfactory formulation of the pattern recognition problem. Moreover, it appears that the key to the solution of these twin problems is the new concept of *inductive class representation,* i.e. a model of a *simultaneously generative and distance-based representation, or encoding, of the (infinite) pattern class based on a small finite training set* (see section 4).

In this paper, based on this new conception of the inductive learning process (section 4), we present a simple explanation of why, we think, the classical, or normed vector-space-based (including ANN) models for pattern recognition, in view of *the limitations imposed by the axiomatic structure of the normed vector space* itself, are in principle incapable of capturing the inductive class structure and therefore of modeling the process of pattern recognition in a realistic environment. For a similar argument, which is based, however, on some very simple basic *necessary* (but not sufficient) requirement for an inductive learning model, see [2]. This intrinsic limitation of the vector-space-based models should partly explain the reasons for the difficulties encountered in reconciling the above two pattern recognition frameworks. The paper is written by the first author who used in section 5 the results of the experiments performed by the second author under the supervision of the first author.

2. OBJECT REPRESENTATION AND THE CORRESPONDING OPERATIONS

The classical (and essentially all known) mathematical structures that offer axiomatic description of a set of objects with some relations among them—e.g. ordered set, group, ring, vector space, topological space—view objects as endowed with a *fixed* structure specified by means of the defining set of axioms. In other words, one might say that the axioms *"force"* the corresponding structure on the individual objects in the set. For example, given a set of three linearly independent vectors, i.e. a basis, in a 3-dimensional vector space over the field of reals, as a result of the axiomatic definition of this space, any given vector in it can be *uniquely* represented as a linear combination of those three vectors, and this decomposition should be viewed as a fixed structural description, or *representation*, of that vector (with respect to the given basis).

The axioms for the concrete mathematical structure characterize *completely* the operations that can be applied to the objects when this structure is imposed on a set of objects. Hence, when adopting a particular mathematical structure to model the actual process in nature, one always has to keep in mind that as far as *other* (than specified by the axioms of the chosen mathematical structure) types of object relations, or *operations*, and thus *the structural object features*, are concerned, they *become absolutely invisible, or nonexistent*. In other words, the adoption of a "wrong", or inappropriate, mathematical structure for modeling of some real phenomenon has very significant implications for our ability to capture the central features of the phenomenon. In this connection, we believe that, as far as the biological processing models are concerned, there are presently no nontrivial satisfactory examples of utilization of any basic mathematical *structures*. The latter may, and as we will argue does, point out to the inadequacy of the existing mathematical structures in this respect. What are the very basic reasons for the last statement?

It appears that the main reason is related to the following fact: classical mathematical structures were abstracted during the development of "numeric" mathematics, while biologically, or biochemically, more relevant mathematical structures should be abstracted during the development of "symbolic" mathematics whose axiomatics is related to symbolic rather than numeric operations. The first author has already outlined the nature of such operations (see for example [3, 4, 5]). In case of a set of strings over a finite alphabet, examples of such operations are substring insertion, deletion, and substitution operations.[1]

The fundamental differences between the "numeric" and "symbolic" mathematical structures become more apparent when one begins to investigate the resulting variety of the admissible distance functions, i.e. the variety of configurations of the corresponding sets under various *distances that are consistent with the underlying (i.e. numeric or symbolic) sets of operations*. This brings us to the next section.

3. SYMBOLIC DISTANCES AS BASED ON THE SYMBOLIC OPERATIONS

Conventionally, in mathematics, when introducing topology into an existing mathematical structure, e.g. into a group or a vector space, the basic criteria is to make sure that this topology "makes" the corresponding operations continuous (as functions) with respect to it [6, Ch. 3]. For example, the vector addition and the scalar multiplication in a normed vector space must be continuous with respect to the metric topology induced by the corresponding distance function. As was discussed in [7], this consistency, on the one hand, is absolutely necessary to ensure the consistency of the local space properties throughout the entire vector space, and on the other hand, it imposes *severe restrictions* on the corresponding class of admissible distance functions. The latter is the necessary price one must pay in order to work in the "nice" spaces that are generalized "numeric" spaces.

The accumulated mathematical experience strongly suggests that when approaching nonnumeric, or symbolic, entities, essentially, the same principle must be applied: to ensure the consistency of the introduced topology with the underlying axiomatic, or operational, structure of the set of objects, the *distance between two objects in the set must be defined by means of the corresponding set of symbolic operations*. By a number of reasons, one of which is to enforce the competitive cooperation, it is useful to assign to each of the symbolic operations a normalized nonnegative weight, i.e. the sum of the weights of all operations for a fixed symbolic structure is 1.

---

[1] Another important path "that points in the right direction" is via a very central in computer science concept of ***abstract data type***, or *ADT*.

Definition 1. A symbolic structure, or a **transformation system (TS)**, is a triple

$$T = (S, O, D)\ ,$$

where

S is a set of structured, or symbolic, object representations called **structs**;

$O = \{o_i\}_{i=1,\ldots,m}$ is a finite set of (reversible) **operations** each of which is a multivalued function that can transform one symbolic object into other(s) and any two structs from S can be transformed into each other by means of them (e.g. deletions/insertions and substitutions);

$D = \{d_\omega\}_{\omega \in \Omega}$ is a **parametric family of distance functions** with the parameter set

$$\Omega = \{\ \omega = (w^1, w^2, \ldots, w^m) \in \mathbf{R}^m \mid \forall i\ \ w^i \geq 0,\ \ \sum w^i = 1\ \}$$

(Ω is called the unit simplex) and, for each parameter vector ω of operation weights, the distance function d_ω is defined as follows

$d_\omega(s_1, s_2)$ = minimum of the numbers, each of which is obtained by adding the weights of the operations in a particular sequence of operations that transforms struct s_1 into struct s_2.

In this definition, the "reversibility" of the set O of operations simply means that the action of any operation on the struct can be reversed by means of another operation (e.g. deletion/insertion). For an axiomatic definition of the transformation system, which has emerged within the framework of evolving transformation system model, see, for example, [3].

Returning to the issue raised at the end of section 2, regarding the fundamental difference between the "numeric" and "symbolic" mathematical structures, we should note that the difference is roughly explicated by the difference between the corresponding families of admissible distance functions. Thus, for example, the initial work [8] has already suggested that, given any fixed finite-dimensional pseudo-Euclidean (more general than Euclidean) vector space and a fixed typical symbolic distance function on the set of strings over a finite alphabet, almost all finite sets of strings cannot be isometrically (preserving the string interdistances) represented in that pseudo-Euclidean space. Even more important, however, is the fact [7] that while in a finite-dimensional vector space all admissible distance functions are equivalent to each other, in a symbolic setting, the last statement is absolutely wrong: even for a set of strings over a finite alphabet there are, in fact, infinitely many nonequivalent classes of distance functions. Basically, what explains the relative richness of the class of symbolic distance functions is the relative richness of the set of various structural paths between a pair of structs (see Definition 1). Moreover, as one moves up the ladder of representational complexity, e.g. from vectors to strings, to labeled trees, to labeled graphs, the richness of the corresponding classes of distance functions grows.

In pattern recognition, the pivotal role of the concept of distance defined on the set of patterns is almost universally recognized (see for example [5]). In the following section we attempt to make this point more explicit by incorporating the concept of distance into a new definition of the inductive learning problem, the problem which appears to be more basic with respect to the pattern recognition problem.

4. INDUCTIVE LEARNING AND INDUCTIVE CLASS REPRESENTATION

Since paper [9] was devoted to this topic, we will restrict ourselves to the *substantially modified* basic definitions whose *present form* was recently proposed by the first author. We note that the following two definitions amount to a radically new understanding of the concept of class, the concept of class generalization, as well as the concept of inductive learning process.

Definition 2. Given some countable representation structure $\boldsymbol{S}$ (specified, as always, axiomatically), by a **class** C we will understand a countable subset of $\boldsymbol{S}$ *whose origin is assumed to be some constructive generative process that, starting from some finite number of elements and using some finite set of operations, allowed by the axioms of* $\boldsymbol{S}$*, generates all of* C.

The assumptions of the above definition are justified based on our present understanding of the physical and chemical processes responsible for *the evolution of objects in the universe* [10, pp 105-111]: it is almost universally accepted in science that all objects have hierarchical *compositional* history and that at each (fixed) hierarchical level an object can be represented as a compositional, or combinative, structure composed of a finite set of "symbolic" primitives according to some fixed set of structural rules.

Definition 3. Given a small finite set C^+ of k (typically $4 \le k \le 15$) **positive** patterns that are randomly chosen from a class C—class to be learned—and a small finite set C^- of **negative** patterns, i.e. not from C, the system has to be able to construct an **inductive class representation of** C **(ICR)** which satisfy the following conditions

- ICR can *generate* from C^+ or its subset *(in a manner consistent with the structure of* $\boldsymbol{S}$*)* an approximation C^* of C such that $C^* \cap C^- = \varnothing$ and
- ICR should also specify *the class distance function* d *on* $\boldsymbol{S}$ *which must be consistent with the structure of* $\boldsymbol{S}$ and such that: for some small nonnegative number ε, the part of C^* contained in the union of k spheres, where each sphere is defined as
$$S(s', \varepsilon) = \{ s \in \boldsymbol{S} \mid d(s, s') < \varepsilon \text{ for a fixed } s' \in C^+ \},$$
coincides with the part of C generated by C^+ and, moreover, the same union has no elements from the complement of C.

The phrase "consistent with the structure of $\boldsymbol{S}$*" simply means that the constructive generative process must rely only on the operations allowed by the axioms of* $\boldsymbol{S}$ *(see section 2).*

The above definition proposes to base our understanding of the nature of inductive learning process on the presence of some general mechanism, the ICR, that is capable: 1) of generating some approximation of the class on the basis of a small training set of patterns, and, more significantly, 2) of producing the class distance function (which is not necessarily metric), which can then serve as a basic tool for a fuzzy but more refined *delineation of the class boundary*. The main source of the present form of the above definition is the concept of ICR proposed by the first author around 1993-94 during the ongoing development of the evolving transformation system (ETS) model [11, Sec. 5] as well as the classical mathematical concept of inductive definition of a set (see, for example, [12, Sec. 3.1]). Paper [11] is particularly recommended as the only *published* brief outline of a more typical ETS learning algorithm. We should also note that, since the early 1970's, an indispensable role of the concept of distance, or inversely similarity, measure in the clarification of the concept of class has gradually become very apparent in cognitive psychology (see, for example, [13, Ch. 5], [14]).

It is not difficult to see that a satisfactory (according to the above definition) inductive learning model simultaneously solves the pattern recognition problem: the corresponding class distance function d offers the sought pattern classification tool with the help of which one can answer the question whether or not a given pattern belongs to class C.

In the ETS model, which suggested the above definitions, the inductive class representation takes on a very revealing and satisfactory form illustrated (condensedly) in the following very simple example (see [4]).

Example. Suppose that the set of patterns is a set of 2-dimensional plane closed shapes composed of three primitives: the straight segment $\boldsymbol{a}$, the convex corner $\boldsymbol{b}$, and the concave corner $\boldsymbol{c}$. Then, the set of structs (Def. 1) could be specified as the set of strings over a three-letter alphabet $\{\boldsymbol{a}, \boldsymbol{b}, \boldsymbol{c}\}$, where any two strings obtained by a circular permutation of each other are equivalent, i.e. they are considered to be identical. Given a small (of size 10-15) training set corresponding to the class of rectangles, at the end of the learning process [2], the resulting ICR (see the definition following the example) may look, for example, as follows

$$(s' = \boldsymbol{abaaababaaab},\ \{ o_1, o_2, o_3 \},\ \omega^* = (0, 1, 0)),$$

or as follows

$$(s' = \boldsymbol{baabaaaabaabaaaa},\ \{ o_1, o_2, o_3 \},\ \omega^* = (0, \tfrac{1}{2}, \tfrac{1}{2})),$$

or as follows

$$(s' = \boldsymbol{aababaabab},\ \{ o_1, o_2, o_3 \},\ \omega^* = (0, 0, 1)),$$

where s' is the generating struct, o_1, o_2, o_3 denote the deletions/insertions of $\boldsymbol{a}, \boldsymbol{b}, \boldsymbol{c}$ respectively, and $\omega^* = (w^1, w^2, w^3)$ is the corresponding weight vector (see Def. 1). As shown in [4], in this case, the corresponding (optimal) family of operation weights forms a 1-dimensional side $w^2 + w^3 = 1$ of a 2-dimensional unit simplex Ω in $\boldsymbol{R}^3$. In the absence of noise, any string s, whose (circular edit) distance $d_{\omega^*}(s, s')$ is 0, is classified as belonging to the class of rectangles.▶

One should note that the above example corresponds to the simplest case, when the construction of the corresponding ICR does not involve the discovery of any new (macro)operations, e.g. deletions/insertions of substrings.

Note that the model name, "evolving transformation system", reflects the fact that the learning process constructs a sequence of transformation systems (each with a more adequate set of operations) resulting in the final ICR.

The general form of ICR in the ETS model is given by the following triple

$$\Pi = (C^{+\prime}, \boldsymbol{O}_{fin}, \Omega_{fin}),$$

where $C^{+\prime}$ is a small subset of C^+ (the set of generators), $\boldsymbol{O}_{fin}$ is the final set of operations at the end of the learning process, and $\Omega_{fin} \subseteq \Omega$ is the set of optimal weight vectors for the final transformation system.

It is not difficult to see that the two conditions in Definition 3 are satisfied (C^* is generated by the operations from $\boldsymbol{O}_{fin}$ acting on the structs from $C^{+\prime}$).

To summarize, the main point of this section is to suggest that the process of inductive learning, and therefore of pattern recognition, cannot be properly understood or satisfactory modeled independently of the two conditions described in Definition 3. In particular, we strongly believe that the failure of the classical, i.e. vector-space-based pattern recognition models, considered next, can be attributed to the inability of the vector space framework to accommodate, for practically all nontrivial useful environments, the inductive learning process *as it was conceived above*.

5. ARE THERE ANY ENVIRONMENTS FOR WHICH THE CLASSICAL PATTERN RECOGNITION MODELS ARE WELL SUITED?

In this section, based on the new understanding of inductive learning outlined in the last section, we first describe *the unrealistic restrictions on the pattern recognition environments* imposed by the structure of the classical, vector-space-based, models. We then discuss the

[2] In this paper we are not considering any ETS learning algorithms that actually construct the ICR (see for example [4], [11]).

implications of ignoring these restrictions and the ongoing, as we believe unproductive, attempts to bypass them. For a related complimentary discussion centered around other examples see [2].

Based on Definitions 2, 3, it is easy to see that, in a vector space framework (the basic operations are vector addition and scalar multiplication), the class that is not a union of several subclasses, first, must lie either in the linear or in the affine subspace generated by the positive training set, C^+, this subspace must not contain any negative training patterns, and second, within this subspace, in some spheres around the patterns from C^+, all the class patterns "related" to the patterns in C^+ (typically all of C) must lie, with *no nonclass patterns present in the spheres*.

Obviously, the above conditions do not hold. Historically, this meant that in order to use the vector-space-based pattern recognition models at all, one had to bring into consideration some classes of nonlinear "decision" functions. However, what do these classes of nonlinear functions have to do with the problem of inductive class representation? In fact, there are uncountably many different classes of nonlinear functions, and, practically, almost all of them are not related to both the structure of the representation space, i.e. to the input vector space, and the "structure" of the training set of vectors.

Thus, if the input representation structure, S, is a vector space, then whether we do or do not add to the vector (or linear) space axioms some nonlinear structure (e.g. for the internal nodes of the corresponding ANN), the following *very important question* arises: *What are we learning during the learning process?* Certainly, the "learned" decision surfaces do not give us anything even remotely resembling the inductive class representation (ICR) as it was outlined in Definition 3. Following further the logic of the new learning framework, one can observe that an essentially unique (up to equivalence [7]) Euclidean distance in the vector space is practically never related to the class distance, but, according to the proposed framework, it is the latter that is directly involved in capturing the class generalization. In other words, the vector space learning framework, whose linear structure "requires" analytically "nice", locally homogeneous and *fixed metric geometry, does not allow one to mold the distance to the ICR*. Hence, *in the light of the learning framework of section 4*, the classical "learning algorithms" in the vector space appear to us now no more than sophisticated games whose aim is to enclose the positive training patterns within some optimal surfaces (chosen from a fixed class of surfaces) in such a way that the negative training patterns are excluded. It is no wonder, then, that, in most cases, *multiple complex surfaces are needed* to accomplish the goal of the "game".

By contrast, in the ETS framework, the class distance function that is being constructed during learning (by searching for the "optimal" *operations* with the "optimal" weights), with each new set of operations, changes "irreversibly" the "configuration" of the pattern space itself.

To illustrate the above points, related to the inadequacy of the classical models (see also [2]), we have performed several simple experiments, the results of which would, probably, not surprise at all anyone sufficiently familiar with the classical vector-space-based learning paradigm. However, in light of the above considerations, we believe that the results might help one to reinforce the above implications of the proposed new understanding of inductive learning and pattern recognition processes.

Figure 1 gives some examples (see [15] for more details) of the experimental pattern recognition results produced by a version of the backpropagation algorithm given in [16] [3]. The binary images are of size 8×12 and the training sets supplied by the authors of [16] are of sizes 30-50 (for each digit). The algorithm has converged successfully for each digit class and correctly classified all training patterns. Moreover, the test patterns, also supplied by the authors of [16], were correctly recognized with the error rate of 9-10%. The patterns given in Figure 1 are the

---

[3] A three layer architecture with the following parameters: input layer size 96 (= 8×12), hidden layer size 8, output layer size 1, temperature 0.9, moment $\mu = 0.5$, $\alpha = 0.1$, error margin 0.01, maximal number of iterations 2250000.

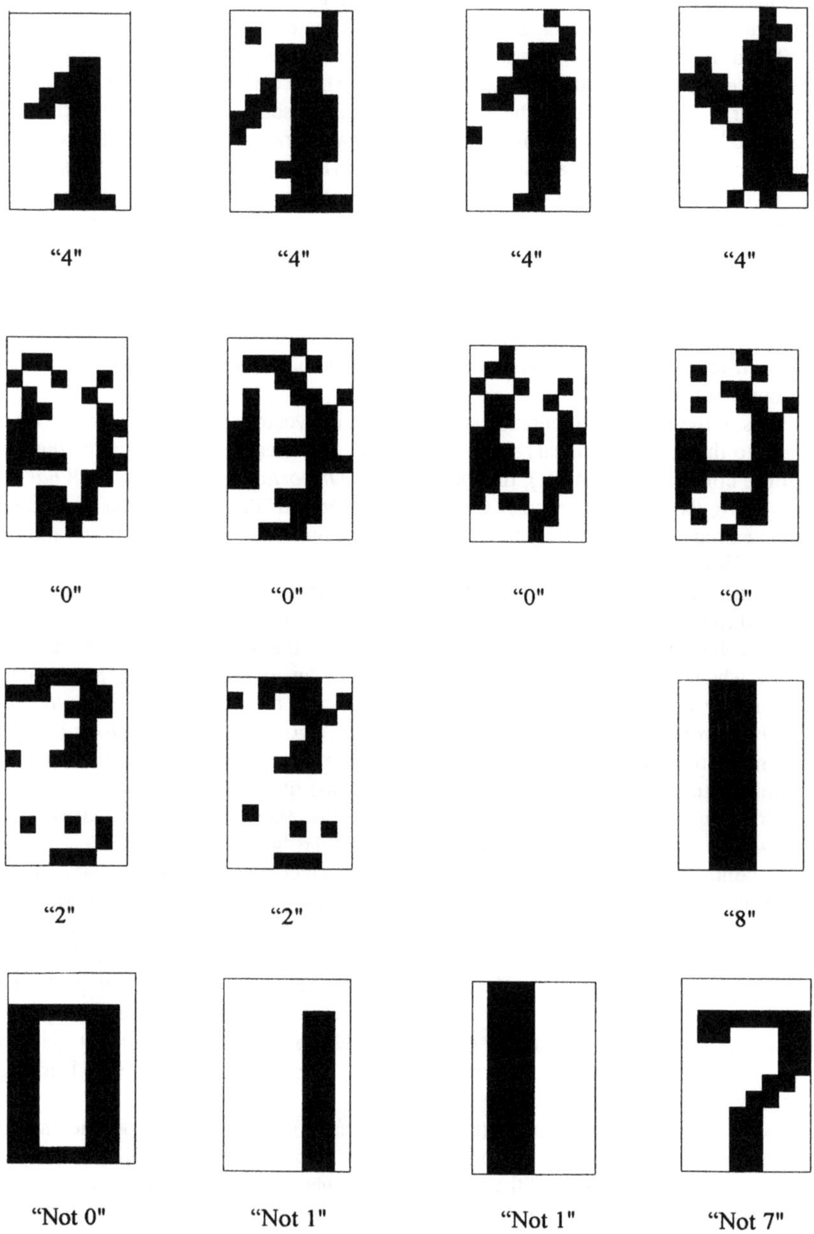

Figure 1: Examples of the binary images classified by the backpropagation algorithm as belonging to the class (or its complement) indicated in " ".

patterns that were constructed by us. These examples do reinforce the above observations: no concept of class has been captured at the end of learning. In particular, one can easily find: 1) the patterns close to each other in the Euclidean metric but belonging to different classes and 2) the patterns distant from each other in the Euclidean metric but belonging to the same class.

Thus, a popular but misleading impression that the classical models are "good enough for practical purposes" is just a tranquillizing illusion which has recently [4] emerged when a virtue has been made of necessity (lack of good models and the resulting need to extensively constrain the original problems).

6. CONCLUSION

In this paper, we very briefly outlined a framework for inductive learning and pattern recognition based on the evolving transformation system (ETS) model [3, 4, 5, 11]. The outlined framework projects the view that the inductive learning process embodies some analytically new form of constructive "activity": the discovery of the appropriate set of weighted "symbolic" operations which capture the class representation based on a *small* training set of patterns. These weighted operations create the connection, or bridge, between the finite set of training patterns and the class generated by the positive training patterns, i.e. they form the core of the *inductive class representation*. The same weighted operations, automatically, modify the representation of the patterns in the class by modifying the corresponding distance function [5]. In particular, the framework suggests a radically new concept of pattern representation: *a pattern representation always involves some finite set of operations,* which, if necessary, are dynamically updated during the learning process. These operations can be thought of as pattern/class features and *the distance between the structurally "compatible" patterns is always computed based on the current set of operations.* The patterns, and therefore the classes, are always viewed as of a generative origin, and the learning process is supposed to find in some chosen operational form, based on a training set, a corresponding (to this operational form) generative inductive class representation: the class consists of those patterns that, first, could be generated (with the help of the operations) from the positive training patterns and, second, are sufficiently close (with respect to the constructed class distance function) to the corresponding positive training patterns.

On the basis of the above framework [6], we suggested that the classical, or vector-space-based, learning framework, in view of the basic axiomatic restrictions of the vector space structure, cannot at all accommodate the inductive learning processes as they emerge from this new framework. This type of axiomatic restrictions is not peculiar to the vector space structure only but are the restrictions that apply to all classical, or of the "numeric" origin, mathematical structures. In other words, what emerges from the above considerations is the need for a fundamentally different class of mathematical structures—"symbolic" mathematical structures, in which the finite set of basic operations is not fixed axiomatically but can be modified dynamically (see for example [3, 5, 8]). The main advantage of such mathematical structures is the ability to modify dynamically their global metric geometry in order to find the optimal class of distance functions that best captures the inductive class representation.

---

[4] This happened after the popularization and the accompanied vulgarization brought by the "connectionists".

[5] I.e. by modifying the distance function (defined on the representation set S) corresponding to the learning class (see Definition 3).

[6] See also another argument based on the *intrinsic* inadequacy of the vector-space-based learning paradigms [2].

Finally, it is interesting to note that if, indeed, as it appears to us, the above new framework, ETS, does capture the essential features of the learning processes, we are faced with a monumental but unavoidable task of designing radically new, *symbolic, measurement devices*, which are, at the same time, *inductive measurement devices* [3]. While all present measurement devices, through their interacting components, produce numbers (with the corresponding essentially unique distance function) as outputs, the symbolic measurement devices, through their interacting components, produce more general entities, "structs" (symbolic entities with the corresponding set of weighted symbolic operations, see Definition 1), as their outputs. Such *autonomous* "intelligent" measurement devices, as is the case with all biological transducers, will be able to interact with the environment in a more direct and evolutionary, i.e. based on the past experience, manner and will be able to capture the *inductive structure* of events/objects. It is the inductive structure that, *in the long run*, appears to be the only reliable structure worth capturing (see [17], particularly pp. 242-245).

REFERENCES

[1] Vapnik VN. and Chervonenkis YaA, Pattern Recognition Theory: Statistical Problems of Learning. Nauka, Moskow, 1974 (in Russian).

[2] Bhavsar VC, Ghorbany AA, Goldfarb L. Artificial neural networks are not learning machines. Internal Technical Report, Faculty of Computer Science, University of New Brunswick.

[3] Goldfarb L, and Deshpande S. What is a symbolic measurement process? In Proceedings of the IEEE Conf. Systems, Man, and Cybernetics, vol 5, IEEE Press, 1997, pp 4139-4145.

[4] Goldfarb L. On the foundations of intelligent processes I: An evolving model for pattern learning. Pattern Recognition 1990; 23: 595-616.

[5] Goldfarb L. What is distance and why do we need the metric model for pattern learning? Pattern Recognition 1992; 25: 431-438.

[6] Taylor AE, Introduction to Functional Analysis. Wiley, New York, 1967.

[7] Goldfarb L, Abela J, Bhavsar VC, Kamat VN. Can a vector space based learning model discover inductive class generalization in a symbolic environment? Pattern Recognition Letters 1995; 16(7): 719-726.

[8] Goldfarb L. A new approach to pattern recognition. In: Kanal LN, Rosenfeld A (eds). Progress in Pattern Recognition 2. North-Holland, Amsterdam, 1983, pp 241-402.

[9] Goldfarb L. Inductive class representation and its central role in pattern recognition. In: Proceedings of the Conference on Intelligent Systems: A Semiotic Perspective, vol 1. NIST, Gaithersberg, Maryland, 1996, pp 53-58.

[10] Reeves H, Malicorne. Earthly reflections of an astrophysicist. Stoddart Pub., Toronto, 1993.

[11] Goldfarb L, Nigam S. The unified learning paradigm: A foundation for AI. In: Honavar V, Uhr L (eds). Artificial Intelligence and Neural Networks: Steps toward Principled Integration. Academic Press, Boston, 1994, pp 533-559.

[12] Hein JL, Discrete Structures, Logic, and Computability. Jones and Bartlett, Boston, 1995.

[13] Bourne LE, Dominovsky RL, Loftus EF, Healy AF, Cognitive processes, 2nd Edition. Prentice-Hall, Englewood Cliffs, New Jersey, 1986.

[14] Hahn U, Chater N. Concepts and similarity. In: Lamberts K, Shanks D (eds). Knowledge, concepts, and categories. MIT Press, Cambridge, Massachusetts, 1997, pp 43 -93.

[15] Hook J, Are artificial neural networks learning machines? Master Thesis, Faculty of Computer Science, University of New Brunswick, Fredericton, Canada, 1998.

[16] Pandya AS, Macy RB, Pattern recognition with neural networks in C++. IEEE Press, 1996.

[17] Plotkin H, Darwin machines and the nature of knowledge. Penguin Books, London, 1995.

PATTERN DISCOVERY IN TIME-ORIENTED DATA

Mohamad Saraee, TimeLab, Dept. of Computation, UMIST, Manchester, UK
George Koundourakis, TimeLab, Dept. of Computation, UMIST, Manchester, UK
Babis Theodoulidis, TimeLab, Dept. of Computation, UMIST, Manchester, UK

ABSTRACT

We present a data mining system, Easy Miner, which has been developed for interactive mining of interesting patterns in time-oriented databases. This system implements a wide spectrum of data mining functions, including generalisation, relevance analysis, classification and discovery of association rules. By integrating these interesting data mining techniques, the system provides a user friendly and interactive environment with good performance. These algorithms were tested on time-oriented medical data and experimental results show that the algorithms are efficient and effective for discovery of patterns in databases.

1 INTRODUCTION

Knowledge Discovery in Databases (KDD) is defined by Fayyad, Piatetsky-Shapiro and Smyth[1] as "the non-trivial process of identifying valid, novel, potentially useful, and ultimately understandable patterns in data". The KDD process is based on a set of tools used to extract patterns from data and a set of processes surrounding the usage of these tools including selection, preprocessing, transformation and interpretation of the results as shown in Figure 1. Data mining is only one step of the process, involving the application of discovery tools to find interesting patterns from targeted data, however in the research community most often the term data mining and KDD have been used interchangeably.

Finding patterns in databases is the fundamental operation behind several data mining tasks, including association rules mining introduced by Agrawal, Imienlinski and Swami[2] and sequential patterns mining introduced by Agrawal and Srikant[3]. The objective of time-oriented data mining is to find and characterise interesting patterns from time-oriented datasets. For example patterns of patients visiting doctors may indicates fraud committed in claiming benefits from health insurance companies. Although demands for such a technique for many application areas are high, the technique itself is in infancy. In this paper we present our approach for mining interesting patterns from time-oriented data. In order to test the appropriateness of our approach, we have been experimenting with a large medical data from register of stroke patients that were collected by GPs and hospitals.

The remainder of this paper is organised as follows. In the next section, we define the problem of discovering patterns in time-oriented data and our approaches for addressing this problem. In Easy Miner pattern discovery components, relevance analysis, association rules mining and in classification rules mining are described in section 3, 4 and 5 respectively. Finally, we present our conclusions in section 6 and identify directions for future research.

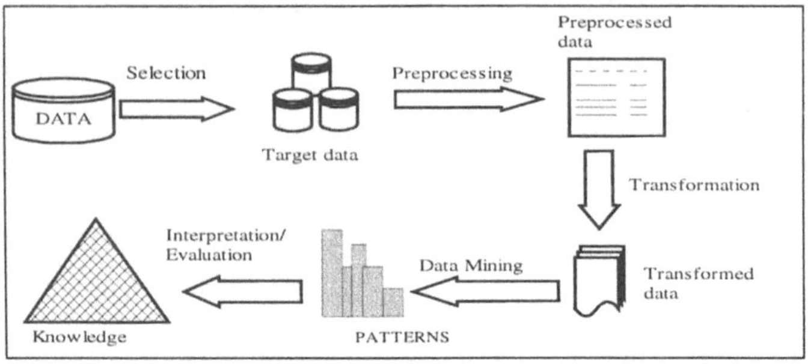

Figure 1. The knowledge discovery process

2 TIME-ORIENTED PATTERN MINING

The discovery of causal relationships within data is one of the most widely investigated forms of pattern discovery. Medical domain is particularly very appropriate for discovering such patterns, since medical staff often interested to know what causes a particular disease. Other form is temporal associations which can detects patterns of behaviour, such as association of purchasing behaviour in particular times of the day. The discovery of trends and cycles in data over time also provide useful information for decision making. In addressing the problem of time-oriented data mining we have worked on two approaches. First, known as pre-processing approach consists of moving from the inherent temporal representation of the domain to an equivalent static one that can be managed by the existing techniques. The second approach is to enhance the existing algorithms or design new ones to handle time-oriented data without any requirement of pre-processing. As the space limited we only discuss the pre-processing approach in this paper.

2.1 RELATED WORK

Maninila, Toivonen and Verkamo[4] introduced temporal patterns in sequences of events with episodes and discovered frequent episodes in sequences. Padmanabham and Tuzhilian [5] used First-Order Temporal Logic (FOTL) to express temporal patterns and then presented technique to discover frequent and most frequent patterns. Also related to our work is mining certain trends in temporal databases using trend dependency by Wijsen and Meersman[6]. Chen, Petrounias and Heathfield[7] defined a SQL-like Mining Language (SML) with the ability to express of task of mining temporal association rules.

2.2 PREPROCESSING APPROACH

As mentioned our first approach to time-oriented pattern discovery process consists of moving from the temporal representation to an equivalent static one that can be managed by the existing algorithms. Valid time intervals are associated with each tuple in time-oriented databases to record the time for which these tuples are valid within the modelled domain. Because these intervals represent important semantics about the application, it may be desirable to include them within the data used to produce generalisation, classification or associations rules. We introduce two concept for integrating temporal semantic into the process: namely the Moving Window clause and the Time_Slice clause.

- The TIME_SLICE Clause: The User specifies a time interval and only those objects in the database whose valid time is contained in this interval get selected for discovery process. Example: Include all patients who have had stroke between 1/10/1995 to 1/10/1997.

- The SLIDING WINDOW Clause: The user specifies a interval width and the objects in the databases are examined through a temporal window, of this width sliding along the temporal axis. Example: Include all patients whose Blood Pressure measurement (BP) have been raised more than 2 times within certain time (1 month, 2 months, 3 months, 6 months, 12 months, 3 years).

In this approach we generate virtual attributes recommended by domain experts to be included in the list of attributes to be used by Easy Miner discovery process. Examples of virtual attributes for our stroke patients data are:

- Average BP from the date of last treatment to the date of last recorded BP before the date of stroke.
- Intervals and average BP during these intervals between the date of first recorded BP and the date of last recorded BP.

3 RELEVANCE ANALYSIS

We perform attribute relevance analysis as defined by Kemper et al.[8]. Example of obvious relevancy amongst database attributes is 'Age' to 'Date of birth'. This kind of knowledge is qualitative and it is quite useful to mine from large databases that hold information about many objects (fields). For example a bank could look in its data and identify the factors that it should take in mind in order to give a credit limit to a customer. Applying Easy Miner to our local bank customers credit history database discovered that Credit Limit is relevant to *Account Status, Monthly Expenses, Marital Status, Monthly Income* and *Gender*.

A number of statistical and machine learning techniques for relevance analysis have been proposed until now. We use an information-theoretic asymmetric measure of relevance introduced by Loether and McTavish [9] known as the *uncertainty coefficient*. If we assume the generated set from the collection of task relevant data is a set *P* of *p* data records and the interesting attribute has *m* distinct values defining by *m* discrete classes P_i (i=1,..., m). Also if we assume that P contains p_i records for each P_i, then a random selected record belongs to class P_i with probability p_i/p. The expected information needed to classify a given sample is given by: $I(p_1, p_2, \ldots, p_m) = -\sum_{i=1}^{m} \frac{p_i}{p} \log_2 \frac{p_i}{p}$

An attribute A with values $\{a_1, a_2, \ldots, a_k\}$ can be used to partition P into $\{C_1, C_2, \ldots, C_k\}$, where C_j contains those records in C that have value a_j of A. Let C_j contain p_{ij} records of class P_i. The expected information based on the partitioning using as split attribute the A, is:

$$E(A) = \sum_{j=1}^{k} \frac{p_{ij} + \ldots + p_{mj}}{p} I(p_{ij} + \ldots + p_{mj})$$

and the information gained by partitioning on attribute A is: $gain(A) = I(p_1, p_2, \ldots, p_m) - E(A)$

Finally the uncertainty coefficient U(A) for attribute A is obtained by normalising the information gain of A so that U(A) ranges from 0 to 1 as follow:

$$U(A) = \frac{I(p_1, p_2, \ldots, p_m) - E(A)}{I(p_1, p_2, \ldots, p_m)}$$

The value 0 means that there is significant independence between attribute A and the interesting attribute, and 1 means that there is strong relevance between the two attributes. Only the *n* most relevant attributes are kept, where *n* is defined by the user.

3 CLASSIFICATION

Classification is an essential issue in data mining. Classification partitions massive quantities of data into sets of common characteristics and properties as discussed by Mehta, Agrawal and Rissanen in [10]. This procedure can be described as follows. In classification a set of example records, acting as *training set,* is analysed in order to produce a model of the given data. Each example/record is assumed to belong to a predefined class, as determined by one of the attributes, called *classifying attribute*. Table 1 shows a part from a sample training set of the medical database, where each record represents a patient and *Lived* is chosen to be the *classifying attribute* of the training set.

Once derived, the classification model can be used to categorise future data samples, as well as providing a better understanding of the database contents. Classification has numerous applications including medical diagnosis, credit approval, and product marketing.

.....	Gender	Date of Birth	Date of Stroke	Lived	.....
...	Male	9/21/1924	9/23/94	Died	...
...	Female	5/8/1921	12/10/94	Died	...
...	Male	1/18/34	2/7/94	Survived	...
...	Male	9/26/1925	11/13/94	Survived	...
...	Female	3/28/51	12/9/94	Died	...
...	Male	1/19/34	2/7/94	Survived	...

Table 1: Sample Training Set

The classification technique developed in Easy Miner is based on the decision tree structure. By using a decision tree, untagged data sample can be classified. This can be performed by testing the attribute values of the sample data against the decision tree. A path is generated from the root to a leaf node, which has the class identification of the sample.

3.1 DECISION TREE CLASSIFIER

A decision tree is a class discriminator that recursively partitions the training set until each partition consists entirely or dominantly of examples from one class. Each non-leaf node of the tree contains a *split point*, which is a test on one or more attributes and determines how the data is partitioned. Figure 2 shows a sample decision-tree classifier based on the training set shown in Figure 2.

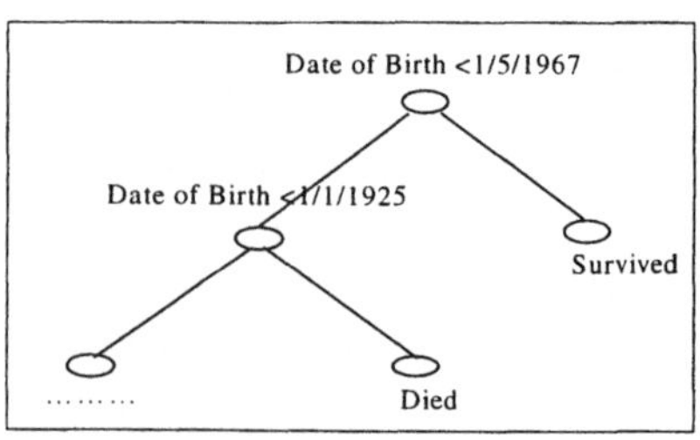

Figure 2: Decision Tree

This decision tree can be used in order to discriminate future patients that had stroke into *Survived* or *Died* categories.

3.2 COLLECTION OF TRAINING SET AND CONSTRUCTION OF DECISION TREE

In order to construct a decision tree classifier, the first step is to retrieve the classification task relevant data and store them in a relation (table). The second step after is to examine the generated training set with the purpose of "purifying" and making it suitable for classification process. Irrelevant attributes in the training set would slow down the classification process and therefore *relevance analysis* is performed to the dataset and only the most relevant attributes are kept. To construct the decision tree classifier we use the following algorithm:

```
MakeTree(Tiraining Data T)
if (all points in S are in the same class) then
        return
EvaluateSplits( )
if (T can not be further partition) then
        Evaluate Each Class Probability(S)
        return
Use best split found to partition S into S1 and S2
Delete(S)
MakeTree(S1)
MakeTree(S2)
```

3.3 DATA STRUCTURE

For each attribute of the training data a separate list is created. An entry of the attribute list has the following fields: (i) attribute value, (ii) class label, (iii) index of the record "id" from which these value has been taken. Initial lists for numeric attributes are sorted when first created.

At first all the entries of the attribute lists are associated with the root of the tree. As the tree grows and nodes are split to create new ones, the attribute lists of each node are partitioned and associated with the children. When this happens, the order of the records in the list is preserved, and resorting is unnecessary. Histograms are another type of data structure introduced by Shafer, Mehta and Agrawal[11]. These histograms are used to capture the class distribution of the attribute records at a given node. So, for numeric attributes, two histograms are associated with each decision-tree node that is under consideration for splitting C_{above} and C_{below}. C_{below} contains the distribution of attributes that have been already processed, and C_{above} contains those not. Categorical attributes also have also a histogram associated with a node an is called *count matrix*. For a numeric attribute the histogram is a list of pairs of the form <class, frequency> and for a categorical attribute, the histogram is a list of triples of the form <attribute value, class, frequency>.

3.4 FINDING SPLIT POINTS

While growing the tree, the goal at each node is to determine the split condition that best divides the training records belonging to the node under examination. Several splitting indices have been proposed elsewhere in [9,10,11] to evaluate the goodness of the split. Two of the most popular and acceptable indexes are the *gini index* and the *entropy index*.

Assuming that we have a dataset T which contains examples from n classes and where p_j is the frequency of class j in dataset T then *gini(T)* is:

$gini(T) = 1 - \sum_{j=1}^{n} p_j^2$ and the entropy index *Ent(T)* is: $Ent(T) = -\sum_{j=1}^{n} p_j \log_2(p_j)$

If a split divides S into subsets S_1 and S_2, then the values of the indexes of the divided data are given by:

$gini_{split}(S) = \frac{n_1}{n} gini(S_1) + \frac{n_2}{n} gini(S_2)$ and $Ent_{split}(S) = \frac{n_1}{n} Ent(S_1) + \frac{n_2}{n} Ent(S_2)$

To find the best split point for a node, we scan each of the attributes lists and evaluate splits based on that attribute. The attribute containing the split point with the lowest value for the split index (*gini or entropy*) is then used to split the node. There are two kinds of attributes for performing a split:

- *Numeric attributes.* If we have a numeric attribute A, a binary split $A<u$ is performed to the set of data it belongs. The candidate-split points are midpoints between every two successive attribute values in the training data. In order to find the split for an attribute on a node, the histogram C_{below} is initialised to zeros and C_{above} is initialised with the class distribution, for all the records for the node. For the root node, this distribution is obtained at the time of sorting. For the other nodes, this distribution is obtained when the node is created. Attribute records are read one at a time and C_{below} and C_{above} are updated for each record read. After each record is read, a split between values we have and we have seen and seen is evaluated. C_{below} and C_{above} have all the information to compute the *gini* or *entropy* index. Since the lists for numeric attributes are kept in sorted order, each of the candidate split points for an attribute is evaluated in a simple scan of the associative attribute list. If a successful point is found, we save it and we reallocate the C_{below} and C_{above} histograms before we continue on the next attribute.

- *Categorical Attributes.* If S(A) is the set of possible values of a categorical attribute A, then the split test is of the form $A \in S'$, where $S' \subset S$. A single scan is made through the attribute list collecting counts in the count matrix for each combination of class label and attribute value found in the data. Once it is completed, all subsets of the attribute values are considered possible split points and the corresponding index are calculated.

3.5 IMPLEMENTATION OF THE SPLIT

When the best split point for a node is found, a split is performed by creating two children nodes and dividing the attribute records between them. The partition of the attribute list of the splitting attribute is straightforward. We simply scan the list, apply the split test and move the records to the two attribute lists of the children nodes. As we partition the list of the splitting attribute, the "id" of each record is inserted into a hash table Once all the "id" are collected, we scan the lists of the remaining attributes and examine the hash table with the "id" of each record. The result of the comparison specifies in which child to place the record. During the splitting operation, class histograms are built for each new leaf. There are some cases that a dataset can not be further partitioned. For example in the training set of Table 2 it is obvious that classifier can not split the first two records into two separate dataset since there all have identical attributes except the classification attribute *Lived.* There is no classification rule that can explain why the two records have different class labels. This is a very usual case in large databases and in particular in time-oriented databases stable where data during the time appears to have the same values in different time-points.

.....	Gender	Date of Birth	Date of Stroke	Lived	.....
...	Female	5/8/1921	12/10/94	Survived	...
...	Female	5/8/1921	12/10/94	Died	...
...	Male	1/18/34	2/7/94	Survived	...
...	Female	3/28/51	12/9/94	Died	...

Table 2: Case of Impossible Partition

In this case, we consider the node with that data set as a leaf of the decision tree with more than one class label. A record of the data set of such a leaf belongs to a class j with probability r_j/r, where r_j is the number of tuples of each class j in that data set and r is the total number of the records of this data set. When an unclassified data set is given as input to the classifier it is possible that some of its records satisfy the classification rule that corresponds to the path from the root to such a leaf. Then these records belong to a class j of that leaf with probability: r_j/r.

3.6 EXAMPLE OF USING CLASSIFICATION

We used Easy Miner to classify records of patients from stroke patients data based on the values

...	Gende	Date of Birth	Date of Stroke	Lived	Predicted Lived	.....
...	Male	9/26/1925	11/13/94	Survived	Survived (Probability = 100%)	.....
...	Male	9/21/1924	9/23/94	Died	Died (Probability = 100%)	....
...	Male	11/1/1921	9/23/94	-	Survived (Probability = 100%)	....
...	Male	10/7/1921	9/23/94	-	Died (Probability = 100%)	....
...	Female	3/28/51	12/9/94	Died	Died (Probability = 100%)	....
...	Female	4/24/51	12/9/94	-	Survived (Probability = 100%)	....
...	Female	5/8/1921	12/10/94	Died	Died (Probability = 100%)	....
...	Female	12/8/1921	12/10/94	-	Survived (Probability = 100%)	....
...	Male	1/18/34	2/7/94	Survived	Survived (Probability = 100%)	....

Table 3: Classified Medical Data

of attribute *Lived*. By using a relatively small training set, we built a classifier for attribute *Lived* and then used the classifier to classify all the records in the medical database. A part of the results of the classification process is shown in Table 3. The attribute *Predicted Lived* contains the prediction/classification for attribute *Lived.*

4. ASSOCIATION RULES

Using formalism provided by Agrawal and Srikant in [8] association rules can be defined as follows: Let $I=\{i_1, i_2,\ldots,i_m\}$ be a set of *items*. Let DB be a database of transactions, where each transaction T consists of a set of items such that $T \subseteq I$. Given an *itemset* $X \subseteq I$, a transaction T *contains* X only and only if $X \subseteq T$. An association rule is an implication of the form $X \Rightarrow Y$, where $X \subseteq I$, $Y \subseteq I$ and $X \cap Y = \varnothing$. The association rule $X \Rightarrow Y$ holds in DB with *confidence c* if the probability of a transaction in DB which contains X also contains Y is *c*. The association rule $X \Rightarrow Y$ has *support s* in DB if the probability of a transaction in DB contains both X and Y is *s*. The task of mining association rules is to find all the association rules whose support is larger than a *minimum support threshold* σ_l' and whose confidence is larger than a *minimum confidence threshold* φ_l'.

4.1 A METHOD FOR MINING ASSOCIATION RULES

As described in previous section, a decision tree classifier is a collection of *IF-THEN* rules that are expressed by its individual paths. This is a semantic characteristic of decision trees and we use this to develop a method for mining association rules from a database. The rules that our method discovers have the form: $X \Rightarrow Y$, where X is a set of conditions upon the values of several attributes and Y a specific value of one attribute. This attribute Y is called *interesting attribute.* Three steps are involved in mining association rules: data preparation, generation of rules and selection of strong rules

4.1.1 Data Preparation

In this stage, the data set is prepared by selecting the *interesting attribute.* If more than one attribute are of interest, then the *interesting attribute* can be constructed by joining these attributes. Next the generalisation induction is performed on the *interesting attribute* by using concept hierarchies. If the *interesting attribute* is of *numeric* type, then its values are being separated into a number of ranges and each value of the numeric attribute is replaced by the range. If among the data set there are categorical attributes (except the *interesting* one) that have a large number of distinct values, then the generalisation induction should be performed on them as well. This process results in viewing the data in abstractions that are more useful and in generating candidate data sets for finding association rules, that have quite significant support.

4.1.2 Generation of Rules and Selection of Strong Rules

The *interesting attribute* now considered to be the classifying attribute as a decision tree classifier is constructed. Each path from the root of the tree to an internal node or a leaf represents one or more association rules of the form:

IF *(sequence of intermediate conditions)* **THEN** *(classifying attribute value)*

The confidence of each generated rule from such a path is r_j /r, where r_j is the number of tuples of each class j that has records in the data set of that internal node or leaf, and r is the total number of the records of the that data set. Strong rules are selected as defined to be the rules of the form A⇒B with the support greater than minimum support and confidence greater than the minimum confidence. In the following tables association rules discovered by Easy Miner from the database of credit for bank customers and also from the stroke patients' data are presented.

Rule's Body	Support	Confidence
IF ((Marital_Status IN {Single})) THEN (Home = Rent)	16.22%	65.15%
IF ((Marital_Status NOT_IN {Single}) (Account_Status IN {60 days late}) (1 < Nbr_Children) (Savings_Account IN {Yes}) (1187< Mo_Income)) THEN (Home = Own)	12.29%	66.00%
IF ((Marital_Status NOT_IN {Single}) (Account_Status IN {Balanced}) (1611.50 < Mo_Income <= 2918.50) (Checking_Account IN {No})) THEN (Home = Own)	14.99%	100.00%

Rule's Body	Support	Confidence
If ((Gender IN {Male}) (Smoking_status In {Smoker})) THEN (Past_Medical History In {Myocardial Infraction})	35.55%	100.00%
If ((High BP >= 2 IN { 2 months}) (Gender IN {female}) (Past_Medical History IN {Atrial fibrillation}) THEN (Lived IN {Died}))	53.99%	100.00%

5. CONCLUSION AND FUTURE WORK

In this paper, our approaches for the discovery of patterns in time-oriented data are introduced. We also presented Easy Miner, our mining tool designed and developed at UMIST. Major components of Easy Miner including relevance analysis, classification rules and discovery of association rules are described in details with examples.

We think the first consideration for constructing an effective pattern discovery system should be given to testing the appropriateness and applicability of the framework. We have started in this direction by experimenting with a large stroke and quality of hypertension control data set.

Several areas exist for further investigation. We like to work on algorithms to discover complex temporal pattern such as "first working day of every month". Also the problem of mining cyclic association rules remains open for research.

We are currently investigating the enhancement to existing techniques for time-oriented data mining. In summary, the work reported in this paper focuses on two areas and their integration. On one side, data mining as a technique for discovery of interesting patterns from database and on the other side time-oriented data as a rich and valuable source of data. We believe that their integration will lead to even higher quality data and discovered patterns.

REFERENCES

[1] Fayyad U, Piatetsky-Shapiro, Smyth Uthurusamy R. Advances in Knowledge Discovery and Data Mining. AAAI/MIT Press, 1995.

[2] Agrawal R, Imienlinski T, Swami A. Database Mining: A Performance Perspective. IEEE Trans. on Knowledge and Data Engineering 1993; 5(6): 914-925.

[3] Agrawal R, Srikant R. Mining Sequential Patterns. In Proceedings of Eleventh International Conf. on Data Engineering, March 1995, Taipie, Taiwan, pp 3-14.

[4] Mannila H, Toivonen H, Verkamo I. Discovering Frequent Episodes in Sequences. In the First International Conference on KDD, pp 210-215.

[5] Padmanabhan B, Tuzhilin A. Pattern Discovery in Temporal Databases: A Temporal Logic Approach. In Proceedings of the 2nd International Conference on Knowledge Discovery and Data Mining, August 1996, Portland, OR.

[6] Wijsen J, Meersman R. On the complexity of mining temporal trends. In Proceedings of the SIGMOD'97 Workshop on Research Issues on Data Mining and Knowledge Discovery (DMKD'97), May 1997

[7] Chen X, Petrounias I, Heathfield H. Discovering Temporal Association Rules in Temporal Databases. In the Proceedings of the International Workshop on Issues and Applications of Database Technology (IADT98), Berlin, Germany, July 1998.

[8] Kamber M, Winstone L, Gong W, Cheng S, Han J. Generalisation and Decision Tree Induction: Efficient Classification in Data Mining. In Proceedings of 1997 International Workshop on Research Issues on Data Engineering (RIDE'97), Birmingham, England, April 1997, pp 111-120.

[9] Loether H.J, McTavish D.G. Descriptive and Inferential Statistics: An Introduction. Allyn and Bacon 1993.

[10] Mehta M., Agrawal R., and Rissanen J. SLIQ: A Fast Scalable Classifier for Data Mining. In Proc. of the Fifth Int'l Conference on Extending Database Technology (EDBT), Avignon, France, March 1996.

[11] Shafer J, Mehta M., Agrawal R. SPRINT: A Scalable Classifier for Data Mining. In Proceedings of the 22nd International Conference on Very Large Data Bases (VLDB), Mumbai (Bombay), India, 1996, pp 544-555.

[12] Rakesh Agrawal and R. Srikant. Fast algorithms for mining association rules. In *Proc. 1994 Int. Conf. Very Large Data Bases*, pages 487-499, Santiago, Chile, September 1994.

ADAPTIVE GRAPHICAL PATTERN RECOGNITION: THE JOINT ROLE OF STRUCTURE AND LEARNING

M. Diligenti, M. Gori, M. Maggini, and E. Martinelli
Dipartimento di Ingegneria dell'Informazione, Università di Siena
Via Roma, 56 - 53100 Siena (Italy)

ABSTRACT

In this paper we introduce methodological and practical issues on *adaptive graphical pattern recognition*, a new approach to process patterns for which neither a purely symbolic nor a purely sub-symbolic representation seems to be adequate. Adaptive graphical pattern recognition is based on appropriate graphical representations of patterns which are subsequently processed by recursive neural networks, equipped with connectionist-based learning algorithms.

The preliminary ideas and results given in [1] are extended and some properties, like the capabilities of incorporating scale and rotation invariance and dealing with noise, are emphasized and related to competing approaches. It turns out that adaptive graphical pattern recognition bridges nicely the gap between traditional connectionist models and syntactic pattern recognition and appears to be a new challenging approach to many pattern recognition problems.

INTRODUCTION

There are several application domains in the field of pattern recognition (see e.g. medical or technical diagnosis, molecular biology, document and image analysis) where the structure of the patterns plays a very important role. As early pointed out by Wiener, patterns can often be regarded as an *arrangement characterized by the order ofthe elements ofwhich they are made, rather than by the intrinsic nature ofthese elements*. Hence, the causal, hierarchical, and topological relations between parts of a given pattern yield a significant information that seems to be useful in most human recognition processes. Among others, these motivations have given rise to the impressive development of approaches to syntactic pattern recognition. Unfortunately, pure symbolic representations do not seem very appropriate whenever the noise plays a major role. On the opposite, adaptive approaches to pattern recognition, like those based on neural networks seem to be very well-suited for dealing with noise and sub-symbolic pattern representations, but can hardly be regarded as good models of patterns which exhibit a significant structure.

In this paper we propose a new approach to pattern recognition which is somewhat in between adaptive pattern recognition (statistical and neural networks sub-symbolic approaches) and syntactic pattern recognition. The basic idea is that of providing graphical representations of patterns where the nodes may contain either symbolic or real-valued features. Special emphasis is placed on representations based on directed ordered graphs (DOAGs) for which the connectionist-based learning algorithms which hold for static data have been recently extended [2, 3]. DOAGs with nodes having real-valued features turn out to be natural representations of many real world patterns and, on the other hand, the constraints on the direction of the links and on the ordering of the children make it possible to cut the complexity of learning significantly.

We present some very promising experimental results for the recognition of company logo under different conditions of noise and under the additional constraints of scale and rotation

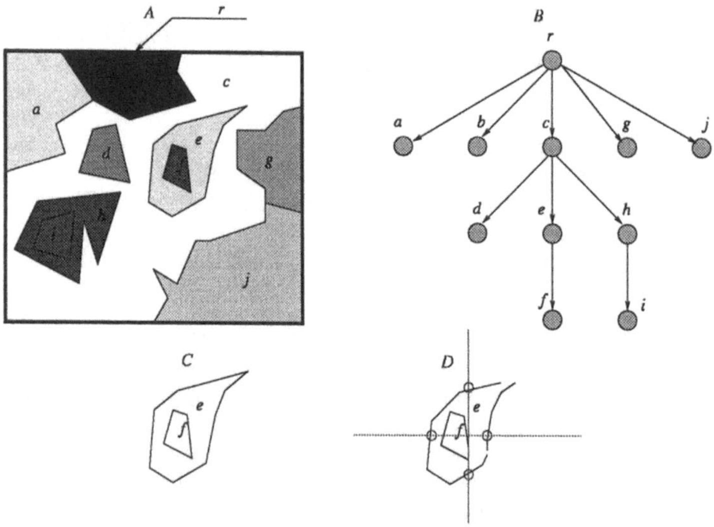

Figure 1: Graphical representations by means of the contour tree algorithm.

invariance. We report a comparison with multilayer perceptrons whose inputs are pre-processed according to several different techniques aimed at incorporating size and rotation invariance.

GRAPHICAL PATTERN REPRESENTATIONS

There are many different ways of expressing the structural properties of patterns that have been studied in the field of syntactic pattern recognition. We consider pattern representations which take into account either the structure or the subsymbolic information.

The picture of Fig 1, which is typically obtained from a given pattern by means of a quantization algorithm, can always be represented by means of a tree by following the contours and expressing the $c_1 \prec c_2$ relationship, which indicates whether a given contour c_1 is inside c_2 [4]. This relationships can also be checked approximately by inspecting the intersection of the outer contour with the vertical and horizontal axes arising from the center of the internal contour (see Fig. 1-D). In so doing, the relationship can be verified more efficiently and the corresponding contour tree algorithm is likely to be more robust with respect to noise than the truly mathematical one. Beginning from the external contour we create the root which is linked to as many subtrees as contours which are inside the external one, and then we continue recursively, that is each subtree is a contour tree itself. The algorithm requires the extraction of the contours and the corresponding domains must properly be extracted by means of a feature-based representation.

A major drawback of the contour tree algorithm is that it focuses on only the $\prec$ relationship and neglects the information arisen from the borders of each domain. This is clearly put forward in Fig. 2, where the contour tree algorithm yields a trivial tree where all the domains of the map are regarded as children at the same level.

Of course, there are many different ways of constructing graphical representations which overcome this limitation. Basically, we need to introduce a sort of relationships which expresses the property that two given domains have part of their border in common. The most

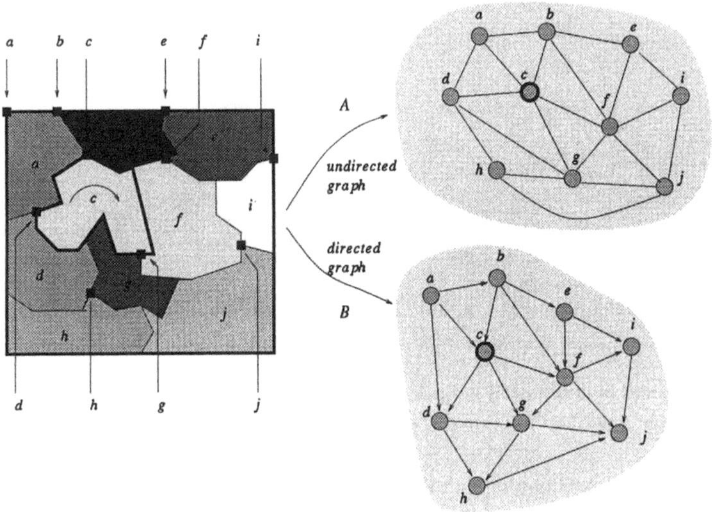

Figure 2: Graphical representations based on the border relationship. A directed ordered graph is created (B).

straightforward way of providing a graphical representation is that of simply expressing that relationship explicitly. As shown in Fig. 2-A, an undirected graph can be created where the pattern structural properties are significantly enhanced with respect to what is produced by the contour tree algorithm. As will be more clear in the following section, however, processing undirected graphs is significantly more difficult than processing trees and directed graphs. A possible extraction of directed graphs is shown in Fig. 2, where the border of each domain is visited so as to identify those domains which partially share the border (see [5] for a detailed analysis).

ADAPTIVE COMPUTATION OF GRAPHS

We propose a general framework for adaptive computation of structured information and focuses attention on connectionist models presenting either architecture or learning issues. This formulation extends recurrent neural networks significantly and makes it possible to conceive graphical models with neuronal units which process data represented by graphs themselves. Let us consider a directed ordered graph so as for any node v one can identify a set, eventually empty, of ordered children $ch[v]$. For each node v we compute a state vector $\boldsymbol{X}_v \in \mathcal{R}^n$ and an output $\boldsymbol{Y}_v \in \mathcal{R}^k$ as follows:

$$\begin{aligned} \boldsymbol{X}_v &= f\left(\boldsymbol{X}_{ch[v]}, \boldsymbol{U}_v, v, \Theta_v^f\right) \\ \boldsymbol{Y}_v &= g\left(\boldsymbol{X}_v, v, \Theta_v^g\right), \end{aligned} \qquad (1)$$

where $\boldsymbol{U}_v \in \mathcal{R}^m$ is the information attached to the node v, $f()$ and $g()$ are functions depending on a set of parameters Θ_v^f and Θ_v^g that are determined through learning.

As shown in Fig. 3, the recursive network - which is essentially a way of expressing the dependence relationships among the variables at the node level - and the given input graph yield the *encoding network* (see [3] for further details). The encoding network makes it possible to unfold the network on the given graph, thus creating a classic feedforward network.

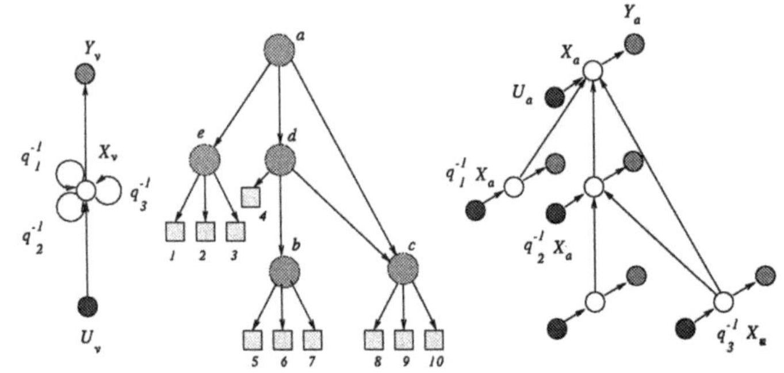

Figure 3: Construction of the encoding network corresponding to a recursive network and a DOAG. Note that $o = 3$ (graph outdegree), and that the nil pointers are represented by proper frontier (initial) states.

Let o be the maximum outdegree of the given directed graph. For a *first-order* recursive network eq. (1) can be written as:

$$\boldsymbol{X}_v = \sigma\left(\sum_{i=1}^{o} \boldsymbol{A}_v(i) \cdot q_i^{-1}\boldsymbol{X}_v + \boldsymbol{B}_v \cdot \boldsymbol{U}_v\right), \tag{2}$$

where the *pointer matrices* $\boldsymbol{A}_v(i) \in \mathcal{R}^{n,n}$, $i = 1, \ldots o$, express the dependence of the state for the node v on the state of its children $ch[v]$, the weight matrix $\boldsymbol{B}_v \in \mathcal{R}^{n,m}$ determines the contribution of the information attached to the node, σ is a sigmoidal function and q_i^{-1} is the *shift operator* that that yields the value of the corresponding variable attached to the i-th child of the current node.

In practice, especially when dealing with graphs having high outdegree, given any node v, the state associated with its corresponding i-th child $q_i^{-1}\boldsymbol{X}_v$ can be conveniently compressed. Hence, the state updating equation (2) becomes

$$\boldsymbol{X}_v = \sigma\left(\sum_{i=1}^{o} \boldsymbol{A}_i \cdot q_i^{-1}\sigma\left(\boldsymbol{P}_v \cdot \boldsymbol{X}_v\right) + \boldsymbol{B}_v \cdot \boldsymbol{U}_v\right). \tag{3}$$

where $\boldsymbol{P}_v \in \mathcal{R}^{n_r,n}$ reduces the dimension n of the pointer information from n to $n_r < n$.

In general, the processing of DOAGs is *node variant*, that is the state updating equation (1) depends explicitly on the node v being processed. Moreover, the graph $\boldsymbol{U}$ can itself affect the computation in the sense that the same node v into two or more different graphs might yield a different output (non-causal transduction). The direct dependence on v and $\boldsymbol{U}$ is typical of problems involving large graphs for which a homogeneous processing of all the nodes seems to be a very restrictive assumption. Most real-world problems supply enough domain knowledge for performing symbolic computation up to a certain level. This kind of computation often involve global properties of graphs and makes it possible to state that some properties hold for a given node. Hence, in order to take these more general requirements into account, equation (1) can be extended to

$$\begin{aligned} \boldsymbol{X}_v &= f\left(\boldsymbol{X}_{ch[v]}, \boldsymbol{U}_v, v, \boldsymbol{U}, \Theta_f\right) \\ \boldsymbol{Y}_v &= g\left(\boldsymbol{X}_v, v, \boldsymbol{U}, \Theta_g\right). \end{aligned} \tag{4}$$

where there is also an explicit dependence on the whole graph $\boldsymbol{U}$. A simple and interesting practical case arises whenever nodes and graphs can be classified by an external algorithm so as the model of equation (4) is replaced by

$$\begin{aligned} c &= \texttt{Class}\,(\boldsymbol{U}, v)\,; \\ \boldsymbol{X}_v &= f\left(\boldsymbol{X}_{ch[v]}, \boldsymbol{U}_v, c, \Theta_f^c\right) \\ \boldsymbol{Y}_v &= g\left(\boldsymbol{X}_v, c, \Theta_g^c\right). \end{aligned} \tag{5}$$

Note that the parameters depend on the class c and, therefore, the external determination of the class makes it possible to learn them from examples using a partition of the given examples. We are basically using the ***divide and conquer*** principle which suggests using a modular architecture in which different models act separately on different classes, created on the basis of stationary requirements. The given set of labelled examples used for learning turns out to be partitioned into $c = 1, \ldots, C$ classes which are determined by purely ***symbolic computation***.
A special case of the $\texttt{Class}(\cdot,\cdot)$ function is that in which one can separate the dependences on the node v and the graph $\boldsymbol{U}$. For instance, cases can be found in which it is useful to operate a partition of the training set into subsets of graphs whose maximum outdegree ranges in a given interval. This requirement arises when dealing with graphs in which the nodes have a significantly different outdegree. In those cases, the computation becomes formally congruent because of the presence of the frontier states but, unfortunately, learning from examples in cases with such a variance is very hard. Likewise, one could also adopt the same criterion of the outdegree on a local basis, that is one could have separate models for nodes with outdegree ranging in different intervals.

The learning of the parameters can be carried out by using the concept of encoding network. In so doing the process of learning is reduced to the case of feedforward networks and is still based on gradient descent. The gradient computation is carried out by means of an algorithm which is referred to as Backpropagation through structure [2], since the delta error is backpropagated through the links of the directed ordered graphs.

EXPERIMENTAL RESULTS

We report some applications in the field of logo recognition, which is a central task for some applications in document classification. A company logo is usually made up of a set of simple geometrical shapes and these shapes are usually nested. Hence, because of their geometrical structure, the logos are well represented by a contour-tree description. In order to validate the proposed classification technique based on graph representation of images and adaptive graphical processing of the extracted graphs, we faced the task of classifying four different logos under different conditions of noise and rotation. The task is particularly challenging because of the presence of high noise levels that alter considerably the structure of the image.

Four types of synthetic noise were added to the original images to model typical degradations introduced by photocopiers and fax machines. The first type of noise was obtained by changing the value of each pixel with a certain probability. The changes for different pixels are uncorrelated. This type of noise is referred to as as the ***salt and pepper noise***. The ***stripe noise*** was created by randomly locating stripes of random thickness on the logo. The ***blob noise*** was produced by means of circular spots with random center and radius. The ***spot noise*** was obtained by superimposing many circular blobs so as to produce complex shapes that look like ink blots. Finally, after the introduction of noise the image was randomly rotated.
Figure 4 shows the results of two intermediate steps performed during the classification of an image. Three different cases are shown to illustrate the effects of noise on the preprocessing. From the images obtained after filtering and edge detection, in the given example, it is clear that the salt and pepper noise is effectively removed and does not affect the contour extraction.

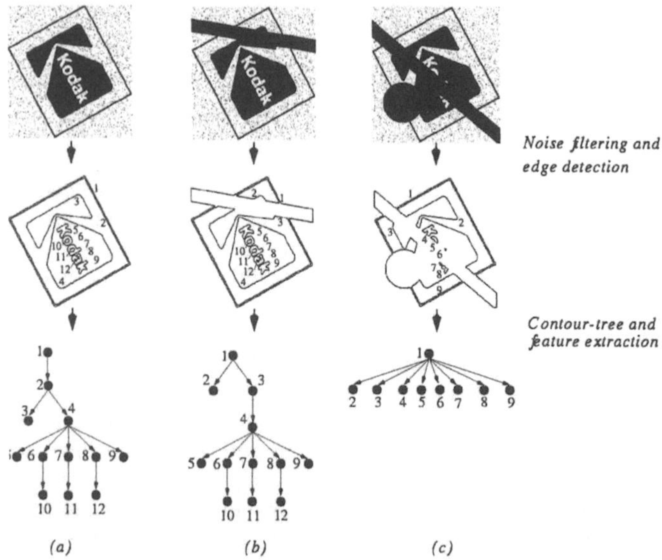

Figure 4: Filtering and contour-tree extraction for three different cases of noise. (a) The logo is corrupted only by salt and pepper noise that is completely removed by filtering the image before edge detection. (b) The logo is corrupted by a single stripe. The structure of the graph extracted by the contour-tree algorithm is only slightly different from the previous one. (c) The logo is corrupted by a stripe and a blob. The structure of the extracted graph is quite different with respect to the original one.

On the opposite, spots and especially stripes affect even the topology of the extracted graph. In any case, also using the simplified algorithm to establish the $\prec$ relationships (see Fig 1-D), the extracted graph is nearly independent of rotations.

Each node of the extracted graph corresponds to a contour in the image. The information attached to the node is a vector of features that describes some geometrical properties of the contour. In particular for these experiments 13 parameters were used to describe each contour[1]: the number of pixels contained inside the contour, the perimeter in pixels, the number of black pixels inside the contour, the distance between the contour and the image barycenters, the angle between the line connecting the image barycenters with the contour barycenter and the horizontal line passing through the image barycenter, the maximum curvature angle for convex sides and for concave sides, the number of points for which the curvature angle is above a given threshold (peaks) both for convex and concave regions, the minimum distance between the contour and the nearest one, and the three minimum distances between the contour and the three contours with the longest perimeter (see [5] for more details).

At each node of the input graph the inputs to the networks are the state vectors computed for the node children and the feature vector stored in the node. These inputs are processed by a layer of hidden neurons. The last layer of neurons compute the node state and output. For these experiments $n = 40$ (hidden neurons) and $n_r = 7$ state neurons were used. The output layer contained four neurons, one for each class.

For each experiment a learning set and a test set were built from the original logo adding the noise and rotating it. Each set contains about 512 instances for each of the four logos.

[1]Many of the following features are normalized with respect to a reference contour in the image.

Stripes and blobs	max. stripes Area	0.11	0.33	0.33
	max. blob Area	0	0	0.2
	salt & pepper	4%	4%	4%
	recognition (%)	100.00%	100.00%	99.77%
Spots	blobs number	0	40	40
	max. blobs dimension	0	0.1	0.2
	salt & pepper	8%	8%	8%
	recognition (%)	100.00%	99.54%	97.11%
Stripes and rotation	max. stripe Area	0.33	0.33	0.33
	salt & pepper	4%	4%	4%
	max. rotation degree	0	± 60	± 180
	recognition(%)	100.00%	99.34%	99.12%

Table 1: Recognition rate for different levels of noise and rotation.

	Max. Rotation	% pixel changed by imp. noise	Max. stripes area (% logo area)	Recog. rate
Autoassociator (no invariants)	± 180	8%	0	93.72%
	± 180	8%	33	80.41%
Autoassociator (Hu-Invariants)	± 180	8%	0	98.97%
	± 180	8%	33	40.32%
Autoassociator (Log-Polar trans.)	± 180	8%	0	99.98%
	± 180	8%	33	79.95%
recursive ANN	± 180	8%	0	100.00 %
	± 180	8%	33	99.12%

Table 2: Comparison between different classifiers with respect to invariance to rotations. In all cases logos can be rotated up to 360 degrees and are corrupted by salt and pepper noise and stripe noise.

Many different experiments were carried on in order to investigate the effects of noise and rotation on the classification performance. Table 1 reports the recognition rate for different levels of noise and rotation. In particular the first two groups of experiments show how the performance is affected by increasing the area covered by spots. The last group clearly shows the effectiveness of the proposed classifier in case of rotations.

Table 2 shows the comparison between the proposed method and other classification techniques based on rotation-invariant features. In particular we tested an autoassociator based classifier using different features as inputs. Neural autoassociators have been applied successfully to classification tasks and also to logo recognition [6]. Two different sets of features were tested beside a simple representation of the logo as a matrix of pixels (no invariants): Hu-invariants are moment based invariants, Log-polar transform converts the X-Y representation of the image to polar coordinates. The results show clearly that recursive networks outperform all the other methods.

CONCLUSIONS

In this paper we have proposed the basic ideas behind adaptive graphical pattern recognition. Unlike traditional connectionist and statistical approaches, which typically rely on a static representation of data composed of vectors of features, the patterns can be properly represented by directed graphs which are subsequently processed according to Backpropagation through structure, a connectionist-based learning procedure which properly unfold the neural network through the given graph.

The idea of performing pattern recognition using recursive neural networks has been recently introduced in [1]. In this paper, we have provided additional indications concerning either methodological or experimental issues. In particular, we have briefly discussed graphical representations which contribute to create more structured representations. Massive experimentation on the given logo data base has demonstrated the importance of properly filtering the logo image before extracting the data structure. This seems to be preferable with respect to the alternative approach proposed in [1], in which the noise is filtered in the created data structure by means of a proper pruning algorithm. The slight modification of the contour tree algorithm herein proposed seems also to play a fundamental role in the creation of data structure which better enhance the structure of the pattern. The experimental results show that, though in theory the contour tree rotation invariance does not longer hold, as a matter of fact, there is a very slight dependence of the performance on the rotation angle. Our preliminary experiments strongly support adaptive graphical pattern recognition in the case in which we need to recognize patterns either under rotation and scale invariance or under noise. These very promising results suggest that the proposed approach might bridge nicely learning approaches based on numerical features and syntactic pattern recognition.

ACKNOWLEDGEMENTS

This research was carried out in the general framework of a joint project between the University of Wollongong (Australia), the University of Pisa (Italy) and the University of Siena (Italy) (see `http://www-dsi.ing.unifi.it/~ paolo/datas`) concerning "Adaptive computation of structured information." We thank P. Frasconi, E. Francesconi, J. Sheng, S. Marinai, G. Soda, and A. Sperduti for very useful discussions.

REFERENCES

[1] E. Francesconi, P. Frasconi, M. Gori, S. Marinai, J. Q. Sheng, G. Soda, and A. Sperduti, "Logo recognition by recursive neural networks," in *Graphics Recognition – Algorithms and Systems* (R. Kasturi and K. Tombre, eds.), pp. 104–117, LNCS, Vol. 1389, Springer Verlag, August 1997.

[2] A. Sperduti and T. Starita, "Supervised neural networks for the classification of structures," *IEEE Transactions on Neural Networks*, vol. 8, no. 3, 1997.

[3] P. Frasconi, M. Gori, and A. Sperduti, "A general framework for adaptive processing of data structures," *IEEE Transactions on Neural Networks*, vol. 9, September 1998.

[4] G. Cortelazzo, G. Mian, G. Vezzi, and P. Zamperoni, "Trademark shapes description by string-maching techniques," *Pattern Recognition*, vol. 27, no. 8, pp. 1005–1018, 1984.

[5] M. Dligenti, M. Gori, M. Maggini, and E. Martinelli, "Adaptive graphical pattern recognition: Foundations and experimental issues," Tech. Rep. 21-98, Dipartimento di Ingegneria dell'Informazione, Università di Siena, Siena, Italy, May 1998.

[6] F. Cesarini, E. Francesconi, M. Gori, S. Marinai, and G. Soda, "A neural-based architecture for spot-noisy logo recognition," in *International Conference on Document Analysis and Recognition*, (Ulm, Germany), pp. 175–179, IEEE Press, August 1997.

TUTORIALS

CLASSIFICATION USING NETWORKS OF NORMALIZED RADIAL BASIS FUNCTIONS.

Guido Bugmann, Centre for Neural and Adaptive Systems,
School of Computing, University of Plymouth, Plymouth PL4 8AA.

ABSTRACT

Normalized Radial Basis Function Networks (NRBF) were invented at the same time as standard RBF nets, in 1989, but went unnoticed until recently, when it was found that they constitute a very interesting tool, especially for pattern classification. NRBF classifiers behave as Nearest Neighbour classifiers and have a functionality similar to Fuzzy Inference Systems but without the Curse of Dimensionality problem. NRBF nets are easy to use, with performances largely insensitive to model parameters and with a very fast training. In this paper the functionality of NRBF nets is compared with those of standard RBF nets. The applications to classification will be illustrated with benchmark problems. For the IRIS classification problem, NRBF match the performances of the best published techniques.

1. INTRODUCTION.

Normalized Radial Basis Functions (NRBF) differ from standard Radial Basis Functions (RBF) by a seemingly minor modification of their equation (section 2). This results in novel computational properties which have attracted little attention in the neural network community. Moody and Darken (1989)[16] were first to mention Normalised RBF nets without elaborating on their functional significance. However. Servin and Cuevas (1993)[20] noted that normalization gave RBF nets the "same classification properties as nets using sigmoid functions". Cha and Kassam (1995)[9] proposed that "a normalized Gaussian basis function features either localized behavior similar to that of a Gaussian or nonlocalized behavior like that of a sigmoid, depending on the location of its centre". Rao et al. (1997)[19] interpreted NRBF nets as mixture of expert models and Jang & Sun (1993)[12] saw similarities with fuzzy inference systems. These multiple views reflect the fact that NRBF nodes in the hidden layer behave more like case indicators rather than basis functions proper, as is elaborated in section 2. This property leads to excellent performances in classification tasks, as shown in section 4. One of the key features of NRBF nets is their excellent generalization, a property that can be exploited to reduce the number of hidden nodes in classification tasks. A new learning rule was proposed to that effect by Bugmann (1998)[5] and is summarized in section 3.

NRBF nets have also given very good results in other classes of application, trajectory learning in robotics (Althoefer and Bugmann, 1995[1], Bugmann et al, 1998[6]) and function mapping (Bugmann, 1998[5]).

2. NORMALIZED RADIAL BASIS FUNCTION NETWORKS

Standard Radial Basis Functions (RBF) nets comprise a hidden layer of RBF nodes and an output layer with linear nodes (Broomhead and Lowe, 1988[7], Moody and Darken, 1989[16]). The function of these nets is given by:

$$y_i(x) = \sum_{j=1}^{n} w_{ij}\,\phi(x - x_j) \qquad (1)$$

where y_i is the activity of the output node i, $\phi(x\text{-}x_j)$is the activity of the hidden node j, with a RBF function centred on the vector x_j, x is the actual input vector and w_{ij} are the weights from the RBF nodes in the hidden layer to the linear output node. Such a net is a universal function approximator according to Powell (1987)[17].

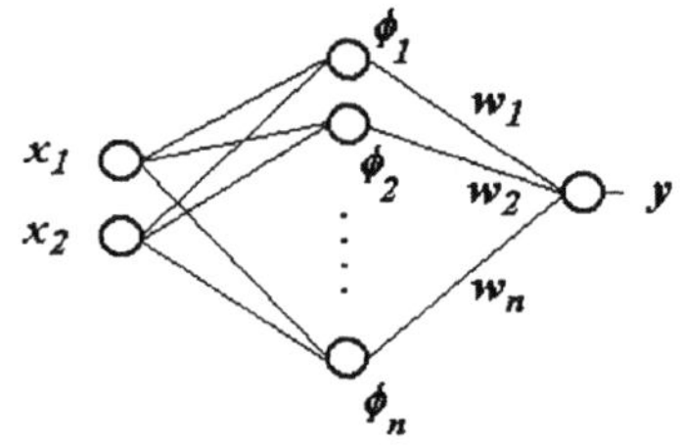

Figure 1: Network architecture for standard RBF nets and Normalized RBF nets (two inputs and one output shown).

The RBF function $\phi(x\text{-}x_j)$ of a hidden node j used here is the Gaussian Radial Basis Function:

$$\phi(x - x_j) = \exp\left(-\frac{\sum_{k=1}^{K}(x_k - w_{jk})^2}{2\sigma^2}\right)$$

where σ is the width of the Gaussian and K is the dimension of the input space. The "weights" w_{jk} between node k in the input layer and node j in the hidden layer do not act multiplicatively as in other neuron models, but define the input vector $x_j = (w_{j1},\ldots,w_{jK})$ eliciting the maximum response of node j (x_j *is* the "centre of the receptive field").

In normalised RBF nets, the output activity is normalised by the total input activity in the hidden layer:

$$y_i(x) = \frac{\sum_j W_{ij}\,\phi(x - x_j)}{\sum_j \phi(x - x_j)} \qquad (2)$$

Moody and Darken (1989)[16] proposed that normalisation be performed by the hidden nodes before the summation stage in the output node. In their approach, normalization is a non-local operation, requiring each hidden node to "know" about the outputs of the other hidden nodes. Hence a computationally costly convergence process is required. A similar view is taken in (Rao et al., 1997[19]). In contrast, in our implementation the normalisation is done in the output layer. As it receives already information from all hidden units, the locality of the computational processes is preserved.

Equation 2 shows that, as a result of the normalization, the output activity becomes an activity-weighted average of the input weights in which the weights from the most active inputs contribute most to the value of the output activity. In other words, the roles of output weights and hidden nodes activities are switched. In standard RBF nets, the weights determine how much each hidden node contributes to the output. In NRBF nets, the activity of the hidden nodes determine which weights contribute most to the output. For instance, in the extreme case where only one of the hidden nodes is active, then the output of the net becomes equal to the weight corresponding to that hidden node, whatever its level of activity.

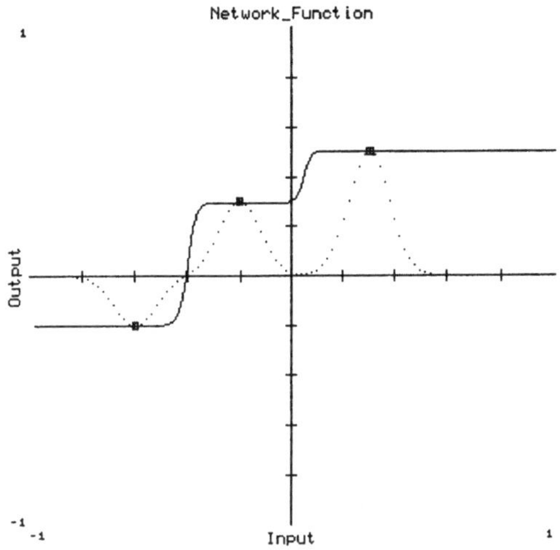

Figure 2. Illustration of the effects of normalization in RBF nets. *Full line:* output y of a NRBF net. *Dotted line:* Output of a standard RBF net. Both nets use three hidden nodes centred on the three training data indicated in the Figure.

Figure 2 shows that hidden nodes have a domain of influence in the input space in which they determine the output of the net. This domain is only limited by conflicts with other hidden nodes and has no limits outside of the domain covered by training data. This explains the "sigmoid-like" behaviour noted by Servin and Cuevas (1993)[20] and Cha and Kassam (1995)[9].

When the size of the Gaussians is small, the decay of the hidden nodes activity with distance is so fast that, for most point of the input space, there is usually only one hidden node that contributes significantly to equation 2. As a result, hidden nodes perform a parcelation of the input space similar to a Voronoi tessellation. This is also illustrated by a two-dimensional example in section 4. Due to normalization, RBF nodes become here case indicators rather than basis functions proper. In that sense, NRBF nets are similar to fuzzy inference systems, as discussed in (Jang & Sun, 1993[12], Andersen et al., 1998[2]). In these systems normalization is a key element of the "centre of gravity defuzzification method (Brown and Harris, 1994, pp 388-404[8]).

In equation 2, normalization is a way to select which weight becomes the output of the net. This is a special case of a more general approach where whole functions are selected. For instance in (Shao et al., 1993[21]) the output y_i is a combination of linear functions $L_{ij}(x)$ weighted by the activity of their respective hidden nodes j.

Two types of networks are compared in this paper: a standard RBF net, as in equation (1) and a net with a normalizing output node as in equation (2). In both nets the hidden nodes have Gaussian receptive fields, with a width σ indicated in figure captions. The networks (Figure 1) have two inputs, one output and a number of hidden nodes determined by the recruitment procedures during training (section 3). Simulations are done on a PC with the neural network development package CORTEX-PRO[1].

3. LEARNING PROCEDURES.

3.1 STANDARD TRAINING PROCEDURE.

For the standard RBF nets, training is done in a standard way (Bishop, 1995, p. 170[4]), by recruiting hidden nodes in the first epoch, then, in subsequent epochs, adjusting the positions of the centres of the nodes and the weights to the output node to minimize the output error, as described below:

i) recruiting a new hidden node centred on an input vector that was beyond a radius of 0.5σ from the centre of an existing node, or slowly shifting the centre $\boldsymbol{x}_j$ of an existing hidden node towards the new vector $\boldsymbol{x}$ using: $\boldsymbol{x}_j(t+1) = 0.8\boldsymbol{x}_j(t) + 0.2\boldsymbol{x}$,

ii) modifying the output weight of the hidden nodes j within a radius 0.5σ of the current input vector $\boldsymbol{x}$ so that the output y_i becomes closer to the desired output y_{id}, using: $w_{ij}(t+1) = w_{ij}(t) + learnrate\ (y_{id} - y)$ (typically, $learnrate = 0.5$).

iii) showing the input vectors repeatedly to the net.

In this procedure, the recruitment of hidden node is purely input-driven, as it depends only on the distribution of training data in the input space. It is a simple procedure that converges rapidly. The number of epoch is indicated in figure captions.

3.2 MODIFIED TRAINING PROCEDURE.

For training the normalized RBF nets, the modified procedure (Bugmann, 1998[5]) is used. Taking advantage of the good interpolation and extrapolation properties of NRBF nets, new nodes are recruited only in crucial points, close to boundaries between two classes. This is achieved by recruiting no new nodes if the network indicates the correct class by using existing nodes. The steps of the modified procedure are:

i). Check if the output vector $\boldsymbol{y}$ of the net is correct, i.e. $|y - y_{desired}| < tolerance$, where a $tolerance = 0.4$ is adequate for classification problems (it may be reduced to much smaller values for mapping problems, where it represents the desired accuracy).

ii). If the output is correct. Do nothing, go to the next training data.

iii). If the output is incorrect and there is no node with its centre close to the current data point, recruit a new node centred on the data point and set its output weights to the desired output vector.

iv). If the output is incorrect and there is a node with centre close to input vector $\boldsymbol{x}$, move its centre $\boldsymbol{x}_j$ closer to the new vector $\boldsymbol{x}$ using: $\boldsymbol{x}_j(t+1) = 0.8\boldsymbol{x}_j(t) + 0.2\boldsymbol{x}$, and modify its output weights using: $w_{ij}(t+1) = w_{ij}(t) + learnrate \cdot (y_{id} - y_i)$.

---

[1]Unistat Ltd, Unistat House, 4 Shirland Mews, London W9 3DY, UK. http://www.unistat.com

The main difference of this procedure with the standard one is that the recruitment of hidden nodes is also output-driven. It results in progressively less new nodes being recruited at each epoch, as the coverage of the class domains is refined. Generally, after 3 epochs, recruitment ceases and performance improvements are solely due to weights and centre modifications. It is not a optimal procedure, because the location of the centres of the recruited nodes depends on the order of presentation of the training data, but this is of no consequences in most applications.

The optimal width of the Gaussian basis functions differs for Normalized and standard RBF nets, and can be estimated by a simple calculation discussed in section 4.1.

4. CLASSIFICATION WITH STANDARD AND NORMALIZED RBF NETS.

4.1 THE PLATEAU-VALLEY CLASSIFICATION PROBLEM

A simple example is used here to illustrate the difference between normalized RBF net and standard RBF nets. In this example, a function $f(x_1,x_2)$ is used to divide the input space into two regions: a "plateau" where the $f(x_1,x_2) = 0.5$ and "valleys" where $f(x_1,x_2) = -0.5$ (Figure 3). The problem is to train a network that classifies the regions of the input space by using 70 data points picked at random from the function $f(x_1,x_2)$. The location of most of these points can be inferred from Figure 4.

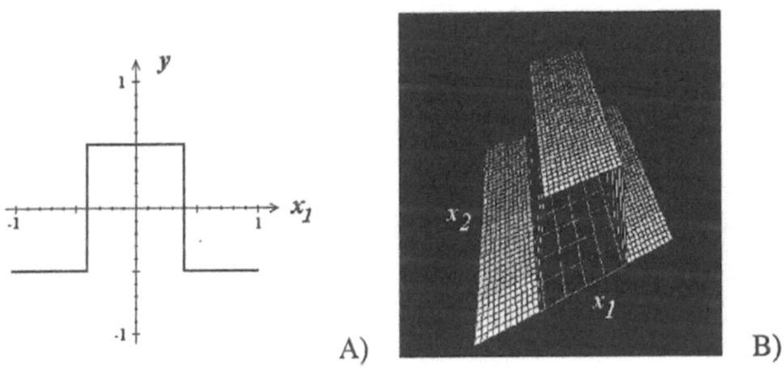

Figure 3. "Plateau" function $y = f(x_1,x_2)$ used in this example. The data are sampled in the domain $-1<x_1<1$, $-1<x_2<1$. The output $y=-0.5$ everywhere except for $-0.4<x_1<0.4$, where $y = 0.5$. **A)** Cross-section of the function along the plane $\{x_1, y\}$. **B)** Perspective view of the function in the sampling domain. The base grid is placed at y = -0.5.

Figures 4B and 5A show the functions learned by the standard RBF net and the NRBF net using a similar same small width for the basis functions. A striking effect of normalization is the improved interpolation. Even in regions of the input space where no RBF hidden node produces a strong response, NRBF nodes with receptive fields in surrounding regions can generate a large output value. In contrast, in standard RBF nets, a significant output requires a hidden node with its centre close to the input vector, or using hidden nodes with wider receptive fields (larger σ).

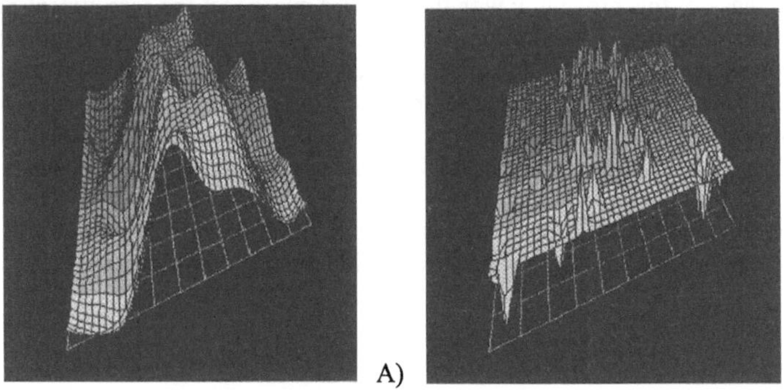

A) B)

Figure 4: A) Function of a standard RBF net (equation 1) trained on 70 points sampled from the function shown in Figure 3. Parameters: $\sigma = 0.21$, Average RMS error < 0.04 after 30 epochs. 50 hidden nodes were recruited by the standard training procedure (section 3.1).
B) Function of a standard RBF net with $\sigma = 0.03$. Figure produced for the purpose of indicating the positions of the 70 training data.

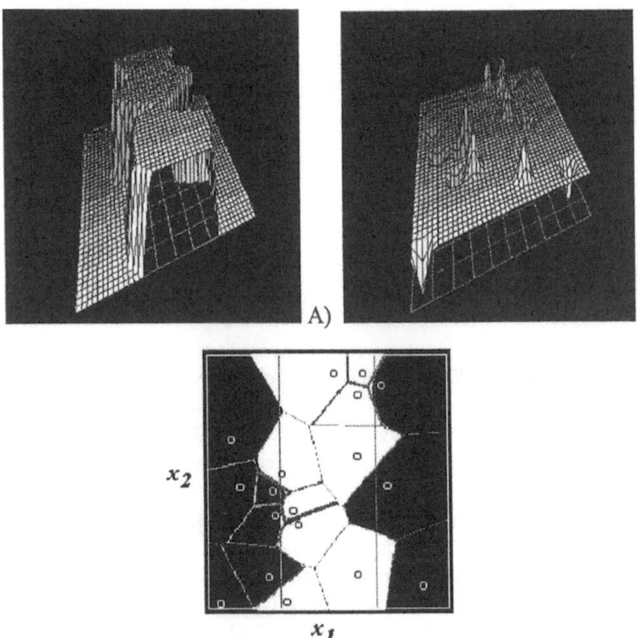

A) B) C)

Figure 5: A) Function of the Normalized RBF net trained with the modified procedure (section 3.2). *Parameters:* $\sigma = 0.05$, Average RMS error = 0.0041 after 2 epochs, 15 hidden nodes recruited. **B)** Non normalized output of the net, plotted to indicate the positions of the recruited nodes. **C)** Partitions of the input space generated by the recruited hidden nodes. The two vertical grey lines indicate the boundaries of the "plateau". Other grey lines indicate regions where neighbouring nodes have similar activities within a 20% margin.

It was shown in Bugmann (1998)[5] that for best interpolation, standard RBF nets require values of σ close to one half of the *largest* distance between nearest neighbours (which is here 0.46), reflecting the need to ensure large enough output values over the largest empty space between training data. Performances are better for larger receptive field sizes. In contrast, NRBF nets trained with the standard procedure show a good performance over a wide range of sizes, with better performances for small sizes. Interestingly, the best performance is achieved for a size $\sigma = 0.12$ which is exactly the *average* distance between a data point and its nearest neighbour in this training set. This size leads also to good generalization in mapping problems (Bugmann, 1998[5]). This points to a simple rule of thumb for an initial selection of the sizes of basis functions for NRBF nets.

Figure 5B shows the location of the recruited nodes. Comparison with Figure 4B indicates that recruited nodes are now mainly located at class boundaries, tending to form polarised pairs, with one member on each side of the boundary. This suggests that anti-symmetric basis functions reminiscent of the Gabor functions observed in visual cortex (Marcelja, 1980[15]; Jones & Palmer, 1987[13]), may constitute ideal oriented basis functions for classification problems with normalizing nets.

4.2 THE TWO-SPIRAL CLASSIFICATION PROBLEM.

Figure 7 illustrates the extrapolation properties of NRBF networks with the two-spirals benchmark problem. The network was trained with all 194 data points shown in Figure 7. It can be seen that areas outside of the immediate neighbourhood of training data are classified according to their nearest neighbour in the training data, or more precisely their nearest hidden node centre. This results in a function very similar to the one obtained with Multi-Layer Perceptrons using sigmoid functions in the hidden layers (Lang & Witbrock, 1988[14]). Indeed training is much faster here, with no classification errors after 4 epochs, and good generalisation may be inferred from Figure 7.

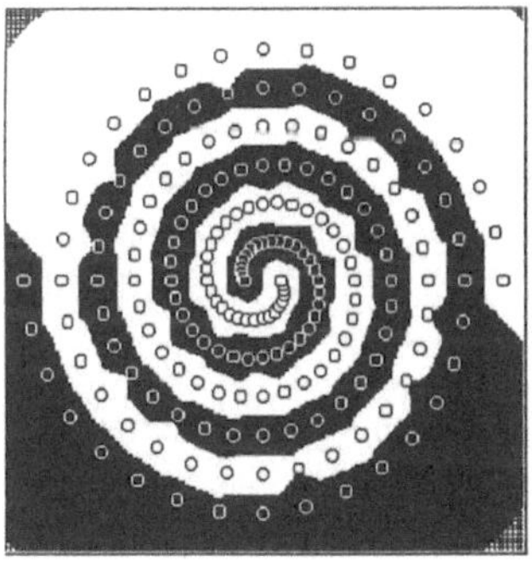

Figure 6: Two spirals classification. White and black areas indicate the two classes assigned to these areas by a Normalised RBF net. The hashed areas indicate unclassified areas due to activities of hidden nodes smaller than the precision of the computer. The 194 training data[2] are indicated by filled and empty symbols . Network parameters: $\sigma = 0.28$, Average RMS error = 0.057 after 4 epochs, 96 nodes recruited using the modified training procedure (section 4.1). Figure range: $-7 < x_1 < 7$, $-7 < x_2 < 7$.

[2] Data from the Carnegie Mellon AI repository: http://www-cgi.cs.cmu.edu/afs/cs/project/ai-repository/ai/areas/neural/bench/cmu/

4.3 THE IRIS BENCHMARK PROBLEM

NRBF nets have also been applied to the IRIS benchmark problem, matching the best published performances (Grant, 1997[10]). These results are summarized below.

Despite there being a huge range of different irises world-wide they can all be classified into one of three distinct classes. The classes are: Iris-Setosa, Iris-Versicolour and Iris-Virginica. The standard method of taxonomy is carried out by measuring four attributes of the flower in centimetres, that is sepal length and width, and petal length and width. Using these measures only one of the classes is linearly separable from the others. The Iris-setosa class to be distinct from the other two. Iris-versicolor and Iris-viginica, however show a high degree of overlap. The database used consisted of 150 samples, 50 for each class. Half of the data in each class were used for training and the other half for testing. A binary output target representation was used where each one of 3 output nodes was true for a particular class of iris and false for all other. The results for the best RBF networks and NRBF network are compared in table 1 with those of other methods. As expected, standard RBF nets exhibit poorer generalisation on the test set.

Classifier	Learning	Testing	Combined
3 Output Weighted RBF	***100%***	***95%***	***97%***
Fuzzy SOFM	100%	95%	97%
Genetic Programming	98%	95%	97%
Optical Thin Film	98%	93%	97%
3 Output Standard RBF	***100%***	***85%***	***93%***

Table 1. Summary of results for various classifier techniques[3].

The results for the Fuzzy Self Organised map are taken from (Hokirawa, 1997[11]). Genetic programming was a technique used by Backer (1996)[3]. Purvis and Li (1995)[18] describe the learning method using an Optical Thin-Film Model. It can be seen that the results achieved using NRBF nets match those of these techniques well.

5. CONCLUSION

These simple examples results suggest that Normalized RBF nets have very good generalisation properties that are beneficial in classification tasks. This is due to the property of normalised RBF nets to produce a significant output even for input vectors far from the centre of the receptive field of any of the hidden nodes.

Taking advantage of this, a modified learning procedure allows NRBF nets to operate with significantly less hidden nodes in classification tasks.

When applied to classification problems, the modified learning procedure results in nodes being recruited mainly along class boundaries. This obviates the need for a dense coverage of class domains, in contrast to standard RBF nets. Thus NRBF nets may contribute to soften the curse of dimensionality associated with networks of localized basis functions.

---

[3]It should be noted that the percentages have been rounded to the nearest percentage point.

It should be pointed out that the modified learning rule also performs well in a function mapping example where the NRBF net outperforms the standard RBF network, in terms of training error and generalization error. Interestingly, it leads to a more uniform performance over the training domain (Bugmann, 1998[5]).

A very positive aspect of NRBF nets is that the size of basis functions is relatively uncritical for the performance in classification and mapping. Further, learning is extremely fast. That makes this type of network very easy to use.

ACKNOWLEDGEMENTS:

Stimulating discussions with Kaspar Althoefer are gratefully acknowledged. The result on the Iris benchmark problem were produced during a student project by David Grant.

REFERENCES

1. Althoefer K. and Bugmann G.(1995) "Planning and Learning Goal-Directed Sequences of Robot-Arm movements", in Fogelman-Soulié F. and Gallinari P. (eds), Proc. of ICANN'95, Paris, Vol. 1, 449-454.
2. Andersen H.C., Lotfi A. & Westphal L. (1998) "Comments on 'Functional Equivalence Between Radial Basis Function Networks and Fuzzy Inference Systems' Submitted to IEEE Trans. on Neural Networks, June, 1997 (http://www.elec.uq.edu.au/~andersen/)
3. Backer G. (1996) Learning with missing data using Genetic Programming. 1st Online Workshop on Soft Computing, http://www.tu-bs.de/institute/psych/gb/gb.html
4. Bishop C.M. (1995) "Neural networks for pattern recognition". Clarendon Press, Oxford, UK.
5. Bugmann G. (1998) "Normalized Radial Basis Function Networks", Neurocomputing, 20, Special Issue on Radial Basis Functions, in press. (Preprint downloadable from: http://www.tech.plym.ac.uk/soc/staff/GuidBugm/Bugmann.html).
6. Bugmann G., Koay K.L., Barlow N., Phillips M. and Rodney D. (1998) "Stable Encoding of Robot Trajectories using Normalised Radial Basis Functions: Application to an Autonomous Wheelchair", To appear in Proc. 29th Intl. Symp. Robotics, 27-30 April, Birmingham, UK (Downloadable from: http://www.tech.plym.ac.uk/soc/staff/GuidBugm/Bugmann.html).
7. Broomhead D.S. and Lowe D. (1988) "Multivariable Functional Interpolation and Adaptive Networks", Complex Systems, 2, pp. 321-355.
8. Brown M. and Harris C. (1994) "Neurofuzzy Adaptive Modelling and Control", Prentice Hall, Hemel Hempstead, UK
9. Cha I. & Kassam S.A. (1995) "Interference Cancelation Using Radial Basis Function Networks", Signal Processing, 47, pp. 247-268.
10. Grant D. (1997) "Iris Classification", Student project, Postgrade Course in Computational Intelligence, accessible at http://freespace.virgin.net/david.grant7/iriscont.htm.
11. Horikawa S. (1997) "Fuzzy Classification System Using Self-Organising Feature Map". Oki Technical Review. Number 159. Vol 63. July 1997.. http://www.obd.com/oki/otr/html/nf/otr-159-05.html
12. Jang J.-S. R. & Sun C.-T. (1993) "Functional Equivalence Between Radial Basis Function Networks and Fuzzy Inference Systems," IEEE Trans. on Neural Networks, vol. 4, pp. 156-159, Jan. 1993. (http://www.cs.nthu.edu.tw/~jang/publication.htm)

13. Jones J.P. & Palmer L.A. (1987) "The two-dimensional spatial structure of simple receptive fields in cat striate cortex". Journal of Neurophysiology, 58, pp. 1187-1211.
14. Lang K.J. & Witbrock M.J. (1988) "Learning to tell two spirals apart". In Touretzky D.S., Hinton G.E. & Sejnowski T.J. (eds). Proc. of the 1988 Connectionist Models Summer School, Morgan Kaufmann Publishers, San Mateo, CA.
15. Marcelja S. (1980) "Mathematical description of the response of simple cortical cells". J. Opt. Soc. Am., 70, pp. 1297-1300.
16. Moody, J. and Darken, Ch. (1989) "Fast learning in networks of locally-tuned processing units.", Neural Computation, 1, 281-294.
17. Powell M.J.D. (1987) "Radial Basis Functions for Multivariate Interpolation: A Review", in Mason J.C. and Cox M.G. (eds) "Algorithms for Approximation", Clarendon Press, Oxford, pp. 143-167.
18. Purvis M. & Li X. (1995) "Connectionist Learning Using an Optical Thin-Film Model". Computer and Information Science. University of Otago, Dunedin. New Zealand.
http://divcom.otago.ac.nz:800/COM/INFOSCI/SECML/lab/publications/pub.html
19. Rao A.V., Miller D., Rose K. & Gersho A. (1997) "Mixture of experts regression modeling by deterministic annealing", IEEE Trans. on Signal Processing, 45, pp. 2811-2820.
20. Servin M. & Cuevas F.J. (1993) "A New Kind of Neural Network Based on Radial Basis Functions", Revista Mexicana de Fisica, 39:2, pp. 235-249.
21. Shao J., Kee Y.C. and Jones R. (1993) "Orthogonal Projection Method for Fast On-Line Learning Algorithm of Radial Basis Function Neural Networks", Proc. INNS World Congress on Neural Networks, Portland Oregon, USA, Vol. 3, pp. 520-535.

PATTERN RECOGNITION- A PILLAR IN THE SENSOR FUSION EDIFICE OR VICE VERSA?

Belur V. Dasarathy, Dynetics, Inc., P. O. Box 5500, Huntsville, Al. 35814-5500

ABSTRACT

Multi-sensor/multi-source information fusion, commonly referred to in the literature as sensor fusion, spans the array of concepts and techniques developed for optimal information processing in distributed environments through intelligent integration of the multi-source data and has gained immense popularity over the past two decades. The objective of this tutorial is to bring out the as-yet-not-well-recognized synergism between the developments in sensor fusion and pattern recognition - the main theme of this conference. Accordingly, the presentation will begin with an overview of the sensor fusion arena and three facets thereof, namely, architectures, algorithms, and applications. The tutorial will first layout the various taxonomies that have been employed to describe the developments in the sensor fusion field. This will help in delineating the significant role played by pattern recognition in the growth of this rapidly evolving field. The key objectives of the sensor fusion process across different applications will be identified. The developments in the pattern recognition field that support meeting various facets of these objectives will be described. This is followed by a review of flexible and self-learning fusion system architectures. Various fusion modes characterized in terms of the inputs and outputs of the fusion process are detailed. The complementary developments in the sensor fusion area that have in essence addressed some of the issues of interest to pattern recognition researchers will also be discussed. The presentation will conclude with illustrations of some real-world applications of these techniques.

1. INTRODUCTION

The pattern recognition community tends to subjectively view the sensor fusion activity as little more than accepting data from multiple sources and processing it in much the same manner as has been done in the past with a single data source, and thus consider the sensor fusion field as a minor facet of the pattern recognition activity. On the other hand, the sensor fusion community often views the pattern recognition activity, albeit once again subjectively, as but one objective among many, of the fusion process depending upon the application on hand. A view, that is more objective than both of these, would be to look upon the two fields as related ones with a significant area of overlap and encourage each community to take note of the developments in the other for mutual benefit. Under such a view, both pattern recognition and sensor fusion are two pillars (along with many others) in the much larger intelligent decision systems edifice. Accordingly, the purpose of this tutorial is to promote the implicit synergism existing between the two fields in a more explicit fashion by delineating the areas of common interest and focus on the reciprocal developments. In order to better appreciate this relationship between pattern recognition and sensor fusion disciplines, it would be helpful to first look at the various taxonomies of the sensor fusion arena.

2. FUSION TAXONOMIES

Multi-sensor/multi-source information fusion spans the array of concepts and techniques developed for optimal information processing in distributed environments through intelligent integration of the multi-source data and has gained popularity over the past two decades. Several books have appeared during the past eight years covering this evolving field, starting with the book by Waltz and Llinas [1], with some offering a broad brush introduction to the field [2, 3] or a review of associated mathematical tools [4], and others dealing in depth with specific aspects such as decision fusion [5], distributed detection [6], and other advance topics [7, 8]. There have been several special issues recently on sensor fusion in the Journal of Optical Engineering [9, 10, 11] as well as in Proceedings of the IEEE [12]. Sensor fusion concepts and techniques can be characterized from several different perspectives, for example: application domain, fusion objective, sensor type, sensor configuration, and fusion process input-output (I/O) Characteristics. Each of these influence the fusion system architecture design and the exploitation of the fusion potential.

2.1 APPLICATION DOMAIN

Sensor fusion models can be characterized on the basis of the domain of their intended application. This is a natural distinction since some concepts may be relevant only in some application environments, as for example non-cooperative target recognition (NCTR) in DOD environments. Further, the studies are driven in most instances by the requirements imposed by the funding source. The major application areas most commonly encountered in the literature are: defense, robotics, medical, and space, although newer domains of application have begun to appear recently, as for example fusion of audio-visual data [13, 14]. Defense applications represent a broad area by themselves and can be further divided into subcategories. These application areas are however not to be viewed as water tight compartments as there is considerable overlap among these areas not only in terms of objectives, but also in terms of fusion concepts and techniques employed to realize those objectives. It is important to note that the research work and examples presented here are not conceptually restricted to any specific application. However, like the majority of studies in this area, they have a flavor of the defense applications at least in terms of the terminology used, as for example, target recognition and tracking.

2.2 FUSION OBJECTIVE

A second principle of characterization is the objective or goals set for the fusion process. One could think of several different goals defined by the different application environments. Typically, the list of fusion objectives for any specific application scenario may include one or more of the following functions: detection of the presence of an object or environmental condition; recognition of an object or delineation of an event; identification (classification) of the specific category thereof; tracking of an object or continued monitoring of an event over a time period; accomplishing physical contact (constructive as in the case of robotics or destructive as in the case of defense applications) with an object; flagging of changes in the environment; conjunction of independent information bits to make an intelligent decision, and so on. One or more of these objectives may be deemed relevant in a specific application or problem environment. For example, in a defense application, one can categorize the objectives as: target acquisition/detection and location; target recognition / classification / identification; target tracking and data association; integration of intelligence from different sources; end game or aim point selection, kill decisions, and last but not the least damage and kill assessment. While many of these objectives are readily distinguishable from one another, multisensor systems designed with one of these objectives in mind may serve the other objectives as well in some cases, depending on the quality and timeliness of the information acquired by the sensors involved. Thus there can be considerable degree of overlap in the goals achieved by multisensor systems originally designed with specific and distinct objectives in mind. The objective of the examples discussed here while not intended to be specific, tends to imply target or object detection and classification as the primary set of goals and are of most likely interest to the pattern recognition community. Thus, the fusion objectives can be categorized as addressing either of the two questions: "what is it?" and "where is it?". By far, pattern recognition represents the tool of choice for addressing the first question and accordingly the presentation here will concentrate on this facet of sensor fusion.

2.3 SENSOR TYPE

This line of characterization is somewhat more specific than the previous ones in the sense that it is limited to the domain of physical sensors and accordingly does not cover other sources of information. However, since in the majority of cases, the sources of information for fusion are indeed the physical sensors and as such this is a significant basis for categorization of the fusion concepts and models. The main categories here are active sensors, passive sensors, and mixed active/passive sensors. The major factors dictating the selection of sensors for fusion are: the compatibility of the sensors for deployment within the same environment, and the complementary nature of the information derived from the sensors. If the sensors were to merely duplicate each other's information acquisition, then the fusion process would merely be the equivalent of building in redundancy for the enhancement of reliability of the overall system. On the other hand, the sensors should be compatible enough, in terms of such variables as data rates, field of view, range, sensitivity to weather conditions, and the like, to make fusion of information from the individual sensors meaningful and practical. Of course, one could go back to the broader definition of sensor as a source of information, in which case more categories, including human sensors, come into play. Although this is a valid generalization of the sensor fusion concept, it is likely to be less tractable to a rigorous analytical treatment. Most studies reported in the literature involve combination of passive and active or passive only sensors. This is mainly because fusion in a sensor suite with multiple active sensors involve more complex timing issues (in terms of achieving congruency along the timeline for receiving the return signals of the different sensors from the object in view) than with the ones with a single active sensor and one or more passive sensors. There do however exist a few studies of this nature reported in the open literature wherein more than one active sensor is deployed within the same problem environment. The fusion system architectures discussed here is however not limited to specific sensor types and is mainly intended to offer the flexibility necessary to encompass all the different sensor options.

2.4 SENSOR SUITE CONFIGURATION

Another perspective commonly encountered in this field is that of sensor suite configurations. Many of these configurations have been developed from theoretical considerations, while a few have been conceived by application environment dictated constraints. Parallel and serial or tandem configurations are by far the most common. Varied complex combinations of the parallel and serial configurations are also possible. Of these, the parallel sensor suite has been the most studied in the literature and represents the scenario wherein the sensors are making observations concurrently. This paradigm is most akin to that of the multiple classifier based pattern recognition systems that are gaining more attention recently [15]. The serial or tandem configuration is of particular interest in scenarios wherein the observations of the different sensors are temporally separated. This temporal separation may be caused by problem scenario constraints such as moving targets, different range and field of view limitations of the sensors and so on. A typical example of such a scenario is one wherein one sensor, say a wide-field-of-view sensor, is used to cue a second narrow-field-of-view sensor. In the real world, the sensor components in tandem, may themselves, consist of sensor suites with multiple sensors in parallel. Thus one can have complex combinations of parallel and tandem sensor suites. Thus sensor configuration has a significant impact on the fusion system architecture since it defines and limits the scope for exploitation of the fusion potential.

2.5 FUSION LEVEL

This has been one of the most popular form of characterization of fusion models and also perhaps the most controversial because of the differences in the sub-cultures within the sensor fusion community as pointed out earlier. Multisensor data integration has been traditionally characterized as fusion at different hierarchical levels depending on the stage of the processing at which such data integration takes place. As stated earlier, it has been common practice (at least within the sensor fusion community dealing with the broad commonalties of defense and civilian applications) to view this as a three-level hierarchy, namely, data fusion, feature fusion, and decision fusion. This three level hierarchy has become fairly accepted terminology although to some extent this is still a matter of individual choice and hence is subjective in nature. An additional dimensionality to the fusion process, that has not been as well recognized, is temporal fusion, that is, fusion of data or information acquired over a period of time. This can occur at any of the three levels listed above and hence is viewed as orthonormal to the three-level categorization. Many other terms, such as spatial and spectral fusion have been occasionally used in the literature to characterize certain specific fusion opportunities. However, these are in essence nothing more than examples of data and/or feature fusion, rather than new categories in themselves. The human brain paradigm is certainly applicable at all the three levels as well as in the temporal fusion sense. Without a doubt, the triumph of the human over the machine is mainly at the decision fusion level because of the innate human ability to take on a global perspective, whereas the machine is most efficient relative to the human, at the data level because of its ability to process large amount of raw data in a short period of time. Information processing at each of these levels of fusion has its own unique set of advantages as well as disadvantages. Also, the input and output to the fusion process need not be at the same level. It is therefore advisable to resolve the ambiguity caused in the characterization of the fusion process by the differences in the level of the inputs and outputs. This resolution of the ambiguity is accomplished here by expanding on this traditional characterization to define the fusion process in terms of the information level of both its input and output as discussed in the next section.

2.6 INPUT-OUTPUT (I/O) BASED CHARACTERIZATION

We expand the three level (data - feature - decision) hierarchy of fusion discussed above into five fusion process input-output (I/O) dependent modes. This accommodates the differing somewhat ambiguous perspectives in the definition of these processing levels. Under one set of conventions, the fusion model has been characterized by the nature of the input components, that is, fusion of specific category of entities, while under another, the fusion model is characterized by the nature of the output. On the other hand, the five I/O modes based characterization discussed below covers without ambiguity both of these two perspectives. Also, this type of taxonomy helps in delineating the correspondence of the developments in sensor fusion with those in pattern recognition.

2.6.1 Data In - Data Out (DAI-DAO) Fusion

This corresponds to pre-feature-extraction processing in the pattern recognition domain. Fusion paradigms in this category are generally based on techniques developed in the traditional signal and image processing domains. As such it is highly dependent on the application domain. This is the most elementary or lowest form of fusion conceivable under this hierarchy. This fusion mode, being one of fusion **of data inputs** resulting in a form of **data output,** has been commonly referred to as data fusion. The way the human eye fuses color information is a typical paradigm of this data level fusion. Multispectral data fusion, such as for example band ratioing of data from different frequency bands of a multispectral scanner (a normalization method commonly used in pre-processing of multi-band data in remote sensing applications), is a good example of this type of fusion process. Many of the processing techniques used in remotely sensed multi-spectral data analysis applications fall under this category. This could conceivably be used in combining information from like sensors such as TV and FLIR, that is, sensors with compatible data rates, data dimensionality and formats, for other application areas as well. Such data level fusion is thus accomplished at the front end of the processing stream, immediately on acquisition (and some possible signal conditioning such as filtering as applicable) of the data from the different sensors. For example, fusion can take place at the pixel level where the intensities sensed by the different sensors can be viewed as being spatially congruent leading to a multispectral approach to pixel data fusion. Of course data registration, both spatial and temporal, is critical to successful data fusion. This type multidimensional data fusion can also be accomplished through principal components analysis or other transform techniques including frequency domain analysis tools. Other types of pixel level fusion can also be construed. This can be useful in extraction of fine details within the data which otherwise would be lost to the final decision process. Fusion paradigms in this category are generally based on techniques developed in the traditional signal and image processing domains.

2.6.2 Data In - Feature Out (DAI-FEO) Fusion

This is the next step in this five step hierarchy. Within the pattern recognition domain, this fusion mode roughly corresponds to the feature extraction process wherein the inputs may come from one or more data sources. Here, data from different sensors (or different bands of the same sensor) are combined to derive some form of a feature of the object in the environment or a descriptor of the phenomenon under observation. Fusion in this mode, depending on one's view point, input - fusion **of data** or output - fusion resulting **in features,** has been looked upon either as data fusion or feature fusion. Feature fusion has also been variously referred to as symbolic fusion, information fusion, fusion at the intermediate level and so on. The manner in which depth perception is achieved in humans, by combining the visual information acquired from the two eyes, can be looked upon as a classical paradigm of this feature or information fusion. Indeed techniques based on this kind of paradigm have been investigated for machine perception of depth in robotic systems. The traditional approach to the computation of object surface temperatures using the intensities from two infrared (IR) bands of a multispectral scanner is another good example of data in- feature out mode of fusion processing. In some cases, this fusion mode may indeed be the first step with the previous mode being totally absent.

2.6.3 Feature In - Feature Out (FEI-FEO) Fusion

In this third stage of the hierarchy, both the **input and output** of the fusion process are **features**. Accordingly, this has been commonly referred to as feature fusion. In the pattern recognition field, this corresponds in a broad sense to the area of transforms commonly employed in the feature extraction process, for example for dimensionality reduction. Typically under feature or discriminant fusion, instead of sensed measurements, derived features are combined either quantitatively, say, in a multi-dimensional feature space sense or qualitatively, within a heuristic decision logic process, or through a combination of such qualitative and quantitative information. This is particularly true when each sensor in the environment has its own set of uniquely different data structure and features obtainable from one are not derivable from the other. For example, shape features obtainable from an imaging sensor may not be available from a non-imaging radar and on the other hand, range information obtainable from the latter may be outside the scope of the former. The two pieces of information can be combined to derive a measure of the volumetric size of a target, a typical fusion activity at the feature level. Tools applicable at this level, in general, can be considered as feature extraction/selection processes. This is typical of the level of fusion reported in many studies involving multiple active and passive sensors such as a millimeter wave (MMW) and infrared (IR) sensor suite. Another study that has some interesting potential for this feature level fusion has been reported previously under the name of super features [16]. The super features approach can synergistically combine features from individual sensors into a set of abstract synthetic or super features. These super features characterize, in some statistical sense, the variations in the individual feature values relative to one another. Depending on the specific super feature employed, the dimensionality of the resulting feature space, that is, the number of super features, can be either dependent or independent of the dimensionality of the individual sensor feature space. Such independence can be of significance in minimizing the computational loads in problems with large number of sensors each with multiple features.

2.6.4 Feature In - Decision Out (FEI-DEO) Fusion

Pattern recognition is indeed the foundation of this fusion mode. It is one of the more common fusion paradigms encountered in a review of the sensor fusion literature. Here, the **inputs** are the **features** from different sensors and the **output** of the fusion process is a **decision** such as target class recognition. Once again depending on the perspective of the researcher, this mode has been referred to as either feature fusion (that is, fusion **of features input**) or decision fusion (fusion resulting in a **decision output**). Most pattern recognition systems involving inputs from multiple sensors have long been performing, in essence, this form of fusion activity (without actually naming it so!) in the recognition phase, where in the feature vector (consisting of feature information from different sensors) is classified on the basis of a priori knowledge and/or training, to arrive at a class label (decision). However, with the advent of sensor fusion as a growing field of interest, this recognition task has also gained currency as a fusion process.

2.6.5 Decision In - Decision Out (DEI-DEO) Fusion

This mode of fusion is the last of the five step hierarchy and has been commonly referred to as decision fusion. Here, both the **inputs** and **output** are **decisions**, and this mode perhaps represents the most studied fusion paradigm. This is applicable across the spectrum of sensors and sensor suite configurations. Depending upon the specific sensors deployed within the sensor suite, fusion with inputs at the data and feature levels, that is, fusion under the previous four modes, may or may not always be practical. For example, fusion with inputs at the data level would require compatible sensors that are appropriately registered to permit such data level integration. In such cases, decisions will have to be made at each sensor based on only the local sensor derived data and these local decisions will have to be passed on to the fusion processor for integrating these individual decisions. Thus, while fusion with inputs at the decision level may not always be necessary or the most advisable approach, it is always at least a feasible approach. The fusion process in such cases would consist in combining at the fusion center the decisions made at the local level. Fusion at this level implies that decisions are derived at a lower level using single or multiple sensors, which may in turn imply that fusion in other previously discussed modes have also been performed. One could arguably visualize an additional mode, DAI-DEO fusion, with inputs at the data level and output at the decision level. This DAI-DEO fusion, while different from the FEI-DEO fusion in terms of the level of pre-processing undergone prior to the fusion process, is very similar to FEI-DEO fusion from the view point of the fusion processing system architecture.

Much of the work in the area of multi-classifiers based character recognition reported in the literature[17, 18] falls into this category. These studies aim at combining the decisions derived from multiple classifiers as a means of improving the classification accuracy and/or the reliability/robustness of the results. An interesting and promising example of these type of studies is the Behavior-Knowledge Space (BKS) approach [19] which was compared with several other methods recently [15]. A related effort reported much earlier, wherein multiple classifiers are utilized not concurrently but through feature-space partitioning that identifies the optimal domain of application of the individual classifiers, is that of the composite classifier [20]. In that study, the composite classifier components consisted of the linear classifier and the nearest neighbor classifier, each operating in its own optimally partitioned feature sub-space.

2.6.6 Temporal (Data/Feature/Decision) Fusion

Typically, any information integration over a period of time can be looked upon as a temporal fusion process. This mode is applicable at any of the levels of the hierarchy discussed earlier and thus represents an orthonormal dimension to the fusion process. Sequential hypothesis testing and other related ideas can be looked upon as temporal fusion of decisions arising from the same or different sensors depending on the application environment.

3. FUSION SYSTEM ARCHITECTURES

3.1 FLEXIBLE SYSTEM ARCHITECTURE

In a practical problem environment, it is likely that fusion in many of the modes discussed above might have to be incorporated into the system design for achieving optimal performance. There exists a persistent school of thought in the sensor fusion field that fusion at the lowest possible level in a given scenario is the best approach since the level of detail in the information is highest at that level. However, it should be noted that the corruption of information due to noise is also the highest at that level. The process of extracting relevant information from the data, in terms of features and decisions, on the one hand may be throwing away valuable information in terms of the details, but on the other may also be reducing the noise that degrade the quality of the ensuing decision. Thus there is an obvious trade-off to be evaluated in choosing the fusion architecture best suited for a given application scenario. Only an exhaustive exploration of the alternatives individually and in combination can help in evaluating such trade-off. One should also take into account the communication needs amongst the sensors and the fusion processor in this trade-off. More detailed discussions of the issues associated with this trade-off can be found in the literature [5, 21]. Recently, an expert system tool has also been developed [22] to aid the uninitiated in the selection of an appropriate architecture for a given application scenario.

3.2 SELF-IMPROVING SYSTEM ARCHITECTURES

Most fusion system architectures discussed in the literature view the fusion system information flow to be a one-way traffic wherein the information flows from the local individual sensor subsystems to the central fusion processor. A recently introduced concept is that of the fusion processor as a teacher with feedback to the local decision makers to improve their performance over time. Improved performance of the sensors (which feed into the fusion process) in turn enhances the performance of the fusion processor. The sensor subsystem performance is improved by using the feedback to fine-tune the decision surfaces as needed to correct its future decision making ability. This cycle of fusion, feedback, and local decision process tuning represents a significantly new concept in the design of fusion system architectures and is offered here to provide new impetus for further research. This mutual reinforcement, can be accomplished by viewing the fusion processor as an ***unfamiliar*** teacher [23], i.e., a teacher whose reliability or level of imperfectness is unknown initially. It is to be noted in this context that earlier teacher models such as probabilistic teacher [24], which viewed the teacher as essentially neutral with an imperfectness of 1/m (where m is the number of decision choices available) and imperfect teacher [25], which viewed the teacher as having a known level of imperfectness, are inadequate since the reliability of the fusion process output is essentially unknown and has to be learnt during the process. The unfamiliar teacher techniques, which implement the concept of "learning under the teacher aids learning about the teacher", have been extended to learning in uncertain or imprecise environments [26] and thus are well-suited for utilization in this context. This concurrent learning - learning under as well as about the unfamiliar teacher - originally conceived for deployment in traditional single sensor based decision processes, can be deployed in a radically different fashion in the context of multi-sensor systems. When so deployed, it enables the fusion system designer to further exploit the fusion process by using the fused output decision (weighted appropriately to reflect the associated confidence) to reward/punish the local decision makers as applicable. This serves to fine-tune the performance of the local decision makers over time which results in further improving the performance of the teacher. These variations of the teacher characteristics, i.e., the vicissitudinous nature of the teacher, can be better modeled using the dynamic variants of the unfamiliar teacher, namely, the VEDIC teacher [27] or its extension to imprecise environments [28]. The specific methodology to be employed for accomplishing this self-improvement is a function of the algorithmic decision processes employed at the local decision maker. Although the fusion processor is deemed in this context specifically as a DEI-DEO processor, one could conceivably have additional feature and/or data level inputs also into the fusion process. Here, the opportunity for fine-tuning the sensor subsystems that provide only data or feature level inputs is somewhat limited as compared to the scope available for fine-tuning the subsystems that provide decision level inputs. In the former cases, one could use the feedback only as a mechanism to flag the less-than -reliable performance of the corresponding sensors as and when they occur and thereby improve the scope for overall system robustness and in the event of problems provide for graceful degradation instead of catastrophic failures.

4. CONCLUDING COMMENTS

The tutorial identifies the areas of common interest between the fields of sensor fusion and pattern recognition to foster better communication between the two communities. Some of the methodologies that have been proposed in the pattern recognition and sensor fusion related publications, although similar in nature, have employed differing terminologies. This lack of commmon terminology has been to some extent a hindrance to cross-pollination of ideas between these two fields. This is particularly significant in the decision in - decision out (DEI-DEO) mode of fusion which is functionally very similar to the developments in the area of multi-classifiers. The two concepts have developed rather independently as can be seen from a perusal of cited references in the corresponding publications. It is hoped that this tutorial will aid in tearing down this invisible barrier between the two communities and promote the natural synergism that exists between these two research domains.

REFERENCES

1. Waltz EL, and Llinas J. Multisensor Data Fusion. Artech House, Boston, 1990.
2. Clark JJ, and Yuille AL. Data Fusion for Sensory Information Processing Systems. Kluwer Academic Publishers, Norwell, MA, 1990.
3. Klein LA. Sensor and Data Fusion Concepts and Applications. SPIE Press Tutorial Text Series, Vol. TT14, SPIE, Bellingham, WA, 1993.
4. Hall DL. Mathematical Techniques in Multisensor Data Fusion. Artech House, Boston, 1992.
5. Dasarathy BV. Decision Fusion. IEEE Computer Society Press, Los Alamitos, CA., 1994.
6. Iyengar SS, Prasad L, Min H. Advances in Distributed Sensor Integration: Applications and Theory. Prentice-Hall Inc., June 1995.
7. Varshney PK. Distributed Detection and Data Fusion. Springer Verlag, New York, 1997.
8. Brooks RR. and Iyengar SS, Multi-Sensor fusion. Prentice Hall, NJ. 1998.
9. Dasarathy BV. (Guest Editor), First Special Section on Sensor Fusion, Optical Engineering 1996; 35(3):601-721.
10. Dasarathy BV. (Guest Editor), Second Special Section on Sensor Fusion, Optical Engineering 1997; 36(3):629-813.
11. Dasarathy BV. (Guest Editor), Third Special Section on Sensor Fusion, Optical Engineering 1998; 37(2):352-531.

12. Varshney PK. (Guest Editor) Special Issue on Sensor Fusion, Proceedings of the IEEE 1997; 85(1):
13. Duc B, Saers Bigun E, Bigun J, Maitre G, and Fischer S. Fusion of audio and video information for multi modal person authentication. Pattern Recognition Letters 1997; 18(9): 835-843.
14. Teissier P, Schwartz J-L, Guerin-Dugue A. Models for Audiovisual Fusion in a Noisy-Vowel Recognition Task. in IEEE Signal Processing Society Workshop on Multimedia Signal Processing, 1997, pp 37-44.
15. Woods K, Kegelmeyer, Jr. WP, Bowyer K. Combination of Multiple Classifiers Using Local Accuracy Estimates. IEEE Transactions on Pattern Analysis and Machine Intelligence1997; 19(4): 405-410.
16. Dasarathy BV. Super Features: A New Tool for Feature Selection. In Proceedings of the IEEE Southeast Conference, 1983, pp 325-329.
17. Xu L, Krzyzak A, Suen CY. Methods of Combining Multiple Classifiers and Their Applications to Handwriting Recognition IEEE Transactions on Systems, Man, and Cybernetics 1992; 22(3): 418-435.
18. Ho TK, Hull JJ, Srihari SN. Decision Combination in Multiple Classifier Systems. IEEE Transactions on Pattern Analysis and Machine Intelligence 1994; 16(1): 66-75.
19. Huang Y, and Suen CY. A Method of Combining Multiple Experts for the Recognition of Unconstrained Handwritten Numerals IEEE Transactions on Pattern Analysis and Machine Intelligence 1995; 17(1): 90-94.
20. Dasarathy BV, and Sheela BV. A Composite Classifier System Design: Concepts and Methodology. Proceedings of the IEEE (special issue on Pattern Recognition and Image Processing) 1979; 67(5): 708-713.
21. Dasarathy BV. Sensor Fusion Potential Exploitation - Innovative Architectures and Illustrative Applications. Proceedings of the IEEE Special Issue on Sensor Fusion - Invited Paper 1997; 85(1): 24-38.
22. Dasarathy BV, and Townsend SD. GIFTS - A Guide to Intelligent Fusion Technology Selection. In Proceedings of the First International Conference on Multisource-Multisensor Information Fusion 1998.
23. Dasarathy BV, and Lakshminarasimhan AL. Sequential Learning Employing Unfamiliar Teacher Hypotheses (SLEUTH) With Concurrent Estimation of Both the Parameters and Teacher Characteristics. International Journal of Computers and Information Sciences 1976; 5(1): 1-7.
24. Agrawala AK. Learning with a Probabilistic Teacher. IEEE Transactions on Information Theory 1970; 16(4): 373-379.
25. Shanmugam K. A Parametric Procedure for Learning with an Imperfect Teacher. IEEE Transactions on Information Theory 1972; 18(2): 300-302.
26. Dasarathy BV. Fuzzy Learning Under and About an Unfamiliar Fuzzy Teacher. in NAFIPS'92, Proceedings of the North American Fuzzy Information Processing Society Conference 1992, pp 368-377.
27. Dasarathy BV, and Lakshminarasimhan AL. Learning Under a VEDIC Teacher International Journal of Computer and Information Sciences 1979; 8(1): 75-88.
28. Dasarathy BV. Fuzzy Learning in Vicissitudinous Environments. In Proceedings of the 11th IAPR International Conference on Pattern Recognition 1992, pp 500-503.

AUTHOR BIOGRAPHIES

The following list contains the brief biographies of the authors whose work was presented at ICAPR'98. Please note that this is not a complete list and it is intended for reference only.

Adnan Amin:
Adnan Amin received the B. Sc. Degree in Mathematics and Diploma in Computer Science from Baghdad University in 1970 and 1973 respectively. He received DEA in Electronics from the University of Paris XI (Orsay) in 1978 and presented his Doctorate D'Etat (D. Sc.) in computer Science to the University of Nancy I (CRIN), France, in 1985. From 1981 to 1985, Dr. Amin was Maitre Assistant at the University of Nancy II. Between 1985 and 1987 he worked in INTEGRO (Paris) as Head of Pattern Recognition Department. From 1987 to 1990, he was an Assistant Professor at Kuwait University and joined the School of Computer Science and Engineering at the University of New South Wales, Australia, in 1991 as a Senior Lecturer. Dr. Amin's research interests are Pattern Recognition and Artificial Intelligence (Document Image understanding ranging from character / word recognition to integrating visual and linguistic information in document composition), Neural networks, Machine learning, and knowledge acquisition. He is a member of the Editorial Board of Pattern Recognition and Artificial Intelligence, and Pattern Analysis and Applications, and has served on the Program and Technical committees of several International Conferences and Workshops. He is serving as Co-chairman of the Second International workshop on Statistical Techniques in Pattern Recognition (SPR98) and seventh International Workshop on Structural and Syntactical Pattern Recognition (SSPR98) to be held in Sydney 1998. Dr. Amin is a member of IEEE, the IEEE Computer Society and the ACM.

Chuan Heng Ang:
Chuan Heng Ang is a senior lecturer in the School of Computing, National University of Singapore. He received a PhD in 1989 in computer science from the University of Maryland ,USA. He has some experience in using a prototype GIS which is implemented based on a linear quadtree. His research interests include the design and analysis of data structures and algorithms, and the applications of spatial data structures in GIS and pattern recognition.

Saf Ashgar:
Saf Ashgar received an MSc in Digital Communications and Signal Processing and a PhD in Electronic Engineering with special emphasis on maximum likelihood detection processes for time varying channels from Loughborough University of Technology. From 1981 to 1084, he worked as a principal signal processing engineer and later project manager for Plessey Telecommunications Ltd. in the advanced data systems group on medium to high speech digital modems for the public switched network. He joined Advances Micro Devices, in CA in 1984 to lead algorithm developments and implementations in embedded digital signal processing based ICs tailored to telecommunications. His current title is of Senior AMD Fellow. He has over 10 publications and contributed in the "Mobile Communication Handbook", CRC Press. He holds 29 patents in signal processing architectures, algorithms and implementations. His current interests are in the areas of voice recognition and development of architectures for very high speed data in wideband applications.

Thiagarajan Balachander:
Thiagarajan Balachander is a Graduate Research Assistant pursuing a doctoral degree at the Artificial Neural Systems Laboratory in the Department of Electrical, Computer Engineering and Computer Science, University of Cincinnati. He received his B.S. from Anna University, India in 1994 and M.S. from University of Cincinnati in 1996, both in Electrical Engineering. His current area of research involves pattern recognition, artificial neural networks, medical image analysis and genetic algorithms. Balachander was a holder of the National Merit Scholarship awarded by the Government of India. He is a member of the IEEE.

Peter N. Belhumeur:
Peter N. Belhumeur graduated in 1985 from Brown University with Highest Honors, receiving a Sc.B. degree in Computer and Information Engineering. He received an S.M. in 1991 and a Ph.D. in 1993 from Harvard University where he studied under a Harvard Fellowship. In 1993 he was a Postdoctoral Fellow at the University of Cambridge's Sir Isaac Newton Institute for Mathematical Sciences. He was appointed Assistant Professor of Electrical Engineering at Yale University in 1994 and was given a joint appointment with the Department of Computer Science in 1998. He is a recipient of the Presidential Early Career Award for Scientists and Engineers, the National Science Foundation Career Award, and the Yale University Junior Faculty Fellowship for the Natural Sciences. He won the ``Best Paper Award" at the 1996 IEEE Conference on

Computer Vision and Pattern Recognition.

Sabine Bergler:
Sabine Bergler received a MS in Computer Science from the University of Massachusetts in Amherst and a Ph.D. In Computer Science from Brandeis University. She is currently Associate Professor in the Computer Science Department at Concordia University in Montreal.. Her research areas center around the automatic exploitation of natural language texts. She has co-edited two books. Her publications range from corpus analysis over machine translation issues to document analysis.

M Bernhardt:
M Bernhardt studied Physics with Mathematics at Southampton University. He then did three years of postgraduate research at Oxford University in the field of localisation of waves propagating in disordered media. For the past five years he has worked at DERA Farnborough in Electro-Optical systems modelling and simulation, and in the fields of TRI algorithms and data fusion for target acquisition using data from EO sensors.

Bir Bhanu:
Bir Bhanu received his S.M. and E.E. degrees in Electrical Engineering and Computer Science from MIT, Ph.D. in Electrical Engineering from USC Image Processing Institute and M.B.A. from UC Irvine. He also received B.S. in Electronics Engineering (with Honors) and M.E. in Electronics Engineering (with Distinction). He came to UCR from his position of Senior Honeywell Fellow at Honeywell Inc. He is a Fellow of the IEEE for contribution to sensor-based navigation, automatic object recognition and closed-loop adaptive techniques for developing robust algorithms. His research interests include Computer Vision, Machine Learning, Robotics, Artificial Intelligence, Signal and Image Processing, Graphics, Visualization, Virtual Reality and Computer Aided Design.

Horst Bischof:
Horst Bischof received his B.S. degree and M.S. degree in computer science from the Vienna University of Technology in 1987 and 1990, respectively. He received his Ph.D. in computer science from the Vienna University of Technology in 1993. In 1998 he got his Habilitation (venia docendi) for applied computer science from Vienna University of Technology. Currently he is an Associate Professor at the Institute for Automation, Pattern Recognition and Image Processing Group. His research interests include neural networks, adaptive methods for computer vision, object recognition, and learning.

Alan N. Bloch:
Alan N. Bloch majored in Languages at Antioch College. He received a Masters in Public Health at Pittsburgh, majoring in Epidemiology and Biostatistics. Following a decade of professional work in hospital and health services planning and educational and health statistics, he took a second Masters in Computer Science at City College in New York, while spending five years on the technical support desk at Lifeboat Associates, then the world's leading publisher of microcomputer software. After installing a computer graphics cinemicro-fluoroscopy system in a cell biology laboratory in Taiwan, he moved to Montreal, where he pursued doctoral studies in Computer Science, and more recently Masters work in Teaching English as a Second Language, at Concordia University, while working part-time teaching English, editing, proof-reading, and pursuing bibliographic research and retrieval.

James Boyce:
James F. Boyce received a first class BSc Honours degree in physics from King's College, University of London, in 1963 and the PhD in theoretical physics from Imperial College of Science and Technology, University of London, in 1966. From 1966 to 1968 he was a research fellow at the International Centre for Theoretical Physics, Trieste, Italy. In 1969 he returned to Imperial College as a research assistant in the Department of Theoretical Physics. In 1970 he became a lecturer in the Department of Physics at Queen Elizabeth College and then moved to the Department of Physics of King's College, University of London, in 1983, where he was appointed reader in physics in 1994. He has research interests in image analysis, machine vision, and seismic processing. Dr Boyce is a member of the Institute of Physics, the British Machine Vision Society, and the International Society for Optical Engineering.

Alberto Broggi:
Alberto Broggi was born in Parma, Italy, in December 1966. He received the Dr. Ing. (Master) degree in Electronic Engineering and the PhD degree both from the University of Parma. Alberto Broggi is currently

holding a permanent Faculty Position (Assistant Professor) at the Dipartimento di Ingegneria dell'Informazione of the University of Parma, and has recently won a position of Associate Professor. He is the coordinator of the ARGO Project, aimed to the development of a computer vision system (GOLD, which stands for Generic Obstacle and Lane Detection) for the automatic driving of a passenger car on highways and freeways. His research interests include Real-Time Computer Vision architectures and algorithms for automated vehicle navigation. He is the author of more than 100 international publications and acted as guest editor and is on the Editorial Board of many international journals and conferences.

Martin Brown:
Martin Brown graduated from Bath University in 1989 with a BSc (Hons) in Applied Mathematics and was awarded a PhD at the University of Southampton for research into learning systems (neural and fuzzy networks) applied to autonomous vehicles. He became a lecturer in the Department of Electronics and Computer Science in 1994 and has continued researching into inductive learning algorithms, support vector machines, land area estimation from remotely sensed data and materials modelling.

Guido Bugmann:
Guido Bugmann studied Physics at the University of Geneva in Switzerland. In 1986 he completed a PhD on "Fabrication of photovoltaic solar cells with a-Si:H produced by anodic deposition in a DC plasma". He has then worked at the Swiss Federal Institute of Technology in Lausanne on the development of a measurement system using an ultra-sound beam and neural networks to measure the size of air bubbles in bacterial cultures. In 1989 he joined the Fundamental Research Laboratories of NEC in Japan and modelled the function of biological neurons in the visual system. In 1992 he joined Prof. John G. Taylor at King's College London to develop applications of the pRAM neuron model and develop a theory of visual latencies. In 1993 he joined the group of Prof. Mike Denham at the University of Plymouth (UK) where he is developing artificial vision systems for robots and investigates path-planning and spatial memory. He supervises 2 PhD students and teaches neural computation to BSc and MSc students. Dr. Bugmann has 3 patents and over 70 publications. He is reviewer for Neural Networks and Biological Cybernetics. He is member of the Swiss Physical Society, The neuroscience Society and the British Machine Vision Association.

Joachim Buhmann
Joachim M. Buhmann received a PhD degree in theoretical physics from the Technical University of Munich in 1988. He held postdoctoral positions at the University of Southern California and at the Lawrence Livermore National Laboratory. Currently, he heads the research group on Computer Vision and Pattern Recognition at the Computer Science department of the University of Bonn, Germany. His research interests cover statistical learning theory and applied statistics with its applications to image understanding and signal processing. Special research topics include exploratory data analysis, stochastic optimization, and computer vision.

Hyung-Gi Byun:
Hyung-Gi Byun graduated with a B.Eng. degree in electrical engineering from Myong Ji University, Korea, in 1984, MSc. degree in Electrical Eng. & Electronics, and Ph.D in Instrumentation and Analytical Science from UMIST, U.K., in 1990 and 1995. He joined the Department of Information & Communication Eng., Samchok National University, Samchok, Korea, where he is currently a lecturer with interests in pattern recognition and signal processing based on artificial neural networks.

Antonella Carbonaro:
Antonella Carbonaro received a degree in Computer Science from the University of Bologna, Italy, in 1992. In 1994 she started her Ph.D. studies working specifically on Learning techniques to solve Computer Vision problems. In 1997 she received the Ph.D. degree on Artificial Intelligent Systems at the University of Ancona, Institute of Informatics. She is a member of groups working in several research projects on Computer Vision and Artificial Intelligence. In particular, she is receiving a fellowship on "Artificial Intelligence", sponsored by Fondazione Cassa dei Risparmi di Cesena, at the faculty of Computer Science of the University of Bologna, and she is collaborating at the Institute of Informatics, University of Ancona. She is author of papers in the Artificial Intelligence field and her current research interests concern perception and learning.

John N. Carter:
John N. Carter is a Lecturer within the Image Speech and Intelligent Systems (ISIS) research group at the Department of Electronics and Computer Science at the University of Southampton. His research interests include 3D analysis, speech analysis, moving feature extraction and biometrics (especially gait).

Ciprian Chelba:
Ciprian Chelba is a graduate student in the Department of Electrical and Computer Engineering of the Johns Hopkins University and is working on his Ph.D. thesis with the Center for Language and Speech Processing there. He received a Diploma Engineer title from the "Politehnica" University, Bucharest, Romania, from the Faculty of Electronics and Telecommunications in 1993. The Diploma Thesis has been developed at Politecnico di Torino, Italy on a Tempus grant awarded by the EC. Ciprian Chelba received an MS degree from The Johns Hopkins University in 1996. He is member of the IEEE and the Association for Computational Linguistics. Ciprian Chelba's current interests are acoustic and language modelling for speech recognition, statistical methods of natural language processing, and information theory.

Yan Rong Chen:
Yan Rong Chen obtained a BSc (Honours) in computer science in 1998 from the National University of Singapore. Her research interests are natural language processing and speech analysis.

Michel Cherbuliez:
Michel Cherbuliez obtained his M.Sc. in computer science in 1997 from the University of Geneva, with a thesis in computer vision and multimedia systems. He is currently Ph.D. student at the Swiss Federal Institute of Technology in Lausanne, where he applies wavelet decomposition techniques to fringe processing.

Lin Cong:
Lin Cong received the PhD in Electrical Engineering from the University of Manchester, Manchester, England, in 1996 in the subject of Robust Speech Recognition. Since 1996, she was an RA in the Dept. of EE, University of Bradford, England, researching in the subject of TMN. Currently she is a senior design engineer at Advances Micro Devices, USA and an IEEE member. Her research interests include digital signal processing and automatic speech recognition in noise environments. She has numerous publications in these areas and 9 patent applications on files She has a First. Class academic record in China before joining the University of Manchester. In 1992, she was awarded a Sino-British Friendship Scheme Scholarship as a visiting scholar to study in the University of Manchester, England. In 1993, she was awarded an ORS Scholarship to undertake her PhD study under the supervision of Prof. Xydeas in the same University.

Patrick Dainty:
Patrick Dainty received a BSc Honours degree in physics from the University of Manchester and an MSc with Distinction in opto-electronics from Newcastle Polytechnic in 1983 and 1985, respectively. He has been a research associate at King's College London since 1994, with research interests in optical communication and processing systems, image analysis, and machine vision. He is an associate member of the Institute of Electrical Engineers.

Belur Dasarathy:
Belur V. Dasarathy, a senior principal engineer at Dynetics, Inc., Huntsville, Alabama, USA, is currently engaged in research and development in the areas of sensor fusion, pattern recognition and related topics for the design and development of automated intelligent decision systems arising in a variety of strategic and tactical DoD problems. He earned his Ph.D from Indian Institute of Science, Bangalore, India. He was honored as the IEEE Region 3 Outstanding Engineer for 1997. He has been the guest editor of Optical Engineering for three special sections on Sensor Fusion. He is the chairman of the annual SPIE Conferences on Sensor Fusion. He has served IEEE Huntsville Section as chairman, vice-chairman, editor of its newsletter. Dr. Dasarathy has over 150 publications and is the author of three IEEE Computer Society Press books: Nearest Neighbor (NN) Norms: NN Pattern Classification Techniques, Decision Fusion and Image Data Compression: Block Truncation Coding.

Renaud de Saint Moulin:
Renaud de Saint Moulin was born in Uccle, Belgium on November 23, 1974. He received the degree of "ingénieur civil électricien" at the Université catholique de Louvain (UCL) in June 1998. He is now with the Dialog Systems research and development centre, an ASCOM company.

Andreas Dengel:
Andreas Dengel is a Professor of Computer Science at the University of Kaiserslautern and Scientific Director of the German Research Centre for Artificial Intelligence (DFKI). From 1980 to 1986 he studied computer science and economics at the University of Kaiserslautern. In 1986 he joined Siemens R&D in Munich where he worked on pattern recognition. From 1987 to 1989 he worked as a research and teaching assistant at the University of Stuttgart where he also finished his Ph.D. in Computer Science. In 1989 he joined DFKI. His

major research activities are in document analysis, pattern recognition and knowledge management. In 1996 he and his group received the Research Innovation Award from the Land Rheinland-Pfalz in Germany. In 1997 he received the ICDAR Young Investigator Award for outstanding contributions to the field of document analysis. He also received the Alcatel SEL Award For Technical Communication in the same year. He is a member of IEEE, GI, and IAPR.

Yves Deville:
Yves Deville is a Professor in the Computer Science Department of the Université Catholique de Louvain, Belgium. He obtained "Licence in Computer Science" from the University of Namur in June 1983; Masters Degree in Computer Science from Syracuse University, U.S.A., in June 1986; and Ph.D. in Computer Science from the University of Namur in February 1987. He was a Research Associate from October 1987 to September 1991 at the Institut d'Informatique, University of Namur. Dr. Deville's initial research focused on methodological issues in logic program development. He elaborated and proposed a method for the systematic development of logic programs. Part of Deville research is now oriented towards logic program synthesis. He is also active in constraint logic programming.

Michelangelo Diligenti:
Michelangelo Diligenti received the Laurea in Telecommunication engineering from Universita' di Siena, Italy, in 1998. His main research interests are in the field of document classification, pattern recognition using neural networks, and user modelling.

C. H. Dimitropoulos:
C. H. Dimitropoulos received a BSc(Eng) with Honours in Electrical and Electronic Engineering from City University, London, in 1990, and an MSc in information processing and neural networks from King's College London in 1991. Since 1994, he has been a Research Associate at King's College London, with research interests in seismic processing, image analysis, and machine vision. He is an associate member of the Institute of Electrical Engineers.

Andrew W.G. Duller:
Andrew W.G. Duller received a BSc in Mathematics in 1981 and a PhD in 1986 on algorithms for fine grained parallel processing both from Bristol University. He continued as a research assistant at Bristol University working on hardware for real-time image processing. In 1988 he received a SERC Research Fellowship and in 1990 was appointed to a lectureship in the School of Electronic Engineering and Computer Systems at the University of Wales, Bangor. His research interests are medical image processing, real-time object tracking, general object recognition and self-organising neural networks.

P Edmundson:
P Edmundson received a BSc Honours degree in Mathematical Physics with Astrophysics from King's College London. He studied for a PhD in X-ray Physics also at King's College. After working at Cap Gemini as an analyst for two years he started work as a Research Associate in the Image Analysis Group at King's College London.

Alessandra Fascioli:
Alessandra Fascioli was born in Parma, Italy, in 1969. In 1996 she received the Dr.Ing. degree in Electronic Engineering from the University of Parma discussing a Master Thesis on Stereo-Vision-Based Obstacle Localization in Automotive Environments. Since 1996 she is a PhD student in Information Technology at the Dipartimento di Ingegneria dell'Informazione of the University of Parma. Her research interests focus on Real-Time Computer Vision for Automated Road Vehicle Guidance. She is one of the investigators of the ARGO Project, aimed to the development of a computer vision system for the automatic driving of a passenger car on highways and freeways. For this purpose she is involved in the study of the image processing techniques based on the Mathematical Morphology computational model.

Ian France:
Ian France received a BSc in Computer Science from the University of York, in 1992 and an MSc in Electronic Engineering from the University of Wales (Bangor) in 1994. He is currently studying for a PhD at U.C.N.W. (Bangor).

Ana Luisa Nobre Fred:
Ana Luisa Nobre Fred was born in Lisbon, Portugal, in 1961. She received the E.E., M.S. and Ph.D. degrees in

electrical and computer engineering from Instituto Superior Técnico (IST), Technical University of Lisbon, Portugal, in 1984, 1989 and 1994, respectively. She is currently Assistant Professor at the Department of Electrical and Computer Engineering, IST, and Researcher with the Communication Theory and Pattern Recognition Group, Institute of Telecommunications. Her research interests include pattern recognition, information theory, image understanding and biomedical applications.

Lev Goldfarb:
Lev Goldfarb received diploma in mathematics/computer science from St-Petersburg University, Russia, in 1973 and Ph.D. degree in systems design from the University of Waterloo, Canada, in 1980. He has been with the School (now Faculty) of Computer science, University of New Brunswick, Canada, since 1982. From 1976 he has been working on the unified, or domain-independent, framework for pattern recognition, a framework that would provide a natural symbiosis of the two main approaches to pattern recognition--the vector-space-based and the syntactic approaches. The efforts has culminated in a radically new mathematical framework--evolving transformation system (ETS) model, the first outline of which appeared in a 1990 paper in journal Pattern Recognition. Careful analysis of the ETS model suggests in particular that the classical sciences have evolved on the basis of the numeric measurement processes which are a very restricted form of the proposed new, "symbolic", or inductive, measurement processes whose outputs are not numbers but the symbolic entities, "structs", with the inter-distances defined by means of the corresponding (inductively learned) set of weighted "symbolic" operations.

Marco Gori:
Marco Gori received the Laurea in electronic engineering from Universita' di Firenze, Italy, in 1984, and the Ph.D. degree in 1990 from Universita' di Bologna, Italy. From October 1988 to June 1989 he was a visiting student at the School of Computer Science (McGill University, Montreal). In 1992, he became an Associate Professor of Computer Science at Universita' di Firenze and, in November 1995, he joint the University of Siena. His main research interests are in neural networks, document analysis and recognition, and multimedia tools for information retrieval in Internet. Dr. Gori is an Associate Editor of the IEEE Trans. Neural Networks, Neurocomputing, and Neural Computing Survey. He is the Italian chairman of the IEEE Neural Network Council (R.I.G.) and is a member of the IAPR, SIREN, and AI*IA Societies. He is also a senior member of the IEEE.

Gregory Hager:
Gregory D. Hager received a B.A. degree in computer science and mathematics from Luther College in 1983, and his MS and Ph.D. in computer science from the University of Pennsylvania in 1985 and 1988, respectively. From 1988 to 1990 he was a Fulbright junior research fellow at the University of Karlsruhe and the Fraunhofer Institute IITB in Karlsruhe Germany. Upon returning to the states he joined the computer science department at Yale University where he is currently an associate professor. He is a member of IEEE and AAAI, and is currently co-chairman of the Robotics and Automation Society Technical Committee on Computer and Robot Vision. His research interests include visual tracking, hand-eye coordination, sensor data fusion and sensor planning. A book on his dissertation work entitled "Task-Directed Sensor Fusion and Planning" is published by Kluwer Academic Publishers, Inc.

Robert M. Haralick:
Robert M. Haralick was born in Brooklyn, New York, on September 30, 1943. He received a B.A. degree in Mathematics from the University of Kansas in 1964, a B.S. degree in Electrical Engineering in 1966 and a M.S. degree in Electrical Engineering in 1967. In 1969, after completing his Ph.D. at the University of Kansas, he joined the faculty of the Electrical Engineering Department there where he last served as Professor from 1975 to 1978. Prof. Haralick now occupies the Boeing Clairmont Egtvedt Professorship in the Department of Electrical Engineering at the University of Washington. Professor Haralick is a Fellow of IEEE for his contributions in computer vision and image processing and a Fellow of IAPR for his contributions in pattern recognition, image processing, and for service to IAPR. He has served on the Editorial Board of IEEE Transactions on Pattern Analysis and Machine Intelligence and has been the computer vision area editor for Communications of the ACM and as an associate editor for Computer Vision, Graphics, and Image Processing and Pattern Recognition. He has published over 450 papers.

Marcus Held:
Marcus Held received the Diploma degree in Computer Science from the University of Bonn, Germany in 1996. In November 1996, he joined the Computer Vision and Pattern Recognition group at the University of Bonn, where he is currently working on his PhD thesis on validation of structures learned by unsupervised learning

algorithms. His research interests include image processing, data analysis, statistical learning theory, and data mining.

Gabor T Herman:
Gabor T Herman received the MSc degree in Mathematics from the University of London, England in 1964, the MS degree in Engineering Science from the University of California, Berkeley, in 1966, and the PhD degree in Mathematics from the University of London, England in 1968. From 1969 to 1981, he was with the Department of Computer Science, State University of New York at Buffalo, where in 1976 he became the Director of the Medical Image Processing Group. Since 1981, he is a Professor in the Medical Imaging Section of the Department of Radiology at the University of Pennsylvania. He is involved editorially in a number of journals-in particular he was for a while Editor-in-Chief of the IEEE Transactions on Medical Imaging-and is the author of numerous articles and books on medical imaging and related topics, including "Geometry of Digital Spaces", to be published by Birkhauser in 1998.

Jaroslav Hook:
Jaroslav Hook after graduating from a high school in Skadovs'k, Ukraine, in 1982 entered Department of Electronics, Kyiv Polytechnic Institute (now National Technical University of Ukraine). He graduated from the Institute in 1988 with a M. Eng. in Solid State Physics and Technology. From 1988 to 1993 he worked as an electronics engineer with company Oktava in Kyiv. In 1994 Jaroslav Hook received a Master's degree in Economics from Central European University in Prague, Czech Republic. He continued the studies in Economics in the Ph.D. program at Brandeis University, USA, until 1996. In 1998 he graduated from the University of New Brunswick with a Master's degree in Computer Science and is currently working as a software designer at Nortel in Ottawa, Canada.

Frederick Jelinek:
Frederick Jelinek is a Professor in the Department of Electrical and Computer Engineering of the Johns Hopkins University and is the Director of the Center for Language and Speech Processing there. A 1962 PhD in electrical engineering from the Massachusetts Institute of Technology (his SB and SM degrees are also from MIT), he has been an instructor at MIT and Harvard and a professor at Cornell. He was a visiting scientist at MIT Lincoln Laboratories (1963 and 1964) and at IBM (1968-69). From 1972 to 1993 he worked at the IBM Watson Research Center at Yorktown Heights, NY where he headed their Continuous Speech Recognition Group. Dr. Jelinek is a Life Fellow of the IEEE and was the 1977 president of the Information Theory Society, having served 4 terms on its Board of Governors. He was named one of the top 100 innovators by Technology Magazine in 1981, and is the recipient of the 1977 IEEE Information Theory Society best paper award, of the 1997 IEEE Speech Processing Society Award, and of the 1998 Information Theory Society Golden Jubilee Paper Award. Jelinek's current interests are acoustic and language modelling for speech recognition, automatic parsing, machine translation, statistical methods of natural language processing, and information theory. He is the author of Probabilistic Information Theory (McGraw-Hill 1968) and of Statistical Methods for Speech Recognition (MIT Press 1998).

Phillis Jones:
Phillis Jones received an MSc in Computer Science from the University of Newcastle. She currently works towards her PhD in the Department of Computer Science at the University of Exeter. Her main research interests are in AI, Knowledge Based Systems and Neural Networks.

Alexander Kadyrov:
Alexander Kadyrov obtained his PhD in Mathematics, in 1983 from St Petersburg University. From 1979 to 1997 he held various research and teaching positions at Penza State University, Russia. Since 1998 he has been working on computer vision at Surrey University, UK, as a research fellow. He has authored or co-authored about 60 papers, textbooks and inventions.

Thomas Kieninger:
Thomas Kieninger, born 1963, is a research scientist at the German Research Center for Artificial Intelligence (DFKI), working in the group of Andreas Dengel. He studied computer science and economics at the University of Kaiserslautern since 1984 and joined the DFKI in 1991. Amongst his work he realized a fast and error tolerant dictionary system for post-processing of OCR text with a high degree of recognition errors. From 1994 to 1996 he developed HyperBraille, a hypertext based information system for blind people which granted uniform access to paper- as well as to Internet documents (WWW, e-mail etc.). HyperBraille won the "Innovation Award from the Land Rheinland-Pfalz" in 1996. He currently works on his Ph.D. where he

investigates all aspects of image based table recognition, ranging from segmentation and layout analysis to evaluation and format conversion.

Josef Kittler:
Josef Kittler graduated from the University of Cambridge in Electrical Engineering in 1971 where he also obtained his Ph.D. in Pattern Recognition in 1974 and the ScD degree in 1991. He joined the Department of Electronic and Electrical Engineering of Surrey University in 1986 where he is a Professor, in charge of the Centre for Vision, Speech and Signal Processing. He has worked on various theoretical aspects of Pattern Recognition and on many applications including automatic inspection, ECG diagnosis, remote sensing, robotics, speech recognition, and document processing. His current research interests include Pattern Recognition, Image Processing and Computer Vision. He has co-authored a book with the title "Pattern Recognition: A statistical approach" published by Prentice-Hall. He has published more than 300 papers. He is a member of the Editorial Boards of Pattern Recognition Journal, Image and Vision Computing, Pattern Recognition Letters, Pattern Recognition and Artificial Intelligence, and Machine Vision and Applications.

Ravi Kothari:
Ravi Kothari is an Assistant Professor in the Department of Electrical & Computer Engineering & Computer Science and Director of the Artificial Neural Systems Laboratory at the University of Cincinnati (UC). His research interests include artificial neural networks, pattern recognition, and image analysis. He received the Eta Kappa Nu Outstanding Professor Award in 1994, and the William E. Restemeyer Teaching Excellence Award in 1993 from the Department of Electrical and Computer Engineering and Computer Science at UC.

George Koundourakis:
George Koundourakis currently working toward his PhD in the Department of Computation at UMIST in the area of development of temporal data mining methods and algorithms within the Timelab research laboratory. Mr Koundourakis received his M.Sc. in Information Systems Engineering from Department of Computation at UMIST and his first degree in Computer Science from the Department of Computer Science, University of Crete in Heraklion, Greece. His experience includes database design and programming and teaching programming languages.

Mihai M. Lazarescu:
Mihai M. Lazarescu received the Bachelor of Science (Computer Science) (Honours First Class) degree in 1996 from the Curtin University, Perth. His research interests include the automatic indexing and retrieval of video, string matching, natural language understanding, model based recognition, incremental machine learning and computer graphics.

Jean-Didier Legat:
Jean-Didier Legat was born in Brussels, Belgium on April 15, 1957. He received his engineering and PhD degrees in microelectronics from the Université Catholique de Louvain, Louvain-la-Neuve, Belgium in 1981 and 1987, respectively. From 1987 to 1990, he was with Image Recognition Integrated Systems (I.R.I.S.), a new company specialised in optical character recognition and automatic document processing. Jean-Didier Legat was co-founder and Vice-President of I.R.I.S. In October 1990, he came back to the UCL Microelectronics Laboratory. He is presently a full professor. His current interests are computer architecture, parallel and distributed systems and design of embedded integrated circuits in the area of artificial neural networks, digital signal processing, computer vision and pattern recognition. He has been an author or co-author of more than 50 publications in the field of microelectronics and he is a member of the IEEE and the SPIE.

José M. N. Leitao:
José M. N. Leitao was born in Aldeia Velha-Avis, Portugal, in 1946. He received the E.E. and Ph.D. degrees in electrical engineering in 1970 and 1983, respectively, both from Instituto Superior Técnico (IST), Technical University of Lisbon, Portugal. He received the "Agregado" degree in electrical and computer engineering, also from the IST, in 1992. He was with the Laboratory of Physiology of the Instituto Gulbenkian de Ciência, Oeiras, Portugal, from 1970 to 1972. After spending three years at the University of Tubingen, Germany, he joined the faculty of IST in 1976, where he is currently Full Professor with the Department of Electrical and Computer Engineering. He is also the coordinator of the Communication Theory and Pattern Recognition Group, Institute of Telecommunications. His main research interests are communication theory, pattern recognition, and signal and image processing.

Ales Leonardis:
Ales Leonardis received his B.S. degree and M.S. degree in electrical engineering from the University of Ljubljana in 1985 and 1988, respectively. He received his Ph.D. in computer science from the University of Ljubljana in 1993. From 1988-1991 he was a visiting researcher in the General Robotics and Active Sensory Perception Laboratory at the University of Pennsylvania. Currently he is an Assistant Professor at the Faculty of Computer and Information Science at the University of Ljubljana. His research interests include robust methods for computer vision, 3-D scene interpretation, recognition, and learning. A. Leonardis is currently serving as the Vice-President of the Slovenian Association for Pattern Recognition and Slovenian representative in the Governing Board of the International Association for Pattern Recognition.

Hugh Lewis:
Hugh Lewis was awarded a BEng (Hons) in Control Engineering in 1992 and a MSc (Eng) in Control Systems in 1993 from The University of Sheffield. In 1998 he completed a PhD at The University of Southampton in remote sensing of clouds using neural networks and is continuing research into neural networks and empirical models for land area estimation from remotely sensed data.

David Lowe:
David Lowe has held a Chair in Neural Computing at Aston University UK since 1993. He has a PhD in quantum transport theory, and previously worked for the UK Defence Research Agency in areas such as automatic speech recognition and the principles of statistical pattern analysis. Although better known for introducing the Radial Basis Function network into the neural network domain in 1988, his main research activity in life is the study of the learning processes in his six children.

Marco Maggini:
Marco Maggini received the Laurea in Electronic Engineering from Universita' di Firenze, Italy, in 1991 and the Ph.D. degree in 1994 from Dipartimento di Sistemi e Informatica, Universita' di Firenze, Italy. He is Assistant Professor of Computer Science at the Dipartimento di Ingegneria dell'Informazione, Universita' di Siena, Italy, since February 1996. He has been collaborating with the NEC Research Institute, Princeton, NJ, USA on parallel processing, neural networks and financial time series prediction. His main research interests concern recurrent neural networks, the relationships between their dynamics and finite state machines, pattern recognition, human computer interaction and WWW applications.

Peter Marcer:
Peter Marcer, BSc, DPhil, FBCS, CEng., a founder and chair of the BCS Cybernetic Machine Specialist Group, began his career at CERN - the European Organization for High Energy Nuclear Research - in the Data Handling Division, is a former Associate Director of the Bristol Computer Centre, South West Universities Computer Network, and a director and a founder member of the European Institute of Quantum Computing and currently a member of the European Commission Pathfinder Project. His presentation discusses the factors which portend the demise of the current silicon superhighway based on CMOS and explains how quantum computing will not just replace it but will bring (and indeed unrecognized has already brought) considerable benefits.

Enrico Martinelli:
Enrico Martinelli graduated cum laude in Electronic Engineering at the University of Pisa. Since 1973 to 1994 he had been with the Institute for Information Processing of the Italian National Research Council, Pisa, where he carried out researches on operating systems, performance evaluation, simulation and logic design of digital circuits, VLSI algorithms and systems, design of special structures for computer graphics and machine arithmetic. In 1995 he joined the Department of Information Engineering of the University of Siena, Italy. His current research interests are focused on logic design of processors for cryptography and neural networks and design of multimedia tools for information retrieval in Internet.

Ruggero Milanese:
Ruggero Milanese obtained his Ph.D. in computer vision in 1993, and was Postdoc Fellow at the International Computer Science Institute, in Berkeley, California. He is currently Assistant Professor in Computer Science at the University of Geneva, where he leads research teams in video databases and in neural networks.

Florica Mindru:
Florica Mindru received her BS degree in computer science from the Technical University of Cluj-Napoca, Romania in 1996; and her MS degree in computer science from the same university in 1997. She is currently a

predoctoral student at the Katholieke Universiteit Leuven (Belgium), at the Department of Electrotechnical Engineering, Centre for Processing Speech and Images. Her research interests include invariant based pattern recognition and aerial image interpretation.

Theo Moons:
Theo Moons received a PhD in mathematics from the Katholieke Universiteit Leuven (Belgium). He then joined the Centre for Processing Speech and Images at the Department of Electrotechnical Engineering of this university. His main research interests include invariants for object recognition, 3D modelling and reconstruction, multiview geometry, and aerial image interpretation.

Nabeel Murshed:
Nabeel Murshed is an Associate Professor in the Department of Applied Informatics at the Pontificia Universidade Catolica do Parana (PUC-PR). He is the co-founder and coordinator of the Lab. of Document Image Analysis and Neural Networks (LADIANN) at PUC-PR, and the founder and program chairman of the Brazilian Symposium on Document Image Analysis (BSDIA'97 and BSDIA'99). He is an active member of the Technical Committee of the IEEE Neural Networks Council and, SPIE. Currently, he is in the program committee of the International Workshop on Statistical Pattern Recognition (SPR'98) and of the IEEE Joint Conference on Neural Networks (IJCNN'99). Prof. Murshed is coordinating research projects devoted to document image analysis, neural networks and data mining. His research interests are computational pattern recognition human visual perception and recognition of handwriting, document image analysis, neural networks and their applications to solving technological problems.

Christine P. Nadal:
Christine P. Nadal received her B.Sc. in computer science from Concordia University, Montreal. Currently she is working as a research assistant in the Centre for Pattern Recognition and Machine Intelligence at Concordia University. She is involved in industrial research projects in the fields handwriting recognition, document identification, and image labelling.

Liang S. Ng:
Liang S. Ng graduated with First class Honours in Electronic Engineering from the University of Southampton in 1995. He was awarded a Special Zepler prize for academic performance in his final year and the Eddie Herman Memorial prize for outstanding design work in Part 2. He has since pursued a PhD concerned with feature vectors in texture recognition.

Mark S. Nixon:
Mark S. Nixon is a Senior Lecturer within the Image Speech and Intelligent Systems (ISIS) research group at the Department of Electronics and Computer Science at the University of Southampton. His research interests include feature and texture extraction, pattern recognition and biometrics (face recognition, and more recently gait). Mark is the Chairman of the ninth British Machine Vision Conference BMVC98, to be held at Southampton this September.

Nicola Nobile:
Nicola Nobile received his Bachelor and Masters of Computer Science degrees from Concordia University. He has held research positions at Industry Canada and at CENPARMI (at Concordia University) and co-founded A.I.A. (Applied Intelligence Atelier), a company specializing in knowledge management, knowledge acquisition, and data mining. He has co-authored conference and journal papers on topics including expert systems, pattern recognition, logic programming, and knowledge management.

Derek Partridge:
Derek Partridge was born in 1945. He received his PhD from Imperial College, London 1972 (computer science), a Diploma of Imperial College 1969 (computer science), and a BSc University College, London, 1968 (Chemistry). Prof. Partridge is current a Professor in the Department of Computer Science at Exeter University. He served as the Head of the Department at the University of Exeter between 1989 and 1994. He has written numerous papers and books in the area of Artificial Intelligence. His main research interests include AI, Neural Networks and Knowledge Based Systems.

Petra Perner:
Petra Perner received her Diploma degree in 1981 form Technical University of Mittweida. From 1981 to 1985, she worked as research assistant in the research group "Industrial robot control" at the Technical University of

Mittweida. She received her PhD degree in computer science in 1985. From 1985 to 1991, she has been a working at the Technical University of Leipzig. From 1986 to 1990, she was the head of the research group "Opto-electronical Inspection Systems". In 1991, she was a visiting scientist at the Fraunhofer-Institute of Non-Destructive Testing in Saarbrücken. In 1992, she worked as a visiting scientist at IBM T.J. Watson Research Center Yorktown Heights/USA. From 1993 to 1995, she was a Scientist and Lecturer at the HTWK Leipzig. Since 1995, she is the director of the Institute of Computer Vision and Applied Computer Sciences in Leipzig.

Krishna C. Persaud:
Krishna Persaud graduated from the University of Newcastle-upon-Tyne, UK, with a BSc Hons. Biochemistry, going on to the University of Warwick, to graduate with a MSc in Molecular Enzymology, 1977, and PhD in Olfactory Biochemistry, 1980. After stays at University of Newcastle-upon-Tyne, UK, University of Pisa, Italy, and the Medical College of Virginia, USA, he joined UMIST in 1989 as a lecturer in Instrumentation and Analytical Science, where he is currently a senior lecturer with research interests in chemical sensing.

Maria Petrou:
Maria Petrou received her BSc in Physics in 1975 from the University of Thessaloniki, Greece, and her PhD in Astronomy in 1981 from the University of Cambridge, United Kingdom. She has been working on Computer Vision since 1986, and has published more than 170 papers, more than 60 of which are in refereed journals, on Astronomy, Low Level Vision, Feature Extraction, Texture Analysis, Markov Random Fields, Probabilistic Relaxation, Colour, Remote Sensing, Industrial Inspection, Medical Signal Processing, etc. She is Professor of Image Analysis at the School of Electronic Engineering, Information Technology and Mathematics of Surrey University, United Kingdom, and a member of the British Machine Vision Association, and of IEEE. She has served as an Associate Editor of IEEE Transactions on Image Processing and she is the Newsletter Editor of IAPR.

Thierry Pun:
Thierry Pun is Professor of Computer Science at the University of Geneva, where he leads the Computer Vision Group since 1989. He obtained his Ph.D. at the Swiss Institute of Technology in Lausanne in 1982. From 1992 to 1985 he was Visiting Fellow at the National Institutes of Health, Bethesda. From 1985 to 1986 he was Research Fellow at the European Laboratory for Particle Physics, Geneva.

Mohamad Saraee:
Mohamad Saraee is currently working toward his PhD in the Department of Computation at UMIST in the area of temporal data mining in medical and clinical domain. Mr Saraee received his M.Sc. in Computer Science from University of Wyoming, Laramie, Wyoming, USA and his BSc degree in Computer Science from Shahid Beheshti University, Tehran, Iran. He is Member of the British Medical Informatics Society, and the British Computer Society. His research interests lie in the areas of Databases, Pattern Discovery in Time-oriented Databases, Medical Informatics and Multimedia Databases. He has published his work in medical and computational journals and conferences and has been supported by the Ministry of Higher Education in Iran and Isfahan University of Technology.

Sameer Singh:
Sameer Singh was born in new Delhi, India and graduated from Birla Institute of Technology with a Bachelor of Engineering degree in Computer Engineering. He received his MSc in IT for Manufacture from the University of Warwick and a PhD from the University of the West of England, UK in speech analysis. He is currently the Director of the Pattern Analysis and Neural Networks group at the Department of Computer Science, University of Exeter, UK. He is the Editor-in-Chief of the Pattern Analysis and Applications journal by Springer, Editor-in-Chief of the Advances in Pattern Recognition book series by Springer, editorial board member of the Perspectives in Neural Computing book series by Springer and editorial board member of the Neural Computing and Applications journal. He is also the Chairman of the British Computer Society Specialist group on Pattern Analysis and Robotics and a Fellow of the Royal Statistical Society.

Ching Y. Suen:
Ching Y. Suen received an M.Sc.(Eng.) degree from the University of
Hong Kong and a Ph.D. degree from the University of British Columbia, Canada. In 1972, he joined the Department of Computer Science of Concordia University, Montreal, where he became Professor in 1979 and served as Chairman from 1980 to 1984. He also served as Associate Dean (Research) of the Faculty of Engineering and Computer Science from 1993 to 1997. Presently he is the Director of CENPARMI, the Centre for Pattern Recognition and Machine Intelligence. Prof. Suen is the author/editor of 11 books on subjects

ranging from Computer Vision and Shape Recognition, Handwriting Recognition and Expert Systems, to Computational Analysis of Mandarin and Chinese. Dr. Suen is the author of more than 250 papers and his current interests include pattern analysis and machine intelligence, character recognition and expert systems, document processing and computational linguistics. An active member of several professional societies and Fellow of the IEEE, IAPR, and the Royal Society of Canada, Dr. Suen is an Associate Editor of several journals related to Pattern Recognition and Artificial Intelligence. During the past 15 years, Dr. Suen has served as President, Vice-President, Governor, and TC Chairman of numerous organizations. He has also organized many international conferences on subjects of his specialities, and is Founder of the Vision Interface conference in Canada, Founder of the International Workshop on Frontiers in Handwriting Recognition, Co-founder of the International Conference on Document Analysis and Recognition. Prof. Suen is the recipient of several awards, including the 1992 ITAC/NSERC award and the 1998 Concordia Research Award for outstanding contributions to pattern recognition, expert systems, and computational linguistics.

Jasjit Suri:
Jasjit Suri was born in India in 1964, received his schooling from Sainik School Rewa, MP, Bachelors in Electronics and Computer Engineering from Maulana Azad College of Technology, Bhopal, Master's in Computer Science from University of Illinois, Chicago, and Doctorate in Electrical Engineering from University of Washington, Seattle, with specialization in Medical Imaging. Dr. Suri has been working in the area of Medical Imaging for last 15 years and has published around 35 publications primarily in the area of Cardiac Imaging, Brain Magnetic Resonance, Abdomen Computer Tomography, Dental Radiograph and Ultrasound Imaging. Dr. Suri has presented his research work at several international conferences in Europe, Australia and United States. Dr. Suri has worked with IBM Scientific Center and Siemens Research Divisions. He has also spent time as a Scientist at University of Wisconsin, Madison and was a faculty member at Maulana Azad College of Technology, Bhopal, India. Currently Dr. Suri is working as a Research Scientist with Transurgical in New York in the area of MR guided High Frequency Ultrasound for tissue ablation to treat benign prostate hyperplasia (BPH). He is a member of IEEE, EMBS, AAAI, RSNA, Siggraph and SPIE societies. He was honored with Indian President's Gold Medal in 1980 and a United States Patent in Cardiac Imaging in 1998.

Chew Lim Tan:
Chew Lim Tan is an associate professor in the School of Computing, National University of Singapore. He is also the Program Director for Research in the School of Computing. His research interests are expert systems, neural networks, computer vision and natural language processing. He obtained a BSc in physics in 1971 from the University of Singapore, an MSc in radiation studies in 1973 from the University of Surrey, UK, and a PhD in computer science in 1986 from the University of Virginia, USA.

John G. Taylor:
John G. Taylor trained in the Universities of London and Cambridge. Positions in UK, USA, Europe. He was appointed Emeritus Professor of Mathematics of London University in 1996. He is presently Guest Scientist at the Research Centre in Juelich, Germany. He is the European Editor-in-Chief of the journal Neural Networks and he has been the President of the International Neural Network Society and the European Neural Network Society. He served as a consultant in the area of Neural Networks to several companies, presently in time series prediction for the financial markets. He has published over 400 scientific papers, authored 12 books, edited 11 others, such as Artificial Neural networks (ed, North-Holland,1992), The Promise of Neural Networks (Springer,1993), Mathematical Approaches to Neural Networks (ed, Elsevier,1994) and Neural Networks (ed, A Waller,1995) and The Race for Consciousness (MIT Press, 1998). He is active in research into financial and industrial applications and higher cognitive brain processes, including consciousness. He has funded research projects from the EC, from EPSRC and from the DRA.

Babis Theodoulidis:
Babis Theodoulidis is senior lecturer of the Department of Computation and Director of the Timelab research laboratory at the University of Manchester Institute of Science and Technology. Dr. Theodoulidis holds a Ph.D. in Computation from the University of Manchester Institute of Science and Technology and M.Sc. in Computer Science from the University of Glasgow, UK, and a Diploma in Computer Engineering and Informatics from the University of Patras, Greece. He is Member of the British Computer Society, Member of the ACM, Member of IEEE Computer Society, Fellow Member of the Greek Computer Society and Fellow Member of the Engineering Council of Greece. His research interests lie in the areas of Databases, Requirements Engineering, System Development Methodologies and Computer-Aided Software Engineering. He has extensively published in these areas and his research work has been supported by the EPSRC, and ESPRIT programme of the

European Union and by British and European industry.

D L Toulson:
D L Toulson received a BSc Honours degree in Physics and a PhD in Neural networks and times series analysis from King's College London. He is author of numerous papers on neural networks applied to time series prediction. After working as a Research Associate in the Image Analysis Group at King's College London he formed his own company Intelligent Financial Systems.

Luc Van Gool:
Luc Van Gool is a professor at the Katholieke Universiteit Leuven in Belgium, Department of Electrotechnical Engineering. There he leads a group of around 30 researchers , working in the area of computer vision at the Centre for Processing Speech and Imaging (formerly known as MI2 - Machine Intelligence and Imaging). He has authored over 150 publications in this area. His main interests include shape recognition and description, 3D acquisition, and grouping. He is a member of the programme committees of several major computer vision conferences. He also is the coordinator of 3 European projects, all dealing with computer vision.

Svetha Venkatesh:
Svetha Venkatesh is a Professor at the School of Computing Science at Curtin University, Perth. Her research is in the areas of active vision, object recognition systems, biologically based vision systems, and the applications of computer vision to image and video database indexing and retrieval. She is the author of over 100 research papers in these areas and is a Senior Member of the IEEE.

Boulos Waked:
Boulos Waked received a B.S. in Computer Science from Beirut University College in Lebanon and a diploma in Computer Science from Concordia University, Montreal. He is currently a research assistant at the Centre for Pattern Recognition and Machine Intelligence (CENPARMI) at the University of Concordia and pursuing a M.S. degree in computer science. His research interests include document image processing, pattern recognition, and parallel computing.

Wenjia Wang:
Wenjia Wang received his BSc in Control Engineering, Feb. 1982 from Northeastern University, (NEU), China. He received his MSc in Electronics and Computing, Nov. 1985, NEU, China and a PhD in Computing and Management from UMIST, UK, in 1996. He worked as a Lecturer at NEU, China, 1985-1992. He current works as a Research Fellow from 1997 in Department of Computer Science, University of Exeter, UK. His main areas of research interest are Neural Networks, AI technology, Process sensing and control and Power electronics.

Geoff A. W. West:
Geoff A. W. West received the BSc (Honours) degree in 1978 and the PhD degree in 1982 from the City University, London. From 1982 to 1988 he was employed as a research fellow and from 1988 as a lecturer at the City University in the School of Engineering investigating techniques for automatic inspection. Since 1990 he has been on the staff of the School of Computing at Curtin University of Technology in Perth, Western Australia where he is currently an Associate Professor. His current research interests include 3D object recognition, active vision, visualisation, computer graphics, automatic visual inspection and related applications. Dr West is a senior member of the IEEE and a member of the IEE (UK) and is a Chartered Engineer. He is on the editorial board of the journal Image and Vision Computing.

Paul Horng Jyh Wu:
Paul Horng Jyh Wu is a senior member at Kent Ridge Digital Labs (KRDL). He obtained a BSE in Electrical Engineering in 1981 from the National Taiwan University. an MSE and a Ph.D. in CSE in 1986 and 1992, respectively from the University of Michigan, USA. He has been engaged in Natural Language Processing R&D for 10 years. His R&D team has developed a multilingual Name Search technology, called FNS, which has found many industrial applications. FNS technology is an integration of several R&D results in text classification and parsing, information retrieval, and text-to-speech transcription, part of the latter, is reported in this paper. The team intends to further commercialise FNS technology and make available text and form processing software for organizations to streamline business processes.

Bo Yuan:
Bo Yuan obtained a BSc in 1985 and an MSc in 1988 both in physics from Peking University, China. He is a

teaching assistant in computer programming and applications at the Department of Physics, National University of Singapore. He is currently pursuing an MSc degree in computer science in the School of Computing, National University of Singapore. His main research interest is in image processing and pattern recognition.

Primo Zingaretti:
Primo Zingaretti received the doctoral degree in electronic engineering from the University of Ancona, Italy, in 1984. From 1985 to 1987 he worked under annual contract at the Computer Science Institute of the Ancona University on the implementation of computer vision and artificial intelligence applications. From 1987 to 1990 he obtained annual grants at INRCA of Ancona, Italy, for developing medical image processing systems. In 1990 he joined the faculty at the University of Ancona, Italy, where he is currently a research and development engineer at the Computer Science Institute. He is author or co-author of more than 50 papers in the computer vision field. His current research interests concern image processing, pattern recognition, image understanding, perception and learning. He is a member of IEEE, IAPR, and AI*IA -Italian Association for Artificial Intelligence.

Author Index

MIX
Papier aus verantwortungsvollen Quellen
Paper from responsible sources
FSC® C105338

If you have any concerns about our products,
you can contact us on
ProductSafety@springernature.com

In case Publisher is established outside the EU,
the EU authorized representative is:
Springer Nature Customer Service Center GmbH
Europaplatz 3, 69115 Heidelberg, Germany

Printed by Libri Plureos GmbH
in Hamburg, Germany